Instructor's Classroom Kit
Volume II

for

Berk

Exploring Lifespan Development

prepared by

Laura E. Berk
Illinois State University

Judy Ashkenaz

Sara Harris
Illinois State University

Trisha Mann
Illinois State University

Pamela Barter

Boston New York San Francisco
Mexico City Montreal Toronto London Madrid Munich Paris
Hong Kong Singapore Tokyo Cape Town Sydney

ISBN-13: 978-0-205-54697-8
ISBN-10: 0-205-54697-8

Printed in the United States of America

10 9 8 7 6 5 4 3 2 1 11 10 09 08 07

CONTENTS

CHAPTER 11
PHYSICAL AND COGNITIVE DEVELOPMENT IN ADOLESCENCE

CHAPTER-AT-A-GLANCE

Chapter Outline	Instruction Ideas	Supplements
Physical Development **Conceptions of Adolescence pp. 283–284**	Learning Objective 11.1	Test Bank Items 1–5 Videos: *Exploring Lifespan Development in Action* and *A Window on Lifespan Development* Please contact your Allyn and Bacon publisher's representative for a wide range of video offerings available to adopters.
Puberty: The Physical Transition to Adulthood pp. 284–288 Hormonal Changes • Body Growth • Motor Development and Physical Activity • Sexual Maturation • Individual Differences in Pubertal Growth • Brain Development	Learning Objectives 11.2–11.4 Lecture Enhancements 11.1–11.2 Learning Activity 11.1	Test Bank Items 6–22
The Psychological Impact of Pubertal Events pp. 288–291 Reactions to Pubertal Changes • Pubertal Change, Emotion, and Social Behavior • Pubertal Timing	Learning Objectives 11.5–11.6 Learning Activities 11.1, 11.3 Ask Yourself p. 291	Transparency 136 Test Bank Items 23–34
Health Issues pp. 291–299 Nutritional Needs • Eating Disorders • Sexual Activity • Sexually Transmitted Diseases • Adolescent Pregnancy and Parenthood • Substance Use and Abuse	Learning Objectives 11.7–11.11 Lecture Enhancement 11.3 Learning Activities 11.4–11.6 Ask Yourself p. 299	Transparency 141 Test Bank Items 35–68
Cognitive Development **Piaget's Theory: The Formal Operational Stage pp. 300–302** Hypothetico-Deductive Reasoning • Propositional Thought • Follow-up Research on Formal Operational Thought	Learning Objectives 11.12–11.13 Learning Enhancement 11.4 Learning Activity 11.7	Transparency 143 Test Bank Items 69–78
An Information-Processing View of Adolescent Cognitive Development pp. 302–303 Scientific Reasoning: Coordinating Theory with Evidence • How Scientific Reasoning Develops	Learning Objective 11.14	Transparency 144 Test Bank Items 79–82
Consequences of Adolescent Cognitive Changes pp. 303–305 Self-Consciousness and Self-Focusing • Idealism and Criticism • Decision Making	Learning Objective 11.15 Ask Yourself p. 305	Test Bank Items 83–89
Learning in School pp. 305–310 School Transitions • Academic Achievement • Dropping Out	Learning Objectives 11.16–11.18 Learning Activities 11.8–11.9 Ask Yourself p. 310	Transparency 149 Test Bank Items 90–105

BRIEF CHAPTER SUMMARY

The beginning of adolescence is marked by puberty: biological changes leading to physical and sexual maturity. Modern research has shown that adolescence is a product of biological, psychological, and social forces.

Genetically influenced hormonal processes regulate pubertal growth. On average, girls reach puberty two years earlier than boys. As the body enlarges, girls' hips and boys' shoulders broaden, girls add more fat, and boys add more muscle. Puberty is accompanied by steady improvement in gross motor performance, but whereas girls' gains are slow and gradual, leveling off by age 14, boys show a dramatic spurt in strength, speed, and endurance that continues through the teenage years.

Menarche, or first menstruation, occurs late in the girl's sequence of pubertal events, following the rapid increase in body size. Among boys, spermarche (first ejaculation) occurs around age 13½, as the sex organs and body enlarge and pubic and underarm hair appears. Heredity, nutrition, and overall health contribute to the timing of puberty. A secular trend in pubertal timing reflects the role of physical well-being. Brain development continues in adolescence, supporting cognitive advances as well as more intense reactions to stimuli.

Puberty is related to a rise in parent–child conflict, but this is usually mild. Parent–child distancing seems to be a modern substitute for the physical departure of young people in nonindustrialized cultures and among nonhuman primates. Reactions to pubertal changes are influenced by prior knowledge, support from family members, and cultural attitudes toward puberty and sexuality. Puberty is related to increased moodiness and a mild rise in parent–child conflict. Early-maturing boys and late-maturing girls, whose appearance closely matches cultural standards of physical attractiveness, have a more positive body image and usually adjust well in adolescence. In contrast, early-maturing girls and late-maturing boys experience emotional and social difficulties.

The arrival of puberty is accompanied by new health issues related to the young person's striving to meet physical and psychological needs. As the body grows, nutritional requirements increase. Eating disorders, sexually transmitted diseases, adolescent pregnancy and parenthood, and substance abuse are some of the most serious health concerns of the teenage years.

During Piaget's formal operational stage, young people develop the capacity for systematic, scientific thinking, arriving at new, more general logical rules through internal reflection. Piaget believed that adolescents become capable of hypothetico-deductive reasoning, in which they begin with a hypothesis, or prediction, from which they deduce logical inferences. Piaget used the term *propositional thought* to refer to adolescents' ability to evaluate the logic of verbal statements without referring to real-world circumstances. Recent research indicates that adolescents are capable of a much deeper grasp of scientific principles than are school-age children. However, even well-educated adults have difficulty with formal operational reasoning, indicating that Piaget's highest stage is affected by specific, school-learning opportunities. Information-processing theorists agree with the broad outlines of Piaget's description of adolescent cognition. But they refer to a variety of specific mechanisms for cognitive change, with metacognition regarded as central to adolescent cognitive development. By coordinating theories with evidence, adolescents develop advanced scientific reasoning skills.

The development of formal operations leads to dramatic revisions in the way adolescents see themselves, others, and the world in general. Using their new cognitive powers, teenagers become more argumentative, idealistic, and critical. Although they show gains in self-regulation, adolescents often have difficulty making decisions in everyday life.

School transitions create adjustment problems for adolescents, especially girls. Teenagers who must cope with added stresses are at greatest risk for adjustment problems following school change. Enhanced support from parents, teachers, and peers eases the strain of school transition.

Adolescent achievement is the result of a long history of cumulative effects. Early on, positive educational environments, both family and school, lead to personal traits that support achievement. The dropout rate in the United States and Canada is particularly high among low-SES ethnic minority youths and is affected by family and school experiences.

LEARNING OBJECTIVES

After reading this chapter, you should be able to:

11.1 Explain how conceptions of adolescence changed over the past century. (pp. 283–284)

11.2 Describe pubertal changes in body size, proportions, motor performance, and sexual maturity. (pp. 284–287)

11.3 Cite factors that influence the timing of puberty. (p. 287)

11.4 Describe brain development in adolescence. (pp. 287–288)

11.5 Discuss adolescents' reactions to the physical changes of puberty, including sex differences, and describe the influence of family and culture. (pp. 288–290)

11.6 Discuss the impact of maturational timing on adolescent adjustment, noting sex differences. (pp. 290–291)

11.7 Describe the nutritional needs, and cite factors related to serious eating disturbances during adolescence. (pp. 291–292)

11.8 Discuss social and cultural influences on adolescent sexual attitudes and behavior. (pp. 292–294)

11.9 Describe factors involved in the development of homosexuality, and discuss the unique adjustment problems of gay and bisexual youths. (pp. 294–296)

11.10 Discuss factors related to sexually transmitted diseases and to teenage pregnancy and parenthood, including interventions for adolescent parents. (pp. 296–298)

11.11 Cite personal and social factors that contribute to adolescent substance use and abuse, and describe prevention and treatment programs. (pp. 298–299)

11.12 Describe the major characteristics of formal operational thought. (pp. 300–301)

11.13 Discuss recent research on formal operational thought and its implications for the accuracy of Piaget's formal operational stage. (pp. 301–302)

11.14 Explain how information-processing researchers account for cognitive change in adolescence, emphasizing the development of scientific reasoning. (pp. 302–303)

11.15 Describe cognitive and behavioral consequences of adolescents' newfound capacity for advanced thinking. (pp. 303–305)

11.16 Discuss the impact of school transitions on adolescent adjustment, and cite ways to ease the strain of these changes. (pp. 305–306)

11.17 Discuss the influence of family, peer, and classroom learning experiences on academic achievement during adolescence. (pp. 306–308)

11.18 Describe personal, family, and school factors related to dropping out, and cite ways to prevent early school leaving. (pp. 308–310)

LECTURE OUTLINE

Physical Development

I. CONCEPTIONS OF ADOLESCENCE (pp. 283–284)
   A. The beginning of adolescence, the transition between childhood and adulthood, is marked by **puberty**, the biological changes leading to an adult-sized body and sexual maturity.
   B. G. Stanley Hall described adolescence as a period so turbulent that it resembled the era in which humans evolved into civilized beings.
   C. Sigmund Freud's daughter, Anna, viewed the teenage years as a biologically based, universal "developmental disturbance."

D. Although certain problems occur more often in adolescence, the overall rate of psychological disturbance rises only slightly from childhood to adolescence.
E. Anthropologist Margaret Mead argued that the social environment is entirely responsible for the entire range of teenage experiences, both negative and positive.
F. Biological, psychological, and social forces combine to influence adolescent development.
G. The demands and pressures of adolescence differ widely among cultures.
   1. Most tribal and village societies have only a brief intervening phase between childhood and adulthood.
   2. In industrialized nations, where successful participation in economic life requires many years of education, adolescence is greatly extended.

II. PUBERTY: THE PHYSICAL TRANSITION TO ADULTHOOD (pp. 284–288)
A. Pubertal growth is regulated by genetically influenced hormonal processes.
B. Girls reach puberty, on average, two years earlier than boys.
C. Hormonal Changes (p. 284)
   1. The hormonal changes underlying puberty are under way by age 8 or 9, when secretions of *growth hormone (GH)* and *thyroxine* increase, leading to enormous gains in body size and to attainment of skeletal maturation. Sexual maturation is controlled by the sex hormones.
      a. Both *estrogens* (thought of as female hormones) and *androgens* (considered to be male hormones) are present in both males and females, but in different amounts.
      b. The boy's testes release large quantities of the androgen *testosterone,* leading to muscle growth, body and facial hair, and other male sex characteristics.
      c. In both sexes, estrogens increase GH secretion, fueling the growth spurt and, in combination with androgens, stimulating gains in bone density that continue into early adulthood.
      d. Estrogens cause girls' breasts, uterus, and vagina to mature, the body to take on feminine proportions, fat to accumulate, and the menstrual cycle to begin.
      e. *Adrenal androgens* influence girls' height spurt and stimulate growth of underarm and pubic hair, but have little impact on boys' physical characteristics.
   2. Pubertal changes are of two broad types: overall body growth and maturation of sexual characteristics.
D. Body Growth (pp. 284–285)
   1. The first outward sign of puberty is the rapid gain in height and weight called the **growth spurt**.
      a. For most girls, the growth spurt begins soon after age 10, for most boys around age 12½
      b. At age 14, the typical girl is surpassed in height and weight by the typical boy.
      c. Growth in body size is complete for most girls by age 16 and for boys by age 17½.
      d. Adolescents add 10 to 11 inches in height and 50 to 75 pounds during the growth spurt.
   2. Body Proportions (pp. 284–285)
      a. At first, growth of the hands, legs, and feet accelerates, and then the torso, reversing the cephalocaudal growth trend of infancy and childhood.
      b. As a result of this pattern, early adolescents often appear awkward and out of proportion.
      c. The most obvious sex differences in body proportions are the broadening of boys' shoulders relative to the hips and the broadening of girls' hips relative to the shoulders and waist.
      d. Because boys have two extra years of preadolescent growth, when the legs are growing the fastest, they end up with proportionally longer legs, relative to girls.
   3. Muscle–Fat Makeup and Other Internal Changes (p. 285)
      a. Around age 8, girls start to add fat on their arms, legs, and trunk, a trend that accelerates from age 11 to 16, while boys' arm and leg fat decreases.
      b. Boys develop larger skeletal muscles, hearts, and lung capacity than girls and, unlike girls, experience an increase in the number of red blood cells.
      c. Boys' greater gain in muscle strength contributes to their superior athletic performance.
E. Motor Development and Physical Activity (pp. 285–286)
   1. Girls' gains in gross motor performance are slow and gradual, leveling off at age 14, whereas boys show a dramatic spurt in strength, speed, and endurance that continues through the teenage years.

2. Among boys, athletic competence is strongly related to peer admiration and self-esteem, leading some adolescent boys to use performance-enhancing drugs, such as anabolic steroids.
3. Besides improving motor performance, sports and exercise influence cognitive and social development.
4. Although sustained physical activity is associated with lifelong health benefits, only 55 percent of U.S. and 65 percent of Canadian students are enrolled in physical education.
5. Required daily physical education, aimed at helping young people find pleasure in sports and exercise, is a vital means of promoting adolescent physical and psychological well-being.

F. Sexual Maturation (pp.286–287)
   1. In adolescence, changes occur in physical features related to sexual functioning.
      a. **Primary sexual characteristics** are the reproductive organs.
      b. **Secondary sexual characteristics** are features that are visible on the outside of the body and serve as additional signs of sexual maturity, such as breast development in females and the appearance of underarm and pubic hair in males and females.
   2. Typically, these characteristics take 4 years to develop, but some adolescents complete sexual maturation in 2 years, whereas others take 5 to 6 years.
   3. Sexual Maturation in Girls (p. 287)
      a. Female puberty usually begins with the budding of the breasts and the growth spurt.
      b. **Menarche,** or first menstruation, typically happens around 12½ years for North American girls and 13 for Western Europeans; the age range extends from 10½ to 15½ years.
      c. Following menarche, pubic hair and breast development are completed, and underarm hair appears.
      d. Nature delays sexual maturity the girl's body is large enough for childbearing.
   4. Sexual Maturation in Boys (p. 287)
      a. The first sign of puberty in boys is the enlargement of the testes, accompanied by changes in the scrotum.
      b. Pubic hair emerges soon after, about the same time the penis begins to enlarge.
      c. The growth spurt occurs much later in the sequence of pubertal events for boys than for girls, reaching its peak at about age 14, when enlargement of the testes and penis is nearly complete.
      d. Facial and body hair also emerge after the peak in body growth, and the voice deepens as the larynx enlarges and the vocal cords lengthen.
      e. **Spermarche**, the first ejaculation of seminal fluid, usually occurs around age 13½.

G. Individual Differences in Pubertal Growth (p. 287)
   1. Identical twins generally reach menarche within a month or two of each other, whereas fraternal twins differ by about 12 months, indicating a substantial contribution from heredity.
   2. In girls, a sharp rise in body weight and fat may trigger sexual maturation as a result of the release from fat cells of a protein called *leptin,* which signals the brain that the girl's energy stores are sufficient for puberty.
      a. This effect explains why menarche and other aspects of sexual maturation occur earlier in heavier and, especially, obese girls.
      b. Girls who eat very little or who begin serious athletic training at early ages usually experience later menarche.
   3. In poverty-stricken regions where malnutrition and infectious disease are widespread, menarche is greatly delayed.
   4. Early family experiences may also contribute to the timing of puberty, with threats to emotional health trending to accelerate puberty.
   5. The existence of a **secular trend**, or generational change, in pubertal timing lends added support to the role of physical well-being in pubertal development.
      a. In industrialized nations, age of menarche declined by about three to four months per decade from 1900 to 1970, a period in which nutrition, health care, sanitation, and control of infectious disease improved greatly.
      b. In North America and some European countries, rising rates of overweight and obesity are sustaining this trend, putting early-maturing girls at risk for unfavorable peer involvements, including sexual activity.

H. Brain Development (pp. 287–288)
   1. Brain-imaging research reveals that continued pruning of unused synapses in the cerebral cortex occurs in adolescence, as do accelerated growth and myelination of stimulated neural fibers.
   2. Linkages between the frontal lobes and other brain areas expand and attain rapid communication, supporting a variety of cognitive advances.
   3. Neurons become more responsive to excitatory neurotransmitters during puberty, leading to more intense reactions to both stressful events and pleasurable stimuli, which, in turn, encourages a drive for novel experiences during this period.
   4. Alterations in neurotransmitter activity may also make adolescents more susceptible to certain disorders, including depression and eating disturbances.
   5. At puberty, changes occur in the brain's regulation of the timing of sleep, so that adolescents go to bed much later than they did as children.
   6. Because teenagers need almost as much sleep as children (about nine hours), when they get up early for school, their sleep needs are not satisfied.
      a. Sleep-deprived adolescents perform poorly on cognitive tasks during morning hours.
      b. They are also more likely to suffer from depressed mood and to engage in high-risk behaviors.
      c. Later school start times can help but do not eliminate sleep deprivation.

III. THE PSYCHOLOGICAL IMPACT OF PUBERTAL EVENTS (pp. 288–291)

A. Reactions to Pubertal Changes (pp. 288–289)
   1. Whereas two generations ago, menarche was often traumatic, today girls commonly react with "surprise" and, typically, a mixture of positive and negative emotions.
   2. Individual differences in girls' response to menarche depend on prior knowledge and support from family members.
      a. For girls with no advance information, menarche can be shocking and disturbing, as was common in the 1950s.
      b. Today, most girls get some information from their mothers, and girls whose fathers know about their pubertal changes adjust especially well, perhaps reflecting a family atmosphere that is accepting of physical and sexual matters.
   3. Boys respond to spermarche with mixed feelings; as with girls, those who feel better prepared tend to react more positively.
      a. Virtually all boys know about ejaculation ahead of time, but few get any information from parents; most obtain it from reading material.
      b. Overall, boys get much less social support than girls for the physical changes of puberty.
   4. The larger cultural context affects the experience of puberty.
      a. Many tribal and village societies celebrate puberty with an *initiation ceremony,* a ritualized announcement to the community that marks an important change in privilege and responsibility.
      b. Western culture grants little formal recognition to movement from childhood to adolescence or from adolescence to adulthood; although certain ethnic and religious ceremonies resemble initiation ceremonies, they seldom lead to a meaningful change in social status.
   5. Western adolescents are granted partial adult status at many different ages—for example, an age for starting employment, for driving, for leaving high school, for voting, and for drinking—making the transition to adulthood especially confusing.

B. Pubertal Change, Emotion, and Social Behavior (pp. 289–290)
   1. Adolescent Moodiness (p. 289)
      a. Although higher pubertal hormone levels are related to greater moodiness, these relationships are not strong.
      b. In several studies tracking mood fluctuations in children, adolescents, and adults, adolescents' negative moods were linked to a greater number of negative life events, including difficulties with parents, disciplinary problems at school, and breaking up with a boyfriend or girlfriend.
      c. Negative events increased steadily from childhood to adolescence, and teenagers also seemed to react to them with greater emotion than did children.

   d. Compared with adults' moods, moods of younger adolescents (ages 12 to 16) were less stable, with a strong relation to situational changes.
      (1) High points were times spent with peers and in self-chosen leisure activities, and coincided with weekend evenings, especially in high school.
      (2) Low points tended to occur in adult-structured settings, such as class, job, and religious services.
      (3) Because going out with friends on weekends is a "cultural script" for adolescents, teenagers who spend weekend evenings at home often feel profoundly lonely.
2. Parent–Child Relationships (pp. 289–290)
   a. Puberty is related to a rise in parent–child conflict, with a surprisingly similar frequency of arguing across North American subcultures, including those whose traditions strongly respect parental authority.
   b. Psychological distancing between parents and children seems to have emerged as a modern substitute for the physical departure from the family that is typical both in nonindustrialized cultures and among nonhuman primates.
   c. Adolescents' new powers of reasoning may contribute to family tensions.
      (1) Parent–adolescent disagreements focus largely on mundane, day-to-day matters.
      (2) Parent–daughter conflict tends to be more intense than conflict with sons.
      (3) Most disputes are mild, with parents and adolescents displaying both conflict and affection, and generally agreeing on important values.

C. Pubertal Timing (pp. 290–291)
1. In studies of pubertal timing, early-maturing boys appeared advantaged in many aspects of emotional and social functioning.
   a. Both adults and peers viewed them as relaxed, independent, self-confident, and physically attractive.
   b. They tended to hold leadership positions in school and to be athletic stars.
   c. Late-maturing boys, in contrast, were viewed as anxious and attention-seeking.
2. Early-maturing girls had emotional and social difficulties.
   a. They were unpopular, withdrawn, lacking in self-confidence, and anxious, and they held few leadership positions.
   b. Late-maturing girls were regarded as physically attractive, lively, sociable, and leaders at school.
3. These trends reflect two factors: how well the adolescent's body matches cultural ideals of physical attractiveness, and how well young people fit in physically with their peers.
4. The Role of Physical Attractiveness (p. 290)
   a. Society's view of the attractive female is thin and long-legged, consistent with the girlish shape that favors the late developer.
   b. The male image—tall, broad-shouldered, and muscular—fits the early-maturing boy.
   c. **Body image** refers to individuals' conception of and attitude toward their own physical appearance.
      (1) Early-maturing girls have a less positive body image than their on-time and late-maturing agemates.
      (2) Although boys are less consistent, early, rapid maturers tend to be more satisfied with their physical characteristics.
   d. These conclusions affect young people's self-esteem and psychological well-being.
5. The Importance of Fitting in with Peers (p. 290)
   a. Adolescents feel most comfortable with peers who match their own level of biological maturity.
   b. As a result, early-maturing girls and late-maturing boys have difficulty because they fall at the extremes of physical development.
   c. Early-maturing adolescents of both sexes tend to seek out older companions—sometimes with unfavorable consequences.

6. Long-Term Consequences (pp. 290–291)
    a. Early-maturing girls are prone to lasting difficulties, tending to remain depressed and to have poorer-quality relationships with family and friends, smaller social networks, and lower life satisfaction into early adulthood, compared to their on-time counterparts.
    b. Early-maturing boys show no lasting problems.
    c. Interventions targeting at-risk early-maturing youths are needed, which include educating parents and teachers and providing adolescents with counseling and social supports.

IV. HEALTH ISSUES (pp. 291–299)
  A. As adolescents attain greater autonomy, their personal decision making becomes important, in health as well as other areas.
  B. Biological, psychological, family, peer, and cultural factors jointly contribute to the health concerns of adolescence.
  C. Nutritional Needs (p. 291)
    1. During the growth spurt, boys require about 2,700 calories a day and much more protein; girls need about 2,200 calories but somewhat less protein.
    2. Teenagers often make unhealthy food choices, especially when they rely on snack bars and vending machines at school and on fast-food eating outside of school.
    3. Frequency of family meals is strongly associated with healthy eating in teenagers, but is less common than with younger children.
  D. Eating Disorders (pp. 291–292)
    1. Girls who reach puberty early, who are very dissatisfied with their body image, and who grow up in homes where concern with weight and thinness is high are at risk for serious eating problems.
    2. Anorexia Nervosa (pp. 291–292)
      a. **Anorexia nervosa** is an eating disturbance in which individuals starve themselves because of a compulsive fear of getting fat.
      b. About 1 percent of North American and Western European teenage girls are affected, and cases have increased sharply in the past 50 years, fueled by cultural admiration of female thinness.
      c. Although anorexia is quite common in all SES groups, Asian-American, Caucasian-American, and Hispanic girls are at greater risk than African-American girls, who tend to be more satisfied with their size and shape.
      d. Boys account for about 10 percent of cases of anorexia, about half in gay or bisexual young men who are uncomfortable with a strong, muscular appearance.
      e. Anorexics have a distorted body image, seeing themselves as too heavy even when severely underweight.
      f. Anorexics generally lose between 25 and 50 percent of their body weight.
        (1) Physical symptoms include cessation of menstruation or nonoccurrence of menarche, pale skin, brittle, discolored nails, appearance of fine dark hairs all over the body, and extreme sensitivity to cold.
        (2) Continued malnutrition can cause the heart muscle to shrink, the kidneys to fail, and irreversible brain damage and loss of bone mass to occur.
      g. About 6 percent of anorexics die of the disorder.
      h. Forces within the person, the family, and the culture give rise to anorexia nervosa.
        (1) Many anorexics have extremely high standards for their own behavior and performance.
        (2) Societal images of "thin is beautiful" contribute to the poorer body image of early-maturing girls, who are at greatest risk for anorexia.
        (3) Often mothers of anorexics have high expectations for their daughters' physical appearance, achievement, and social acceptance and are overprotective and controlling, while fathers are emotionally distant.
        (4) It is unclear whether maladaptive parent–child relationships precede or follow the development of anorexia, or both.
      i. Treatment usually involves a combination of hospitalization and family therapy.
        (1) Hospitalization is often necessary to prevent life-threatening malnutrition.
        (2) Medication can reduce anxiety and neurotransmitter imbalances.
        (3) Less than 50 percent of patients recover fully.

3. Bulimia Nervosa (p. 292)
    a. **Bulimia nervosa** is an eating disorder in which young people, usually girls, engage in strict dieting and excessive exercise accompanied by binge eating, often followed by deliberate vomiting and purging with laxatives.
    b. The repeated vomiting erodes tooth enamel and can also cause life-threatening damage to the throat and stomach.
    c. Bulimia is more common than anorexia, affecting about 2 to 3 percent of teenage girls, of whom only 5 percent have previously been anorexic.
    d. Bulimia, like anorexia, is influenced by heredity, as well as by overweight and early puberty.
    e. Some bulimics are perfectionists, but others lack self-control in other areas of their lives as well.
    f. Like anorexics, bulimics feel pathological anxiety about gaining weight, but they may have experienced their parents as emotionally unavailable rather than controlling.
    g. Unlike anorexics, bulimics usually feel depressed and guilty about their abnormal eating habits, making bulimia easier to treat than anorexia.
    h. Treatment may include support groups, nutrition education, training in changing eating habits, and medication to control anxiety, depression, and appetite.

E. Sexual Activity (pp. 292–296)
1. The Impact of Culture (pp. 292–293)
    a. Typically, North American parents give children little information about sex, discourage sex play, and rarely talk about sex in their presence.
    b. If young people do not get information about sex from their parents, they generally turn to friends, books, magazines, movies, television, and the Internet.
    c. Prime-time TV shows tend to depict sexual partners as spontaneous and passionate, and as experiencing no negative consequences.
    d. Adolescents receive contradictory and confusing messages about sex: Adults emphasize that sex at a young age and outside of marriage is wrong, but the broader social environment extols the excitement and romanticism of sex.
2. Characteristics of Sexually Active Adolescents (pp. 293–294)
    a. Although the overall rates of teenage sexual activity are similar in the United States, Canada, and other Western countries, the quality of sexual experiences differs.
    b. A substantial number of young people are sexually active by age 15, with males tending to have their first intercourse earlier than females.
    c. American youths begin sexual activity earlier than their Canadian counterparts, but most have had only one or two sexual partners by the end of high school.
    d. Teenage sexual activity is linked to personal, family, peer, and educational characteristics, including early pubertal timing, parental divorce, single-parent and stepfamily homes, large family size, little or no religious involvement, weak parental monitoring, disrupted parent–child communication, sexually active friends and older siblings, poor school performance, lower educational aspirations, and tendency to engage in norm-violating acts.
    e. Early sexual activity is more common among young people who grow up in low-income families, where many of these factors may exist.
    f. Living in a hazardous neighborhood also increases the likelihood that teenagers will be sexually active, largely accounting for the high rate of premarital intercourse among African-American teenagers.
    g. Early, prolonged father absence predicts higher rates of intercourse and pregnancy among adolescent girls.
3. Contraceptive Use (p. 294)
    a. Adolescent contraceptive use has increased in recent years, but 27 percent of sexually active U.S. teenagers and 13 percent in Canada do not use contraception consistently.
    b. Adolescents' failure to apply their reasoning capacities to everyday situations may explain why many youths do not use contraception consistently.

c. Teenagers who lack the rewards of meaningful education and work are especially likely to engage in irresponsible sex, sometimes in exploitative relationships.
d. Teenagers who talk openly with their parents about sex are more likely to use birth control, but many parents do not engage in such discussions.
e. Sex education classes often provide incomplete or incorrect knowledge, and many teens do not know where to get birth control counseling and devices.

4. Sexual Orientation (pp. 294–296)
   a. About 2 to 3 percent of young people identify as lesbian, gay, or bisexual.
   b. Heredity makes an important contribution to homosexuality.
      (1) Identical twins are much more likely than fraternal twins to share a homosexual orientation; the same is true for biological as opposed to adoptive relatives.
      (2) Male homosexuality tends to be more common on the maternal than paternal side of families, suggesting that it might be X-linked.
   c. According to some researchers, certain genes may affect the level or impact of prenatal sex hormones, which modify brain structures in ways that induce homosexual feelings and behavior.
      (1) Both genetic and environmental factors, such as maternal exposure to very high levels of estrogens or androgens, can alter prenatal hormones.
      (2) Homosexual men also tend to be later in birth order and to have a higher-than-average number of older brothers.
   d. Stereotypes and misconceptions about homosexuality continue to be widespread.
      (1) Most homosexual adolescents are not "gender deviant" in dress or behavior.
      (2) About 50 to 60 percent of adolescents who report having engaged in homosexual acts identify as heterosexual.

F. Sexually Transmitted Diseases (p. 296)
1. Sexual active adolescents have the highest rates of sexually transmitted diseases, or STDs, of all age groups; one out of six sexually active teenagers contracts an STD each year.
2. STDs, left untreated, can lead to sterility and life-threatening complications.
3. The most serious STD is AIDS.
   a. In the United States, one-fifth of AIDS cases occur in young people between ages 20 and 29; in contrast, Canada has a low incidence of AIDS among people under age 30.
   b. Drug-abusing and homosexual adolescents account for most cases, but heterosexual spread of the disease has increased.
4. As a result of school courses and media campaigns, about 60 percent of middle school students and 90 percent of high school students are aware of the basic facts of AIDS, but most have limited information about other STDs and about how to protect themselves.

G. Adolescent Pregnancy and Parenthood (pp. 296–298)
1. Each year, about 900,000 U.S. teenage girls become pregnant, 30,000 of them younger than age 15.
2. The U.S. adolescent pregnancy rate is higher than that of most other industrialized countries, and about twice the Canadian rate, because of several factors:
   a. Effective sex education reaches too few teenagers.
   b. Convenient, low-cost contraceptive services for adolescents are scarce.
   c. Many families live in poverty, which encourages young people to take risks.
3. Because 40 percent of U.S. and 50 percent of Canadian teenage pregnancies end in abortion, the number of teenage births in North America is lower than it was 35 years ago.
4. However, teens who do give birth are far less likely to marry before childbirth.
   a. Today, 85 percent of teenage births were to unmarried females, compared with 15 percent in 1960.
   b. One out of five births to adolescents are repeat births.
   c. Only a small number of girls give up their infants for adoption.
5. Correlates and Consequences of Adolescent Parenthood (p. 297)
   a. Teenage parents are much more likely to be poor than agemates who postpone childbearing.
   b. A high percentage of out-of-wedlock births are to low-income minority teenagers—African-American, Native-American, Hispanic, and Canadian-Aboriginal.

c. After the birth of a child, adolescents' lives often worsen in at least three respects:
   (1) *Educational attainment:* Only about 70 percent of U.S. adolescent mothers graduate from high school, compared with 95 percent of those who wait to become parents.
   (2) *Marital patterns:* Teenage motherhood reduces the chances of marriage, and these mothers are more likely to divorce than their peers who delay childbearing.
   (3) *Economic circumstances:* Teenage mothers are likely to be on welfare or, if employed, to work at unsatisfying, low-paid jobs.

d. Because teenage girls often do not receive early prenatal care, their babies have high rates of prenatal and birth complications, especially low birth weight.

e. Compared to adult mothers, adolescent mothers know less about child development and interact less effectively with their babies.

f. If the teen mother finishes high school, avoids additional births, and finds a stable marriage partner, long-term disruptions are less severe.

6. Prevention Strategies (pp. 297–298)
   a. Preventing teenage pregnancy means addressing the many factors underlying sexual activity and lack of contraceptive use.
   b. Today, more effective programs teach adolescents skills for handling sexual situations, promote the value of abstinence to those who are not yet sexually active, and provide information about contraceptives and ready access to them.
   c. The most controversial aspect of adolescent pregnancy prevention involves providing easy access to contraceptives, but an abstinence-only focus has been shown to be ineffective in preventing sexual activity among those who have already had intercourse.
   d. In Canada and Western Europe, where contraceptives are available to teenagers and subsidized by universal health insurance, teenage sexual activity is no higher than in the United States—but pregnancy, childbirth, and abortion rates are lower.
   e. Teenagers who look forward to a promising future are far less likely to engage in early and irresponsible sex.

7. Intervening with Adolescent Parents (p. 298)
   a. Young parents need health care, encouragement to stay in school, job training, instruction in parenting and life-management skills, and high-quality, affordable child care.
   b. Adolescent mothers benefit from relationships with family members and other adults who are sensitive to their developmental needs.
   c. Fathers need encouragement to increase their financial and emotional commitment to the baby.
      (1) Effective interventions are those that legally establish paternity and child support, help fathers become financially self-sufficient, and give them training in parenting skills.
      (2) Teenage mothers who receive practical and emotional support from their child's father are more likely to sustain a relationship with him, which, in turn, predicts greater paternal involvement in caregiving.

H. Substance Use and Abuse (pp. 298–299)

1. By tenth grade, 40 percent of U.S. young people have tried cigarette smoking, 63 percent drinking, and 38 percent at least one illegal drug (usually marijuana)—figures that represent a substantial decline since the mid-1990s, probably resulting from greater parent, school, and media focus on the hazards of drug use.
2. In part, drug taking reflects the sensation seeking of the teenage years, and adolescents live in drug-dependent cultural contexts.
3. Cigarette and alcohol ads designed to appeal to teenagers also play a role.
4. The majority of substance *experimenters* are psychologically healthy, sociable, curious young people.
5. Poverty is linked to family and peer contexts that promote illegal drug use.
6. A minority of adolescent experimenters move from use to *abuse* of drugs.
7. Correlates and Consequences of Adolescent Substance Abuse (p. 299)
   a. In contrast to experimenters, drug abusers are seriously troubled adolescents who express their unhappiness through antisocial acts, often developing an impulsive, disruptive style in early childhood.

   b. Their drug taking starts earlier than other adolescents' and may have genetic roots, but it is also promoted by environmental factors, including low SES, family mental health problems, parental and older sibling drug abuse, lack of parental involvement, abuse, and poor school performance.
   c. Peer encouragement is a strong predictor of substance abuse, especially among teenagers with family problems.
   d. Adolescent substance abuse often has lifelong consequences, including higher rates of chronic anxiety, depression, antisocial behavior, divorce, and job loss.

8. Prevention and Treatment (p. 299)
   a. School and community programs that reduce drug experimentation typically teach adolescents skills for resisting peer pressure, emphasize health and safety risks of drug taking, and get adolescents to commit to not using drugs.
   b. Interventions that teach teenagers about the dangers of drugs and prevent them from harming themselves and others when they do experiment are essential.
   c. Preventing drug abuse requires different strategies, including working with parents and teaching at-risk teenagers strategies for handling life stressors.
   d. For adolescent drug abusers, family and individual therapy are usually needed, along with academic and vocational training to improve life success.
   e. Because even comprehensive programs have high relapse rates, one recommendation is to start treatment gradually, in order to increase young people's motivation to make lasting changes.

Cognitive Development

V. PIAGET'S THEORY: THE FORMAL OPERATIONAL STAGE (pp. 300–302)
   A. According to Piaget, around age 11 young people enter the **formal operational stage**, in which they develop the capacity for systematic, scientific thinking, coming up with new, more general logical rules through internal reflection.
   B. Hypothetico-Deductive Reasoning (pp. 300–301)
      1. In Piaget's view, adolescents become capable of **hypothetico-deductive reasoning**, a problem-solving strategy in which they begin with a *hypothesis,* a prediction about variables that might affect an outcome, and then *deduce* logical, testable inferences from that hypothesis, isolating and combining variables to see which of these inferences are confirmed in the real world.
      2. Unlike concrete operational children, who begin with reality in making predictions about a situation, adolescents are able to begin with possibility and proceed to reality, as in their approach to Piaget's famous *pendulum problem,* in which they try to figure out what influences the speed at which a pendulum swings through its arc.
   C. Propositional Thought (p. 301)
      1. **Propositional thought**, a second important characteristic of Piaget's formal operational stage, refers to adolescents' ability to evaluate the logic of propositions (verbal statements) without referring to real-world circumstances, in contrast to younger children, who can evaluate the logic of statements only by referring to real-world circumstances.
      2. Formal operational thought requires language-based and other symbolic systems that do not stand for real things, as well as verbal reasoning about abstract concepts.
   D. Follow-Up Research on Formal Operational Thought (pp. 301–302)
      1. Are Children Capable of Hypothetico-Deductive and Propositional Thinking? (p. 301)
         a. School-age children can understand hypotheses in simplified situations involving no more than two variables, but they cannot sort out evidence bearing on three or more variables at once.
         b. They also have difficulty explaining why a pattern of observations supports a hypothesis, even when they recognize the connection between the two.
         c. In an entirely verbal model, children have difficulty reasoning from premises that contradict reality or their own beliefs.
         d. Unlike adolescents, they have difficulty inhibiting knowledge that casts doubt on the truthfulness of hypothetical premises and, as a result, fail to grasp the *logical necessity* of propositional reasoning.

e. Gains in the capacity to analyze the logic of propositions occurs gradually from childhood on, calling into question the emergence of a discrete new stage of cognitive development at adolescence.

2. Do All Individuals Reach the Formal Operational Stage? (pp. 301–302)
    a. Even many well-educated adults have difficulty with formal operational reasoning.
    b. People are most likely to think systematically in situations in which they have had extensive experience, as supported by evidence that taking college courses leads to improvements in formal reasoning related to course content.
    c. In many village and tribal societies, formal operational tasks are not mastered at all, raising further questions about Piaget's stage sequence.
    d. Questions of how young people make the transition to formal operational thought have prompted many researchers to adopt an information-processing view.

VI. AN INFORMATION-PROCESSING VIEW OF ADOLESCENT COGNITIVE DEVELOPMENT (pp. 302–303)

A. Information-processing theorists refer to a variety of specific mechanisms:
    1. *Attention* becomes more selective.
    2. *Inhibition* improves, supporting gains in attention and reasoning.
    3. *Strategies* become more effective, improving storage, representation, and retrieval of information.
    4. *Knowledge* increases, easing strategy use.
    5. *Metacognition* expands, leading to new insights into effective strategies for acquiring information and solving problems.
    6. *Cognitive self-regulation* improves, yielding better moment-by-moment monitoring, evaluation, and redirection of thinking.
    7. *Speed of thinking and processing capacity* increase.

B. One of these mechanisms of change—*metacognition*—is central to adolescent cognitive development.

C. Scientific Reasoning: Coordinating Theory with Evidence (p. 302)
    1. The heart of scientific reasoning is coordinating theories with evidence.
    2. In experiments, the youngest participants (third grade) often ignored conflicting evidence or distorted it in ways consistent with their theory.
    3. The ability to distinguish theory from evidence and to use logical rules to examine their relationship in complex, multivariable situations improves from childhood into adolescence and adulthood.

D. How Scientific Reasoning Develops (pp. 302–303)
    1. Greater working-memory capacity permits a theory and the effects of several variables to be compared at once.
    2. Adolescents benefit from exposure to increasingly complex problems and instruction highlighting critical features of tasks and effective strategies.
    3. As a result, scientific reasoning is strongly influenced by years of schooling.
    4. Researchers believe that because sophisticated *metacognitive understanding* is at the heart of scientific reasoning, the ability to *think about* theories, *deliberately isolate* variables, and *actively seek* disconfirming evidence is rarely present before adolescence.
    5. Adolescents and adults vary widely in scientific reasoning skills, often applying logic more effectively to ideas they doubt than to those they favor.
        a. Scientific reasoning requires the metacognitive capacity to evaluate one's own objectivity.
        b. This flexible, open-minded approach is both a cognitive attainment and a personality disposition.
    6. Information-processing findings confirm that scientific reasoning develops gradually out of many specific experiences.

VII. CONSEQUENCES OF ADOLESCENT COGNITIVE CHANGES (pp. 303–305)

A. Self-Consciousness and Self-Focusing (pp. 303–304)
    1. As adolescents' ability to reflect on their own thoughts improves, along with physical and psychological changes, they start to think more about themselves.
    2. Followers of Piaget suggested that two distorted images of the relation between self and other appear.
        a. The **imaginary audience** refers to adolescents' belief that they are the focus of everyone else's attention and concern.

b. The **personal fable** is adolescents' belief that they are special and unique, so that others cannot possibly understand their thoughts and feelings; it may promote a sense of invulnerability to danger.

3. The imaginary audience and personal fable are strongest during early adolescence, and then decline.
4. Research confirms that these distorted visions of the self are an outgrowth of advances in perspective taking, leading young teenagers to be more concerned with what others think.

B. Idealism and Criticism (p. 304)

1. Because adolescents are able to think about possibilities, they can imagine an ideal world and want to explore alternative family, religious, political, and moral systems.
2. The disparity between adults' and teenagers' worldviews creates tension between parent and child as adolescents become fault-finding critics.
3. Teenage idealism and criticism are advantageous, overall, because through their awareness of others' strengths and weaknesses, adolescents develop a capacity to form lasting relationships and to work constructively for social change.

C. Decision Making (pp. 304–305)

1. Adolescents are able to handle cognitive tasks more effectively than younger children, but they often do not follow the steps of rational thinking: (1) identifying the pros and cons of each alternative, (2) assessing the likelihood of various outcomes, (3) evaluating their choice in terms of whether their goals were met, and, if not, (4) learning from the mistake.
2. Adults are better than adolescents at making decisions about hypothetical dilemmas and are less likely to fall back on intuitive judgments.
3. Teenagers find decision making difficult because they do not have sufficient knowledge to predict potential outcomes, and they often confront complex situations involving competing goals.
4. Adolescents may feel overwhelmed by their expanding range of options; when this happens, they resort to habit, act on impulse, or postpone decision making.
5. As they learn from their successes and failures, adolescents' decision-making confidence and performance improve.

VIII. LEARNING IN SCHOOL (pp. 305–310)

A. School Transitions (pp. 305–306)

1. Impact of School Transitions (p. 305)
   a. School transitions can create adjustment problems that lead to a decline in adolescents' grades with each school change.
   b. Tighter academic standards are partly responsible; other factors include less personal attention, more whole-class instruction, and less chance to participate in classroom decision making.
   c. Students must readjust their feelings of self-confidence and self-worth as school becomes more impersonal and academic expectations change.
   d. Distressed young people whose school performance drops sharply often show a persisting pattern of poor self-esteem, motivation, and achievement.
   e. For some, school transition initiates a downward spiral in academic performance and school involvement that leads to dropping out.
2. Helping Adolescents Adjust to School Transitions (pp. 305–306)
   a. School transitions often lead to environmental changes that fit poorly with adolescents' developmental needs, disrupting close relationships with teachers, emphasizing competition, reducing decision making, and interfering with peer networks at a time when all of these are important.
   b. Enhanced support from parents, teachers, and peers is important in easing the strain of school transition.
   c. Forming smaller units within larger schools can be helpful, as can homerooms in which teachers offer academic and personal counseling, and assignment of students to classes with a group of familiar peers or a constant group of new peers.
   d. Successful transitions are most likely to occur in schools that minimize competition and differential treatment based on ability.

B. Academic Achievement (pp. 306–308)
   1. Positive educational environments, both family and school, lead to personal traits that support achievement—intelligence, confidence in one's abilities, the desire to succeed, and high educational aspirations.
   2. Child-Rearing Practices (p. 306)
      a. Authoritative parenting is linked to achievement in adolescence for young people varying widely in SES.
      b. Authoritarian and permissive styles are associated with lower grades, and an uninvolved style predicts the poorest school performance.
      c. The link between authoritative parenting and academic competence is found in countries with diverse value systems.
   3. Parent–School Partnerships (pp. 306–307)
      a. High-achieving adolescents typically have parents who keep tabs on their child's progress, communicate with teachers, and make sure that their child is enrolled in challenging, well-taught classes.
      b. Creation of stronger home–school links can relieve some of the stress that exists for parents who live in low-income, high-risk neighborhoods.
   4. Peer Influences (p. 307)
      a. Adolescents whose parents value achievement are likely to choose friends who share those values.
      b. Peer support for high achievement also depends on the overall climate of the peer culture, which, for ethnic minority youths, is powerfully affected by the surrounding social order.
         (1) Discriminatory treatment by teachers and peers, often resulting from stereotypes, often trigger anger, anxiety, self-doubt, and declines in achievement among African-American adolescents.
         (2) Even middle-SES black teenagers may react against working hard, convinced that getting good grades will have little future payoff.
      c. In one study, poverty-stricken African-American teenagers were high-achieving and optimistic, with a belief that they could alter their social position through their own agency—a perspective that had come from parents, relatives, and teachers.
   5. Classroom Learning Experiences (pp. 307–308)
      a. In large, departmentalized secondary schools, many adolescents report that their classes lack warmth and supportiveness—a circumstance that dampens their motivation.
      b. Because of the uneven quality of instruction in American schools, a great many seniors graduate from high school poorly equipped with basic academic skills.
      c. By middle school, large numbers of poverty-stricken minority students have been placed in low academic tracks, compounding their learning difficulties.
      d. High school students are separated into academic and vocational tracks in virtually all industrialized nations, often by means of a national examination that fixes future possibilities for the young person.
      e. In contrast, educational decisions in North America are more fluid, but SES differences in educational quality and academic achievement result in a more drastic sorting process than in these other countries.
      f. Compared with other Western nations, the United States and Canada have a higher percentage of young people who regard themselves as educational failures and drop out of high school.

C. Dropping Out (pp. 308–310)
   1. In the United States and Canada, 11 percent of young people leave high school without a diploma, with a particularly high rate of dropout among low-SES ethnic minority youths, especially Hispanic and Canadian-Aboriginal teenagers.
   2. Dropouts have much lower literacy scores than high school graduates and lack the skills employers value; as a result, they are far less likely to be employed than are high school graduates who do not go to college.

3. Factors Related to Dropping Out (p. 308)
   a. Many dropouts are poor achievers who engage in many norm-violating acts.
   b. Many others have few behavior problems but simply experience academic difficulties and quietly disengage from school, becoming alienated from all aspects of school life.
   c. Students who drop out are more likely to have parents who are uninvolved in their education.
   d. Large, impersonal schools and classes, unsupportive teachers, and a lack of opportunities for active participation undermine the chances for success of academically marginal students.
   e. Students in general education and vocational tracks are three times more likely to drop out as those in a college preparatory track.
4. Prevention Strategies (pp. 308–310)
   a. High-quality vocational training that integrates academic and job-related instruction helps students see the relevance of what happens in the classroom to their future goals.
   b. Remedial instruction and counseling that offer personalized attention can help overcome the negative psychological effects of repeated school failure.
   c. Efforts must be made to address the many factors in students' lives related to leaving school early.
   d. Participation in extracurricular activities can draw some marginal students into the community life of the school.
5. Over the past 50 years, the percentage of North American young people completing high school by age 24 increased from less than 50 percent to nearly 90 percent.
6. About one-third of high school dropouts return on their own to finish their education within a few years.

LECTURE ENHANCEMENTS

LECTURE ENHANCEMENT 11.1
More on the Use of Performance-Enhancing Substances in Adolescence (pp. 285–286)

Time: 5–10 minutes

Objective: To highlight recommendations for identifying and treating users and potential users of performance-enhancing substances.

As noted in the text, some adolescents become so obsessed with physical prowess that they turn to performance-enhancing drugs. Although a wealth of research exists on the effects of performance-enhancing drugs on adults, few studies have focused on individuals younger than 18 years (American Academy of Pediatrics, 2005). Research with adult participants shows that many performance-enhancing substances, such as anabolic steroids and stimulants, pose serious health risks, particularly when used for long periods of time. Moreover, the health risks may be especially high for adolescents, who often feel invincible to the consequences of risky behavior.

The American Academy of Pediatrics (2005) provides the following recommendations for identifying and treating adolescent users and potential users of performance-enhancing substances:

1. Coaches and athletic trainers should strongly discourage the use of performance-enhancing substances.

2. Parents should educate themselves on the dangers of performance-enhancing substances and strongly discourage their children from using them.

3. Schools and sports organizations should not only discourage the use of performance-enhancing substances, but they should also incorporate this message into educational materials for parents, athletes, and coaches.

4. Instead of focusing on punitive interventions (for example, an athlete is suspended for several games after testing positive for steroids), educators and coaches should promote the importance of sound nutrition and exercise.

5. Instead of promoting the "win-at-all-costs" philosophy, coaches should focus on wholesome and fair competition. Moreover, the value of fair competition should be instilled early on—when children first become interested in sports and other competitive activities.
6. When adolescents admit to using performance-enhancing substances, they should be provided with unbiased medical information, including the benefits and risks associated with those substances. A physician should also assess for other high-risk behaviors and provide safer alternatives for improving athletic performance.
7. Parents, teachers, and coaches should reinforce and praise nonusers of performance-enhancing drugs and communicate openly about the dangers of these substances.

In small groups, have students review ecological systems theory (Chapter 1, pp. 19–21). How might intervening at various levels of the environment help prevent the use of performance-enhancing substances in teenagers?

American Academy of Pediatrics (2005). Policy statement: Use of performance-enhancing substances. *Pediatrics, 115,* 1103–1106.

LECTURE ENHANCEMENT 11.2
Factors Underlying Body Dissatisfaction in Adolescent Girls (pp. 290–291)

Time: 10–15 minutes

Objective: To highlight factors underlying body dissatisfaction in adolescent girls.

As noted in the text, adolescents with a distorted body image are at risk for serious eating disturbances. Although a negative body image does not always result in an eating disorder, a large percentage of adolescent girls engage in dieting and other weight-loss techniques in the hopes of becoming thinner. To better understand factors that underlie body dissatisfaction, Tiggemann, Gardiner, and Slater (2001) recruited 67 girls who were in their junior year of high school. Participants were not selected on the basis of an eating disorder or risk for an eating disorder. The researchers were simply interested in adolescent girls' beliefs and feelings about thinness and body satisfaction. Focus groups of 10 to 16 girls were held in high school classrooms and lasted approximately 50 minutes.

A moderator, who was also a clinical psychologist, attended each focus group and used four open-ended questions to guide the group discussion: "Why do women and girls wish to be thinner?" "Does indicating you want to be thinner mean that you are dissatisfied with your current size?" "Do guys like women as thin as women think guys like them to be?" "Is it OK to talk about these things as we have been doing today, or does it make things worse?" To help yield more in-depth responses, the moderator sometimes added transition questions, asked for clarification, or challenged statements. Each focus group was audio-recorded for later coding and analyses.

Results indicated that the media and the fashion industry contribute substantially to participants' desire to be thinner. Media portrayals of thin, attractive women led many of the participants to believe that thinness and attractiveness are the cultural norm. Interestingly, although the participants understood that media and fashion portrayals of women are unrealistic and are often manipulated by airbrushing and lighting, they continued to strive toward a thin ideal. The participants also indicated a desire for the kind of attention that thin, attractive women seem to attract. At the same time, though, they pointed out that this kind of attention does not usually lead to genuine friendships. Although participants felt they would feel more confident and self-assured if they were thinner, they realized that losing weight does not necessarily make a woman more confident. The majority of participants indicated that discussing beliefs and feelings about thinness was important. They stated that the discussion helped them understand that they are not alone in their desire to be thinner. It also allowed them to express their frustration about the media and fashion industry's portrayal of women.

Regarding men's perceptions of very thin women, the participants thought that men usually desire more voluptuous women. At the same time, this belief did not counteract their desire to be thinner. Perhaps the most important finding was that although many of the girls wished to be thinner, few of them reported being dissatisfied with their bodies. Therefore, a desire to lose weight is not necessarily associated with body dissatisfaction. Taken together, these findings indicate that the media and the fashion industry strongly influence adolescent girls' perceptions of thinness and ideal body size. However, the ambiguities in the participants' answers suggest that although adolescent girls desire thinness and attractiveness, they also realize that media and fashion images of women do not provide a realistic portrayal of the appearance of most women. Instead of waiting for eating disorders to develop, Tiggemann and colleagues (2001) suggest that schools capitalize on girls' understanding of the unreality of media and fashion portrayals. It is also important for girls to learn how to feel positive about themselves in other ways so that they do not equate thinness with happiness, confidence, or success.

As a class, discuss media and fashion images currently directed at adolescent boys and girls. What images have students recently encountered, and how might these images contribute to body satisfaction? Have students encountered any images that counteract cultural valuing of extreme thinness? Explain.

Tiggemann, M., Gardiner, M., & Slater, A. (2001). I would rather be a size 10 than have straight A's: A focus group study on adolescent girls' wish to be thinner. *Journal of Adolescence, 23,* 645–659.

LECTURE ENHANCEMENT 11.3
Promoting Adolescent Health and Well-Being (pp. 291–292)

Time: 10–15 minutes

Objective: To highlight strategies for promoting the health and well-being of adolescents.

Because many health-promoting and health-compromising behaviors begin in adolescence, the teenage years are an especially crucial time for health education. Call and collaborators (2002) propose the following strategies for increasing the health and well-being of adolescents:

1. Because leading causes of adolescent injury and mortality in industrialized nations are accidents, homicide, and suicide, most health care systems currently provide crisis care rather than preventive services. To facilitate a shift from crisis care to preventive care, communities and organizations must make health care resources, such as school-based health and social service programs, available to all adolescents. Non-school-based programs should be placed in easily accessible locations throughout the community.
2. Because teenagers in high-poverty, high-crime areas have few if any health and social services at their disposal, parents, educators, and community organizations must advocate for those services. Adolescents who have access to resources and to caring adults are more resilient than teenagers without such access.
3. Adolescents should be included in efforts to establish health education programs. Young people who help create and share responsibility for health programs are more likely to engage in health-promoting behavior.
4. Providing service learning opportunities, including volunteer work, enables adolescents to participate in their community, and helps them learn how to function effectively in the adult world.
5. Because adolescents spend a significant amount of time watching television and using computers, the media can be an effective tool for promoting healthy behavior. For example, television programs can highlight important adolescent concerns, such as resistance to peer pressure to drink alcohol or to have sex. Television characters that deal with difficult situations provide teenagers with positive models. Auahi Kore, an anti-tobacco media campaign in New Zealand, has substantially reduced adolescent smoking.
6. Although it is unlikely that dramatic shifts in the distribution of wealth will take place any time in the near future, new health-conscious policies may be a more readily obtainable goal. For example, the government heavily invests in numerous non-health-related policies, such as policies on education, commerce, housing, and military defense. Highlighting the expense of these non-health-related policies may encourage lawmakers to rethink current health policies, particularly when they consider the enormous cost of crisis care. After all, investing in the health and well-being of adolescents results in less expenditure in the future. Specifically, young people who establish healthy lifestyles early on tend to require less medical care later in

life. Moreover, adolescents ultimately represent the intellectual, educational, and economic resources of a nation. According to the United Nations Population Fund (2003), the consequences of not investing in adolescent health can be devastating for a nation's future well-being. For instance, early pregnancy and childbearing are linked to higher infant and maternal mortality, higher health care costs, higher welfare costs, underemployment, and reduced prospects for eradicating poverty. Sexually transmitted diseases overburden health care systems, and alcohol and drug abuse contribute to increased health care costs, unwanted pregnancies, and underemployment.

Call, K. T., Riedel, A. A., Hein, K., McLoyd, V., Petersen, A., & Kipke, M. (2002). Adolescent health and well-being in the twenty-first century: A global perspective. *Journal of Research on Adolescence, 12,* 69–98

United Nations Population Fund. (2003). State of world population 2003. Retrieved from http://www.unfpa.org/swp/2003/swpmain.htm.

LECTURE ENHANCEMENT 11.4
A Unique Approach to Correcting Common Thinking Errors in Adolescents (pp. 299–300)

Time: 10–15 minutes

Objective: To explore a game designed to exercise adolescents' reasoning and life skills.

The text mentions that at adolescence, young people first become capable of hypothetico-deductive reasoning. That is, when faced with a problem, they start with a general theory of all possible factors that might affect the outcome and deduce from it specific hypotheses (or predictions) about what might happen. Then they test these hypotheses in an orderly fashion to see which ones work in the real world. However, adolescents sometimes commit thinking errors when faced with a problem. These errors include self-centered thinking, minimizing or mislabeling situations, assuming the worst, and blaming others (Horn, Shively, & Gibbs, 2001).

In a unique approach to helping teenagers develop skills for correcting thinking errors, Horn, Shively, and Gibbs (2001) developed EQUIPPED for Life, a board game in which two to four players are presented with real-life scenarios pertaining to difficult situations. The players elect an adult or another individual who is familiar with the game as the group facilitator. The facilitator, along with other players who function as peer-helpers, guides each participant through various scenarios and helps identify thinking errors and propose more accurate and constructive responses. The goal of the game is to answer questions correctly in each of six areas: Community, Education, Employment, Daily Living, Relationships, and Substance Abuse, and to obtain two "EQUIP chips" from the facilitator for each of the six categories.

Players start by rolling the dice, and whoever rolls the highest number begins. Players then take turns rolling the dice and moving their game markers to the corresponding spaces on the game board. To earn an EQUIP chip, a player must land on a space that instructs him or her to select a Situation Card. Most of the Situation Cards present a scenario involving one of the thinking errors (Self-Centered, Minimizing/Mislabeling, Assuming the Worst, or Blaming Others). Others are "good deeds" and "bad deeds," which direct the player to move forward or backward on the board, to roll again, or to go to a specific space on the board. If a player draws a typical Situation Card, he or she must identify the thinking error presented on the card and may use the Thinking Error Card to help identify the particular error. Following identification of the thinking error and presentation of an accurate way to react in the situation, the facilitator and the other players determine whether the player accurately named and corrected the thinking error. If they determine that the player has successfully dealt with the situation, he or she earns an EQUIP chip. The first player to acquire all 12 EQUIP chips wins the game.

This game was designed to help adolescents of varying life experiences learn to think and act responsibly. It can be used as an enjoyable instructional tool or supplement in schools, in mental health facilities, and even in the correctional system. EQUIPPED for Life can be ordered from Research Press at *www.researchpress.com.*

Horn, M., Shively, R., & Gibbs, J. C. (2001). *EQUIPPED for Life: A Game for Helping Youth Think and Act Responsibly.* Champaign, IL: Research Press.

LEARNING ACTIVITIES

LEARNING ACTIVITY 11.1
"Facts on Puberty" Quiz (pp. 284–291)

Before introducing the text discussion on puberty, present students with the following exercise:

Directions: Read each of the following statements and indicate whether it is *True* (T) or *False* (F).

Statements:

_____ 1. Menarche takes place immediately before the peak of the height spurt.
_____ 2. In the sequence of pubertal events, the growth spurt occurs at approximately the same age for both boys and girls.
_____ 3. Both heredity and physical health contribute to pubertal growth.
_____ 4. Research indicates that adolescence is a period of storm and stress for most teenagers.
_____ 5. Both biological and social forces contribute to the experience of adolescence.
_____ 6. Girls adjust especially well to puberty when their fathers are aware of pubertal changes.
_____ 7. Compared to girls, boys tend to get less social support for the physical changes of puberty.
_____ 8. Most researchers agree that high sex hormone levels are primarily responsible for adolescent moodiness.
_____ 9. Psychological distancing between parents and children is normal during adolescence, and most parent–child conflict is mild.
_____ 10. Late-maturing boys and early-maturing girls tend to be popular, self-confident, and sociable.

Answers:

1. F
2. F
3. T
4. F
5. T
6. T
7. T
8. F
9. T
10. F

LEARNING ACTIVITY 11.2
Interviewing Parents and Grandparents About Secular Trends in Physical Growth (p. 287)

Have students interview parents and grandparents about their height and weight and the approximate age at which they reached adult stature. Girls might also ask their mothers and grandmothers to report how old they were when menarche occurred. To help interpret their findings, students should ask about diet and health during the childhood years and any other factors that parents and grandparents think might have influenced secular change. Data from the entire class can be pooled for an overall look at secular trends in physical growth.

LEARNING ACTIVITY 11.3
Making Naturalistic Observations of Young Adolescents (pp. 284–291)

To better understand the various aspects of adolescent physical development, students can visit a junior high school before or after school. Instruct them to watch for examples of developmental patterns discussed in the text—for example, sex differences in athletic skill, changes in body proportions during early adolescence, and the tendency among teenagers to seek companions whose level of biological maturity is similar to their own. After students have completed the activity, spend some class time discussing their observations.

LEARNING ACTIVITY 11.4
Evaluating the Role of Media in Teenage Girls' Views of Themselves (pp. 290–294)

About-Face is a San Francisco–based, nonprofit organization devoted to changing negative and distorted images of women in the media. Using media education, outreach, and activism, About-Face promotes self-esteem in girls and women of all ages, sizes, and racial backgrounds. Have students explore the website *http://www.about-face.org/* and respond to the following questions: What evidence is there for a connection between the media's depiction of women and low self-esteem, depression, and eating disorders? List five suggestions for empowering girls and women against negative media images. How hard is it to find positive images of women in the media? Do you think that the media also depict boys and men in an unfavorable and unrealistic fashion? Why or why not?

LEARNING ACTIVITY 11.5
Critiquing an Adolescent Magazine (p. 290)

Have students locate and critique a magazine geared toward adolescents using the following questions: Does the magazine primarily target teenage boys or girls? Is there an advice column in the magazine? If so, does the column provide advice about puberty or sexuality? Is the information consistent with research in the text? What types of images are portrayed in the magazines? Are the images supportive of healthy development? Why or why not? As a parent, would you encourage your children to read such magazines? Explain.

LEARNING ACTIVITY 11.6
Advice from the Popular Press Regarding Parent–Child Communication About Sexuality (pp. 292–298)

North American parents tend to give their children little information about sex. Although both parents and adolescents express a desire for open communication about sexual issues, parents often feel that they lack the knowledge and communication skills to talk openly about sex. One source of information for parents is the popular press. Magazines such as *Parents, Ladies' Home Journal*, and *Redbook* sometimes offer information on adolescent sexuality and advice for discussing sex with adolescents and younger children.

Ask students to locate one or two articles in the popular press that give parents information on adolescent sexuality or advice on discussing sex with their children. Next, have students critique the articles they find. For example, what topics are covered? Are values discussed in addition to the biological details of sex? Are the more difficult topics, such as homosexuality, contraception, and STDs, discussed? What is the quality of the information in the articles? Does the information seem accurate (supported by research in the text)? What specific advice, if any, is given for improving communication between parents and children? Are the articles culturally sensitive? Explain.

LEARNING ACTIVITY 11.7
Assessing Propositional Thinking (p. 301)

Have students locate two children (preferably a child under the age of 10 and an adolescent) and present the following statement: "If dogs are bigger than elephants and elephants are bigger than mice, then dogs are bigger than mice." Students should record each child's answer and compare it with research in the text. Did the younger child judge the statement to be false? What factors allow older children and adolescents to grasp the logical necessity of prepositional reasoning?

LEARNING ACTIVITY 11.8
Helping Adolescents Adjust to School Transitions (pp. 305–306)

Ask students to pretend they must speak to a group of parents and teachers about helping adolescents adjust to school transitions. Using research in the text as a guide, students should create a list of recommendations for both parents and teachers. What can be done to support adolescents who have an especially difficult time after a school transition?

LEARNING ACTIVITY 11.9
Analyzing Letters to the Editor in Junior High and High School Newspapers (pp. 305–306)

Have students obtain several copies of junior high and high school newspapers and read the "Letters to the Editor" section. Do any of the letters address problems associated with the transition to secondary school, such as increased whole-class instruction, less individualized attention, less chance to participate in classroom decision making, or overly strict, inflexible rules? Students should explain why teenagers react strongly to these issues, referring to developmental tasks of adolescence.

ASK YOURSELF . . .

REVIEW: Summarize the consequences of pubertal timing for adolescent development. (pp. 290–291)

The timing of puberty influences adolescent psychological adjustment. Early-maturing boys and later-maturing girls, whose appearance closely matches cultural ideals of physical attractiveness, have a more positive image, feel more self-confident, and hold more positions of leadership. In contrast, early-maturing girls and later-maturing boys, who fit in least well physically with peers, are more likely to experience emotional and social difficulties. Early-maturing girls, in particular, are prone to lasting difficulties.

APPLY: As a school-age child, Chloe enjoyed leisure activities with her parents. Now, as a 14-year-old, she spends hours in her room and resists going on weekend family excursions. Explain Chloe's behavior. (pp. 289–290)

Among nonhuman primates, the young typically leave the family around the time of puberty. The same is true in many nonindustrialized cultures. Departure of young people from the family is adaptive in that it discourages sexual relations between close blood relatives. But because children in industrialized societies remain economically dependent on parents long after they reach puberty, they cannot physically leave the family. Consequently, a modern substitute for physical departure seems to have emerged—psychological distancing. This may explain why Chloe prefers to spend so much time alone and no longer wants to join in weekend family activities.

REFLECT: Think back to your own reactions to the physical changes of puberty. Are they consistent with research findings? Explain. (pp. 288–289)

This is an open-ended question with no right or wrong answer.

REVIEW: Compare risk factors for anorexia nervosa and bulimia nervosa. How do treatments and outcomes differ for the two disorders? (pp. 291–292)

Forces within the person, the family, and the larger culture give rise to anorexia nervosa. The societal image of "thin is beautiful" contributes to the poorer body image of early-maturing girls, who are at greatest risk for anorexia. In addition, many anorexics have extremely high standards for their own behavior and performance, are emotionally inhibited, and avoid intimate ties outside the family. Consequently, these girls tend to be excellent students who are responsible and well-behaved—ideal daughters in many respects. Yet parent–adolescent interactions reveal problems related to adolescent autonomy. Often mothers of these girls have high expectations for physical appearance, achievement, and social acceptance and are overprotective and controlling; fathers tend to be emotionally distant. Instead of rebelling openly, anorexic girls seem to do so covertly—by fiercely pursuing perfection in achievement, respectable behavior, and thinness.

Twin studies show that bulimia, like anorexia, is influenced by heredity. Although bulimics share with anorexics a pathological fear of getting fat, they may have experienced their parents as disengaged and emotionally unavailable rather than controlling. Overweight and early puberty increase the risk. Some bulimics, like anorexics, are perfectionists. Others lack self-control not just in eating but also in other areas of their lives, engaging in petty shoplifting and alcohol abuse.

Because anorexic girls typically deny that any problem exists, treating the disorder is difficult. Hospitalization is often necessary to prevent life-threatening malnutrition. Common treatments include family therapy, as well as medication to reduce anxiety and neurotransmitter imbalances. Even so, only about 50 percent of anorexics fully recover. Bulimics, by contrast, generally feel depressed and guilty about their abnormal eating habits. As a result, bulimia is usually easier to treat than anorexia, through support groups, nutrition education, training in changing eating habits, and anti-anxiety, antidepressant, and appetite-control medication.

APPLY: After 17-year-old Veronica gave birth to Ben, her parents told her they didn't have room for the baby. Veronica dropped out of school and moved in with her boyfriend. A few months later, he left. Why are Veronica and Ben likely to experience long-term hardships? (pp. 296–298)

Teenage parents have both life conditions and personal attributes that interfere with their ability to parent effectively. They are far more likely to be poor than agemates who postpone childbearing, and their backgrounds often include low parental warmth and involvement, domestic violence and child abuse, repeated parental divorce and remarriage, adult models of unmarried parenthood, and residence in neighborhoods where these risks are typical. After the baby is born, adolescents' lives tend to worsen in at least three respects:

(1) *Educational attainment:* Only about 70 percent of U.S. adolescent girls who give birth before age 18 finish high school, compared with 95 percent of girls who wait to become parents.

(2) *Marital patterns:* Teenage motherhood reduces the chances of marriage. When these young mothers do marry, they are more likely to divorce than their peers who delay childbearing. As a result, they spend more of their parenting years as single parents.

(3) *Economic circumstances:* Many teenage mothers are on welfare. If they are employed, their limited education restricts them to unsatisfying, low-paid jobs. Adolescent fathers, too, are likely to be unemployed or to work at unskilled jobs, earning too little to provide their children with basic necessities.

Because teenage girls often do not get early prenatal care, their babies have high rates of prenatal and birth complications, especially low birth weight. Teenage mothers also know less about child development and interact less effectively with their babies than older mothers. Their children tend to score low on intelligence tests, achieve poorly in school, and engage in disruptive social behavior. Too often, the cycle of adolescent pregnancy is repeated in the next generation.

REFLECT: Describe your experiences with peer pressure to experiment with alcohol and drugs. What factors influenced your response? (pp. 298–299)

This is an open-ended question with no right or wrong answer.

REVIEW: Describe research findings that challenge Piaget's notion of a new, discrete stage of cognitive development at adolescence. (pp. 301–302)

Piaget believed that around age 11, young people enter the *formal operational stage,* a new stage in which they develop the capacity for abstract, systematic, scientific thinking. In contrast to children at the concrete operational stage, who can only "operate on reality," formal operational adolescents can "operate on operations," coming up with general logical rules through internal reflection, without the need for concrete things and events as objects of thought.

Piaget also believed that at adolescence, young people first become capable of *hypothetico-deductive reasoning.* When faced with a problem, they start with a *hypothesis,* or prediction about the variables that might affect an outcome. From the hypothesis, they *deduce* logical, testable inferences. By systematically isolating and combining variables, they discover which of their inferences are confirmed in the real world. Instead of starting with reality as concrete operational children do, their thinking starts with possibility and proceed to reality. Going along with this, in Piaget's scheme, adolescents become capable of *propositional thought*—the ability to evaluate the logic of propositions (verbal statements) without referring to real-world circumstances.

In fact, school-age children already show the glimmerings of hypothetico-deductive reasoning, although they are less competent at it than adolescents. In simplified situations involving only two possible causal variables, 6-year-olds understand that hypotheses must be confirmed by appropriate evidence. Similarly, when a simple set of premises runs contrary to real-world knowledge, even 4- to 6-year-olds are able to use propositional thought to reason logically in make-believe play.

In early adolescence, young people become better at both hypothetico-deductive reasoning and propositional thought. As they get older, they can handle problems that involve more complex sets of mental operations. They also become better able to explain the logical rules on which their reasoning is based. However, these capacities do not appear suddenly, around the time of puberty. Rather, gains occur gradually from childhood on. These findings call into question the emergence of a discrete new stage of cognitive development at adolescence.

APPLY: Thirteen-year-old Rosie had a crush on a boy who failed to return her affections. After her mother assured her that there would be other boys, Rosie snapped, "Mom! You don't know what it's like to be in love!" Which cognitive distortion of adolescence does Rosie's thinking illustrate? Explain. (pp. 303–304)

Rosie's thinking is an example of the *personal fable.* Because teenagers are so sure that others are observing and thinking about them, they develop an inflated opinion of their own importance. They start to feel that they are special and unique. Many adolescents view themselves as reaching great heights of glory and also, alternatively, as sinking to unusual depths of despair—experiences that others could not possibly understand. This is reflected in Rosie's comments to her mother: "You don't know what it's like to be in love!"

REFLECT: Do you recall engaging in idealistic thinking or poor decision making as a teenager? Describe examples. (pp. 304–305)

This is an open-ended question with no right or wrong answer.

REVIEW: List ways that parents can promote their adolescent's academic achievement, and explain why each is effective. (pp. 306–307)

Authoritative parenting, which combines acceptance and involvement with reasonable demands for maturity and gradual autonomy granting, is linked to achievement in adolescence, just as it predicts mastery-oriented behavior during the school years. Authoritative parents who engage in joint decision making with adolescents, gradually permitting more autonomy with age, have youngsters who achieve especially well. Warmth, open discussion, firmness, and monitoring of the adolescents' whereabouts and activities make young people feel cared about and valued, encourage reflective thinking and self-regulation, and increase awareness of the importance of doing well in school. These factors, in turn, are related to mastery-oriented attributions, effort, achievement, and high educational expectations. The authoritative style is linked to higher grades for young people varying widely in SES. Moreover, the connection between authoritative parenting and achievement is seen in countries with diverse value systems.

High-achieving students typically have parents who keep tabs on their child's progress, communicate with teachers, and make sure that their child is enrolled in challenging, well-taught classes. Parents who are in frequent contact with their child's school send a message to their teenager about the value of education, promote wise educational decisions, and model constructive solutions to academic problems.

APPLY: Tanisha is finishing sixth grade. She could either continue in her current school though eighth grade or switch to a much larger junior high school. What would you suggest she do, and why? (pp. 307–308)

Adolescents need school environments that are responsive to their expanding powers of reasoning and emotional and social needs. Those who attend large, departmentalized secondary schools often perceive their classes and teachers as lacking warmth and supportiveness. The structure of such schools also makes it difficult for teachers and students to get to know one another well.

However, an advantage of separate classes in each subject is that adolescents can be taught by subject-matter experts, who are more likely to encourage high-level thinking and to emphasize content relevant to students' experiences—approaches that promote interest, effort, and achievement. Therefore, if Tanisha is a high-achieving student with well-developed academic interests, the larger junior high school might offer valuable opportunities. But secondary school classrooms do not consistently provide challenging, interesting teaching. For most students, the advantages of attending a smaller school with more personal, flexible instruction outweigh the advantages of specialization at this age. Weighing all of these factors, Tanisha should most likely stay in her current school through eighth grade.

REFLECT: Describe your own experiences in making the transition to middle or junior high school and then to high school. What did you find stressful? What helped you adjust? (pp. 305–306)

This is an open-ended question with no right or wrong answer.

SUGGESTED STUDENT READINGS

Brown, J. D., Steele, J. R., & Walsh-Childers, K. (Eds.). (2002). *Sexual teens, sexual media.* Mahwah, NJ: Erlbaum. Examines the influence of the media on adolescent sexual attitudes, gender roles, sexual orientation, standards of beauty, and romantic relationships.

Carskadon, M. A. (2003). *Adolescent sleep patterns: Biological, social, and psychological influences.* New York: Cambridge University Press. A collection of chapters focusing on adolescent wake and sleep patterns, including the role of sleep deprivation in risky driving behavior, the effects of school and work on sleep habits, severe disturbances in adolescent sleep cycles, and benefits of starting school later in the day.

Hayward, C. (Ed.). (2003). *Gender differences at puberty.* New York: Cambridge University Press. An ecological examination of the effects of puberty, this book focuses on the impact of puberty on physical, social, and psychological development. Other topics include changes in body image, aggression, sexual abuse, and romantic relationships.

Ogbu, J. U. (2003). *Black American students in an affluent suburb: A study of academic disengagement.* Mahwah, NJ: Erlbaum. Explores factors that contribute to academic disengagement in black students of all socioeconomic backgrounds, including the impact of school race relations, discipline, culture, language, and peer relations.

TRANSPARENCIES

T-136 **Younger and Older Adolescents' Emotional Experiences Across the Week**
Figure 11.2 (p. 289)

T-141 **Teenage Pregnancy Rate in Eight Industrialized Nations**
Figure 11.4 (p. 296)

T-143 **Piaget's Pendulum Problem**
Figure 11.5 (p. 300)

T-144 **Which Features of These Sports Balls—Size, Color, Surface Texture, or Presence or Absence of Ridges—Influence the Quality of a Player's Serve?**
Figure 11.6 (p. 303)

T-149 **High School Graduation Rates in Ten Industrialized Nations**
Figure 11.8 (p. 308)

MEDIA MATERIALS

EXPLORING LIFESPAN DEVELOPMENT IN ACTION

Adolescence

This section opens with the dramatic physical changes of puberty, which lead to an adult-sized body and sexual maturity. When adolescents become sexually active without using contraception, the consequences can be profound, as Rhiannon and Joel's story reveals. After dating Joel for a year, Rhiannon discovered that she was pregnant. Joel and Rhiannon share their reactions to the pregnancy and describe how the arrival of their son, Jacob, has changed their lives. Ray and Laurie relate their concerns about the effect of adolescent parenthood on their son's future.

Next, the Observation Program turns to cognitive development. During adolescence, young people become better at thinking abstractly. Piaget's formal operational stage is illustrated through visits to high school social studies and math classes, where students engage in hypothetico-deductive reasoning and propositional thought.

During adolescence, peer groups become important contexts for social learning. The impact of puberty and of perspective taking on gender-role development in early adolescence is evident as eighth graders talk about their own and their peers' capacities and behaviors. For adolescent boys and girls alike, friendship plays an important role in the development of self-esteem and identity.

As adolescents' cognitive and social experiences expand, they think more about themselves. Teenagers combine their various personality traits into an organized self-concept, which provides a foundation for identity development. Jean, Phil, and Carla, high school seniors, discuss their experiences in constructing an identity. Mark, a college student, looks back on his struggle to formulate a sexual identity in adolescence. Best friends Mari and Sarah talk about the meaning and importance of friendship.

A WINDOW ON LIFESPAN DEVELOPMENT

A High School History Class

In this segment, high school students discuss the Protestant Reformation that took place in Europe in the sixteenth century. Martin Luther, a key figure in the Reformation, believed the Catholic Church to be corrupt. He was upset that the Church sold high-priced indulgences—tickets that ensured the buyer forgiveness of sins, participation in the grace of God, and freedom from purgatory. Luther published a list of grievances against the Church called the *Ninety-Five Theses*. In the list, Luther harshly criticized the Church's conduct and demanded reform. His actions eventually led to a split in the Catholic Church. Watch as students discuss Martin Luther and the Reformation. They not only express their own viewpoints but also engage in sophisticated debate with one another.

Friendship and Popularity: Mari and Sarah, Age 13

In this segment, Mari and Sarah discuss the meaning and importance of friendship and popularity. They begin by explaining how their friendship developed: They initially met at school and soon discovered they had similar interests and personalities. Sarah illustrates how adolescents regard intimacy and loyalty as important ingredients of friendship as she talks about how lies, dishonesty, and lack of communication can destroy a friendship. Next, Mari and Sarah give their perspectives on sex differences in friendship. Finally, the girls talk about cliques, crowds, and their perceptions of what makes people popular or unpopular. Notice how they mention various influences on clique and crowd membership, such as culture, parenting practices, and personality traits.

Identity and Relationships with Parents: High School Seniors

In this segment, a group of high school students discuss their identity development and talk about the role of parents in this developmental process. Notice how students credit their parents with their early identity and sense of self. However, they also point out that as they have grown and matured, their views have changed and are now quite different from those of their parents. The students mention peers, the desire to be an individual, and exploring others' viewpoints as important influences on their current identity.

VIDEOTAPES AND DVDs

Adolescence: Cognitive & Moral Development (1995, Magna Systems, 25 min.). This program examines changes in thinking and moral reasoning that accompany the physical changes of puberty. It discusses the cognitive developments of adolescence, including the capacity for logical, abstract thinking, the limitations of adolescent egocentrism, and the impact of schooling, home life, and the larger culture on adolescent cognitive processes.

Adolescence: Current Issues I (1995, Magna Systems, 32 min.). This program presents a realistic look at some of today's most serious teenage challenges—pregnancy, sexually transmitted diseases, sexual harassment and abuse, and alcohol and substance abuse. It uses insights from recognized authorities in the field of adolescent development and from teenagers themselves to give the viewer meaningful and constructive suggestions to meet these challenges.

Adolescence: Physical Growth & Development (1995, Magna Systems, 30 min.). This program looks at the physical changes that occur during puberty, including the impact of early or late maturation on the adolescent's self-concept. It also covers a number of problems associated with the teenage years—eating disorders, adolescent pregnancy, sexually transmitted diseases, and drug and alcohol use.

Adolescent Cognition: Thinking in a New Key (2004, Insight Media, 30 min.). This program explores the cognitive changes that occur during adolescence. David Elkind cites the work of Jean Piaget, Erik Erikson, and Erving Goffman as he examines the intellectual, emotional, and social consequences of the changes in thinking that characterize this period of life.

Assessment of Growth and Puberty (1993, Films Media Group, 20 min.). This program examines how measurements of physical growth are used to monitor a child or adolescent's overall well-being. The program provides information about the assessment of pubertal status and the correct techniques for evaluating a child's stature, body proportions, and growth rate.

Baby Love (1996, Films Media Group, 57 min.). This documentary looks at the issue of unintended teenage pregnancy through interviews with a diverse group of adolescent mothers, some as young as 13, who speak out on topics including love, virginity, sex, pregnancy, birth, parenting, their families, and their babies' fathers. Their own accounts of their experiences provide a compellingly personal view of this complex social problem. This program, which contains explicit language, is an indispensable resource for use in teen pregnancy prevention, intervention, and parenting programs. The program is a presentation of the Independent Television Service, with funding provided by the Corporation for Public Broadcasting.

Battling Eating Disorders (2006, Films Media Group/A Meridian Production, 29 min.). This program examines the impact of anorexia and other eating disorders on teenagers, especially young women, and explores their origins in issues of body image and self-esteem. Hosted by *The Sopranos'* Jamie-Lynn Sigler, a survivor of teenage anorexia, the program looks at the rise of so-called Pro-Ana websites, which promote anorexia, bulimia, and binge eating. It emphasizes the importance of identifying these disorders as actual diseases, not simply misguided lifestyle choices—a realization that is essential for effective treatment.

Body Image for Boys (2002, Films Media Group/A Cambridge Educational Production, 18 min.). This program explores some of the issues faced by young men today as idealized images of the male physique are widely promoted in the media, fostering a growing preoccupation with appearance among young men and teenagers and leading to a rise in anorexia and body dysmorphic disorder among men as well as women. The program presents the views of experts and of young patients dealing with problems that include steroid abuse, eating disorders, and exercise addiction.

Eating Disorders: The Inner Voice (2000, Films Media Group/A Cambridge Educational Production, 30 min.). This feature-style program is dedicated to demonstrating that eating disorders are not simply about the desire to be thin but, rather, are severe psychological disorders that take years to overcome and can have devastating physical consequences. Interviews with young survivors of anorexia nervosa, bulimia nervosa, and so-called exercise bulimia portray the physical and emotional suffering associated with these disorders. Experts from the fields of medicine, psychology, and nutrition talk about the various types of eating disorders, the risks for developing them, treatment options, and the definition of a healthy lifestyle.

Fat Like Me: How to Win the Weight War (2003, Films Media Group, 43 min.). This *ABC News* special looks at the causes of obesity from the viewpoint of nutritionists, psychologists, pediatricians, and other experts. The program explores the physical and emotional damage resulting from obesity and offers ideas for parents and schools to use as they work together to help children improve their health. Hidden-camera coverage documents a social experiment in which a slim teen who has been professionally made up to look obese is subjected to the type of abuse that is often directed at overweight people. The hidden-camera segment is followed by a discussion of the stigmatizing effects of intolerance. A teacher's guide is included.

Me and My Hormones (1996, Films Media Group, 45 min.). This program, an ABC *After School Special,* illustrates biological changes through the stories of women of three generations living in the same house. A daughter experiences menarche at the same time as her mother is going through menopause and her grandmother is preparing to move to a senior living community. The program shows how, in response to these changes, the three women recognize a need to support one another.

Not Exactly Nirvana: Young Women and Self-Esteem (1997, Aquarius Health Care Videos, 38 min.). This program focuses on the shifts in self-image that boys and girls experience during adolescence. The program illustrates how boys tend to continue to build confidence and self-esteem in the teenage years, while girls of a similar age are more likely to develop a poor self-image and low self-esteem. It offers suggestions for ways that young women can develop their self-esteem by setting and achieving goals, with an emphasis on participation in such activities as theater and sports.

Nutrition for Teens (2000, Films Media Group, 25 min.; not available in French-speaking Canada). In this program, a registered dietitian identifies the nutrients that are essential for adolescents to meet their physical, mental, and emotional needs. Healthy eating habits are identified and distinguished from unsafe "diets," and the causes, symptoms, and physical effects of eating disorders are explored. A supplement, including quizzes, goals, and objectives, is included.

Puberty (1996, Films Media Group/A BBC Production, 18 min.). This program examines the hormone-driven changes that occur in male and female adolescents as they reach physical, sexual, and emotional maturity. It includes a detailed examination of body changes in boys and girls, as well as topics that affect both sexes, such as acne, growth spurts, and the emergence of body hair. The program, which contains explicit language and material, also features microscopic, endoscopic, and thermal imaging of hormone crystals and components of the male and female reproductive systems.

The Science of Addiction (1999, Films Media Group, 17 min.). This program features the stories of four teenagers—Luis, Jennifer, Dan, and Mike—as they confront the addictions that have taken over their lives. Experts talk about the psychological, medical, and social aspects of chemical dependence. Computer animation and PET imaging are used to illustrate how drugs affect the chemistry of the brain.

Secret Life of the Brain, Episode 3: The Teenage Brain: A World of Their Own (2002, PBS Home Video, 60 min.). This program offers comfort to parents who are convinced their teenagers are different from other human beings. In fact, as the program illustrates, adolescents' brains really are different. The teenage brain is a work in progress, teeming with hormones, while the areas that guide reasoning and impulse control are still developing. The program shows why adolescents are especially susceptible to addiction and schizophrenia, two areas of research that can benefit from increased understanding of how the brain functions.

Sexually Transmitted Infections (2003, Films Media Group, 27 min.). This program demonstrates how teens can protect themselves from sexually transmitted infections (STIs) through an emphasis on prevention, including both abstinence and safe sex. Topics covered include the ways these infections are carried and spread, their symptoms, current testing procedures, available treatments, and advice for talking with a sexual partner about STIs. A 15-page facilitator's guide is included.

The Silent Hunger: Anorexia and Bulimia (1994, Films Media Group, 46 min.). This program attempts to define eating disorders and to identify their causes. It specifically investigates anorexia nervosa, bulimia nervosa, and binge-eating syndrome, using interviews with seven females who have suffered from eating disorders, the father of a woman who died as a result of such a disorder, and health professionals. In addition to the interviews, dramatic sequences are used to promote greater understanding of the issues and strong emotions associated with eating disorders.

Smoking Out the Truth: Teens and Tobacco (2006, Films Media Group/A Cambridge Educational Production, 24 min.). This program emphasizes the misconceptions and faulty reasoning that lead teenagers to start smoking or continue the habit. Through conversations with both smoking and nonsmoking students, it offers convincing rationales and workable strategies for quitting or abstaining. Topics covered include peer pressure, cigarette marketing and advertising schemes targeted at teens, the physical damage done by nicotine and tobacco, and the difficulty of quitting.

Spin the Bottle: Sex, Lies & Alcohol (2004, Media Education Foundation, 45 min.). This film examines the role of contemporary popular culture in glamorizing excessive drinking and other high-risk behaviors. Through numerous examples, it shows the difficulties students encounter as they navigate a cultural environment saturated with seductive media images that play a powerful role in linking gender identity and alcohol use. Through interviews with campus health professionals, the program vividly portrays the effects of drinking on student health and academic performance. Commentary by Jean Kilbourne (creator of the *Killing Us Softly* film series) and others focuses on the gender messages associated with different types of alcohol. *Spin the Bottle* concludes by offering some concrete strategies young people can use to counter media messages about alcohol.

The Strength to Resist: Media's Impact on Women and Girls (2000, Cambridge Documentary Films, 33 min.; formerly titled *Beyond Killing Us Softly: The Strength to Resist*). This film uses media clips to highlight the relationship between advertising images and the cultural obsession with dieting and thinness, especially among young women. With appearances by Carol Gilligan, Catherine Steiner-Adair, Gail Dines, and others, the film explores what it means to grow up in a society that bombards children and teens with images of "perfection," encouraging the belief that one's body size is a measure of self-worth. It also offers some possible solutions for young women—finding positive role models, being physically active, resisting stereotypical images, avoiding fashion media, and respecting those who have fought for women's rights. A study guide is available.

Teen Dads' Point of View (1994, Magna Systems, 40 min.). This program addresses teen pregnancy from the viewpoint of teenage fathers, who discuss their attitudes toward sex, birth control, pregnancy, and fatherhood. The program also explores changes in society's attitudes toward teen fathers, the societal cost of teen pregnancy, involvement of a new father, the importance of developing parenting skills, incentives for establishing paternity, and the legal responsibilities of the young father.

Teen Dreams (2001, Films Media Group/A Discovery Channel Production, 46 min.). Through a "first love" scenario that tells the story of 14-year-old Darren and 13-year-old Natalie, this program looks at the anatomical and physiological changes of puberty, including pimples, hormonal fluctuations, the development of body hair and body odor, and changes in body shape and in the vocal cords.

Teen Mothers (1999, Magna Systems, 26 min.). This program deals with the main issues surrounding teenage pregnancy—guilt, love, co-dependency, support, independence, the impact on the teen and her current family, and how to make realistic decisions for the future.

Teen Parents: Making It Work (1996, Films Media Group, 19 min.). This program profiles teenage parents raising their children in an urban setting, including both young couples and single parents. The program examines the factors that promote success in child rearing for teen parents, including love for their babies, self-respect, family support, and determination to succeed in all areas of their lives. It also looks at the stresses faced by teenage mothers living with their own parents, and offers advice on dealing with differences of opinion and well-intentioned interference. A profile of the Laurence G. Paquin School for Expectant Teen Mothers, in Baltimore, is included.

Teen Sex (2004, Films Media Group/A Discovery Channel Production, 46 min.). This program explores contemporary changes in sexual mores through interviews with teens 13 to 19, who talk about peer pressure, the double standard, media influence, sexual intercourse, oral sex, sexually transmitted diseases, birth control, pregnancy—and how these issues affect them and their families. The program, which contains mature themes and explicit language and imagery, presents onscreen statistics from the Kaiser Family Foundation to highlight important trends. It also includes interviews with parents and commentary by experts, including adolescent medicine specialist Gale Burstein, Leslee Unruh of the National Abstinence Clearinghouse, and *Seventeen* magazine editor Atoosa Rubenstein.

Young Men as Fathers: For Teens and Young Parents (2003, Films Media Group, 20 min.). In light of increasing evidence that involvement of both parents promotes children's emotional and physical development, this program is aimed at young men, especially teenage fathers. Through interviews in which teen fathers and other young men share their real-life experiences, the program highlights the important role of fathers in a child's life.

TEST BANK

MULTIPLE CHOICE

1) Sanga has started experiencing a flood of biological changes. At the end of these changes, she will have an adult-sized body and have reached sexual maturity. Sanga is
   A) starting puberty.
   B) beginning menarche.
   C) experiencing spermarche.
   D) developing an identity.

   Answer: A
   Page Ref: 282, 283
   Skill: Applied
   Objective: 11.1

2) According to G. Stanley Hall, adolescence is
   A) a period of calm before the storm of adulthood.
   B) concerned with physical but not emotional growth.
   C) the least important phase of development.
   D) an extremely turbulent phase of growth.

Answer: D
Page Ref: 283
Skill: Factual
Objective: 11.1

3) Margaret Mead viewed adolescent adjustment as heavily influenced by
   A) individual behavior.
   B) the social environment.
   C) Freudian impulses and desires.
   D) Piagetian cognitive operations.

Answer: B
Page Ref: 283
Skill: Factual
Objective: 11.1

4) Most researchers today agree that adolescence is
   A) biologically determined.
   B) socially determined.
   C) affected by biological, psychosocial, and social forces.
   D) not a distinct stage of human development.

Answer: C
Page Ref: 283–284
Skill: Factual
Objective: 11.1

5) Derek lives in the United States. Dala lives in a small tribal society in Brazil. Which of the following statements is correct?
   A) Derek's adolescence will start much earlier, but not last as long as Dala's.
   B) The period of adolescence should last roughly the same amount of time for both young people.
   C) Dala will experience a much longer period of adolescence than Derek.
   D) Derek will experience a much longer period of adolescence than Dala.

Answer: D
Page Ref: 284
Skill: Applied
Objective: 11.1

6) Which of the following statements is true?
   A) Boys reach puberty an average of two years earlier than girls do.
   B) Girls reach puberty an average of two years earlier than boys do.
   C) Boys and girls reach puberty at approximately the same time.
   D) Culture impacts whether boys or girls reach puberty first.

Answer: B
Page Ref: 284
Skill: Factual
Objective: 11.2

7) Eleven-year-old Ellen has hit a growth spurt and notices that she has developed underarm and pubic hair. Which of the following hormones is responsible for this change?
   A) estrogen
   B) testosterone
   C) adrenal androgens
   D) thyroxine
   Answer: C
   Page Ref: 284
   Skill: Applied
   Objective: 11.2

8) Which of the following would be the LAST to experience the growth spurt of puberty?
   A) hands
   B) feet
   C) legs
   D) torso
   Answer: D
   Page Ref: 284
   Skill: Conceptual
   Objective: 11.2

9) An increased number of red blood cells as well as larger skeletal muscles, hearts, and lung capacity are all reasons that
   A) boys need an extra two years of preadolescent growth.
   B) boys show superior athletic performance during the teenage years.
   C) girls need an extra two years of preadolescent growth.
   D) girls show superior athletic performance during the teenage years.
   Answer: B
   Page Ref: 285
   Skill: Factual
   Objective: 11.2

10) Which of the following statements is true of physical skill in adolescence?
   A) Boys and girls are evenly matched.
   B) Few girls perform as well as the average boy.
   C) Low-performing girls have skills equal to high-performing boys.
   D) Girls perform better in athletics until about age 15, when boys surpass them.
   Answer: B
   Page Ref: 285
   Skill: Factual
   Objective: 11.2

11) Todd is a star high school athlete, who has recently exhibited severe mood swings and aggressiveness. An initial health screening also indicates that Todd has acne and high blood pressure. Todd is exhibiting symptoms indicative of
   A) typical adolescent stress.
   B) lack of sleep.
   C) anabolic steroid use.
   D) a previously undetected traumatic brain injury, probably acquired during football.
   Answer: C
   Page Ref: 285
   Skill: Applied
   Objective: 11.2

12) Which of the following statements about adolescent physical fitness is INACCURATE?
A) In high school, only 55 percent of U.S. students are enrolled in physical education.
B) Athletics provide important lessons in teamwork, problem solving, and assertiveness.
C) Substantial physical activity in high school is not associated with any lifelong health benefits.
D) Sports and exercise influence cognitive development.
Answer: C
Page Ref: 286
Skill: Conceptual
Objective: 11.2

13) Twelve-year-old Doris has just started her first menstrual cycle. She is experiencing
A) spermarche.
B) menarche.
C) menopause.
D) this maturational process much later than the average North American female.
Answer: B
Page Ref: 287
Skill: Applied
Objective: 11.2

14) In girls, menarche occurs __________ the peak of the height spurt __________.
A) after; to ensure that the body is large enough for childbearing
B) after; because there isn't enough energy for menstruation while the body is growing rapidly
C) before; because breast development cannot occur while a female is menstruating
D) before; as menstruation is necessary to enhance bone development
Answer: A
Page Ref: 287
Skill: Factual
Objective: 11.2

15) In boys, the onset of puberty begins with
A) penile enlargement.
B) enlargement of the testes.
C) the appearance of pubic hair.
D) spermarche.
Answer: B
Page Ref: 287
Skill: Factual
Objective: 11.2

16) A teenage boy's first ejaculation is known as
A) testogenesis.
B) menarche.
C) spermarche.
D) spermuration.
Answer: C
Page Ref: 287
Skill: Factual
Objective: 11.2

17) The timing of menarche in girls is affected by
   A) society's attitudes toward sex.
   B) the girl's feelings about sex.
   C) the girl's feelings of self-esteem.
   D) the pubertal rise in body fat.

Answer: D
Page Ref: 287
Skill: Factual
Objective: 11.3

18) All of the adolescent girls below are the same age. Who will probably be the first to reach menarche?
   A) Tania, a long distance runner
   B) Brooke, who is overweight
   C) Imarin, who comes from a low-income family and is malnourished
   D) Marina, who suffers from frequent illness

Answer: B
Page Ref: 287
Skill: Applied
Objective: 11.3

19) The major factor that makes girls in one region of the world reach menarche earlier than those in another region is most likely their
   A) physical well-being.
   B) social attitudes.
   C) genetic differences.
   D) educational levels.

Answer: A
Page Ref: 287
Skill: Factual
Objective: 11.3

20) A secular trend in the timing of puberty is a tendency for
   A) boys to mature later than girls do.
   B) girls to mature earlier than their mothers.
   C) menarche to occur after the growth spurt.
   D) puberty to begin with breast enlargement.

Answer: B
Page Ref: 287
Skill: Factual
Objective: 11.3

21) During puberty, the neurons become more responsive to excitatory neurotransmitters. What effect does this have on adolescents?
   A) The typical brain functions that support planning and self-regulation are interrupted, resulting in an increase in "thrill-seeking" behaviors.
   B) They experience pleasurable stimuli less intensely, causing them to seek enhanced stimulation through artificial means (e.g., illicit drug use).
   C) They react more strongly to stressful events.
   D) Brain regulation of sleep is altered, resulting in a need for three to four additional hours of sleep per night.

Answer: C
Page Ref: 288
Skill: Factual
Objective: 11.4

22) Imagine that you are a high school principal who is cognizant of the changes in the adolescent brain's regulation of sleep. Assuming all of the options below are within your power, which are you most likely to implement to improve student performance?
A) Institute an afternoon siesta hour, modeled after Spanish tradition.
B) Start school an hour earlier in the mornings.
C) Administer any state- and federally required "high stakes" tests in the afternoon.
D) Increase the length of morning classes to coincide with the alertness cycles of teenagers.
Answer: C
Page Ref: 288
Skill: Applied
Objective: 11.4

23) Tammy has just experienced menarche and had a very negative reaction to it. Which of the following is likely to be true about Tammy?
A) Her mother told her in advance about menstruation.
B) Her father was informed about what was happening.
C) Her parents do not like to talk openly about menstruation.
D) Her school gave her information about sexual maturity.
Answer: C
Page Ref: 288
Skill: Applied
Objective: 11.5

24) Which of the following statements is correct?
A) Most boys brag about spermarche as a sign of approaching adulthood.
B) Most boys obtain information on spermarche from parents.
C) Boys get more social support for the physical changes of puberty than do girls.
D) Many boys report being unprepared for spermarche.
Answer: D
Page Ref: 288
Skill: Conceptual
Objective: 11.5

25) Fourteen-year-old Baska has just undergone a community-wide ceremony initiating him into adulthood. His responsibilities within his village will shift substantially as he takes a more active role in the hunt for food. He has just experienced a(n)
A) transition marker.
B) social institution.
C) initiation ceremony.
D) manhood ceremony.
Answer: C
Page Ref: 288–289
Skill: Applied
Objective: 11.5

26) Which of the following is an event that typically indicates partial adult status?
A) receipt of a driver's license
B) entering high school
C) beginning to date
D) menarche or spermarche
Answer: A
Page Ref: 289
Skill: Conceptual
Objective: 11.5

27) Which statement below most accurately reflects teenagers' emotional experiences?
   A) Adolescence is a time of deeper valleys and higher peaks in emotional experience.
   B) Adolescence is a period of relative calm, marked with infrequent emotional mood swings.
   C) Adolescence is a period of relative calm, but perceived as a period of storm and stress.
   D) While adolescents perceive their emotional peaks and valleys as being more extreme, they are actually consistent with those experienced by adults.

Answer: A
Page Ref: 289
Skill: Factual
Objective: 11.5

28) Silas, a 16-year-old male, is more likely to have positive emotions when he
   A) is involved in adult-structured activities.
   B) is spending time with peers.
   C) has just completed a difficult job successfully.
   D) is waiting quietly for someone else to do something.

Answer: B
Page Ref: 289
Skill: Applied
Objective: 11.5

29) In industrialized nations, children do not leave the family group at puberty, but they do trigger increased parent–child conflicts. This __________ is a modern substitute for the actual physical departure that takes place in nonindustrialized cultures.
   A) greatly under reported phenomenon
   B) highly stressful period
   C) psychological distancing
   D) assertion of adult roles by adolescents

Answer: C
Page Ref: 289
Skill: Factual
Objective: 11.5

30) Mr. and Mrs. Duran are having more frequent disagreements with their teenage daughter. If they argue over typical parent–adolescent issues, these disagreements are most likely
   A) over important values such as honesty or the importance of education.
   B) less intense than arguments over similar issues with their teenage son.
   C) the most intense when their viewpoint on a matter is actually relatively similar to that of their daughter's.
   D) on mundane, daily matters such as driving and curfew.

Answer: D
Page Ref: 289
Skill: Applied
Objective: 11.5

31) Child X is popular with agemates, holds many leadership positions in school, and is an athletic star. Child X displays characteristics consistent with
   A) an early-maturing girl.
   B) a late-maturing boy.
   C) an early-maturing boy.
   D) an early-maturing child of either sex.

Answer: C
Page Ref: 290
Skill: Applied
Objective: 11.6

52) Research has shown which of the following to be factors linked to the development of homosexuality?
   A) prenatal exposure to high levels of sex hormones
   B) a later birth order with higher-than-average number of sisters
   C) early interactions with homosexual adults
   D) a mother who smokes during pregnancy

Answer: A
Page Ref: 296
Skill: Conceptual
Objective: 11.9

53) Which of the following statements is a true statement regarding adolescents and homosexuality?
   A) Most homosexual adolescents are "gender-deviant" in the way they dress.
   B) Most homosexual adolescents are "gender-deviant" in the way they behave.
   C) Many heterosexual adolescents participate in homosexual acts.
   D) Attraction to members of the same sex is limited to gay and lesbian teenagers.

Answer: C
Page Ref: 296
Skill: Conceptual
Objective: 11.9

54) Within a group of 30 sexually active adolescents, about how many will contract an STD this year?
   A) 5
   B) 10
   C) 15
   D) 20

Answer: A
Page Ref: 296
Skill: Applied
Objective: 11.10

55) Roughly how many cases of AIDS originate during adolescence?
   A) 1 out of 2
   B) 1 out of 5
   C) 1 out of 10
   D) 1 out of 100

Answer: B
Page Ref: 296
Skill: Factual
Objective: 11.10

56) Many gay men and women first sensed their sexual orientation between the ages of __________ when they discovered __________.
   A) 6 and 12; their play interests were more like those of the other gender
   B) 12 and 14; strong attractions to members of the same sex
   C) 3 and 4; preference for their same-sex parent
   D) 6 and 12; preferences for quiet activities and hobbies

Answer: A
Page Ref: 295
Skill: Factual
Objective: Box SI: Gay, Lesbian, and Bisexual Youths

57) Homosexual adolescents and adults typically move through a three-phase sequence in coming out. Those three phases (in order) are
   A) questioning, information seeking, satisfaction.
   B) feeling different, confusion, self-acceptance.
   C) worry, self-acceptance, happiness.
   D) confusion, embarrassment, resignation.
   Answer: B
   Page Ref: 295
   Skill: Factual
   Objective: Box SI: Gay, Lesbian, and Bisexual Youths

58) Sienna is a 16-year-old who has reached self-acceptance about being a lesbian. The greatest predictor of her favorable adjustment will be
   A) the level of understanding and support provided by her parents.
   B) her friends' initial reactions to the news.
   C) the level of acceptance received from her peers.
   D) whether her school provides support for gay and lesbian students, either in the form of individual counseling or support groups.
   Answer: A
   Page Ref: 295
   Skill: Applied
   Objective: Box SI: Gay, Lesbian, and Bisexual Youths

59) Studies show that 90 percent of high school students are aware of the basic facts about AIDS
   A) but most believe that AIDS happens to "other people" and that they are somehow immune to its effects.
   B) but still believe that birth control pills provide some protection from STDs.
   C) and therefore take necessary precautions when engaging in sexual activities.
   D) but are poorly informed about how to protect themselves against other STDs.
   Answer: D
   Page Ref: 296
   Skill: Conceptual
   Objective: 11.10

60) Teenage pregnancies are a far greater problem today than several decades ago because
   A) the majority of pregnancies end in abortion.
   B) the stigma of teenage parenthood is much worse.
   C) adolescent parents are far less likely to marry, increasing the negative consequences for both mother and baby.
   D) federal benefits for teenage mothers have been cut drastically.
   Answer: C
   Page Ref: 296–297
   Skill: Factual
   Objective: 11.10

61) Which of the statements below is true of teenage mothers?
   A) They have fewer complications during pregnancy due to age.
   B) They are rarely on welfare.
   C) They are less likely to divorce if they do marry.
   D) They have a 30 percent likelihood of dropping out of school.
   Answer: D
   Page Ref: 297
   Skill: Conceptual
   Objective: 11.10

62) Compared with older mothers, teenage mothers
A) interact less effectively with their children.
B) are less likely to punish their children.
C) have more academically talented children.
D) are more likely to be Caucasian American.
Answer: A
Page Ref: 297
Skill: Factual
Objective: 11.10

63) Which of the following is typically a component of basic sex education programs, but does little to promote responsible sexual behavior?
A) teaching skills for handling sexual situations
B) promoting the value of abstinence to teenagers who are not yet sexually active
C) providing facts about anatomy and reproduction
D) providing information about contraceptives and easy access to them
Answer: C
Page Ref: 297
Skill: Conceptual
Objective: 11.10

64) Research indicates that easy access to contraceptives for teenagers results in
A) reduced pregnancy rates.
B) higher rates of sexual activity.
C) an increase in childbirth rates.
D) higher abortion rates.
Answer: A
Page Ref: 297
Skill: Conceptual
Objective: 11.10

65) Which substance do adolescents experiment with most during the teenage years?
A) cigarettes
B) alcohol
C) marijuana
D) cocaine
Answer: B
Page Ref: 298
Skill: Factual
Objective: 11.11

66) By the end of high school, over 50 percent of teenagers have experimented with illegal drugs. These numbers
A) are considered to be low estimates, as many teenagers do not accurately report their drug use.
B) show a substantial increase since the mid-1990s, despite decreased attention in the media.
C) are considered to be overly high estimates, as many teenagers "fake" data on questionnaires in an attempt to appear more involved than they really are.
D) represent a substantial decline since the mid-1990s, probably resulting from increased focus on the hazards of drug use.
Answer: D
Page Ref: 298
Skill: Factual
Objective: 11.11

67) Which of these is most likely to increase substance abuse among teenagers with family problems?
A) tendency of doctors to prescribe medications to treat children's problems
B) parental drug use
C) poor grades in school
D) peer encouragement
Answer: D
Page Ref: 299
Skill: Factual
Objective: 11.11

68) One recommendation provided in your text for treating teenage drug abusers is to
A) have them arrested so they can see the possible long-term consequences if they don't stop their drug use.
B) start treatment gradually, through support-group sessions that focus on reducing drug taking.
C) provide medical intervention, often in the seemingly contradictory form of drug therapy.
D) link them up with a group of other drug-abusing teens.
Answer: B
Page Ref: 299
Skill: Factual
Objective: 11.11

69) __________ adolescents are able to come up with new, general logical rules through internal reflection.
A) Concrete operational
B) Concrete propositional
C) Formal propositional
D) Formal operational
Answer: D
Page Ref: 300
Skill: Factual
Objective: 11.12

70) In preparing for a competition, 12-year-old Robi tries to think of all possible factors that might affect the distance that his remote-controlled car can jump off a ramp. He lists them and then tests them in an orderly fashion. Robi is using
A) hypothetico-deductive reasoning.
B) concrete propositional thought.
C) cognitive intuition.
D) operational thought.
Answer: A
Page Ref: 300
Skill: Applied
Objective: 11.12

71) Bonnie is concrete operational and Katie is formal operational. When asked to solve the pendulum problem, Bonnie will
A) be completely unable to solve the problem.
B) systematically test alternative hypotheses.
C) solve it intuitively, without experimentation.
D) unsystematically test some of the variables affecting the pendulum speed.
Answer: D
Page Ref: 300
Skill: Applied
Objective: 11.12

72) Teenagers Zia and Helena love to play word games, where they evaluate the logical validity of statements ("Most zups like to eat crups. Mup is a zup. Does Mup like to eat crups?"). They are able to do this without any reference to real-world circumstances. The girls are demonstrating
   A) propositional thought.
   B) hypothetico-deductive reasoning.
   C) the scientific method.
   D) cognitive intuition.
   Answer: A
   Page Ref: 301
   Skill: Applied
   Objective: 11.12

73) A researcher hides a poker chip in her hand and asks children to indicate whether this statement is true, false, or uncertain: "Either the chip is green or it is not green." A concrete operational child will say it is __________. A formal operational child will say it is __________.
   A) true; uncertain
   B) uncertain; true
   C) uncertain; false
   D) true; false
   Answer: B
   Page Ref: 301
   Skill: Factual
   Objective: 11.12

74) Six-year-old Tynnique is asked to evaluate evidence about a hypothesis. She will probably
   A) be unable even to understand this kind of problem.
   B) do as well as an adult if the researcher motivates her with candy.
   C) handle only problems that relate to her familiar world.
   D) deal with only one or two possible variables and be unable to deal with three or more.
   Answer: D
   Page Ref: 301
   Skill: Applied
   Objective: 11.13

75) Young children are unable to grasp the __________ of propositional reasoning—that the validity of conclusions drawn from premises rests on the rules of logic, not on real-world confirmation.
   A) obvious contradictions
   B) concrete examples
   C) logical necessity
   D) single foundation
   Answer: C
   Page Ref: 301
   Skill: Factual
   Objective: 11.13

76) Warren is 17 years old. When faced with propositional thought problems, he is likely to
   A) justify his answer using fictional or make-believe responses.
   B) use manipulatives to explain his answer.
   C) be unable to answer them, as this process does not become fully developed until the early twenties.
   D) justify his reasoning by explaining the rules on which it is based.
   Answer: D
   Page Ref: 301
   Skill: Applied
   Objective: 11.13

77) The primary factor that keeps college students and adults from displaying formal operational thinking in some situations is that
    A) they do not have enough experience in those situations.
    B) their cognitive development is delayed by biological factors.
    C) this kind of thinking is not especially useful in our society.
    D) there is a cultural stigma associated with formal operations.
    Answer: A
    Page Ref: 301
    Skill: Factual
    Objective: 11.13

78) Which individual is LEAST likely to master formal operational tasks at all?
    A) George, an American high school student
    B) Gus, a high school student in Tonga
    C) Ghenniaa, the chief of a tribal society in Tonga
    D) Grady, the custodian at George's high school
    Answer: C
    Page Ref: 301–302
    Skill: Applied
    Objective: 11.13

79) Which of the following explains the cognitive impact of increased processing capacity?
    A) Strategy use is decreased.
    B) More information can be held at once in working memory and combined into increasingly complex, efficient representations.
    C) Storage, representation, and retrieval of information is improved.
    D) Attention becomes better adapted to the demands of tasks.
    Answer: B
    Page Ref: 302
    Skill: Factual
    Objective: 11.14

80) Joshua is a third grader. When presented with conflicting evidence in a problem, he will probably
    A) pay close attention to conflicting evidence.
    B) distort the evidence so that it is consistent with his preferred theory.
    C) use logical rules to examine the situation.
    D) interpret evidence as multiple representations of "the way things are."
    Answer: B
    Page Ref: 302
    Skill: Conceptual
    Objective: 11.14

81) Researchers consider __________ to be at the heart of scientific reasoning.
    A) increased processing capacity
    B) an improved attention span
    C) strategy development
    D) metacognition
    Answer: D
    Page Ref: 302
    Skill: Factual
    Objective: 11.14

82) Adolescents develop scientific reasoning skills
A) in a non-sequential fashion.
B) by experimenting with various strategies, reflecting on and revising them, and then becoming aware of the nature of logic so they can apply it to new situations.
C) by consciously applying evidence from many specific experiences.
D) through direct instruction in the higher grades.
Answer: B
Page Ref: 303
Skill: Conceptual
Objective: 11.14

83) Although Suzanna desperately wants to learn how to dive, she refuses to practice at the pool because "everyone will be watching me and laugh because I'm the only one who can't do it." Her thinking reflects
A) the imaginary audience.
B) the personal fable.
C) idealism.
D) cognitive self-regulation.
Answer: A
Page Ref: 303
Skill: Applied
Objective: 11.15

84) The imaginary audience characteristic of adolescent thinking is most likely responsible for adolescents'
A) increased argumentativeness with their parents.
B) extreme sensitivity to public criticism.
C) greater willingness to engage in risky behavior.
D) ability to solve problems with many variables.
Answer: B
Page Ref: 303
Skill: Factual
Objective: 11.15

85) Carl is sure that his romantic passion for his girlfriend, his deep concern over the poor and homeless, and his poetic appreciation of nature are far beyond anything anyone has felt before. This thinking is characterized by
A) juvenile obsession.
B) cognitive dissonance.
C) the personal fable.
D) the imaginary audience.
Answer: C
Page Ref: 304
Skill: Applied
Objective: 11.15

86) Kasim takes more sexual risks, uses more drugs, and commits more delinquent acts than his peers. Which of the following sets of scores can contribute to this behavior?
A) low personal-fable, low sensation-seeking
B) high personal-fable, low sensation-seeking
C) low personal-fable, high sensation-seeking
D) high personal-fable, high sensation-seeking
Answer: D
Page Ref: 304
Skill: Applied
Objective: 11.15

87) Fourteen-year-old Liam has become increasingly critical of his parents and siblings, which has created a great deal of family tension. This is typical of the __________ that manifests during the development of abstract reasoning.

A) idealism
B) imaginary audience
C) personal fable
D) metacognition

Answer: A
Page Ref: 304
Skill: Applied
Objective: 11.15

88) Sixteen-year-old Asma and a group of friends are trying to decide whether to see a newly released movie tonight. The newspaper contains a review, complete with an informal survey of 50 people who saw the movie. Most of the viewers rated the movie very favorably. On the other hand, two of Asma's classmates saw it and said it was kind of boring. Based on information in your text, what will be the outcome of the group's decision-making process?

A) They will use data to decide and will choose to see the movie.
B) They will fall back on intuitive judgments and decide not to see the movie.
C) They will take a vote and go with the majority's wishes.
D) They will determine that the decision is too hard and choose to hang out at the mall instead.

Answer: B
Page Ref: 304
Skill: Applied
Objective: 11.15

89) What is one way to enhance a teenager's ability to make rational decisions?

A) Provide her with a large number of possible solutions to a problem.
B) Prompt her to think logically.
C) Make sure she understands the potential negative outcomes of a poor decision.
D) Provide her with only real-life, rather than hypothetical, decision-making opportunities.

Answer: B
Page Ref: 304
Skill: Conceptual
Objective: 11.15

90) You are on a committee charged with restructuring a school district to minimize the strain of school transitions in adolescents. Which of these should you recommend most?

A) Make sure academic expectations in junior high are tougher than in elementary school.
B) Encourage large classes to help shy students fit in better with their peers.
C) Cut back on extracurricular activities offered to avoid distracting students from their classes.
D) Assign new students to classes with several familiar peers or a constant group of new peers.

Answer: D
Page Ref: 305
Skill: Applied
Objective: 11.16

91) Barton Middle School tries to minimize competition between the students, and avoids differential treatment based on ability. Which of the following outcomes would you expect?
   A) Parents of high-achieving students will be upset at the lack of differentiated instruction for their children.
   B) Students will feel unchallenged and performance will decrease.
   C) Students will perceive the sensitivity and flexibility of their environment positively and will be less likely to exhibit problem behaviors.
   D) Students will say that they like the learning environment better, but no actual academic or behavioral gains will be evident.

Answer: C
Page Ref: 306
Skill: Applied
Objective: 11.16

92) Which parents will probably have teenagers with superior school performance?
   A) the Berrys, who have an authoritative parenting style
   B) the Roberts, who have an authoritarian parenting style
   C) the Kidmans, who have a permissive parenting style
   D) the Bates, who have an inconsistent parenting style

Answer: A
Page Ref: 306
Skill: Applied
Objective: 11.17

93) Which statement about parent-school partnerships is accurate?
   A) Home-school communication is less important during middle and high school than during the elementary years.
   B) High-achieving students typically have parents who keep tabs on their progress and communicate with teachers.
   C) Low-income parents are less interested in their children's school achievement than higher income parents.
   D) Increasing parent involvement in school governance can create tension when trying to balance the interests of both parties.

Answer: B
Page Ref: 306
Skill: Factual
Objective: 11.17

94) Research has shown that inner-city African-American adolescents who are high-achieving and optimistic about their futures in the face of peer pressures
   A) have an unrealistic world view.
   B) developed the philosophy that injustice can be overcome through discussions with parents, relatives, and teachers.
   C) are targets of school violence.
   D) tend to complete high school, but drop out of college.

Answer: B
Page Ref: 307
Skill: Factual
Objective: 11.17

95) Which group of students is most likely to experience poor mastery of basic skills due to underfunded schools, outdated equipment, and shortages of textbooks?
   A) low-income ethnic minority students
   B) high school students
   C) students in small, departmentalized schools
   D) students in rural and remote regions of the country

Answer: A
Page Ref: 307
Skill: Factual
Objective: 11.17

96) The open, flexible system for making educational decisions for students in North America
   A) results in fewer low-income students being placed in lower course levels or tracks.
   B) is impacted by SES to the degree that it more drastically sorts students than systems in other countries.
   C) is being emulated by countries that currently use a national examination to determine high school course placements.
   D) was initially devised in an attempt to better serve students with mild cognitive disabilities.

Answer: B
Page Ref: 308
Skill: Factual
Objective: 11.17

97) The dropout rate from American high schools is highest for teenagers who are
   A) Hispanic.
   B) white.
   C) African-American.
   D) Asian-American.

Answer: A
Page Ref: 308
Skill: Factual
Objective: 11.18

98) Typically, parents of students who drop out of high school
   A) try to encourage achievement but don't know how.
   B) show little involvement in their children's education.
   C) successfully completed high school themselves.
   D) have serious emotional and personality problems.

Answer: B
Page Ref: 308
Skill: Factual
Objective: 11.18

99) Students placed in vocational tracks
   A) are much more likely to graduate from high school than those placed in lower-level academic tracks.
   B) are less likely to finish high school, as they are often hired without a diploma as a result of business internships.
   C) are three times more likely to drop out than students in college preparatory tracks.
   D) generally choose these classes because they are more interesting and stimulating than academic courses.

Answer: C
Page Ref: 308
Skill: Factual
Objective: 11.18

100) Luigi is a marginal high school student who wants to be a car mechanic and who sees schoolwork as a waste of time. He would probably benefit most from
A) being given more homework as punishment.
B) expulsion from school until his attitude improves.
C) strict teachers who make sure he drills on the basic skills.
D) a combination of vocational training and academic work.
Answer: D
Page Ref: 308
Skill: Applied
Objective: 11.18

101) Which of these is generally most helpful in keeping potential dropouts in school?
A) remedial instruction with social support
B) greater emotional distance from their teachers
C) cutting back on job-related instruction
D) putting them in larger classes
Answer: A
Page Ref: 309
Skill: Factual
Objective: 11.18

102) Which activity would have the most lasting and positive impact on 16-year-old Jason's life?
A) an after-school program that matches adolescent tutors with elementary students from low-income backgrounds
B) playing ping-pong at the YMCA
C) a video game tournament sponsored by a local youth recreation center
D) watching TV with his friends
Answer: A
Page Ref: 309
Skill: Applied
Objective: Box LS: Extracurricular Activities

103) Extracurricular activities have the greatest benefit for youths with academic, emotional, and social problems when
A) they have a trusting relationship with an activity adviser who validates their skills and strengthens their motivation.
B) the activities are provided at little or no cost to students.
C) the activities occur not only after school, but on weekends as well.
D) they incorporate counseling services for both students and families.
Answer: A
Page Ref: 309
Skill: Factual
Objective: Box LS: Extracurricular Activities

104) The most powerful influence on extracurricular involvement is
A) the school's win/loss sports record.
B) small school size.
C) the variety of opportunities available for both academic and sports pursuits.
D) funding for after-school activities.
Answer: B
Page Ref: 309
Skill: Factual
Objective: 11.18

105) The good news about American high school dropouts is that about one-third of them
   A) compete successfully for rewarding, well-paying jobs.
   B) are happily married and satisfied with their lives.
   C) advance rapidly in their careers, though they must start low.
   D) return on their own to finish their education within a few years.

Answer: D

Page Ref: 310

Skill: Factual

Objective: 11.18

ESSAY

106) List the five basic tasks of adolescence.

Answer: Accept one's full-grown body.
Acquire adult ways of thinking.
Attain greater independence from one's family.
Develop more mature ways of relating to peers of both sexes.
Begin to construct an identity (a secure sense of who one is in terms of sexual, vocational, moral, ethnic, religious, and other life values and goals).

Page Ref: 283

107) Describe the major changes in the brain during adolescence.

Answer: Brain-imaging research reveals continued pruning of unused synapses in the cerebral cortex, especially in the frontal lobes—the "governor" of thought and action. In addition, growth and myelination of stimulated neural fibers accelerate, strengthening connections among various brain regions—especially the frontal lobes and other areas, which attain rapid communication. This sculpting of the adolescent brain supports diverse cognitive advances, including attention, planning, capacity to integrate information, and self-regulation. In addition, neurons become more responsive to excitatory neurotransmitters during puberty. As a result, adolescents react more strongly to stressful events and also experience pleasurable stimuli more intensely.

Page Ref: 287–288

108) Describe girls' reactions to menarche and boys' reactions to spermarche during puberty. What factors influence the way adolescents respond?

Answer: Today, girls commonly react with "surprise," undoubtedly due to the sudden onset of the event. Otherwise, they typically report a mixture of positive and negative emotions. Yet wide individual differences exist that depend on prior knowledge and support from family members. For girls who have no advance information, menarche can be shocking and disturbing. Today, few are uninformed, a shift that is probably due to modern parents' greater willingness to discuss sexual matters and more widespread health education classes. Almost all girls get some information from their mothers. And girls whose fathers are told about pubertal changes adjust especially well, perhaps reflecting a family atmosphere that is highly understanding and accepting of physical and sexual matters.

Boys' responses to spermarche reflect mixed feelings. Virtually all boys know about ejaculation ahead of time, but many say that no one spoke to them before or during puberty about physical changes. Usually they get their information from reading material. Even boys who had advance information often say that their first ejaculation occurred earlier than they expected and that they were unprepared for it. As with girls, boys who feel better prepared tend to react more positively. Few boys tell anyone about spermarche.

The experience of puberty is affected by the larger culture in which boys and girls live. Many tribal and village societies celebrate puberty with an *initiation ceremony,* a ritualized announcement to the community that marks an important change in privilege and responsibility. Consequently, young people know that pubertal changes are honored and valued in their culture. In contrast, Western societies grant little formal recognition to movement from childhood to adolescence or from adolescence to adulthood. The absence of a widely accepted marker of physical and social maturity makes the process of becoming an adult especially confusing.

Page Ref: 287

109) Describe the impact of puberty on parent–child interaction and the adaptive value of this change in adolescents' relationships with their parents.

Answer: Many studies show that puberty is related to a rise in parent–child conflict. Researchers believe the association may have some adaptive value. Among nonhuman primates, the young typically leave the family group around puberty. The same is true in many nonindustrialized cultures. But because children in industrialized societies remain economically dependent on parents long after puberty, they cannot leave the family. Consequently, a modern substitute for physical departure seems to have emerged—psychological distancing between parents and children. As children become physically mature, they demand to be treated in adultlike ways. Adolescents' new powers of reasoning may also contribute to a rise in family tensions. Parent–adolescent disagreements focus largely on mundane, day-to-day matters—driving, dating partners, curfews, and the like. But beneath these disputes lie serious concerns: parental efforts to protect teenagers from harm. Most disputes are mild. In reality, parents and adolescents display both conflict and affection, and tend to agree on the more important values.

Page Ref: 289–290

110) Mr. and Mrs. Faber wonder what they should do to have a healthy discussion of sexuality with their teenage daughter. What can you recommend?

Answer: Answers should include information from the *Applying What We Know: Communicating with Adolescents About Sexual Issues* box on page 293.

Foster open communication.
Use correct terms for body parts.
Use effective discussion techniques.
Reflect before speaking.
Keep conversations going.

Page Ref: 293

111) What are the three primary factors that heighten the numbers of adolescent pregnancies in North America?

Answer:
1. Effective sex education reaches too few teenagers.
2. Convenient, low-cost contraceptive services for adolescents are scarce.
3. Many families live in poverty, which encourages teenagers to take risks.

Page Ref: 296

112) Describe the three areas in the lives of pregnant teenagers that tend to worsen after the baby is born.

Answer: The lives of pregnant teenagers are often troubled in many ways, and after the baby is born, their circumstances tend to worsen in at least three respects:

- *Educational attainment.* Giving birth before age 18 reduces the likelihood of finishing high school. Only 70 percent of adolescent mothers graduate, compared with 95 percent of girls who wait to become parents.
- *Marital patterns.* Teenage motherhood reduces the chances of marriage. When these mothers do marry, they are more likely to divorce than are their peers who delay childbearing. Consequently, teenage mothers spend more of their parenting years as single parents.
- *Economic circumstances.* Many teenage mothers are on welfare. If they are employed, their limited education restricts them to unsatisfying, low-paid jobs. Many adolescent fathers, too, are unemployed or work at unskilled jobs. Usually they earn too little to provide their children with basic necessities.

Page Ref: 297

113) Briefly discuss why pregnant teenage girls often experience birth complications, and the concerns regarding their parenting skills and subsequent impact on their children.

Answer: Many pregnant teenage girls do not receive early prenatal care, so their babies have high rates of prenatal and birth complications—especially low birth weight. Compared with adult mothers, adolescent mothers know less about child development and interact less effectively with them. Their children tend to score low on intelligence tests, achieve poorly in school, and engage in disruptive social behavior. Too often, the cycle of adolescent pregnancy is repeated in the next generation.

Page Ref: 302

Pubertal Timing

1. Describe the effects of maturational timing on the following groups of adolescents. (p. 290)

   Early-maturing boys: ______

   Late-maturing boys: ______

   Early-maturing girls: ______

   Late-maturing girls: ______

2. Cite two factors that contribute to boys' and girls' adjustment to early versus late pubertal maturation. (p. 290)

   A. ______

   B. ______

3. What is *body image*? How does pubertal timing affect body image? (p. 290)

   A. ______

   B. ______

4. Describe the importance of physical status in relation to peers for early and late maturers. (p. 290)

   Early maturers: ______

   Late maturers: ______

5. Discuss the long-term consequences of early and late maturation. (pp. 290–291)

   Early maturation: ______

   Late maturation: ______

Health Issues

Nutritional Needs

1. True or False: Of all age groups, adolescents are the most likely to skip breakfast, consume empty calories, and eat on the run. (p. 291)

2. List two factors that are associated with consumption of high-fat foods and soft drinks. (p. 291)

   A. ______

   B. ______

3. What factor strongly predicts healthy eating in teenagers? (p. 291)

____

Eating Disorders

1. What three factors put adolescents at high risk for serious eating problems? (p. 291)

   A. ______________________________

   B. ______________________________

   C. ______________________________

2. Describe characteristics of *anorexia nervosa*. (p. 291)

   ____

   ____

   ____

3. Cite forces within the person, the family, and the larger culture that give rise to anorexia nervosa. (pp. 291–292)

   Individual: ______________________________

   ____

   Family: ______________________________

   ____

   Culture: ______________________________

   ____

4. Why is treating anorexia nervosa so difficult? (p. 292)

   ____

   ____

   ____

5. Describe characteristics of *bulimia nervosa*. (p. 292)

   ____

   ____

   ____

6. True or False: Bulimia is far less common than anorexia nervosa. (p. 292)

7. How are bulimics similar to anorexics? How are they different? (p. 292)

   Similar: ______________________________

   Different: ______________________________

Sexual Activity

1. Explain how hormonal changes contribute to an increased sex drive in adolescence. (p. 292)

   ____

   ____

   ____

2. Why do many parents avoid meaningful discussions about sex? (p. 293)

3. True or False: Adolescents tend to receive contradictory messages about sex from their parents and the media. Explain your answer. (p. 293)

4. Describe trends in the sexual behavior of adolescents in the United States and Canada. (pp. 293–294)

5. True or False: American youths tend to begin sexual activity at a younger age than their Canadian and Western European counterparts. (p. 293)

6. Cite at least six factors that are linked to early and frequent teenage sexual activity. (p. 294)

   A.

   B.

   C.

   D.

   E.

   F.

7. Why do many sexually active adolescents fail to use contraception consistently? (p. 294)

8. What factors increase the likelihood that teenagers will use birth control? (p. 294)

9. Explain how heredity might contribute to homosexuality. (p. 296)

10. True or False: Most gay, lesbian, and bisexual youths are "gender deviant" in dress or behavior, meaning they dress and behave quite differently than their heterosexual peers. (p. 296)

Social Issues: Gay, Lesbian, and Bisexual Youths: Coming Out to Oneself and Others

1. True or False: In North America, homosexuals are rarely stigmatized. (p. 295)
2. Describe the three-phase sequence adolescents go through in coming out to themselves and others. (p. 295)

   A. ____

   ____

   B. ____

   ____

   C. ____

   ____

3. For most gay and lesbian individuals, a first sense of their sexual orientation appears between the ages of __________ and __________. In what context does this commonly occur? (p. 295)

   ____

   ____

4. What are some potential outcomes for adolescents who are extremely troubled or guilt-ridden about their sexual orientation? (p. 295)

   ____

   ____

5. What factors increase the likelihood that gay and lesbian youths will reach self-acceptance? (p. 295)

   ____

   ____

6. Explain how coming out can enhance development of gay and lesbian adolescents. (p. 295)

   ____

   ____

Sexually Transmitted Diseases

1. True or False: Adolescents have the highest rates of sexually transmitted diseases (STDs) of all age groups. (p. 296)
2. What are the consequences of untreated STDs? (p. 296)

   ____

3. By far, the most serious STD is __________. (p. 296)
4. True or False: It is at least twice as easy for a female to infect a male with any STD, including AIDS, as it is for a male to infect a female. (p. 296)

Adolescent Pregnancy and Parenthood

1. True or False: The adolescent pregnancy rate in Canada is nearly double that of the United States. (p. 296)
2. List three factors that heighten the incidence of adolescent pregnancy. (p. 296)

   A. ______

   B. ______

   C. ______
3. Why is teenage pregnancy a much greater problem today than it was 35 years ago? (pp. 296–297)

   ______

   ______
4. Describe common background characteristics of teenage parents. (p. 297)

   ______

   ______

   ______
5. Summarize the consequences of adolescent parenthood in the following areas: (p. 297)

   Educational attainment: ______

   ______

   Marital patterns: ______

   ______

   Economic circumstances: ______

   ______
6. Cite a birth complication that is common among babies of teenage mothers. (p. 297)

   ______
7. List three common characteristics of children born to adolescent mothers. (p. 297)

   A. ______

   B. ______

   C. ______
8. What factors protect adolescent parents and their children from long-term difficulties? (p. 297)

   ______

   ______

   ______
9. List three components of effective sex education programs. (p. 297)

   A. ______

   B. ______

   C. ______

10. Cite the most controversial aspect of adolescent pregnancy prevention. (p. 297)

____

11. Efforts to prevent adolescent pregnancy and parenthood must go beyond improving sex education to build ____________ and ____________. (p. 298)

12. What are some characteristics of effective interventions for adolescent parents? (p. 298)

____

____

____

____

13. Nearly half of young fathers visit their children during the first few years after birth, and contact usually (diminishes / increases) over time. (p. 298)

Substance Use and Abuse

1. By tenth grade, ____________ percent of U.S. young people have tried cigarette smoking, ____________ percent drinking, and ____________ percent at least one illegal drug. Canadian rates of teenage alcohol and drug use are (similar / much lower). (p. 298)

2. Cite factors that may explain recent trends in adolescent substance use. (p. 298)

____

____

____

3. True or False: Teenagers who experiment with alcohol, tobacco, and marijuana are headed for a life of addiction. (p. 298)

4. How do experimenters differ from drug abusers? (p. 298)

____

____

5. What environmental factors are associated with adolescent drug abuse? (p. 299)

____

____

____

6. List three lifelong consequences of adolescent drug abuse. (p. 299)

   A. ____

   B. ____

   C. ____

7. List three characteristics of successful drug prevention programs. (p. 299)

   A. ____

   B. ____

   C. ____

Cognitive Development

Piaget's Theory: The Formal Operational Stage

1. Summarize the basic differences between concrete and formal operational reasoning. (p. 300)

Hypothetico-Deductive Reasoning

1. What is *hypothetico-deductive reasoning*? (p. 300)

2. Describe adolescents' performance on Piaget's *pendulum problem.* (pp. 300–301)

Propositional Thought

1. Define *propositional thought,* and provide an example. (p. 301)

   A.

   B.

2. True or False: Piaget maintained that language plays a more central role in children's than in adolescents' cognitive development. (p. 301)

Follow-Up Research on Formal Operational Thought

1. Cite examples illustrating that school-age children show signs of *hypothetico-deductive reasoning* and *propositional thought* but are not as competent as adolescents. (p. 301)

   Hypothetico-deductive reasoning:

   Propositional thought:

2. True or False: Hypothetico-deductive reasoning and propositional thought appear suddenly, around the time of puberty. (p. 301)

3. What is one reason why many adults are not fully formal operational? (p. 301)

4. True or False: In many villages and tribal societies, formal operational tasks are not mastered at all. Explain your answer. (pp. 301–302)

____

____

An Information-Processing View of Adolescent Cognitive Development

1. List mechanisms of cognition change according to information-processing theorists. (p. 302)

   A. ____

   B. ____

   C. ____

   D. ____

   E. ____

   F. ____

   G. ____

2. Which mechanism is central to adolescent cognitive development? (p. 302)

____

Scientific Reasoning: Coordinating Theory with Evidence

1. How does scientific reasoning change from childhood into adolescence and adulthood? (p. 302)

____

____

How Scientific Reasoning Develops

1. Identify three factors that support adolescents' skill at coordinating theory with evidence. (p. 302)

   A. ____

   B. ____

   C. ____

2. Scientific reasoning is (strongly / weakly) influenced by years of schooling. (p. 302)

3. True or False: Like Piaget, information-processing theorists maintain that scientific reasoning results from an abrupt, stagewise change. Briefly explain your response. (p. 303)

____

____

Consequences of Adolescent Cognitive Changes

Self-Consciousness and Self-Focusing

1. What developmental changes contribute to adolescents' ability to think more about themselves? (p. 303)

____

____

____

2. Describe two distorted images of the self and others that appear during adolescence. (pp. 303–304)

   Imaginary audience: ______________________________

   ____

   Personal fable: ______________________________

   ____

3. When are the imaginary audience and personal fable the strongest? (p. 304)

   ____

4. How do gains in perspective taking contribute to adolescents' distorted visions of the self? (p. 304)

   ____

   ____

Idealism and Criticism

1. How are *idealism* and *criticism* advantageous to teenagers? (p. 304)

   ____

   ____

Decision Making

1. List four components of decision making. (p. 304)

   A. ______________________________

   B. ______________________________

   C. ______________________________

   D. ______________________________

2. True or False: When making decisions, adolescents, more often than adults, fall back on well-learned, intuitive judgments. (p. 304)

3. Why is decision making so challenging for adolescents? (pp. 304–305)

   ____

   ____

   ____

   ____

Learning in School

School Transitions

1. With each school change, adolescents' grades (decline / increase). Why is this so? (p. 305)

   ____

   ____

   ____

2. Cite adjustment problems that can occur with school transitions. (p. 305)

   ____

   ____

3. Which adolescents are at greatest risk for developing self-esteem and academic difficulties during school transitions? (p. 305)

____

4. List four environmental changes during school transitions that fit poorly with adolescents' developmental needs. (p. 305)

   A. ____

   B. ____

   C. ____

   D. ____

5. Discuss ways that parents, teachers, and peers can ease the strain of school transitions. (p. 306)

____

____

____

Academic Achievement

1. How do authoritative, authoritarian, permissive, and uninvolved child-rearing styles contribute to adolescent academic achievement? Which style is the most effective, and why? (p. 306)

   Authoritative: ____

   Authoritarian: ____

   Permissive: ____

   Uninvolved: ____

   Most effective: ____

2. How do parent–school partnerships foster academic achievement? (pp. 306–307)

____

____

3. What role do peers play in academic achievement? (p. 307)

____

____

4. How does the surrounding peer climate and social order influence ethnic minority youths' academic achievement? (p. 307)

____

____

____

5. Compare the academic progress of students who are assigned to a college preparatory track with those who are assigned to a vocational or general education track. (pp. 307–308)

   College: ____

____

   Vocational/General Education: ____

____

6. True or False: Among the industrialized countries, only the United States and Canada assign high school students into academic and vocational tracks. (p. 308)

Dropping Out

1. List two consequences of dropping out of school. (p. 308)

   A. ______________________________

   ____

   B. ______________________________

   ____

2. Cite characteristics of students who are at risk for dropping out of high school. (p. 308)

   ____

   ____

   ____

3. How does family background contribute to dropping out of school? (p. 308)

   ____

   ____

   ____

4. List four strategies for helping teenagers who are at risk for dropping out of high school. (pp. 308–309)

   A. ______________________________

   B. ______________________________

   C. ______________________________

   D. ______________________________

5. Over the past half century, the percentage of American and Canadian adolescents completing high school has (increased / decreased) steadily. (p. 310)

A Lifespan Vista: Extracurricular Activities: Contexts for Positive Youth Development

1. What types of extracurricular activities promote diverse academic and social skills and have a lasting positive impact on adjustment? (p. 309)

   ____

   ____

2. Cite benefits of extracurricular involvement that extend into adult life. (p. 309)

   ____

   ____

3. True or False: Adolescents who spend many afternoons and evenings engaged in unstructured activities resemble adolescents who engage in structured, goal-oriented activities in adjustment outcomes. (p. 309)

4. Which teenagers are especially likely to benefit from extracurricular participation? (p. 309)

   ____

PUZZLE 11.1

Across

1. First menstruation
3. __________ sexual characteristics: features visible on the outside of the body that serve as signs of sexual maturity but do not involve reproductive organs
5. Growth __________: rapid gain in height and weight during adolescence
6. Personal __________: adolescents' belief that they are special and unique and that others cannot understand their thoughts and feelings
8. __________ nervosa: eating disorder in which individuals go on eating binges followed by deliberate vomiting, other purging techniques, and strict dieting
9. __________ nervosa: eating disorder in which individuals starve themselves because of a compulsive fear of getting fat
11. __________ thought: type of formal operational reasoning in which adolescents evaluate the logic of verbal statements without referring to real-world circumstances
13. In Piaget's __________ operational stage, adolescents develop the capacity for abstract, scientific thinking.
14. __________ trend: change in body size and rate of growth from one generation to the next

Down

2. __________-deductive reasoning: formal operational problem-solving strategy in which adolescents begin with a general theory of all possible factors that could affect an outcome and deduce specific hypotheses, which they test systematically
4. Period of development in which the individual crosses the dividing line between childhood and adulthood
5. First ejaculation of seminal fluid
7. __________ audience: adolescents' belief that they are the focus of everyone else's attention and concern
10. Body __________: conception of and attitude toward one's physical appearance
11. __________ sexual characteristics: physical features that involve the reproductive organs
12. Biological changes at adolescence that lead to an adult-sized body and sexual maturity

CROSSWORD PUZZLE SOLUTION

PUZZLE 11.1

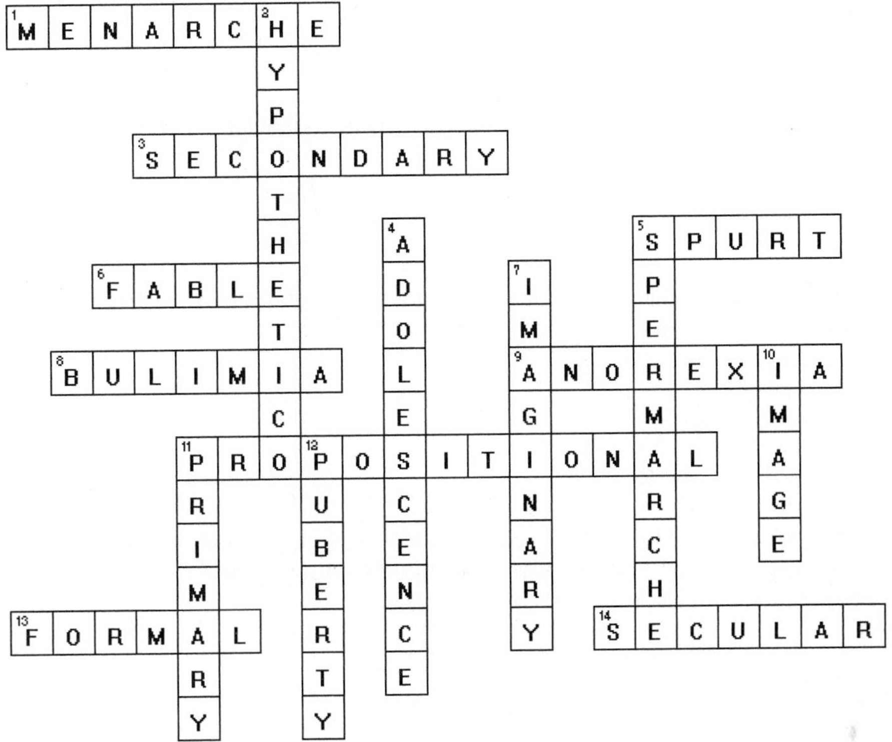

PRACTICE TEST #1

1. The beginning of adolescence is marked by (p. 283)
   a. the tenth birthday.
   b. becoming a teenager.
   c. puberty.
   d. adulthood.

2. The first outward sign of puberty is the rapid gain in height and weight known as the (p. 284)
   a. growing phase.
   b. adolescent surge.
   c. expansion stage.
   d. growth spurt.

3. Girls, who have been advanced in physical maturity since the prenatal period, reach puberty, on average, (p. 284)
   a. two years earlier than boys.
   b. six years earlier than boys.
   c. at the same time as boys.
   d. two years later than boys.

4. Physical growth in adolescence (p. 285)
   a. occurs at a slow, steady pace.
   b. follows the cephalocaudal trend that is also characteristic of infancy and childhood.
   c. leads to large differences in the body proportions of boys and girls.
   d. causes boys to add more fat, while girls add more muscle.

5. Nature delays sexual maturity in girls until (p. 287)
   a. pubic and underarm hair appears.
   b. the girl's body is large enough for childbearing.
   c. the secular trend has taken place.
   d. the stage of menopause.

6. Changes in the brain during adolescence (p. 288)
   a. are less extensive than were previously believed.
   b. play a role in teenagers' drive for novel experiences.
   c. allow teenagers to get along with very little sleep.
   d. cause a decrease in the ability to experience pleasurable stimuli, which in turn leads to moodiness.

7. Adolescent moodiness is generally (p. 289)
   a. strongly linked to higher pubertal hormonal levels.
   b. the result of alcohol or drug abuse.
   c. no different from moodiness in adults.
   d. linked to negative life events.

8. Beneath most parental–adolescent disputes about mundane, day-to-day matters lie parental efforts to (p. 290)
   a. protect teenagers from harm.
   b. control teenagers' unruly behavior.
   c. initiate psychological distancing.
   d. develop teenagers' powers of reasoning.

9. In contrast to those with anorexia, adolescents with bulimia nervosa (p. 292)
   a. do not have a pathological fear of getting fat.
   b. feel guilty about their eating habits.
   c. are afraid of becoming too thin.
   d. do not want help for their problem.

10. Which of the following factors is linked to increased contraceptive use among sexually active adolescents? (p. 294)
    a. Having sexual contact with multiple partners
    b. Imitating the sexually responsible role models seen in many prime-time TV shows
    c. Being able to talk openly with parents about sex and contraceptives
    d. Participating in sex education courses

11. Why do adolescents have higher rates of STDs than any other age group? (p. 296)
    a. Most teens have limited understanding of many STDs and are poorly informed about how to protect themselves.
    b. Teenagers are biologically ill-equipped to fight off many of these aggressive diseases.
    c. Only a very small percentage of high school students are aware of basic facts about AIDS.
    d. Contraceptives are not available to most teenagers.

12. Adolescent mothers (p. 297)
    a. are just as likely as other adolescent girls to finish high school.
    b. usually have a good understanding of child development.
    c. tend to have children who achieve poorly in school and who engage in disruptive social behavior.
    d. rarely experience complications of pregnancy or birth.

13. Research on adolescent drug use and abuse shows that (p. 298)
    a. the majority of adolescents completely abstain from using drugs and alcohol.
    b. many adolescents who engage in limited experimentation with drugs and alcohol are psychologically healthy, sociable, and curious individuals.
    c. experimentation with drugs often leads to long-term abuse and dependency.
    d. parents and teachers should not worry about drug experimentation because it is a normal part of adolescent development.

14. A researcher hides a poker chip in her hand and asks participants to indicate whether the following statement is true, false, or uncertain: "Either the chip in my hand is green or it is not green." An adolescent responds by using __________ to conclude that the "either-or" statement must be true. (p. 301)
    a. hypothetico-deductive reasoning
    b. propositional thought
    c. concrete operational reasoning
    d. relativistic reasoning

15. The adolescent capacity for scientific reasoning (p. 302)
    a. develops as an abrupt, stagewise change, similar to earlier Piagetian stages.
    b. results from an increase in working-memory capacity, regardless of years of schooling or other experiences.
    c. develops out of many specific experiences that require children and adolescents to match theories against evidence and evaluate their thinking.
    d. is a purely cognitive attainment that is unrelated to the individual's personality.

16. Thirteen-year-old Peter has become extremely self-conscious because he believes he is the focus of everyone else's attention and concern. Peter's distorted view is called (p. 303)
    a. the imaginary audience.
    b. the personal fable.
    c. propositional thought.
    d. metacognitive reasoning.

17. Adolescent idealism often leads teenagers to be (p. 304)
    a. more cooperative at home.
    b. better students at school.
    c. more realistic in their evaluations of others.
    d. more critical of parents and siblings.

18. Students are at especially great risk for academic and social difficulties after a school transition if they (p. 305)
    a. move from a larger school to a smaller one.
    b. had very high grades in their old school.
    c. have to cope with additional life transitions at the same time.
    d. come from a K–8 school.

19. A(n) __________ parenting style predicts higher grades for adolescents of varying SES. (p. 306)
    a. uninvolved
    b. permissive
    c. authoritarian
    d. authoritative

20. Approximately __________ of school dropouts return to finish their secondary education within a few years. (p. 310)
    a. one-quarter
    b. one-third
    c. 50 percent
    d. 65 percent

PRACTICE TEST #2

1. Margaret Mead was the first researcher to demonstrate that adolescent adjustment is greatly influenced by (p. 283)
    a. the age at which children reach puberty.
    b. social and cultural forces.
    c. diet and exercise.
    d. biological predispositions.

2. Side effects of steroid use include (p. 285)
    a. lack of body hair.
    b. low blood pressure.
    c. passive behavior.
    d. mood swings.

3. In boys, the first sign of puberty is (p. 287)
    a. enlargement of the penis.
    b. emergence of facial and body hair.
    c. enlargement of the testes.
    d. deepening of the voice.

4. Delayed menarche in poverty-stricken regions of the world reflects (p. 287)
    a. the role of physical well-being in pubertal development.
    b. the effects of emotional stress.
    c. a secular change in pubertal timing.
    d. the effects of overweight and obesity due to an unhealthy diet.

5. Compared to school-age children and adults, adolescents (p. 289)
    a. experience decreased moodiness.
    b. report less favorable moods.
    c. have more stable moods.
    d. are more likely to report negative mood during times of a day spent with friends.

6. Many studies show that puberty is related to a rise in parent–child (p. 289)
   a. conflict.
   b. interaction.
   c. closeness.
   d. interdependency.

7. Parent–adolescent conflicts typically focus on (p. 290)
   a. substance abuse.
   b. mundane, day-to-day matters such as driving or curfews.
   c. early sexual activity.
   d. long-term goals such as college or vocational training.

8. Compared with their on-time and late-maturing agemates, early-maturing girls usually report (p. 290)
   a. a more positive body image.
   b. a less positive body image.
   c. an indifferent attitude toward their body.
   d. a healthier outlook on puberty.

9. Which of the following statements about anorexia and bulimia is true? (p. 292)
   a. Bulimia is more common than anorexia nervosa.
   b. Individuals with bulimia rarely feel depressed or guilty about their eating habits.
   c. Neither anorexia nor bulimia is influenced by heredity.
   d. Most individuals with anorexia only worsen their health by refusing to exercise.

10. Mothers of girls with anorexia tend to be (p. 292)
    a. obese.
    b. overprotective and controlling.
    c. uninvolved.
    d. uninterested in physical appearance.

11. Which of the following statements about adolescent sexual activity is true? (p. 294)
    a. Adolescent contraceptive use has increased in recent years.
    b. A recent trend toward liberal sexual attitudes has resulted in a greater frequency of premarital sex.
    c. Females tend to have their first sexual intercourse earlier than males.
    d. Income level is unrelated to amount or type of adolescent sexual activity.

12. In North America, which of the following risky behaviors is engaged in by the highest percentage of students at the end of high school? (p. 298)
    a. heavy drinking during the past two weeks
    b. ingestion of at least one highly addictive and toxic substance
    c. regular cigarette smoking
    d. experimentation with illegal drugs

13. In Piaget's famous *pendulum problem,* children at the concrete operational stage (p. 300)
    a. perform better than either older or younger children.
    b. cannot separate the effects of each variable.
    c. usually notice variables that are not immediately suggested by the concrete materials of the task.
    d. do not acknowledge the difference in string lengths.

14. The thinking of many college students and adults is not fully formal operational because (p. 301)
    a. they lack the types of experiences necessary for solving formal operational tasks.
    b. they are not motivated to solve formal operational tasks.
    c. only the most intelligent people reach the formal operational stage.
    d. they are more interested in socializing than thinking.

15. Which of the following statements reflects the imaginary audience? (p. 303)
    a. "I don't care if my new haircut is bad. I'm going to the party anyway."
    b. "I can't go to the party with a huge pimple on my cheek! Everyone will make fun of me!"
    c. "My parents don't understand how hard school is for me!"
    d. "No one will care if I can't afford a new dress for the prom. I'll just wear the same one I wore last year."

16. In decision making, adolescents (p. 304)
    a. outperform adults, making good use of their newly developed ability to think rationally and evaluate various alternatives.
    b. are more likely than adults to suggest seeking advice in solving a real-world problem.
    c. are more likely than adults to fall back on well-learned intuitive judgments.
    d. are especially good at predicting potential outcomes because of their growing capacity to think about possibilities.

17. When schools minimize competition and differential treatment based on ability, (p. 306)
    a. many otherwise competitive students develop a feeling of ineptitude.
    b. their orderly atmosphere is replaced with a feeling of anarchy.
    c. students in middle and junior high school are less likely to feel angry and depressed.
    d. those with greater abilities are stifled, leading to a decline in their abilities.

18. Which of the following supports academic achievement in adolescence? (p. 307)
    a. authoritarian parenting
    b. reduced parental involvement in school-related issues
    c. having close friends who value school achievement
    d. large, departmentalized secondary schools

19. Typically, parents of students who drop out of school (p. 308)
    a. encourage achievement but just aren't successful.
    b. completed high school themselves.
    c. have serious emotional problems.
    d. show little involvement in their teenagers' education.

20. Among adolescents, the most powerful influence on involvement in extracurricular activities is (p. 309)
    a. small school size.
    b. academic achievement.
    c. level of SES.
    d. a mentoring program.

POWERPOINT SLIDES

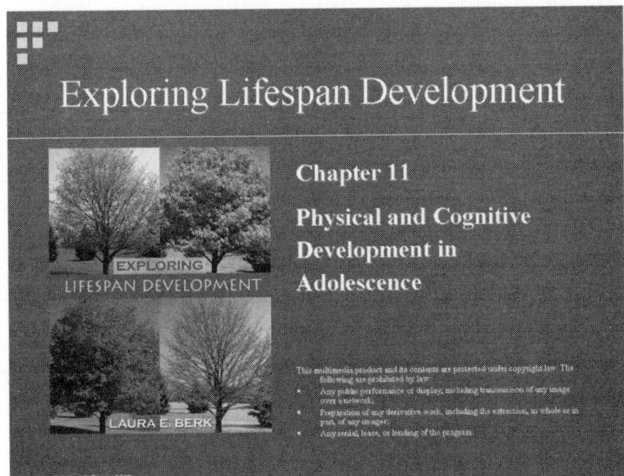

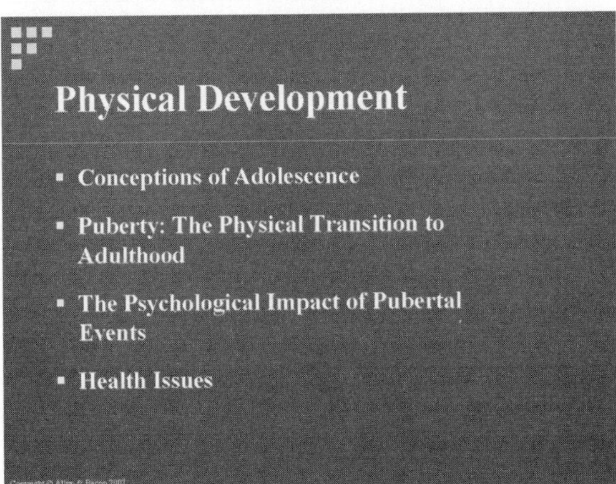

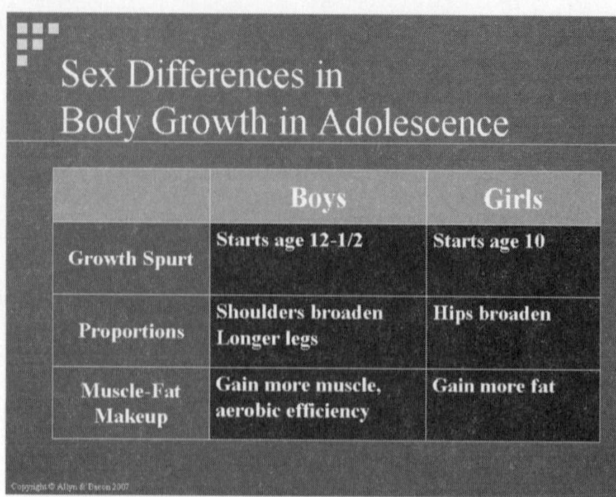

	Boys	Girls
Growth Spurt	Starts age 12-1/2	Starts age 10
Proportions	Shoulders broaden Longer legs	Hips broaden
Muscle-Fat Makeup	Gain more muscle, aerobic efficiency	Gain more fat

Sexual Maturation

Primary Sexual Characteristics

- Maturation of the reproductive organs
  - **Girls**: menarche
  - **Boys**: spermarche

Secondary Sexual Characteristics

- Other visible parts of the body that signal sexual maturity
  - **Girls:** breasts
  - **Boys:** facial hair, voice change
  - **Both:** underarm hair

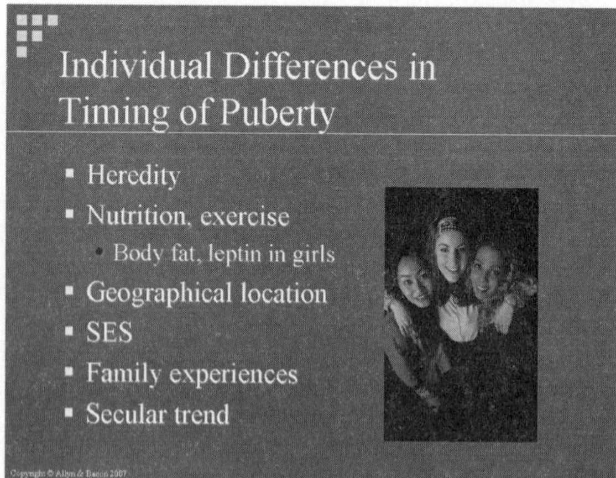

Adolescent Brain Development

Pruning continues	Frontal lobes	Cognitive advances: ▪ Attention ▪ Planning ▪ Integrating information ▪ Self-regulation
Growth & myelination speed up	Strengthen connections among regions	
Neurotransmitter response changes	More sensitive to excitatory messages	Intensifies reactions to ▪ Stress ▪ Pleasure, novelty

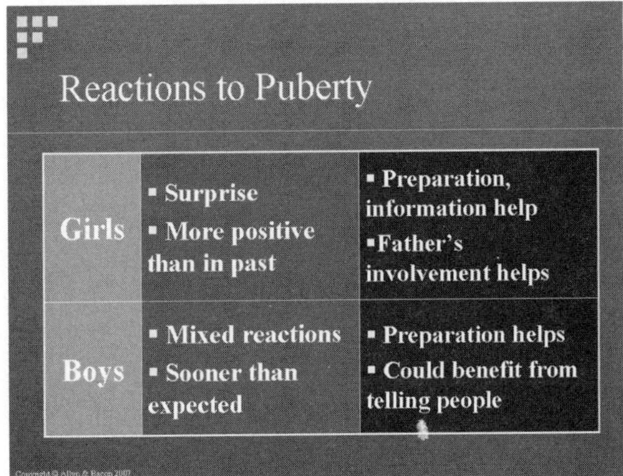

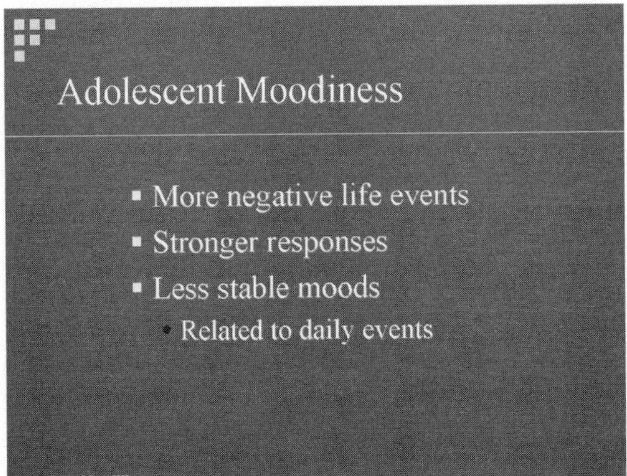

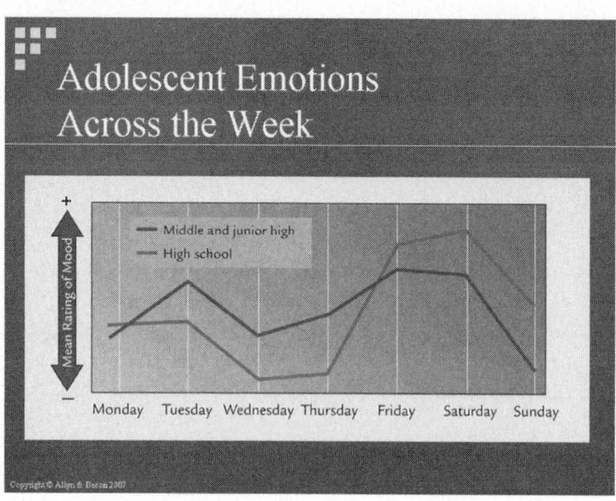

Parent–Child Relationships During Adolescence

- **Rise in conflict**
  - Psychological distancing
  - Different views of teen readiness for responsibility
- **Most conflict is mild**
  - Also affection, support

Consequences of Timing of Puberty

	Girls	Boys
Early Maturing	• Unpopular, withdrawn, low confidence • More deviant behavior • Negative body image • More long-term problems	• Popular • Confident, independent • Positive body image
Late Maturing	• Popular • Sociable, lively, school leaders • Positive body image	• Unpopular • Anxious, talkative, attention-seeking • Negative body image

Factors in Reactions to Timing of Puberty

- **Physical attractiveness – body image**
  - **Girls: most want to be thinner, smaller**
  - **Boys: most want to be bigger**
- **Fitting in with peers**
  - **Prefer similar level of physical maturity**

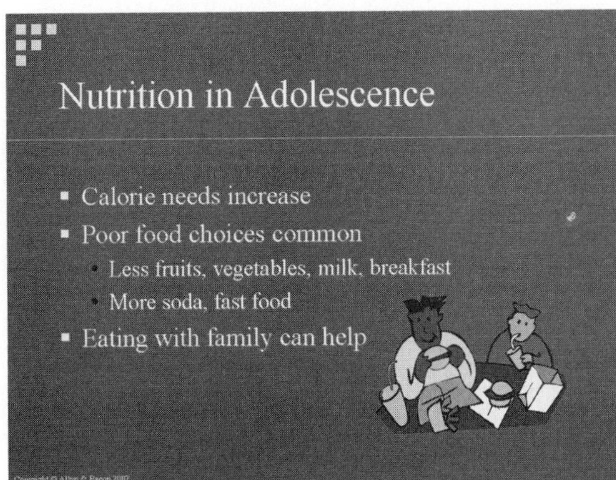

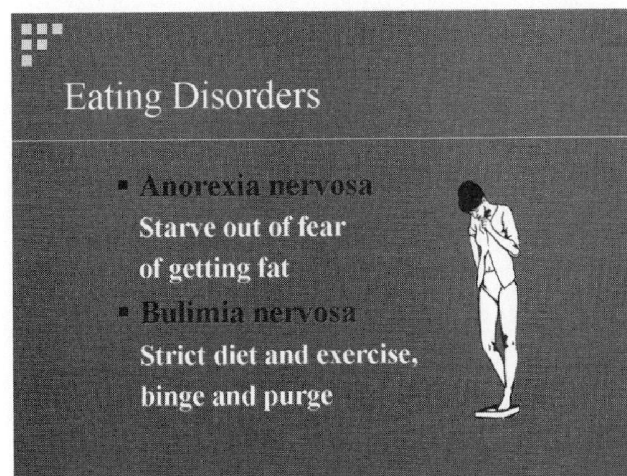

Talking to Adolescents About Sex

- Foster open communication
- Use correct terms
- Listen, discuss, collaborate
- Think before talking
- Keep conversations going

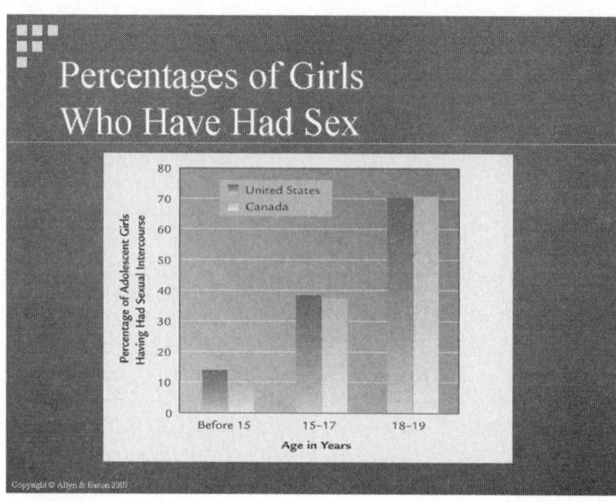

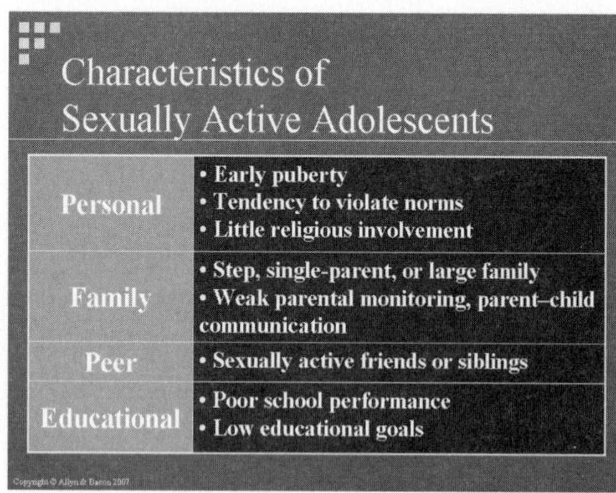

Personal	• Early puberty • Tendency to violate norms • Little religious involvement
Family	• Step, single-parent, or large family • Weak parental monitoring, parent–child communication
Peer	• Sexually active friends or siblings
Educational	• Poor school performance • Low educational goals

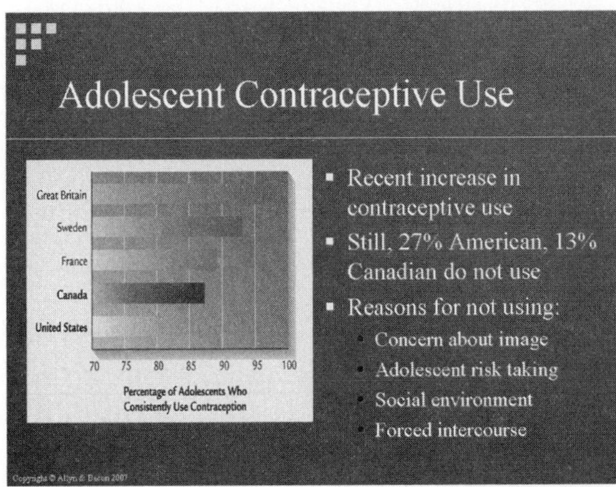
Adolescent Contraceptive Use
Great Britain
Sweden
France
Canada
United States
70 75 80 85 90 95 100
Percentage of Adolescents Who Consistently Use Contraception
Recent increase in contraceptive use
Still, 27% American, 13% Canadian do not use
Reasons for not using:
Concern about image
Adolescent risk taking
Social environment
Forced intercourse

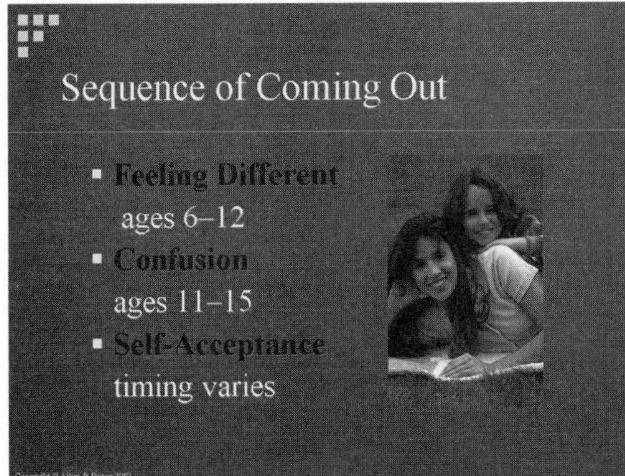
Sequence of Coming Out
Feeling Different
ages 6–12
Confusion
ages 11–15
Self-Acceptance
timing varies

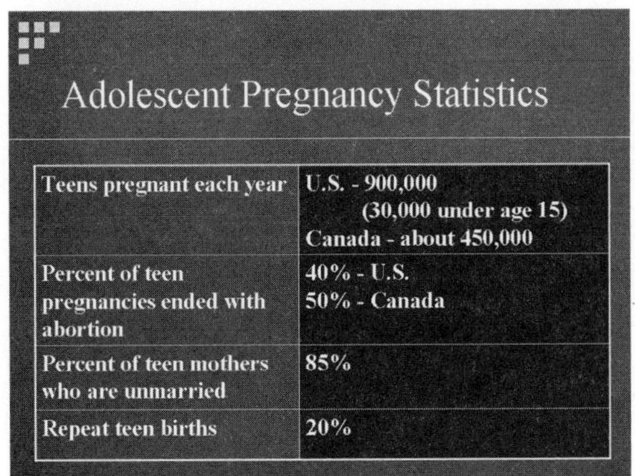
Adolescent Pregnancy Statistics
Teens pregnant each year
U.S. - 900,000 (30,000 under age 15)
Canada - about 450,000
Percent of teen pregnancies ended with abortion
40% - U.S.
50% - Canada
Percent of teen mothers who are unmarried
85%
Repeat teen births
20%

Risks for Teen Mothers

- Less educational achievement
- More time as single parents
- Economic problems
- Pregnancy and birth complications
- Lack of parenting skills

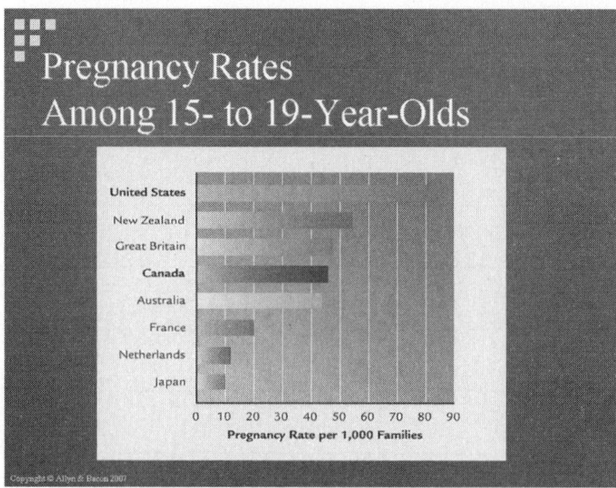

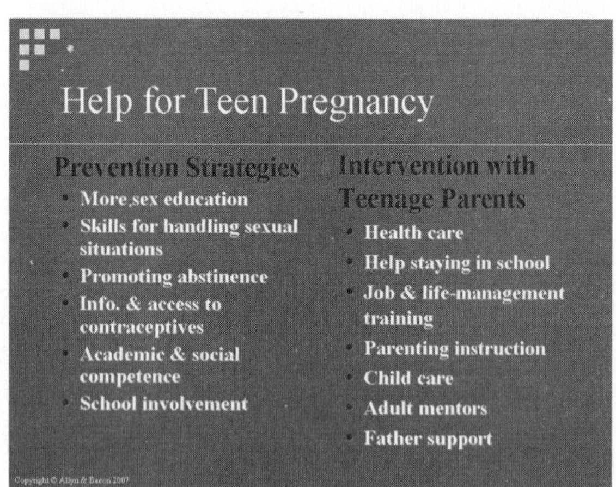

Adolescent Substance Abusers

Compared to experimenters

- More antisocial, impulsive acts
- Start earlier
- More likely to be affected by genetic and environmental factors

Piaget's Theory: Formal Operational Stage

- **Hypothetico-deductive reasoning**
  - **Deducing hypotheses from a general theory**
  - **Pendulum problem**
- **Propositional Thought**
  - **Evaluating the logic of verbal propositions**

Piaget's Pendulum Problem

Follow-up Research on Formal Operational Thought

- **School-age children start developing abstract thinking skills**
  - Problems with propositional thinking
    - Logical necessity
- **Formal operations may not be universal**
  - Training, context contribute
  - Often fall back on easier thinking

Information Processing Improvements in Adolescence

- Attention
- Inhibition
- Memory strategies
- Knowledge
- Metacognition
- Cognitive self-regulation
- Processing capacity
- Speed of thinking

Scientific Reasoning

- **Coordinating Theory with Evidence**
- **Improves with Age**
  - **From childhood through adulthood**
  - **Individuals vary**
- **Contributing Factors**
  - **Working memory capacity**
  - **Exposure to complex problems**
  - **Metacognitive understanding**
  - **Open-mindedness**

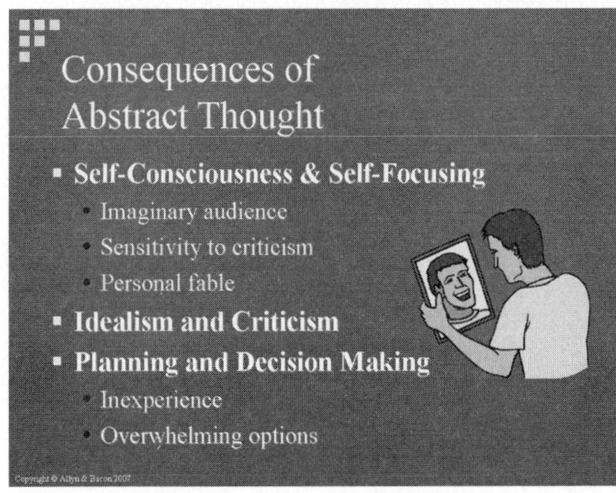
Consequences of
Abstract Thought
Self-Consciousness & Self-Focusing
Imaginary audience
Sensitivity to criticism
Personal fable
Idealism and Criticism
Planning and Decision Making
Inexperience
Overwhelming options
Copyright © Allyn & Bacon 2007

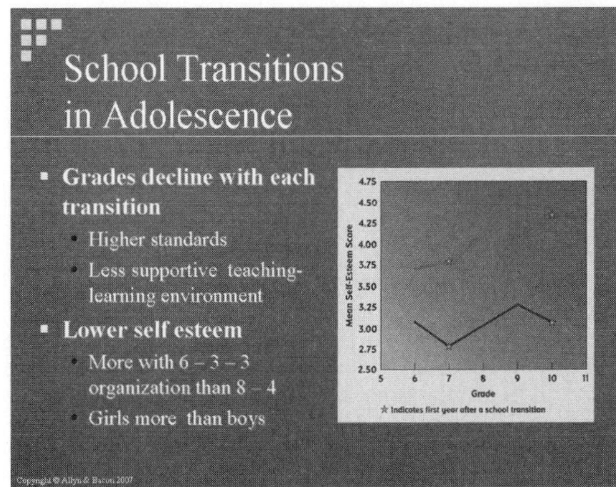
School Transitions
in Adolescence
Grades decline with each transition
Higher standards
Less supportive teaching-learning environment
Lower self esteem
More with 6 – 3 – 3 organization than 8 – 4
Girls more than boys
Mean Self-Esteem Score
4.75
4.50
4.25
4.00
3.75
3.50
3.25
3.00
2.75
2.50
5
6
7
8
9
10
11
Grade
☆ Indicates first year after a school transition
Copyright © Allyn & Bacon 2007

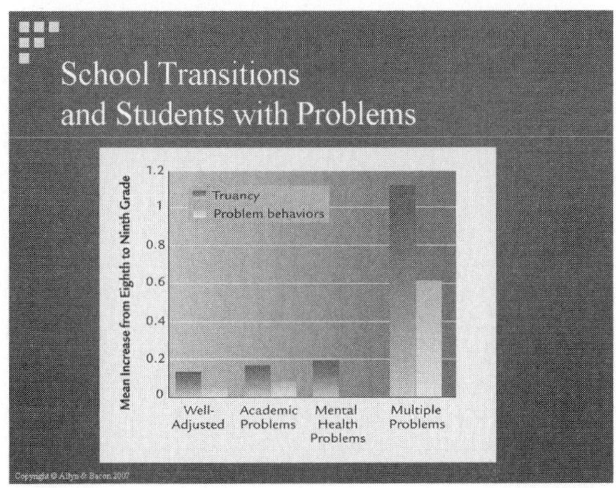
School Transitions
and Students with Problems
Mean Increase from Eighth to Ninth Grade
1.2
1
0.8
0.6
0.4
0.2
0
Truancy
Problem behaviors
Well-Adjusted
Academic Problems
Mental Health Problems
Multiple Problems
Copyright © Allyn & Bacon 2007

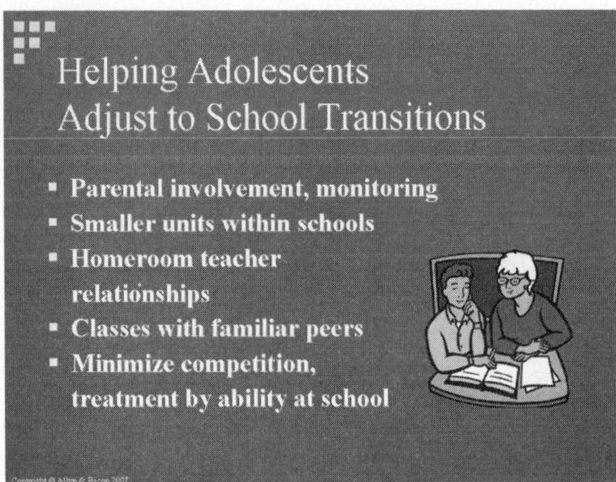
Helping Adolescents
Adjust to School Transitions
Parental involvement, monitoring
Smaller units within schools
Homeroom teacher relationships
Classes with familiar peers
Minimize competition, treatment by ability at school
Copyright © Allyn & Bacon 2007

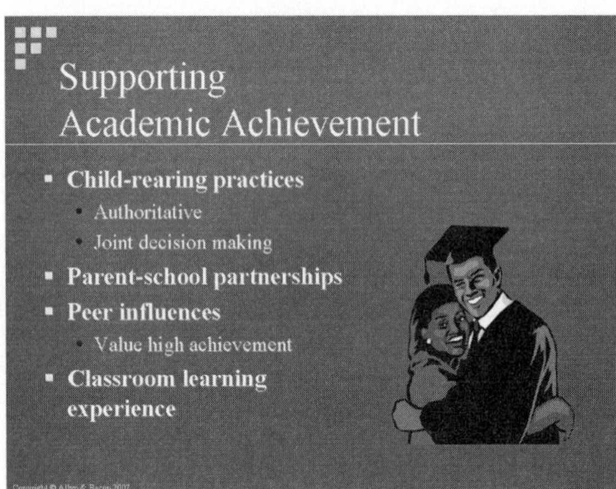
Supporting
Academic Achievement
Child-rearing practices
Authoritative
Joint decision making
Parent-school partnerships
Peer influences
Value high achievement
Classroom learning experience
Copyright © Allyn & Bacon 2007

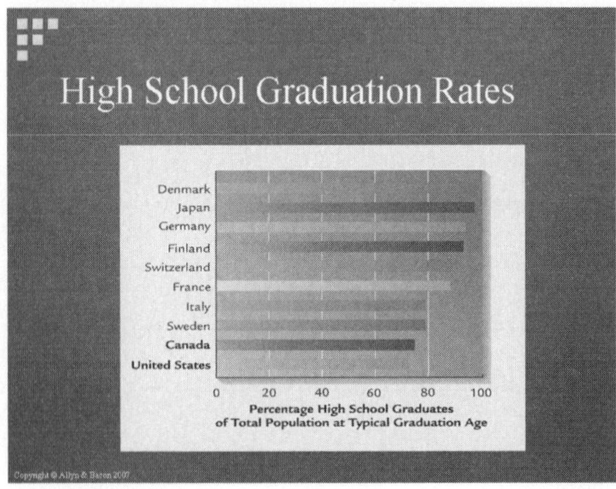
High School Graduation Rates
Denmark
Japan
Germany
Finland
Switzerland
France
Italy
Sweden
Canada
United States
0
20
40
60
80
100
Percentage High School Graduates
of Total Population at Typical Graduation Age
Copyright © Allyn & Bacon 2007

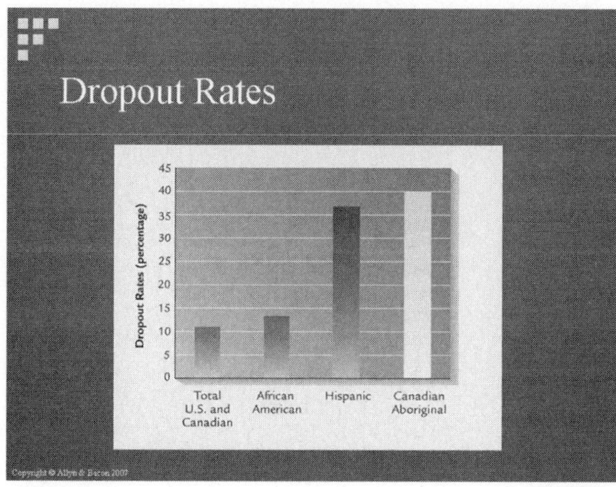
Dropout Rates
Dropout Rates (percentage)
45
40
35
30
25
20
15
10
5
0
Total U.S. and Canadian
African American
Hispanic
Canadian Aboriginal

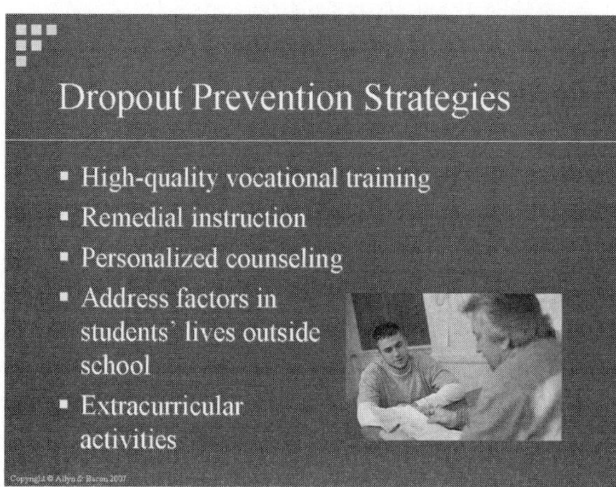
Dropout Prevention Strategies
High-quality vocational training
Remedial instruction
Personalized counseling
Address factors in students' lives outside school
Extracurricular activities

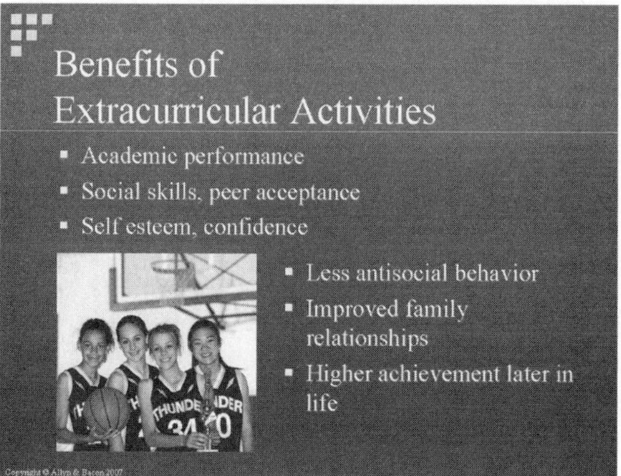
Benefits of Extracurricular Activities
Academic performance
Social skills, peer acceptance
Self esteem, confidence
Less antisocial behavior
Improved family relationships
Higher achievement later in life

CHAPTER 12
EMOTIONAL AND SOCIAL DEVELOPMENT IN ADOLESCENCE

CHAPTER-AT-A-GLANCE

Chapter Outline	Instruction Ideas	Supplements
Erikson's Theory: Identity versus Role Confusion pp. 314–315	Learning Objective 12.1	Test Bank Items 1–8 Videos: *Exploring Lifespan Development in Action* and *A Window on Lifespan Development* Please contact your Allyn and Bacon publisher's representative for a wide range of video offerings available to adopters.
Self-Understanding pp. 315–318 Changes in Self-Concept • Changes in Self-Esteem • Paths to Identity • Identity Status and Psychological Well-Being • Factors Affecting Identity Development	Learning Objectives 12.2–12.3 Lecture Enhancements 12.1–12.2 Learning Activities 12.1–12.2 Ask Yourself p. 317	Test Bank Items 9–28
Moral Development pp. 319–324 Kohlberg's Theory of Moral Development • Are There Sex Differences in Moral Reasoning? • Coordinating Personal Choice with Morality • Influences on Moral Reasoning • Moral Reasoning and Behavior • Religious Involvement and Moral Development	Learning Objectives 12.4–12.6 Lecture Enhancement 12.3 Learning Activities 12.3–12.5	Test Bank Items 29–54
Gender Typing p. 324	Learning Objective 12.7 Ask Yourself p. 324	Test Bank Items 55–59
The Family pp. 325–326 Parent–Child Relationships • Family Circumstances • Siblings	Learning Objective 12.8 Lecture Activity 12.6	Test Bank Items 60–69
Peer Relations pp. 326–329 Friendships • Cliques and Crowds • Dating	Learning Objective 12.9 Lecture Enhancement 12.4 Learning Activities 12.7–12.8 Ask Yourself p. 329	Transparency 154 Test Bank Items 70–87
Problems of Development pp. 330–333 Depression • Suicide • Delinquency	Learning Objectives 12.10–12.11 Learning Activity 12.9 Ask Yourself p. 332	Test Bank Items 88–100

BRIEF CHAPTER SUMMARY

Erikson was the first to recognize identity as the major personality achievement of adolescence and as a crucial step toward becoming a productive, happy adult. Young people who successfully resolve the psychological conflict of identity versus role confusion construct a solid self-definition based on self-chosen values and goals. During adolescence, cognitive changes transform the young person's vision of the self into a more complex, well-organized, and consistent picture. For most young people, self-esteem rises over the teenage years, influenced by factors in the family, at school, and in the larger social environment.

Adolescents' well-organized self-descriptions and differentiated sense of self-esteem provide the cognitive foundation for identity development. Researchers have derived four identity statuses that reflect adolescents' progress toward developing a mature identity. Two of these—identity achievement and moratorium—are adaptive, associated with positive personality characteristics. Adolescents who remain in one of the other statuses—identity foreclosure or identity diffusion—tend to have adjustment difficulties.

Lawrence Kohlberg, continuing the research of Piaget, identified six distinct stages of moral development. According to Kohlberg, moral development is a gradual process that extends into adulthood as the individual actively grapples with moral issues and achieves gains in perspective taking, which lead to more effective ways of resolving moral conflicts. Child-rearing practices, schooling, peer interaction, and culture all contribute to moral development. As individuals advance through Kohlberg's stages, moral reasoning becomes more closely related to behavior.

Biological, social, and cognitive factors all play a role in making early adolescence a period of gender intensification—increased gender stereotyping of attitudes and behavior, and movement toward a more traditional gender identity, especially for girls. Development at adolescence involves striving for autonomy—a sense of oneself as a separate, self-governing individual. Over the adolescent years, relationships with parents and siblings change as teenagers strive to establish a healthy balance between connection to and separation from the family. As adolescents spend more time with peers, intimacy and loyalty become central features of friendship. Adolescent peer groups are organized into tightly knit groups called cliques; as teenagers become interested in dating, several cliques come together to form a crowd.

Although most young people move through adolescence with little difficulty, some encounter major disruptions, such as premature parenthood, substance abuse, and school failure. The most common psychological problem of the teenage years, depression, is influenced by a diverse combination of biological and environmental factors. The suicide rate increases dramatically at adolescence. Many teenagers become involved in some delinquent activity, but only a few are serious or repeat offenders. Family, school, peer, and neighborhood factors are related to delinquency.

LEARNING OBJECTIVES

After reading this chapter, you should be able to:

12.1 Discuss Erikson's theory of identity development. (pp. 314–315)

12.2 Describe changes in self-concept and self-esteem during adolescence. (pp. 315–316)

12.3 Describe the four identity statuses, the adjustment outcomes of each status, and factors that promote identity development. (pp. 316–318)

12.4 Describe Kohlberg's theory of moral development and evaluate its accuracy. (pp. 319–321)

12.5 Summarize research on Gilligan's claim that Kohlberg underestimated the moral maturity of females. (pp. 321–322)

12.6 Describe influences on moral reasoning and its relationship to moral behavior. (pp. 322–324)

12.7 Explain why early adolescence is a period of gender intensification. (p. 324)

12.8 Discuss changes in parent–child and sibling relationships during adolescence. (pp. 325–326)

12.9 Describe adolescent friendships, peer groups, and dating relationships and their consequences for development. (pp. 326–329)

12.10 Discuss factors related to adolescent depression and suicide, along with approaches for prevention and treatment. (pp. 330–331)

12.11 Summarize factors related to delinquency, and describe strategies for prevention and treatment. (pp. 331–333)

LECTURE OUTLINE

I. ERIKSON'S THEORY: IDENTITY VERSUS ROLE CONFUSION (pp. 314–315)
   A. Erik Erikson was the first to recognize **identity** as the major personality achievement of adolescence and as a crucial step toward becoming a productive, happy adult.
   B. Constructing an identity involves defining who you are, what you value, and the directions you choose to pursue in life.
      1. It is an explicit theory of oneself as a rational agent—one who acts on the basis of reason, takes responsibility for those actions, and can explain them.
      2. The search for identity drives many choices—vocation, interpersonal relationships, community involvement, ethnic-group membership, and expression of one's sexual orientation, as well as moral, political, and religious ideals.
   C. Erikson called the psychological conflict of adolescence **identity versus role confusion**.
      1. Successful outcomes of earlier stages pave the way to its positive resolution.
         a. Young people who reach adolescence with a weak sense of *trust* have trouble finding ideals to have faith in.
         b. Those with little *autonomy* or *initiative* do not engage in the active exploration required to choose among alternatives.
         c. Those who lack a sense of *industry* fail to select a vocation that matches their interests and skills.
      2. Erikson believed that teenagers in complex societies experience an *identity crisis*.
         a. In Erikson's view, this crisis is a temporary period of distress and inner soul-searching before settling on values and goals.
         b. Current theorists agree that questioning of values, plans, and priorities is necessary for a mature identity, but they see this process not as a "crisis," for most young people, but simply as a process of *exploration* followed by *commitment.*
      3. The negative outcome of adolescence is *role confusion.*
         a. If young people's earlier conflicts were resolved negatively or if society limits their choices to ones that do not match their abilities and desires, they may appear directionless and unprepared for the psychological challenges of adulthood.
         b. Young people who lack a firm identity will find it difficult to risk the *intimacy* of early adulthood.

II. SELF-UNDERSTANDING (pp. 315–318)
   A. During adolescence, the young person's vision of the self becomes more complex, well organized, and consistent.
   B. Changes in Self-Concept (p. 315)
      1. In describing themselves, adolescents unify separate traits ("smart," "talented") into more abstract descriptors ("intelligent").
      2. At first, these generalizations are not interconnected and are often contradictory, as teenagers display different selves in different relationships—with parents, classmates, close friends, and romantic partners.
      3. Gradually, cognitive changes enable teenagers to combine their traits into an organized system.
         a. Their ability to use qualifiers ("I have a *fairly* quick temper") reveals their awareness that psychological qualities can vary in different situations.
         b. Older adolescents also add integrating principles ("I'm very adaptable") that make sense out of apparent contradictions.

4. Compared with school-age children, teenagers place more emphasis on social virtues, such as being friendly, considerate, kind, and cooperative.
5. Among older adolescents, personal and moral values are key themes, as young people revise their views of themselves to include enduring beliefs and plans.

C. Changes in Self-Esteem (pp. 315–316)
1. In adolescence, young people add several new dimensions of self-concept to their self-evaluations: close friendship, romantic appeal, and job competence.
2. For most young people, self-esteem rises, and they see themselves as more mature, capable, personable, and attractive than previously, but individual differences in self-esteem also become increasingly stable in adolescence.
3. Positive relationships among self-esteem, valuing of various activities, and success at those activities strengthen.
4. Authoritative parenting and encouragement from teachers predict high self-esteem in adolescence, whereas feedback that is negative or not contingent on performance triggers, at best, uncertainty about the self's capacities and, at worst, a sense of being incompetent and unloved.

D. Paths to Identity (p. 316)
1. Researchers evaluating progress in identity development have derived four *identity statuses* on the basis of two key criteria derived from Erikson's theory: *exploration* and *commitment.*
   a. **Identity achievement**: Commitment to values, beliefs, and goals following a period of exploration
   b. **Identity moratorium**: Exploration without having reached commitment
   c. **Identity foreclosure**: Commitment in the absence of exploration
   d. **Identity diffusion**: An apathetic state characterized by lack of both exploration and commitment
2. Some young people remain in one identity status, while others experience many status transitions, with most young people moving from "lower" statuses (foreclosure or diffusion) to higher ones (moratorium or achievement) between their mid-teens and mid-twenties, although some move in the reverse direction.
3. The pattern often varies across *identity domains,* such as sexual orientation, vocation, and religious and political values.
4. Attending college promotes identity development by providing students with expanded opportunities to explore career options and lifestyles, compared with those who do not go to college.
   a. After college, graduates can often sample a broad range of life experiences before choosing a life course.
   b. Those who go to work immediately after high school graduation settle on a self-definition earlier than college-educated youths but are at risk for identity diffusion if they encounter difficulty realizing their occupational goals because of lack of training or vocational choices.

E. Identity Status and Psychological Well-Being (pp. 316–317)
1. Identity achievement and moratorium are both psychologically healthy routes to a mature self-definition.
   a. Adolescents in moratorium, though anxious about the challenges that lie before them, resemble identity-achieved individuals in their use of an active, *information-gathering cognitive style* to make personal decisions and solve problems.
   b. Young people who are identity achieved or exploring have greater self-esteem, feel more in control of their own lives, are more likely to view school and work as feasible avenues for realizing their aspirations, and are more advanced in moral reasoning.
2. Adolescents who get stuck in either foreclosure or diffusion tend to be passive in the face of identity concerns and to have adjustment difficulties.
   a. Foreclosed individuals display a *dogmatic, inflexible cognitive style.*
      (1) They usually internalize the values and beliefs of parents and others without deliberate evaluation.
      (2) Most fear rejection by people on whom they depend for affection and self-esteem.
   b. Least mature in identity development are long-term diffused individuals.
      (1) They typically use a *diffuse-avoidant cognitive style,* allowing situational pressures to dictate their reactions instead of dealing with personal decisions and problems.

(2) Compared with other young people, they are more likely to entrust themselves to luck or fate, to go along with the crowd, to experience time management and academic difficulties, and to use and abuse drugs.

F. Factors Affecting Identity Development (pp. 317–318)

1. Adolescent identity formation is the beginning of a lifelong, dynamic process that is influenced by many factors related to both personality and context.
2. Identity status is both cause and consequence of personality.
   a. Adolescents who assume that absolute truth is always attainable tend to be foreclosed.
   b. Those who doubt that they will ever feel certain about anything are more often identity diffused.
   c. Those who appreciate that they can use rational criteria to choose among alternatives are likely to be in a state of moratorium or identity achievement.
3. Parenting practices are associated with identity status.
   a. Adolescents who feel attached to their parents but also free to voice their own opinions tend to be in a state of moratorium or identity achievement.
   b. Foreclosed teenagers usually have close bonds with parents but lack opportunities for healthy separation.
   c. Diffused young people report the lowest levels of parental support and of warm, open communication.
4. Interaction with a variety of peers expands adolescents' exposure to ideas and values.
5. Schools can help by offering rich and varied opportunities for exploration, both within and outside the classroom.
6. Societal forces are responsible for the special problems faced by gay, lesbian, and bisexual youths and by some ethnic minority adolescents in forming a secure identity.
   a. For minority adolescents, **ethnic identity**—a sense of ethnic-group membership and attitudes and feelings associated with that membership—is central to the quest for identity.
   b. Forming a **bicultural identity**—by exploring and adopting values from both the adolescent's subculture and the dominant culture—offers added benefits.

III. MORAL DEVELOPMENT (pp. 319–324)

A. Kohlberg's Theory of Moral Development (pp. 319–321)

1. Early work on the judgment of the child inspired Lawrence Kohlberg's more comprehensive theory of the development of moral understanding.
2. Using a clinical interviewing procedure, Kohlberg presented a sample of 10- to 16-year-old boys with hypothetical *moral dilemmas*—stories presenting a conflict between two moral values.
3. For each dilemma, Kohlberg asked participants what the main actor should do and why, then followed them longitudinally, reinterviewing them at intervals over the next 20 years.
4. Kohlberg's "Heinz dilemma" pits the value of obeying the law (not stealing) against the value of human life (saving a dying person).
   a. Kohlberg emphasized that moral maturity depends on *the way an individual reasons* about the dilemma, not on *the content of the response* (whether or not to steal).
   b. Only at Kohlberg's two highest stages do moral reasoning and content come together in a coherent ethical system in which, given a choice between obeying the law and preserving individual rights, the most advanced moral thinkers support individual rights—in the case of the Heinz dilemma, stealing in order to save a life.
5. Kohlberg's Stages (pp. 320–321)
   a. Kohlberg's six stages are organized into three general levels of moral development.
   b. Kohlberg believed that moral understanding is promoted by the same factors Piaget thought were important for cognitive growth: actively grappling with moral issues and noticing weaknesses in one's current reasoning, and gain in perspective taking, which permit individuals to resolve moral conflicts in more effective ways.
   c. The Preconventional Level (p. 320)
      (1) At the **preconventional level**, morality is externally controlled; children accept the rules of authority figures and judge actions by their consequences, viewing behaviors that result in punishment as bad, those that lead to rewards as good.

(2) *Stage 1: The punishment and obedience orientation* (p. 320): Children at this stage find it difficult to consider two points of view in a moral dilemma; they ignore people's intentions and focus instead on fear of authority and avoidance of punishment as reasons for behaving morally.

(3) *Stage 2: The instrumental purpose orientation* (p. 320): Children become aware that people can have different perspectives in a moral dilemma, but at first this understanding is very concrete; they view right action as flowing from self-interest and understand reciprocity as equal exchange of favors.

d. The Conventional Level (pp. 320–321):

(1) At the **conventional level**, individuals regard conformity to social rules as important because they believe that actively maintaining the current social system ensures positive relationships and societal order.

(2) *Stage 3: The "good boy–good girl" orientation, or the morality of interpersonal cooperation* (p. 320): The individual obeys rules in order to promote social harmony, based on an understanding of *ideal reciprocity* and on the capacity to view a two-person relationship from the vantage point of an impartial outside observer.

(3) *Stage 4: The social-order-maintaining orientation* (p. 321): The individual takes societal laws into account and believes that rules must be enforced evenhandedly and that each member of society has a personal duty to uphold the rules in order to maintain societal order.

e. The Postconventional or Principled Level (p. 321)

(1) Moving beyond unquestioning support for their own society's rules and laws, individuals at the **postconventional level** define morality in terms of abstract principles and values that apply to all situations and societies.

(2) *Stage 5: The social contract orientation* (p. 321): Individuals view laws and rules as flexible instruments for furthering human purposes; they can imagine alternatives to their own social order, and they emphasize fair procedures for interpreting and changing the law. When laws are consistent with individual rights and the interests of the majority, each person follows them because of a *social contract orientation*—free and willing participation in the system because it brings about more good for people than if it did not exist.

(3) *Stage 6: The universal ethical principle orientation* (p. 321): At this highest stage, right action is defined by self-chosen ethical principles of conscience that are valid for all people, regardless of law and social agreement, and are abstract, including such principles as equal consideration of the claims of all human beings and respect for the worth and dignity of each person.

6. Research on Kohlberg's Stage Sequence (p. 321)

a. Kohlberg's original research and other longitudinal studies provide the most convincing evidence for his stage sequence.

b. With few exceptions, individuals move through the first four stages in the predicted order, at a slow and gradual pace.

(1) Reasoning at Stages 1 and 2 decreases in early adolescence.

(2) Stage 3 increases through midadolescence and then declines.

(3) Stage 4 reasoning rises over the teenage years and, by early adulthood, is the typical response.

c. Few people move beyond Stage 4 to Kohlberg's postconventional stages.

(1) A key challenge to Kohlberg's theory is the absence of clear evidence that his Stage 6 actually follows Stage 5.

(2) Moral maturity can be seen in a revised understanding of Stages 3 and 4, which are not based on social conformity (as Kohlberg assumed) but, rather, require profound moral constructions—an understanding of ideal reciprocity as the basis for relationships (Stage 3) and for widely accepted moral standards, set forth in rules and laws (Stage 4).

(3) In this view, "postconventional" morality is a highly reflective endeavor limited to a handful of people who have attained advanced education, usually in philosophy.

7. Real-life conflicts often elicit moral reasoning below a person's actual capacity because they mix cognition with intense emotion.
8. Like Piaget's cognitive stages, Kohlberg's moral stages do not develop in a neat stepwise fashion; instead, people draw on a range of moral responses that vary with context.

B. Are There Sex Differences in Moral Reasoning? (pp. 321–322)
  1. Carol Gilligan and others have argued that Kohlberg's theory, formulated on the basis of interviews with males, does not adequately represent the morality of girls and women.
  2. Gilligan believes that feminine morality emphasizes an "ethic of care" that Kohlberg's system devalues—a *different* but no less valid basis for moral judgment than a focus on impersonal rights.
  3. Many studies have tested Gilligan's claim that Kohlberg's approach underestimates the moral maturity of females, and most do not support it.
     a. On both hypothetical dilemmas and everyday moral problems, adolescent and adult females display reasoning at the same or a higher stage as their male agemates.
     b. Themes of justice and caring appear in the responses of both sexes.
     c. When girls raise interpersonal concerns, these are not downgraded in Kohlberg's system.
  4. Gilligan does make a powerful claim that research on moral development has been limited by too much attention to rights and justice (a "masculine" ideal) and too little to care and responsiveness (a "feminine" ideal).
     a. Some evidence shows that females do tend to emphasize care, while males either stress justice or focus equally on justice and care.
     b. This difference in emphasis may reflect women's greater involvement in daily activities involving care and concern for others.

C. Coordinating Personal Choice with Morality (p. 322)
  1. Adolescents' moral advances are evident in their reasoning about situations that raise competing moral, social-conventional, and personal issues.
  2. As adolescents enlarge the range of issues they regard as personal, they think more intently about conflicts between personal choice and community obligation—for example, laws restricting speech, religion, marriage, childbearing, group membership, and other individual rights.
  3. Compared with school-age children, teenagers allow for more circumstances when excluding someone (more often on the basis of gender than of race) would be acceptable either as an expression of personal choice or because of concerns about effective group functioning.
  4. As they integrate personal rights with ideal reciprocity, adolescents demand that the protections they want for themselves extend to others as well.

D. Influences on Moral Reasoning (pp. 322–323)
  1. Moral understanding is influenced by various factors, including child-rearing practices, schooling, peer interaction, and culture.
  2. Evidence suggests that, as Kohlberg believed, these experiences work by presenting young people with cognitive challenges, which stimulate them to think about moral problems in more complex ways.
  3. Parenting Practices (p. 322)
     a. Moral understanding in adolescence is fostered by warm parenting and discussion of moral concerns.
     b. Teenagers whose parents listen sensitively, ask clarifying questions, and present higher-level reasoning gain most in moral development.
     c. Those whose parents lecture, use threats, or make sarcastic remarks show little or no change.
  4. Schooling (p. 322)
     a. Years of schooling is a powerful predictor of movement to Kohlberg's Stage 4 or higher.
     b. Attending college introduces young people to social issues that range beyond personal relationships to entire political or cultural groups.
     c. College students who report more academic perspective-taking opportunities (such as classes that emphasize open discussion of opinions) and who indicate that they have become more aware of social diversity tend to be advanced in moral reasoning.

5. Peer Interaction (p. 322)
   a. Research supports Piaget's belief that moral understanding is promoted by interaction among peers, who confront one another with differing viewpoints.
   b. Through negotiating and compromising with agemates, children and adolescents realize that social life can be based on cooperation between equals rather than authority relations.
   c. Young people who report more close friendships and who more often participate in conversations with their friends are advanced in moral reasoning.
   d. The mutuality and intimacy of friendship, which fosters decisions based on consensual agreement, may be particularly important for moral development.
6. Culture (p. 323)
   a. People in industrialized nations move through Kohlberg's stages more quickly and advance to a higher level than those in village societies, who rarely move beyond Stage 3.
      (1) In village societies, moral cooperation is based on direct relations between people and does not allow for the development of advanced moral understanding (Stages 4 to 6), which depends on appreciating the role of larger social structures, such as laws and government institutions.
      (2) Responses to moral dilemmas in collectivist cultures (including village societies) are often more other-directed than in Western Europe and North America.
   b. In cultures that highly value interdependency, statements portraying the individual as vitally connected to the social group are common.
      (1) In one study, Japanese male and female adolescents, who almost always integrated caring and justice-based reasoning, placed greater weight on caring, which they saw as a communal responsibility.
      (2) In research conducted in India, even highly educated people (expected to have attained Kohlberg's Stages 4 and 5) less often held individuals accountable for moral transgressions because they viewed solutions to moral dilemmas as the responsibility of the entire society, not of a single person.
   c. These findings raise the question of whether Kohlberg's highest level represents a culturally specific way of thinking, limited to individualistic Western societies that emphasize an appeal to an inner, private conscience.
   d. However, a common justice-based morality is clearly evident in the dilemma responses of people from vastly different cultures.

E. Moral Reasoning and Behavior (p. 323)
1. According to Kohlberg, moral thought and action should come together at the higher levels of moral understanding.
   a. Mature moral thinkers realize that behaving according to their beliefs is vital for creating and maintaining a just social world.
   b. Higher-stage adolescents more often act prosocially by helping, sharing, and defending victims of injustice and less often engage in cheating, aggression, and other antisocial behaviors.
2. However, the connection between advanced moral reasoning and action is only modest.
   a. Moral behavior is influenced by factors besides cognition, including emotions (empathy, sympathy, and guilt), temperament, and a history of experiences that affect moral decision making.
   b. Morality is also affected by **moral self-relevance**—the degree to which morality is central to self-concept.
   c. Research has yet to discover the origins of a sense of moral self-relevance.
      (1) Close relationships with parents, teachers, and friends may play vital roles by modeling prosocial behavior and fostering emotional processes of empathy and guilt, which combine with moral cognition to motivate moral action.
      (2) *Just educational environments*—in which teachers guide students in democratic decision making and rule setting, resolving disputes civilly, and taking responsibility for others' welfare—may also be influential, and schools may also foster students' moral self-relevance by expanding opportunities for civic engagement.

F. Religious Involvement and Moral Development (pp. 323–324)
   1. Religion is especially important in in North American families.
      a. Nearly two-thirds of Americans and about one-half of Canadians reported being religious, compared with one-third of people in Great Britain and Italy, and even fewer elsewhere in Europe.
      b. Formal religious involvement declines in adolescence, but teenagers who remain part of a religious community are advantaged over nonaffiliated youths in moral values and behavior.
      c. Religious affiliation encourages involvement in community service activities, promotes responsible academic and social behavior, and discourages misconduct.
   2. Factors contributing to these favorable outcomes:
      a. In a study of inner-city high school students, religiously involved young people were more likely to report trusting relationships with parents, other adults, and friends who held similar world views.
      b. The more activities they shared with this network, the higher they scored in empathy and prosocial behavior.
      c. Religious education and youth activities teach concern for others and provide opportunities for moral discussions and community volunteering.
      d. Adolescents who feel connected to a higher being may develop certain inner strengths, including moral self-relevance, that help translate their thinking into action.
      e. An exception is seen in religious cults, where rigid indoctrination into the group's beliefs, suppression of individuality, and estrangement from society all work against moral maturity.

IV. GENDER TYPING (p. 324)
   A. Early adolescence is a period of **gender intensification**—increased gender stereotyping of attitudes and behavior, and movement toward a more traditional gender identity.
   B. Gender intensification occurs in both sexes but is stronger for girls, who feel less free to experiment with "other-gender" activities and behavior than in middle childhood.
   C. Biological, social, and cognitive factors are involved in gender intensification.
      1. Puberty magnifies sex differences in appearance, so teenagers spend more time thinking about themselves in gender-linked ways.
      2. Pubertal changes prompt gender-typed pressures from others, especially parents, who may encourage "gender-appropriate" activities and behavior more than in middle childhood.
      3. When adolescents start to date, they often become more gender typed as a way of increasing their attractiveness.
      4. Cognitive changes, especially greater concern with what others think, make young teenagers more responsive to gender-role expectations.
   D. By middle to late adolescence, gender intensification declines, but not all young people move beyond it to the same degree.
      1. Teenagers who are encouraged to explore non-gender-typed options and to question the value of gender stereotypes for themselves and society are more likely to build an androgynous gender identity.
      2. Androgynous adolescents, especially girls, tend to be psychologically healthier—more self-confident, more willing to speak their own mind, better liked by peers, and identity achieved.

V. THE FAMILY (pp. 325–326)
   A. Adolescent development involves striving for **autonomy**—a sense of oneself as a separate, self-governing individual.
      1. Teenagers strive to rely more on themselves and less on parents for decision making.
      2. Parent–child relationships remain vital for helping adolescents become autonomous, responsible individuals.
   B. Parent–Child Relationships (p. 325)
      1. Adolescent autonomy is supported by a variety of changes within the adolescent.
         a. Puberty triggers psychological distancing from parents.
         b. As young people look more mature, parents give them more independence and responsibility.

c. Cognitive development paves the way for autonomy as adolescents become able to solve problems and make decisions more effectively.
d. Improved ability to reason about social relationships leads teenagers to *deidealize* their parents, so that they may question parental authority.

2. Because teenagers still need guidance and sometimes protection from dangerous situations, autonomy is fostered by warm, supportive parent–adolescent ties that permit young people to explore ideas and social roles.
   a. In diverse ethnic groups, positive relationships with parents predict high self-reliance, work orientation, academic competence, and favorable self-esteem.
   b. Research in many cultures shows that parents who are coercive or psychologically controlling interfere with the development of autonomy, with links to low self-esteem, depression, and antisocial behavior persisting into early adulthood.
3. The rapid physical and psychological changes of adolescence trigger conflicting expectations in parent–child relationships that affect the entire family system—a major reason that many parents find rearing teenagers to be stressful.
4. Parents and teenagers—especially young teenagers—differ sharply on the appropriate age for granting certain privileges, such as control over clothing, school courses, and going out with friends.
   a. Favorable adjustment is related to consistent parental monitoring of the young person's daily activities, through a cooperative relationship in which the adolescent willingly discloses information.
   b. Parental monitoring is also linked to other positive outcomes—a reduction in sexual activity, improved school performance, and positive psychological well-being.
5. Throughout adolescence, the quality of the parent–child relationship is the single most consistent predictor of mental health.
   a. In well-functioning families, teenagers remain attached to parents and seek their advice, but in a context of greater freedom.
   b. Mild parent–child conflict facilitates adolescent identity and autonomy by giving family members practice at expressing and tolerating disagreement and by signaling the need for adjustments in the parent–child relationship.
   c. By the end of adolescence, most parents and children achieve this mature, mutual relationship, and harmonious interaction is on the rise.

C. Family Circumstances (pp. 325–326)
1. Parents who are financially secure, not overloaded with job pressures, and content with their marriages usually find it easier to grant teenagers appropriate autonomy and experience less conflict with them.
2. Less than 10 percent of families with adolescents have seriously troubled relationships.
3. Teenagers who develop well despite family stresses benefit from the same factors that fostered resiliency in earlier years: an appealing, easygoing disposition, a parent who combines warmth with high expectations, or (if parental supports are lacking) bonds with prosocial adults outside the family who care deeply about the adolescent's well-being.

D. Siblings (p. 326)
1. Like parent-child relationships, sibling interactions adapt to change at adolescence.
   a. Younger siblings accept less direction from older brothers and sisters as they become more mature, so sibling influence declines.
   b. As teenagers become more involved in friendships and romantic relationships, they invest less time and energy in siblings, who are part of the family from which they are trying to establish autonomy.
   c. Despite a drop in companionship, attachment between siblings remains strong in most cases.
2. Siblings who established a positive bond in early childhood and whose parents continue to be warm and involved are more likely to express affection and caring.
3. Mild sibling differences in perceived parental affection no longer trigger jealousy but, instead, predict increasing sibling warmth, perhaps because adolescents now interpret a unique parental relationship as a sign of their own individuality.

VI. PEER RELATIONS (pp. 326–329)
   A. As adolescents spend less time with family members, peers become increasingly important.
   B. In industrialized nations, young people spend most of each weekday with agemates in school, and they also spend much out-of-class time together.
   C. Friendships (pp. 326–328)
      1. Characteristics of Adolescent Friendships (pp. 326–327)
         a. Adolescents seek psychological closeness, trust, and mutual understanding from their friends.
         b. Self-disclosure between friends increases steadily over the adolescent years.
         c. More than younger children, teenagers want their friends to be *loyal.*
         d. Adolescent friends tend to be alike in identity status, educational aspirations, political beliefs, and willingness to try drugs and engage in lawbreaking acts—and become more similar in these ways over time—though occasionally teenagers befriend agemates with differing attitudes and values.
         e. Cooperation and mutual affirmation between friends rise in adolescence, reflecting greater effort and skill at preserving the relationship and increased sensitivity to friends' needs and desires.
         f. Adolescents are less possessive of their friends than in childhood because they desire some autonomy for themselves and recognize that friends need this, too.
      2. Sex Differences in Friendships (p. 327)
         a. In line with gender-role expectations, girls' friendships typically focus on communal concerns, boys' on achievement and status.
         b. Emotional closeness is more common between girls, who engage in more *self-disclosure* (sharing of innermost thoughts and feelings) and supportive statements.
         c. Boys more often gather for sports and competitive games, and their discussions usually focus on accomplishments and involve more competition and conflict.
         d. Closeness in friendship, though usually beneficial, can have costs.
            (1) Adolescent friends sometimes *coruminate,* or repeatedly mull over problems and negative feelings, an activity that sparks anxiety and depression.
            (2) When conflicts arise between intimate friends, more potential exists for one party to harm the other through relational aggression.
      3. Friendships on the Internet (p. 327)
         a. Use of the Internet to communicate, especially through instant messaging, seems to support friendship closeness in adolescence.
         b. Besides communicating with friends they know, adolescents use the Internet to meet new people.
         c. The Internet's value for facilitating convenient and satisfying communication between teenage friends must be weighed against its potential for facilitating harmful social experiences.
      4. Friendships and Adjustment (pp. 327–328)
         a. Close adolescent friendships—as long as they are not characterized by jealousy, relational aggression, or attraction to antisocial behavior—are related to many aspects of psychological health and competence into early adulthood.
            (1) Close friendships provide opportunities to explore the self and develop a deep understanding of another person, supporting the development of self-concept, perspective taking, and identity.
            (2) They provide a foundation for future intimate relationships, which may help adolescents establish and work out problems in romantic partnerships.
            (3) They help young people deal with the stresses of adolescence, contributing to involvement in constructive youth activities, avoidance of antisocial acts, and psychological well-being.
            (4) They can improve attitudes toward and involvement in school, leading teenagers to view all aspects of school life more positively.
   D. Cliques and Crowds (pp. 328–329)
      1. In early adolescence, tightly knit *peer groups* tend to form, organized around **cliques**—groups of five to seven members who are good friends and, therefore, usually resemble one another in family background, attitudes, and values.

a. At first, cliques are limited to same-sex members, and, among girls but not boys, clique membership predicts academic and social competence.
b. Clique membership is more important to girls, who use it as a context for expressing emotional closeness.
c. By midadolescence, mixed-sex cliques are common.

2. Often several cliques with similar values form a larger, more loosely organized group called a **crowd**.
   a. Membership in a crowd is based on reputation and stereotype, giving the adolescent an identity within the larger social structure of the school.
   b. Typical high school crowds include "brains," "jocks," "populars," "partyers," "nonconformists," and "burnouts."
   c. Crowd affiliations are linked to strengths in adolescents' self-concepts, which reflect their interests and abilities, as well as family factors, suggesting that many peer-group values are extensions of values acquired at home.
      (1) Adolescents with authoritative parents are more likely to be members of "brain," "jock," and "popular" groups that accept both adult and peer reward systems.
      (2) Boys with permissive parents are more apt to align themselves with the "partyers" and "burnouts," suggesting lack of identification with adult reward systems.
3. As interest in dating increases, boys' and girls' cliques come together into mixed-sex cliques, which provide models for how to interact with the opposite sex and a chance to do so without having to be intimate.
   a. Gradually, the larger group divides into couples, several of whom spend time going out together.
   b. By late adolescence, as boys and girls become comfortable approaching each other directly, the mixed-sex clique disappears.
4. From tenth to twelfth grade, about half of young people switch crowds, mostly in favorable directions associated with rewarding friendships and gains in self-esteem.
5. "Brains" and "normal" crowds grow, and deviant crowds lose members as teenagers focus more on their future.

E. Dating (p. 329)
   1. With the hormonal changes of puberty, sexual interest increases, but cultural expectations determine when and how dating begins.
      a. Asian youths start dating later and have fewer dating partners than young people in Western societies, which encourage romantic involvements between teenagers from middle school on.
      b. Early relationships (at age 12 to 14) last only briefly, but by age 16 they continue, on average, for nearly two years.
      c. Young adolescents tend to mention recreation and achieving peer status as reasons for dating.
      d. By late adolescence, young people are ready for greater psychological intimacy and look for someone who offers companionship, affection, and social support.
      e. The achievement of intimacy between dating partners typically lags behind that of friends.
   2. Consistent with ethological theory and the idea that early attachment bonds lead to an *internal working model*—a set of expectations about attachment figures that guides later close relationships—secure models of parental attachment and supportive interactions with parents predicted secure models of friendship in high school seniors, which, in turn, were related to the security of their romantic relationships.
   3. These findings suggest that experiences with parents influence the quality of adolescents' friendships, and that teenagers then transfer what they have learned in their friendships to the romantic arena.
   4. Perhaps because early adolescent dating relationships are shallow and stereotyped, early dating is related to drug use, delinquency, and poor academic achievement.
      a. These factors, along with a history of aggression in family and peer relationships, increase the likelihood of dating violence.
      b. Young teenagers are better off sticking with group activities, such as parties and dances, before becoming involved with a steady boyfriend or girlfriend.

5. Homosexual youths face special challenges in initiating and maintaining visible romances.
    a. Their first dating relationships seem to be short-lived and to involve little emotional commitment, because they fear peer harassment and rejection.
    b. Many have difficulty finding a same-sex partner because their homosexual peers have not yet come out.
    c. Often their first contacts with other sexual minority youths occur in support groups, where they are free to date publicly.
6. As long as it does not begin too soon, dating provides lessons in cooperation, etiquette, and dealing with people in a wider range of situations.
    a. Among older teenagers, close romantic ties promote enhanced sensitivity, empathy, social support, and identity development.
    b. About half of first romances do not survive high school graduation, and those that do typically become less satisfying, because young people are still forming their identities, and are likely to find that they have little in common later on.

VII. PROBLEMS OF DEVELOPMENT (pp. 330–333)

A. Depression (p. 330)

1. The most common psychological problem of adolescence is depression—feeling sad, frustrated, and hopeless about life, accompanied by loss of pleasure in most activities and disturbances in sleep, appetite, concentration, and energy.
2. Rates of depression:
    a. About 15 to 20 percent of teenagers have had one or more major depressive episodes, a rate comparable to that of adults.
    b. From 2 to 8 percent are chronically depressed—gloomy and self-critical for many months and sometimes years.
3. Depressive symptoms increase sharply between ages 13 and 15, when sex differences emerge in industrialized nations, with adolescent girls twice as likely as boys to report persistent depression—a difference sustained throughout the lifespan.
4. Factors Related to Depression (p. 330)
    a. Kinship studies of twins and other close relatives reveal that heredity plays an important role in depression.
    b. Depression may also result from maladaptive parenting by the depressed parent, leading to impairment of the child's emotional self-regulation, attachment, and self-esteem.
    c. Depressed youths usually display a learned-helpless attributional style, viewing positive academic and social outcomes as beyond their control.
5. Sex Differences (p. 330)
    a. Biological changes associated with puberty cannot be responsible for depression because the gender difference is limited to industrialized nations.
    b. In developing countries, rates of depression are similar for males and females and occasionally higher in males.
    c. Gender-typed coping styles seem to be responsible for this difference.
        (1) Early-maturing girls are especially prone to depression.
        (2) Gender intensification in early adolescence often strengthens girls' passivity and dependency, which are maladaptive approaches to the tasks expected of teenagers in complex cultures.
        (3) Consistent with this explanation, adolescents who identify strongly with "feminine" traits are more depressed, regardless of their sex.
        (4) Girls who repeatedly feel overwhelmed develop an overly reactive physiological stress response and cope more poorly with future challenges.
        (5) In this way, stressful experiences and stress reactivity feed on one another, sustaining depression.
    d. Profound depression can lead to suicidal thoughts and, all too often, to suicide attempts.

B. Suicide (pp. 330–331)
   1. The suicide rate increases over the lifespan, from childhood to old age, but it jumps sharply at adolescence.
      a. Suicide is the third-leading cause of death (after motor vehicle collisions and homicides) among American youths and the second-leading cause (after motor vehicle collisions) among Canadian youths.
      b. In other industrialized nations, adolescent suicide rates vary widely, for reasons that remain unclear.
   2. Factors Related to Adolescent Suicide (pp. 330–331)
      a. Despite girls' higher rates of depression, 4 or 5 times as many boys as girls kill themselves.
         (1) Girls make more unsuccessful suicide attempts, using methods from which they are more likely to be revived, such as a sleeping pill overdose, while boys tend to choose techniques that lead to instant death, such as firearms or hanging.
         (2) Gender-role expectations may be responsible; less tolerance exists for feelings of helplessness and failed efforts in males than in females.
      b. African Americans and Hispanics have lower suicide rates than Caucasian Americans. However, the suicide rate among African-American adolescent males has risen recently.
      c. Native-American and Canadian-Aboriginal youths commit suicide at rates 2 to 7 times national averages, probably influenced by high rates of profound family poverty, school failure, alcohol and drug use, and depression.
      d. Gay, lesbian, and bisexual youths attempt suicide three times as often as other adolescents, as a result of more family conflict, inner turmoil about their sexuality, and peer rejection due to their sexual orientation.
   3. Suicide tends to occur in two types of young people.
      a. The first group includes highly intelligent adolescents who are solitary, withdrawn, and unable to meet their own high standards or those of important people in their lives.
      b. The second, larger group includes teenagers who show antisocial tendencies, and besides being hostile and destructive to others, they turn their anger and disappointment inward.
   4. Suicidal teenagers often have family backgrounds that include emotional and antisocial disorders, as well as a history of stressful life events, including economic disadvantage, parental divorce, frequent parent–child conflict, and abuse and neglect.
   5. Events that may trigger suicide attempts include parental blaming of the teenager for family problems, the breakup of an important peer relationship, or the humiliation of getting caught engaging in antisocial acts.
   6. Cognitive changes leading to an increase in suicide rates in adolescence:
      a. Teenagers are better able to plan ahead than younger children.
      b. Belief in the personal fable leads many depressed young people to conclude that no one could possibly understand their intense pain, and their despair and hopelessness deepen.
   7. Prevention and Treatment (p. 331)
      a. To prevent suicides, parents and teachers must be trained to pick up on the signals a troubled teenager sends.
      b. Schools and recreational and religious organizations can provide sympathetic counselors, peer support groups, and information about telephone hot lines.
      c. Once a teenager takes steps toward suicide, essential help includes staying with the young person, listening, and expressing compassion and concern until professional help arrives.
   8. Treatments for depressed and suicidal adolescents range from antidepressant medication to individual, family, and group therapy.
   9. Gun control legislation that limits adolescents' access to the most frequent and deadly suicide method in the United States would greatly reduce both the number of suicides and the high teenage homicide rate.
   10. Teenage suicides often occur in clusters, with one death increasing the likelihood of others among peers who knew the young person or heard about the suicide through the media.
   11. In view of this trend, a watchful eye must be kept on vulnerable adolescents after a suicide happens, and journalists should use restraint in publicizing teenage suicides.

C. Delinquency (pp. 331–333)
   1. Although North American youth crime has declined since the mid-1990s, U.S. and Canadian 12- to 17-year-olds account for a substantial proportion of police arrests—about 17 percent in the United States and 23 percent in Canada.
   2. Almost all teenagers, when asked directly and confidentially, admit to having committed an offense of some sort—usually a minor crime, such as petty stealing or disorderly conduct.
   3. Both police arrests and self-reports show that delinquency rises over adolescence, then declines into early adulthood.
      a. Among young teenagers, antisocial behavior increases as a result of the desire for peer approval.
      b. Over time, peers become less influential, moral reasoning improves, and young people enter social contexts (such as marriage, work, and career) that are less conducive to lawbreaking.
   4. For most adolescents, a brush with the law does not forecast long-term antisocial behavior, but repeated arrests are cause for concern.
      a. Teenagers are responsible for 13 percent of violent offenses in the United States and for 8 percent in Canada.
      b. A small percentage become recurrent offenders, who commit most of these crimes, and some enter a life of crime.
   5. Factors Related to Delinquency (p. 332)
      a. In adolescence, the gender gap in aggression widens: Although girls account for about 18 percent of adolescent violence—a larger proportion than a decade ago—their offenses are largely limited to simple assault (pushing or spitting), the least serious category, while violent crime continues to be mostly the domain of boys.
      b. Although SES and ethnicity are strong predictors of arrests, they are only mildly related to teenagers' self-reports of antisocial acts; arrest rates reflect primarily the tendency to arrest, charge, and punish low-SES ethnic minority youths more often than their higher-SES white and Asian counterparts.
      c. Difficult temperament, low intelligence, poor school performance, peer rejection in childhood, and association with antisocial peers are linked to delinquency.
         (1) Families of delinquent youths tend to be low in warmth, high in conflict, and characterized by harsh, inconsistent discipline and low monitoring, especially with boys.
         (2) When children who are extreme in these characteristics are also exposed to inept parenting, aggression rises during childhood, leads to violent offenses in adolescence, and persists into adulthood.
      d. Teenagers commit more crimes in poverty-stricken neighborhoods with limited recreational and employment opportunities and high adult criminality.
         (1) In such neighborhoods, adolescents have easy access to deviant peers, drugs, and firearms and are likely to be recruited into antisocial gangs, whose members commit the vast majority of violent delinquent acts.
         (2) Schools in these locales typically fail to meet students' developmental needs but, instead, are characterized by large classes, weak instruction, and lax enforcement of rules, all factors that increase teenagers' inclination toward aggression and violence.
   6. Prevention and Treatment (p. 332)
      a. Effective prevention of delinquency should start early and take place at multiple levels to address factors that include family relationships, parenting style, the quality of teaching in schools, and economic and social conditions in communities.
      b. Treating serious offenders also requires an intensive, often lengthy approach that recognizes the multiple determinants of delinquency.
      c. Efforts to create nonaggressive environments—at the family, community, and cultural levels—are needed to help delinquent youths and to foster healthy development of all young people.

LECTURE ENHANCEMENTS

LECTURE ENHANCEMENT 12.1
Age-Related Changes and Gender Differences in Perceptions of Self-Competence and Values (p. 315)

Time: 15–20 minutes

Objective: To examine age-related changes and gender differences in children's perceptions of self-competence and values.

As discussed in the text, children's beliefs about their own competence influence both achievement motivation and self-esteem. Children who perceive themselves as competent perform better in school and are more motivated to tackle challenging tasks than children who perceive themselves as incompetent. Researchers have found that perceptions of self-competence often change over time and differ among boys and girls. Whereas boys usually feel more competent in math and science, girls usually feel more competent in spelling and English. To extend existing research, Jacobs and colleagues (2002) recruited 761 children who were involved in the Childhood and Beyond longitudinal study. Using a sequential design, they followed three cohorts of children across the elementary, middle school, and high school years. During year one, participants were in grades 1, 2, and 4. At the end of the study, participants were in grades 9, 10, and 12. All were from middle- and high-income families; 95 percent were Caucasian. The researchers collected the following information:

1. Competence belief items. During the spring of each year, participants were asked to rate their competence in math, language arts, and sports.
2. Subjective task value items. During the spring of each year, participants were asked how interesting and how much fun math, language arts, and sports were. They were also asked how important it was to be good at each activity and how useful each activity was.
3. Performance measures. In year one, all participants took an intelligence test. Although the test measures general cognitive ability, the researchers were primarily interested in items assessing knowledge of math and language arts. Participants also completed a test of motor proficiency, which assesses performance on gross motor tasks (such as running, throwing a ball, and jumping) generally important for most sports activities.

Results indicated that self-perceptions of competence and subjective task values declined in all three areas (math, language arts, and sports) as children got older. Because young children's self-perceptions tend to be unrealistically high, the researchers expected a decline from early to middle childhood. However, the continuing decline into the high school years was unexpected. In response to this finding, Jacobs and colleagues (2002) suggested that as students get older, they encounter larger pools of potential competitors on sports teams and in advanced placement classes and that, as a result, their options for involvement in certain activities become increasingly limited. The best elementary school math student or athlete may transition to middle school and find that his or her skills are less developed than those of many other students.

Findings also indicated that over time, changes in competence beliefs predicted changes in value and usefulness ratings in all three areas. Participants who felt less competent in math, language arts, or sports placed less value on the importance and usefulness of those activities. Interestingly, gender differences in perceptions of competence and rates of change in those perceptions were largest among younger participants. Younger children felt more competent in gender-stereotyped activities (boys felt more competent in math and sports, and girls felt more competent in language arts). However, by middle school, both boys and girls had similar competence beliefs about math and sports. That is, they reported similar levels of competence in these two areas. The only significant gender difference was in language arts: Boys' feelings of competence and values decreased more rapidly than girls' feelings. Therefore, for this particular sample, the gender gap in math and sports actually narrowed over time, whereas the gender gap in language arts increased. Because these findings are not consistent with studies in which the gender gap for math and sports increases as children get older, it is possible that some unknown variable, such as socialization experiences, contributed to these results. It is also important to note that the majority of the participants came from middle- and upper-SES families and were not representative of the general population.

Taken together, these findings indicate that children's perceptions of competence show a steady decline from the elementary to the high school years. The results also suggest that the gender gap in math and sports is narrowing. It is possible that parents and teachers are encouraging girls to participate more in "nontraditional" activities. However, the finding that boys felt less competent in language arts as they got older suggests that language arts continues to be a gender-typed activity.

In small groups, have students list child-rearing practices that might contribute to self-perceptions of competence at academic and other activities during childhood and adolescence. Which practices support and which ones undermine children's sense of competence?

Jacobs, J. E., Lanza, S., Osgood, D. W., Eccles, J. S., & Wigfield, A. (2002). Changes in children's self-competence and values: Gender and domain differences across grades one through twelve. *Child Development, 73,* 509–527.

LECTURE ENHANCEMENT 12.2
Ethnic Identity and Academic Achievement (p. 318)

Time: 10 minutes

Objective: To highlight three aspects of ethnic identity, including the relationship between ethnic identity and academic achievement.

As noted in the text, a strong ethnic identity is associated with higher self-esteem, greater optimism, and a sense of mastery over one's environment. Compared to adolescents with a negative attitude toward their ethnic group, adolescents with a positive attitude seem to be better adjusted. Perhaps one of the most important benefits of a secure ethnic identity is higher academic achievement. In a longitudinal study, Chavous and colleagues (2003) examined the relationship between ethnic identity and academic outcomes among African-American teenagers. The study focused on three aspects of ethnic identity:

1. *Centrality*—the extent to which being African American is central to respondents' definitions of themselves (for example, "Being black is a major part of my identity"; "I feel close to other black people").
2. *Private regard*—one's positive or negative feelings toward African Americans and one's membership in that group (for example, "I am happy that I am black"; "I am proud of black people").
3. *Public regard*—the extent to which respondents feel that others view African Americans positively or negatively (for example, "In general, other groups view blacks in a positive manner"; "Blacks are considered to be good by society").

In general, findings showed that these three components of ethnic identity were related to academic beliefs and outcomes. Participants with high centrality, strong group pride (private regard), or positive beliefs about society's views of blacks (public regard) expressed greater confidence in their own academic ability. Participants with positive beliefs about societal views of African Americans also showed stronger attachment to school, in that they placed a higher value on education and had more positive relationships with teachers and other students. In addition, participants who scored higher on centrality and private regard had better school attendance, were more likely to complete high school, and were more likely to complete college. The researchers suggested that even though all three components of ethnic identity seem to be important influences, identifying with other African Americans and having a strong personal sense of ethnic pride seem to be especially important for academic behavior, aspirations, and attainment.

Chavous, T. M., Bernat, D. H., Schmeelk-Cone, K., Caldwell, C. H., Kohn-Wood, L., & Zimmerman, M. A. (2003). Racial identity and academic attainment among African-American adolescents. *Child Development, 74,* 1076–1090.

LECTURE ENHANCEMENT 12.3
More on Moral Development in Adolescence: Involvement in Religious Cults (pp. 323–324)

Time: 5–10 minutes

Objective: To examine why adolescents decide to join cults.

Research shows that involvement in religion generally seems to benefit an adolescent's moral development. However, religious cults do not supply this benefit. They can suppress adolescents' individuality or isolate them from the larger society. What makes some teenagers want to join these cults? According to Richmond (2004), some teenagers are especially likely to be attracted to a cult for the following reasons:

1. Conformity. Adolescents need to feel that they belong to a group and that they are cared for and important to others. Cults often serve this function.
2. Rebellion. Although adolescents express a need for conformity, they are also rebellious at times. When adolescents sense hypocrisy in parents and society, they may reject what others (particularly parents) tell them to do.
3. Confusion. The rapid series of changes associated with puberty and the developmental tasks of adolescence, including identity and autonomy, can be stressful and confusing for some adolescents. Cult leaders may appear to provide the direction, purpose, and leadership that confused adolescents crave.
4. Altruism. Adolescents often want to be devoted to a cause—to feel that they are making a difference in the world. Many cult organizations respond to this need because they appear to the teenager to be making the world "right," even though in actuality they are often destructive.
5. Intimacy. Cults and their leaders may serve as substitutes for parents. Young people who have no warm, involved relationships with parents may bond easily with cult leaders, who serve as influential authority figures and role models.

Of course, not all "dissenting religious groups" are harmful. Richmond (2004) maintains that asking several key questions can help determine whether a particular cult is dangerous: Does the group use mind control? Does it financially exploit its members? Does it claim to have an exalted status? Does it attempt to isolate itself from mainstream society? Does it have a history of committing acts of violence?

Richmond, L. J. (2004). When spirituality goes awry: Students in cults. *Professional School Counseling, 7,* 367–375.

LECTURE ENHANCEMENT 12.4
Peer Influences and Adolescent Risk Behavior (pp. 328–329)

Time: 15–20 minutes

Objective: To examine the influence of peers on adolescent sexual activity and binge drinking.

Peers influence adolescent risk-taking. However, researchers have also found that adolescents tend to select friends with whom they share values and personality traits. Therefore, teenagers with a predisposition toward high-risk behavior may engage in that behavior regardless of who their friends are.

To further examine the influence of peers on adolescent risk behavior, Jaccard, Blanton, and Dodge (2005) recruited 1,700 friendship dyads in grades 7 through 11. The study lasted one year and focused on the extent to which close friends encourage sexual activity and binge drinking in each other. The researchers collected the following information:

1. *Nominations and peer linking.* Each participant was asked to list five same-sex friends. To determine how close the participant was to each friend, the researchers asked a series of such questions, such as "Did you go to [name]'s house during the past week?" "Did you talk to [name] on the phone during the past week?" Questions were scored a 0 for a no and 1 for yes. The higher scores represented the participant's closest friends. The friend with the highest score became the participant's target friend.

2. *Adolescent satisfaction with maternal relationship.* Participants were asked to respond on a 5-point agree/disagree scale to the following question: "Overall, I am satisfied with my relationship with my mother."

3. *Adolescent perceptions of parental control.* To determine how controlling participants perceived their parents to be, the researchers asked, "Do your parents let you make your own decisions about (1) the time you come home on weekend nights, (2) the people you hang out with, (3) what you wear, (4) how much TV you watch, (5) which TV programs you watch, (6) what time you go to bed on weeknights, and (7) what you eat?" Questions were scored 1 for a no and 0 for a yes, with higher scores indicating greater parental control.

4. *Physical development.* Participants reported on their physical maturity by responding to several statements about pubertal development—for example, extent of body hair (boys) and degree of breast development (girls).

5. *Adolescent perceptions of mothers' attitudes about sex.* Participants were asked to rate their perceptions of their mother's attitudes toward sex and contraception, using the following questions: "How would your mother feel about your having sex at this time in your life?" "How would your mother feel about your using birth control at this time in your life?" Answers were scored on a scale of 1 to 5 from strongly approve to strongly disapprove.

6. *Academic achievement.* To measure academic achievement, the researchers obtained self-reported grades during the previous grading period.

7. *Involvement in romantic relationships.* Participants were asked to provide the first and last initials of individuals with whom they had a romantic relationship during the past 18 months.

8. *Behavioral outcomes.* Participants were asked if they had yet engaged in sexual intercourse and, if so, how recently. To determine if participants had engaged in binge drinking, they were asked, "Over the past 12 months, on how many days did you drink five or more drinks in a row?"

9. *Peer similarity on the surrounding dimension.* If both the participant and the target friend reported engaging in sexual activity or binge drinking, they were classified as similar on that dimension.

Results indicated that although friend behavior did have some impact on participants' sexual activity and binge drinking, the effects were small. According to Jaccard and colleagues (2005), unlike clothing preferences and extracurricular activities, sexual activity and binge drinking often represent fundamental value systems. Previous research indicates that adolescents are less vulnerable to peer pressure when personal values are at stake. At the same time, the small number of participants who engaged in binge drinking were very similar to their target friend in behavioral outcomes (how often they engaged in binge drinking) and in reports of low maternal warmth. This is consistent with other research in which peer influences are greater when parental bonds are strained.

Using information in this study, research in the text, and their own experiences, ask students to discuss factors that contribute to adolescent risk taking. Some students may even be willing to discuss their own experiences with peer pressure and risky behavior.

Jaccard, J., Blanton, H., & Dodge, T. (2005). Peer influences on risk behavior: An analysis of the effects of a close friend. *Developmental Psychology, 41,* 135–147.

LEARNING ACTIVITIES

LEARNING ACTIVITY 12.1
True or False: Self-Understanding in Adolescence (pp. 315–317)

Present the following exercise to students as a quiz or in-class activity:

Directions: Read each of the following statements and indicate whether it is *True* (T) or *False* (F).

Statements:

_____ 1. As adolescents' social world expands, contradictory self-descriptions increase.
_____ 2. Compared with school-age children, teenagers place less emphasis on social virtues, such as being friendly, considerate, kind, and cooperative.
_____ 3. For the majority of young people, level of self-esteem drops drastically in adolescence.
_____ 4. Individualized differences in self-esteem become increasingly stable in adolescence.
_____ 5. In a study of adolescents in 13 industrialized nations, most were pessimistic about the future.
_____ 6. Authoritarian parenting predicts high self-esteem in adolescence, just as it did in childhood.
_____ 7. Identity development often varies across identity domains, such as sexual orientation, vocation, and religious and political values.
_____ 8. Young people in long-term foreclosure and diffusion are more likely to view school and work as feasible avenues for realizing their aspirations and are more advanced in moral reasoning.
_____ 9. Foreclosed teenagers usually have close bonds with parents but lack opportunities for healthy separation.
_____ 10. Minority youths often feel caught between the standards of the larger society and those of their culture of origin.

Answers:

1. T
2. F
3. F
4. T
5. F
6. F
7. T
8. F
9. T
10. T

LEARNING ACTIVITY 12.2
Supporting Adolescent Identity Development (pp. 317–319)

As discussed in the text, supportive home and school environments can enhance identity development in adolescence. Ask students to respond to one of the following scenarios:

1. Provide advice to parents who want to nurture their teenager's identity development. In addition, cite parenting practices that are associated with a foreclosed or diffused identity status. Reflecting on your own adolescence, in what ways did your parents support or hinder your identity development?

2. Provide advice to high school personnel for nurturing students' identity development. What teaching practices, school services, and activities would be helpful? Reflecting on your own adolescence, in what ways did your high school experience foster or hinder your identity development?

LEARNING ACTIVITY 12.3
Matching: Moral Development in Adolescence (pp. 319–324)

Present the following exercise as an in-class activity or quiz:

Directions: Match each of the following terms with its correct definition.

Terms:

1. Moral dilemmas
2. Preconventional level
3. Conventional level
4. Postconventional/Principled level
5. Moral self-relevance

Definitions:

A. Individuals believe that actively maintaining the current social system ensures positive relationships and social order.
B. The degree to which morality is central to self-concept.
C. Morality is externally controlled: Behaviors that result in punishment are viewed as bad, and those that lead to rewards are seen as good.
D. Individuals define morality in terms of abstract principles and values that apply to all situations and societies.
E. Stories that present a conflict between two moral values.

Answers:

1. E
2. C
3. A
4. D
5. B

LEARNING ACTIVITY 12.4
Assessing Moral Reasoning (pp. 319–323)

Have students visit the website *http://www.haverford.edu/psych/ddavis/p109g/kohlberg.dilemmas.html*, which presents four moral dilemmas and a series of questions. Students should select one dilemma, answer the questions, and evaluate their level of moral reasoning on the basis of research in the text. Next, have students select a moral dilemma and ask a friend, roommate, or family member to read it and respond to the questions. Students should then classify that individual's level of moral reasoning. Finally, ask students to reflect on the activity. Do they think these moral dilemmas accurately assess moral reasoning? Why or why not?

LEARNING ACTIVITY 12.5
Analyzing Letters to the Editor in Your Local Newspaper for Maturity of Moral Reasoning (pp. 319–321)

Letters to the editor in newspapers often present reasoning on moral issues. For example, the U.S. war in Iraq is a "hot" topic for debate and is sometimes objected to on moral grounds. Abortion, political corruption, and the death penalty are other topics that often appear in the newspaper. Have students select one or two letters, identify the moral issues raised, and attempt to classify the maturity of moral reasoning expressed in each according to Kohlberg's stages. Once students have completed the activity, discuss their findings. What level of moral reasoning is reflected most often in the letters?

LEARNING ACTIVITY 12.6
Parent–Child Relationships in Adolescence (p. 325)

Tell students to pretend they have been asked to speak to a local parent organization about parent–child relationships in adolescence. Using research from Chapters 11 and 12, students should list topics to include in their presentation. For example, what are some myths about parent–child relationships during adolescence? Are high levels of parent–child conflict common in most families? What behavioral changes can parents expect as children transition from middle childhood to adolescence? How should parents respond to their child's growing need for autonomy? What parenting behaviors should parents avoid, and why?

LEARNING ACTIVITY 12.7
Internet Friendships (p. 327)

Have students interview two or three college-age friends about using the Internet to meet new people. The following questions may be helpful:

1. How do you feel about meeting new people on the Internet?
2. Have you ever met a friend or romantic partner on the Internet? If so, are you still in contact with that person? Was the individual honest and straightforward about him- or herself? Explain.
3. If you have met someone on the Internet, did you feel safe and supported by this person? Why or why not?
4. If you have not used the Internet to meet new people, will you do so in the future? Why or why not?
5. If you have used the Internet to meet new people, will you continue to do so in the future? Why or why not?
6. What are the benefits of meeting new people on the Internet? What are some potential risks?

After completing this activity, ask students to bring the interviews to class for discussion. For example, did the majority of respondents indicate that they had met new people on the Internet? Did they experience any problems with their online friend or romantic partner? For respondents who have never used the Internet to meet new people, what reasons did they give for this decision? Did the respondents seem to understand the potential dangers of meeting people online? Were students surprised by any of the findings?

LEARNING ACTIVITY 12.8
Observing Adolescent Peer Groups (pp. 326–329)

Suggest that students visit a typical teenage gathering place, such as a mall, arcade, fast-food restaurant, or movie theater, and answer the following questions: Are peer groups large or small? Same-sex or mixed? Are there differences in the ways boys and girls interact? How close do same-sex groups stand? How about mixed-sex groups? Is there anything noteworthy about group members' dress? What age differences are apparent? Once students have completed this activity, ask them to share some of their observations in class.

LEARNING ACTIVITY 12.9
Creating a Pamphlet About Problems of Development (pp. 330–333)

As noted in the text, most young people move through adolescence with little disturbance. However, some encounter major disruptions in development. In small groups, have students create a pamphlet for parents and teachers about problems of development. For example, what information do parents and teachers need to know about depression, suicide, and delinquency? What symptoms do depressed, suicidal, and delinquent youths often display? Do boys and girls display different symptoms? What biological and environmental factors contribute to problems of development? How can adults prevent and intervene with depressed, suicidal, and delinquent adolescents?

ASK YOURSELF . . .

REVIEW: List personal and contextual factors that contribute to identity development. (pp. 316–317)

Identity status is both cause and consequence of personality. Adolescents who have a flexible, open-minded approach to grappling with competing beliefs and values and who feel attached to parents but free to voice their own opinions are likely to be advanced in identity development. Interaction with peers expands adolescents' exposure to a variety of ideas and values, and attachment to friends is associated with greater involvement in exploring both relationship and career issues. Schools can promote identity development by offering rich and varied opportunities for exploration, both in the classroom and through extracurricular options. Because attending college expands young people's opportunities to explore career options and lifestyles, college students make more progress toward formulating an identity than they did in high school. Finally, larger societal forces also affect identity development, particularly for some ethnic minority adolescents and for gay, lesbian, and bisexual youths.

APPLY: Return to the conversation between Louis and Darryl in the opening of this chapter. Which identity status best characterizes each of the two boys, and why? (pp. 314, 316)

Both Louis and Darryl can be characterized as in a state of *identity moratorium*—exploration without having reached commitment to a path. They have begun to question who they are, what they value, and what their goals are in life. Neither Louis nor Darryl has committed himself to an identity. Their questioning is a start on the road to self-discovery.

REFLECT: How would you characterize your identity status? Does it vary across the domains of sexuality, close relationships, vocation, religious beliefs, and political values? Describe your identity development in an important domain, along with factors that may have influenced it. (p. 316)

This is an open-ended question with no right or wrong answer.

REVIEW: How does an understanding of ideal reciprocity contribute to moral development? Why might Kohlberg's Stages 3 and 4 be morally mature constructions? (pp. 320–321)

Kohlberg's Stage 3, described as the morality of interpersonal cooperation, depends on an understanding of ideal reciprocity as the basis for relationships. To attain this stage of moral development, an individual must have the capacity to view a two-person relationship from the vantage point of an impartial outside observer. Stage 4, expanding this orientation beyond close relationships, takes into account the larger perspective of societal laws that must be enforced evenhandedly in order to ensure societal order and cooperative relations between individuals.

Both of these stages require profound moral constructions that go beyond the mere social conformity implied by the term "conventional." Since very few people ever move beyond Stage 4, Kohlberg's "postconventional" morality may, in fact, be a highly reflective endeavor limited to a handful of people with advanced education in philosophy, while moral maturity may be found in a revised understanding of Stages 3 and 4.

APPLY: Tam grew up in a small village culture, Lydia in a large industrial city. At age 15, Tam reasons at Kohlberg's Stage 3, Lydia at Stage 4. What factors might account for the difference? (p. 323)

Young people in industrialized nations move through Kohlberg's stages more quickly and advance to higher levels than do individuals in nonindustrialized, village societies, who rarely move beyond Stage 3. In village societies, moral cooperation is based on direct relations between people. In Stages 4 to 6, reasoning depends on understanding the role of larger structures, such as laws and government institutions, in resolving moral conflict. Because individuals who are not exposed to these structures cannot reason at the higher stages, Tam reasons at a lower stage than Lydia does.

REFLECT: In early adolescence, did you and your friends display gender intensification? Cite examples. When did this concern with gender appropriateness decline? (p. 324)

This is an open-ended question with no right or wrong answer.

REVIEW: Cite the distinct positive functions of friendships, cliques, and crowds in adolescence. What factors lead some friendships and peer-group ties to be harmful? (pp. 326–329)

Teenagers, more than younger children, seek intimacy and loyalty in friendships. Adolescent friends tend to be alike in identity status, educational aspirations, political beliefs, and willingness to try drugs and engage in lawbreaking acts. As long as adolescent friendships are not characterized by jealousy, relational aggression, or a common attraction to antisocial behavior, they are related to many aspects of psychological health and competence into early childhood, for several reasons:

1. Close friendships provide opportunities to explore the self and develop a deep understanding of another person. Through open, honest communication, adolescent friends become sensitive to each other's strengths and weaknesses, needs and desires—a process that supports the development of self-concept, perspective taking, and identity.
2. Close friendships provide a foundation for future intimate relationships. Sexuality and romance are common topics of discussion between teenage friends. These conversations, along with the intimacy of friendship itself, may help adolescents establish and solve problems in romantic partnerships.
3. Close friendships help young people deal with the stresses of adolescence. Supportive, prosocial friendships promote empathy, sympathy, and prosocial behavior. As a result, friendships contribute to involvement in constructive youth activities, avoidance of antisocial acts, and psychological well-being.
4. Close friendships can improve attitudes toward and involvement in school. Teenagers who enjoy interacting with friends at school may begin to view all aspects of school life more positively.

In similar fashion, both cliques and crowds serve vital functions in adolescence. The *clique* provides a context for expressing emotional closeness, especially among girls, and predicts academic and social competence among girls, though not among boys. The *crowd,* a larger, more loosely organized group, provides adolescents with a temporary identity within the larger social structure of their school at an age when they are separating from family and constructing a coherent sense of self.

When adolescent friendships are based on a shared attraction to antisocial behavior, they can have a negative impact on psychological health and competence. Teenagers whose parents are permissive and uninvolved often affiliate with "partyer" or "burnout" crowds, suggesting lack of identification with adult reward systems. Furthermore, the impact of having antisocial, drug-using friends is strongest for teenagers whose parents use less effective child-rearing styles.

APPLY: Thirteen-year-old Mattie's parents are warm, firm in their expectations, and consistent in monitoring her activities. At school, Mattie met some girls who want her to tell her parents she's going to a friend's house and then, instead, join them at the beach for a party. Is Mattie likely to comply? Explain. (pp. 328–329)

Mattie is not likely to comply with her friends' suggestion that she lie to her parents. Her parents' warmth, firm expectations, and consistent monitoring of her activities are characteristics of an authoritative child-rearing style. Adolescents who describe their parents as authoritative tend to be members of peer groups (such as "brain," "jock," or "popular" groups) that accept both adult and peer reward systems—evidence that many peer-group values are extensions of values acquired at home. Although peer interaction exposes adolescents to a broader range of ideas and values than those they encounter at home, adolescents like Mattie are likely to feel attached to their parents but also free to voice their own opinions, giving them less reason to break their parents' rules. As a result, Mattie will probably say no to her friends' request.

REFLECT: How did family experiences influence your crowd membership in high school? How did your crowd membership influence your behavior? (pp. 328–329)

This is an open-ended question with no right or wrong answer.

REVIEW: Why are adolescent girls at greater risk for depression and adolescent boys at greater risk for suicide? (pp. 330–331)

Gender differences in rates of depression are seen only in industrialized nations, so they cannot be the result of biological changes associated with puberty. Research suggests that gender-typed coping styles are responsible for girls' higher depression rates. The gender intensification of early adolescence often strengthens girls' passivity and dependency—maladaptive approaches to the challenges encountered by teenagers in complex cultures. Consistent with this finding, adolescents who identify strongly with "feminine" traits are more likely to be depressed, regardless of their sex. Girls who repeatedly feel overwhelmed develop an overly reactive physiological stress response and cope poorly with future challenges. In this way, stressful experiences and stress reactivity feed on one another, sustaining depression.

Despite girls' higher rates of depression, far more boys than girls kill themselves, by a ratio of 4 or 5 to 1. Girls make more unsuccessful suicide attempts than boys, using methods from which they are more likely to be revived, such as an overdose of sleeping pills. In contrast, boys tend to choose techniques that lead to instant death, such as firearms. As with the female tendency toward depression, gender role expectations may be responsible: Less tolerance exists for feelings of helplessness and failed efforts in males than in females.

APPLY: Zeke had been a well-behaved child in elementary school, but at age 13 he started spending time with the "wrong crowd." At age 16, he was arrested for property damage. Is Zeke likely to become a long-term offender? Why or why not? (pp. 331–333)

Zeke is not likely to become a long-term offender. Adolescent delinquency follows two paths of development—one with an onset of conduct problems in childhood, the second with an onset in adolescence. Zeke, who did not have conduct problems in childhood, is following the second path. Longitudinal research reveals that the early-onset type is far more likely than the late-onset type, such as Zeke, to have a lifelong pattern of aggression and criminality. In youths who begin to display antisocial behavior around the time of puberty, conduct problems arise from the peer context of early adolescence, not from biological deficits or a history of unfavorable development as seen in early-onset children. The late-onset type of antisocial behavior usually does not persist beyond the transition to young adulthood.

SUGGESTED STUDENT READINGS

Kruger, J. (2005). *Identity in adolescence: The balance between self and other.* New York: Routledge. Presents a thorough overview of identity development in adolescence, including theories of identity development, the process of forming an identity, and up-to-date research.

Ladd, G. W. (2005). *Children's peer relations and social competence: A century of progress.* New Haven: Yale University Press. Using over a century's worth of research, this book examines the importance of peer relations for healthy child and adolescent development. Topics include early research on peer relations, friendship, the origins of social competence, and the role of gender, emotion, and culture in peer relationships.

Marcovitz, H. (2004). *Teens and family issues.* Folcroft, PA: Mason Crest Publishers. Based on results from the Gallup Youth Study, which surveys U.S. teenagers' perspectives on family, peers, school, social issues, and other relevant topics, this book examines the importance of family relationships for healthy development.

Underwood, M. (2003). *Social aggression among girls.* New York: Guilford. A collection of chapters highlighting the development and unique features of aggression in girls. The author also includes up-to-date research on the consequences of girls' aggression and approaches to intervention.

TRANSPARENCIES

T-154 Age Changes in Reported Self-Disclosure to Parents and Peers, Based on Data from Several Studies
Figure 12.1 (p. 327)

MEDIA MATERIALS

EXPLORING LIFESPAN DEVELOPMENT IN ACTION

Adolescence

This section opens with the dramatic physical changes of puberty, which lead to an adult-sized body and sexual maturity. When adolescents become sexually active without using contraception, the consequences can be profound, as Rhiannon and Joel's story reveals. After dating Joel for a year, Rhiannon discovered that she was pregnant. Joel and Rhiannon share their reactions to the pregnancy and describe how the arrival of their son, Jacob, has changed their lives. Ray and Laurie relate their concerns about the effect of adolescent parenthood on their son's future.

Next, the Observation Program turns to cognitive development. During adolescence, young people become better at thinking abstractly. Piaget's formal operational stage is illustrated through visits to high school social studies and math classes, where students engage in hypothetico-deductive reasoning and propositional thought.

During adolescence, peer groups become important contexts for social learning. The impact of puberty and of perspective taking on gender-role development in early adolescence is evident as eighth graders talk about their own and their peers' capacities and behaviors. For adolescent boys and girls alike, friendship plays an important role in the development of self-esteem and identity.

As adolescents' cognitive and social experiences expand, they think more about themselves. Teenagers combine their various personality traits into an organized self-concept, which provides a foundation for identity development. Jean, Phil, and Carla, high school seniors, discuss their experiences in constructing an identity. Mark, a college student, looks back on his struggle to formulate a sexual identity in adolescence. Best friends Mari and Sarah talk about the meaning and importance of friendship.

A WINDOW ON LIFESPAN DEVELOPMENT

A High School History Class

In this segment, high school students discuss the Protestant Reformation that took place in Europe in the sixteenth century. Martin Luther, a key figure in the Reformation, believed the Catholic Church to be corrupt. He was upset that the Church sold high-priced indulgences—tickets that ensured the buyer forgiveness of sins, participation in the grace of God, and freedom from purgatory. Luther published a list of grievances against the Church called the *Ninety-Five Theses*. In the list, Luther harshly criticized the Church's conduct and demanded reform. His actions eventually led to a split in the Catholic Church. Watch as students discuss Martin Luther and the Reformation. They not only express their own viewpoints but also engage in sophisticated debate with one another.

Friendship and Popularity: Mari and Sarah, Age 13

In this segment, Mari and Sarah discuss the meaning and importance of friendship and popularity. They begin by explaining how their friendship developed: They initially met at school and soon discovered they had similar interests and personalities. Sarah illustrates how adolescents regard intimacy and loyalty as important ingredients of friendship as she talks about how lies, dishonesty, and lack of communication can destroy a friendship. Next, Mari and Sarah give their perspectives on sex differences in friendship. Finally, the girls talk about cliques, crowds, and their perceptions of what makes people popular or unpopular. Notice how they mention various influences on clique and crowd membership, such as culture, parenting practices, and personality traits.

Identity and Relationships with Parents: High School Seniors

In this segment, a group of high school students discuss their identity development and talk about the role of parents in this developmental process. Notice how students credit their parents with their early identity and sense of self. However, the students point out that as they have grown and matured, their views have changed and are now quite different from those of their parents. They mention peers, the desire to be an individual, and exploring others' viewpoints as important influences on their current identity.

VIDEOTAPES AND DVDs

Adolescence: Social and Emotional Development (1998, Child Development Media/Magna Systems, 30 min.). This program explores one of the major tasks of adolescence—the search for identity in various domains: political, sexual, religious, and vocational. The program includes a discussion of the relationship between teenagers' values and ideals and those of their parents, illustrating how adolescents tend to follow their parents' values in serious matters, while looking to their peer group in such areas as music, dress, dating, and social patterns.

Adolescence: The Prolonged Transition (1993, GPN, 30 min.). This program, Module 19 of the Worlds of Childhood series, explores the extent to which "adolescence" as a period of increased autonomy, identity development, and risk taking is a socially constructed phenomenon. The program examines the rites of passage adolescents experience in a variety of cultures. It also addresses the universal aspects of adolescence—the biological changes of puberty and emerging sexuality, as well as the transition from childhood to a role in the broader adult world.

American Adolescence (1999, Films Media Group, 30 min.). This program looks at the factors—a rising divorce rate, frequent relocation of families, and preoccupation with television, video games, and computers—that account for the sense of isolation and detachment many contemporary teenagers feel in relation to traditional values and lifestyles. Through interviews with experts, including top officials of the Families and Work Institute, the National Teen Pregnancy Prevention Research Center, and the National Center on Addiction and Substance Abuse Control, the program considers the question of how this generation's hopes, fears, and expectations will shape U.S. society.

Childhood Depression (2000, Films Media Group/A Dartmouth-Hitchcock Medical Center Production, 29 min.). This program focuses on the 4 to 8 percent of American children—including up to 16 percent of teenage girls—who experience an episode of major depression. The program, part of the series The Doctor Is In, shows how early diagnosis and treatment are crucial in preventing patterns of repeated depression from occurring later in life and also in preventing related problems such as substance abuse and suicide. Children talk about their own experiences in coping with depression, and child psychiatrist David G. Fassler, author of *Help Me, I'm Sad,* and Dartmouth Medical School psychologist Steven Atkins provide professional insights.

Coming of Age: Ethnographic Profiles from a Global Perspective (2005, Films Media Group/A BBCW Production, 60 min.). This program examines the lives of six children and adolescents in a variety of cultures as each one experiences an important rite of passage in the transition from childhood to adulthood. Through portrayals of widely varying experiences, including an Inuit boy's first hunt, a young Russian's involvement in a right-wing hate group, and a 15-year-old Chinese girl's obligatory attendance at a weeklong military boot camp, the program illustrates both universal qualities and differences in human development around the world.

Dealing with Teens: A Guide to Survival (1994, Films Media Group, 47 min.). This program offers suggestions for dealing with some the issues faced by today's teens and preteens: experimentation with sex and drugs, relationships, sexuality, and moods and emotions. Moderated by actor Howard Hesseman and featuring a panel of medical experts, the program provides a list of warning signs for parents and others who want to try to define the limits of normal teenage behaviors.

Dear Mom and Dad, I'm Gay (1993, Films Media Group, 28 min.). In this specially adapted Phil Donahue program, gay teens and their parents discuss how parents react when they learn that they have a homosexual child, with scenarios ranging from acceptance to anger.

"Don't Kill Yourself": One Survivor's Message (1997, Films Media Group, 23 min.). This program tells the story of one young man, David, who survived a suicide attempt at age 16. Interviewed six years later, he talks about the events that led him to try to commit suicide. He describes how low self-esteem led him to become addicted to drugs, which in turn reinforced his sense that his life was not worth living. The program goes on to show how David recovered from addiction and changed his life in other ways after the suicide attempt.

From Depression to Discovery: A Teenager's Guidebook (2005, Films Media Group, 25 min.). This program exposes common myths and misconceptions about clinical depression, such as the idea that it does not affect young people. It portrays the outer and inner signs of depression and explores current forms of treatment. Interviews with teens who are living successfully with depression and commentary by adolescent psychologist Harold S. Koplewicz are woven together with graphics reinforcing essential information. A teacher's guide includes activities, discussion questions, and vocabulary terms.

Feel Good about Failure: The Dark Side of Self-Esteem Classes (1998, Films Media Group, 13 min.). In this program, *ABC News* anchors Diane Sawyer and Sam Donaldson and correspondent John Stossel look at the negative consequences of the self-esteem movement. The program points out that research evidence does not confirm any benefits of self-esteem classes, while empirical evidence suggests that too much praise can undermine students' interest in seeking out greater academic challenges. The program addresses the question of whether children are inadvertently being taught that there is no connection between effort and excellence. Finally, it notes that the American Psychological Association has stated that inflated self-esteem can actually set the stage for school violence.

Growing Up Fast (2004, Films Media Group, 35 min.). In this documentary, filmmaker and author Joanna Lipper tracks six teenage mothers and several young fathers during their last six months of high school. Going beyond a portrayal of the challenges of teen parenthood, the film reveals the strength, resilience, self-awareness, and insight these adolescents display as they reflect on their past decisions. Through the stories of these six teens, the film explores the emotional and psychological factors that lead to teen pregnancy. It challenges stereotypical assumptions about teen mothers by showing the young women working at minimum-wage jobs to support their families while simultaneously striving to complete the requirements for high school graduation. This program has been recognized by the Academy of Motion Picture Arts and Sciences as an outstanding short documentary. Additional information is online at *www.growingupfast.com.*

Kids and Crime: Keeping Kids Out of Trouble (1995, Films Media Group, 26 min.). This program examines successful efforts in various U.S. communities to help teenagers stay out of trouble. Examples include the stories of a former gang member in Texas, teens who run their own juvenile court in Florida, and Arizona schools that have instituted a longer school day in an effort to keep kids off the streets. The program also looks at community responses to gang violence and at a Connecticut initiative aimed at teaching young people nonviolent approaches to conflict resolution.

Moral Development I—Concept & Theory (1998, Magna Systems, 29 min.). Using live-action video examples and interviews, this program explains the concept of morality and defines key terms such as "moral code," "moral judgment," and "moral intelligence." The program discusses the complex issues involved in helping young people develop a sense of right and wrong. It illustrates how the essential values fundamental to most moral codes—empathy, duty, self-reliance, justice, and self-control—are developed throughout childhood and adolescence. In addition, the program reviews major theories of moral development, including psychoanalytic, sociobiological, social learning, and cognitive learning.

Moral Development II—Learning to Be Moral (1998, Magna Systems, 29 min.). This program reviews the emergence of moral behavior from infancy through adolescence. A detailed discussion of the roles of parents emphasizes how they nurture and stimulate their children's moral development. Through interviews and live-action video, the program, which includes the insights of both professionals and parents, examines the types of experiences and environmental factors that inhibit the unfolding of moral development.

Teen and Child Depression (1992, Films Media Group, 19 min.). This program looks at the common symptoms of depression, including oversleeping or insomnia, difficulties with concentration and memory, and lack of pleasure in life. It examines the possible causes of bipolar disorder, offers evidence for a biological basis for depression, and explores the role of environmental factors, such as child abuse, in activating depression. The program also discusses available treatments for depression.

Teens: What Makes Them Tick? (1999, Films Media Group, 41 min.). In this *ABC News* special, John Stossel interviews teens and their parents to examine what is really going on with adolescents during the years of "raging hormones." Through a visit to Harvard Medical School's Brain Imaging Center, Stossel explores the physiological explanations for teen behavior and describes the social hierarchy behind teenage fads. A psychologist and a therapist offer parents a few ideas for successfully nurturing teens: Have rules, but not too many; allow room for mistakes; listen more than you lecture.

3 Girls I Know: Intimate Stories of Personal Responsibility (2004, Films Media Group, 54 min.). This documentary looks at adolescent issues, including sexuality, relationships, and HIV/AIDS, through the stories of three teenage girls from various ethnic backgrounds. The girls talk about their sexual identities, their fears, and the consequences of their choices, and advocate for personal responsibility and for expanded sex education and AIDS awareness. A teacher's guide is included.

What's Health Got to Do with It? Young Women Speak Out (2002, Films Media Group, 53 min.). In this program, a diverse group of 16 teenage girls share observations on their own physical, mental, and emotional health, including such topics as body image, depression, eating disorders, relationships, sexual orientation, sexuality, and violence. The program, filmed over a four-week course at Smith College, portrays the relentless pressures in the lives of today's adolescent females.

TEST BANK

MULTIPLE CHOICE

1) According to Erikson, the major personality achievement during adolescence is
   A) identity.
   B) autonomy.
   C) intimacy.
   D) trust.
   Answer: A
   Page Ref: 314
   Skill: Factual
   Objective: 12.1

2) Yaya is trying to construct her identity. Based on Erikson's theory, which of the following would be of little concern to her?
   A) defining who she is
   B) defining what she values
   C) defining what directions she chooses to pursue in life
   D) helping her friends define what their values are
   Answer: D
   Page Ref: 314
   Skill: Applied
   Objective: 12.1

3) Erikson called the psychological conflict of adolescence
   A) self-esteem versus identity.
   B) identity versus role confusion.
   C) identity versus desires.
   D) desires versus reality.
   Answer: B
   Page Ref: 314
   Skill: Factual
   Objective: 12.1

4) Indigo has reached adolescence with a weak sense of trust. According to Erikson, she will
   A) have trouble finding ideals to have faith in.
   B) not engage in active exploration required to choose among alternatives.
   C) fail to select a career that matches her interests and skills.
   D) develop this trust over time through her involvement in cliques and peer groups.
   Answer: A
   Page Ref: 314
   Skill: Applied
   Objective: 12.1

5) Leslie is unable to select a vocation that matches her interests and skills. She probably
   A) has a weak sense of trust.
   B) has little autonomy.
   C) lacks a sense of industry.
   D) has no initiative.
   Answer: C
   Page Ref: 314
   Skill: Applied
   Objective: 12.1

6) Sixteen-year-old Isaac is going through a temporary period of confusion and distress. He is experimenting with alternatives and will finally settle on his own personal values and goals. Erikson would say that Issac is undergoing
   A) identity confusion.
   B) identity exploration.
   C) an identity crisis.
   D) an identity breakdown.
   Answer: C
   Page Ref: 314
   Skill: Applied
   Objective: 12.1

7) Alba is a young adult who has not achieved a firm sense of self. According to Erikson, she will
   A) experience role confusion until her early twenties and then eventually develop an identity.
   B) find it difficult to risk intimacy.
   C) probably work in a vocation that her parents select for her.
   D) have little religious faith or belief in a higher being.
   Answer: B
   Page Ref: 315
   Skill: Applied
   Objective: 12.1

8) According to Erikson, someone who suffers a negative outcome to the psychological conflict of adolescence will experience
   A) restricted exploration.
   B) personality crisis.
   C) basic commitment.
   D) role confusion.
   Answer: D
   Page Ref: 314
   Skill: Factual
   Objective: 12.1

9) Mr. and Mrs. Azpeitia notice that their 13-year-old daughter describes herself to her grandmother as "pretty smart," but refers to herself as "an airhead" around her friends. Similarly, she talks at dinner of the difficulties of being shy, but then laughs in agreement when her friends tease her about being very outgoing. If Mr. and Mrs. Azpeitia came to you for advice about their daughter, what could you tell them (based on information in your text)?
   A) As she gets older, their daughter's cognitive changes will allow her to combine her traits into an organized system.
   B) The traits that she exhibits around her family are probably indicative of her true self.
   C) The traits that she exhibits around her friends are probably an indication of who she really wants to be.
   D) She will eventually resolve these inconsistencies by integrating principles that make sense out of the contradictions, but this typically does not occur until early adulthood.
   Answer: A
   Page Ref: 315
   Skill: Applied
   Objective: 12.2

10) Which statement below exemplifies an adolescent's awareness that psychological qualities often change from one situation to the next?
   A) "I have a fairly good sense of humor."
   B) "I'm smart."
   C) "I'm not shy."
   D) "I think I'm a good person."

   Answer: A

   Page Ref: 315
   Skill: Conceptual
   Objective: 12.2

11) Compared to those of her 10-year-old sister, 15-year-old Lillie's self-descriptions will place more emphasis on
   A) physical appearance.
   B) social virtues.
   C) favorite activities.
   D) school performance.

   Answer: B

   Page Ref: 315
   Skill: Applied
   Objective: 12.2

12) As DeJuan enters adolescence, he is likely to add which dimensions of self-evaluation?
   A) athletic ability, academic ability, social awareness
   B) friendship, honesty, integrity
   C) physical attractiveness, romantic appeal, relationships with family members
   D) close friendship, romantic appeal, job competence

   Answer: D

   Page Ref: 315
   Skill: Applied
   Objective: 12.2

13) Landon's parents wonder how his self-esteem will change during adolescence. They would be interested to know that it will probably
   A) differentiate and rise steadily.
   B) become more negative.
   C) fluctuate a great deal.
   D) remain stable.

   Answer: A

   Page Ref: 315
   Skill: Applied
   Objective: 12.2

14) Which of the following is a powerful predictor of teenagers' judgments of the importance and usefulness of school subjects, their willingness to exert effort, their achievement, and their eventual career choices?
   A) job competence
   B) academic self-esteem
   C) athletic self-esteem
   D) positive peer relationships

   Answer: B

   Page Ref: 315
   Skill: Factual
   Objective: 12.2

15) Which of the following factors is predictive of high self-esteem in adolescence?
   A) conditional support from parents and peers
   B) "acting phony" to avoid peer disapproval
   C) authoritative parenting
   D) living in a neighborhood with many people of different ethnicities

Answer: C
Page Ref: 315
Skill: Factual
Objective: 12.2

16) Tony has thought hard and talked to many people before selecting a career in music. When asked if he'd change his mind if something better comes along, he said, "I doubt it." He is characterized by
   A) identity moratorium.
   B) identity diffusion.
   C) identity foreclosure.
   D) identity achievement.

Answer: D
Page Ref: 316
Skill: Applied
Objective: 12.3

17) Katarina accepts her family's political and religious beliefs without question. She is characterized by
   A) identity foreclosure.
   B) identity diffusion.
   C) identity moratorium.
   D) identity achievement.

Answer: A
Page Ref: 316
Skill: Applied
Objective: 12.3

18) When asked about his career plans, Simon says, "Haven't thought about it. Doesn't make too much difference what I do." He is characterized by
   A) identity achievement.
   B) identity diffusion.
   C) identity moratorium.
   D) identity foreclosure.

Answer: B
Page Ref: 316
Skill: Applied
Objective: 12.3

19) Shannon has begun to question her parents' religious beliefs and is visiting other churches to find out about alternatives. She is characterized by
   A) identity diffusion.
   B) identity foreclosure.
   C) identity moratorium.
   D) identity achievement.

Answer: C
Page Ref: 316
Skill: Applied
Objective: 12.3

20) Shirin has made more progress toward formulating an identity in the last three years than in the previous four years. Shirin will probably also sample a broad range of life experiences before choosing a life course. Shirin probably
   A) is a college student.
   B) dropped out of high school.
   C) started working immediately after finishing high school.
   D) is identity diffused.
   Answer: A
   Page Ref: 316
   Skill: Applied
   Objective: 12.3

21) Shane gets upset when his classmates disagree with him and regards their behavior as a threat. Shane is in which identity status?
   A) identity diffusion
   B) identity conventionalism
   C) identity foreclosure
   D) identity moratorium
   Answer: C
   Page Ref: 316
   Skill: Applied
   Objective: 12.3

22) Sixteen-year-old Nico tends to go along with whatever his friends are doing, has trouble with time management, and has a sense of hopelessness about the future. He has probably spent a long time in which identity status?
   A) identity foreclosure
   B) identity diffusion
   C) identity moratorium
   D) identity achievement
   Answer: B
   Page Ref: 316
   Skill: Applied
   Objective: 12.3

23) The possibility for reformulating identity exists
   A) primarily during the later teenage years.
   B) only during middle childhood.
   C) for diffused and foreclosed adolescents only.
   D) whenever the individual or his or her situational context changes.
   Answer: D
   Page Ref: 316
   Skill: Factual
   Objective: 12.3

24) Roberto insists that the absolute truth is always attainable. Roberto is probably
   A) identity foreclosed.
   B) identity diffused.
   C) in a state of identity moratorium.
   D) identity achieved.
   Answer: A
   Page Ref: 316
   Skill: Applied
   Objective: 12.3

25) Halleli is an adolescent who is identity achieved. As such, she will tend to
   A) assume that absolute truth can always be achieved.
   B) doubt that anything can ever be known with certainty.
   C) believe rational criteria can be used to make choices.
   D) display more concrete and fewer formal operations.
Answer: C
Page Ref: 316
Skill: Applied
Objective: 12.3

26) Mr. and Mrs. Zhao want to help their son develop a more mature identity. They can support this by
   A) developing very close bonds with little chance for separation.
   B) providing low levels of warmth or open communication.
   C) providing more specific direction about how he should behave.
   D) developing close bonds while allowing freedom to voice his own opinions.
Answer: D
Page Ref: 316–317
Skill: Applied
Objective: 12.3

27) Teenagers with warm, trusting peer ties are
   A) more likely to demonstrate career interests similar to their friends', reducing the amount of career exploration that they do.
   B) less likely to be involved in vocational training programs.
   C) more likely to be in academically challenging classes and aspire to higher-paying careers.
   D) more involved in exploring relationship issues, such as what they value in close friends and in a life partner.
Answer: D
Page Ref: 317
Skill: Conceptual
Objective: 12.3

28) Which of the following is a strategy for helping minority adolescents resolve identity conflicts constructively?
   A) Encourage ethnic pride and separation from other ethnic groups.
   B) Promote effective parenting that discourages students to explore the meaning of ethnicity in their own lives.
   C) Respect native language and unique learning styles in school.
   D) Prevent contact between ethnic groups.
Answer: C
Page Ref: 318
Skill: Conceptual
Objective: Box CI: Identity Development Among Ethnic Minority Adolescents

29) Kohlberg assessed moral maturity by describing a moral dilemma and analyzing a person's responses to it. His analysis focused primarily on which aspect of the response?
   A) content
   B) emotions
   C) reasoning
   D) length
Answer: C
Page Ref: 319
Skill: Factual
Objective: 12.4

30) In response to the Heinz dilemma, Juanita explains, "He shouldn't steal it, because if he does he could go to jail." She is at which of Kohlberg's stages of moral development?
   A) Stage 1
   B) Stage 2
   C) Stage 3
   D) Stage 4
Answer: A
Page Ref: 320
Skill: Applied
Objective: 12.4

31) In response to the Heinz dilemma, Tom states, "The druggist can do what he wants and Heinz can do what he wants to do." He is at which of Kohlberg's stages of moral development?
   A) Stage 1
   B) Stage 2
   C) Stage 3
   D) Stage 4
Answer: B
Page Ref: 320
Skill: Applied
Objective: 12.4

32) When individuals express the same concern for the welfare of another as they do for themselves, they understand a standard of fairness called
   A) ideal reciprocity.
   B) a moral dilemma.
   C) instrumental purpose.
   D) universal ethics.
Answer: A
Page Ref: 320
Skill: Factual
Objective: 12.4

33) In response to the Heinz dilemma, Maria says, "The law was written to protect people, but in this case it's hurting his wife. So he should steal it, since by breaking the law he is really following its original meaning." She is at which of Kohlberg's stages of moral development?
   A) Stage 3
   B) Stage 4
   C) Stage 5
   D) Stage 6
Answer: C
Page Ref: 321
Skill: Applied
Objective: 12.4

34) In response to the Heinz dilemma, Jodie states, "If he doesn't do everything he can to save his wife, his family and friends will be ashamed of him, so I think he should steal it." She is at which of Kohlberg's stages of moral development?
   A) Stage 3
   B) Stage 4
   C) Stage 5
   D) Stage 6
Answer: A
Page Ref: 320
Skill: Applied
Objective: 12.4

35) In response to the Heinz dilemma, Amos says, "His wife's life is important, but society can't exist if people break the laws any time they want to. Heinz should not steal it because it would undermine society." He is at which of Kohlberg's stages of moral development?
A) Stage 3
B) Stage 4
C) Stage 5
D) Stage 6
Answer: B
Page Ref: 321
Skill: Applied
Objective: 12.4

36) In response to the Heinz dilemma, Martin explains, "A human life has more value than any sort of property. He should steal the drug to protect that life." He is at which of Kohlberg's stages of moral development?
A) Stage 3
B) Stage 4
C) Stage 5
D) Stage 6
Answer: D
Page Ref: 321
Skill: Applied
Objective: 12.4

37) Although Kohlberg proposes six stages of moral development,
A) current research suggests there are at least eight stages.
B) his research was only able to verify the first three stages.
C) most people never move beyond Stage 4.
D) there is no evidence to support his theory.
Answer: C
Page Ref: 321
Skill: Factual
Objective: 12.4

38) Kohlberg's Stage 6 is a matter of speculation that might only be achieved (theoretically) by
A) people who have devoted their lives to religious thought and prayer.
B) world leaders whose experiences have allowed them to make hundreds of moral decisions, all of which affect the fate of many.
C) individuals who have had training in Kohlberg's theories.
D) individuals with advanced education, usually with training in philosophy.
Answer: D
Page Ref: 321
Skill: Factual
Objective: 12.4

39) Because everyday decisions are complicated by real-world factors and emotions, the moral reasoning exhibited in such situations is generally
A) lower than that measured by Kohlberg's dilemmas.
B) higher than that measured by Kohlberg's dilemmas.
C) easier for people to grapple with than hypothetical situations.
D) determined by a "majority rules" mentality of those involved.
Answer: A
Page Ref: 321
Skill: Factual
Objective: 12.4

40) Consider the following statement: "An ethic of care should be considered when evaluating moral reasoning." The statement is consistent with the beliefs of which person?
   A) Erikson
   B) Kohlberg
   C) Piaget
   D) Gilligan
   Answer: D
   Page Ref: 321–322
   Skill: Factual
   Objective: 12.5

41) Dr. Maya wants to test Gilligan's claim that Kohlberg's approach to morality underestimates the moral maturity of females. If her research results are consistent with others who tested this claim,
   A) she will find little evidence to support this belief as females reason at the same or a higher stage as their male agemates.
   B) her evidence will find that Gilligan is correct in her criticism of Kohlberg.
   C) she will find that Kohlberg's approach overestimates the morality of females.
   D) she will find that themes of both justice and caring appear in the responses of males but not females.
   Answer: A
   Page Ref: 322
   Skill: Factual
   Objective: 12.5

42) When differences in male and female morality do appear, they
   A) occur most often in real-life rather than hypothetical dilemmas.
   B) are opposite of Gilligan's viewpoint.
   C) show that women actually stress justice over care.
   D) provide differing and often contradictory results.
   Answer: A
   Page Ref: 322
   Skill: Factual
   Objective: 12.5

43) Which of the following issues will teenager Zandile argue are the province of the individual and not subject to control by authority figures?
   A) dress and hairstyle
   B) establishing a business
   C) behavioral expectations in school settings
   D) wages and taxes
   Answer: A
   Page Ref: 322
   Skill: Applied
   Objective: 12.5

44) Parents can help their adolescents achieve greater gains in moral understanding by
   A) asking clarifying questions.
   B) remaining silent when adolescents struggle with exercises in reasoning.
   C) stating their own personal opinions frequently.
   D) listening critically to adolescents' ideas.
   Answer: A
   Page Ref: 322
   Skill: Conceptual
   Objective: 12.6

45) Aida makes little or no gains in moral reasoning as a teenager. Her parents probably
   A) lecture, use threats, and make sarcastic remarks.
   B) have made good progress in their own moral reasoning.
   C) listen sensitively and ask clarifying questions.
   D) foster discussion of moral concerns.

Answer: A
Page Ref: 322
Skill: Applied
Objective: 12.6

46) Why are an individual's years of schooling such a powerful predictor of movement to Kohlberg's Stage 4 of moral reasoning?
   A) Post-secondary education is strongly affiliated with household income, which in turn correlates to moral development.
   B) Most colleges and universities require at least three undergraduate level classes on moral reasoning.
   C) Moral reasoning increases with age; the more years of schooling an individual has, the older they are.
   D) Attending college introduces young people to social issues that broaden their perspective-taking opportunities.

Answer: D
Page Ref: 322
Skill: Factual
Objective: 12.6

47) Which interaction is more likely to increase levels of moral reasoning?
   A) Two friends confront and critique each others' viewpoints on a controversial topic.
   B) A teenager heckles a woman who is protesting outside the state's capitol building.
   C) An adolescent listens quietly to her friend's viewpoint and then says she agrees.
   D) A class watches a televised debate between two political candidates on a controversial subject.

Answer: A
Page Ref: 322
Skill: Conceptual
Objective: 12.6

48) People in tribal and village cultures rarely move beyond Kohlberg's Stage 3 because
   A) moral reasoning at Stages 4 through 6 depends on an understanding of the role of larger societal structures in resolving conflict and such structures do not exist in these cultures.
   B) they are not capable of moral reasoning at higher levels.
   C) they do not have access to higher education, crucial to the development of higher moral reasoning.
   D) only individuals from Western cultures can attain higher moral reasoning.

Answer: A
Page Ref: 323
Skill: Factual
Objective: 12.6

49) In response to the Heinz dilemma, an elderly gentleman states, "The entire community is to blame for this situation. Heinz should not be facing this problem alone. It is everyone's responsibility to join in and get help for his wife." We can deduce from this statement that the gentleman
   A) is permanently stuck in Kohlberg's Stage 2.
   B) probably did not understand the question.
   C) probably comes from a small village or collectivist culture.
   D) has achieved Kohlberg's Stage 6.

Answer: C
Page Ref: 323
Skill: Applied
Objective: 12.6

50) Dan and Leon are both college sophomores. Leon is functioning at a higher moral reasoning level than Dan. What conclusion can we draw based on that knowledge?
   A) Leon is just as likely to cheat on tests as Dan.
   B) Dan is actually more honest.
   C) Dan is more likely to display behavior that is in line with his beliefs.
   D) Leon is more likely to help, share, and defend victims of injustice.
Answer: D
Page Ref: 323
Skill: Applied
Objective: 12.6

51) Azure works hard to behave in ways that she sees as moral and decent. Her sense of morality is very important to her self-concept. Azure's characteristics can be thought of as
   A) moral self-relevance.
   B) ideal reciprocity.
   C) autonomy.
   D) moral identity.
Answer: A
Page Ref: 323
Skill: Applied
Objective: 12.6

52) Which statement best explains the development of moral self-relevance?
   A) Research has yet to discover the origins of a sense of moral self-relevance.
   B) Close peer relationships have the greatest impact on moral self-relevance.
   C) Just educational environments are most predictive of moral self-relevance as an adult.
   D) Authoritarian parenting is strongly linked to the development of moral self-relevance.
Answer: A
Page Ref: 323
Skill: Factual
Objective: 12.6

53) Teenagers from which country are most likely to report being religious?
   A) Italy
   B) Great Britain
   C) Canada
   D) United States
Answer: D
Page Ref: 323–324
Skill: Factual
Objective: 12.6

54) Which type of religious involvement has been shown to hinder the development of moral maturity?
   A) religious education
   B) involvement in church youth groups
   C) indoctrination into a religious cult
   D) personal feelings of connection to a higher being
Answer: C
Page Ref: 324
Skill: Factual
Objective: 12.6

55) Marla, who used to wear work shoes, jeans, and loose flannel shirts, suddenly starts dressing in skirts and heels and wearing makeup. She is showing evidence of
A) gender intensification.
B) social androgyny.
C) the Oedipal conflict.
D) identity foreclosure.
Answer: A
Page Ref: 324
Skill: Applied
Objective: 12.7

56) Which individual will likely show stronger gender intensification?
A) Evan, a 10-year-old boy
B) Eve, a 10-year-old girl
C) Reece, a teenage boy
D) Tamar, a teenage girl
Answer: D
Page Ref: 324
Skill: Applied
Objective: 12.7

57) Which of the following contributes to gender intensification in adolescence?
A) the magnification of sex differences in appearance caused by puberty
B) decreased concern for what others think
C) course offerings (home economics or shop classes) of high schools
D) sexual content in R-rated movies
Answer: A
Page Ref: 324
Skill: Conceptual
Objective: 12.7

58) Which child is likely to be psychologically healthier?
A) Maria, who has a strong feminine gender identity
B) Luis, who has a strong masculine gender identity
C) Gabriella, who has an androgynous gender identity
D) Gordon, who has a strong feminine gender identity
Answer: C
Page Ref: 325
Skill: Applied
Objective: 12.7

59) Shobana wants to rely more on herself than on her parents when decisions come up that affect her. She feels more independent from her parents than at any other time of her life. Shobana is developing
A) individuality.
B) identity foreclosure.
C) autonomy.
D) identity diffusion.
Answer: C
Page Ref: 325
Skill: Applied
Objective: 12.7

60) During adolescence, an improved ability to reason about social relationships leads teenagers to __________ their parents.
   A) deidealize
   B) idolize
   C) lose respect for
   D) feel sorry for
   Answer: A
   Page Ref: 325
   Skill: Factual
   Objective: 12.8

61) Mr. and Mrs. McDermott's three children all have low self-esteem, struggle with depression, and exhibit antisocial behavior. Mr. and Mrs. McDermott probably incorporate which of the following parenting techniques?
   A) coercive or controlling behaviors
   B) psychologically supportive behaviors
   C) firm monitoring of children's activities
   D) permissiveness and noninterference
   Answer: A
   Page Ref: 325
   Skill: Conceptual
   Objective: 12.8

62) In the parent–adolescent relationships, __________ predicts favorable adjustment of young people and __________ predicts their mental health.
   A) deidealization; autonomy
   B) gender intensification; moral self-relevance
   C) focus on the family; focus on peers
   D) consistent parental monitoring; quality of the relationship
   Answer: D
   Page Ref: 325
   Skill: Factual
   Objective: 12.8

63) Mr. and Mrs. Santistevan wonder what they can do to promote the mental health of their two teenage children. They should know that __________ is the single most consistent predictor of mental health.
   A) the quality of the parent-child relationship
   B) the level of moral self-relevance achieved
   C) early granting of autonomy
   D) strong sibling affection
   Answer: A
   Page Ref: 325
   Skill: Applied
   Objective: 12.8

64) Which of the following is a positive outcome of mild family conflict?
   A) Occasional conflicts signal that the parents are probably slightly overprotective and need to consider greater autonomy granting.
   B) Mild conflicts help everyone in the family appreciate nonconflict-ridden times.
   C) Conflicts inform parents of the changing needs and expectations of their children, signaling that adjustments in the parent–child relationship are necessary.
   D) Conflicts during the teenage years are expected by parents, who would be worried that something were amiss if they did not surface occasionally.
   Answer: C
   Page Ref: 325
   Skill: Factual
   Objective: 12.8

65) Renata lives in a dangerous neighborhood. As a result, her parents maintain tighter control and put more pressure on her to behave in a safe manner. Renata is likely to
   A) resent the lack of freedom that she has in comparison to her friends.
   B) experience more conflict due to their controlling parenting style.
   C) interpret her parents' behavior as a sign of parental caring.
   D) exhibit more anxiety and depression than her peers whose parents are not as strict.
   Answer: C
   Page Ref: 325
   Skill: Applied
   Objective: 12.8

66) Which family is likely to grant its teenager an appropriate degree of autonomy?
   A) Martina's parents both hold time-consuming, stressful jobs.
   B) Karina is being raised by her grandmother, who has been out of work for nearly seven months.
   C) Serena's parents are financially secure, invested in their work, and content in their marriage.
   D) Bettina's parents are divorcing and fighting over custody.
   Answer: C
   Page Ref: 326
   Skill: Applied
   Objective: 12.8

67) Teenagers who develop well despite family stresses tend to have
   A) high self-esteem.
   B) a firm parent who combines structure with strong discipline.
   C) an intense, driven personality.
   D) a bond with an adult outside the family who cares deeply for their well-being.
   Answer: D
   Page Ref: 327
   Skill: Conceptual
   Objective: 12.8

68) As younger siblings mature and become more self-sufficient,
   A) they depend more on the advice of older siblings on wardrobe and dating issues than on their parents.
   B) they accept less direction from their older brothers and sisters.
   C) the relationships of same-sex siblings strengthen, while opposite-sex sibling relationships become more distant.
   D) girls work harder than boys to maintain relationships with siblings.
   Answer: B
   Page Ref: 326
   Skill: Factual
   Objective: 12.8

69) Smita and Shailaja have always had a very strong sibling relationship. As they enter the teenage years, we can expect their relationship to become
   A) more unequal.
   B) hostile and quarrelsome.
   C) more intense.
   D) less intense.
   Answer: D
   Page Ref: 326
   Skill: Applied
   Objective: 12.8

70) Teenagers in the United States spend more time together outside the classroom than do teenagers in East Asia, because
   A) more teens in the United States come from large families.
   B) of a shorter school year and less demanding academic standards.
   C) the United States has fewer public gathering places for teens.
   D) there is greater flexibility in school hours in East Asia.
   Answer: B
   Page Ref: 326
   Skill: Factual
   Objective: 12.9

71) The number of "best friends"
   A) is the marker by which adolescents measure popularity.
   B) is generally larger for girls than for boys.
   C) declines during adolescence to about one or two in adulthood.
   D) steadily increases during adolescence as teenagers fine-tune their social skills.
   Answer: C
   Page Ref: 326
   Skill: Factual
   Objective: 12.9

72) When asked about the meaning of friendship, teenagers stress which of the following characteristics?
   A) attractiveness and popularity
   B) common interests and activities
   C) intimacy and loyalty
   D) kindness and happiness
   Answer: C
   Page Ref: 326
   Skill: Factual
   Objective: 12.9

73) Which pair is typical of adolescent friends?
   A) Jayme and Somer, who are alike in identity status, educational aspirations, and political beliefs
   B) Autumn and Skye, who are very different in identity status, educational aspirations, and political beliefs
   C) Bella and Kate, who argue a lot
   D) Connor—a boy and Lizzy—a girl
   Answer: A
   Page Ref: 326
   Skill: Applied
   Objective: 12.9

74) Which of the following activities among friends can spark anxiety or depression?
   A) self-disclosure
   B) formation of a clique
   C) co-rumination
   D) competition for similar goals
   Answer: C
   Page Ref: 327
   Skill: Factual
   Objective: 12.9

106) Describe the functions that cliques and crowds serve, and explain the factors that cause the importance of crowds to decline over time.

Answer: Cliques are small groups of about five to seven members who are good friends and similar in family background, attitudes, and values. Sometimes several cliques with similar values form a larger, more loosely organized group called a crowd. Unlike the more intimate clique, membership in a crowd is based on reputation and stereotype. Whereas the clique serves as the main context for direct interaction, the crowd grants the adolescent an identity within the larger social structure of the school. Cliques offer models for how to interact with the other sex and a chance to do so without having to be intimate. By late adolescence, boys and girls feel comfortable enough about approaching each other directly that the mixed-sex clique is no longer needed and disappears. Crowds also decline in importance, as adolescents formulate personal values and goals.

Page Ref: 329

107) Describe the challenges facing homosexual adolescents as they enter into dating relationships.

Answer: The first dating relationships of homosexual youths seem to be short-lived and to involve little emotional commitment for different reasons from those of heterosexuals: They fear peer harassment and rejection. In addition, many have difficulty finding a same-sex partner because their homosexual peers have not yet come out.

Page Ref: 329

108) Describe behaviors characteristic of depression in adolescents, and differentiate between typical patterns of boys and girls.

Answer: Depression—feeling sad, frustrated, and hopeless about life, accompanied by a loss of pleasure in most activities and disturbances in sleep, appetite, concentration, and energy—is the most common psychological problem of adolescence. Gender-typed coping styles seem to be responsible for the different rates of depression among boys and girls. Early-maturing girls, who often have a negative body image and are less well-liked by peers, are prone to depression. At the same time, the gender intensification of early adolescence often strengthens girls' passivity and dependency—maladaptive approaches to the tasks expected of teenagers in complex cultures. Adolescents who identify strongly with "feminine" traits are more depressed than their "masculine" and "androgynous" agemates, regardless of their sex.

Page Ref: 330

STUDY QUESTIONS

Erikson's Theory: Identity versus Role Confusion

1. Explain how adolescents construct an identity. (p. 314)

____

____

____

2. Discuss Erikson's notion of *identity crisis.* (p. 314)

____

____

____

3. Current theorists (do / do not) agree with Erikson that the process of identity development constitutes a "crisis." (p. 314)

4. What did Erikson describe as the negative outcome of adolescence? Explain how this develops. (pp. 314–315)

   A. ______________________________

   B. ______________________________

   ____

Self-Understanding

Changes in Self-Concept

1. True or False: Young adolescents often provide contradictory self-descriptions—for example, describing themselves as both shy and outgoing. (p. 315)
2. Compared to school-age children, teenagers place (more / less) emphasis on social virtues, such as being friendly, considerate, kind, and cooperative. Why is this so? (p. 315)

   ____

   ____

Changes in Self-Esteem

1. List three new dimensions of self-evaluation that are added during adolescence. (p. 315)

   A. ______________________________

   B. ______________________________

   C. ______________________________
2. Except for temporary declines after ______________, self-esteem rises for most young people. (p. 315)
3. Differentiate factors associated with high versus low self-esteem in adolescence. (pp. 315–316)

   High: ______________________________

   ____

   Low: ______________________________

   ____

Paths to Identity

1. Match each of the following identity statuses with its appropriate description. (p. 316)

   _____ Committed to values and goals without taking time to explore alternatives
   _____ Have not yet made definite commitments and are still exploring alternatives
   _____ Committed to self-chosen values and goals after having already explored alternatives
   _____ Lack clear direction; are not committed to values and goals and are not actively seeking them

   1. Identity achievement
   2. Moratorium
   3. Identity foreclosure
   4. Identity diffusion
2. Most adolescents start out at "lower" identity statuses, such as ______________ and ______________, but by the time they reach their twenties, they have moved toward "higher" statuses, including ______________ and ______________. (p. 316)

Identity Status and Psychological Well-Being

1. True or False: Research supports the conclusion that identity achievement and moratorium are psychologically healthy routes to a mature self-definition, whereas identity foreclosure and identity diffusion are maladaptive. (p. 316)

2. How do adolescents in moratorium resemble identity-achieved individuals? (pp. 316–317)

____

____

3. Long-term (diffused / foreclosed) individuals are the least mature in identity development. Explain your answer. (p. 317)

____

____

Factors Affecting Identity Development

1. Match the following identity statuses with the appropriate description. Descriptions may apply to more than one identity status. (p. 317)

______	Assumes that absolute truth is always attainable	1. Identity achievement
______	Lacks confidence in the prospect of ever knowing anything with certainty	2. Moratorium
______	Appreciates that they can use rational criteria to choose among alternatives	3. Identity foreclosure
______	Feels attached to parents but are also free to voice their own opinions	4. Identity diffusion
______	Has close bonds with parents but lack healthy separation	
______	Reports the lowest levels of warm, open communication at home	
______	Fostered by classrooms that promote high-level thinking, as well as extracurricular and community activities that permit teens to take on responsible roles	

2. How do peers help adolescents explore their identity options? (p. 317)

____

____

3. How can schools foster adolescent identity development? (p. 317)

____

____

____

Cultural Influences: Identity Development among Ethnic Minority Adolescents

1. What is an *ethnic identity*? (p. 318)

____

____

____

2. What unique problems do ethnic-minority adolescents experience during identity development? (p. 318)

3. Explain the special challenges faced by young people with parents of different ethnicities. (p. 318)

4. List three ways society can help minority adolescents to resolve identity conflicts constructively. (p. 318)

   A.

   B.

   C.

5. What is a *bicultural identity,* and how does it benefit minority adolescents? (p. 318)

   A.

   B.

Moral Development

Kohlberg's Theory of Moral Development

1. What are *moral dilemmas,* and what do they reveal about moral reasoning? (p. 319)

2. True or False: Kohlberg emphasized that *the way an individual reasons* about a dilemma, not *the content of the response,* determines moral maturity. (p. 319)

3. List two factors that both Piaget and Kohlberg believed promoted moral understanding. (p. 320)

   A.

   B.

4. Explain the basic characteristics of moral reasoning at each of Kohlberg's three levels. (p. 320)

   Preconventional:

   Conventional:

   Postconventional or Principled:

5. Match each of the following moral orientations with its appropriate description. (pp. 320–321)

_____ Laws must be obeyed under all circumstances; rules must be enforced in the same even-handed manner for everyone, and each member of society has a personal duty to uphold them

_____ Right action is defined by self-chosen ethical principals of conscience that are valid for all humanity, regardless of law and social agreement

_____ Ignores people's intentions and focuses on fear of authority and avoidance of punishment as reasons for behaving morally

_____ Obeys rules because they promote social harmony

_____ Regards rules and laws as flexible and emphasizes fair procedures for interpreting and changing the law in order to protect individual rights and the interests of the majority

_____ Views right action as flowing from self-interest; reciprocity is understood as equal exchange of favors

1. Punishment and obedience orientation
2. Instrumental purpose orientation
3. "Good boy–good girl" orientation
4. Social-order-maintaining orientation
5. Social contract orientation
6. Universal ethical principle orientation

6. True or False: Longitudinal research suggests that individuals do not move through the stages of moral development in the order in which Kohlberg suggested. (p. 321)

7. True or False: Few people move beyond Kohlberg's Stage 4, the social-order-maintaining orientation. Briefly explain your response. (p. 321)

____

____

8. Moral maturity can be found in a revised understanding of Stages 3 and 4, which require profound moral constructions. Describe what those are. (p. 321)

____

____

____

9. Moral reasoning about real-life problems tends to fall (above / below) a person's actual moral capacity. Explain your answer. (p. 321)

____

____

____

10. True or False: Kohlberg's stages develop in a neat, stepwise fashion. (p. 321)

Are There Sex Differences in Moral Reasoning?

1. Carol Gilligan believes that feminine morality emphasizes an ethic of care that is devalued in Kohlberg's model. Explain what she means by this. (p. 321)

____

____

____

2. True or False: Research supports Gilligan's claim that Kohlberg's approach underestimates females' moral maturity. (pp. 321–322)

3. True or False: Females tend to emphasize care, whereas males either stress justice or focus equally on justice and care. (p. 322)

Coordinating Personal Choice with Morality

1. True or False: In diverse Western and non-Western cultures, teenagers express great concern with matters of personal choice. (p. 322)
2. By tenth grade, young people indicate that exclusion of another peer is "OK." How do adolescents justify this exclusion? (p. 322)

____

____

3. Teenagers display more subtle thinking than school-age children on certain issues. Describe two of these issues. (p. 322)

   A. ____

   ____

   B. ____

   ____

Influences on Moral Reasoning

1. Describe child-rearing practices that promote gains in moral understanding. (p. 322)

____

____

____

2. True or False: Years of schooling is one of the most powerful predictors of moral maturity. (p. 322)
3. Cite two aspects of peer discussions that stimulate moral development. (p. 322)

   A. ____

   B. ____

4. True or False: Cross-cultural research shows that individuals in industrialized nations move through Kohlberg's stages more quickly and advance to higher levels than individuals in village societies. Briefly explain your answer. (p. 323)

____

____

____

Moral Reasoning and Behavior

1. A (weak / modest / strong) relationship exists between advanced moral reasoning and action. (p. 323)
2. Besides cognition, what factors influence moral behavior in adolescence? (p. 323)

____

____

3. What is *moral self-relevance*? (p. 323)

____

4. How can close relationships and schools foster adolescents' sense of moral self-relevance? (p. 323)

   Close relationships: ______________________________

   ____

   Schools: ______________________________

   ____

Religious Involvement and Moral Development

1. In recent national polls, nearly ______ of Americans and about ______ of Canadians reported being religious. As adolescents search for a personally meaningful identity, formal religious involvement (declines / increases). (pp. 323–324)

2. How do religious communities promote adolescents' moral values and behaviors? (p. 324)

   ____

   ____

   ____

Gender Typing

1. What is *gender intensification*? (p. 324)

   ____

   ____

2. Gender intensification is stronger for (boys / girls). (p. 324)

3. Cite biological, social, and cognitive factors associated with gender intensification. (p. 324)

   Biological: ______________________________

   ____

   Social: ______________________________

   ____

   Cognitive: ______________________________

   ____

   ____

4. Gender intensification (declines / increases) during middle to late adolescence. (p. 324)

5. (Androgynous / Gender-typed) adolescents tend to be psychologically healthier. (p. 324)

The Family

1. During adolescence, ______________—establishing oneself as a separate, self-governing individual—becomes a salient task. (p. 325)

Parent–Child Relationships

1. Describe parenting practices that foster adolescent autonomy. (p. 325)

   ____

   ____

   ____

2. What is a major reason that many parents find rearing teenagers to be stressful? (p. 325)

____

____

3. True or False: The quality of the parent–child relationship is the most consistent predictor of mental health throughout adolescence. (p. 325)

4. Explain how mild parent–child conflict is beneficial during adolescence. (p. 325)

____

____

____

Family Circumstances

1. True or False: Maternal employment or a dual-earner family reduces the amount of time that parents spend with their teenagers and is harmful to adolescent development. Explain your response. (p. 326)

____

____

____

2. What factors promote resilience in adolescents who have seriously troubled relationships with their families? (p. 326)

____

____

____

Siblings

1. During adolescence, teenagers invest (more / less) time and energy in siblings. Explain your answer. (p. 326)

____

____

____

2. Sibling relationships become (more / less) intense during adolescence, in both positive and negative feelings. (p. 326)

3. True or False: In adolescence, mild sibling differences in perceived parental affection no longer trigger jealousy but, instead, predict increasing sibling warmth. (p. 326)

Peer Relations

Friendships

1. Cite the two characteristics of adolescent friendship. (p. 326)

   A. ____

   B. ____

2. List ways in which adolescent friends are likely to resemble one another. (p. 326)

____

____

____

3. Adolescents are (less / more) possessive of their friends than they were in childhood. (p. 327)

4. Briefly summarize sex differences in adolescents' close friendships. (p. 327)

____

____

____

5. When can closeness in friendship be problematic? (p. 327)

____

____

____

6. How do adolescents use the Internet to build and support relationships? (p. 327)

____

____

____

7. Cite four reasons why adolescent friendships are related to psychological health and competence into early adulthood. (pp. 327–328)

   A. ______________________________

   ____

   B. ______________________________

   ____

   C. ______________________________

   ____

   D. ______________________________

   ____

Cliques and Crowds

1. Differentiate between cliques and crowds, noting the characteristics of each. (p. 328)

   Cliques: ______________________________

   ____

   Crowds: ______________________________

   ____

2. Provide some examples of typical high school crowds. (p. 328)

3. True or False: Peer group values are often an extension of values learned in the home. Explain your answer. (p. 328)

4. Describe the function of mixed-sex cliques in early adolescence. (pp. 328–329)

5. True or False: Crowds increase in importance from early to late adolescence. (p. 329)

Dating

1. Differentiate younger and older adolescents' reasons for dating. (p. 329)

   Younger: _____

   Older: _____

2. How do experiences with parents influence the quality of adolescents' friendships and romantic relationships? (p. 329)

3. True or False: Early dating is positively associated with social maturity. (p. 329)

4. What factors increase the likelihood of dating violence? (p. 329)

5. Describe the unique challenges faced by homosexual adolescents in initiating and maintaining visible romances. (p. 329)

6. Describe the benefits of close romantic relationships among older teenagers. (p. 329)

Problems of Development

Depression

1. True or False: Depression is the most common psychological problem of adolescence. (p. 330)
2. About _______ to _______ percent of U.S. teenagers have experienced one or more depressive episodes, and _______ to _______ percent are chronically depressed. (p. 330)
3. List three events that might spark depression in a vulnerable young person. (p. 330)

   A. ______________________________

   B. ______________________________

   C. ______________________________
4. Biological changes associated with puberty (can / cannot) account for sex differences in depression. Explain your answer. (p. 330)

   ____

   ____

   ____
5. Explain how the gender intensification of early adolescence can contribute to higher rates of depression in girls. (p. 330)

   ____

   ____

   ____

Suicide

1. True or False: Suicide is currently the leading cause of death among young people in the United States and Canada. (p. 330)
2. True or False: Adolescent suicide rates are roughly equivalent in all industrialized countries. (p. 330)
3. Discuss sex differences in adolescent suicide. (pp. 330–331)

   ____

   ____

   ____
4. Compared with their Caucasian peers, African-American and Hispanic adolescents have (lower / higher) suicide rates. (p. 331)
5. True or False: Gay, lesbian, and bisexual youth are three times more likely than other adolescents to attempt suicide. (p. 331)
6. Describe two types of young people who tend to commit suicide. (p. 331)

   A. ______________________________

   ____

   B. ______________________________

   ____

7. Describe the family backgrounds of suicidal teenagers. (p. 331)

8. Why does suicide increase in adolescence? (p. 331)

9. What types of treatments are available for depressed and suicidal adolescents? (p. 331)

10. True or False: Teenage suicides often take place in clusters. Explain your answer. (p. 331)

Delinquency

1. Explain why delinquency rises over adolescence, then declines into young adulthood. (p. 331)

2. For most adolescents, a brush with the law (does / does not) forecast long-term antisocial behavior. (p. 332)

3. Describe gender differences in delinquent and aggressive behavior. (p. 332)

   Males:

   Females:

4. List personal, family, neighborhood, and school factors associated with delinquency. (p. 332)

   Personal:

   Family:

   Neighborhood:

   School:

5. Describe characteristics of effective treatment programs for adolescent delinquency. (p. 332)

____

____

____

A Lifespan Vista: Two Routes to Adolescent Delinquency

1. Persistent adolescent delinquency follows two paths of development, one with an onset of ____________________ problems in childhood, the second with an onset in ______________. Longitudinal research reveals that the (early / late) onset type is far more likely to lead to a life course pattern of aggression and criminality. (p. 333)

2. Describe characteristics that distinguish early-onset from late-onset delinquent youth. (p. 333)

   Early-onset: ____

   ____

   ____

   Late-onset: ____

   ____

   ____

PUZZLE 12.1

Across

3. __________ identity: identity constructed by adolescents who explore and adopt values from both their subculture and the dominant culture
7. Identity status of individuals who are exploring alternatives in an effort to find values and goals to guide their life
10. Kohlberg's highest level of moral development; individuals define morality in terms of abstract principles and values that apply to all situations and societies
11. __________ identity: sense of ethnic group membership and the attitudes and feelings associated with that membership
12. __________ self-relevance: the degree to which morality is central to self-concept
13. A well-organized conception of the self, made up of values, beliefs, and goals to which the individual is solidly committed
14. A large, loosely organized peer group in which membership is based on reputation and stereotype
15. A sense of oneself as a separate, self-governing individual
16. A small group of about five to seven peers who are friends
17. Identity _________: identity status of individuals who do not have firm commitments to values and goals and are not actively trying to reach them

Down

1. __________ morality: Piaget's second stage of moral development in which children view rules as flexible, socially agreed-upon principles that can be revised to suit the will of the majority
2. Identity versus role __________: Erikson's psychological conflict of adolescence
4. Kohlberg's second level of moral development; moral understanding is based on conforming to social rules to ensure positive relationships and social order
5. Identity __________: identity status of individuals who have accepted ready-made values and goals that authority figures have chosen for them
6. __________ morality: Piaget's first stage of moral development in which children view rules as permanent and unchangeable
8. Identity __________: identity status of individuals who have explored and committed themselves to self-chosen values and goals
9. Gender __________: increased stereotyping of attitudes and behavior; movement toward a more traditional gender identity
10. Kohlberg's first level of moral development; moral understanding is based on rewards, punishment, and the power of authority figures

CROSSWORD PUZZLE SOLUTION

PUZZLE 12.1

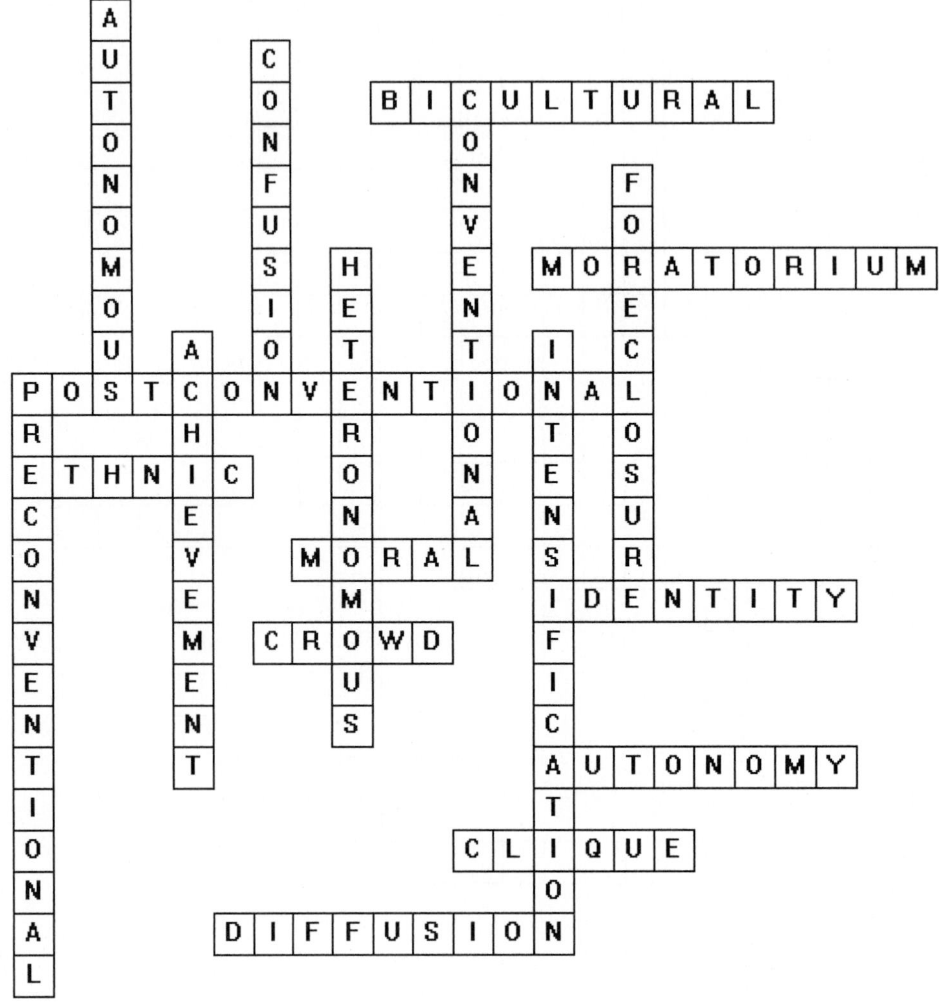

PRACTICE TEST #1

1. According to Erikson, young people have trouble finding ideals to have faith in when they reach adolescence with a weak sense of (p. 314)
   a. humor.
   b. trust.
   c. hope.
   d. ideals.

2. In adolescence, young people add _________ as a new dimension of their self-concept. (p. 315)
   a. close friendship
   b. membership in social groups
   c. individual interests
   d. personal preferences

3. Individuals who have difficulty realizing their occupational goals because of lack of training or vocational choices are likely to be at risk for (p. 316)
   a. identity achievement.
   b. identity moratorium.
   c. identity diffusion.
   d. identity foreclosure.

4. Research on identity construction indicates that (p. 316)
   a. most adolescents experience a serious identity crisis.
   b. adolescents typically retain the same identity status across adolescence and early adulthood.
   c. adolescents in high school make more progress toward identity formation than college students.
   d. adolescents who go to work after high school settle on an identity status earlier than do college-bound youths.

5. Kieran has followed the religious path of his family without exploring alternatives and tends to be defensive when his teenage friends bring up the subject. Kieran is (p. 317)
   a. identity foreclosed.
   b. identity diffused.
   c. in moratorium.
   d. identity achieved.

6. According to Kohlberg, moral maturity is determined is determined by (p. 319)
   a. adherence to laws.
   b. whether an individual understands a moral dilemma.
   c. the way an individual reasons about a moral dilemma.
   d. the content of the response to a moral dilemma.

7. Which of the following is true, based on research on Kohlberg's stage sequence? (p. 321)
   a. By early adulthood, Stage 5 is the typical response.
   b. Stages 3 and 4 require a profound understanding of ideal reciprocity.
   c. Postconventional morality is less mature than originally thought.
   d. People rely only on cognition to resolve moral dilemmas.

8. When individuals are faced with real-life, as opposed to hypothetical, moral dilemmas, their moral reasoning tends to (p. 321)
   a. become more mature.
   b. become less mature.
   c. remain at the same level of maturity.
   d. follow no predictable pattern.

9. Yolanda's greater propensity to get involved in community service than her agemates' (though she does not differ from them in moral reasoning) is an example of (p. 323)
   a. moral development.
   b. moral behavior.
   c. moral self-relevance.
   d. moral involvement.

10. During early adolescence, gender intensification is (p. 324)
    a. stronger for boys.
    b. stronger for girls.
    c. equally strong for both boys and girls.
    d. not yet an important issue.

11. Teenagers who are encouraged to explore non-gender-typed options and to question the value of gender stereotypes for themselves and society are more likely to build a(n) ____________ gender identity. (p. 324)
    a. erroneous
    b. androgynous
    c. intensified
    d. gender-specific

12. Which of the following fosters adolescent autonomy? (p. 325)
    a. parents who are assertive enough to use psychological control
    b. teenagers' unquestioning admiration of their parents
    c. parents who are warm, supportive, and permit teenagers to explore ideas
    d. parents who delay granting certain privileges, such as driving and dating

13. Throughout adolescence, the most consistent predictor of mental health is (p. 325)
    a. the quality of the parent–child relationship.
    b. development of positive peer relationships.
    c. popularity and social status.
    d. success in academic efforts.

14. During adolescence, siblings (p. 326)
    a. have a more unequal relationship, with younger siblings showing greater willingness to accept direction from older siblings.
    b. devote more time to each other.
    c. have less intense interactions.
    d. experience a decline in the quality of their relationship.

15. John, Gerry, Samuel, Suzanne, and Karen spent much of their free time in and out of school together. They often did things together on weekends, and even began to dress alike. The closely knit group they formed would be considered a (p. 328)
    a. clique.
    b. crowd.
    c. bunch.
    d. pact.

16. The assortment of teenagers into cliques and crowds is influenced by (p. 328)
    a. teacher preference.
    b. parenting style.
    c. stress of school transition.
    d. desire to date.

17. In early adolescence, dating (p. 329)
    a. is done for recreational purposes, as well as to achieve status among agemates.
    b. is focused on psychological intimacy, shared interests, and the search for a good permanent partner.
    c. fosters social maturity.
    d. protects teens against drug use, delinquency, and poor school performance.

18. Studies on the effects of depression on adolescents show that adolescent girls (p. 330)
    a. almost never report persistent depression.
    b. are much less likely than boys to report persistent depression.
    c. are just as likely as boys to report persistent depression.
    d. are twice as likely as boys to report persistent depression.

19. Youth crime (p. 331)
    a. has declined over the past decade.
    b. accounts for a minimal proportion of police arrests—less than 5 percent.
    c. is most often serious in nature.
    d. forecasts a long-term pattern of antisocial behavior for most adolescents.

20. On the path to adolescent delinquency for those with early-onset antisocial behavior, which of the following characteristics defines early childhood rather than middle childhood? (p. 332)
    a. academic failure
    b. commitment to deviant peer group
    c. difficult and fearless temperamental styles
    d. rejection by normal peers

PRACTICE TEST #2

1. According to Erikson, young people who lack a firm sense of self (an identity) to which they can return will find it difficult to risk (p. 315)
    a. intimacy.
    b. security.
    c. shame.
    d. scrutiny.

2. Which of the following parenting styles is linked with positive outcomes in adolescence, including high self-esteem, self-reliance, academic achievement, and work orientation? (pp. 315, 325)
    a. authoritarian
    b. authoritative
    c. permissive
    d. uninvolved

3. When asked about his career plans, Simon says, "Haven't thought about it. Doesn't make too much difference what I do." Simon's identity status is best characterized as (p. 316)
    a. identity achievement.
    b. identity diffusion.
    c. identity moratorium.
    d. identity foreclosure.

4. Adolescents who lack confidence in the prospect of ever knowing anything with certainty and who report low levels of warm, open communication in the home are likely to have which identity status? (p. 316)
    a. identity achievement
    b. identity moratorium
    c. identity foreclosure
    d. identity diffusion

5. __________ typically have close parent–child bonds but lack opportunities for healthy separation. (p. 317)
    a. Identity-achieved adolescents
    b. Adolescents in a state of moratorium
    c. Foreclosed young people
    d. Diffused teenagers

6. Morality is externally controlled at the (p. 320)
   a. preconventional level.
   b. principled level.
   c. conventional level.
   d. postconventional level.

7. When an individual's moral reasoning stems from self-interest, which stage of Kohlberg's theory would best characterize his or her level of moral understanding? (p. 320)
   a. Stage 2: The instrumental purpose orientation
   b. Stage 3: The "good boy–good girl" orientation
   c. Stage 4: The social-order-maintaining orientation
   d. Stage 6: The universal ethical principle orientation

8. In Kohlberg's theory, the __________ individual believes that laws should never be disobeyed because they are vital for ensuring societal order and cooperative relations between individuals. (p. 321)
   a. Stage 1
   b. Stage 2
   c. Stage 4
   d. Stage 6

9. Because situational factors influence moral judgments, Kohlberg's moral stages are shown to be (p. 321)
   a. loosely organized.
   b. tightly organized.
   c. frequently achieved out of order.
   d. inaccurate beyond Stage 3.

10. Which of the following is true with regard to the influences on moral reasoning? (p. 322)
    a. A rigid, closed-minded approach to new information and experiences is linked to gains in moral reasoning.
    b. Peer conflict facilitates moral reasoning by making children aware of others' perspectives.
    c. Strict, authoritarian parenting is associated with more mature moral reasoning.
    d. Movement through Kohlberg's stages is the same in all cultures throughout the world.

11. Research shows that the connection between advanced moral reasoning and moral action is best described as (p. 323)
    a. nonexistent; one does not influence the other.
    b. only modest; moral behavior is influenced by many factors besides cognition.
    c. significant; higher-stage individuals generally report high moral self-relevance.
    d. powerful; mature moral thinkers almost always behave morally.

12. Which adolescent is likely to be psychologically healthiest? (p. 324)
    a. Jasmine, who has a strong feminine gender identity
    b. Luis, who has a strong masculine gender identity
    c. Gabriella, who has an androgynous gender identity
    d. Gordon, who has a feminine gender identity

13. When asked about the meaning of friendship, teenagers stress two characteristics: (p. 326)
    a. intimacy and loyalty.
    b. honesty and loyalty.
    c. intimacy and generosity.
    d. generosity and sincerity.

14. In adolescent friendships, (p. 327)
    a. young people look for common interests and sense of trust, more than any other qualities.
    b. boys engage in more self-disclosure than girls.
    c. cooperation and mutual affirmation increase, while possessiveness of friends decreases.
    d. intimacy has many benefits, and no costs.

15. The first dating relationships of homosexual youths tend to be short-lived and involve little emotional commitment. This is largely because (p. 329)
    a. they are not emotionally ready for more mature, emotionally intense relationships.
    b. they fear peer harassment and rejection.
    c. they are still questioning their sexual identity.
    d. they are looking for relationships that are fun and recreational, with little interest in forming close, long-lasting relational ties.

16. The most common psychological problem of adolescence is (p. 330)
    a. delinquency.
    b. identity diffusion.
    c. gender confusion.
    d. depression.

17. Research examining why girls are more prone to depression than are boys shows that (p. 330)
    a. the biological changes associated with puberty are primarily responsible for the gender gap.
    b. rates of depression for males and females are similar in all developing and industrialized countries around the world.
    c. gender-typed coping styles account for girls' higher rates of depression.
    d. girls with an androgynous or masculine gender identity are as likely as girls with a strong feminine identity to show signs of depression.

18. Which of the following is true of suicide among teenagers? (p. 330)
    a. Boys are four to five times more likely to kill themselves than girls.
    b. African Americans have higher suicide rates than Caucasian Americans.
    c. Rates of teenage suicide are the same among all industrialized nations.
    d. Boys make more unsuccessful suicide attempts than girls.

19. Children or adolescents who engage in illegal acts are considered to be (p. 331)
    a. clinically depressed.
    b. juvenile delinquents.
    c. suicidal.
    d. autonomous.

20. All of the following are associated with successful prevention of juvenile delinquency EXCEPT (p. 332)
    a. authoritative parenting.
    b. high-quality teaching in schools.
    c. positive family relationships.
    d. low monitoring.

POWERPOINT SLIDES

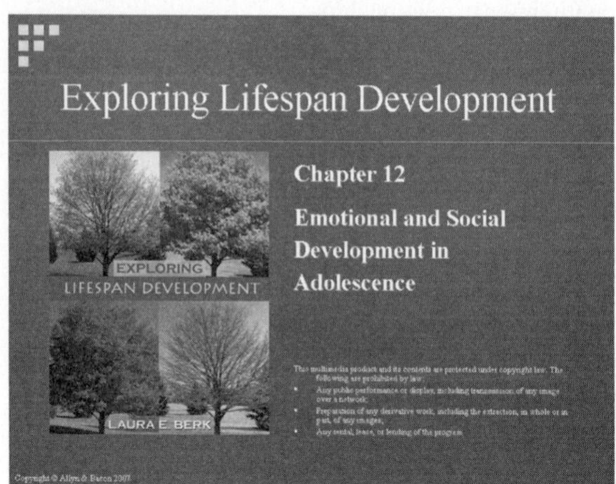

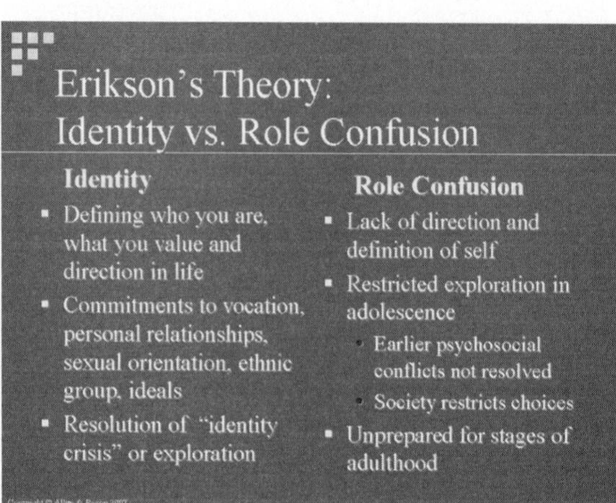

Self-Concept in Adolescence

- Unify separate traits into larger, abstract ones
- May describe contradictory traits; social situations
- Gradually combine traits into organized system
  - Qualifiers
  - Integrating principles

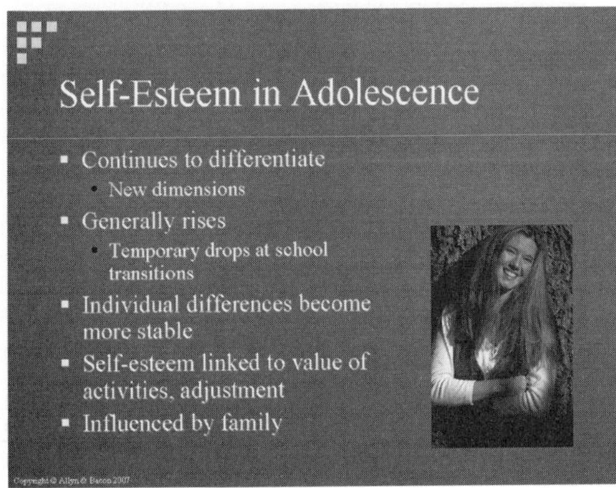
Self-Esteem in Adolescence
Continues to differentiate
New dimensions
Generally rises
Temporary drops at school transitions
Individual differences become more stable
Self-esteem linked to value of activities, adjustment
Influenced by family

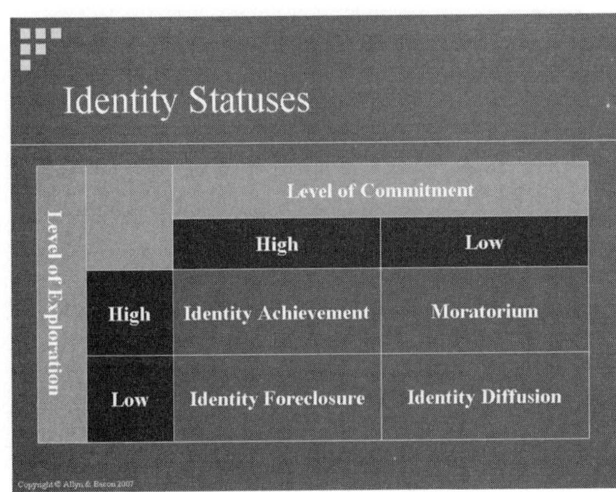
Identity Statuses
Level of Commitment
High
Low
Level of Exploration
High
Identity Achievement
Moratorium
Low
Identity Foreclosure
Identity Diffusion

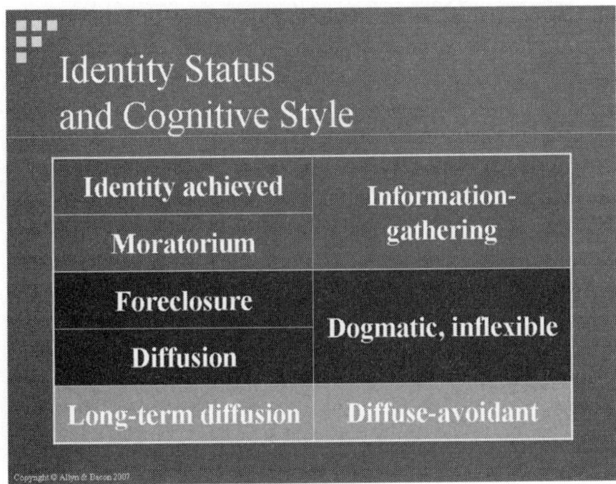
Identity Status and Cognitive Style
Identity achieved
Moratorium
Information-gathering
Foreclosure
Diffusion
Dogmatic, inflexible
Long-term diffusion
Diffuse-avoidant

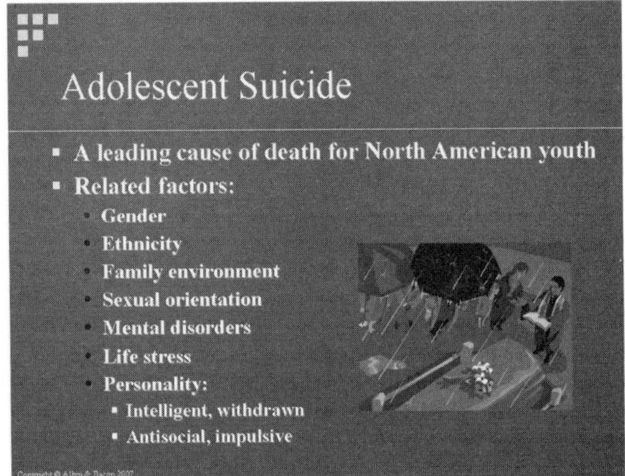
Adolescent Suicide
A leading cause of death for North American youth
Related factors:
Gender
Ethnicity
Family environment
Sexual orientation
Mental disorders
Life stress
Personality:
Intelligent, withdrawn
Antisocial, impulsive
Copyright © Allyn & Bacon 2007

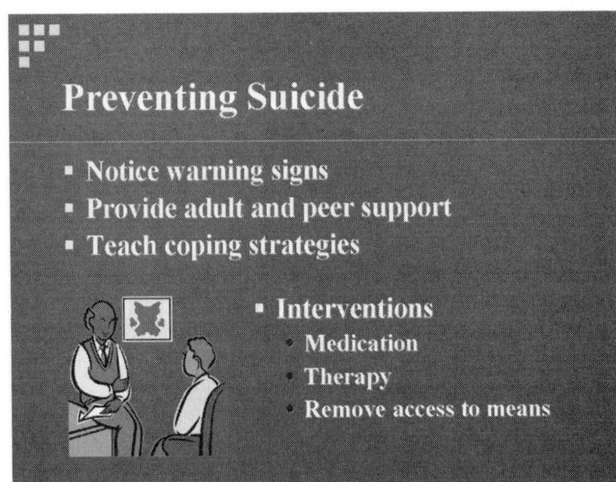
Preventing Suicide
Notice warning signs
Provide adult and peer support
Teach coping strategies
Interventions
Medication
Therapy
Remove access to means
Copyright © Allyn & Bacon 2007

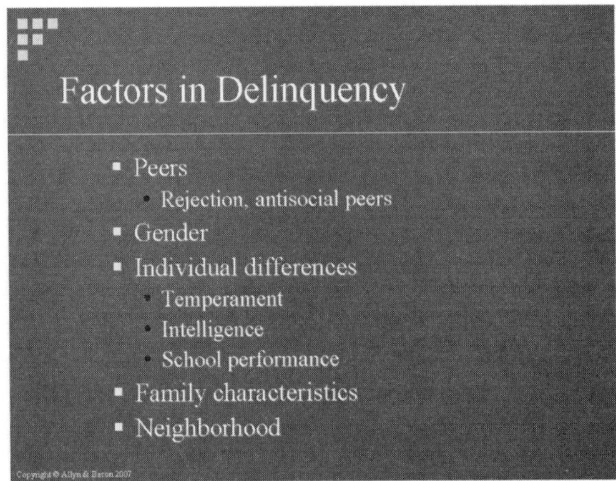
Factors in Delinquency
Peers
Rejection, antisocial peers
Gender
Individual differences
Temperament
Intelligence
School performance
Family characteristics
Neighborhood
Copyright © Allyn & Bacon 2007

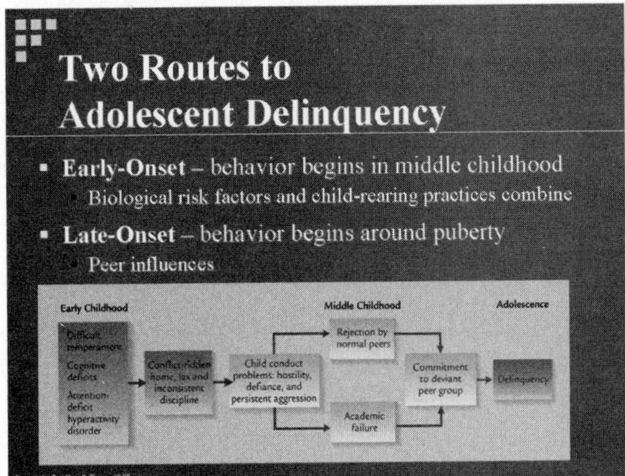
Two Routes to
Adolescent Delinquency
Early-Onset – behavior begins in middle childhood
Biological risk factors and child-rearing practices combine
Late-Onset – behavior begins around puberty
Peer influences
Early Childhood
Middle Childhood
Adolescence
Difficult temperament
Cognitive deficits
Attention-deficit hyperactivity disorder
Conflict-ridden home, lax and inconsistent discipline
Child conduct problems: hostility, defiance, and persistent aggression
Rejection by normal peers
Academic failure
Commitment to deviant peer group
Delinquency

CHAPTER 13
PHYSICAL AND COGNITIVE DEVELOPMENT IN EARLY ADULTHOOD

CHAPTER-AT-A-GLANCE

Chapter Outline	Instruction Ideas	Supplements
***A Gradual Transition: Emerging Adulthood* pp. 339–340**	Learning Objective 13.1 Learning Activity 13.1	Transparency 161 Test Bank Items 1–4 Videos: *Exploring Lifespan Development in Action* and *A Window on Lifespan Development* Please contact your Allyn and Bacon publisher's representative for a wide range of video offerings available to adopters.
Physical Development **Biological Aging Is Under Way in Early Adulthood pp. 340–342** Aging at the Level of DNA and Body Cells • Aging at the Level of Organs and Tissues	Learning Objective 13.2	Test Bank Items 5–18
Physical Changes pp. 342–345 Cardiovascular and Respiratory Systems • Motor Performance • Immune System • Reproductive Capacity	Learning Objective 13.3 Ask Yourself p. 345	Test Bank Items 19–34
Health and Fitness pp. 345–354 Nutrition • Exercise • Substance Abuse • Sexuality • Psychological Stress	Learning Objectives 13.4–13.7 Lecture Enhancement 13.1 Learning Activities 13.2–13.4 Ask Yourself p. 354	Transparency 166 Test Bank Items 35–78
Cognitive Development **Changes in the Structure of Thought pp. 354–357** Perry's Theory: Epistemic Cognition • Labouvie-Vief's Theory: Pragmatic Thought and Cognitive-Affective Complexity	Learning Objective 13.8 Lecture Enhancement 13.2 Learning Activity 13.5	Test Bank Items 79–86
Expertise and Creativity p. 357	Learning Objective 13.9 Learning Activity 13.6 Ask Yourself p. 357	Test Bank Items 87–91
The College Experience p. 358 Psychological Impact of Attending College • Dropping Out	Learning Objective 13.10	Test Bank Items 92–96
Vocational Choice pp. 358–362 Selecting a Vocation • Factors Influencing Vocational Choice • Vocational Preparation of Non–College-Bound Young Adults	Learning Objectives 13.11–13.12 Lecture Enhancements 13.3–13.4 Learning Activities 13.7–13.8 Ask Yourself p. 362	Test Bank Items 97–112

BRIEF CHAPTER SUMMARY

In the modern developed world, the transition to adult roles is prolonged in a new, transitional phase of development, emerging adulthood, which allows for further exploration and identity development before taking on adult roles.

Once body structures reach maximum capacity and efficiency, biological aging begins. The combined result of many causes, it can be modified through behavioral and environmental interventions. In early adulthood, gradual changes occur in physical appearance and body functioning, including declines in athletic skills, in the immune system's protective function, and in reproductive capacity.

SES variations in health over the lifespan reflect differences in both environmental risks and health-related behaviors. Overweight and obesity, strongly associated with serious health problems, have increased dramatically in many Western nations. Young adults are more likely than younger or older people to smoke cigarettes, use marijuana, take stimulants, or engage in binge drinking.

Monogamous, emotionally committed relationships are more typical than casual sex among young adults, and attitudes toward homosexuality have become more accepting as a result of political activism and greater openness on the part of homosexuals. A significant percentage of North American women have endured rape; many more have experienced other forms of sexual aggression, sometimes with lasting psychological effects. Women's menstrual cycle presents unique health concerns, including premenstrual syndrome, an array of symptoms preceding the monthly period. The unique challenges of early adulthood make it a particularly stressful time of life. Social support can provide a buffer against psychological stress, which is related to unfavorable health outcomes, including both unhealthy behaviors and direct physical consequences.

The cognitive-developmental changes of childhood and adolescence extend into adulthood, as seen in the development of epistemic cognition (reflection on one's own thinking process); a movement from dualistic, right-or-wrong thinking toward relativistic thinking; and a shift from hypothetical to pragmatic thought, with greater use of logic to solve real-world problems.

Expertise develops in adulthood as individuals master specific complex domains. College serves as a formative environment in which students can devote their attention to exploring alternative values, roles, and behaviors. Personality, family influences, teachers, and gender stereotypes all influence vocational choice as young adults explore possibilities and eventually settle on an occupation. Non-college-bound young people have a particular need for apprenticeships and other forms of preparation for productive, meaningful lives.

LEARNING OBJECTIVES

After reading this chapter, you should be able to:

13.1 Define emerging adulthood, noting cultural changes that have contributed to the emergence of this period. (pp. 339–340)

13.2 Describe current theories of biological aging, including those at the level of DNA and body cells, and those at the level of tissues and organs. (pp. 340–342)

13.3 Describe the physical changes of aging, paying special attention to the cardiovascular and respiratory systems, motor performance, the immune system, and reproductive capacity. (pp. 342–345)

13.4 Describe the impact of SES, nutrition, and exercise on health, and discuss obesity in adulthood. (pp. 345–348)

13.5 Describe trends in substance abuse in early adulthood, and discuss the health risks of each. (pp. 348–350)

13.6 Summarize young adults' sexual attitudes and behaviors, including sexual orientation, sexual coercion, and premenstrual syndrome. (pp. 350–354)

13.7 Explain how psychological stress affects health. (p. 354)

13.8 Describe characteristics of adult thought, highlighting the theories of Perry and Labouvie-Vief. (pp. 354–357)

13.9 Discuss the development of expertise and creativity in adulthood. (p. 357)

13.10 Describe the impact of a college education on young people's lives, and discuss the problem of dropping out. (p. 358)

13.11 Trace the development of vocational choice, and cite factors that influence it. (pp. 358–361)

13.12 Summarize the problems that North American non-college-bound young people face in preparing for a vocation. (pp. 362)

LECTURE OUTLINE

I. A GRADUAL TRANSITION: EMERGING ADULTHOOD (pp. 339–340)
   A. Today's young people move into these widely accepted markers of adulthood more slowly than those of a generation ago.
   B. This prolonged transition to adult roles has led to the identification of a new, transitional phase of development, extending from the late teens to the mid-twenties, called **emerging adulthood**, when most young people have left adolescence but not yet taken on full adult responsibilities.
      1. Released from the oversight of parents but not yet immersed in adult roles, emerging adults can explore alternatives more intensely than they did as teenagers, a process that prolongs identity development.
      2. Routes to adult responsibilities are diverse in timing and order across individuals, with very little that is normative or socially expected.
         a. Many more college students than in past generations pursue their education in a drawn-out, nonlinear way.
         b. About one-third of North American college graduates enter graduate school before settling into a career track.
      3. Rapid cultural changes explain the recent appearance of emerging adulthood.
         a. Entry-level positions in many fields require more education than in the past.
         b. Nations with abundant wealth and longer-lived populations have no pressing need for young people's labor.
      4. Emerging adulthood is limited or nonexistent for many low-SES young people who are burdened by early parenthood, did not finish high school, are otherwise academically unprepared for college, or have no avenue to vocational training.
      5. As emerging adults experiment, they often encounter uncertainties and disappointments in relationships, education, and work that require them to adjust, and sometimes radically change, their paths.

Physical Development

II. BIOLOGICAL AGING IS UNDER WAY IN EARLY ADULTHOOD (pp. 340–342)
   A. Once body structures reach maximum capacity and efficiency, **biological aging**, or **senescence**, begins—genetically influenced declines in the functioning of organs and systems that are universal in human beings.
      1. Like physical growth, biological aging is *multidimensional* and *multidirectional.*
         a. The changes of aging vary widely across parts of the body.
         b. Aging is characterized by individual differences that reflect genetic makeup, lifestyle, environment, and historical period.
      2. Biological aging can be modified substantially through behavioral and environmental interventions, such as improvements in nutrition, medical treatment, sanitation, and safety, which have added 25 to 30 years to average life expectancy in industrialized nations over the past century.
      3. Biological aging is the combined result of many causes, some operating at the level of DNA, others at the level of cells, and still others at the level of tissues, organs, and whole organisms.
      4. The popular *"wear-and-tear" theory* of aging is an oversimplification.
         a. Worn-out body parts usually repair or replace themselves, and no relationship exists between physical work and early death.

b. Regular, moderate to vigorous exercise predicts a healthier, longer life for people varying widely in SES and ethnicity.

B. Aging at the Level of DNA and Body Cells (p. 341)

1. Current explanations are of two types, a combination of which may eventually prove to be correct.
   a. Some emphasize the *programmed effects of specific genes.*
   b. Others emphasize the *cumulative effects of random events,* both internal and external, that damage genetic and cellular material.
2. Evidence for and against programmed effects of specific genes:
   a. Evidence for the heritability of longevity is seen in the fact that people with long-lived parents tend to live longer themselves, and the lifespans of identical twins are more similar than those of fraternal twins.
   b. Rather than inheriting longevity directly, people probably inherit one or more risk factors.
   c. One "genetic programming" theory, which proposes that "aging genes" control certain biological changes, such as menopause, gray hair, and deterioration of body cells, is based on research evidence showing that human cells allowed to divide in the laboratory have a lifespan of 50 divisions, plus or minus 10.
      (1) With each duplication, a special type of DNA called *telomeres* shortens, until so little remains that the cells no longer duplicate.
      (2) Telomere shortening acts as a brake against somatic mutations (like those involved in cancer), which become more likely as cells duplicate.
      (3) However, an increase in the number of cells with short telomeres also contributes to age-related disease and loss of function.
3. Evidence for and against the theory of cumulative effects of random events (gradual damage to DNA in body cells through spontaneous or externally caused mutations that accumulate, making cell repair and replacement less efficient or producing abnormal cancerous cells):
   a. Animal studies confirm an increase in DNA breaks and deletions and damage to other cellular material with age, and similar evidence is accruing for humans.
   b. One probable cause of age-related DNA and cellular abnormalities is the release of **free radicals**, naturally occurring, highly reactive chemicals that form in the presence of oxygen or may be triggered by the presence of radiation and certain pollutants and drugs.
      (1) Free radicals are thought to be involved in cardiovascular disease, neurological disorders, cancer, cataracts, arthritis, and other disorders of aging.
      (2) Although our bodies produce substances that neutralize free radicals, some harm occurs and accumulates over time.
   c. Some researchers believe that genes for longevity work by defending against free radicals, as do foods rich in vitamins C and E and beta-carotene.

C. Aging at the Level of Organs and Tissues (pp. 341–342)

1. The **cross-linkage theory of aging**:
   a. Over time, protein fibers that make up the body's connective tissue form bonds, or links, with one another, and tissue becomes less elastic, leading to loss of flexibility in the skin and other organs, clouding of the lens of the eye, clogging of arteries, damage to the kidneys, and other negative effects.
   b. Cross-linking can be reduced by external factors, including regular exercise and a vitamin-rich, low-fat diet.
2. Gradual failure of the endocrine system:
   a. Disruptions in the endocrine system can have widespread effects on health and survival (as an example, decreased estrogen production in women culminates in menopause).
   b. Research indicates that a gradual drop in growth hormone (GH) is associated with loss of muscle and bone mass, addition of body fat, thinning of the skin, and decline in cardiovascular functioning.
   c. Diet and physical activity can limit these aspects of biological aging, as can hormone therapy, but the latter has serious side effects, including increased risk of fluid retention in tissues, muscle pain, and cancer.

3. Declines in immune system functioning:
    a. Immune system declines contribute to many conditions of aging, including increased susceptibility to infectious disease and cancer, and changes in blood vessel walls associated with cardiovascular disease.
    b. Decreased vigor of the immune response seems to be genetically programmed but can be intensified by other aging processes, such as weakening of the endocrine system.

III. PHYSICAL CHANGES (pp. 342–345)
  A. During the twenties and thirties, the physical changes of aging are so gradual that they are hardly noticeable.
  B. Cardiovascular and Respiratory Systems (pp. 342–344)
    1. Heart disease is a leading cause of death throughout adulthood, leading to as many as 11 percent of U.S. male and 6 percent of U.S. female deaths between ages 20 and 34—figures that more than double in the following decade and, thereafter, rise steadily with age.
        a. *Hypertension,* or high blood pressure, occurs 12 percent more often in the U.S. black than in the U.S. white population.
        b. The rate of death from heart disease among African Americans is 28 percent higher than among whites.
        c. In healthy individuals, the heart's ability to meet the body's oxygen requirements under typical conditions does not change during adulthood.
        d. Heart performance during stressful exercise declines with age as a result of a decrease in maximum heart rate and greater rigidity of the heart muscle.
        e. *Atherosclerosis* is a serious disease of the cardiovascular system in which heavy deposits of plaque containing cholesterol and fats collect on the walls of the main arteries.
            (1) Because atherosclerosis is multiply determined, it is hard to separate the contributions of biological aging from individual genetic and environmental influences.
            (2) Animal research indicates that before puberty, a high-fat diet produces only fatty streaks on the artery walls, while in sexually mature adults, it leads to serious plaque deposits—suggesting that sex hormones may heighten the effects of a high-fat diet.
        f. Heart disease has decreased considerably since the mid-twentieth century, with a larger drop in the last 20 years due to a decline in cigarette smoking, improved diet and exercise among at-risk individuals, and better medical detection and treatment of high blood pressure and cholesterol.
    2. Like the heart, lung capacity decreases during physical exertion.
        a. Maximum vital capacity (amount of air that can be forced in and out of the lungs) declines by 10 percent per decade after age 25.
        b. Connective tissue in the lungs, chest muscles, and ribs stiffens with age, making it harder for the lungs to expand to full volume.
        c. Aging of the lungs makes it harder for older adults to meet the body's oxygen needs while exercising.
  C. Motor Performance (p. 344)
    1. Declines in heart and lung functioning during exertion, combined with gradual muscle loss, lead to changes in motor performance.
    2. In ordinary people, the impact of biological aging on motor skills is difficult to separate from decreases in motivation and practice, so it is valuable to study outstanding athletes, whose attainments at each age approach the limits of what is biologically possible.
    3. In investigations charting the mean ages for best performance of Olympic and professional athletes in a variety of sports over time, absolute performance in most events improved over the past century as athletes continually set new world records, suggesting improved training methods, but ages of best performance remained relatively constant.
        a. Athletic tasks that require speed of limb movement, explosive strength, and gross body coordination (sprinting, jumping, and tennis) typically peak in the early twenties.
        b. Those that depend on endurance, arm–hand steadiness, and aiming (long-distance running, baseball, and golf) take longer to perfect and usually peak in the late twenties and early thirties.

4. The upper biological limit of motor capacity is reached in the first part of early adulthood.
    a. Longitudinal research on master runners reveals that as long as practice continues, speed drops only slightly from the mid-thirties into the sixties.
    b. For long-distance swimmers, the decline in speed with advancing age occurs even later, in the seventies.
5. Biological aging accounts for only a small part of age-related decline until advanced old age; before that, lower levels of performance largely reflect reduced capacities resulting from adaptation to a less physically demanding lifestyle.

D. Immune System (pp. 344–345)
1. The immune response is the combined work of specialized cells that neutralize or destroy antigens (foreign substances) in the body.
2. Two types of white blood cells play vital roles:
    a. *T cells,* which originate in the bone marrow and mature in the thymus (a small gland located in the upper part of the chest), attack antigens directly.
    b. *B cells,* manufactured in the bone marrow, secrete antibodies into the bloodstream that multiply, capture antigens, and permit the blood system to destroy them.
3. Because receptors on their surfaces recognize only a single antigen, T and B cells come in great variety and join with additional cells to produce immunity.
4. The immune system's capacity to offer protection against disease increases through adolescence but declines after age 20 as a result of changes in the thymus that compromise the immune response, which is also weakened by both psychological and physical stress.

E. Reproductive Capacity (p. 345)
1. First births to women in their thirties have increased greatly over the past two decades, as many people have delayed childbearing until their education is complete, their careers are well established, and they know they can support a child.
2. Women's fertility declines with age, especially in the late thirties and forties, largely because of a reduced number and quality of ova.
3. In males, semen volume and sperm concentration and motility gradually decrease after age 40, contributing to reduced fertility rates in older men.
4. These fertility declines place individuals who postpone childbearing until their late thirties or their forties at risk of having fewer children than they desired or none at all.

IV. HEALTH AND FITNESS (pp. 345–354)

A. Death rates in early adulthood for all causes are lower for Canadians than Americans, probably as a result of a combination of factors, including Canada's lower rates of poverty and extreme obesity, stricter gun control policies, and system of universal, government-sponsored health insurance.

B. Income, education, and occupational status show strong, continuous relationships with almost every disease and health indicator.
1. Economically advantaged and well-educated individuals sustain better health over most of their adult lives, while the health of lower-income individuals with limited education steadily declines.
2. These differences can be largely attributed to SES differences in health-related circumstances and habits, including stressful life events, crowding, pollution, diet, exercise, overweight and obesity, substance abuse, availability of supportive social relationships, and (in the United States) access to affordable health care.

C. Several factors account for the greater SES disparities in the United States than in Canada.
1. The United States does not provide universal health insurance.
2. Poverty-stricken U.S. families have lower incomes than their Canadian counterparts.
3. SES groups are more likely to be segregated by neighborhood in U.S. than in Canadian large cities, resulting in greater inequalities in environmental factors that affect health.

D. Nutrition (pp. 346–348)
1. An abundance of food, combined with a heavily scheduled life, means that most North Americans eat because they feel like it or because it is time to do so rather than to maintain the body's function.
2. Overweight and Obesity (pp. 346–347)
    a. Obesity (a greater than 20 percent increase over average body weight, based on age, sex, and physical build) has increased dramatically in many Western nations.

b. Today, 31 percent of U.S. adults and 23 percent of Canadian adults are obese, with higher rates among Hispanic, Canadian-Aboriginal, African-American, and Native-American adults.
c. An additional 34 percent of Americans and 36 percent of Canadians are overweight.
d. Obesity rates rise steadily between ages 20 and 60, because overweight children tend to become overweight adults, while many others experience large weight gains in adulthood.
e. Causes and Consequences (pp. 346–347)
  (1) With the decline in need for physical labor in the home and workplace, people's lives have become more sedentary.
  (2) The average number of calories and amount of sugar and fat consumed by North Americans rose throughout the twentieth century, with a sharp increase after 1970.
f. Between ages 25 and 50, some weight gain is normal, reflecting a gradual decline in **basal metabolic rate (BMR)**, the amount of energy the body uses at complete rest.
g. However, excess weight is strongly associated with serious health problems—including high blood pressure, circulatory difficulties, atherosclerosis, stroke, adult-onset diabetes, liver and gallbladder disease, arthritis, sleep and digestive disorders, and most forms of cancer—and with early death.
h. Overweight adults also suffer enormous social discrimination that can affect success in seeking employment, renting apartments, finding mates, and other aspects of life.
i. Treatment (p. 347)
  (1) Even moderate weight loss reduces health problems substantially.
  (2) Treatment for obesity should promote lasting behavior change:
    (a) A well-balanced diet lower in calories and fat, plus exercise
    (b) Training participants to keep an accurate record of what they eat
    (c) Social support
    (d) Teaching problem-solving skills
    (e) Extended intervention

3. Dietary Fat (pp. 347–348)
  a. Although public awareness of health risks has led to a slight drop in fat consumption by North American adults, about 60 percent of adults still eat more than recommended by U.S. and Canadian national dietary guidelines.
  b. Reasons for limiting dietary fat include the strong connection of total fat consumption with obesity and of saturated fat with cardiovascular disease, as well as possible links with breast and colon cancers.
  c. Moderate fat consumption is essential for normal body functioning, but excess fat may be converted to cholesterol, which accumulates as plaque on the arterial walls in atherosclerosis.
  d. Excess fat consumption is a major contributor to the high rate of heart disease in the U.S. black population, compared with Africans in West Africa and the Caribbean.
  e. Regular exercise can reduce the harmful influence of dietary fat by creating chemical byproducts that help eliminate cholesterol from the body.

E. Exercise (p. 348)
  1. Benefits of exercise:
    a. Regular exercise reduces body fat, builds muscle, and fosters resistance to disease by enhancing the immune response and by reducing the incidence of obesity.
    b. People who exercise are likely to adopt other healthful behaviors, such as changes in diet, alcohol consumption, and smoking.
    c. Exercise strengthens the heart muscle, lowers blood pressure, and produces "good cholesterol" (high-density lipoproteins, or HDLs), which helps remove "bad cholesterol" (low-density lipoproteins, or LDLs) from the artery walls.
    d. Regular physical activity can also reduce anxiety and depression, improve mood, enhance alertness and energy, and reduce stress, which strengthens immunity to disease.
    e. Physical activity promotes self-esteem, ability to cope with stress, on-the-job productivity, and overall life satisfaction.
  2. Currently, the U.S. government recommends 30 minutes of moderate-intensity physical activity on five or more days per week, or 20 or more minutes of vigorous-intensity exercise on three or more days per week; Canadian recommendations are even more stringent.

F. Substance Abuse (pp. 348–349)
  1. Drug taking peaks among 19- to 22-year-olds, then declines during the twenties.
    a. Young adults are more likely than younger or older individuals to smoke cigarettes, chew tobacco, use marijuana, and take stimulants to enhance performance.
    b. Binge drinking and experimentation with prescription drugs and "party drugs" increase, at times with tragic consequences.
    c. As many as 20 percent of North American 21- to 25-year-olds are substance abusers; cigarette smoking and alcohol consumption are the most common substance disorders.
  2. Risks of drug use:
    a. Risks include brain damage, lasting impairments in mental functioning, and unintentional injury and death.
    b. Chronic alcohol and drug taking intensify the psychological problems that underlie addiction.
  3. Cigarette Smoking (p. 348)
    a. Dissemination of information on the harmful effects of cigarette smoking has reduced its prevalence dramatically in North America since 1965, but change has been slow.
      (1) Most of the drop in smoking has occurred among college graduates, with very little change for those who did not finish high school.
      (2) Although more men than women smoke, the gender gap is much smaller today than in the past, reflecting a sharp increase in smoking among young women who did not finish high school.
      (3) The earlier people start smoking, the greater their daily cigarette consumption and likelihood of continuing.
    b. Nicotine, tar, carbon monoxide, and other chemicals found in cigarette smoke damage many body structures, including the cardiovascular system, and the retina of the eye, as well as skin abnormalities (premature aging, poor wound healing, and hair loss), a decline in bone mass, a decrease in reserve ova and earlier menopause in women, and a reduced sperm count and higher rate of sexual impotence in men.
    c. Other deadly outcomes include increased risk of heart attack, stroke, acute leukemia, melanoma, and cancer of the mouth, throat, larynx, esophagus, lungs, stomach, pancreas, kidneys, and bladder.
    d. Preventive efforts with adolescents and young adults are vital.
      (1) The chances of premature death rise with the number of cigarettes consumed; benefits of quitting include return of most disease risks to nonsmoker levels within 3 to 8 years.
      (2) Although millions of people have stopped smoking without help, those who enter treatment programs or use cessation aids (such as nicotine gum, nasal spray, or patches) have a 70 to 90 percent failure rate.
      (3) To be effective, treatments need to last long enough or teach skills for avoiding relapse.
  4. Alcohol (pp. 349–350)
    a. About 13 percent of men and 3 percent of women in the United States and Canada are heavy drinkers, and about one-third of this group are *alcoholics*—people who cannot limit their alcohol use.
      (1) In men, alcoholism usually begins in the teens and early twenties and worsens over the following decade.
      (2) In women, alcoholism usually begins in the twenties and thirties and takes a more variable course.
    b. Although twin studies support a genetic contribution to alcoholism, half of hospitalized alcoholics have no family history of problem drinking.
    c. Alcoholism crosses SES and ethnic lines but is higher in some groups than others.
      (1) Less alcoholism is seen in cultures where alcohol is a traditional part of religious or ceremonial activities.
      (2) Dependency is more likely where access to alcohol is carefully controlled and viewed as a sign of adulthood, explaining in part why college students drink more heavily than young people not enrolled in college.
      (3) Poverty and hopelessness also promote excessive drinking.

- d. Negative physical and psychological effects of alcohol:
  - (1) Alcohol acts as a depressant, impairing the brain's ability to control thought and action.
  - (2) In heavy drinkers, drinking relieves anxiety at first but then induces it as the effects wear off, prompting the alcoholic to drink again.
  - (3) Heavy drinking is linked to liver disease, cardiovascular disease, inflammation of the pancreas, irritation of the intestinal tract, bone marrow problems, disorders of the blood and joints, and some forms of cancer.
  - (4) Over time, alcohol causes brain damage, leading to confusion, apathy, inability to learn, and impaired memory.
  - (5) About 40 percent of fatal motor vehicle crashes in the United States and Canada involve drivers who have been drinking.
  - (6) Nearly half of convicted felons are alcoholics, and about half of police activities in large cities involve alcohol-related offenses.
  - (7) Alcohol frequently plays a part in sexual coercion, including date rape, and in domestic violence.
- e. Treatment:
  - (1) The most successful treatments combine personal and family counseling, group support, and aversion therapy (use of medication that produces a physically unpleasant reaction to alcohol, such as nausea and vomiting).
  - (2) About 50 percent of alcoholics relapse within a few months.

G. Sexuality (pp. 350–354)

1. Sexual activity and lifestyles:
   - a. By the end of their teenage years, more than 70 percent of young people have had sexual intercourse; by age 22, the figure rises to 90 percent.
   - b. Compared with earlier generations, contemporary adults display a wider range of sexual choices and lifestyles, including cohabitation, marriage, extramarital experiences, and orientation toward a heterosexual or homosexual partner.
2. Heterosexual Attitudes and Behavior (pp. 350–351)
   - a. The National Health and Social Life Survey, the first in-depth study of U.S. adults' sex lives based on a nationally representative sample, surveyed 3,400 randomly chosen 18- to 59-year-olds about their sex lives.
     - (1) Findings were remarkably similar to those of surveys conducted at about the same time in France, Great Britain, and Finland, and to a more recent U.S. survey.
     - (2) The sexual practices of adults are diverse, but most are far less sexually active than we have come to believe.
     - (3) Monogamous, emotionally committed couples are more typical (and more satisfied) than couples who engage in casual sex.
   - b. Sexual partners usually do not select each other arbitrarily.
     - (1) They tend to be within 5 years in age and of similar education, ethnicity, and (to a lesser extent) religion.
     - (2) People who establish lasting relationships usually meet in conventional ways—through family members or friends, or at work, school, or social events.
     - (3) Internet dating services have become an increasingly popular way to initiate relationships, and adults who form an online relationship and then meet face-to-face often go on to see each other again, with 18 percent of such ties lasting for more than a year.
   - c. Americans today have more sexual partners over their lifetimes than they did a generation ago.
     - (1) Whereas one-third of adults over age 50 have had five or more partners, half of 30- to 50-year-olds have accumulated that many in much less time.
     - (2) About 70 percent of adults of any age report that they have had just one sexual partner in the past year.
     - (3) Dating today is more likely to lead first to cohabitation rather than marriage, while cohabitation leads either to marriage or to breakup—meaning that people will have a larger number of sexual partners in a lifetime.

(4) People are marrying later, and the divorce rate remains high—additional factors that create more opportunities for new sexual partners.
(5) However, most people spend the majority of their lives with one partner, and only 3 percent of Americans, most of them men, report five or more partners in a single year.

d. Frequency of sexual intercourse is typically unaffected by education, SES, or ethnicity.
(1) One-third of 18- to 59-year-olds report that they have intercourse as often as twice a week, another third a few times a month, and the remaining third a few times a year or not at all.
(2) Factors affecting frequency of sexual activity include age, whether people are cohabiting or married, and how long the couple has been together.
(3) Sexual activity increases through the twenties as people either cohabit or marry, then declines around age 30 in response to the demands of daily life—working, commuting, taking care of home and children.

e. Findings on sexual satisfaction challenge two stereotypes: that marriage is sexually dull and that people with many partners have more satisfying sex lives.
(1) More than 80 percent of adults in committed relationships (and 88 percent of married couples) say they feel "extremely physically and emotionally satisfied."
(2) As number of sex partners increases, satisfaction declines sharply.

f. A minority of adults—women more often than men—report persistent sexual problems; the risk of sexual dysfunction is higher for those with a history of unfavorable personal relationships and sexual experiences.
(1) For women, the two most frequent difficulties are lack of interest in sex and inability to achieve orgasm.
(2) The most common male difficulties are climaxing too early and anxiety about performance.
(3) Sexual difficulties are linked to low SES and psychological stress and are more common among people who are not married, have had more than five partners, and have experienced sexual abuse during childhood or (for women) sexual coercion in adulthood.

3. Homosexual Attitudes and Behavior (pp. 351–352)

a. The majority of Americans support civil liberties and equal employment opportunities for gay men, lesbians, and bisexuals.

b. Attitudes toward sexual relations between two adults of the same sex have become more accepting in the past decade, partly as a result of homosexuals' political activism and greater openness about their sexual orientation.

c. Perhaps because they are especially concerned with gender-role conformity, heterosexual men judge homosexuals (especially gay men) more harshly than do heterosexual women.

d. In the National Health and Social Life Survey, 2.8 percent of men and 1.4 percent of women identified themselves as homosexual or bisexual—figures similar to those of other national surveys conducted in the United States, France, and Great Britain.
(1) An estimated 30 percent of same-sex couples do not report themselves as such in survey research.
(2) This unwillingness to answer questions, engendered by a climate of persecution, has limited researchers' access to information about the sex lives of gay men and lesbians.

e. The little evidence available indicates that homosexual sex follows many of the same rules as heterosexual sex:
(1) People tend to seek out partners similar in education and background to themselves.
(2) Partners in committed relationships have sex more often and are more satisfied.
(3) The overall frequency of sex is modest.

f. Homosexuals tend to live in large cities, where many others share their sexual orientation, or in college towns, where attitudes are more accepting.

g. Living in small communities where prejudice is intense and no social network exists through which to find compatible homosexual partners is isolating, lonely, and predictive of mental health problems.

4. Sexual Coercion (pp. 352–353)

a. An estimated 6 to 15 percent of North American women have endured *rape,* legally defined as intercourse by force, by threat of harm, or when the victim is incapable of giving consent (because of mental illness, mental retardation, or alcohol consumption).

b. From 22 to 57 percent of women have experienced other forms of sexual aggression, usually by men they know well; 8 out of 10 victims are under age 30.
c. Sexual coercion crosses SES and ethnic lines, and personal characteristics of the man with whom a woman is involved are far better predictors of her chances of becoming a victim than her own characteristics.
   (1) Men who engage in sexual assault tend to believe in traditional gender roles, approve of violence against women, and accept common myths that women are responsible for being raped.
   (2) Perpetrators tend to interpret women's social behavior inaccurately, viewing friendliness as seductiveness, assertiveness as hostility, and resistance as desire.
   (3) Predators express little remorse.
   (4) Sexual abuse in childhood, promiscuity in adolescence, and alcohol abuse in adulthood are associated with sexual coercion.
   (5) Approximately half of all sexual assaults take place while people are intoxicated.
d. Cultures in which men are taught from an early age to be dominant, competitive, and aggressive and women to be submissive, cooperative, and passive reinforce the themes of rape.
   (1) Men may view a date not as a chance to get to know a partner but as a potential sexual conquest.
   (2) Societal acceptance of violence sets the stage for rape, which typically occurs in relationships in which other forms of aggression are commonplace.
e. About 15 to 30 percent of North American young adult samples report female-initiated coercive sexual behavior against men; 3 to 10 percent of male responses indicating threats of physical force or actual force.
   (1) Victimized men often say that women who committed these acts encouraged them to get drunk and threatened to end the relationship unless they complied.
   (2) Authorities rarely recognize female-initiated forced sex as illegal, and few men report these crimes.
f. Consequences (p. 353)
   (1) Women's psychological reactions to rape resemble those of survivors of extreme trauma.
   (2) Immediate responses—shock, confusion, withdrawal, and psychological numbing—eventually give way to chronic fatigue, tension, disturbed sleep, depression, and suicidal thoughts.
   (3) Victims of ongoing sexual coercion may fall into a pattern of extreme passivity and fear.
   (4) One-third to one-half of female rape victims are physically injured, some contract sexually transmitted diseases, and about 5 to 20 percent become pregnant.
   (5) Women victimized by rape (and other crimes) report more symptoms of illness across almost all body systems and are more likely to engage in negative health behaviors, including smoking and alcohol use.
g. Prevention and Treatment (p. 353)
   (1) Community services, including safe houses, crisis hotlines, support groups, and legal assistance, exist to help women take refuge from abusive partners, but most are underfunded and cannot reach out to everyone in need.
   (2) Practically no services exist for victimized men, who are often too embarrassed to come forward.
   (3) Therapy to address the trauma induced by rape may include individual treatment aimed at reducing anxiety and depression, as well as group sessions where contact with other survivors can help counter isolation and self-blame.
   (4) Other features that foster recovery include routine screening for victimization during health-care visits, validation of the experience, and safety planning.

5. Menstrual Cycle (pp. 353–354)
   a. **Premenstrual syndrome (PMS)** refers to an array of physical and psychological symptoms, seen in nearly 40 percent of women, that usually appear 6 to 10 days prior to menstruation, generally starting after age 20.
   b. The most common symptoms are abdominal cramps, fluid retention, diarrhea, tender breasts, backache, head ache, fatigue, tension, irritability, and depression.

c. Most women have mild symptoms, but for 10 to 20 percent, PMS is severe enough to interfere with academic, occupational, and social functioning.

d. Causes of PMS:

(1) PMS is a worldwide phenomenon affecting women of varying SES levels, nationalities, and cultures.

(2) Identical twins are twice as likely as fraternal twins to share the syndrome, providing evidence of a genetic predisposition.

e. Although PMS is related to hormonal changes that follow ovulation and precede menstruation, hormone therapy is not consistently effective, suggesting that sensitivity of brain centers to these hormones, rather than the hormones themselves, is probably responsible.

f. No method has been devised for curing PMS, but some common treatments that may be helpful include analgesics, antidepressant medication, diuretics for fluid buildup, limiting caffeine intake, a diet low in fat and high in fiber, vitamin/mineral supplements, exercise, and other strategies for reducing stress.

H. Psychological Stress (p. 354)

1. Psychological stress—measured in terms of adverse social conditions, negative life events, or daily hassles—is related to a wide variety of unfavorable health outcomes through both behavioral and direct physical consequences.

2. Cardiovascular responses to stress:

a. Because stress elevates blood pressure, chronic stress resulting from economic hardship and inner-city living is consistently linked to hypertension, contributing to the high incidence of heart disease in low-income groups, especially African Americans.

b. Compared with higher-SES individuals, low-SES adults show a stronger cardiovascular response to stress, perhaps because they more often perceive stressors as unsolvable.

3. Other health effects:

a. Psychological stress interferes with immune system functioning, a link that may underlie its relationship to several forms of cancer.

b. By reducing digestive activity as blood flows to the brain, heart, and extremities, stress can cause gastrointestinal difficulties (constipation, diarrhea, colitis, and ulcers).

4. The many challenging tasks of early adulthood make it a particularly stressful time of life.

a. Young adults more often report depressive feelings than middle-aged people, who are better than young adults at coping with stress because of their longer life experience and greater sense of personal control over their lives.

b. Because social support has a lifelong mitigating effect on stress, helping stressed young adults establish and maintain satisfying social ties is an important health intervention.

Cognitive Development

V. CHANGES IN THE STRUCTURE OF THOUGHT (pp. 354–357)

A. Piaget acknowledged the possibility that important advances in thinking follow the attainment of formal operations.

1. He observed that adolescents place excessive faith in abstract systems, preferring a logical, internally consistent—but inaccurate—perspective on the world to one that is vague, contradictory, and adapted to particular circumstances.

2. Researchers who have studied **postformal thought** have observed that cognitive development occurs beyond Piaget's formal operations, as personal effort and social experiences spark increasingly rational, flexible, and practical ways of thinking that accept uncertainties and vary across situations.

B. Perry's Theory: Epistemic Cognition (pp. 355–356)

1. William Perry's work provided the starting point for a growing research literature on the development of **epistemic cognition**—our reflections on how we arrived at facts, beliefs, and ideas.

2. Mature, rational thinkers consider the justifiability of their conclusions and, when they cannot justify their approach, revise it in favor of a more balanced, adequate route to acquiring knowledge.

3. Development of Epistemic Cognition (p. 355)

a. Perry interviewed Harvard University students at the end of each of their four years of college to discover why young adults respond in dramatically different ways to the diversity of ideas they encounter in college.

b. Students' responses to Perry's question about "what stood out" during the previous year showed how their reflections on knowing changed as they experienced the complexities of university life and moved closer to adult roles—findings confirmed in many subsequent studies.
c. Younger students, who regarded knowledge as consisting of separate units (beliefs and propositions) whose truth could be determined by comparing them to abstract standards, engaged in **dualistic thinking**, dividing information, values, and authority into right and wrong or good and bad.
d. Older students, in contrast, had moved toward **relativistic thinking**—viewing all knowledge as embedded in a framework of thought.
   (1) Aware of a diversity of opinions on many topics, they gave up the possibility of absolute truth in favor of multiple truths, each relative to its context, and their thinking became more flexible and tolerant.
   (2) The relativistic thinker is aware that each person, in arriving at a position, chooses one of many possible positions, each a defensible version of "truth."
e. Eventually, the most mature individuals progress to **commitment within relativistic thinking**.
   (1) Instead of choosing between opposing views, they try to formulate a more satisfying perspective that synthesizes contradictions.
   (2) Although few college students reach this extension of relativism, adults who attain it often display a more sophisticated approach to learning, actively seeking out differing perspectives to advance their knowledge and understanding.

4. Importance of Peer Interaction and Reflection (pp. 355–356)
   a. Advances in epistemic cognition depend on further gains in metacognition, which occur in situations that challenge young people's perspectives and prompt them to reflect on the rationality of their thought processes—something that is more likely to happen during group problem-solving processes.
   b. In a comparison of the college learning experiences of seniors who scored low and high in Perry's scheme, the high scoring students frequently reported activities that encouraged them to struggle with realistic but ambiguous problems in a supportive environment where faculty offered encouragement and guidance.
   c. Reflection on one's own thinking can occur individually, but peer interaction can foster the necessary type of individual reflection: arguing with oneself over competing ideas and strategies and coordinating opposing perspectives into a new, more effective structure.

C. Labouvie-Vief's Theory: Pragmatic Thought and Cognitive-Affective Complexity (pp. 356–357)
   1. Like Perry, Labouvie-Vief points out that whereas adolescents operate within a world of possibility, adulthood involves movement from hypothetical to **pragmatic thought**—a structural advance in which logic becomes a tool for solving real-world problems.
   2. According to Labouvie-Vief, the need to specialize motivates this change.
      a. As adults choose one path from many alternatives, they become more aware of the constraints of everyday life.
      b. As they balance various roles, adults give up their earlier discomfort with contradictions, accept inconsistencies as part of life, and develop ways of thinking that thrive on imperfection and compromise.
   3. Young adults' enhanced reflective capacities also alter the dynamics of their emotional lives as they become more adept at integrating cognition with emotion and, in doing so, at making sense of discrepancies.
   4. Analyzing the self-descriptions of several hundred 10- to 80-year-olds diverse in SES, Labouvie-Vief found that from adolescence through middle adulthood, people gained in **cognitive-affective complexity**—coordination of positive and negative feelings into a complex, organized structure.
      a. Cognitive-affective complexity promotes awareness of one's own and others' perspectives and motivations.
      b. It helps people regulate intense emotion and think rationally about real-world dilemmas, even those containing negative information.

VI. EXPERTISE AND CREATIVITY (p. 357)

A. Because it takes many years for a person to master any complex domain, **expertise**—acquisition of extensive knowledge in a field or endeavor—is supported by the specialization that begins with selecting a college major or an occupation.

B. Characteristics of experts:

1. Compared with novices, experts remember and reason more quickly and effectively, know more domain-specific concepts, and represent them in at a deeper and more abstract level and as having more features that can be linked to other concepts.
2. While novices' understanding is superficial, experts approach problems with underlying principles in mind.
3. Experts can use what they know to arrive at many solutions automatically through quick and easy remembering.
4. Whereas the novice takes a trial-and-error approach to problem solving, experts, when confronted with a challenging problem, tend to plan ahead, systematically analyzing and categorizing elements and selecting the best from many possibilities.

C. Expertise is necessary for creativity as well as problem solving.

D. Case studies support the 10-year rule in development of master-level creativity—a decade between initial exposure to a field and sufficient expertise to produce a creative work.

1. Creative accomplishment rises in early adulthood, peaks in the late thirties or early forties, and gradually declines, although a creative person rarely becomes noncreative.
2. Those who get an early start in creativity tend to peak and drop off sooner, while "late bloomers" hit their stride at older ages, suggesting that creativity is more a function of "career age" than of chronological age.

E. The course of creativity varies across disciplines.

1. Artists and musicians typically show an early rise in creativity, perhaps because they do not need extensive formal education before they begin to produce.
2. Academic scholars and scientists usually display their achievements later and over a longer time.

F. Creativity is rooted in expertise, but not all experts are creative—only those who also have an innovative thinking style, tolerance of ambiguity, a special drive to succeed, and a willingness to experiment and try again after failure.

G. Especially for women, the investment of time and energy that creativity demands can be postponed or disrupted by child rearing, divorce, or an unsupportive partner.

VII. THE COLLEGE EXPERIENCE (p. 358)

A. About two-thirds of North American high school graduates enroll in an institution of higher education.

B. Besides offering a route to a high-status career with personal and monetary rewards, colleges and universities serve as a "developmental testing ground" for young people—an opportunity to devote full attention to exploring alternative values, roles, and behaviors.

C. Psychological Impact of Attending College (p. 358)

1. Research shows that from the first to the last year of college, students become better at reasoning about problems that have no clear solution, identifying the strengths and weaknesses of opposing sides of complex issues, and reflecting on the quality of their thinking.
2. College students' attitudes and values also broaden.
   a. They show increased interest in literature, the performing arts, and philosophical and historical issues, and greater tolerance for ethnic and cultural diversity.
   b. Their moral reasoning advances as they develop a concern with individual rights and human welfare.
   c. Exposure to multiple worldviews encourages young people to look more closely at themselves, which promotes the development of greater self-understanding, enhanced self-esteem, and a firmer sense of identity.
3. Residence hall living is one of the most consistent predictors of cognitive change because it maximizes involvement in the institution's educational and social systems.
   a. These findings underscore the importance of programs that integrate commuting students into campus life outside of class.

   b. Quality of academic experiences also affects outcomes: Psychological benefits increase with students' effort and willingness to participate in class and with challenging teaching that integrates learning in separate courses, offers extensive contact with faculty, and connects course work with real workplace activities.

D. Dropping Out (p. 358)
   1. Forty-five percent of North American students at two-year institutions and 30 percent of those at four-year institutions drop out, most within the first year and many within the first 6 weeks.
   2. Both personal and institutional factors play a role in college leaving.
      a. Dropout rates are higher (up to 50 percent of freshmen) in colleges with less selective admission requirements.
      b. Ethnic minority students from low-SES families are at increased risk for dropping out.
      c. Entering freshmen who have trouble adapting—because of lack of motivation, poor study skills, financial pressures, or emotional dependence on parents—quickly develop negative attitudes toward the college environment.
      d. Colleges that do little to help high-risk students through developmental courses and other support services have a higher percentage of dropouts.
      e. Students who report experiencing "disrespect" on campus because of their ethnicity or religion are more likely to drop out.
   3. Reaching out to first-year college students is crucial to prevent dropout.
      a. Programs that forge bonds between teachers and students and that provide academic support, part-time work opportunities, and meaningful extracurricular roles increase retention.
      b. Membership in campus-based social and religious organizations is especially helpful in strengthening minority students' sense of belonging.
      c. Young people who feel that they have entered a college community that is concerned about them as individuals are far more likely to graduate.

VIII. VOCATIONAL CHOICE (pp. 358–362)

A. Selecting a Vocation (p. 359)
   1. In societies with an abundance of career possibilities, occupational choice is a gradual process that begins long before adolescence.
   2. Major theorists view the young person as moving through several periods of vocational development.
      a. The **fantasy period**: In early and middle childhood, children fantasize about career options; their preferences, guided largely by familiarity, glamour, and excitement, bear little relation to the decisions they will eventually make.
      b. The **tentative period**: Between ages 11 and 16, adolescents think about careers in more complex ways, at first in terms of their *interests,* and soon—as they become more aware of personal and educational requirements for different vocations—in terms of their *abilities* and *values.*
      c. The **realistic period**: By the late teens and early twenties, young people start to narrow their options.
         (1) They may engage in further *exploration*—gathering more information about possibilities that blend with their personal characteristics.
         (2) In the final phase, *crystallization,* they focus on a general vocational category and experiment for a time before settling on a single occupation.

B. Factors Influencing Vocational Choice (pp. 359–361)
   1. A few young people know from an early age just what they want to be and follow a direct path to a career goal, some decide and later change their minds, while still others remain undecided for an extended period.
   2. College students have additional time to explore various options, while many low-SES youths face a restricted range of choices.
   3. Making an occupational choice, like other developmental milestones, is the result of a dynamic interaction between person and environment, affected by a many influences, including personality, family and teachers, and gender stereotypes.

4. Personality (pp. 359–360)
   a. John Holland identified six personality types that affect vocational choice:
      (1) The *investigative person,* who enjoys working with ideas, is likely to select a scientific occupation (for example, anthropologist, physicist, or engineer).
      (2) The *social person,* who likes interacting with people, gravitates toward human services (counseling, social work, or teaching).
      (3) The *realistic person,* who prefers real-world problems and working with objects, tends to choose a mechanical occupation (construction, plumbing, or surveying).
      (4) The *artistic person,* who is emotional and high in need for individual expression, looks toward an artistic field (writing, music, or the visual arts).
      (5) The *conventional person,* who likes well-structured tasks and values material possessions and social status, has traits well suited to certain business fields (accounting, banking, or quality control).
      (6) The *enterprising person,* who is adventurous, persuasive, and a strong leader, is drawn to sales and supervisory positions or to politics.
   b. Research confirms a moderate relationship between these six personality types and vocational choice in diverse cultures.
   c. Many people are blends of several personality types and can do well at more than one kind of occupation; actual career decisions are made in the context of family influences, educational opportunities, and current life circumstances.
5. Family Influences (p. 360)
   a. Individuals who grew up in higher-SES homes are more likely to select high-status, white-collar occupations, such as doctor, lawyer, scientist, or engineer. Those with lower-SES backgrounds tend to choose less prestigious, blue-collar careers, such as plumber, construction worker, food service employee, or secretary.
   b. Parent–child vocational similarity is partly a function of similarity in personality, intellectual abilities, and—especially—educational attainment.
   c. Number of years of schooling completed powerfully predicts occupational status.
   d. Other factors also promote family resemblance in occupational choice.
      (1) Higher-SES parents are more likely to give their children important information about the world of work and to have connections with people who can help the young person obtain a high-status position.
      (2) Higher-SES parents tend make use of parenting practices that promote curiosity and self-direction, which are required in many high-status careers, while lower-SES parents are more likely to emphasize conformity and obedience.
   e. Parental pressure to do well in school and encouragement toward high-status occupations predict vocational attainment beyond family SES.
6. Teachers (p. 360)
   a. Young adults who choose careers requiring extensive education often report that teachers influenced their choice—yet another reason to promote positive teacher–student relations, especially for high school students from low-SES families.
   b. College-bound high school students tend to have closer relationships with teachers than do other students—relationships that are especially likely to foster high career aspirations in young women.
7. Gender Stereotypes (pp. 360–361)
   a. Over the past three decades, young women have expressed increasing interest in occupations largely held by men, as a result of changes in gender-role attitudes and a dramatic rise in numbers of employed mothers, who serve as career-oriented models for their daughters.
   b. Women's progress in entering and excelling at male-dominated professions has been slow.
      (1) The percentage of women engineers, lawyers, doctors, and business executives increased between 1983 and 2004 in the United States but remains far from equal representation.
      (2) Women are concentrated in traditionally feminine—and less well-paid—professions such as social work, education, and nursing.

(3) In virtually all fields, women's achievements lag behind those of men, who write more books, make more discoveries, hold more positions of leadership, and produce more works of art.

c. Gender-stereotyped messages play a key role in making girls less confident of their abilities and more likely to underestimate their achievement as they begin secondary school—even though girls' grades are higher than boys'.

d. During college, women's low self-confidence about succeeding in male-dominated fields further limits their occupational choices.
   (1) Many mathematically talented college women settle on non-science majors.
   (2) Those who remain in the sciences are more likely than their male counterparts to choose a health profession over engineering or a math or physical science career.

e. A pressing need exists for programs that sensitize high school and college personnel to the special problems women face in developing and maintaining high vocational aspirations and selecting nontraditional careers.

f. Young women who continue to achieve usually have four experiences in common:
   (1) A college environment that values women's accomplishments and attempts to enhance women's experiences in its curriculum
   (2) Frequent interaction with faculty and professionals in their chosen fields
   (3) The opportunity to test their abilities in a supportive environment
   (4) Models of accomplished women who have successfully dealt with family–career role conflict

g. Compared to women, men have changed little in their interest in nontraditional occupations.

C. Vocational Preparation of Non-College-Bound Young Adults (p. 362)

1. Approximately one-third of North American young people graduate from high school with no current plans to go to college and face challenges in finding meaningful work opportunities.
   a. Although they are better able than high school dropouts to find a job, North American non-college-bound high school graduates typically have fewer work opportunities than high school graduates of several decades ago.
   b. About 15 percent of Canadian and 20 percent of U.S. recent high school graduates who do not continue their education are unemployed, and many others work in temporary, low-paid, unskilled jobs.
   c. North American employers regard recent high school graduates as poorly prepared for skilled business and industrial occupations and manual trades.

2. Unlike European nations, the United States and Canada have no widespread training systems for non-college-bound youths.
   a. As a result, most graduate without work-related skills and experience a "floundering period" that lasts for several years.
   b. Inspired by programs in Austria, Denmark, Switzerland, and several East European countries, youth apprenticeship strategies that coordinate on-the-job training with classroom instruction are being considered as an important dimension of U.S. and Canadian educational reforms.
   c. Benefits of bringing together the worlds of schooling and work:
      (1) These programs help non-college-bound young people establish productive lives right after graduation.
      (2) They motivate at-risk youths to stay in school.
      (3) They contribute to a nation's economic growth.
   d. Implementing an apprenticeship system poses major challenges, including the following:
      (1) Employers are reluctant to assume part of the responsibility for vocational training.
      (2) Cooperation between schools and businesses is vital for the success of these programs.
      (3) It is important to prevent low-SES youths from being concentrated in the lowest-skilled apprenticeship placements—an obstacle that Germany itself has not yet fully overcome.
   e. Small-scale school-to-work projects in the United States and Canada are attempting to solve these problems and build bridges between learning and working.

LECTURE ENHANCEMENTS

LECTURE ENHANCEMENT 13.1
Is There a Relationship Between Sleep Duration and Obesity? (pp. 346–347)

Time: 5–10 minutes

Objective: To examine the relationship between short sleep duration and obesity in young adults.

As noted in the text, overweight and obesity is a major health concern for children and adults in many Western nations. Some researchers have found a link between short sleep duration and obesity and body mass index (BMI). To further examine this relationship, Hasler and colleagues (2004) recruited 496 young adults and followed them from age 19 to age 40. The researchers collected the following information six times throughout the study:

1. A diagnostic interview was used to assess general health, the presence of any psychiatric conditions, and somatic syndromes (such as sleep problems, obesity, chronic headaches, and stomach ailments).
2. Body Mass Index.
3. Participants completed self-reports of sleep duration, which included the time they went to bed, the time they arose, and the amount of time needed to fall asleep. Additional questions addressed daytime fatigue, awakenings during the night, and quality of sleep.

Findings indicated a strong relationship between short sleep duration and obesity in young adults. Specifically, sleeping less than six hours a night predicted obesity in adults at ages 27, 29, and 34, even after controlling for general health, the presence of psychiatric conditions, and somatic syndromes. Interestingly, short sleep duration did not predict obesity at age 40. Therefore, sleep deprivation—as it relates to weight gain—seems to be more problematic for young adults than for middle-aged adults. According to Hasler and colleagues (2004), since sleep is a potentially modifiable risk factor, these findings may have important implications for obesity prevention and treatment.

Hasler, G., Buysse, D. J., Klaghefer, R., Gamma, A., Ajdacic, V., Eich, D., Rossler, W., & Angst, J. (2004). The association between short sleep duration and obesity in young adults: A 13-year prospective study. *Sleep, 27,* 661–666.

LECTURE ENHANCEMENT 13.2
Age-Related Changes in Cognitive Development (pp. 354–357)

Time: 10–15 minutes

Objective: To highlight age-related changes in cognitive development.

As discussed in the text, cognitive development continues throughout adulthood. To further examine the relationship between age and cognitive development, Hood and Deopere (2002) recruited 165 adults between the ages of 18 and 87 years. Approximately three-fourths of the sample were either attending college, had completed some college, or had graduated from college. All participants completed the following assessments:

1. *Quick Test* (*QT*). To control for varying levels of intelligence, participants completed an IQ test that was designed to provide a quick measure of verbal-perceptual intelligence.
2. *Scale of Intellectual Development* (*SID*). Based on Perry's theory of epistemic cognition, the SID assesses Dualism, Relativism, and Commitment.
3. *Life Experiences Survey.* The Life Experiences Survey was used to gather relevant demographic information, such as age, occupation, marital status, religious involvement, and educational background.

Results indicated that certain aspects of cognitive development changed substantially with age. For example, older participants scored higher on the Dualism scale than younger participants. That is, older participants were more likely to perceive the world in terms of "Us-Right-Good" versus "Them-Wrong-Bad." This relationship remained strong even after controlling for IQ and educational background. The researchers also found an inverse relationship between age and Relativism scores: As age increased, relativism decreased. Younger participants, regardless of education or intelligence, were more relativistic than older participants. Although the researchers were unable to determine why younger participants were more relativistic, the findings suggest that younger adults may be more flexible in their thinking than older adults.

It is important to note that even though the researchers found age-related differences in thinking, education did play an important role. Overall, participants with higher levels of education scored lower on the Dualism scale and higher on the Relativism scale. As with previous research, these findings support the importance of formal education for the development of complex thought in adulthood.

Hood, A. H., & Deopere, D. L. (2002). The relationship of cognitive development to age, when education and intelligence are controlled for. *Journal of Adult Development, 9,* 229–234.

LECTURE ENHANCEMENT 13.3
Do Personal Interests and Knowledge in High School Affect Adult Intellect and Vocational Choice? (pp. 358–361)

Time: 10–15 minutes

Objective: To explore how personal interests and knowledge in high school might influence adult intellect and vocational choice.

As noted in the text, cognitive development in adulthood is influenced by many factors, such as formal education and peer interaction and reflection. But what role do personal interests and knowledge in high school play in the development of adult intellect and vocational choice? To find out, Reeve and Hakel (2001) conducted a meta-analysis of 330,154 high school students throughout the United States. All students completed a battery of tests designed to measure general knowledge, vocabulary level, and interests in various academic subjects (for example, physical science, math, biology, literature, art, music, farming, sports, accounting, and social studies). Students also completed a 205-item occupational interests survey in which they were asked to rate how appealing they found each occupation. For instance, if presented with "lawyer," participants could chose: *I would like this very much, I would like this a little, I don't know if I would like this, I would dislike this a little,* or *I would dislike this very much.*

Not surprisingly, the researchers found that participants tended to have greater knowledge of subjects that matched their interests. This finding was especially strong for older students. That is, as they advanced in age, participants' interest and knowledge profiles became more similar—the more interested they were in a given subject, the greater their knowledge was of the content. This makes sense given that freshman and sophomores are exposed to a diverse range of academic subjects. As they move through high school, students have more opportunities to pursue electives, which likely reflect their personal interests. According to Reeve and Hakel (2001), as their interests and knowledge converge, high school students build the foundation for future vocational pursuits. Although the researchers did not follow the sample to determine if their personal interests influenced later vocational choices, participants tended to respond more favorably to occupations that were consistent with their knowledge and interests. Taken together, these findings suggest that personal interests and knowledge in high school have important implications for adult development and vocational choice.

Spend some class time discussing these findings. Do students agree that their personal interests in high school shaped their current vocational decisions? Why or why not?

Reeve, C. L., & Hakel, M. D. (2001). Toward an understanding of adult intellectual development: Investigating within-individual convergence of interest and knowledge profiles. *Journal of Applied Psychology, 85,* 897–908.

LECTURE ENHANCEMENT 13.4
Is Career Choice in Early Adulthood Affected by Parents' Early Gender Beliefs? (pp. 359–361)

Time: 10–15 minutes

Objective: To investigate the long-term impact of parents' early gender beliefs on children's academic achievement and future career choice.

As noted in previous chapters, the social environment (parents, teachers, peers, media) exerts a strong influence on children's gender development. According to Bleeker and Jacobs (2004), parental beliefs not only influence academic achievement but also contribute to gender differences in children's perceptions of their own ability. For example, in families where girls have been encouraged to pursue math- and science-related activities, girls tend to have more confidence in their ability to excel in these domains. In families where girls are encouraged to pursue "feminine"-stereotyped activities (such as reading and spelling), math and science self-efficacy tends to be much lower.

To further investigate the relationship between parents' early gender beliefs and adolescents' math and science achievement and future career choices, Bleeker and Jacobs (2004) conducted a follow-up with participants from the Michigan Study of Adolescent Life Transitions, which began in 1983 (when children were in sixth grade). A total of 354 mothers and children participated. The researchers collected the following information:

1. Adolescent and parent questionnaires included a variety of questions about parents' and adolescents' attitudes toward math and science. For example:

   Adolescent

(1) How good at math are you?	1 = not at all good	7 = very good
(2) How well do you think you would do in a science- or math-related field?	1 = not do well at all	7 = would do very well

   Parent

(1) In general, to whom do you believe math is more important?	1 = females	7 = males
(2) How successful do you think your child would be in a career requiring math ability?	1 = not at all	7 = very successful

2. Several additional adolescent measures were also used: a scale measuring adolescents' self-perceptions of math ability during tenth grade (for example, "How good at math are you?"), a scale measuring math and science self-efficacy two years after high school (for example, "How well do you think you would do in a math- or science-related field?"), and a single-item question about current career or occupation when participants were 24 or 25 years old.

Results indicated that mothers' early gender beliefs about math and science achievement had long-term implications for children's self-perceptions of ability and ultimately influenced their career choice. For example, mothers who regarded their children as capable of succeeding in math careers (reported during middle school) were more likely to have adolescents with high self-perceptions of math ability in the tenth grade. They were also more likely to have adolescents with high math–science self-efficacy two years after high school. These findings were true for both boys and girls.

Perhaps the most compelling finding was that female adolescents, whose mothers predicted that they were not likely to excel in math or science careers, were 66 percent less likely to enter a science-related occupation. This was true for both women who attended college and those who entered the work force after high school. It is important to note that this finding was significant only for girls—that is, mothers' perceptions of career ability seemed to have a much greater impact on girls than on boys. Taken together, these results highlight the long-term implications of parents' gender beliefs on both academic achievement and later career choice.

Ask students to reflect on these findings as they relate to their own vocational choices. Were students encouraged to pursue traditionally masculine or feminine subjects in school? Did parental beliefs influence students' choice of a college major? Using findings from this study and Lecture Enhancement 13.3, how might gender expectations influence personal interests and knowledge?

Bleeker, M. M., & Jacobs, J. E. (2004). Achievement in math and science: Do mothers' beliefs matter 12 years later? *Journal of Educational Psychology, 96,* 97–109.

LEARNING ACTIVITIES

LEARNING ACTIVITY 13.1
Interviewing College-Age Students About Emerging Adulthood (pp. 339–340)

Have students pose the following question to four or five college-age friends: "Do you consider yourself to have reached adulthood? Why or why not?" Students should record the answers and compare them with research in the text. For example, did the respondents give an ambiguous answer? What information did respondents give to justify their answer? Were students surprised by any of the answers? Explain.

LEARNING ACTIVITY 13.2
The National Heart, Lung, and Blood Institute (pp. 341–344, 345–348)

To extend students' knowledge about the relationship between nutrition, lifestyle, and heart disease, have them visit a website sponsored by the National Heart, Lung, and Blood Institute (NHLBI): *http://www.nhlbisupport.com/chd1/how.htm#quiz*. Ask students to complete the *Heart Disease IQ and Cholesterol Quiz*. How many questions did they answer correctly? Were they surprised with how much or how little they knew? Next, instruct students to click on Therapeutic Lifestyle Changes (TLC), which focuses on how changes in lifestyle, regular exercise, and weight management can reduce the chances of having a heart attack or related complications. TLC presents a variety of short activities designed to facilitate a healthy adult lifestyle.

1. Students should complete a Personal Eating Plan. Based on their responses to a few short questions, the program will calculate recommended nutritional levels (calories, saturated fat, and total fat) for lowering cholesterol.
2. Students can visit the Virtual Grocery Store in which they will learn about shopping for foods low in saturated fat and cholesterol. Based on the information provided, did students find the suggestions to be helpful? How about practical? Why or why not?
3. The Cyberkitchen presents a series of food images (for example, ice cream, roast beef, cereal) and asks the respondent to indicate if each image represents a standard serving size. If not, the respondent is asked to decide whether the quantity is larger or smaller than a standard serving size. After responses have been entered, students can determine if they are able to recognize standard servings and if they tend to eat more or less than recommended amounts.
4. In the Create-A-Diet Activity, students will be asked to select food items for breakfast, lunch, dinner, and snacks. Once selections have been made, the program will provide a summary of nutritional values and compare it with their Personal Eating Plan completed in Step 1. Did students select foods that were within their personal eating plan (recommended number of calories, saturated fat, and total fat)? Were they surprised by the nutritional values of the foods they selected? How helpful was this activity? Would students use a plan such as this to modify their eating habits? Why or why not?

LEARNING ACTIVITY 13.3
Recording Exercise Participation and Food Intake (p. 348)

Ask students to keep a daily log of their exercise participation and food intake for at least one week. Students should record (a) the type of exercise, (b) the intensity of exercise (heart rate), and (c) the duration of the exercise session. Food intake should be recorded as (a) what was eaten, (b) when and where it was eaten, and when possible, (c) the total and saturated fat content of the food item. Fat content should be recorded as the "percentage of daily value based on a 2,000-calorie diet." Values for fat content can be found on the labels of packaged foods. Students who eat meals primarily in college cafeterias may wish to discuss the fat content of their "dorm food" with food service personnel. Pamphlets containing nutrition information may also be available to students upon request.

Following the recording period, discuss students' daily logs. Did they meet the exercise prescription of 20 minutes, three to five times a week, with relatively vigorous use of the large muscles of the body, in which heart rate was elevated to 60 to 90 percent of its maximum? What types of exercise did students participate in? Did they use college exercise facilities for their workouts? If not, where did they go? What were the benefits of the exercise? What barriers did students encounter? How could these barriers be overcome?

Next, discuss the food intake logs. Did students limit their fat intake to 30 percent of caloric intake? What proportions of total fat intake was comprised of saturated fat? Did students eat more, less, or the same amount of food as they normally do? What other discoveries did students make concerning their exercise and dietary habits?

LEARNING ACTIVITY 13.4
Creating a Pamphlet for Young Adults About Physical Health and Development (pp. 340–354)

Have students pretend they have been asked by the Campus Health Center to create a pamphlet on the importance of physical health and development in early adulthood. Students should make a list of topics they would include in their pamphlets. For example, what physical changes typically occur during early adulthood? What are some common health risks? How can lifestyle choices in early adulthood affect health and well-being later in life? How can psychological stress affect physical health and development?

LEARNING ACTIVITY 13.5
Matching: Cognitive Development in Early Adulthood (pp. 355–357)

Present the following exercise as an in-class activity or quiz:

Directions: Match each of the following terms with its correct description.

Terms:

1. Postformal thought
2. Epistemic cognition
3. Dualistic thinking
4. Relativistic thinking
5. Commitment within relativistic thinking
6. Pragmatic thought
7. Cognitive-affective complexity
8. Expertise

Descriptions:

A. Awareness and coordination of positive and negative feelings into a complex, organized structure
B. Viewing all knowledge as embedded in a framework of thought
C. A structural advance in which logic becomes a tool for solving real-world problems
D. Acquisition of extensive knowledge in a filed or endeavor
E. Instead of choosing between opposing views, the most mature individuals try to formulate a more satisfying perspective that synthesizes contradictions
F. Refers to our reflections on how we arrived at facts, beliefs, and ideas
G. Cognitive development beyond Piaget's formal operations
H. Dividing information, values, and authority into right and wrong, good and bad, we and they

Answers:

1. G
2. F
3. H
4. B
5. E
6. C
7. A
8. D

LEARNING ACTIVITY 13.6
Selecting College-Level Courses That Foster or Enhance Creativity (p. 357)

Have students locate a course registration book, read the course descriptions, and make a list of classes that might foster or enhance creativity. Using research discussed in the text, what are some characteristics of creative people? How might these courses appeal to creative students? Have students taken any classes that have enhanced their problem-solving skills? If so, what were those classes? What made those classes stand out? Did the instructors have characteristics commonly associated with creativity and expertise? Explain.

LEARNING ACTIVITY 13.7
Phases of Vocational Development (p. 359)

Have students locate a child, adolescent, and adult for an interview on vocational development. If some students lack access to all three age groups, you may encourage them to work in groups. The following questions can help guide the interview:

- For children: "What do you want to be when you grow up, and why?"
- For adolescents: "What are your career plans?" "Why have you chosen this particular career path?"
- For adults: "What is your present career?" or "What are your career plans?" "Why did you choose this particular career path?" "Do you see yourself changing careers in the future? If so, why?"

Students can also ask participants to describe how their vocational choices or preferences have changed over time.

Next, students should compare the answers with the phases of vocational development described in the text. Did the interviews reveal age-related differences in vocational choice? Were students surprised by any of their findings? Did students' own vocational development move through these phases? Explain.

LEARNING ACTIVITY 13.8
Finding Out about Vocational Guidance on Your Campus (pp. 360–361)

Invite a representative from the Office of Career Planning and Placement (or someone associated with a similar office) to your class for a discussion of vocational resources on campus. You may also ask the speaker to discuss theories of vocational testing and development. Descriptions of specific tests and samples of test items (without violating test security) should be of interest to students.

Prior to the classroom visit, have students prepare two or three questions to ask the guest speaker. For example: Which vocational tests are available? Why are these tests important? How accurate are these tests? What services are available to students for finding appropriate job placements? What are the procedures for utilizing these services?

ASK YOURSELF . . .

REVIEW: What cultural changes have led to the appearance of the period known as emerging adulthood? (pp. 339–340)

Emerging adulthood describes a transitional period of development, extending from the late teens to the mid-twenties, when young people have left adolescence but have not yet taken on adult responsibilities. Compared to a generation ago, young people in the developed world move more slowly into widely accepted markers of adulthood—marriage, career, and full economic independence.

Rapid cultural changes explain the recent appearance of emerging adulthood. Schooling is prolonged because young people need more education to prepare for entry-level positions in many fields. Also, nations with abundant wealth and longer-lived populations have no pressing need for young people's labor, freeing 18- to 25-year-olds to enter into a "moratorium" period in which they can explore alternatives in jobs, educational paths, and love partners.

APPLY: Penny is a long-distance runner for her college track team. She wonders what her running performance will be like thirty years from now. What factors will affect Penny's long-term athletic skill? (pp. 342–344)

Long-distance runners generally reach their peak performance in their late twenties and early thirties. Longitudinal research on master runners reveals that as long as practice continues, speed drops only slightly from the mid-thirties into the sixties, when performance falls off at an accelerating pace. Sustained training leads to adaptations in body structures that minimize motor decline. If Penny remains an active runner, her performance should fall off only slightly over the next thirty years.

REFLECT: Before reading this chapter, had you thought of early adulthood as a period of aging? Why is it important for young adults to be conscious of factors that contribute to biological aging? (pp. 340–341)

This is an open-ended question with no right or wrong answer.

REVIEW: Why are people in committed relationships likely to be more sexually active and satisfied than those who are dating several partners? (pp. 350–352)

Although Americans today have more sexual partners over their lifetimes than they did a generation ago, most adults report that they have had just one sexual partner in the past year. More than 80 percent of adults in committed relationships report that they are physically and emotionally satisfied with their sex lives. In contrast, as number of sex partners increases, satisfaction declines—challenging the stereotypes of marriage as sexually dull and of people with many partners having "hotter" sex. Surveys of adults, both heterosexual and homosexual, repeatedly show that satisfying sex involves more than technique; it is attained in the context of love, affection, and fidelity, which is more likely to be found within a committed relationship.

APPLY: Tom began going to a health club three days a week after work. Soon the pressures of his job convinced him that he no longer had time for regular exercise. Explain to Tom why he should keep up his exercise regimen, and suggest ways to fit it into his busy life. (p. 348)

Besides reducing body fat and building muscle, exercise fosters resistance to disease. Frequent bouts of moderate-intensity exercise enhance the immune response, lowering the risk of colds or flu and promoting faster recovery when these illnesses do strike. Furthermore, in several longitudinal studies extending over 10 to 20 years, physical activity was linked to reduced incidence of cancer at all body sites except the skin, with the strongest findings for cancer of the rectum and colon. Physically active people are also less likely to develop diabetes and cardiovascular disease. If they do, these illnesses typically occur later and are less severe than among their inactive agemates.

Tom should also be reminded of the mental health benefits of regular exercise. Physical activity reduces anxiety and depression, improves mood, and enhances alertness and energy. The stress-reducing properties of exercise undoubtedly strengthen immunity to disease. As physical activity enhances psychological well-being, it promotes self-esteem, ability to cope with stress, on-the-job productivity, and life satisfaction.

To fit exercise into his busy lifestyle, Tom might try exercising over the lunch hour rather than after work. This will give him an added burst of energy in the afternoon. Another option might be exercising first thing in the morning, before going to work. Also, he should make sure that his exercise regimen is enjoyable, perhaps substituting some vigorous weekend activities such as bicycling or hiking with friends for one of his health club sessions.

REFLECT: List three strategies that you can implement now to enhance your health in future decades, noting research that supports the importance of each change in your behavior. (pp. 345–350)

This is an open-ended question with no right or wrong answer.

REVIEW: How does expertise affect information processing? Why is expertise necessary for, but not the same as, creativity? (p. 357)

Expertise is the acquisition of extensive knowledge in a field or endeavor. Once expertise is attained, it has a profound impact on information processing. For example, compared with novices, experts remember and reason more quickly and effectively. Experts approach problems with underlying principles in mind, whereas novices' understanding is only superficial. Experts can use what they know to arrive at solutions automatically, through quick and easy remembering. When a problem is especially challenging, they tend to plan ahead, systematically analyzing and categorizing elements and selecting the best from many possibilities, whereas the novice proceeds more by trial and error.

Expertise is also necessary for creativity. Mature creativity requires a unique cognitive capacity—the ability to formulate new, culturally meaningful problems and to ask significant questions that have never been posed before. But although creativity is rooted in expertise, not all experts are creative. Creativity also requires other qualities, including an innovative thinking style, tolerance of ambiguity, and a willingness to experiment and try again after failure. In addition, creativity requires time and energy.

APPLY: For her human development course, Marcia wrote a paper in which she discussed differing implications of Piaget's and Vygotsky's theories for education. Then she presented evidence that combining both perspectives yields a more effective approach than either position by itself. Explain how Marcia's reasoning illustrates advanced epistemic cognition. (pp. 355–356)

Epistemic cognition refers to our reflections on how we arrived at facts, beliefs, and ideas. Mature, rational thinkers are able to consider the justifiability of their conclusions when these differ from those of others. When they cannot justify their approach, they revise it, seeking a more balanced route to acquiring knowledge.

Whereas younger students engage in *dualistic thinking*—dividing information, values, and authority into right and wrong or good and bad—older students move toward *relativistic thinking.* Understanding that all knowledge is embedded in a framework of thought, they become aware that diverse opinions exist on many topics. They give up the possibility of absolute truth in favor of multiple truths, each relative to its context. As a result, their thinking becomes more flexible and tolerant.

The most mature individuals progress to a approach described as *commitment within relativistic thinking.* Instead of choosing between opposing views, they try to synthesize contradictions into a more satisfying perspective. This is the approach Marcia has taken in writing a paper in which she presents evidence that combining the perspectives of Piaget and Vygotsky yields a more effective approach to education than either position alone. Adults who, like Marcia, attain this extension of relativism display a more sophisticated approach to learning, in which they actively seek out differing perspectives to advance their knowledge and understanding.

REFLECT: Describe a classroom experience or assignment in one of your college courses that promoted relativistic thinking. (p. 355)

This is an open-ended question with no right or wrong answer.

REVIEW: What student and college-environment characteristics contribute to favorable psychological changes during the college years? (p. 358)

During the college years, students typically experience broad psychological changes. They become better at reasoning about problems that have no clear solution, identifying strengths and weaknesses in opposing sides of complex issues, and reflecting on the quality of their thinking. Their attitudes and values broaden as they develop increased interest in literature, the performing arts, and philosophical and historical issues. College students also tend to develop greater tolerance for ethnic and cultural diversity, along with greater concern for individual rights and human welfare. As they are exposed to multiple worldviews, young people are likely to look more closely at themselves, developing greater self-understanding and self-esteem, as well as a firmer sense of identity.

Both academic and nonacademic activities during the college years influence these changes. The more students interact with peers in academic and extracurricular settings, the more they benefit. Living on a residence hall is one of the most consistent predictors of cognitive change, because it maximizes involvement in the institution's educational and social systems. Programs that integrate commuting students into out-of-class campus life are a vital part of promoting these changes. Quality of academic experience also matters; psychological benefits increase with students' effort and willingness to participate in class and with challenging teaching.

APPLY: Diane, a high school senior, knows that she wants to "work with people" but doesn't yet have a specific career in mind. Diane's father is a chemistry professor, her mother a social worker. What steps can Diane's parents take to broaden her awareness of the world of work and help her focus on an occupational goal? (pp. 358–359)

Parents who have professional careers, as Diane's mother and father do, are in a good position to give their children important information about the world of work. They are also likely to have connections with people who can help the young person obtain a high-status position. In Diane's case, both of her parents "work with people," though in very different ways. Diane can benefit from talking with her father about college teaching, or perhaps sitting in on one of his classes. From her mother, she can learn about the satisfactions and frustrations of working with clients as a social worker. Through their professional connections, Diane's parents may be able to help her seek out

3) The developmental phase called *emerging adulthood* developed because
   A) the transition to adult roles has become so prolonged that an additional developmental period appeared.
   B) teenagers began assuming adult roles, but did not yet have the legal status to recognize them as adults.
   C) researchers could not agree on when adulthood actually began, so they compromised with the "in-between" period of emerging adulthood.
   D) there was no way to define the "gray" area between adolescence and adulthood.

Answer: A
Page Ref: 339–340
Skill: Factual
Objective: 13.1

4) Which young person will probably not experience emerging adulthood, but rather a "floundering period"?
   A) Yusung, who will be attending a nationally renowned university several thousand miles away from home
   B) Tyi-sanna, a low-SES teenager who dropped out of high school
   C) Loana, a low-SES teenager who has an academic scholarship to attend a local university next fall
   D) Kent, who has just finished college but does not yet have a job in his chosen field

Answer: B
Page Ref: 340
Skill: Applied
Objective: 13.1

5) All members of our species experience __________, genetically influenced declines in the functioning of organs and systems.
   A) secular trends
   B) senescence
   C) gender intensification
   D) free radicalization

Answer: B
Page Ref: 340
Skill: Factual
Objective: 13.2

6) The leader of a small, developing nation wants to increase the average lifespan of her citizens. Based on research in industrialized countries, which of the following has been found to be clearly beneficial?
   A) Improve food processing procedures.
   B) Develop better trade policies with foreign countries.
   C) Increase educational standards.
   D) Improve nutrition and sanitation.

Answer: D
Page Ref: 340
Skill: Applied
Objective: 13.2

7) Which of these facts is the strongest evidence to CONTRADICT the theory that aging occurs as the body wears out from use?
   A) Overweight individuals have shorter lifespans.
   B) Moderate-to-vigorous exercise is related to longer lifespans.
   C) Heart disease is a major factor in premature death.
   D) Faces typically show aging before the rest of the body.

Answer: B
Page Ref: 341
Skill: Conceptual
Objective: 13.2

8) Earle's grandfather lived to be 87 and his father is still alive at the age of 92. Earle concludes that longevity is inherited and anticipates a very long life. Earle should know that

A) there is no reliable data on the heritability of longevity, and random factors probably contributed to the long lives of his relatives.
B) current generations are actually experiencing shorter lifespans than previous generations, due to environmental toxins and careers that require very little physical activity.
C) rather than inheriting longevity directly, people probably inherit risk factors that influence their chances of dying earlier or later.
D) the heritability of longevity is approximately .95, indicating that longevity is directly related to genetic factors.

Answer: C
Page Ref: 341
Skill: Applied
Objective: 13.2

9) While telomere shortening causes cells to die, it also

A) helps prevent disease-causing mutations, which become more likely as cells duplicate.
B) increases disease-causing mutations, which decrease as cells duplicate.
C) increases the lifespan of heart, liver, and kidney cells.
D) subsequently increases nerve regeneration and neural myelinization.

Answer: A
Page Ref: 341
Skill: Factual
Objective: 13.2

10) The "random events" theory of biological aging attributes aging primarily to

A) the programmed action of specific genes.
B) accidental injuries, such as pulled muscles.
C) wear and tear caused by excessive use.
D) spontaneous or externally caused mutations to DNA.

Answer: D
Page Ref: 341
Skill: Factual
Objective: 13.2

11) Which of the following evidence has been found to support the "random events" theory of biological aging?

A) Genetic engineering that manipulates telomere activity has extended the lifespan of human cells.
B) Both animal and human studies confirm an increase in DNA breaks and deletions and damage to other cellular material with age.
C) Free radical activity has been verified in at least 600 plant and animal species to date.
D) Humans who maintain higher levels of physical activity over several decades show increased "wear and tear" on all body organs that subsequently reduces their maximum lifespan.

Answer: B
Page Ref: 341
Skill: Factual
Objective: 13.2

12) In the chemistry of aging, a free radical is

A) a highly reactive chemical produced naturally by the body that forms in the presence of oxygen.
B) a form of pollution that is produced by chemical factories.
C) a nutritional supplement that can reduce visible aging.
D) the form of DNA that is found inside cancerous cells.

Answer: A
Page Ref: 341
Skill: Factual
Objective: 13.2

13) Free radicals are thought to be involved in which of the following?
   A) disorders of aging
   B) osteoporosis
   C) Down syndrome
   D) sickle-cell disease
   Answer: A
   Page Ref: 341
   Skill: Conceptual
   Objective: 13.2

14) Preston has begun eating more foods rich in vitamins C and E and beta-carotene. He believes this will help him to live longer. Preston should know that
   A) the free radical theory is widely disputed in the scientific community, and there is questionable proof as to the efficacy of his new diet.
   B) these ingredients forestall free-radical damage, so his new diet may improve his life expectancy.
   C) current research tends to support the genetic programming theory of aging, in which his diet plays no significant role.
   D) a healthy diet will reduce the rate of cardiovascular disease and improve his overall chances for a longer life, but eating the specific foods he has chosen will have no proven value.
   Answer: B
   Page Ref: 341
   Skill: Applied
   Objective: 13.2

15) According to the cross-linkage theory of aging, bonds between protein fibers in connective tissue can lead to
   A) the strengthening of skin and bone to reduce aging.
   B) the ability of the body to use nutrients more efficiently.
   C) loss of flexibility in the skin and clogging of arteries.
   D) reduced production of many hormones, especially estrogen.
   Answer: C
   Page Ref: 341
   Skill: Factual
   Objective: 13.2

16) In adults, the loss of growth hormone is associated with
   A) the development of bone cancer.
   B) loss of muscle and bone mass.
   C) thickening of the skin.
   D) increased heart rate.
   Answer: B
   Page Ref: 342
   Skill: Conceptual
   Objective: 13.2

17) Because hormones affect many body functions, disruptions to the endocrine system can have widespread effects on health and survival. To date, __________ is the safest approach to limit biological aspects of aging in the endocrine system.
   A) a program including a healthy diet and physical activity
   B) hormone therapy
   C) genetic reconstruction
   D) cellular therapy
   Answer: A
   Page Ref: 342
   Skill: Factual
   Objective: 13.2

18) The declines in immune system functioning that contribute to many conditions of aging appear to be
    A) caused by the random events.
    B) caused by cross-linkage breakdown of connective tissues.
    C) genetically programmed, but intensified by other aging processes.
    D) caused by random DNA breakdowns and exacerbated by free radicals, except in cases of genetic programming.

Answer: C
Page Ref: 342
Skill: Factual
Objective: 13.2

19) The physical changes that take place in early adulthood are typically
    A) gradual and difficult to notice.
    B) related to improved performance.
    C) focused on taste and smell.
    D) involved in reproductive abilities.

Answer: A
Page Ref: 342
Skill: Factual
Objective: 13.3

20) Which person has a higher risk of hypertension and heart disease?
    A) Erica, a white female
    B) Ida, an African-American female
    C) Ming, an Asian-American female
    D) any young adult who engages in stressful exercise

Answer: B
Page Ref: 342
Skill: Applied
Objective: 13.3

21) The ability of a person's heart to meet the body's oxygen requirements during normal, everyday activity shows which of these patterns of change during adulthood?
    A) It declines gradually and steadily after age 30.
    B) It increases gradually and steadily until age 50.
    C) It remains unchanged throughout adulthood.
    D) It increases slightly until age 40, then drops rapidly.

Answer: C
Page Ref: 342
Skill: Factual
Objective: 13.3

22) Jacqui is an avid athlete. She believes that her physical activity will protect her heart from age-related performance declines. Jacqui should know that
    A) these declines are genetically programmed and cannot be avoided.
    B) there are no age-related declines in heart performance, but she should continue to exercise anyway because of the other health benefits involved.
    C) age-related performance declines are most evident under typical conditions, as measured by heart rate in relation to volume of blood pumped.
    D) the only heart performance declines related to age occur during stressful exercise.

Answer: D
Page Ref: 342
Skill: Applied
Objective: 13.3

23) When an adult suffers from atherosclerosis, or deposits of fatty plaque on the walls of the arteries, it typically develops
A) very slightly before age 60, but can become serious after that.
B) after age 40 in individuals who showed no signs of it earlier.
C) very rapidly in extreme old age, leading to sudden heart failure.
D) early in life and progresses to become a serious illness.
Answer: D
Page Ref: 342
Skill: Factual
Objective: 13.3

24) Attempts to improve diet and exercise and decrease cigarette smoking
A) are failing and the North American population is becoming increasingly unhealthy.
B) have resulted in a considerable decrease in heart disease.
C) have resulted in some decreases in lung disease, but heart disease continues to rise.
D) have improved the overall health of individuals from high-SES backgrounds only.
Answer: B
Page Ref: 342
Skill: Factual
Objective: 13.3

25) Yao is 45 years old. How has the maximum vital capacity of his lungs changed from when he was 25?
A) It has decreased by about 20 percent.
B) It has remained constant.
C) It has decreased by about 50 percent.
D) The maximum vital capacity has remained unchanged while at rest, but has increased by about 15 percent during physical exertion.
Answer: A
Page Ref: 342
Skill: Applied
Objective: 13.3

26) Imagine that you are a researcher who wants to study the impact of biological aging on motor skills. What type of people are you most likely to study?
A) outstanding athletes
B) people who exercise frequently
C) individuals who exercise occasionally
D) people who never exercise
Answer: A
Page Ref: 344
Skill: Applied
Objective: 13.3

27) Which type of motor skills peak latest in life?
A) speed of limb movement
B) skills that require either stamina or precise motor control
C) explosive strength
D) gross body coordination
Answer: B
Page Ref: 344
Skill: Factual
Objective: 13.3

28) Juan is a tennis player; Miguel is a golfer. Which statement below is correct?
   A) Both athletes' skills will peak in their early twenties.
   B) Juan's athletic skills will peak in his early thirties.
   C) Miguel's athletic skills will peak in his late twenties or early thirties.
   D) Both athletes' skills will peak in their late thirties.

Answer: C
Page Ref: 344
Skill: Applied
Objective: 13.3

29) Which statement best summarizes age-related changes in athletic skills?
   A) Athletic skills peak during early adulthood, then decline at a steady rate over the rest of the lifespan.
   B) Athletic skills usually peak during early adulthood, with certain skills peaking later in life, and all skills showing marked decline after the age of 40.
   C) The age at which athletic skills peak gets older with each generation, and superb athletes are generally the only individuals who notice age-related declines in performance.
   D) Biological aging accounts for only a small part of age-related decline in athletic skills.

Answer: D
Page Ref: 344
Skill: Factual
Objective: 13.3

30) Object A is a white blood cell that originates in the bone marrow and matures in the thymus. Object A attacks foreign substances in the body and is referred to as a(n)
   A) T cell.
   B) B cell.
   C) antigen.
   D) biodefense.

Answer: A
Page Ref: 344
Skill: Factual
Objective: 13.3

31) One factor that contributes to the loss of efficiency of the immune system as we age is the
   A) enlargement of the pituitary gland.
   B) shrinkage of the thymus gland.
   C) overproduction of thymic hormones.
   D) enlargement of the prostate gland.

Answer: B
Page Ref: 344
Skill: Factual
Objective: 13.3

32) Which of the following illustrates the relationship between stress and the immune system?
   A) Denny gets sick right before a vacation he was greatly anticipating.
   B) Benny smokes and is a heavy drinker, yet rarely gets sick.
   C) Jenny has a nagging cold throughout semester finals.
   D) Kenny is in excellent health, yet has very bad allergies.

Answer: C
Page Ref: 344
Skill: Applied
Objective: 13.3

33) The most important cause of the age-related drop in female fertility is
   A) a decline in reserve ova.
   B) chromosomal disorders.
   C) a decreased sperm concentration in the male partner.
   D) the inability of the uterus to support a developing fetus.

Answer: A
Page Ref: 345
Skill: Factual
Objective: 13.3

34) Mr. and Mrs. Izzo are in their early forties and wish to start a family. They realize their reduced chances of becoming pregnant, and are willing to use reproductive technologies such as in vitro fertilization in order to start their family. The Izzos should know that
   A) the success rates of reproductive technologies drop sharply after age 35.
   B) reproductive capacity does not tend to decline until the mid-forties, so their chances for getting pregnant without additional support are still high.
   C) even if in vitro fertilization is successful, Mrs. Izzo's chances of carrying the baby past the first trimester are slim, due to her advanced age.
   D) reproductive technologies have helped thousands of couples in their forties and beyond become parents, and scientific discoveries are advancing the age for successful childbearing even further.

Answer: A
Page Ref: 345
Skill: Applied
Objective: 13.3

35) Which of the following contributes to the differences in Canadian and American health and mortality rates?
   A) the existence of a national health insurance system in Canada
   B) better medical technology and care available in America
   C) lax gun registration, safety, and control policies in Canada
   D) higher SES level overall for the American population

Answer: A
Page Ref: 345
Skill: Conceptual
Objective: 13.4

36) __________ show strong and continuous relationships with almost every disease and health indicator.
   A) Gender and personality
   B) Income, education, and occupational status
   C) Quality of family and peer relationships
   D) Size of family and number of marriages

Answer: B
Page Ref: 346
Skill: Factual
Objective: 13.4

37) Calvin has a 20 percent greater body weight than he should have, based on his age, sex, and physical build. Calvin is considered to be
   A) overweight, but not obese.
   B) obese.
   C) heavy, but not overweight or obese.
   D) typical for the average North American male.

Answer: B
Page Ref: 346
Skill: Applied
Objective: 13.4

38) Obesity is much more common among
   A) middle-aged middle-income men.
   B) many ethnic minority groups.
   C) women in their early twenties.
   D) people with high income levels.
   Answer: B
   Page Ref: 346
   Skill: Factual
   Objective: 13.4

39) When overweight and obesity rates are combined, __________ percent of Americans are considered to be at an unhealthy weight.
   A) 85
   B) 65
   C) 45
   D) 25
   Answer: B
   Page Ref: 346
   Skill: Factual
   Objective: 13.4

40) Which statement is TRUE of American weight gain?
   A) Many people show large weight gains between the ages of 25 and 40.
   B) Most people gain weight during the childhood years, lose it during the teenage years, and regain it after age 25.
   C) Although the number of obese and overweight individuals has increased, Americans still rank 15th among industrialized nations in percentage of adults at risk for weight-related health problems.
   D) The number of Americans who are obese and overweight has decreased slightly during the last decade, due to increased public awareness about diet and exercise.
   Answer: A
   Page Ref: 346
   Skill: Factual
   Objective: 13.4

41) Nadine gained 10 pounds between the ages of 25 and 50. She should know that
   A) the only reason for this gain is a lack of physical activity.
   B) obesity like hers is a serious cause of major health problems.
   C) this is normal, because of a drop in the basal metabolic rate.
   D) her children are likely to suffer problems from being overweight.
   Answer: C
   Page Ref: 346
   Skill: Applied
   Objective: 13.4

42) Joshua is curious about the amount of energy his body uses when he is completely at rest. Joshua is wondering about his BMR, or
   A) basal metabolic rate.
   B) basic metabolism requirements.
   C) beginning, median, and resting requirements.
   D) body's measurement at rest.
   Answer: A
   Page Ref: 346
   Skill: Applied
   Objective: 13.4

43) Compared with people of normal weight, obese individuals are more likely to be
   A) victims of severe hormonal imbalances.
   B) cheerful and optimistic in outlook on life.
   C) middle- or upper-income individuals.
   D) denied apartments, college loans, and jobs.

Answer: D
Page Ref: 346–347
Skill: Factual
Objective: 13.4

44) Two years ago, Mr. and Mrs. Dworet and their teenage son, Russell, were all obese and started a weight-loss program. Based on current research findings, we can anticipate that today
   A) they have returned to, or are above, their previous weights.
   B) they are all at their ideal weights.
   C) Russell has maintained his weight loss, but his parents have rebounded to their original weights.
   D) Russell lost and then regained his weight, while his parents were never able to lose more than a few pounds.

Answer: A
Page Ref: 347
Skill: Applied
Objective: 13.4

45) Baru wants to go on a diet. Based upon research findings, she should
   A) go on a high-carbohydrate diet.
   B) restrict her calorie and fat intake while increasing her physical activity.
   C) start a high-protein diet.
   D) learn not to think too much about what or when to eat.

Answer: B
Page Ref: 347
Skill: Applied
Objective: 13.4

46) __________ fat is solid at room temperature and generally comes from meat and dairy products.
   A) Unsaturated
   B) Saturated
   C) Partially hydrogenated
   D) Polysaturated

Answer: B
Page Ref: 347
Skill: Factual
Objective: 13.4

47) The low rate of heart disease among West Africans
   A) is evidence that the high incidence of heart disease among African Americans is most likely due to excess fat consumption combined with societal conditions.
   B) has confounded researchers who study the genetic tendencies toward heart disease.
   C) can be attributed to social factors that stress extreme thinness.
   D) is indicative of a lifestyle with too much physical activity.

Answer: A
Page Ref: 347–348
Skill: Factual
Objective: 13.4

48) Studies of the exercise habits of North Americans find that
   A) over half do not know the benefits of regular exercise.
   B) most know its value, but 30 percent of Canadians and 38 percent of Americans are inactive.
   C) 75 percent of all North Americans engage in some regular physical fitness program.
   D) physically active individuals are no healthier than inactive ones.

Answer: B
Page Ref: 348
Skill: Factual
Objective: 13.4

49) Which individual would enjoy the best outcomes from physical exercise?
   A) Yulika, who is at risk for skin cancer
   B) Gwiok, who is at risk for lung cancer
   C) Tom, who is at risk for colon cancer
   D) Suzette, who is at risk for breast cancer

Answer: C
Page Ref: 348
Skill: Applied
Objective: 13.4

50) Regular physical activity has the psychological effect of
   A) creating depression and anxiety.
   B) increasing levels of emotional stress.
   C) making people relaxed and sleepy.
   D) enhancing alertness and energy.

Answer: D
Page Ref: 348
Skill: Factual
Objective: 13.4

51) Dorota wants to exercise at a level that will provide the best level of protection against illnesses such as cardiovascular disease, diabetes, and colon cancer. She should exercise
   A) daily, with enough intensity to build up a sweat.
   B) for 20 minutes, 3 times per week.
   C) for 30 minutes, 2 times per week.
   D) for at least an hour, once a week.

Answer: A
Page Ref: 348
Skill: Applied
Objective: 13.4

52) Mr. Jochim has talked frequently with his teenage children about the hazards of illicit drug use, but feels he needs to do a better job discussing the more common substance abuses. If he wants to focus on the two most commonly abused substances with his children in a discussion this week, he should focus on
   A) cigarette smoking and prescription medication abuse.
   B) alcohol consumption and over-the-counter medications.
   C) cigarette smoking and alcohol consumption.
   D) alcohol consumption and abuse of household cleaning products.

Answer: C
Page Ref: 349
Skill: Applied
Objective: 13.5

53) The U.S. Surgeon General wants to target an anti-smoking campaign at the group of individuals for whom smoking rates have decreased very little in the last few decades. The campaign should be geared towards
   A) high school dropouts.
   B) high school graduates.
   C) college students.
   D) college graduates.
   Answer: A
   Page Ref: 349
   Skill: Applied
   Objective: 13.5

54) The ingredients of cigarette smoke cause all of the following EXCEPT
   A) deterioration of the retina of the eye.
   B) higher rate of male impotence.
   C) more rapid wrinkling of the skin.
   D) higher sperm count.
   Answer: D
   Page Ref: 349
   Skill: Conceptual
   Objective: 13.5

55) Thirty young people start to smoke before the age of 21. Statistically, how many will die from a smoking-related disease?
   A) 5
   B) 10
   C) 15
   D) 30
   Answer: B
   Page Ref: 349
   Skill: Applied
   Objective: 13.5

56) One hundred smokers have just joined a treatment program to stop smoking. Based on statistical averages, you can predict that
   A) more than half will successfully stop smoking for good.
   B) 70 to 90 of them will be smoking again after one year.
   C) at least 60 of them are men over the age of 45.
   D) 30 to 40 of them began smoking before the age of 21.
   Answer: B
   Page Ref: 349
   Skill: Applied
   Objective: 13.5

57) One difference in the development of alcoholism between men and women is that
   A) men's alcoholism often starts with beer-drinking, while women start with mixed drinks.
   B) women usually start experimenting earlier, while alcoholism in men typically develops in the late twenties and early thirties.
   C) men typically start drinking in their teens and early twenties, while women typically experience onset in the twenties and thirties.
   D) alcoholism among men usually starts with social drinking, while women primarily drink alone.
   Answer: C
   Page Ref: 349
   Skill: Factual
   Objective: 13.5

58) Alcoholism is a more common problem among cultures in which alcohol is
   A) regularly served to and around children.
   B) a traditional part of ceremonial activities.
   C) forbidden for everyone of any age in society.
   D) a carefully controlled sign of adulthood.

Answer: D
Page Ref: 349
Skill: Factual
Objective: 13.5

59) Which statement explains alcohol's effects on feelings of anxiety?
   A) Alcohol relieves anxiety, and then the alcoholic is no longer worried about getting drunk, so he or she continues to drink excessively.
   B) While many alcoholics say they drink to relieve stress, alcohol in fact induces anxiety in heavy drinkers, but its effects make them unaware of their increased anxiety level.
   C) In a heavy drinker, alcohol relieves anxiety at first but then induces it as the effects wear off, so the alcoholic drinks again.
   D) Alcohol has no effects on anxiety, except an indirect effect on the family members of the alcoholic.

Answer: C
Page Ref: 349
Skill: Factual
Objective: 13.5

60) Large percentages of highway fatalities, criminal activity, date rape, and domestic violence can be attributed to
   A) alcohol abuse.
   B) cigarette smoking.
   C) pornography.
   D) obesity.

Answer: A
Page Ref: 350
Skill: Factual
Objective: 13.5

61) The most successful treatments for alcohol problems emphasize
   A) a combination of personal, family, group, and aversion therapies.
   B) treating the alcoholic individual in isolation.
   C) providing strict punishment for the misuses of alcohol.
   D) accepting and supporting the alcoholic's need for alcohol.

Answer: A
Page Ref: 350
Skill: Factual
Objective: 13.5

62) Which of the following is a method through which the majority of couples in lasting relationships meet each other?
   A) at night clubs
   B) through personal ads
   C) through work
   D) in singles bars

Answer: C
Page Ref: 350
Skill: Conceptual
Objective: 13.6

63) Moira is frustrated by her lack of success in meeting romantic partners at work and in singles clubs, and is interested in online dating services. Moira needs to know that
   A) success rates are higher than with conventional strategies with 39 percent of relationships that begin online lasting more than a year.
   B) online romances are generally more successful than those that started conventionally, as people tend to be more open and honest in written communication than in face-to-face interactions.
   C) success rates are lower than with conventional strategies, with only 18 percent of the relationships that actually evolve lasting for more than a year.
   D) though success rates are lower than with conventional strategies, most adults who finally meet face-to-face develop relationships that last for more than a year.

Answer: C
Page Ref: 350
Skill: Applied
Objective: 13.6

64) Which person is likely to engage in higher rates of sexual activity?
   A) Ted, who is single and dating
   B) Tony, a teenager
   C) Torrie, who is married
   D) Tanya, who is divorced and dating

Answer: C
Page Ref: 350
Skill: Applied
Objective: 13.6

65) Which person is likely to report the lowest level of satisfaction with his sex life?
   A) Billy Ray, who has just started having sex with his girlfriend
   B) Mark, who has been living with his girlfriend for the last four months
   C) Christopher, who is single and has had five different partners in the last year
   D) James, who has been married to his wife for 15 years

Answer: C
Page Ref: 350
Skill: Applied
Objective: 13.6

66) Sexual difficulties are more common among all of the following groups of people EXCEPT
   A) unmarried people.
   B) those who have had more than five partners.
   C) victims of sexual abuse or coercion.
   D) married couples.

Answer: D
Page Ref: 350–351
Skill: Conceptual
Objective: 13.6

67) Researchers have found that satisfying sex generally involves
   A) good technique.
   B) an emotionally fulfilling relationship.
   C) spontaneity.
   D) some type of fantasy fulfillment.

Answer: B
Page Ref: 350–351
Skill: Conceptual
Objective: 13.6

68) Studies of the differences between men and women with respect to sexual activity have found that, when the small number of men with very many partners is excluded, the number of lifetime sexual partners is
   A) basically the same for men and women.
   B) much higher for men than for women.
   C) much lower for men than for women.
   D) lower for men in their teens, but climbs steadily for men thereafter.
   Answer: A
   Page Ref: 351
   Skill: Factual
   Objective: Box SI: Sex Differences in Attitudes Toward Sexuality

69) Which of the following is INCONSISTENT with the research findings on fidelity and long-term commitments between men and women?
   A) Men are more upset at the thought of their partner having sex with another person.
   B) Men see infidelity as a potential loss of investment in the children by their partner.
   C) Women are more upset at the thought of their partner feeling affection for someone else.
   D) Conflicting goals and attitudes between men and women are greatest for young adults.
   Answer: B
   Page Ref: 351
   Skill: Conceptual
   Objective: Box SI: Sex Differences in Attitudes Toward Sexuality

70) Which statement most accurately reflects the sentiments of most Americans toward gay men, lesbians, and bisexuals?
   A) Most Americans are opposed to homosexuality.
   B) Most Americans support civil liberties and equal employment opportunities for gay men, lesbians, and bisexuals.
   C) Most Americans approve of same-sex marriages and would advocate on behalf of gay men, lesbians, and bisexuals if asked.
   D) Most Americans are bisexual.
   Answer: B
   Page Ref: 351
   Skill: Factual
   Objective: 13.6

71) The majority of rape victims are __________, and the abusers are __________.
   A) under age 30; under age 20
   B) under age 30; men they know well
   C) unwilling to prosecute their attacker; knowledgeable in the legal defense system
   D) intoxicated at the time of their attack; sober
   Answer: B
   Page Ref: 352
   Skill: Factual
   Objective: 13.6

72) Jenny and Jessie work in a large business office. Jenny can be characterized as a friendly person, while Jessie is assertive. Jake, who also works in the office and has committed several unreported sexual assaults, is likely to
   A) interpret Jenny's friendliness as seductiveness and Jessie's assertiveness as hostility.
   B) interpret both women's interactions as displaying a desire for sexual intimacy.
   C) attempt a sexual assault on Jessie but not on Jenny.
   D) admit responsibility for an attempted assault on either woman.
   Answer: A
   Page Ref: 352
   Skill: Applied
   Objective: 13.6

73) All of the following are important parts of fostering recovery for rape victims EXCEPT
   A) routine screenings by doctors for signs of victimization.
   B) contact with a group of other rape survivors.
   C) intensive questioning by police to file criminal charges.
   D) planning to prevent reassault by the abuser.
Answer: C
Page Ref: 353
Skill: Factual
Objective: 13.6

74) The array of physical and psychological symptoms that often appear 6 to 10 days before menstruation is referred to as __________ syndrome.
   A) dysmenorrheal
   B) intrauterine
   C) premenstrual
   D) malobstetrical
Answer: C
Page Ref: 353–354
Skill: Factual
Objective: 13.6

75) Worldwide studies of the occurrence of premenstrual syndrome find that
   A) it is much more common in the United States than in other countries.
   B) it is more common in Western, industrialized countries.
   C) it is more common in underdeveloped, non-industrial countries.
   D) it is equally common all over the world.
Answer: D
Page Ref: 354
Skill: Factual
Objective: 13.6

76) A successful cure for PMS
   A) includes hormone therapy.
   B) uses a combination of hormone therapy and sensitivity training for particular centers of the brain.
   C) must incorporate analgesics for pain, antidepressant medication, vitamin/mineral supplements, exercise, and stress-reducing measures.
   D) has not yet been discovered.
Answer: D
Page Ref: 354
Skill: Factual
Objective: 13.6

77) A strong cardiovascular response, immune system interference, and reduced digestive activity are all symptoms of
   A) hypertension.
   B) alcoholism.
   C) psychological stress.
   D) genetically programmed aging.
Answer: C
Page Ref: 354
Skill: Conceptual
Objective: 13.7

78) Moniqua has just moved to another city after her divorce and is dealing with stress. Which of the following suggestions would have the highest probability of helping her to buffer the effects of stress?
   A) Hit the singles clubs and bars after work.
   B) Actively seek out a satisfying sexual relationship.
   C) Take anti-depressants.
   D) Develop and maintain satisfying social ties.
   Answer: D
   Page Ref: 354
   Skill: Applied
   Objective: 13.7

79) According to some theorists, cognitive development continues past the stages identified in Piaget's theory, leading to a stage called
   A) postformal thought.
   B) advanced reasoning.
   C) nonoperational cognition.
   D) mensa mentation.
   Answer: A
   Page Ref: 355
   Skill: Factual
   Objective: 13.8

80) Torri and her team at work are trying to determine the direction in which their division should focus. Because Torri's viewpoint is so different from everyone else's, she takes some time to reflect on the facts she analyzed, and how she arrived at her conclusion. Torri is engaged in
   A) preformal thought.
   B) epistemic cognition.
   C) dualistic thinking.
   D) meta-awareness.
   Answer: B
   Page Ref: 355
   Skill: Applied
   Objective: 13.8

81) According to Perry's study of adult thinking, which of the following statements is an example of dualistic thinking?
   A) "Well, at first I thought I liked the movie, but then I decided I didn't."
   B) "I think my college professor is great, and really believe everything she says."
   C) "Her answers are very embedded in the framework of her thoughts."
   D) "There is no absolute truth because there are multiple truths, each relative to its own context."
   Answer: B
   Page Ref: 355
   Skill: Applied
   Objective: 13.8

82) According to Perry's work, when older students view knowledge as embedded in a framework of thought with multiple truths, each relative to its own context, they are engaged in
   A) postformal thought.
   B) dualistic thinking.
   C) relativistic thinking.
   D) adaptive cognition.
   Answer: C
   Page Ref: 355
   Skill: Factual
   Objective: 13.8

83) Tyson has listened to his uncle rail against the "evils of immigration." On the other hand, his boss constantly discusses how our country is very dependent upon immigrant labor, and how citizens should work together to end the unfair treatment these workers receive. Instead of choosing between these opposing views, Tyson formulates his own perspective that synthesizes components of both arguments. Tyson's cognitive development reflects
A) relativistic thinking.
B) dualistic thinking.
C) commitment within relativistic thinking.
D) metacognition.
Answer: C
Page Ref: 355
Skill: Applied
Objective: 13.8

84) Professor Peabody wants to develop the epistemic cognition of his engineering students. Which of the following would you recommend?
A) Allow students time to reflect on how they worked together as a team, and what problematic aspects of their communication could have improved the outcome.
B) Give them realistic and highly defined problems, but allow them complete freedom in working through to the solutions.
C) Give them realistic but ambiguous problems, and offer them encouragement and guidance as they work.
D) Ask students to develop problems based upon situations that are meaningful or problematic for them.
Answer: C
Page Ref: 356
Skill: Applied
Objective: 13.8

85) According to Labouvie-Vief's theory of adult cognitive development, the change that occurs from adolescence to adulthood is primarily in the direction of
A) increasing pragmatism.
B) increasing abstraction.
C) decreasing logic.
D) nothing; in this theory, thinking doesn't change during adulthood.
Answer: A
Page Ref: 356
Skill: Factual
Objective: 13.8

86) Shelton has just started his own business. While he feels elation at the prospect of being able to do the work he has always dreamed of, he also acknowledges feelings of concern, fear, and disappointment at various aspects of his new life. Shelton's ability to reconcile these various issues reflects
A) cognitive-affective complexity.
B) expertise.
C) pragmatism.
D) dualistic thinking.
Answer: A
Page Ref: 356
Skill: Applied
Objective: 13.8

87) __________ is/are supported by the specialization that begins with selecting a college major or an occupation.
A) Information
B) Expertise
C) Hypotheses
D) Algorithms
Answer: B
Page Ref: 357
Skill: Factual
Objective: 13.9

88) One difference between an expert and a novice is that, when faced with a challenging problem to solve, the expert is more likely to
A) focus on specific surface features of the problem.
B) solve it in a less creative, more mechanical way.
C) analyze and categorize it before trying to solve it.
D) already know the answers to all meaningful problems.
Answer: C
Page Ref: 357
Skill: Conceptual
Objective: 13.9

89) A unique cognitive capacity that is required for mature creativity is the ability to
A) put ideas together at random to see what comes out.
B) apply standard solutions in ways that are unusual.
C) ignore the practical issues involved in a solution.
D) formulate new, significant, and meaningful problems.
Answer: D
Page Ref: 357
Skill: Factual
Objective: 13.9

90) Barbara is a musician, Chris is an artist, and Dennis is an engineer. Which of the following statements is probably true?
A) Dennis's creativity will peak later than that of the other two.
B) Chris's creativity will be the last to peak.
C) Barbara will be the last to show a rise in creativity.
D) Creativity will diminish equally among all three people.
Answer: A
Page Ref: 357
Skill: Applied
Objective: 13.9

91) Which of the following is a reason that creativity in women may be postponed or disrupted?
A) lack of drive to succeed
B) child rearing
C) insecure gender identity
D) a supportive partner
Answer: B
Page Ref: 357
Skill: Conceptual
Objective: 13.9

92) In addition to gaining academic knowledge from their courses, college students also experience psychological changes, including
A) the ability to apply reasoning to problems with no clear answer.
B) an exposure to so many new ideas it leads to moral confusion.
C) confusion and uncertainty about their own inner identity.
D) a decreased tolerance for people from diverse backgrounds.
Answer: A
Page Ref: 358
Skill: Factual
Objective: 13.10

93) College attendance will have the most psychological impact on which student?
   A) Terryn, who attends a four-year institution and lives at home
   B) Sara, who attends a four-year institution and lives on campus
   C) Kristen, who attends a two-year institution and lives at home
   D) Allyson, who attends a prestigious university and commutes

Answer: B
Page Ref: 358
Skill: Applied
Objective: 13.10

94) Which student is most at risk for dropping out of college?
   A) a sophomore at a large state university
   B) a freshman in his second semester at a highly selective school
   C) a freshman in her first month at a school with low admission requirements
   D) a junior who lives on campus with three sophomores as dorm mates

Answer: C
Page Ref: 358
Skill: Applied
Objective: 13.10

95) Which of the following factors has been shown to REDUCE college ethnic minority students' desire to remain in school?
   A) lack of educational aspirations
   B) lack of transportation to attend off-campus events
   C) experiencing disrespect on campus because of their ethnicity or religion
   D) too much interference by college officials

Answer: C
Page Ref: 358
Skill: Factual
Objective: 13.10

96) A college that wishes to reduce substantially the number of students who drop out should most probably do which of the following?
   A) Offer students more privacy and freedom to explore.
   B) Encourage students to live off-campus in apartments.
   C) Focus more attention on students who are about to graduate.
   D) Reach out to students in their first few weeks and months.

Answer: D
Page Ref: 358
Skill: Conceptual
Objective: 13.10

97) Seven-year-old Kadeija fantasizes about becoming a detective when she grows up. Her desires stem from a television show about a young teenage sleuth. According to vocational development theorists, her current career preference
   A) will probably bear little relation to the career decisions that she will eventually make.
   B) will probably be actualized, because she has already committed to a career at such a young age.
   C) is atypical of most young children, who base their preferences on what jobs their parents have.
   D) is unrealistic, as it is impossible to get a detective license as a teenager.

Answer: A
Page Ref: 359
Skill: Applied
Objective: 13.11

98) The tentative period of occupational choice, during early and middle adolescence, begins with a focus on __________ and shifts to a focus on __________.

A) fantasy; crystallization
B) interests; abilities and values
C) social value; income level
D) parental values; personal values

Answer: B
Page Ref: 359
Skill: Factual
Objective: 13.11

99) Twenty-year-old Dominic explored the possibility of becoming a teacher by tutoring in an after-school program. He then chose to major in education. Dominic is in the __________ of vocational development.

A) fantasy period
B) tentative period
C) realistic period
D) acquisition period

Answer: C
Page Ref: 359
Skill: Factual
Objective: 13.11

100) Lauren enjoys working with ideas; Julia prefers interacting with people. According to Holland's six personality types, Lauren is considered __________ and Julia is considered __________.

A) investigative; social
B) realistic; conventional
C) enterprising; effusive
D) mastery-oriented; network-oriented

Answer: A
Page Ref: 359
Skill: Applied
Objective: 13.11

101) Katie enjoys solving important everyday problems and Mary enjoys emotion and individual expression. According to Holland's theory of six personality types, Katie is __________ and Mary is __________.

A) investigative; social
B) realistic; artistic
C) conventional; unconventional
D) focused; diffuse

Answer: B
Page Ref: 359
Skill: Applied
Objective: 13.11

102) Of the six personality types that affect vocational choice identified by Holland, someone who enjoys material possessions and social status is considered __________ and someone who enjoys adventure and is a strong leader is considered __________.

A) social; realistic
B) neurotic; compulsive
C) conventional; enterprising
D) demanding; encouraging

Answer: C
Page Ref: 359
Skill: Factual
Objective: 13.11

103) __________ powerfully predicts occupational status.

A) Parents' income
B) Personality type
C) Ethnic identity
D) Educational level

Answer: D
Page Ref: 360
Skill: Factual
Objective: 13.11

104) Jamie is a low-SES student who has earned a college scholarship to study political science. Based on the research reported in the text, which of the following factors probably most influenced her situation?

A) being a volunteer in a tutoring program for low-SES students
B) having a close relationship with her high school social studies teacher
C) attending political debates as part of a class field trip
D) watching news coverage of Condoleezza Rice

Answer: B
Page Ref: 360
Skill: Applied
Objective: 13.11

105) A dramatic rise in the numbers of employed mothers, who serve as models for their daughters, has resulted in

A) a reduced number of high school students who are prepared for the transition to college.
B) a renewed interest in one-income families where the mother stays home and manages the household and children.
C) increased interest by young women in occupations largely held by men.
D) an intolerance for male-dominated office dynamics among the current generation of workers.

Answer: C
Page Ref: 360
Skill: Factual
Objective: 13.11

106) Which of these facts most strongly CONTRADICTS the idea that women do not often succeed in male-dominated professions such as engineering or physics?

A) There are no known biological differences in these abilities.
B) No one can measure the abilities needed for these professions.
C) Many male supervisors are reluctant to hire women for these jobs.
D) Even mathematically talented women choose not to enter these fields.

Answer: D
Page Ref: 360
Skill: Conceptual
Objective: 13.11

107) Rachel is an academically gifted young woman with an interest in the sciences. Which career path is she more likely to take?

A) medicine
B) engineering
C) astrophysics
D) architecture

Answer: A
Page Ref: 360
Skill: Applied
Objective: 13.11

108) Bobby Joe is a high school graduate from the United States who chose not to go on to college. He is likely to
   A) have received vocational training while in high school.
   B) be working in a temporary, unskilled job.
   C) have received job placement services during his transition from high school to the world of work.
   D) have been involved in an apprenticeship program.
   Answer: B
   Page Ref: 362
   Skill: Applied
   Objective: 13.12

109) Rashid is a 24-year-old male nurse. Research on men in nontraditional careers would suggest that Rashid
   A) has more liberal social attitudes than his peers in traditionally masculine occupations.
   B) rates occupational prestige as important to his job choice.
   C) is likely to aspire to graduate education.
   D) is less self-assured than other males his age.
   Answer: A
   Page Ref: 361
   Skill: Applied
   Objective: Box SI: Masculinity at Work

110) Jesse is a 24-year-old male nurse. Based on information in your text, which person can we anticipate to have the most negative reaction to Jesse's career choice?
   A) Jesse's girlfriend
   B) Jesse's supervisor
   C) a woman who is Jesse's coworker
   D) a man in a traditionally masculine field
   Answer: D
   Page Ref: 361
   Skill: Applied
   Objective: Box SI: Masculinity at Work

111) North American employers regard the recent high school graduate as
   A) poorly prepared for skilled business and industrial occupations and for manual trades.
   B) far better prepared for the world of work than in past generations.
   C) overly prepared in academic areas that do not relate to the business arena.
   D) uninterested in jobs that require physical exertion in outdoor locations.
   Answer: A
   Page Ref: 362
   Skill: Factual
   Objective: 13.12

112) Which of the following would be considered a benefit of rather than a challenge to the implementation of an apprenticeship program?
   A) ensuring cooperation between schools and businesses
   B) overcoming the reluctance of employers to assume part of the responsibility for vocational training
   C) contributing to the nation's economic growth
   D) preventing low-SES youths from being concentrated in the lowest-skilled apprenticeship placements
   Answer: C
   Page Ref: 362
   Skill: Factual
   Objective: 13.12

ESSAY

113) List the common set of tasks usually associated with early adulthood.

Answer: Leaving home, completing education, beginning full-time work, attaining economic independence, establishing a long-term sexually and emotionally intimate relationship, and starting a family.

Page Ref: 339–340

114) Explain the factors that contribute to the appearance of the emerging adulthood developmental phase.

Answer: Rapid cultural changes explain the recent appearance of the bridge between adolescence and adulthood. First, entry-level positions in many fields require more education than in the past, prompting young adults to seek higher education in record numbers. Second, nations with abundant wealth and longer-lived populations have no pressing need for young people's labor. This frees 18- to 25-year-olds for this extended "moratorium."

Page Ref: 339–340

115) Describe two major theories of aging at the level of DNA and body cells. Include examples of evidence that support each theory.

Answer: Current explanations of biological aging at the level of DNA and body cells are of two types: (1) those that emphasize the *programmed effects of specific genes*, and (2) those that emphasize the *cumulative effects of random events*, both internal and external, that damage genetic and cellular material. Genetically programmed aging receives some support from kinship studies indicating that longevity is a family trait. People whose parents had long lives tend to live longer themselves, and there is greater similarity in the lifespans of identical than fraternal twins. But the heritability of longevity is quite modest-between .15 and .25 for age at death and from .27 to.57 for various measures of current biological age (for example, blood pressure, bone density). Rather than inheriting longevity directly, people probably inherit one or more risk factors, which influence their chances of dying earlier or later. One "genetic programming" theory proposes the existence of "aging genes" that control certain biological changes, such as menopause, gray hair, and deterioration of body cells. The strongest evidence for this view comes from research showing that human cells allowed to divide in the laboratory have a lifespan of 50 divisions plus or minus 10. With each duplication, a special type of DNA called *telomeres*, located at the ends of chromosomes, shortens. Eventually, so little remains that the cells no longer duplicate at all. Telomere shortening acts as a brake against somatic mutations, which become more likely as cells duplicate. But an increase in the number of senescent cells also contributes to age-related disease and loss of function.

According to an alternative, "random events" view, DNA in body cells is gradually damaged due to spontaneous or externally caused mutations. As these accumulate, cell repair and replacement are less efficient, or abnormal cancerous cells are produced. Studies of various animal species confirm an increase in DNA breaks and deletions and damage to other cellular material with age. Among humans, similar evidence is accumulating.

One probable cause of age-related DNA and cellular abnormalities is the release of free radicals, naturally occurring, highly reactive chemicals that form in the presence of oxygen. When oxygen atoms break down within the cell, the reaction strips away an electron, creating a free radical. As it seeks a replacement from its surroundings, it destroys nearby cellular material, including DNA, proteins, and fats essential for cell functioning. Free radicals are thought to be involved in more than 60 disorders of aging, including heart disease, cancer, cataracts, and arthritis. Although our bodies produce substances that neutralize free radicals, some harm occurs and accumulates.

Some researchers believe that genes for longevity work by defending against free radicals. In this way, a programmed genetic response may limit random DNA and cellular deterioration. Foods rich in vitamins C and E and beta-carotene forestall free-radical damage as well.

Page Ref: 340–342

3. How does emerging adulthood prolong identity development? (p. 340)

4. Cite two cultural changes that have contributed to emerging adulthood. (p. 340)

   A.

   B.

5. True or False: Emerging adulthood is limited or nonexistent for many low-SES young people. Explain your answer. (p. 340)

Physical Development

1. Describe *biological aging,* or *senescence.* (p. 340)

2. List four contextual factors that influence biological aging. (p. 340)

   A.

   B.

   C.

   D.

Biological Aging Is Under Way in Early Adulthood

1. Briefly explain and evaluate the "*wear-and-tear*" theory of biological aging. (p. 341)

Aging at the Level of DNA and Body Cells

1. List two current explanations of biological aging at the level of DNA and body cells. (p. 341)

   A.

   B.

2. Discuss evidence supporting the "genetic programming" theory, which proposes the existence of "aging genes" that control certain biological changes. Note the role of *telomeres* in your response. (p. 341)

3. Briefly summarize the "random events" theory of biological aging. (p. 341)

____

____

____

4. One probable cause of age-related DNA and cellular abnormalities, implicated in more than 60 disorders of aging, is the release of _______________—naturally occurring, highly reactive chemicals that form in the presence of oxygen. (p. 341)

Aging at the Level of Organs and Tissues

1. According to the _______________ *theory of aging,* protein fibers that make up the body's connective tissue form bonds with one another over time. When these normally separate fibers link, tissue becomes less elastic, leading to many negative outcomes. (p. 341)

2. Gradual failure of the _______________ system, which produces and regulates hormones, is another route to biological aging. List two examples of decreased hormone production, along with their consequences. (pp. 341–342)

   A. _______________

   B. _______________

3. Declines in _______________ system functioning, which result in increased susceptibility to infectious disease, are related to many conditions of aging. (p. 342)

Physical Changes

Cardiovascular and Respiratory Systems

1. The rate of death from heart disease among (African Americans / Caucasian Americans) is 28 percent higher than among (African Americans / Caucasian Americans). (p. 342)

2. True or False: In healthy individuals, the heart's ability to meet the body's oxygen needs under typical conditions does not change during adulthood. (p. 342)

3. What is *atherosclerosis,* and how does it progress? (p. 342)

   A. _______________

   B. _______________

4. Explain why rates of heart disease have declined considerably since the mid-twentieth century. (p. 342)

____

____

5. Cite two ways in which lung functioning changes with age. (pp. 342, 344)

   A. _______________

   B. _______________

Motor Performance

1. Which athletic skills peak in the early twenties, and which ones usually peak in the late twenties and early thirties? (p. 344)

   Early twenties: ______________________________

   ____

   Late twenties and early thirties: ______________________________

   ____

2. What does research on outstanding athletes reveal about the upper biological limit of motor capacity? (p. 344)

   ____

   ____

   ____

3. True or False: Age-related declines in athletic skill are almost entirely attributable to biological aging. (p. 344)

Immune System

1. Describe two types of white blood cells that are vital in immune system functioning. (p. 344)

   A. ______________________________

   ____

   B. ______________________________

   ____

2. One factor that contributes to age-related declines in the immune response is shrinkage of the ____________, which results in decreased production of certain hormones. (p. 344)

3. Explain how stress can weaken the immune response. (pp. 344–345)

   ____

   ____

   ____

Reproductive Capacity

1. Explain why many women experience a decline in fertility across early and middle adulthood. (p. 345)

   ____

   ____

   ____

2. True or False: Male reproductive capacity is unaffected by age. (p. 345)

Health and Fitness

1. Death rates in early adulthood for all causes are (lower / higher) for Canadians than Americans. What factors contribute to this difference? (p. 345)

   ____

   ____

2. Briefly summarize SES variations in health during adulthood, noting factors responsible for these differences. (p. 346)

   Variations: ______________________________

   ____

   Factors responsible: ______________________________

   ____

Nutrition

1. Today, ______ percent of U.S. adults and ______ percent of Canadian adults are obese. (p. 346)
2. True or False: In the United States and Western Europe, 5 to 7 percent more women than men suffer from obesity. In Canada, obesity rates for the two sexes are equal. (p. 346)
3. A (large / small) number of people show large weight gains in adulthood, most often between ages 25 to 40. (p. 346)
4. Define basal metabolic rate (BMR), and describe changes in the BMR during early adulthood that contribute to weight gain. (p. 346)

   Definition: ______________________________

   ____

   Changes: ______________________________

   ____

5. List several health problems associated with being overweight or obese. (p. 346)

   ____

   ____

6. List five elements of effective treatment for obesity. (p. 347)

   A. ______________________________

   B. ______________________________

   C. ______________________________

   D. ______________________________

   E. ______________________________

7. Summarize the detrimental effects of excess dietary fat consumption, noting specific consequences of saturated fat. (pp. 347–348)

   ____

   ____

Exercise

1. Although most North Americans are aware of the health benefits of exercise, about ___ percent in Canada and ___ percent in the United States are inactive. (p. 348)
2. True or False: Exercise helps prevent serious illnesses, such as cancer, adult-onset diabetes, and cardiovascular disease. (p. 348)

3. List five ways that exercise helps prevent serious illnesses. (p. 348)

   A. ______________________________

   B. ______________________________

   C. ______________________________

   D. ______________________________

   E. ______________________________

4. How much exercise is recommended for a healthier and longer life? (p. 348)

   ____

   ____

Substance Abuse

1. True or False: Drug taking peaks among 19- to 22-year-olds and then declines throughout the twenties. (p. 348)
2. What are the two most common substance disorders in early adulthood? (p. 349)

   A. ______________________________

   B. ______________________________

3. Smoking rates have declined very (slowly / rapidly) over the past 40 years. (p. 349)
4. Discuss the consequences of smoking on health. (p. 349)

   ____

   ____

   ____

5. True or False: One out of every three young people who become regular smokers will die from a smoking-related disease. (p. 349)
6. Summarize the benefits of quitting smoking, noting the success rate of those who use cessation aids. (p. 349)

   ____

   ____

7. Describe gender differences in the development and chronicity of alcoholism. (p. 349)

   Men: ______________________________

   Women: ______________________________

8. Twin studies (do / do not) support a genetic contribution to alcoholism. (p. 349)
9. List personal and cultural factors associated with alcoholism. (p. 349)

   Personal: ______________________________

   ____

   Cultural: ______________________________

   ____

10. List some of the health problems associated with chronic alcohol use. (pp. 349–350)

    ____

    ____

11. Cite components of successful treatment programs for alcoholism. (p. 350)

____

____

Sexuality

1. True or False: Sexual partners tend to be alike in age, education, ethnicity, and religion. (p. 350)
2. True or False: Internet dating services are a successful way for young adults to meet a compatible partner, although conventional strategies for initiating relationships have higher success rates. (p. 350)
3. True or False: Consistent with popular belief, Americans today have more sexual partners than they did a generation ago. Briefly explain your response. (p. 350)

   ____

   ____

4. List three factors that affect frequency of sexual activity. (p. 350)

   A. ____

   B. ____

   C. ____

5. True or False: As the number of sexual partners increases, satisfaction with one's sex life also increases. (p. 350)
6. List the two sexual difficulties most frequently reported by men and by women. (p. 351)

   Men: ____

   Women: ____

7. The majority of Americans (do / do not) support civil liberties and equal employment opportunities for gay men, lesbians, and bisexuals. (p. 351)
8. Heterosexual (women / men) judge homosexuals more harshly. (pp. 351–352)
9. What major factor has limited researchers' access to information about the sex lives of gay men and lesbians? (p. 352)

   ____

10. Explain how the rules for homosexual sex are similar to the rules for heterosexual sex. (p. 352)

    ____

    ____

11. Describe characteristics of gay and lesbian couples, noting living arrangements and level of education. (p. 352)

    ____

    ____

12. An estimated ______ to ______ percent of North American women have experienced rape. (p. 352)
13. Women are most often raped by (strangers / men they know well). (p. 352)
14. Describe the personal characteristics of men who commit sexual assault. (p. 352)

    ____

    ____

    ____

15. Briefly describe three cultural forces that contribute to sexual coercion. (p. 352)

    A. ______________________________

    ____

    B. ______________________________

    ____

    C. ______________________________

    ____

16. True or False: Authorities are just as likely to recognize female-initiated forced sex as illegal as male-initiated forced sex. (pp. 352–353)

17. Summarize the immediate and long-term consequences of rape. (p. 353)

    Immediate: ______________________________

    ____

    Long-term: ______________________________

    ____

18. Cite three critical features in the treatment of rape victims that help foster recovery. (p. 353)

    A. ______________________________

    B. ______________________________

    C. ______________________________

19. List five ways to prevent sexual coercion. (p. 353)

    A. ______________________________

    B. ______________________________

    C. ______________________________

    D. ______________________________

    E. ______________________________

20. List common symptoms of premenstrual syndrome (PMS). (pp. 353–354)

    ____

    ____

    ____

21. Nearly ______ percent of women worldwide experience some form of PMS, but only ____ to ____ percent of women experience symptoms severe enough to interfere with academic, occupational, or social functioning. (p. 354)

22. List common treatments for PMS. (p. 354)

    ____

    ____

Biology and Environment: Sex Differences in Attitudes Toward Sexuality

1. Summarize psychoanalytic, evolutionary, and social-learning perspectives on sex differences in attitudes toward sexuality. (p. 351)

   Psychoanalytic: ______________________________

   ____

   Evolutionary: ______________________________

   ____

   Social-learning: ______________________________

   ____

2. True or False: Women are more opposed to casual sex than men and are only half as likely to engage in it. (p. 351)

3. True or False: Young women's complaints that many men are not interested in long-term commitments are generally unfounded. (p. 351)

Psychological Stress

1. Describe several physical consequences of psychological stress. (p. 354)

   ____

   ____

   ____

2. Explain why early adulthood is a particularly stressful time of life. (p. 354)

   ____

   ____

Cognitive Development

Changes in the Structure of Thought

1. Cognitive development beyond Piaget's formal operational stage is known as ____________ *thought.* (p. 355)

Perry's Theory: Epistemic Cognition

1. What is *epistemic cognition*? (p. 355)

   ____

   ____

   ____

2. Using Perry's research, describe the structure of thought in younger and older college students. Refer to *dualistic* and *relativistic thinking* in your response. (p. 355)

   Younger college students: ______________________________

   ____

   Older college students: ______________________________

   ____

3. Define *commitment within relativistic thinking,* and provide an example. (p. 355)

   A. ____

   ____

   B. ____

4. True or False: Almost all college students reach the stage of *commitment within relativistic thinking.* (p. 355)

5. How do peers contribute to development of epistemic cognition in early adulthood? (pp. 355–356)

   ____

   ____

6. Explain how peer interaction facilitates individual reflection in early adulthood. (p. 356)

   ____

   ____

Labouvie-Vief's Theory: Pragmatic Thought and Cognitive-Affective Complexity

1. According to Labouvie-Vief, adulthood marks a shift from hypothetical to ____________ *thought*—a structural advance in which logic becomes a tool for solving real-world problems. What motivates this change? (p. 356)

   ____

   ____

2. Define *cognitive-affective complexity,* noting how it changes in adulthood. Describe its consequences. (p. 356)

   A. ____

   ____

   B. ____

   ____

   C. ____

   ____

Expertise and Creativity

1. Describe *expertise,* noting factors that support it. (p. 357)

   A. ____

   ____

   B. ____

   ____

2. Summarize differences in problem solving among experts and novices. (p. 357)

   Experts: ____

   ____

   Novices: ____

   ____

3. True or False: Expertise is necessary for creativity. (p. 357)
4. Describe general trends in the development of creativity across adulthood. (p. 357)

____

____

5. In addition to expertise, what other personal qualities foster the development of creativity? (p. 357)

____

____

The College Experience

Psychological Impact of Attending College

1. Describe psychological changes that take place during the college years. (p. 358)

____

____

____

2. Cite two factors that jointly contribute to the impact of college. (p. 358)

   A. ____

   B. ____

Dropping Out

1. True or False: Forty-five percent of North American students at two-year institutions and 30 percent of students at four-year institutions drop out, most within the first year and many within the first six weeks. (p. 358)
2. Summarize personal and institutional characteristics that contribute to young people's decision to drop out of college. (p. 358)

   Personal: ____

   ____

   Institutional: ____

   ____

3. True or False: Reaching out to college students, especially during the early weeks and throughout the first year, is critical. Explain your answer. (p. 358)

____

____

____

Vocational Choice

Selecting a Vocation

1. Briefly summarize the three periods of vocational development, noting age range at which each occurs. (p. 359)

   Fantasy period: ______________________________

   ____

   Tentative period: ______________________________

   ____

   Realistic period: ______________________________

   ____

Factors Influencing Vocational Choice

1. Match each of the following personality types that affect vocational choice with the appropriate description. (p. 359)

   _____ Likes well-structured tasks and values social status; tends to choose business occupations
   _____ Prefers real-world problems and work with objects; tends toward mechanical occupations
   _____ Is adventurous, persuasive, and a strong leader; drawn toward sales and supervisory positions
   _____ Enjoys working with ideas; drawn toward scientific occupations
   _____ Has a high need for emotional and individual expression; drawn to artistic fields
   _____ Likes interacting with people; drawn toward human services

   1. Investigative
   2. Social
   3. Realistic
   4. Artistic
   5. Conventional
   6. Enterprising

2. Research confirms a (weak/moderate/strong) relationship between Holland's personality types and vocational choice. (p. 359)

3. Identify two reasons, other than educational attainment, why young people's vocational aspirations correlate strongly with the jobs of their parents. (p. 360)

   A. ______________________________

   ____

   B. ______________________________

   ____

4. Teachers (do / do not) play a powerful role in young adults' career decisions. (p. 360)

5. True or False: Over the past three decades, young women's career preferences have remained strongly gender stereotyped. (p. 360)

6. Women's progress in entering and excelling at male-dominated professions has been (slow / rapid). (p. 360)

7. True or False: Sex differences in vocational achievement can be directly attributed to differences in ability. Explain your response. (p. 360)

   ____

   ____

8. List three experiences common to young women who show high achievement during college. (p. 361)

   A. ______________________________

   B. ______________________________

   C. ______________________________

Social Issues: Masculinity at Work: Men Who Choose Nontraditional Careers

1. Describe characteristics of men who choose traditionally feminine occupations compared to those who choose traditionally masculine jobs. (p. 361)

   Traditionally Feminine: ______________________________

   ____

   Traditionally Masculine: ______________________________

   ____

2. True or False: Because of their male minority status in traditionally female occupations, co-workers often assume men are more knowledgeable than they actually are. (p. 361)

3. True or False: Many men in female-dominated occupations express anxiety about being stigmatized for their career choice—by other men, not by women. (p. 361)

Vocational Preparation of Non-College-Bound Young Adults

1. Non-college-bound high school graduates have (more / fewer) work opportunities than they did several decades ago. (p. 362)

2. Summarize the challenges faced by non-college-bound young adults in trying to gain employment, and describe the type of jobs they are likely to find. (p. 362)

   Challenges: ______________________________

   ____

   Type of jobs: ______________________________

   ____

3. Describe the challenges of implementing an apprenticeship program for non-college-bound young adults. (p. 362)

   ____

   ____

   ____

PUZZLE 13.1

Across

2. Cognitive development beyond Piaget's formal operational stage is referred to as __________ thought
4. ___________ cognition refers to our reflections on how we arrived at facts, beliefs, and ideas
6. _________ adulthood: a transitional phase of development, extending from the late teens to the mid-twenties
7. __________ thinking: dividing information, values, and authority into right and wrong, good and bad, we and they
8. __________ thinking: viewing all knowledge as imbedded in a framework of thought; favoring multiple truths relative to the context of evaluation
9. During the _________ period of vocational development, children fantasize about career options through make-believe play
11. _________ within relativistic thinking: when one resists choosing between opposing views and instead tries to formulate a more satisfying perspective that synthesizes contradictions
15. __________ aging: genetically influenced, age-related declines in the functioning of organs and systems that are universal in all members of our species
16. __________-__________ theory: the formation of bonds between normally separate protein fibers causes the body's connective tissue to become less elastic
17. During the __________ period of vocational development, adolescents weigh vocational options against their interests, abilities, and values

Down

1. __________-__________ complexity is the awareness and coordination of positive and negative feelings into a complex, organized structure
3. _________ thought: logic becomes a tool for solving real-world problems
5. During the _________ period of vocational development, individuals focus on a general career category and eventually settle on a single occupation
10. The amount of energy the body uses at complete rest (abbr.)
12. Acquisition of extensive knowledge in a field or endeavor
13. Free __________: naturally occurring, highly reactive chemicals that form in the presence of oxygen and destroy cellular material
14. Array of physical and psychological symptoms that usually appear 6 to 10 days prior to menstruation (abbr.)

CROSSWORD PUZZLE SOLUTIONS

PUZZLE 13.1

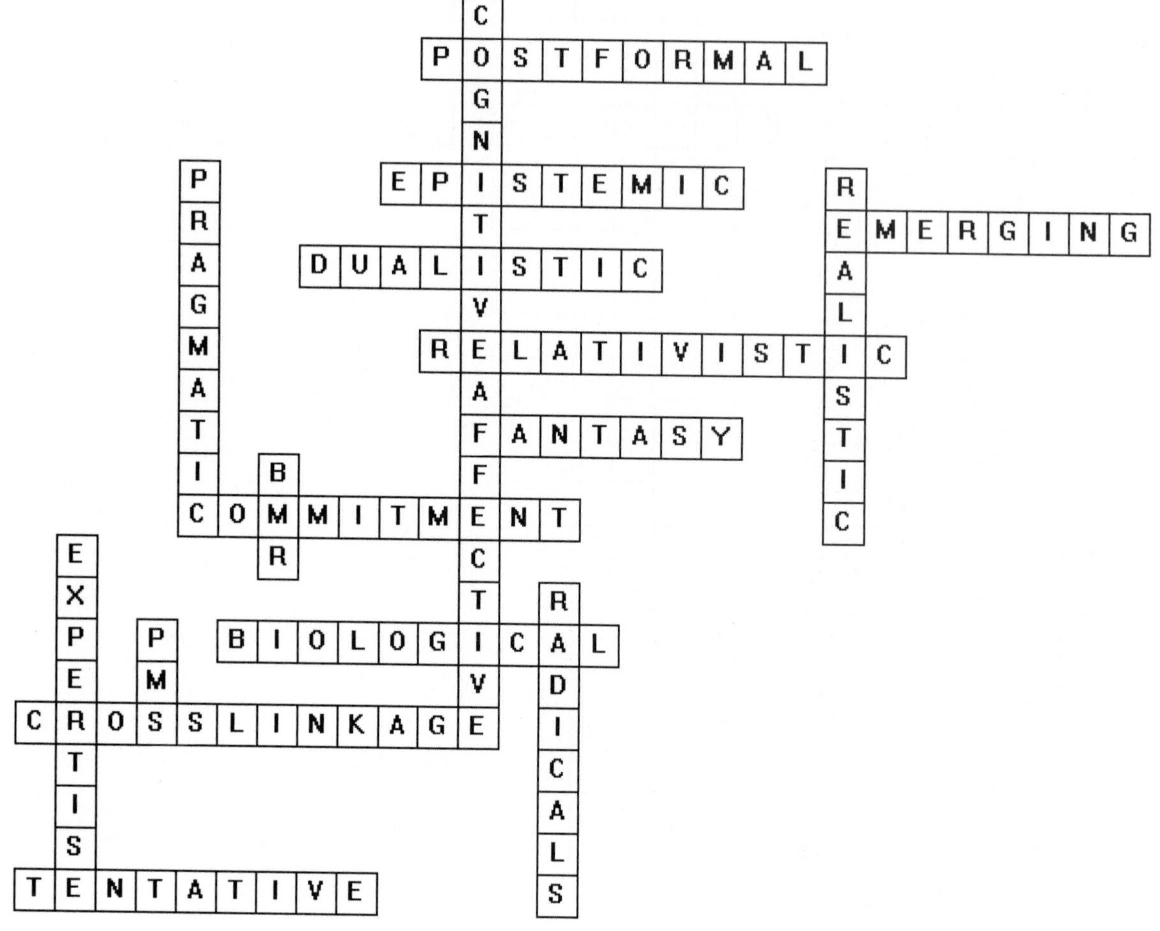

PRACTICE TEST #1

1. The transition to adult roles includes a phase of development known as emerging adulthood, which (p. 339)
   a. **greatly prolongs identity development.**
   b. typically extends from about age 18 until the early thirties.
   c. begins after young people have completed their education, regardless of age.
   d. first became common a generation ago.

2. Over the past century in industrialized nations, improved nutrition, medical treatment, sanitation, and safety have resulted in an increase in average life expectancy of about (p. 340)
   a. 10 to 15 years.
   b. 15 to 25 years.
   c. **25 to 30 years.**
   d. 50 to 60 years.

3. Biological aging (p. 340)
   a. is the result of "wear and tear" on the body's tissues and organs.
   b. **begins in the early twenties.**
   c. takes place more rapidly in people who engage in physical work.
   d. is largely the result of heredity, with little influence from environmental factors.

4. According to the "random events" theory of aging, spontaneous or externally caused mutations cause gradual damage to (p. 341)
   a. **DNA.**
   b. essential vitamins.
   c. the skin.
   d. bone structure.

5. In males, semen volume and sperm concentration and motility gradually decrease after age (p. 345)
   a. 20.
   b. 30.
   c. **40.**
   d. 50.

6. Research on health and fitness indicates that (p. 346)
   a. heart disease is the leading cause of death among individuals between ages 25 and 44.
   b. death rates for all causes are essentially equivalent in industrialized nations throughout the world.
   c. **income, education, and occupational status show a strong relationship with almost every disease and health indicator.**
   d. SES disparities in health and mortality are lesser in the United States than in other industrialized countries.

7. Rising rates of obesity in industrialized nations are the result of (p. 346)
   a. hereditary vulnerability to weight gain.
   b. reduced basal metabolic rate among individuals between ages 25 and 50.
   c. **reduced physical labor and increased fat intake.**
   d. poor-quality health care and lack of universal health insurance.

8. Adding some weight between ages 25 and 50 is a normal part of aging, resulting from a gradual decline in (p. 346)
   a. **basal metabolic rate.**
   b. T and B cells.
   c. motor performance.
   d. free radicals.

9. To maintain normal body function and better health, the best rule of thumb is to (p. 348)
   a. eliminate all fat from the diet.
   b. eliminate all unsaturated fats from the diet.
   c. eat less fat of all kinds and substitute unsaturated for saturated fat.
   d. eat less fat of all kinds and substitute saturated for unsaturated fat.

10. Which of the following statements about the value of exercise is accurate? (p. 348)
    a. People who exercise can feel free to eat diets rich in fat, consume alcohol, and smoke, without negative health effects.
    b. Exercise reduces the incidence of obesity.
    c. Regular exercise has not been shown to reduce stress.
    d. Exercise weakens the heart muscle, increasing the risk of cardiovascular disease.

11. The ingredients of cigarette smoke leave their damaging mark (p. 349)
    a. only in the lungs.
    b. only in the mouth and lungs.
    c. only in the lungs and digestive tract.
    d. throughout the body.

12. Which of the following statements about cigarette smoking is true? (p. 349)
    a. Smoking rates have increased among North American adults over the last several decades.
    b. The later people start smoking, the greater their likelihood of continuing.
    c. One out of every three young people who becomes a regular smoker will die from a smoking-related disease.
    d. Despite some improvement in health, those who quit smoking will never return to nonsmoker levels of disease risk.

13. Research on sexual behavior shows that (p. 350)
    a. sexual partners tend to be similar in age, education, ethnicity, and religion.
    b. nearly 50 percent of adults who eventually marry meet at bars, through personal ads, or on vacation.
    c. Americans today have fewer sexual partners than those of a generation ago.
    d. the majority of Americans report having five or more sexual partners in a single year.

14. Men who engage in sexual assault (p. 352)
    a. are less likely to endorse traditional gender roles.
    b. have difficulty accurately interpreting women's social behavior.
    c. usually acknowledge their own responsibility.
    d. are most likely to be from low-SES, ethnic minority groups.

15. According to Perry's work on epistemic cognition, which skill is the first to develop? (p. 355)
    a. Individuals formulate a perspective that synthesizes contradictions.
    b. Individuals give up the possibility of absolute truth.
    c. Individuals choose between many possible, opposing views.
    d. Individuals separate information into right and wrong.

16. Most students who drop out of college (p. 358)
    a. do so during their sophomore or junior year because they are unable to decide on a major.
    b. do not have the ability to succeed at the institution to which they were admitted.
    c. have serious problems with alcohol or drugs.
    d. have problems that are typical rather than catastrophic in nature.

17. Twenty-year-old Dominic explored the possibility of becoming a teacher by tutoring in an after-school program and interviewing several of his previous teachers about their career choice. He then decided to major in education. Dominic is in the ______________ period of vocational development. (p. 359)
    a. fantasy
    b. tentative
    c. realistic
    d. acquisition

18. The relationship between personality and vocational choice is (p. 359)
    a. weak, as people rarely choose occupations that complement their personality.
    b. moderate, as most people are a blend of personality types and could do well at more than one kind of occupation.
    c. strong, as career choice, success, and satisfaction are almost entirely attributable to personality factors.
    d. inconclusive, with research findings varying widely on this topic.

19. Young people's vocational aspirations (p. 360)
    a. are generally much higher than their parents'.
    b. are influenced by their fathers' occupations but not by their mothers'.
    c. reflect genetic similarities between parent and child but are unrelated to parenting style.
    d. tend to correlate with their parents' occupations because of similarities in personality, intellectual abilities, and educational attainment.

20. Non-college-bound North American students (p. 362)
    a. are even less likely to find employment than students who drop out of high school.
    b. are typically well prepared for skilled business and industrial occupations.
    c. are better able to find skilled jobs than their counterparts in European nations.
    d. are typically unable to find a job better than the ones they held as students.

PRACTICE TEST #2

1. Which of the following provides support for the programmed effects of "aging genes"? (p. 341)
    a. Human cells that are allowed to divide in the laboratory have a lifespan of 50 divisions, plus or minus 10.
    b. DNA in body cells is gradually damaged through spontaneous or externally caused mutations.
    c. Free radicals released by the body's cells destroy nearby cellular material.
    d. Biological aging does not appear to be affected by environmental factors.

2. Research on the role of key hormones in aging indicates that a gradual drop in growth hormone (GH) is associated with (p. 342)
    a. thickening of the skin.
    b. loss of muscle and bone mass.
    c. reduction in body fat.
    d. increase in cardiovascular functioning.

3. During the twenties and thirties, physical changes of aging (p. 342)
    a. occur only if an individual develops a serious illness.
    b. occur more rapidly than at any other time in the life cycle.
    c. have not yet begun to occur.
    d. occur so gradually that most are hardly noticeable.

4. In healthy individuals, the heart's ability to meet the body's oxygen requirements under normal conditions (as measured by heart rate in relation to volume of blood pumped) (p. 342)
    a. decreases slightly during adulthood.
    b. decreases greatly during adulthood.
    c. does not change during adulthood.
    d. actually increases during adulthood.

5. Studies of outstanding athletes show that (p. 344)
    a. as they begin to age, their attainments fall short of what is biologically possible, even with intensive training.
    b. athletic tasks that depend on endurance peak in the early twenties, while those involving speed, strength, and gross body coordination peak in the late twenties and early thirties.
    c. age-related decline in athletic skill is largely attributable to biological aging.
    d. the upper biological limit of motor capacity is reached in the first part of early adulthood.

6. The immune system declines after age 20 because (p. 344)
   a. production of the thymus hormone increases.
   b. the thymus shrinks, becoming less able to promote full maturity and differentiation of T cells.
   c. the thymus increases in size throughout adulthood.
   d. the stresses of adult life contribute to weakening of the immune system.

7. Treatment for obese adults should (p. 347)
   a. be brief—no more than a few weeks—in order to encourage individuals to take control of their diet and exercise habits on their own.
   b. focus only on changing dietary habits, not on exercise, because it is difficult for obese adults to exercise enough to have any effect.
   c. begin as soon as possible.
   d. focus only on exercise, because regular exercise is more effective than dieting in controlling weight.

8. Which of the following statements about fat consumption is true? (p. 347)
   a. U.S. and Canadian dietary guidelines suggest that dietary fat should make up no more than 30 percent of total caloric intake.
   b. Unsaturated fats are more unhealthy than saturated fats.
   c. To maximize healthy body functioning, dietary fats should be avoided entirely.
   d. Behavioral interventions, such as regular exercise, are largely ineffective in reducing the harmful influence of dietary fats.

9. Among the following groups of North Americans, who is more likely to be inactive compared to their counterparts? (p. 348)
   a. high-SES adults
   b. women
   c. individuals who live in safe neighborhoods
   d. Canadians

10. Which of the following statements about alcoholism is true? (p. 350)
    a. About 50 percent of recovering alcoholics relapse within a few months.
    b. In men, alcoholism usually begins in the late thirties or early forties.
    c. Alcoholism affects more women than men.
    d. The physical effects of alcohol abuse are limited to the liver.

11. The group reporting the highest rates of physical and emotional satisfaction with their sex lives are (pp. 350–351)
    a. individuals in committed relationships who are not yet married.
    b. individuals who have had a large number of sexual partners.
    c. young adults involved in casual dating relationships.
    d. married couples.

12. Victims of sexual coercion (p. 353)
    a. are usually over the age of 30.
    b. rarely know their abusers.
    c. show reactions similar to those of survivors of extreme trauma, including shock, withdrawal, and psychological numbing.
    d. are typically quick to confide in trusted family members and friends about the assault.

13. Premenstrual syndrome (p. 354)
    a. is much more common in women living in industrialized nations than in the developing world.
    b. shows no evidence of having a genetic link.
    c. affects nearly 40 percent of women.
    d. is entirely the result of a genetic predisposition.

14. With regard to epistemic cognition, (p. 355)
    a. students only rarely reach the level of dualistic thinking.
    b. students typically move from relativistic thinking toward dualistic thinking.
    c. as students continue through college, they tend to become less flexible and less tolerant.
    d. the most mature students eventually progress to commitment within relativistic thinking.

15. Compared with novices, experts (p. 357)
    a. reason less effectively.
    b. remember and reason more quickly and effectively.
    c. know fewer domain-specific concepts, because they are focused on underlying principles.
    d. show a more superficial understanding of a larger amount of information.

16. Which of the following statements about expertise and creativity is true? (p. 357)
    a. Experts and novices show remarkably similar reasoning and problem-solving skills.
    b. Creativity takes essentially the same form in childhood and adulthood.
    c. Creativity tends to peak in early adulthood, approximately five years after initial exposure to a field.
    d. Although expertise is necessary for creativity, creativity requires other qualities besides expertise.

17. Those who get an early start in creativity tend to peak and drop off sooner, whereas "late bloomers" reach their full stride at older ages. This suggests that creativity is more a function of ____________ than of chronological age. (p. 357)
    a. "actual age"
    b. "career age"
    c. "adult age"
    d. "old age"

18. Cognitive growth during the college years is promoted when (p. 358)
    a. students take online classes rather than enrolling in a postsecondary institution.
    b. students choose a major during their freshman year.
    c. students live in college residence halls and become involved in campus life.
    d. students live at home in order to minimize distractions and promote a higher-quality environment for serious study.

19. Which of the following statements about influences on young people's vocational choices is true? (p. 360)
    a. Because children have considerable knowledge of the drawbacks of their parents' careers, they are likely to choose radically different occupations for themselves.
    b. Teachers are more influential than parents in the career decisions of non-college-bound youths.
    c. Young adults tend to choose occupations that are consistent with their family values, but teachers also play an important role in career decision making.
    d. Neither parents nor teachers have much influence on young adults' career decisions; rather, personality type is the strongest predictor of occupational choice.

20. Teenagers who do not plan to go to college after high school graduation (p. 362)
    a. have a much easier time finding employment than do many college graduates.
    b. are typically limited to temporary, low-paid, unskilled jobs.
    c. often have high-quality vocational preparation, which enables them to enter high-paying, high-skill occupations.
    d. do not have well-developed career aspirations.

POWERPOINT SLIDES

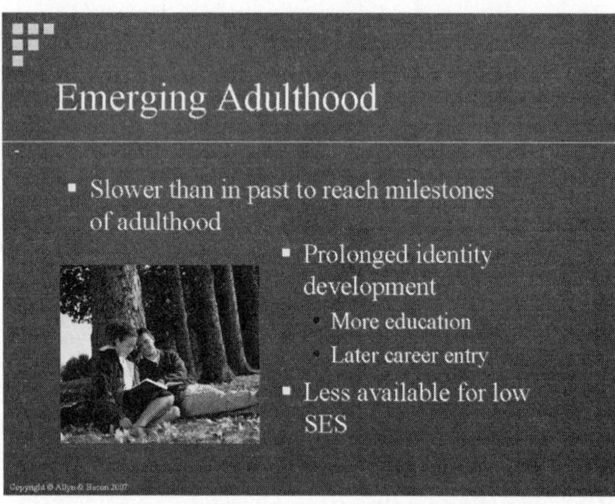

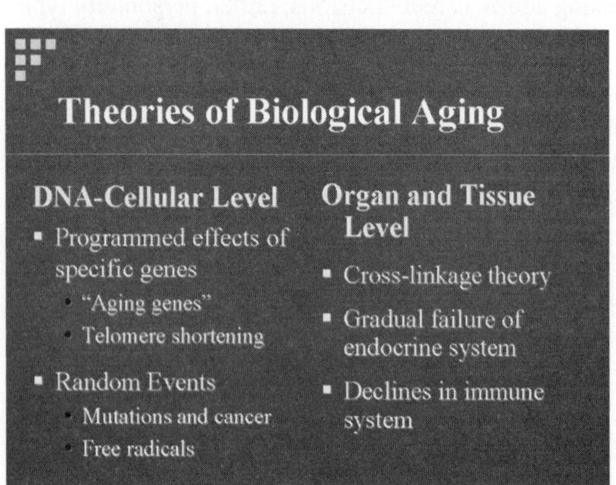

Cardiovascular & Respiratory Changes

- **Heart**
  - Few resting changes, lower performance under stress
  - Hypertension, atherosclerosis
  - Diseases declining - better lifestyle
- **Lungs**
  - Maximum vital capacity declines after 25
  - Stiffness makes breathing harder with age

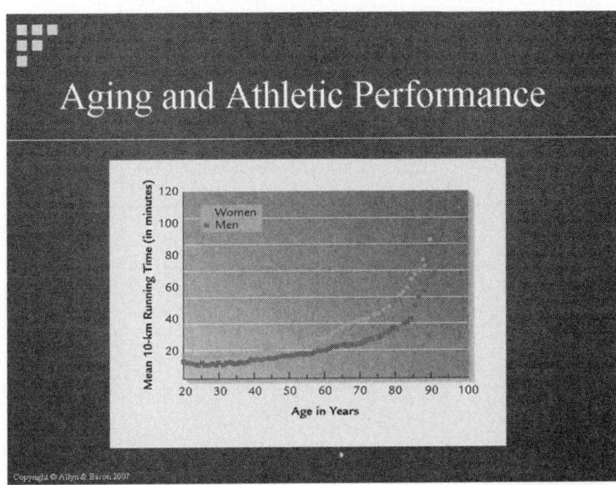

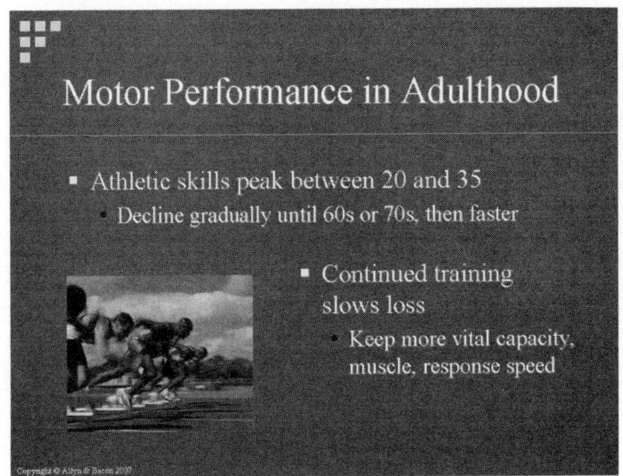

The Immune System in Early Adulthood

Declines after age 20:

- Fewer T cells from shrinking thymus
- B cells don't work as well without T cells
- Stress weakens immune response

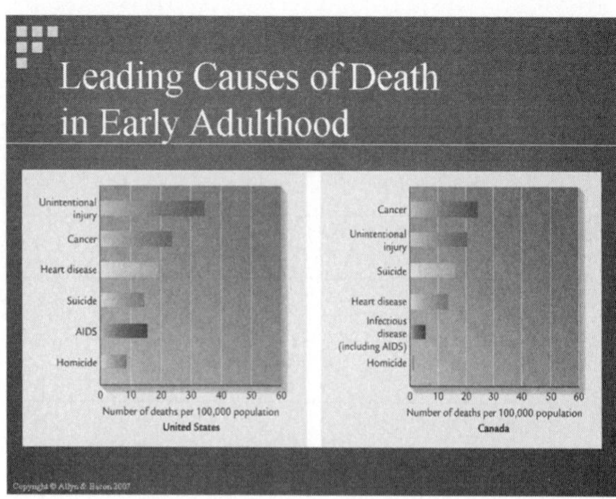

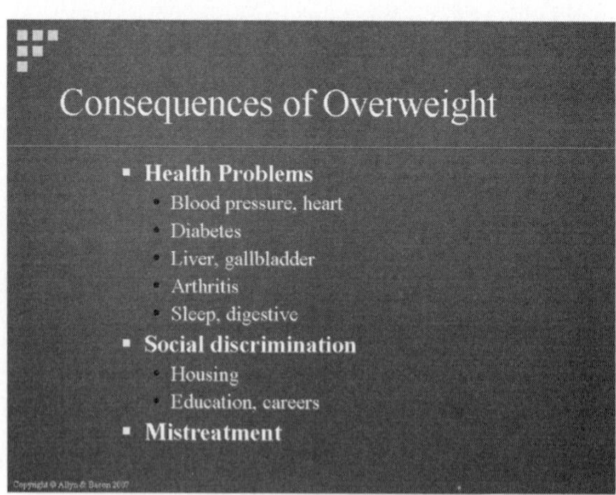

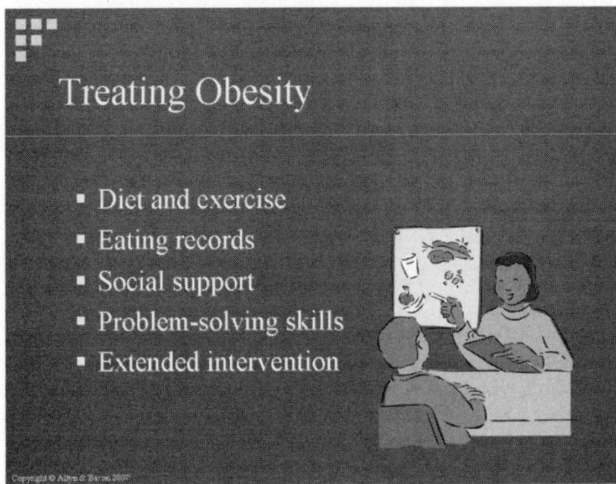

Dietary Fat

- **Saturated Fat**
  - From meat and dairy
  - Solid at room temperature
  - No more than 10% of daily calories
- **Total fat**
  - 30% or less of daily calories

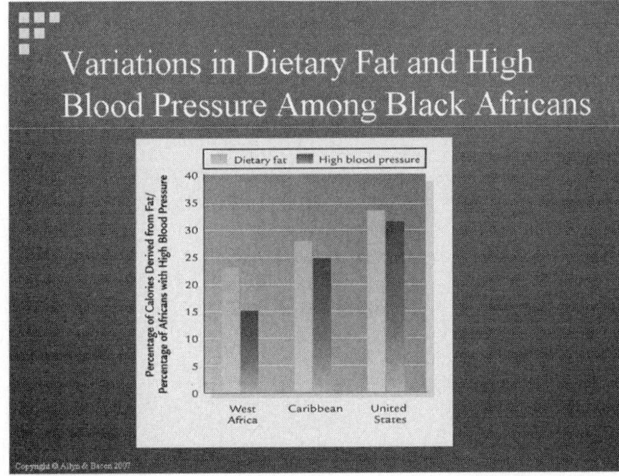

Exercise
Only one third get enough
At least 30 minutes moderate five or more days a week
More often, more vigorous is better
Around one third of North Americans are inactive
Women
Low SES
Copyright © Allyn & Bacon 2007

Benefits of Exercise
Reduces fat, builds muscle
Boosts immune system, prevents some diseases
Cardiovascular benefits
Mental health benefits
Stress reduction
Self-esteem
Longer life
Copyright © Allyn & Bacon 2007

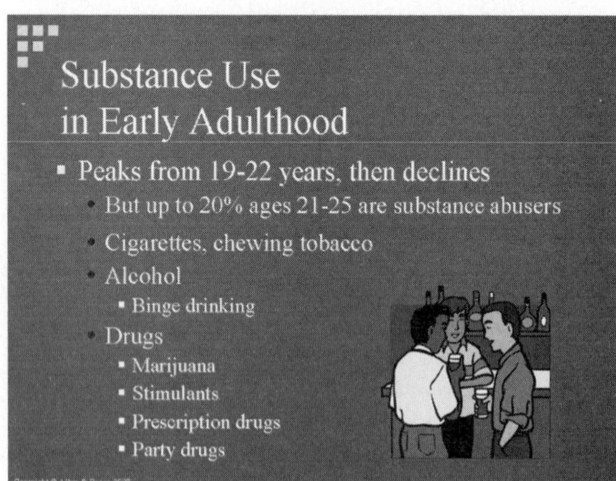
Substance Use in Early Adulthood
Peaks from 19-22 years, then declines
But up to 20% ages 21-25 are substance abusers
Cigarettes, chewing tobacco
Alcohol
Binge drinking
Drugs
Marijuana
Stimulants
Prescription drugs
Party drugs
Copyright © Allyn & Bacon 2007

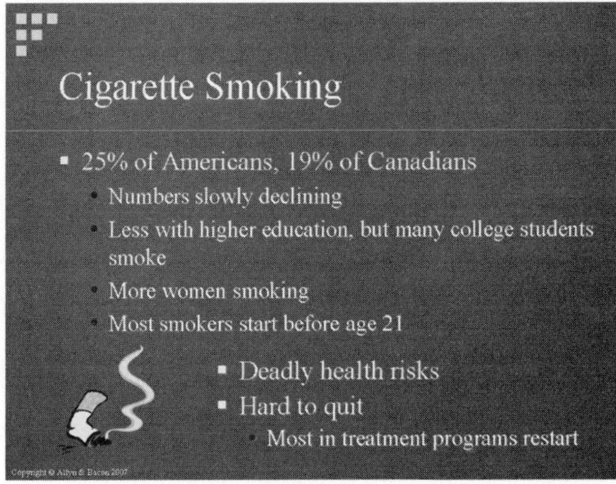
Cigarette Smoking
25% of Americans, 19% of Canadians
Numbers slowly declining
Less with higher education, but many college students smoke
More women smoking
Most smokers start before age 21
Deadly health risks
Hard to quit
Most in treatment programs restart
Copyright © Allyn & Bacon 2007

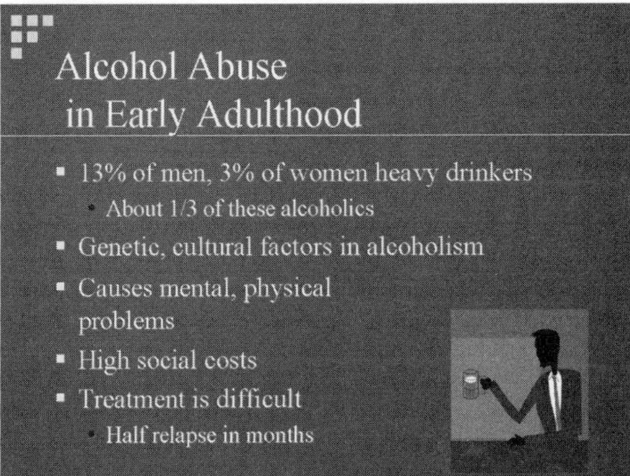
Alcohol Abuse in Early Adulthood
13% of men, 3% of women heavy drinkers
About 1/3 of these alcoholics
Genetic, cultural factors in alcoholism
Causes mental, physical problems
High social costs
Treatment is difficult
Half relapse in months
Copyright © Allyn & Bacon 2007

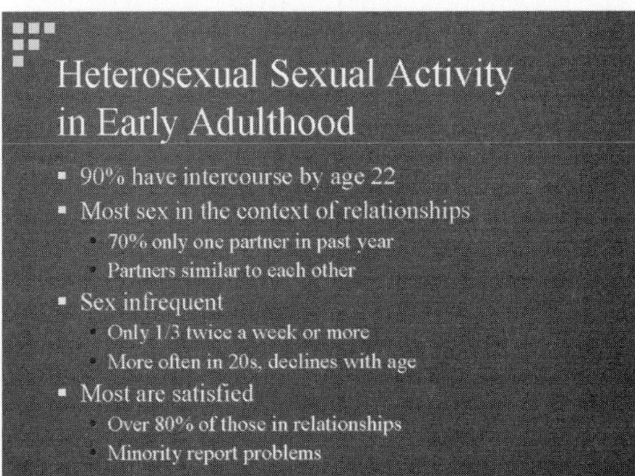
Heterosexual Sexual Activity in Early Adulthood
90% have intercourse by age 22
Most sex in the context of relationships
70% only one partner in past year
Partners similar to each other
Sex infrequent
Only 1/3 twice a week or more
More often in 20s, declines with age
Most are satisfied
Over 80% of those in relationships
Minority report problems
Copyright © Allyn & Bacon 2007

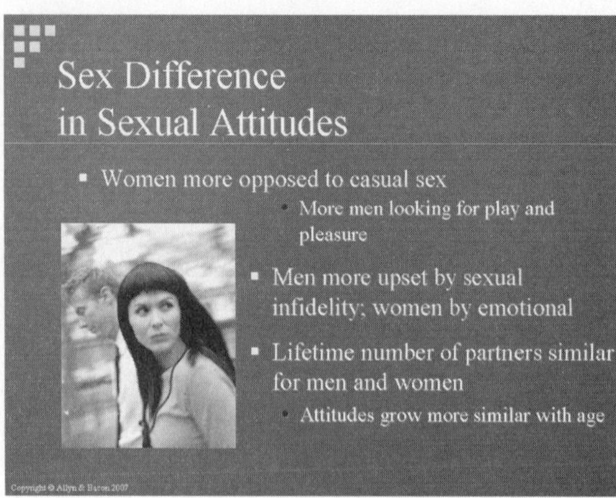

Homosexuality and Bisexuality in Early Adulthood

- 2.8% of men, 1.4% of women
  - Estimated 30% same-sex couples do not report
- Similar behavior to heterosexuals
- Public acceptance growing
  - Majority say it's "OK," support civil liberties, job opportunities
- Most well-educated; live in larger cities, college towns

Factors Related to Sexual Coercion

Perpetrator Characteristics	Cultural Forces
▪ Believe traditional gender roles ▪ Approve violence against women; accept rape myths ▪ Perceive behavior inaccurately ▪ History of own abuse, promiscuity ▪ Alcohol abuse	▪ Men taught dominance, competition, aggression ▪ Women submission ▪ Acceptance of violence ▪ Aggressive pornography

Consequences of Rape and Sexual Abuse

- Trauma response
  - Immediate shock
  - Long-term problems
    - Depression
- Physical injury
- STDs
- General ill health
- Negative behaviors

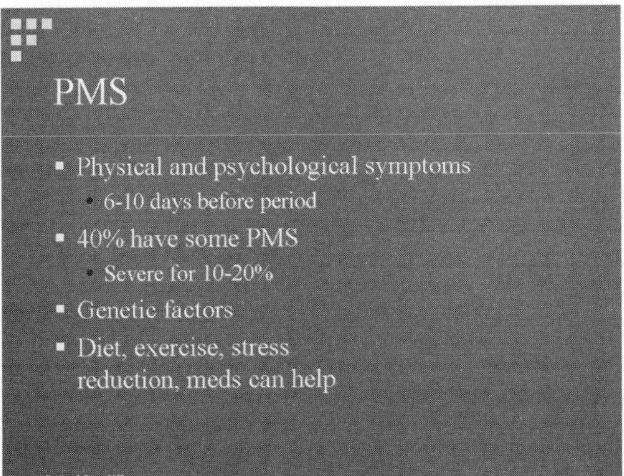

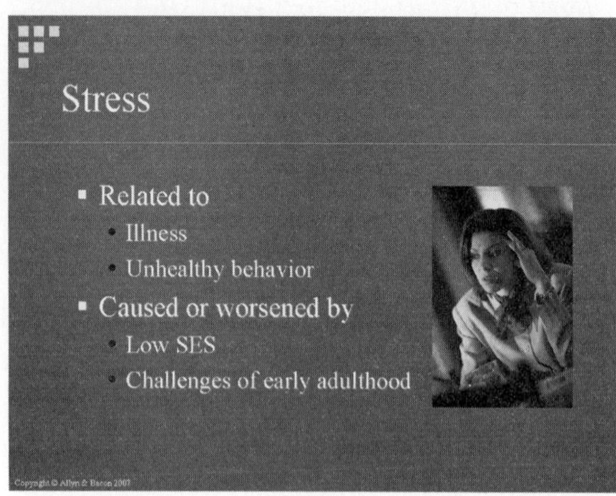
Stress
Related to
Illness
Unhealthy behavior
Caused or worsened by
Low SES
Challenges of early adulthood

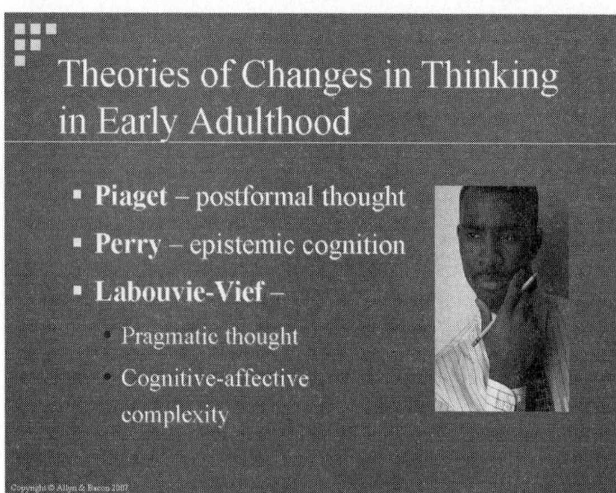
Theories of Changes in Thinking in Early Adulthood
Piaget – postformal thought
Perry – epistemic cognition
Labouvie-Vief –
Pragmatic thought
Cognitive-affective complexity

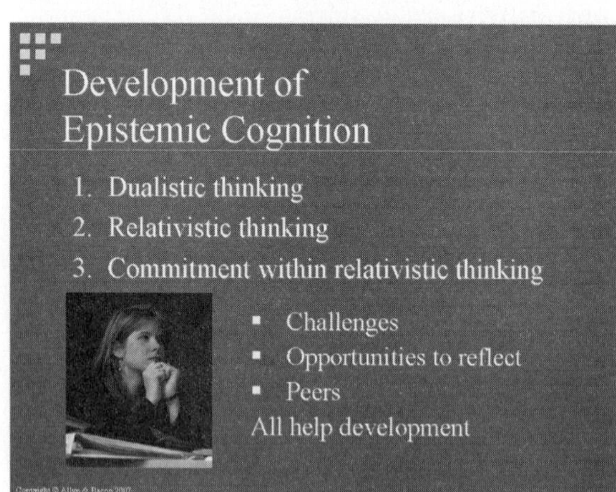
Development of Epistemic Cognition
1. Dualistic thinking
2. Relativistic thinking
3. Commitment within relativistic thinking
Challenges
Opportunities to reflect
Peers
All help development

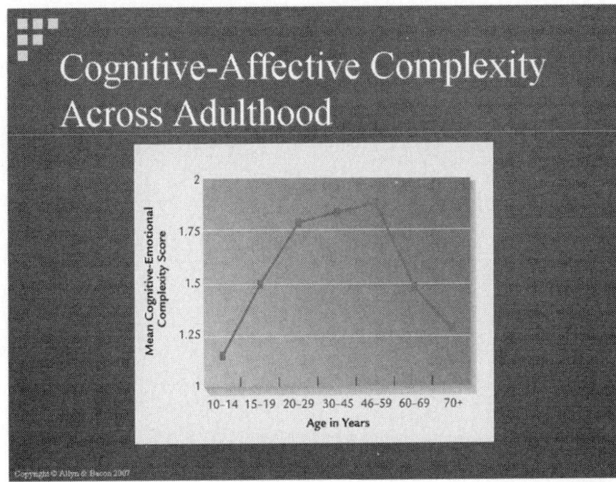
Cognitive-Affective Complexity Across Adulthood
Mean Cognitive-Emotional Complexity Score
2
1.75
1.5
1.25
1
10-14 15-19 20-29 30-45 46-59 60-69 70+
Age in Years
Copyright © Allyn & Bacon 2007

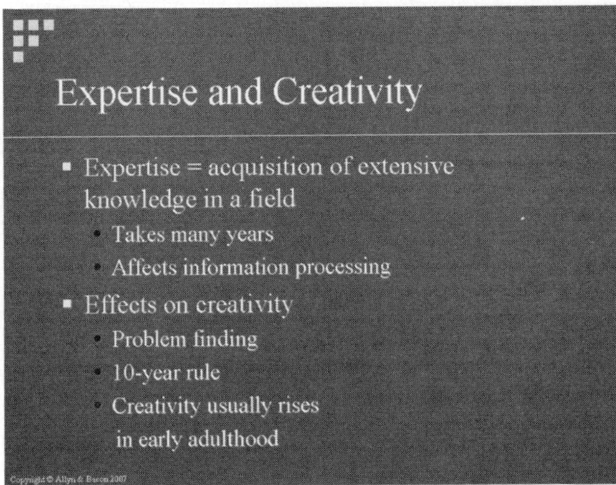
Expertise and Creativity
Expertise = acquisition of extensive knowledge in a field
Takes many years
Affects information processing
Effects on creativity
Problem finding
10-year rule
Creativity usually rises in early adulthood
Copyright © Allyn & Bacon 2007

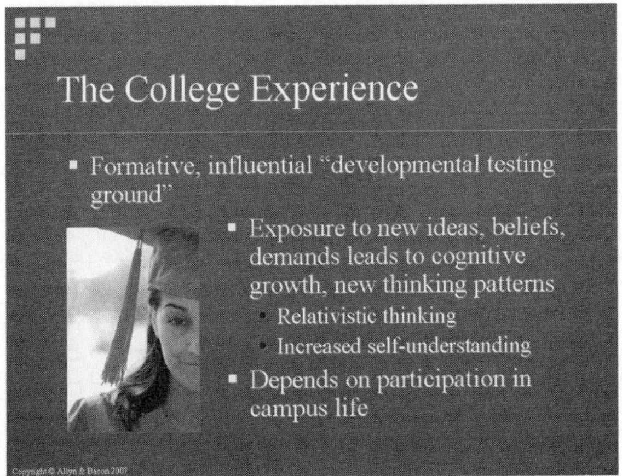
The College Experience
Formative, influential "developmental testing ground"
Exposure to new ideas, beliefs, demands leads to cognitive growth, new thinking patterns
Relativistic thinking
Increased self-understanding
Depends on participation in campus life
Copyright © Allyn & Bacon 2007

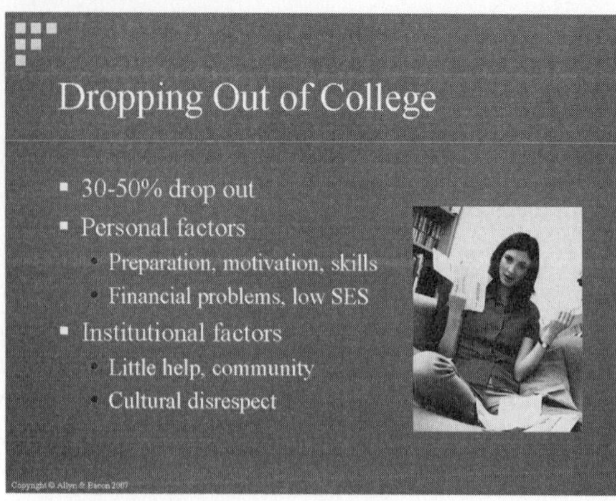
Dropping Out of College
30-50% drop out
Personal factors
Preparation, motivation, skills
Financial problems, low SES
Institutional factors
Little help, community
Cultural disrespect

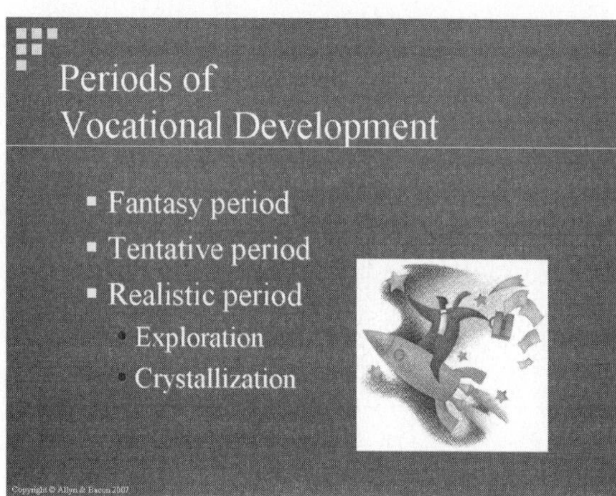
Periods of Vocational Development
Fantasy period
Tentative period
Realistic period
Exploration
Crystallization

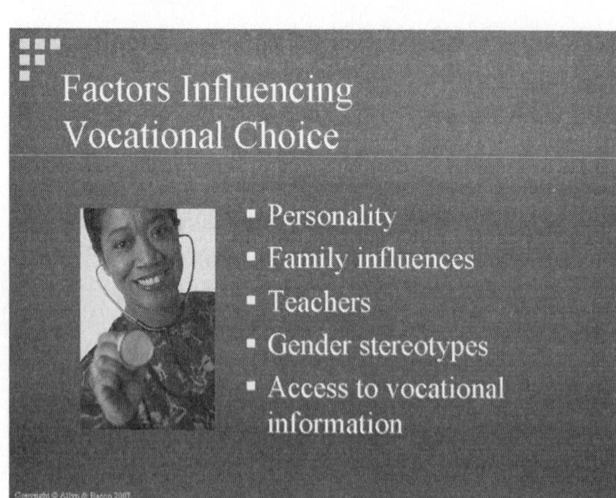
Factors Influencing Vocational Choice
Personality
Family influences
Teachers
Gender stereotypes
Access to vocational information

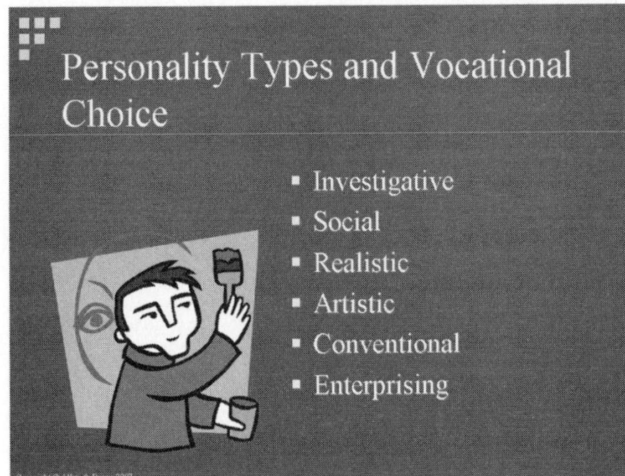
Personality Types and Vocational Choice
Investigative
Social
Realistic
Artistic
Conventional
Enterprising
Copyright © Allyn & Bacon 2007

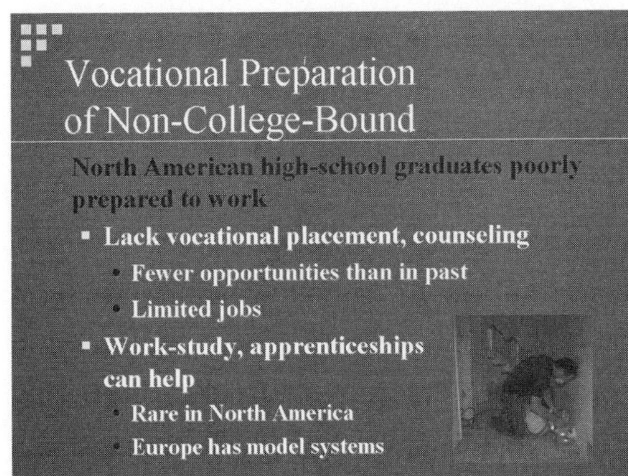
Vocational Preparation of Non-College-Bound
North American high-school graduates poorly prepared to work
Lack vocational placement, counseling
Fewer opportunities than in past
Limited jobs
Work-study, apprenticeships can help
Rare in North America
Europe has model systems
Copyright © Allyn & Bacon 2007

CHAPTER 14
EMOTIONAL AND SOCIAL DEVELOPMENT IN EARLY ADULTHOOD

CHAPTER-AT-A-GLANCE

Chapter Outline	Instruction Ideas	Supplements
Erikson's Theory: Intimacy versus Isolation pp. 366–367	Learning Objective 14.1	Test Bank Item 1 Videos: *Exploring Lifespan Development in Action* and *A Window on Lifespan Development* Please contact your Allyn and Bacon publisher's representative for a wide range of video offerings available to adopters.
Other Theories of Adult Psychosocial Development pp. 367–369 Levinson's Seasons of Life • Vaillant's Adaptation to Life • Limitations of Levinson's and Vaillant's Theories • The Social Clock	Learning Objectives 14.2–14.3 Learning Activities 14.1–14.2 Ask Yourself p. 369	Test Bank Items 2–18
Close Relationships pp. 370–374 Romantic Love • Friendships • Loneliness	Learning Objectives 14.4–14.7 Lecture Enhancement 14.1 Learning Activity 14.3 Ask Yourself p. 374	Transparency 163 Test Bank Items 19–48
The Family Life Cycle pp. 374–381 Leaving Home • Joining of Families in Marriage • Parenthood	Learning Objective 14.8 Lecture Enhancement 14.2 Learning Activities 14.4–14.7 Ask Yourself p. 381	Transparency 171 Test Bank Items 49–82
The Diversity of Adult Lifestyles pp. 381–386 Singlehood • Cohabitation • Childlessness • Divorce and Remarriage • Variant Styles of Parenthood	Learning Objectives 14.9–14.11 Lecture Enhancement 14.3 Learning Activities 14.8–14.9 Ask Yourself p. 386	Transparency 173 Test Bank Items 83–106
Career Development pp. 386–389 Establishing a Career • Women and Ethnic Minorities • Combining Work and Family	Learning Objective 14.12 Lecture Enhancement 14.4 Learning Activity 14.10 Ask Yourself p. 389	Test Bank Items 107–115

BRIEF CHAPTER SUMMARY

Erikson described the psychological conflict of early adulthood as intimacy versus isolation. In his view, successful resolution of this conflict prepares the individual for the middle adulthood stage, which focuses on generativity, or caring for the next generation and helping to improve society. Levinson suggested that development consists of a series of qualitatively distinct "seasons" in which individuals revise their life structure to meet changing needs. Vaillant refined Erikson's stages, confirming Erikson's stages but filling in the gaps between them.

Although societal expectations have become less rigid, conformity to or departure from the social clock—age-graded expectations for major life events—can be a major source of personality change in adulthood. Following a social clock fosters confidence in young adults, whereas deviating from it can lead to psychological distress.

Although young adults are especially concerned with romantic love and the establishment of an intimate tie with another person, they also satisfy the need for intimacy through relationships with friends, siblings, and co-workers that involve mutual commitment. Romantic partners tend to resemble one another in age, ethnicity, SES, religion, and various personal and physical attributes. Loneliness, as long as it is not overwhelming, can be a motivating factor in healthy personality development.

The family life cycle is a sequence of phases characterizing the development of most families around the world, but wide variation exists in the sequence and timing of these phases. Departure from the parental home is a major step toward assuming adult responsibilities, although nearly half of young adults return home for a brief time after initial leaving. Young adults also delay marriage more today than a half-century ago. Same-sex marriages are recognized in Canada and several other countries, and in the state of Massachusetts; evidence suggests that the factors contributing to happiness for cohabiting same-sex couples are similar to those in other-sex marriages. Women's workplace participation affects both traditional and egalitarian marriages in defining marital roles, with most couplings arriving at a form of marriage somewhere between traditional and egalitarian. Modern couples are having fewer children and postponing parenthood longer than in past generations. Marriages that are gratifying and supportive tend to remain so after childbirth, while troubled marriages usually become more distressed. Parent education programs can help parents clarify their child-rearing values and use more effective strategies.

Today, more adults are single than in the past, and cohabitation without marriage is much more common. The number of couples who choose to remain childless has risen as well. Although childlessness may be distressing when it is involuntary, voluntarily childless adults are just as satisfied with their lives as are parents who have good relationships with their children. Nearly half of all marriages end in divorce, and many people later remarry, often creating blended families that pose their own unique challenges. Never-married parenthood has increased and, for low-SES women, often increases financial hardship. Families headed by homosexuals generally fare well, except for difficulties related to living in an unsupportive society.

Men's career paths are usually continuous, while women's are often discontinuous because of child rearing and other family demands. Although women and ethnic minorities have entered nearly all professions, they still tend to be concentrated in occupations that are less well-paid and that offer little opportunity for advancement. Couples in dual-earner marriages often face complex career decisions and challenges in meeting both work and family responsibilities. When dual-earner couples cooperate to surmount difficulties, they benefit from higher earnings, a better standard of living, and women's self-fulfillment and improved well-being.

LEARNING OBJECTIVES

After reading this chapter, you should be able to:

14.1 Describe Erikson's stage of intimacy versus isolation, noting personality changes that take place during early adulthood. (pp. 366–367)

14.2 Summarize Levinson's and Vaillant's psychosocial theories of adult personality development, including how they apply to both men's and women's lives and their limitations. (pp. 367–369)

14.3 Describe the social clock and how it affects personality in adulthood. (p. 369)

14.4 Discuss factors that affect mate selection, and explain the role of romantic love in young adults' quest for intimacy. (pp. 370–371)

14.5 Explain how culture influences the experience of love. (p. 371)

14.6 Cite characteristics of adult friendships and sibling relationships, including differences between same-sex, other-sex, and sibling friendships. (pp. 371–373)

14.7 Cite factors that influence loneliness, and explain the role of loneliness in adult development. (pp. 373–374)

14.8 Trace phases of the family life cycle that are prominent in early adulthood, noting factors that influence these phases. (pp. 374–381)

14.9 Discuss the diversity of adult lifestyles, focusing on singlehood, cohabitation, and childlessness. (pp. 381–383)

14.10 Discuss today's high rates of divorce and remarriage, and cite factors that contribute to them. (pp. 383–384)

14.11 Summarize challenges associated with variant styles of parenthood, including stepparents, never-married parents, and gay and lesbian parents. (pp. 384–386)

14.12 Describe patterns of career development, and cite difficulties faced by women, ethnic minorities, and couples seeking to combine work and family. (pp. 386–389)

LECTURE OUTLINE

I. ERIKSON'S THEORY: INTIMACY VERSUS ISOLATION (pp. 366–367)
   A. According to Erikson, the psychological conflict of early adulthood is **intimacy versus isolation**, reflected in the young person's thoughts and feelings about making a permanent commitment to an intimate partner.
      1. Intimacy requires that young adults redefine their identity to include both partners' values and interests at a time when they are still grappling with identity issues.
      2. Maturity involves balancing the desire for self-determination with the desire for intimacy.
   B. A secure identity fosters attainment of intimacy.
      1. For both men and women, identity achievement is positively correlated with fidelity and love, while identity moratorium—a state of searching prior to commitment—is negatively associated with fidelity and love.
      2. For women, coordination of identity and intimacy is more complex than for men, because women are more likely to consider the impact of their personal goals on important relationships.
   C. Erikson believed that successful resolution of intimacy versus isolation prepares the individual for the middle adulthood stage, which focuses on *generativity*—caring for the next generation and helping to improve society.

II. OTHER THEORIES OF ADULT PSYCHOSOCIAL DEVELOPMENT (pp. 367–369)
   A. Levinson's Seasons of Life (pp. 367–368)
      1. Through in-depth biographical interviews with men and women age 35 to 45, Daniel Levinson identified a common path of change within which men and women approach developmental tasks in somewhat different ways.
      2. Like Erikson, Levinson saw development as a sequence of qualitatively distinct eras (stages or seasons), in each of which biological and social forces introduce new psychological challenges.
      3. A key concept in Levinson's theory is the **life structure**, the underlying design of a person's life, consisting of relationships with significant individuals, groups, and institutions.
      4. Men's and women's accounts of their lives confirm Levinson's description of the life course and his view of early adulthood as a stage that can bring rich satisfaction in love, sexuality, family life, occupational advancement, and realization of life goals, but that also involves serious life decisions at a time when many people do not yet have enough experience to choose wisely.
      5. Dreams and Mentors (pp. 367–368)
         a. Levinson found that during the early adult transition (age 17 to 22), most people construct a *dream*—an image of themselves in the adult world that guides their decision making.
            (1) For men, the dream usually has an individualistic focus, with significant others seen in supporting roles.

LEARNING ACTIVITIES

LEARNING ACTIVITY 14.1
True or False: Theories of Adult Psychosocial Development (pp. 366–369)

Present the following exercise to students as a quiz or in-class activity:

Directions: Read each of the following statements and indicate whether it is *True (T)* or *False (F).*

Statements:

_____ 1. Erikson's theory has had little impact on the study of adult personality development.
_____ 2. Research confirms that a secure identity fosters attainment of intimacy.
_____ 3. People with a sense of isolation tend to compete rather than cooperate, are not accepting of differences, and are easily threatened when others get too close.
_____ 4. In Levinson's theory, the life structure has little to do with one's happiness and psychological well-being.
_____ 5. Most career-oriented women display "split dreams" in which both marriage and career are prominent.
_____ 6. "Settling down" accurately describes women's experiences during their thirties.
_____ 7. Both Vaillant and Levinson agree that quality of relationships with important people shape the life course.
_____ 8. According to Vaillant, during their forties, men focus on career consolidation and individual achievement.
_____ 9. Few societies have time tables for accomplishing major developmental tasks.
_____ 10. A major source of personality change in adulthood is conformity to or departure from the social clock.

Answers:

1. F
2. T
3. T
4. F
5. T
6. F
7. T
8. F
9. F
10. T

LEARNING ACTIVITY 14.2
Exploring Perceived Developmental Tasks of Young Adulthood (pp. 366–369)

Ask students to list the major life events that they anticipate occurring in their own lives in their twenties and thirties. Nontraditional students can list events they have already experienced. Next, students should pose the same question to two or three friends and record their answers. In class, discuss students' lists. How well do they correspond to the developmental tasks proposed by Erikson, Levinson, and Vaillant? Is there evidence for a "feminine" social clock and a "masculine" social clock? Explain.

LEARNING ACTIVITY 14.3
Preferred Characteristics of Romantic Partners Found in Newspaper or Internet Advertisements (p. 370)

Students can examine preferred characteristics of romantic partners by analyzing personal advertisements (ads) in the newspaper or on the Internet. If the selected newspaper or Internet site has a large number of personal ads, students can systematically sample the ads by reading every fifth, tenth, or another selected number of ads. Students should compare the preferred characteristics of partners in the ads with research on mate selection. Discussion questions might include: What characteristics do women seek in a partner? What characteristics do men seek? Are there age differences in preferred characteristics? What characteristics do men and women reveal about themselves? Do people seek partners like themselves? Are people seeking partners of a similar age? Are there gender differences in preferred age for partners? Do the advertisers seem to be seeking long-term or short-term relationships? Are the ads representative of the general population's preferred characteristics for romantic partners? Explain.

LEARNING ACTIVITY 14.4
Interviewing Friends or Relatives About Experiences with Leaving Home (pp. 374–375)

Have students interview three or four friends or relatives about experiences with leaving home. For example, at what age did the individual leave home? What were the circumstances surrounding the departure (for example, work, college, marriage)? Has the individual returned home since the initial departure? If so, why? Was leaving home a stressful event? Explain. Next, students should compare the answers with research in the text. Did most people leave home in their late teens and early twenties? Did timing of departure vary with the reason for leaving? Did individuals return home at least once after their initial departure?

LEARNING ACTIVITY 14.5
Completing a Marriage Contract (pp. 375–377)

To help students understand the multitude of decisions that must be made during a marriage, have them complete a marriage contract with a significant other or friend. The goal of the contract is to clearly define one another's expectations about marriage and identify areas of disagreement. Some questions to address in the contract include: Where will you live? Where will you work? If one of you is promoted, what circumstances will affect your decision to take the promotion (for example, willingness to move far away)? Do you plan to attend church? If so, what religion will you follow? Do you plan to pursue more education or vocational training? Who will be responsible for household bills? How will household chores be divided? What type of transportation will you use? Do you plan to rent or buy a house? Will finances be combined or kept separate? How will money be managed? What kind of budget will you keep? How will you spend holidays (for example, split holidays between both sides of the family)? How much time will you spend with one another's family? Do you plan to have children? If so, how many children will you have? Who will be in charge of child care? Will both parents continue to work after a baby is born? If so, who will take care of the child while you're at work? If not, who will stay home? How will you account for the difference in income if one parent stays home? What kind of discipline will you use? Will one parent be more responsible for discipline? If so, why? Where will your children go to school? Do you plan to send your children to college? If so, how will you finance college? How much time do you plan to spend together? How will you handle marital conflict? What will you do for leisure time activities? How much time will be spent with friends and co-workers? Will you have a prenuptial agreement? If so, how will it be arranged?

Once students have completed their contracts, ask them to reflect on the activity. Did they learn anything new about their partner? Were there any areas of disagreement? Did they discuss these areas as they were completing the contract? Why or why not? Was this a difficult activity to complete? Would students use a contract like this? Explain.

LEARNING ACTIVITY 14.6
Examining Popular Books on Parenting (pp. 377, 379–381)

Ask students to visit a local library or bookstore and examine two popular books on parenting. As they explore the books, students should respond to the following questions: What parenting topics are available (for example, balancing work and family, changes in roles after the arrival of a new baby, parent education, single parenthood, divorce)? Is the advice presented in the books supported by research in the text? Why or why not?

LEARNING ACTIVITY 14.7
Inviting a Guest Speaker or Panel to Discuss Issues of Domestic Violence (pp. 378–379)

Contact a community mental health center or domestic violence shelter and invite a counselor, caseworker, or panel of professionals to speak to your class about services available to victims and perpetrators of domestic violence. Students should prepare a list of questions for the speaker(s), such as: What is domestic violence? How often does it occur? What are characteristics of abusers and their victims? What services are available to men who are victims of domestic violence? Are services directed toward the family unit or do victims receive separate services from perpetrators? What are some policies about pressing charges against abusers?

LEARNING ACTIVITY 14.8
Speaking to Young Adults About Cohabitation (pp. 382–383)

Tell students to consider the following scenario:

> Your close friends, Alex and Meredith, have been dating for nearly two years. They have talked about marriage for several months but wonder if they should test their relationship and get used to living together first. The couple has come to you for advice. Using research in the text to support your answer, what would you tell Alex and Meredith about cohabitation? Based on the available research, would you recommend that the couple proceed with a trial marriage? Why or why not?

LEARNING ACTIVITY 14.9
Conducting a Mock Seminar for Stepparents and Their Spouses (pp. 384–385)

Ask students to pretend they must speak at a seminar for new stepparents and their partners. Using research from this chapter and Chapter 10 as a guide, what information would students include in the seminar? For example, what topics should be addressed? How might blended families work together to make a smooth transition? What conflicts might arise between stepparents and parents, and between stepparents and children, and how should they be dealt with? How can stepparents develop a warm bond with their stepchildren? Where can family members go to get help if problems persist?

LEARNING ACTIVITY 14.10
Families and Work Institute (pp. 386–388)

The Families and Work Institute is a nonprofit organization that conducts research on the relationship between work and family. Have students review the website *http://www.familiesandwork.org* and answer the following questions: What is the Fatherhood Project? Click on *Overwork in America: When the Way We Work Becomes Too Much*. Why was this study conducted? Using information presented in the text, explain how the results of this study might benefit employed mothers. How might they influence quality of parenting? How could the results be used to support public policy for equal pay and equal employment opportunities for women?

ASK YOURSELF . . .

REVIEW: According to Levinson, how do the life structures of men and women differ? (pp. 367–368)

The life structure is the underlying design of a person's life, consisting of relationships with significant others—individuals, groups, and institutions. During the adult transition, most young adults construct a *dream,* an image of themselves in the adult world that guides their decision making. For men, the dream usually is individualistic, emphasizing an independent achiever in an occupational role, with significant others supporting their goals. In contrast, most career-oriented women display "split dreams" in which both marriage and career are prominent. Also, women's dreams tend to define the self in terms of relationships with husband, children, and colleagues.

To create the culminating life structure of early adulthood, men usually "settle down" by focusing on certain relationships and aspirations while setting others aside. They try to establish a stable niche in society that is consistent with their values. In contrast, women are less likely to "settle down" in their thirties, when many are adding an occupational or relationship commitment to their lives. Not until middle age do many women attain the stability typical of men in their thirties—reaching career maturity and taking on more authority in the community.

APPLY: Using the concept of the social clock, explain Sharese's conflicted feelings about marrying Ernie after she finished graduate school. (p. 369)

The *social clock* refers to age-graded expectations for major life events, such as beginning a first job, getting married, the birth of a first child, buying a home, and retiring. All societies have such timetables. Being on time or off time can profoundly affect self-esteem because adults (like children and adolescents) make social comparisons, measuring the their own progress against that of their agemates.

When Sharese compares her life with the lives of her friends Heather and Christy, she wonders if it is possible for a woman to have both family and career. Realizing that she is not yet established either in her career or in a marriage, Sharese wonders if she is off time in her development. She feels conflicted about getting married because, on the one hand, she fears losing her freedom, and yet, having achieved independence from her family, she still wants and needs the close, affectionate ties that marriage and family can bring.

REFLECT: Describe your early adulthood dream (see page 367). Then ask a friend or classmate of the other gender to describe his or her dream and compare the two. Are they consistent with Levinson's findings? (pp. 367–368)

This is an open-ended question with no right or wrong answer.

REVIEW: Describe gender differences in traits usually desired in a long-term partner. What findings indicate that *both* biological and social forces contribute to those differences? (p. 370)

In choosing a long-term partner, men and women differ in the importance placed on certain characteristics. In research carried out in diverse industrialized and developing countries, women assign greater weight to intelligence, ambition, financial status, and moral character, whereas men place more emphasis on physical attractiveness and domestic skills. In addition, women prefer a same-age or slightly older partner, men a younger partner.

Evolutionary theory helps explain these differences. Because their capacity to reproduce is limited, women seek a mate with traits such as earning power and emotional commitment that will help ensure children's survival and well-being. In contrast, men look for a mate with traits that signal youth, health, sexual pleasure, and ability to give birth and care for offspring. As further evidence for this difference, men often want a relationship to move more quickly toward physical intimacy, while women typically prefer to take the time to achieve psychological intimacy first.

From an alternative, social learning perspective, gender roles profoundly influence criteria for mate selection. Beginning in childhood, men learn to be assertive and independent—behaviors they will need for success in the work world. Women acquire nurturant behaviors, which facilitate caregiving. Then each sex learns to value traits in the other that fit with a traditional division of labor. In support of this theory, in cultures and in younger generations characterized by greater gender equity, men and women are more alike in their mate preferences. For example, men may place more emphasis on their mate's financial prospects and less on her domestic skills, and both sexes care somewhat less about their mate's age relative to their own. Instead, they place a high value on relationship satisfaction.

APPLY: After dating for two years, Mindy and Graham reported greater love and relationship satisfaction than during their first few months of dating. What features of communication probably deepened their bond, and why is it likely to endure? (pp. 370–371)

As romantic involvements are transformed from relationships based on passionate love to ones based on companionate love, *commitment* may be the aspect of love that determines whether a relationship survives. The ability to communicate commitment—through warmth, sensitivity, empathy, caring, acceptance, and respect—probably played a large role in the deepening of Mindy and Graham's bond. Intimate partners who consistently express their commitment report higher-quality and longer-lasting relationships. An important feature of such couples' communication is constructive conflict resolution—directly expressing wishes and needs, listening patiently, asking for clarification, compromising, accepting responsibility, and avoiding the escalation of negative interaction sparked by criticism, contempt, defensiveness, and stonewalling. The way Graham handles conflict is particularly important, because men tend to be less skilled than women at negotiating it.

REFLECT: Do you have a nonromantic, close other-sex friendship? If so, how has it enhanced your emotional and social development? (pp. 371, 373)

This is an open-ended question with no right or wrong answer.

REVIEW: What strategies can couples use to ease the transition to a first birth? How about a second birth? (pp. 379–380)

The early weeks after a baby enters the family are full of profound changes: new caregiving and household responsibilities, disrupted sleep, less time for the couple's relationship, and added financial responsibilities. In response to these demands, the roles of husband and wife usually become more traditional, even for couples who are committed to gender equality and accustomed to sharing household tasks. Postponing childbearing until the late twenties or thirties eases the transition to parenthood by giving couples time to first pursue occupational goals and gain life experience. Under these circumstances, men are more enthusiastic about becoming fathers and therefore more willing to participate actively. And women whose careers are under way are more likely to encourage their husbands to share housework and child care.

A second birth typically requires that fathers take an even more active role in parenting—by caring for the firstborn while the mother is recuperating and by sharing in the high demands of tending to both a baby and a young child. Consequently, well-functioning families with a newborn second child typically show a pulling back from the traditional division of responsibilities that occurred after the first birth. Fathers' willingness to put greater emphasis on the parenting role is strongly linked to mothers' adjustment after the arrival of a second baby.

Generous, paid employment leave—less available in the United States than in most other industrialized nations—is crucial for parents of newborns, but new mothers often do not use unpaid work leave because they cannot afford the income loss, while new fathers tend to take little or none. Favorable workplace policies can help keep a couple's stress at a manageable level after the birth of a baby.

APPLY: After her wedding, Sharese was convinced she had made a mistake. Cite factors that sustained her marriage and led it to become especially happy. (pp. 376–377)

Sharese and Ernie married after their education was complete. By delaying marriage, each had developed a secure enough identity and sufficient independence to be ready to create a mature marital bond. They also postponed having children until their careers were under way and they had built a sense of togetherness that allowed each to thrive as an individual. Waiting to bear children gives couples time to pursue occupational goals and gain life experience. Under these circumstances, men are more enthusiastic about becoming fathers and therefore more willing to participate actively. Women whose careers are underway are more likely to encourage their husbands to share housework and child care. Shared parenting leads to marital satisfaction.

Patience, caring, shared values, enjoyment of each other's company, and good conflict resolution skills also contributed to their compatibility. Sharese and Ernie seem to be working toward an egalitarian marriage in which husband and wife relate as equals.

REFLECT: Do you live with your parents or on your own? What factors contributed to your current living arrangements? If you live independently, has your relationship with your parents changed in ways that match the findings of research? (pp. 374–375)

This is an open-ended question with no right or wrong answer.

REVIEW: Why is never-married single parenthood especially high among African Americans? What conditions affect parent and child well-being in these families? (p. 385)

African-American women postpone marriage more and childbirth less than women in other U.S. ethnic groups. Job loss, persisting unemployment, and consequent inability of many black men to support a family have contributed to the postponement of marriage and the resulting greater prevalence of African-American never-married, single-mother families.

Never-married black mothers may get help with child rearing from their extended family, especially their own mothers and sometimes male relatives, and about one-third marry within nine years after birth of the first child. But for low-SES women, never-married parenthood generally increases financial hardship. Children of never-married mothers who lack involvement of a father achieve less well in school and display more antisocial behavior than children in low-SES, first-marriage families—problems that also make life more difficult for mothers. When a mother marries an antisocial father, her child is at greater risk for conduct problems than if she had reared the child alone. Strengthening social support, education, and employment opportunities for low-SES parents would greatly enhance the well-being of unmarried mothers and their children.

APPLY: After dating for a year, Wanda and Scott decided to live together. Their parents worried that cohabitation would reduce Wanda and Scott's chances for a successful marriage. Is this fear justified? Why or why not? (pp. 382–383)

Wanda and Scott's parents' concerns are justified. For young people who are not ready for marriage, as may be the case with Wanda and Scott, cohabitation combines the rewards of a close relationship with the opportunity to limit their degree of commitment. North American couples who cohabit before they are engaged to be married are more prone to divorce than couples who wait to live together until after they have made a commitment to each other—an association that is less strong or not present in Western European nations, where cohabitation is thoroughly integrated into society and is not necessarily associated with less conventional values, as it is in North America. Also, formerly cohabiting married couples tend to have poorer-quality relationships, perhaps because the open-ended quality of the cohabiting relationship reduces their motivation to develop effective conflict-resolution skills.

REFLECT: Do your own experiences or those of your friends match research findings on cohabitation, singlehood, never-married parents, or gay and lesbian parents? Select one instance and discuss. (pp. 381–386)

This is an open-ended question with no right or wrong answer.

REVIEW: Why do professionally accomplished women, especially those who are members of economically disadvantaged minorities, typically display high self-efficacy? (pp. 387–388)

Women who pursue nontraditional careers usually have "masculine" traits—high achievement orientation, self-reliance, and belief that their efforts will result in success. Ethnic minority women face special challenges in realizing their career potential because they must surmount combined gender and racial discrimination. Those who succeed often display unusually high self-efficacy, attacking problems head-on despite encountering repeated obstacles to achievement. In an interview study of African-American women who had become leaders in diverse fields, all reported intense persistence, fueled by supportive relationships with other women, including teachers, colleagues, and friends who countered their sense of professional isolation. Many described their mothers as inspiring role models who had set high standards for them. Others mentioned support from their African-American communities, stating that a deep sense of connection to their people had empowered them.

APPLY: Heather climbed the career ladder of her company quickly, reaching a top-level executive position by her early thirties. In contrast, Sharese and Christy did not attain managerial roles in early adulthood. What factors account for this disparity in career progress? (pp. 387–388)

Sharese and Christy had *discontinuous career paths*—ones that were interrupted or deferred by childbearing and child rearing. Their career planning was necessarily short-term and subject to considerable change. Sharese, and most likely Christy, experienced a sense of role overload. Both faced the challenge of combining work and family. Work–family role conflict negatively affects quality of life in both work and home settings.

Heather, in contrast, is unattached and free to pursue the full range of career options before her. Her career path has been continuous—beginning after completion of her formal education and most likely to end at retirement. She has not had to interrupt her career to bear and raise children, and she has not faced the demands of balancing career and family. For these reasons, singlehood is strongly associated with career achievement in women.

REFLECT: Contact a major employer in your area and ask what policies it has to assist workers in combining work and family roles. What improvements would you suggest? Why are family-friendly policies "win-win" situations for both workers and employers? (p. 388)

This is an open-ended question with no right or wrong answer.

SUGGESTED STUDENT READINGS

Church, E. (2004). *Understanding stepmothers: Women share their struggles, successes, and insights.* Tornoto: HarperCollins. Presents an extensive overview of research on stepmothers, including the rewards, challenges, and diverse experiences of women who have encountered stepparenthood. An excellent resource for students, teachers, parents, and anyone interested in working with children and families.

Jacobs, J. A., & Gerson, K. (2005). *The time divide: Work, family, and gender inequality.* Cambridge, MA: Harvard University Press. Examines the multitude of benefits and challenges facing dual-earner families. The authors also explore how public policies in the United States and other industrialized nations affect family and work, including gender inequalities in the workplace.

McCarthy, B., & McCarthy, E. J. (2004). *Getting it right the first time.* New York: Brunner-Routledge. Using up-to-date research, detailed case studies, and applied activities, this book examines the most important ingredients for building a successful marriage. The authors also present common marital myths, explain why the early years are so critical, and provide strategies for promoting respect, trust, and intimacy.

TRANSPARENCIES

T-163 Changes in Loneliness Over the Lifespan
Figure 14.1 (p. 374)

T-171 Average Hours Per Week of Housework Reported by Men and Women in Four Nations
Figure 14.2 (p. 376)

T-173 Generational Increase in First Conjugal Unions Beginning as Cohabitations in the United States and Canada
Figure 14.5 (p. 382)

MEDIA MATERIALS

EXPLORING LIFESPAN DEVELOPMENT IN ACTION

Early Adulthood

This section opens with 24-year-old Elizabeth and 25-year-old Joel discussing whether they have truly reached adulthood. Elizabeth and Joel are recent college graduates and are both teachers of young children. Notice how they feel more mature and capable than they did as adolescents but still have not yet fully assumed adult responsibilities. They discuss the transition to adulthood, including how they will know when they reach this milestone.

Katie and Pete, both juniors in college, discuss events leading up to and following Katie's diagnosis of Hodgkin's disease, including changes in Katie's activity level, the impact of her illness and treatment on their relationship, and their hopes and fears for the future. Pete credits Katie's positive attitude with not only contributing to her favorable recovery but also giving him the strength to support her throughout the illness and treatment. At a time of life when most young people are experiencing health and vitality, Katie and Pete illustrate how a serious illness can exert a powerful impact on the life structure.

Brad, a sales representative for a large textbook publishing company, and Julie, marketing and community relations director for a large health care facility, illustrate cognitive and vocational development in young adulthood. Brad notes the importance of practical know-how and experience, time management, and personal relationships with customers. He discusses the influence on his career progress of his parents and important mentors at the company. He also describes his dream of adulthood. Over the next couple of years, some of Brad's dream is realized, and he discusses the challenges that have accompanied his career advancement. Currently a senior marketing manager, Brad shares his desire to serve as a mentor for other company employees. Although Julie had few mentors, she reports other on-the-job supports for learning. She emphasizes the importance of business know-how and communications skills for success.

For most young people, the quest for intimacy leads to marriage. Sarah and Dennis describe their extended courtship, strong rapport with each other, and parental models of a happy, lasting marriage. Matthew and Grant, two gay men who live in a small midwestern town, also had a long courtship and recently celebrated their union. Strong communication serves as the foundation for their relationship. Both couples discuss how they have worked out a household division of labor.

Bill, a custodial parent of two sons, describes the pain of his divorce; why he took custody of Dylan and Jeremy; and his efforts to develop a career that will offer Jeremy, who is severely disabled with cerebral palsy, a secure future.

Deb and Ron represent the dual-earner marriage, the dominant family form today. The Observation Program depicts their busy schedule, the role of social supports in the workplace and extended family, and the challenges and rewards of combining career with parenthood.

A WINDOW ON LIFESPAN DEVELOPMENT

Identity and Dreams: Casey, Age 22

Casey discusses the development of her identity, people who have influenced it, and her dreams for the future. As she describes her goals, notice how she incorporates aspects of her identity into her future plans. For instance, Casey has aspirations to establish a career prior to starting a family. As a result, she has decided to go to graduate school and enter the field of gerontology before settling down. Casey also discusses the importance of lasting friendships as she faces the challenges of emerging adulthood.

Mentoring in the Workplace: Julie, Age 38

When she changed fields, Julie found few mentors within her own company. She describes her search for mentors through networking and membership in professional organizations.

A Dual-Earner Marriage: Challenges and Rewards: Deb and Ron

Deb and Ron describe the rewards and challenges of being in a dual-earner family. Despite their hectic lifestyle, they find gratification in watching their children grow and in succeeding in the struggle together.

VIDEOTAPES AND DVDs

And Baby Makes Two: Single Motherhood (1998, Films Media Group, 29 min.). This program examines the effects on society as a growing number of women choose to have and rear their children as single parents. The program looks at the cultural costs of this trend toward a fatherless society and considers the responsibility we all share for helping children grow into confident and responsible adults.

The Changing Family and Its Implications: T. Berry Brazelton (1988, Films Media Group, 50 min.). In this program, T. Berry Brazelton talks with Bill Moyers about the changing American family, with a special focus on the challenges faced by working parents.

The Child in the Family (2004, Magna Systems, 29 min.). Through interviews with parents and video profiles, this program explores the roles of parents and the functions the family serves for children in today's society, as well as how these roles and functions have changed over time. It considers the diversity of family types in today's world and examines stresses within the family and the importance of parenting styles.

Daddy & Me: A Father's Role (2001, Aquarius Health Care Media, 27 min.). This program addresses the significant role of a father in a child's life, as seen through the eyes of both children and adults. Noting that 27 million children in America currently live apart from their fathers, the program considers the issue of father absence and its effects on individuals and society. It offers advice from experts, including those from the National Center on Fathering, on the father's role in the family.

Dear Mom and Dad, I'm Gay (1993, Films Media Group, 28 min.). In this specially adapted Phil Donahue program, gay teens and their parents discuss how parents react when they learn that they have a homosexual child, with scenarios ranging from acceptance to anger.

Disappearance of the Father (1996, Concept Media, 28 min.). This program focuses on the reasons many noncustodial fathers drop out of their children's lives and on the detrimental effects this has on children and society as a whole. The program also examines the role of stepfathers in children's lives.

Early Adulthood: Love, Marriage, and Divorce (1999, Insight Media, 29 min.). This program examines the issues that young adults face as they choose a mate and prepare for the commitment of marriage. The program looks at various types of relationships and discusses the high prevalence of divorce.

Early Adulthood: Parenthood (1999, Magna Systems, 29 min.). This program looks at how young adults adjust to the new responsibilities that parenthood brings. It explores some common myths and misconceptions about parenting and covers issues of concern to all parents, including step, foster, and adoptive parents. Finally, the program describes and assesses various child-rearing styles.

Ending Domestic Violence: Healing the Family (1996, Films Media Group, 28 min.). This program examines the issue of family violence through the story of a victims' rights advocate, who talks about her 18-month marriage to an abusive husband. The advocate, who is seen counseling a mother of three who is also involved in an abusive relationship, provides insight into the dynamics of domestic abuse.

Families Matter (1992, Films Media Group, 60 min.). This program with Bill Moyers examines the changes in the United States that have made it an unfriendly culture for children and families. The program, featuring both experts and parents, looks at a variety of efforts to rebuild a web of support for families.

Fatherless in America (1994, Films Media Group, 26 min.). This program examines the causes and effects of the problem of fatherless families. It also looks at some efforts that have been made to reverse the growing trend toward fatherlessness in the United States.

Florence and Robin: Lesbian Parenthood (1994, Films Media Group, 52 min.). This program explores attitudes toward lesbianism from the perspective of the difficulties faced by a lesbian couple who are trying to become parents. The program includes interviews with children of lesbian and gay couples.

Gender and Communication: She Talks, He Talks (1994, Insight Media, 22 min.). This program explores the different ways in which men and women converse. Topics include why males tend to emphasize the literal meaning of words, why women may weaken their speech patterns, and male and female motivations for asking questions.

Juggling Work and Family (2001, Films Media Group, 120 min.). In this documentary, Pulitzer Prize-winning journalist Hedrick Smith considers the implications of the workforce changes that have made dual-career couples and single parents the norm, leading to work–family conflicts that affect both children and parents. Using case studies and expert insights, the program looks at how individuals struggle to reconcile workplace expectations with family commitments.

Life with Father (1996, Concept Media, 28 min.). This program, Part 1 of the series Human Development: Importance of Fatherhood, examines the unique contribution of fathers to their children's development. David Blankenhorn discusses issues such as protection, sponsorship, and breadwinning.

Life without Father (1996, Concept Media, 28 min.) This program, Part 3 of the series Human Development: Importance of Fatherhood, addresses the emotional effects of fatherlessness, citing Judith Wallerstein's long-term study of divorced families.

Long Road Home: A Stepfamily Reaches Out (1994, Films Media Group, 46 min.). In this ABC Afterschool Special, a teenager learns the importance of family when he reluctantly drives from Los Angeles to Denver with his new stepmother. The program shows how 16-year-old Hank learns the value of family and is able to open his heart to his father again.

Men and Women: Talking Together (1993, Insight Media, 58 min.). In this program, Deborah Tannen and Robert Bly discuss gender differences in communication styles before a live audience. They explore such topics as male and female conversational rituals, the politics of shame, and the use of comforting as a power device.

Portraits in Human Sexuality: Meeting, Dating, and Maintaining Relationships (2006, Films Media Group, 35 min.). This program focuses on developmental issues in sexuality through four segments that focus in turn on children, adolescents, adults, and a couple who are persevering in their efforts to have children. The program, which contains clinically explicit language, examines the various factors that shape our perceptions of sex and reproduction, including parents, friends, sex education classes, and the media. Contains clinically explicit language.

Single Parenting: One-Parent Families (1995, Magna Systems/A United Learning Video, 29 min.). This program looks at the unique challenges facing single parents. It explores ways to minimize the negative effects on children of a divorce or a death in the family. A Facilitator's Guide is included.

Values and the Traditional Family (1994, Insight Media, 15 min.). In this program, historian Stephanie Coontz talks about the effects on the American family of domestic violence, divorce, poverty, and joblessness.

Who's Raising Our Children? (1996, Films Media Group, 29 min.). This program examines the changes in parental roles that have resulted from modern economic, social, and technological developments. Examples include dual-income families, changes in gender roles, "miracle babies" born as a result of new reproductive technologies, and the effects of family disintegration.

Women and Men Unglued: Marriage and Relationships in the 21st Century (2003, Films Media Group, 87 min.). This program looks at changes in contemporary gender relations and expectations. Through portraits and interviews, it explores the reasons that so many men and women today are choosing to remain single. Men and women talk about issues such as dating, marriage, money, parenting, romantic love, feminism, and commitment.

TEST BANK

MULTIPLE CHOICE

1) Jack and Kate work for the same law firm and have been dating for several years. As they work to coordinate aspects of identity and intimacy, they are each now confronted with the possibility of a promotion and reassignments to different cities. Which of the following is probably true?
   A) Kate is more likely to consider the impact of her personal goals on their relationship.
   B) Jack is more likely to turn down the promotion in order to maintain his relationship with Kate.
   C) Jack is more likely to struggle with the decision, while Kate will take a more problem-solving approach to make her decision.
   D) If they are unable to resolve their personal and professional relationships positively, both are at risk for identity moratorium.

   Answer: A
   Page Ref: 366
   Skill: Applied
   Objective: 14.1

2) According to Levinson's theory, each era of adult development begins with a(n) __________, which is then followed by a stable period in which individuals build a life structure.
   A) culminating life structure
   B) transition
   C) enlightenment
   D) anticlimax

   Answer: B
   Page Ref: 367
   Skill: Factual
   Objective: 14.2

3) In Levinson's theory of adult development, the underlying design of a person's life at a given time is called the
   A) ego integrity.
   B) internal map.
   C) life structure.
   D) transition.
   Answer: C
   Page Ref: 367
   Skill: Factual
   Objective: 14.2

4) According to Levinson, someone who characterizes their life as full of energy and abundance, contradiction, and stress is probably in the life structure for
   A) late childhood.
   B) early adulthood.
   C) middle adulthood.
   D) late adulthood.
   Answer: B
   Page Ref: 367
   Skill: Conceptual
   Objective: 14.2

5) When she graduated from college, Andrea imagined herself progressing through the levels in a business until she had an upper-management job. Levinson would describe this image as her
   A) dream.
   B) transition.
   C) mentor.
   D) fantasy.
   Answer: A
   Page Ref: 367
   Skill: Applied
   Objective: 14.2

6) Endia has what Levinson would characterize as "split dreams." This means that Endia
   A) has several career paths or options available to her, and is unable to decide between them.
   B) has images of herself in the adult world in which both marriage and career are prominent.
   C) is unable to decide whether her marriage, motherhood, or career should be the focus of her life.
   D) is probably identity diffused.
   Answer: B
   Page Ref: 367
   Skill: Applied
   Objective: 14.2

7) Once Andrea began working in the business world, she formed a close relationship with Muriel, who was a few years older and had worked with the company for five years. Muriel showed Andrea the ropes and, with her help, Andrea quickly received a promotion and was given more responsibility. According to Levinson, Muriel
   A) was acting out her dream.
   B) was probably going through age-30 transition.
   C) acted as a mentor to Andrea.
   D) acted inappropriately and probably jeopardized her own job.
   Answer: C
   Page Ref: 368
   Skill: Applied
   Objective: 14.2

8) Priyanka, who is single, spent her twenties building up a successful career as a clinical psychologist. According to Levinson, as she reaches the age-30 transition, she will
   A) begin to feel a loss of identity as she increasingly defines herself by her vocation rather than other personal characteristics.
   B) consider adoption or in vitro fertilization using donor sperm, in order to fulfill her increasingly strong yearning for motherhood.
   C) question whether she made the right career decision.
   D) focus on finding a life partner.

Answer: D
Page Ref: 368
Skill: Applied
Objective: 14.2

9) For which of these people is the age-30 transition most likely to be a psychological crisis?
   A) Miles, who has no romantic relationships and a boring job
   B) Roberta, a successful office manager with a good marriage
   C) Carlos, a divorced man who runs an expanding chain of stores
   D) Grace, happily married with three children but no outside job

Answer: A
Page Ref: 368
Skill: Applied
Objective: 14.2

10) According to Levinson's theory of adult psychosocial development, which individual is most likely to be in a stage of settling down and advancing?
   A) Leslie, a 30-year-old nurse
   B) Tony, a 35-year-old engineer
   C) Ida, a 33-year-old teacher
   D) Ken, a 25-year-old doctoral student

Answer: B
Page Ref: 368
Skill: Applied
Objective: 14.2

11) Nasim stayed at home with her two children for ten years before resuming her career in her early thirties. She is likely to reach career maturity
   A) at the same time that most men do.
   B) during her mid-thirties.
   C) during middle age.
   D) just before she retires.

Answer: C
Page Ref: 368
Skill: Applied
Objective: 14.2

12) The major difference between Levinson's and Vaillant's psychosocial theories of adult development is that Vaillant's theory
   A) denies a strict age-related schedule of change.
   B) focuses more on the transitions than the eras.
   C) was based primarily on research with women.
   D) is more relevant to development in other countries.

Answer: A
Page Ref: 368
Skill: Factual
Objective: 14.2

13) Both Levinson and Vaillant agree that adult psychosocial development is primarily shaped by
A) psychological changes that happen with age.
B) the quality of sustained relationships with others.
C) the kind of education and training a person has.
D) the unconscious forces laid down in childhood.
Answer: B
Page Ref: 368
Skill: Conceptual
Objective: 14.2

14) Fifty-four-year-old Abdul has become concerned about the values of the new generation and the state of our current society. He becomes a tutor and mentor for a program at a local community center that works with at-risk youth. His actions are consistent with
A) Vaillant's ego integrity stage.
B) Erikson's intimacy versus isolation stage.
C) Levinson's age-30 transition stage.
D) Vaillant's theories regarding the "keepers of meaning" and guardians of culture.
Answer: D
Page Ref: 368
Skill: Applied
Objective: 14.2

15) Dr. Therrian wants to replicate the work of Levinson and Vaillant and address some of the sampling limitations of their studies. In order to do this, she needs to
A) include a large number of people born in the first few decades of the twentieth century.
B) include a larger sample of men.
C) include more lower-SES men and women of diverse backgrounds.
D) interview the individuals later in life so that they can compare their recollections over a greater timespan.
Answer: C
Page Ref: 369
Skill: Applied
Objective: 14.2

16) Samera and Addison are a married couple in their early thirties who feel increasing pressure to buy a home and have children. This age-related expectation for what they should accomplish during this period of their lives is
A) stronger for men than for women.
B) a primary reason for divorces that occur during the age-30 transition period.
C) based on the social clock.
D) no longer applicable in today's society.
Answer: C
Page Ref: 369
Skill: Conceptual
Objective: 14.3

17) As Matthias gets older he is more sociable, independent, and intellectually effective. Matthias probably
A) followed an occupational timetable typical for men.
B) started a family earlier than the typical social clock.
C) has a lifestyle that is incongruent with the social clock expectations for a man his age.
D) neither married nor became successful in his career.
Answer: A
Page Ref: 369
Skill: Applied
Objective: 14.3

18) Aida is looking for a long-term partner. She is most likely to find a successful match
   A) with someone who is her opposite in many traits.
   B) with someone she initially met in a singles club or bar.
   C) by dating someone much younger than she is.
   D) in someone who is quite similar to herself.

   Answer: D
   Page Ref: 370
   Skill: Applied
   Objective: 14.3

19) When Sheila and Robert select their mates, research suggests that Sheila will place more weight on __________, while Robert will emphasize __________.
   A) intelligence and financial status; physical attractiveness and domestic skills
   B) health and strength; career plans and physical attractiveness
   C) physical attractiveness and moral character; intelligence and sense of humor
   D) physical attractiveness and athletic ability; moral character and manners

   Answer: A
   Page Ref: 370
   Skill: Applied
   Objective: 14.4

20) Talli finds that she is attracted to men who are intelligent, ambitious, financially secure, and have a strong moral character. According to evolutionary theory, Talli is instinctively drawn to this type of man because these traits will ensure that he can
   A) father a large number of children.
   B) help raise their children successfully.
   C) be physically healthier than other potential mates.
   D) be a satisfying sexual partner.

   Answer: B
   Page Ref: 370
   Skill: Applied
   Objective: 14.4

21) The fact that men more often desire a relationship that moves quickly to physical intimacy while women desire psychological intimacy
   A) provides further evidence for the evolutionary theory of mate selection.
   B) indicates that men and women start relationships with incompatible need fulfillment issues.
   C) provides support for the theory that men are unable to psychologically commit to a monogamous relationship.
   D) shows that gender roles influence criteria for mate selection.

   Answer: A
   Page Ref: 370
   Skill: Factual
   Objective: 14.4

22) In cultures with greater gender equity, which of the following is evidence of the social learning perspective that gender roles influence criteria for mate selection?
   A) Men are more concerned with a woman's domestic skills.
   B) Women place less emphasis on a man's financial status.
   C) Both sexes place a high value on relationship satisfaction.
   D) Men and women place a high value on sexual satisfaction.

   Answer: C
   Page Ref: 370
   Skill: Conceptual
   Objective: 14.4

23) According to Sternberg's triangular theory of love,
   A) monogamy is unlikely with this generation's increased lifespan, so most individuals are likely to have more than one long-term partner.
   B) intimacy, passion, and commitment shift in emphasis as romantic relationships develop.
   C) intimacy is strongest at the beginning of a relationship.
   D) most adults have been involved in a polygamous relationship at some time in their lives.

Answer: B
Page Ref: 370
Skill: Conceptual
Objective: 14.4

24) Viggo and Olivia communicate with each other in warm and tender ways and frequently express concern for each other's well-being. According to Sternberg, they are displaying the __________ component of love.
   A) passion
   B) commitment
   C) intimacy
   D) possession

Answer: C
Page Ref: 370
Skill: Applied
Objective: 14.4

25) Pedro and Sierra have a relationship in which the desire for sexual activity and romance is very strong. Which component of love reflects this?
   A) commitment
   B) intimacy
   C) desire
   D) passion

Answer: D
Page Ref: 370
Skill: Applied
Objective: 14.4

26) Raj has realized that he is in love with his girlfriend and wants to maintain their relationship by getting married. This is characteristic of the __________ component of love.
   A) commitment
   B) intimacy
   C) passion
   D) control

Answer: A
Page Ref: 370
Skill: Applied
Objective: 14.4

27) Paige has had a few dates with Timothy. __________ is a strong predictor of whether they will keep dating.
   A) Companionate love
   B) Passionate love
   C) Intimate love
   D) Monogamous love

Answer: B
Page Ref: 370
Skill: Applied
Objective: 14.4

28) Paige and Timothy have been dating for over a year. Their romance will most likely break up without
   A) companionate love.
   B) passionate love.
   C) intimate love.
   D) monogamous love.

Answer: A
Page Ref: 370
Skill: Applied
Objective: 14.4

29) Paige and Timothy have been married for 30 years. When asked to compare their current relationship to when they were newlyweds, they are most likely to say that
   A) their marriage has more passion than earlier.
   B) they love each other more now than they did earlier.
   C) they love each other less than they did earlier.
   D) their relationship gradually transformed from companionate to passionate.

Answer: B
Page Ref: 370
Skill: Applied
Objective: 14.4

30) Because Paige and Timothy have been married for 30 years, we can anticipate that
   A) they infrequently verbalize expressions of their love and commitment to each other.
   B) any conflicts are not addressed immediately, and stonewalling tactics are used until each of the partners is calm enough to talk about the problem.
   C) they use constructive conflict resolution to solve differences of opinion.
   D) they avoid discussions rather than negotiate conflicts communicatively.

Answer: C
Page Ref: 370
Skill: Applied
Objective: 14.4

31) Ariana developed secure attachments to her parents when she was small. Chances are high that her love relationship will be characterized in terms of
   A) jealousy, possessiveness, and control.
   B) dependency, insecurity, and sacrifice.
   C) desperation, anxiety, and fear.
   D) trust, friendship, and happiness.

Answer: D
Page Ref: 372–373
Skill: Applied
Objective: Box LS: Attachment Patterns and Adult Romantic Relationships

32) Because Asa's past relationships have been characterized by jealousy and emotional distance, he feels a great deal of mistrust for his love partners. He feels anxiety about people "getting too close" and stresses the need for independence in his relationships. Based on this information, we can conclude that Asa has a(n) __________ attachment history.
   A) resistant
   B) secure
   C) trusting
   D) avoidant

Answer: D
Page Ref: 372–373
Skill: Applied
Objective: Box LS: Attachment Patterns and Adult Romantic Relationships

83) In recent years, the number of young adults who are not living with an intimate partner has
   A) remained quite constant.
   B) increased substantially.
   C) decreased substantially.
   D) varied unpredictably.
   Answer: B
   Page Ref: 381
   Skill: Factual
   Objective: 14.9

84) Which groups of people are overrepresented among singles after age 30?
   A) women in prestigious careers and high-income ethnic minority men
   B) women in traditional career roles like teaching and nursing and men in prestigious careers
   C) men in blue-collar occupations and unemployed women
   D) men in blue-collar occupations and women in prestigious careers
   Answer: D
   Page Ref: 381–382
   Skill: Factual
   Objective: 14.9

85) __________ is one reason for the higher rate of never-married African Americans.
   A) The high unemployment rate among black men
   B) Cultural views on the unimportance of marriage
   C) Increased rates of cross-race marriages
   D) Higher numbers of black female professionals
   Answer: A
   Page Ref: 382
   Skill: Factual
   Objective: 14.9

86) Why are single men more likely to experience physical and mental health problems than single women?
   A) Women depend less on their partners for emotional support, so they can remain psychologically healthier in the absence of a relationship.
   B) They have less social support than women, who rely on their intimate same-sex friendships.
   C) Single men tend to ignore their health concerns more, whereas married men's wives help them maintain a healthier lifestyle.
   D) Single women are forced to take a greater stand against the social clock, which promotes mental and psychological strength.
   Answer: B
   Page Ref: 382
   Skill: Factual
   Objective: 14.9

87) Matt and India are involved in an intimate, sexual relationship and they share an apartment. Their relationship is referred to as
   A) noncommitted.
   B) paralegal.
   C) cohabitation.
   D) informal.
   Answer: C
   Page Ref: 382
   Skill: Applied
   Objective: 14.9

88) Which person is more likely to cohabit than get married?
A) Trevor, who is divorced
B) Tyler, who is very conservative
C) Tracy, who is very religious
D) Tia, who has had few sexual partners
Answer: A
Page Ref: 382
Skill: Applied
Objective: 14.9

89) When couples in North America live together before they get married, they are more likely to
A) feel a strong commitment.
B) own a house jointly.
C) become divorced.
D) have children.
Answer: C
Page Ref: 382
Skill: Factual
Objective: 14.9

90) One important difference between cohabiting couples and couples who are married is that cohabiters are more likely to
A) feel a strong commitment to their partners.
B) be liberal and unconventional.
C) be politically conservative and religious.
D) have warm, close ties with their parents.
Answer: B
Page Ref: 382
Skill: Conceptual
Objective: 14.9

91) Which couple is least likely to work on their relationship and more likely to experience the negative outcomes often associated with cohabitation?
A) a couple who is testing the relationship after a divorce in order to avoid a second failure
B) a same-sex couple
C) a low-SES couple
D) a couple in their twenties who sees cohabitation as an alternative to marriage
Answer: D
Page Ref: 383
Skill: Conceptual
Objective: 14.9

92) The number of couples who choose not to have any children is difficult to determine because
A) many couples actually have children from previous marriages.
B) childlessness is not always a permanent condition.
C) many deceptively tell researchers that would like to have children someday to avoid the social stigma associated with childlessness.
D) nobody has really studied this phenomenon thoroughly.
Answer: B
Page Ref: 383
Skill: Factual
Objective: 14.9

93) All of the following are frequent characteristics of individuals who are voluntarily childless EXCEPT
A) only children.
B) minimally committed to their chosen careers.
C) highly educated.
D) prestigious occupations.
Answer: B
Page Ref: 383
Skill: Conceptual
Objective: 14.9

94) Kaipo and Noelani were not able to have children due to infertility. Their overall life contentment will depend on
A) the degree to which they find compensating rewards in other areas of their lives.
B) whether they are able to adopt a child.
C) the number of friends they have who are also childless.
D) how their friends and family react to their childlessness.
Answer: A
Page Ref: 383
Skill: Applied
Objective: 14.9

95) Which of the following is a strong predictor of divorce?
A) strong religious beliefs
B) drinking or using drugs
C) having more than one child within the first three years of marriage
D) poverty
Answer: B
Page Ref: 383
Skill: Conceptual
Objective: 14.10

96) Nyree and Kyle are divorcing. Research results from following families over two decades show that
A) chances are they will eventually remarry after several years.
B) their divorce negatively influences their grandchildren's chances for divorce.
C) their children are unlikely to marry.
D) they are unlikely to end up in another long-term relationship.
Answer: B
Page Ref: 383–384
Skill: Applied
Objective: 14.10

97) The number of divorces initiated by well-educated, career-oriented women is often caused by
A) a lack of willingness to compromise at home for women who are used to giving orders on the job.
B) disagreements between husband and wife on who should take time off from work to care for children.
C) career-related social interactions for women that lead to infidelity.
D) a husband's lack of support for his wife's career.
Answer: D
Page Ref: 384
Skill: Factual
Objective: 14.10

98) Which of these individuals is likely to have the most difficult time after a divorce?
   A) Anna, who does not remarry soon after the divorce
   B) Abigail, who remarries shortly after the divorce
   C) Abe, who does not remarry soon after the divorce
   D) Adam, who remarries shortly after the divorce

Answer: C
Page Ref: 384
Skill: Applied
Objective: 14.10

99) Which of the following is a reason why many remarriages end in divorce?
   A) Divorce is seen as a more acceptable solution by those who have already been divorced once.
   B) Continued involvement of non-custodial parents in the lives of their children places additional stress on the marriage.
   C) Stepfamily situations create strong bonds among siblings.
   D) Practical matters like finances and child rearing are typically more important to one spouse than another.

Answer: A
Page Ref: 384
Skill: Conceptual
Objective: 14.10

100) Because there is no warm attachment bond to build on,
   A) a new stepparent often has difficulty disciplining a stepchild.
   B) couples in remarriages have a more difficult time developing intimacy.
   C) stepparents often try to spoil a stepchild in an attempt to win affection.
   D) new stepparents often focus their attentions on the new spouse and ignore the stepchild.

Answer: A
Page Ref: 384
Skill: Factual
Objective: 14.11

101) Which of these stepparents is likely to have the easiest time establishing a positive relationship with the stepchildren?
   A) a stepfather with no biological children
   B) a stepfather who has biological children
   C) a stepmother with no biological children
   D) a stepmother who has biological children

Answer: B
Page Ref: 385
Skill: Applied
Objective: 14.11

102) __________ is a crucial component for stepparent adjustment.
   A) A caring relationship between step-grandparents and the step-grandchildren
   B) The increased involvement of the absent biological parent
   C) The absence of the noncustodial parents in the lives of the children
   D) The children's willingness to accept the parent's new spouse

Answer: D
Page Ref: 385
Skill: Conceptual
Objective: 14.11

103) When a young African-American woman has a child and then, several years later, marries a man—not the child's father—the typical result is that

A) the couple functions like other first-marriage parents.
B) the children never fully accept the stepfather into the family.
C) the marriage is less successful than other first marriages.
D) the extended family does not fully accept the marriage.

Answer: A
Page Ref: 385
Skill: Factual
Objective: 14.11

104) Children of __________ are more likely to display antisocial behavior and do poorly in school because they __________.

A) never-married mothers; lack the discipline a father provides
B) never-married mothers; lack the involvement of a father
C) twice-divorced mothers; are frustrated by the instability of their home life
D) never-married fathers; are unable to learn cooperative and caring behavior without proper modeling by a mother

Answer: B
Page Ref: 385
Skill: Factual
Objective: 14.11

105) Research suggests that

A) gay fathers are less responsive to their children's needs than heterosexual fathers.
B) gay fathers are less consistent in setting limits than heterosexual fathers.
C) gay parents are as committed and effective as heterosexual parents.
D) homosexual parents are more committed and effective than heterosexual parents.

Answer: C
Page Ref: 385
Skill: Conceptual
Objective: 14.11

106) Trisha's mother is a lesbian. Trisha will most likely be

A) a lesbian as well.
B) psychologically maladjusted.
C) more traditional in her gender roles.
D) heterosexual and well adjusted.

Answer: D
Page Ref: 386
Skill: Applied
Objective: 14.11

107) The Mitras are both college professors. Based upon career research, we can expect Mr. Mitra's career path to be __________ and Mrs. Mitra's career path to be __________.

A) discontinuous; continuous
B) continuous; discontinuous
C) traditional; unconventional
D) unconventional; traditional

Answer: B
Page Ref: 386
Skill: Applied
Objective: 14.12

108) After just 18 months on her first post-college job, Cecile has resigned. Information in your text would suggest that this is probably
   A) because her degree program did not adequately prepare her for real-life employment.
   B) due to her unwillingness to work as hard as her supervisors require.
   C) because she has experienced a gap between her expectations of what the job would be like and its reality.
   D) due to her frustration with her older colleagues and their inability to keep up with the latest technology.
   Answer: C
   Page Ref: 387
   Skill: Applied
   Objective: 14.12

109) Jonas has just started his career. Which person would probably make the most effective mentor for Jonas?
   A) a coworker with more experience than Jonas who is not a top executive
   B) another young graduate just starting his or her career
   C) a female, rather than a male, mentor
   D) one of the top executives in the company
   Answer: A
   Page Ref: 387
   Skill: Applied
   Objective: 14.12

110) Investigations of earning in the North American workplace indicate that
   A) the gender gap decreases as employees move through a company's ranks.
   B) the gap between men's and women's earnings increases with age.
   C) salaries are relatively equal for men and women.
   D) when the discontinuous nature of women's careers are taken into account, women *seem* to have been working longer than they really have, increasing the appearance of salary inequities.
   Answer: B
   Page Ref: 387
   Skill: Factual
   Objective: 14.12

111) Women who pursue careers in fields that are considered traditionally "masculine" are more likely to
   A) be dissatisfied with their work when they get it.
   B) be less committed to their jobs and resign easily.
   C) have "masculine" qualities with respect to work.
   D) be more "feminine" in their attitudes toward life.
   Answer: C
   Page Ref: 387
   Skill: Factual
   Objective: 14.12

112) Which person is likely to face the most discrimination in the workplace?
   A) Neva, an African-American woman
   B) Ned, an African-American man
   C) Nell, a white female
   D) Nathan, a white male
   Answer: A
   Page Ref: 388
   Skill: Applied
   Objective: 14.12

113) In a study of highly successful African-American women, the common themes that emerged from their experiences were
   A) relatively little discrimination, prejudice, and pain.
   B) sacrifice, self-doubt, and regret.
   C) persistence and a connection to others.
   D) love, truth, and honesty.
   Answer: C
   Page Ref: 388
   Skill: Factual
   Objective: 14.12

114) The major source of stress in dual-career families is
   A) role overload from job and family pressures.
   B) conflict with traditional gender-role patterns.
   C) negative attitudes from the extended family.
   D) interference from family members and friends.
   Answer: A
   Page Ref: 388
   Skill: Factual
   Objective: 14.12

115) Emmanuel is the human resources person for a small company. He notices that many of his young, working parents are experiencing role overload, and feels that this negatively affects productivity. Which of the following recommendations could Emmanuel follow in order to improve employee performance while maintaining the company's bottom line?
   A) Meet with the employees and let them know he understands their struggles, as his children were once young too.
   B) Hire additional staff to support his struggling employees.
   C) Implement flexible work-hour options.
   D) Hire only people without children.
   Answer: C
   Page Ref: 388
   Skill: Applied
   Objective: 14.12

ESSAY

116) What is meant by the "social clock"? Describe evidence indicating that the social clock is a major source of personality change in adulthood.
   Answer: The term "social clock" refers to age-graded expectations for life events, such as beginning a first job, getting married, birth of the first child, buying a home, and retiring. All societies have timetables for accomplishing major developmental tasks. Being on time or off time can profoundly affect self-esteem because adults (like children and adolescents) make social comparisons, measuring the progress of their lives against their friends', siblings', and colleagues'. A major source of personality change in adulthood is conformity to or departure from the social clock. In a study of college women born in the 1930s who were followed up at ages 27 and 43, researchers determined how closely participants followed a "feminine" social clock (marriage and parenthood in the early or mid-twenties) or a "masculine" social clock (entry into a high-status career and advancement by the late twenties). Those who started families on time became more responsible, self-controlled, tolerant, and nurturant but declined in self-esteem and felt more vulnerable as their lives progressed. Those who followed an occupational timetable typical for men became more dominant, sociable, independent, and intellectually effective, a trend also found in a cohort born a decade later. Women not on a social clock—who had neither married nor begun a career by age 30—were doing especially poorly. They suffered from self-doubt, feelings of incompetence, and loneliness.
   Page Ref: 369

117) Describe how circumstances and personal characteristics contribute to loneliness.

Answer: Separated, divorced, or widowed adults are lonelier than their married, cohabiting, or single counterparts, suggesting that loneliness is intense after the loss of an intimate tie. Men not involved in a romantic relationship feel lonelier than women, perhaps because they have fewer alternatives for satisfying intimacy needs. And immigrants from collectivist cultures report higher levels of loneliness than people born in the United States and Canada. Leaving a large, close-knit family system for an individualistic society seems to prompt intense feelings of isolation.

Personal characteristics also contribute to loneliness. Young adults who are socially anxious or who have insecure working models of attachment to parents are more often intensely lonely.

Page Ref: 373–374

118) Kaci and Hunter met and fell in love when they were both 22 years old. They married after knowing each other for four months, and had their first baby 10 months after their wedding. Although they struggled financially for a few years, Hunter finished college and now has a good job as a sales representative for a pharmaceutical company. Kaci wants to finish her education but will not return to college until their children are older, as she is the primary caregiver due to Hunter's travel schedule. Kaci's mother and stepfather live nearby, while her father and his third wife live in another state. Hunter's mother lives in the same town, but hasn't spoken to him since he married Kaci, and Hunter's father has been uninvolved in his life since he was a child. Based on information in your text, what can you predict about the long-term outcomes for this marriage?

Answer: There are a number of factors that predict a happy marriage, and Kaci and Hunter have very few of them. Happy marriages most often have partners with similar backgrounds (SES, education, religion, age) who marry after age 23 after dating for at least six months and who wait at least a year before having children. Furthermore, their relationships with extended family members, who also have stable marital patterns, are positive. Financial and employment status is secure and family responsibilities are shared.

In Kaci and Hunter's case, they married and had children at an early age, after a short period of dating. Both extended families are fraught with instability and, in Hunter's case, negativity. While Hunter's job now provides financial stability, the fact that Kaci has not been able to fulfill her dream presents an obstacle, as does the fact that the family responsibilities are primarily hers.

Page Ref: 376

119) What are strategies that can successfully help couples promote better mate selection and enhance marital satisfaction?

Answer: Courses in family life education in high schools and colleges can promote better mate selection. Premarital counseling aimed at helping couples discuss their desires openly and use positive, respectful conflict-resolution strategies can ease adjustment to marriage and enhance relationship quality.

Page Ref: 377–378

120) Describe changes in the marital relationship after the birth of a baby. What steps can couples take to preserve marital happiness during this time?

Answer: **Changes**: Childbirth profoundly alters the lives of husband and wife. Disrupted sleep schedules, less time to devote to each other and to leisure activities, and new financial responsibilities often lead to a mild decline in marital happiness. In addition, entry of children into the family usually causes the roles of husband and wife to become more traditional. Movement toward traditional roles is hardest on new mothers who have been involved in a career. The larger the difference in men's and women's responsibilities, the greater the rise in conflict and decline in marital satisfaction and mental health after childbirth, especially for women. Violated expectations about jointly caring for a new baby contribute to the decline in marital happiness. Women, especially, count on far more help from their husbands than usually occurs.

Possible steps to take: Postponing childbearing until the late twenties or thirties, as more couples are doing today, eases the transition to parenthood. Waiting permits couples to pursue occupational goals and gain life experience. Under these circumstances, men are more enthusiastic about becoming fathers and therefore more willing to participate actively. And women whose careers are under way are more likely to encourage their husbands to share housework and child care.

Page Ref: 379–380

121) Describe characteristics of individuals who are voluntarily childless, and their long-term happiness with the lifestyle.

Answer: Besides marital satisfaction and freedom from child-care responsibilities, common reasons for not having children include the woman's career and economic security. Consistent with these motives, the voluntarily childless are usually college-educated, have prestigious occupations, and are highly committed to their work. Many were only or firstborn children whose parents encouraged achievement and independence. Voluntarily childless women are more self-reliant and assertive. Voluntarily childless adults are just as content with their lives as are parents who have rewarding relationships with their children. Childlessness interferes with adjustment and life satisfaction only when it is beyond a person's control.

Page Ref: 383

122) Describe predictors of and factors relating to divorce. How do these factors impact the decision to end a marriage?

Answer: In a nine-year longitudinal study of 2,000 married people, wives reported more problems than husbands, with the gender difference largely involving the wife's emotions, such as anger, hurt feelings, and moodiness. Husbands seemed to have difficulty sensing their wives' distress, which contributed to the wives' view of their marriages as problematic. Regardless of which spouse reported the problem or was judged responsible for it, the strongest predictors of divorce during the following decade were infidelity, spending money foolishly, drinking or using drugs, jealousy, irritating habits, and moodiness. Other studies show that younger age at marriage, not attending religious services, being previously divorced, and having parents who had divorced increased the chances of divorce, in part because these background factors were linked to marital difficulties. Not going to religious services may raise divorce odds by subtracting an influential context for instilling positive marital behaviors. And parental divorce elevates certain problems in the next generations.

Page Ref: 383–384

STUDY QUESTIONS

Erikson's Theory: Intimacy versus Isolation

1. According to Erikson, what is the psychological conflict of early adulthood? (p. 366)

____

2. Explain how a secure identity fosters attainment of intimacy. (pp. 366–367)

____

____

____

3. Describe the characteristics of individuals who have achieved a sense of intimacy versus those affected by isolation. (p. 366)

Intimacy: ____

____

Isolation: ____

____

Other Theories of Adult Psychosocial Development

Levinson's Seasons of Life

1. True or False: Like Erikson, Levinson regarded development as a sequence of qualitatively distinct eras (stages or seasons). (p. 367)

2. Each era begins with a _______________, lasting about five years, which concludes the previous era and prepares the person for the next. (p. 367)

3. Describe the *life structure,* including its central components. (p. 367)

____

____

4. Describe differences in the life dreams of men and women. (p. 367)

   Men: ____

   ____

   Women: ____

   ____

5. How do mentors facilitate realization of young adults' dreams? Who are mentors likely to be? (p. 368)

   A. ____

   ____

   B. ____

   ____

6. Explain how young people reevaluate their life structure during the age-30 transition. (p. 368)

____

____

____

7. True or False: For men and women without satisfying relational or occupational accomplishments, the age-30 transition can be a relief. (p. 368)

8. Describe women's experiences with "settling down" during their thirties. How do their experiences compare to those of men? (p. 368)

   Women's experiences: ____

   ____

   Men's experiences: ____

   ____

Vaillant's Adaptation to Life

1. Using Vaillant's theory, explain how men alter themselves and their social world to adapt to life at the following ages: (p. 368)

   Twenties: ____

   Thirties: ____

   Forties: ____

   Fifties and Sixties: ____

   Seventies: ____

2. True or False: When he eventually studied the development of bright, well-educated women, Vaillant found that their development differed sharply from men's. (p. 368)

Limitations of Levinson's and Vaillant's Theories

1. Identify three limitations of Levinson's and Vaillant's theories. (p. 369)

   A. ______________________________

   B. ______________________________

   C. ______________________________

The Social Clock

1. What is the *social clock,* and how does it influence adult development? (p. 369)

   A. ______________________________

   ____

   B. ______________________________

   ____

2. Describe characteristics of college women born in the 1930s who followed a "feminine" social clock, a "masculine" social clock, or no social clock. (p. 369)

   Feminine: ______________________________

   Masculine: ______________________________

   No social clock: ______________________________

3. How does following a social clock foster confidence during early adulthood? (p. 369)

   ____

   ____

Close Relationships

Romantic Love

1. True or False: In selecting a mate, research suggests that "opposites attract." Explain your answer. (p. 370)

   ____

   ____

2. In choosing a long-term partner, men and women differ in the importance they place on certain characteristics. How do evolutionary and social-learning perspectives explain this difference? (p. 370)

   Evolutionary: ______________________________

   ____

   ____

   Social learning: ______________________________

   ____

3. True or False: For romance to lead to a lasting partnership, it must happen at the right time for both individuals. (p. 370)

4. List and define the three components of Sternberg's *triangular theory of love.* (p. 370)

   A. ______________________________

   B. ______________________________

   C. ______________________________

5. In the transformation of romantic involvements from passionate to companionate, ________________ may be the aspect of love that determines whether a relationship survives. (p. 370)

6. Describe important features of communication that contribute to high-quality intimate relationships. (pp. 370–371)

____

____

____

7. How does the Eastern perspective of love differ from the perspectives of Western cultures? (p. 371)

____

____

____

A Lifespan Vista: Childhood Attachment Patterns and Adult Romantic Relationships

1. Early attachment bonds lead to the construction of a(n) ____________________, or set of expectations about attachment figures, that serve as a guide for close relationships. (p. 372)

2. Explain how attachment security in childhood influences adult experiences with romantic partners. (pp. 372–373)

   Secure attachment: ____

   ____

   Avoidant attachment: ____

   ____

   Resistant attachment: ____

   ____

3. In addition to child attachment patterns, what other factors contribute to later internal working models and intimate ties? (p. 373)

____

____

Friendships

1. Cite three benefits of adult friendship. (p. 371)

   A. ____

   B. ____

   C. ____

2. What features characterize adult friendships? (p. 371)

____

____

____

3. Compare characteristics of women's same-sex friendships with those of men. (p. 371)

   Women: ______________________________

   ____

   Men: ______________________________

   ____

4. What group of adults has the largest number of other-sex friends? (p. 371)

   ____

5. What are some benefits of other-sex friendships? (p. 371)

   ____

6. True or False: The majority of other-sex friendships turn into romance. (p. 373)

7. Explain why friend and sibling roles often merge in early adulthood, noting how adult sibling ties resemble friendships. (p. 373)

   ____

   ____

   ____

Loneliness

1. Describe situations in which adults experience *loneliness.* (p. 373)

   ____

   ____

2. True or False: Loneliness peaks during the teens and early twenties, after which it declines steadily into the seventies. Explain your answer. (p. 373)

   ____

   ____

   ____

3. Under what circumstances are adults likely to experience loneliness? (p. 374)

   ____

   ____

4. When not involved in a romantic relationship, (men / women) feel lonelier, perhaps because they have fewer alternatives for satisfying intimacy needs. (p. 374)

5. Describe personal characteristics that contribute to loneliness. (p. 374)

   ____

   ____

   ____

6. How can loneliness be motivating? (p. 374)

   ____

   ____

The Family Life Cycle

1. What is the *family life cycle*? Describe characteristics of individuals in the early adulthood phase. (p. 374)

   A. ____________________

   ____

   B. ____________________

   ____

Leaving Home

1. The average age of leaving the family home has (increased / decreased) in recent years. (p. 374)
2. Nearly ______ percent of young adults return home for a brief time after initial leaving. Those who departed to marry are (most / least) likely to return. Those who left because of family conflict (usually / rarely) return. (p. 375)
3. How do SES and ethnicity contribute to early departure from the family home? (p. 375)

   ____

   ____

Joining of Families in Marriage

1. Currently, the average age of marriage in the United States is ____ for women and ____ for men. In Canada, the average age of marriage is ____ for women and ____ for men. (p. 375)
2. The number of first and second marriages in the United States and Canada has (increased / declined) over the last few decades. What are some possible reasons for this trend? (p. 375)

   ____

   ____

3. Nearly ______ percent of North Americans marry at least once. (p. 375)
4. Why is research on same-sex marriages scant? (p. 375)

   ____

   ____

5. What is the most consistent predictor of marital stability? (p. 376)

   ____

6. Cite differences between *traditional* and *egalitarian* marriages. (p. 376)

   Traditional: ____________________

   ____

   Egalitarian: ____________________

   ____

7. In Western nations, men in dual-earner marriages participate much (less / more) in child care than they did in the past. (p. 376)
8. True or False: North American women spend nearly twice as much time as men on housework. (p. 376)

9. List three relationship qualities that contribute to marital satisfaction. (pp. 376–377)

   A. ______________________________

   B. ______________________________

   C. ______________________________

10. True or False: Most couples spend little time reflecting on the decision to marry before their wedding day. (p. 377)

Social Issues: Partner Abuse

1. Partner abuse in which (husbands / wives) are perpetrators and (husbands / wives) are physically injured is the type most likely to be reported to authorities. Why might this not accurately reflect true rates of abuse? (p. 378)

   ____

   ____

   ____

2. True or False: Partner abuse occurs at about the same rate in same-sex relationships as in heterosexual relationships. (p. 378)

3. List three reasons both men and women give for abusing their partner. (p. 378)

   A. ______________________________

   B. ______________________________

   C. ______________________________

4. Describe factors that contribute to partner abuse. (p. 378)

   Psychological: ______________________________

   ____

   ____

   Family: ______________________________

   ____

   ____

   Cultural: ______________________________

   ____

   ____

5. List reasons why many people do not leave destructive relationships before abuse escalates. (p. 378)

   ____

   ____

   ____

6. Describe treatment for victims and perpetrators of partner abuse. (p. 379)

   Victims: ______________________________

   ____

   Perpetrators: ______________________________

   ____

Parenthood

1. Family size in industrialized nations has (increased / declined). (p. 377)
2. List three factors that affect the decision to have children. (p. 377)

   A. ______________________________

   B. ______________________________

   C. ______________________________

3. True or False: Women with high-status, demanding careers less often choose parenthood and, when they do, more often delay it than women with less time-consuming jobs. (p. 377)
4. Describe reasons for having children that are most important to all groups of people. (pp. 377, 379)

   ____

   ____

   ____

5. Cite two disadvantages of parenthood mentioned most often by young adults. (p. 379)

   A. ______________________________

   B. ______________________________

6. After the arrival of a new baby, the roles of husbands and wives become (more / less) traditional. (p. 379)
7. List factors that contribute to marital satisfaction after childbirth. (p. 379)

   ____

   ____

   ____

   ____

8. How does postponing childbearing ease the transition to parenthood? (p. 380)

   ____

   ____

9. Describe changes in parental roles and responsibilities after the birth of a second child. (p. 380)

   ____

   ____

   ____

10. True or False: Generous, paid employment leave after the birth of a child is widely available in industrialized nations, but not in the United States. (p. 380)
11. In today's complex world, men and women are (more/less) sure about how to rear children than in previous generations. (p. 380)
12. Cite a major struggle for employed parents. Is this more of a problem for men or women? Explain. (p. 380)

    A. ______________________________

    B. ______________________________

    ____

13. Identify some benefits of child rearing for adult development. (p. 380)

____

____

14. Briefly describe how adolescence brings changes in parental roles. (p. 380)

____

____

15. Cite differences in the way mothers and fathers seek information and learn about child rearing. (pp. 380–381)

Mothers: ____

____

Fathers: ____

____

16. Parent education courses exist to help parents in the following four areas. (p. 381)

A. ____

B. ____

C. ____

D. ____

The Diversity of Adult Lifestyles

Singlehood

1. Cite two factors that have contributed to the growing numbers of single adults. (p. 381)

A. ____

B. ____

2. Because they marry later, more young adult (men / women) are single. But (men / women) are far more likely than (men / women) to remain single for many years or their entire lives. Explain your answer. (p. 381)

____

____

3. List the two most often mentioned advantages of singlehood, as well as drawbacks of singlehood. (p. 382)

Advantages: ____

____

Drawbacks: ____

____

____

4. Single (men / women) have more physical and mental health problems than single (men / women). Why is this so? (p. 382)

____

____

Cohabitation

1. Define *cohabitation,* and explain which group of young people has experienced an especially dramatic rise in this type of lifestyle. (p. 382)

   A. ______________________________

   B. ______________________________

2. True or False: Among people in their twenties, cohabitation is now the preferred mode of entry into a committed intimate partnership, with more than 50 percent of North American couples choosing it. (p. 382)

3. How do Western European attitudes toward cohabitation differ from those of North Americans? (p. 382)

   ____

   ____

   ____

4. American and Canadian couples who cohabit before marriage are (more / less) prone to divorce than married couples who did not cohabit. (p. 382)

5. List three types of couples who do not experience the negative outcomes of cohabitation. (p. 383)

   A. ______________________________

   B. ______________________________

   C. ______________________________

Childlessness

1. List reasons couples choose to remain childless. (p. 383)

   ____

   ____

2. (Involuntarily / Voluntarily) childless adults are just as content with their lives as parents who have warm relationships with their children. However, (involuntarily / voluntarily) childless adults are likely to be dissatisfied. (p. 383)

Divorce and Remarriage

1. Explain why divorce rates have stabilized since the mid-1980s. (p. 383)

   ____

   ____

   ____

   ____

2. During which periods of adult life are divorces especially likely to occur, and why? (p. 383)

   ____

   ____

3. Describe maladaptive communication patterns that contribute to divorce. (p. 383)

   ____

   ____

   ____

4. Cite background factors that increase the chances of divorce. (p. 383)

____

____

5. Parental divorce (elevates / reduces) risk of divorce in at least two succeeding generations. What explains this trend? (pp. 383–384)

____

____

____

6. True or False: When a woman's workplace status and income exceed her husband's, the risk of divorce decreases. (p. 384)

7. Discuss the consequences of divorce for men and women. (p. 384)

   Men: ____

   ____

   Women: ____

   ____

8. How do men and women differ in their adjustment after divorce? (p. 384)

   Men: ____

   ____

   Women: ____

   ____

9. True or False: On average, people remarry within four years of divorce, women somewhat faster than men. (p. 384)

10. List four reasons that remarriages are especially vulnerable to breakup. (p. 384)

    A. ____

    B. ____

    C. ____

    D. ____

Variant Styles of Parenthood

1. Why are stepmothers especially likely to experience conflict? (p. 385)

____

____

2. Cite reasons that stepfathers with children of their own have less difficulty adjusting to their role as a stepparent. (p. 385)

____

____

____

3. What are three crucial ingredients of positive stepparent adjustment? (p. 385)

   A. ____________________

   B. ____________________

   C. ____________________

4. In the United States, the largest group of never-married parents is ____________________. Explain this finding. (p. 385)

   ____

   ____

   ____

5. How do children of never-married parents usually fare? What factors affect their well-being? (p. 385)

   A. ____________________

   ____

   B. ____________________

   ____

6. True or False: Gay and lesbian parents are as committed to and effective at child rearing as heterosexual parents. (p. 385)

7. Overall, families headed by homosexuals can be distinguished from other families only by issues related to living in a ____________ society. (p. 386)

Career Development

Establishing a Career

1. Men typically have ____________ careers—beginning after completion of formal education and ending with retirement. Many women have ______________ career paths—ones that were interrupted or deferred by child rearing and other family needs. (p. 386)

2. Why can entry into the workforce be discouraging, even for those who enter their chosen field? (pp. 386–387)

   ____

   ____

3. How do personal characteristics affect career progress? (p. 387)

   ____

   ____

   ____

4. Access to an effective mentor is jointly affected by what two factors? (p. 387)

   A. ____________________

   B. ____________________

Women and Ethnic Minorities

1. True or False: Women generally remain concentrated in occupations that offer little opportunity for advancement. (p. 387)

2. Describe reasons why career planning is often short-term and subject to change, especially for women in traditionally feminine occupations. (p. 387)

3. Describe women's career progress in male-dominated fields. (p. 387)

4. Cite examples of racial bias in the labor market. (pp. 387–388)

Combining Work and Family

1. Define *dual-earner marriage.* What are the main sources of strain in these families? (p. 388)

   A.

   B.

2. Role overload is greater for (men / women). Explain your answer. (p. 388)

3. What strategies can help dual-earner couples combine work and family roles in ways that promote mastery and pleasure in both spheres of life? (p. 388)

PUZZLE 14.1

Across

2. According to Sternberg's __________ theory of love, love has three components—intimacy, passion, and commitment—that shift in emphasis as the romantic relationship develops
4. Feelings of unhappiness that result from a gap between actual and desired social relationships
6. Social __________: age-graded expectations for life events, such as beginning a first job, getting married, birth of a first child, etc.
9. __________ marriage: form of marriage involving clear division of husband's and wife's roles
10. __________ marriage: form of marriage in which husband and wife share power and authority
11. In a __________-__________ marriage, both husband and wife are employed
12. Lifestyle of unmarried individuals who have an intimate, sexual relationship and share a residence

Down

1. Love based on intense sexual attraction
3. Love based on warm, trusting affection and caregiving
5. __________ versus isolation: Erikson's psychological conflict of youth
7. In Levinson's theory, the underlying pattern or design of a person's life at a given time is called the __________ structure
8. __________ life cycle: sequence of phases that characterizes the development of most families around the world

CROSSWORD PUZZLE SOLUTION

PUZZLE 14.1

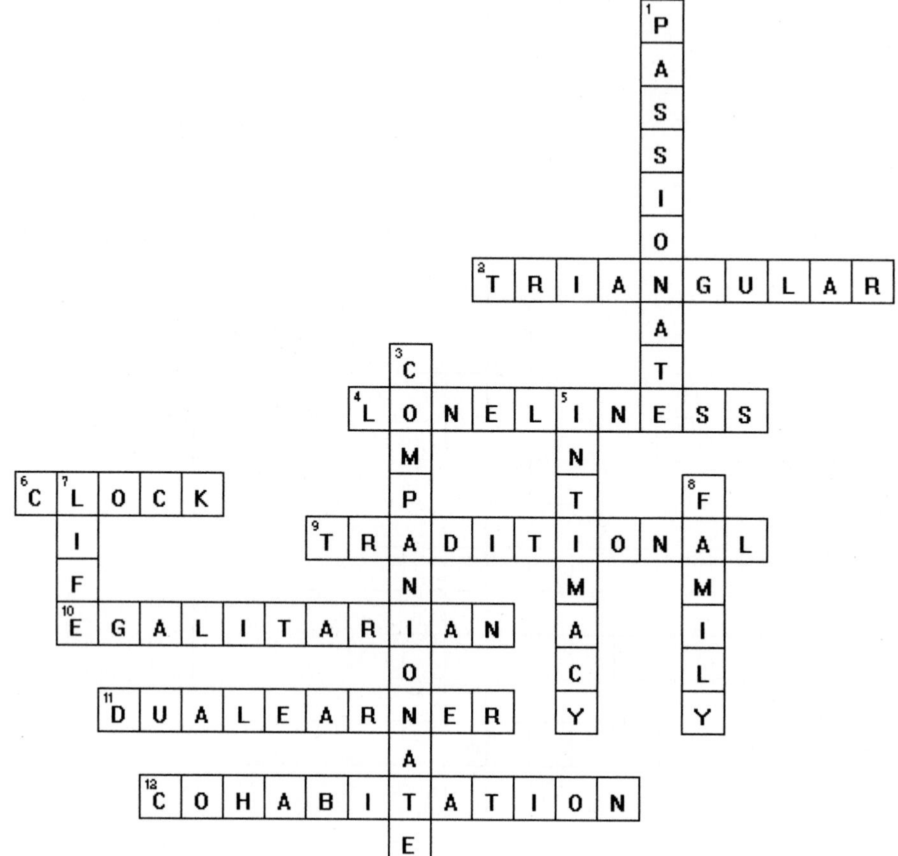

PRACTICE TEST #1

1. When 18- to 25-year-olds are asked what it means to become an adult, most emphasize (p. 366)
   a. career goals.
   b. family goals.
   c. physical qualities.
   d. psychological qualities.

2. The conflict of intimacy versus isolation is successfully resolved when a young adult (p. 366)
   a. establishes a committed, mutually gratifying close relationship.
   b. graduates from a two- or four-year college.
   c. is offered a desirable job in his or her chosen field of work.
   d. leaves the childhood home and begins living independently.

3. In Levinson's concept of the life structure, (p. 367)
   a. men and women typically approach developmental tasks in very similar ways.
   b. ideally, individuals find a desirable life structure in early adulthood and make very few changes after that.
   c. only a few components, related to marriage/family and occupation, are central.
   d. career-oriented women typically construct a dream that is focused entirely on occupational goals, not on relationships.

4. Who among the following is most likely to become a mentor? (p. 368)
   a. a senior colleague to a new coworker
   b. a brother to his older sister
   c. a grandmother to her grandson
   d. a husband to his wife

5. During the age-30 transition, young people reevaluate their (p. 368)
   a. childhood.
   b. sexuality.
   c. life structure.
   d. physical health.

6. According to the social learning perspective, gender roles (p. 370)
   a. profoundly influence criteria for mate selection among individuals of both sexes.
   b. influence men's criteria for mate selection but not women's.
   c. influence women's criteria for mate selection but not men's.
   d. have little influence on criteria for mate selection.

7. At the very beginning of a relationship, the strongest component of love is (p. 370)
   a. passionate love.
   b. compassionate love.
   c. intimacy.
   d. commitment.

8. Couples who report having higher-quality long-term relationships (p. 370)
   a. have sex much more often than the average couple.
   b. somehow manage to keep the mystery in their relationship.
   c. credit their success to being very different, because opposites attract.
   d. consistently communicate their commitment to each other.

9. As people age, intimate, same-sex friendships (p. 371)
   a. increase for both men and women.
   b. increase only for men.
   c. are more numerous for men than they are for women.
   d. are more numerous for women than they are for men.

10. Which of the following have the largest number of other-sex friends? (p. 371)
    a. highly educated, employed women
    b. highly educated, employed men
    c. college-age women
    d. college-age men

11. ________________ of young adults return home to live for a brief time after initial leaving. (p. 375)
    a. About one-third
    b. Nearly half
    c. About two-thirds
    d. More than three-fourths

12. Among North Americans, the average age of first marriage is (p. 375)
    a. lower than it was 40 years ago.
    b. the same for men and women.
    c. a little higher in Canada than in the United States.
    d. the same as a generation ago.

13. When asked about the disadvantages of parenthood, young adults most often mention (p. 379)
    a lack of spousal support.
    b. inability to save for their child's college education.
    c. loss of freedom.
    d. unwanted child-rearing advice from in-laws.

14. North American couples who cohabit before becoming engaged are (p. 382)
    a. more committed to each other and display more adaptive patterns of communication than couples who did not cohabit.
    b. more likely to divorce than married couples who did not cohabit.
    c. better prepared for the demands of marriage than couples who did not cohabit.
    d. likely to have conventional values, because cohabitation is widely accepted.

15. When a woman's workplace status and income exceed her husband's, (p. 384)
    a. the couple's likelihood of having children dramatically increases.
    b. the couple's gender-role beliefs are said to be in sync.
    c. the risk of divorce increases.
    d. the risk of divorce decreases.

16. For most divorced adults, negative reactions to divorce subside within (p. 384)
    a. one month.
    b. six months.
    c. two years.
    d. five to seven years.

17. On average, people remarry within (p. 384)
    a. one year of divorce.
    b. two years of divorce.
    c. three years of divorce.
    d. four years of divorce.

18. In the United States, the largest group of never-married parents are young (p. 385)
    a. Asian women.
    b. Mexican-American men.
    c. African-American women.
    d. Caucasian men.

19. Research on gay and lesbian parents indicates that they (p. 385)
    a. have maladjusted children.
    b. are as committed to and effective at child rearing as heterosexual parents.
    c. are less committed to child rearing than heterosexual parents.
    d. are often inconsistent and harsh with their children.

20. Career-oriented, successful ethnic minority women (p. 388)
    a. face racial but not gender discrimination.
    b. rarely receive support from other women.
    c. tend to have mothers who had low expectations for them.
    d. often display unusually high self-efficacy.

PRACTICE TEST #2

1. Like Erikson, Levinson viewed development as (p. 367)
   a. a continuous sequence extending into late adulthood.
   b. especially turbulent for women.
   c. a sequence of qualitatively distinct eras.
   d. biologically determined.

2. Levinson found that during the early adult transition, most individuals construct a(n) (p. 367)
   a. occupational identity.
   b. conceptual identity.
   c. dream.
   d. social clock.

3. Mentors (p. 368)
   a. are usually related to those they guide or educate.
   b. are more readily available to men than to women.
   c. are usually younger than the person they are advising.
   d. usually focus on job training rather than on the values or customs of the occupational setting.

4. In his study of 250 men, Vaillant found that in their fifties and sixties, the men (p. 368)
   a. devoted themselves to intimacy concerns.
   b. became "keepers of meaning."
   c. focused on career consolidation.
   d. pulled back from individual achievement in favor of giving to and guiding others.

5. Ellie's same-age friends all seemed to be getting married and starting families, while Ellie was still single. As a consequence, Ellie felt lonely, had a negative opinion of herself, and questioned her future. The best explanation of Ellie's situation is the (p. 369)
   a. life structure.
   b. social clock.
   c. age-30 transition.
   d. family life cycle.

6. In choosing a long-time partner, men are more apt than women to emphasize (p. 370)
   a. intelligence.
   b. physical attractiveness.
   c. financial status.
   d. moral character.

7. Warm, trusting affection and caregiving in a relationship is (p. 370)
   a. companionate love.
   b. passionate love.
   c. commitment.
   d. intimacy.

8. Compared to Eastern cultural perspectives, Western views of mature love are more likely to focus on (p. 371)
   a. lifelong dependence on one's chosen partner.
   b. obligations to others, particularly parents.
   c. companionship and practical matters, such as similarity of background, career promise, and likelihood of being a good parent.
   d. autonomy, appreciation of the partner's unique qualities, and intense emotion.

9. Highly educated, employed women (p. 371)
   a. have the fewest other-sex friends.
   b. have the greatest number of other-sex friends.
   c. rarely have time for either same-sex or other-sex friends.
   d. often look to other-sex friends for romantic involvement.

10. Loneliness usually peaks in the (p. 373)
    a. mid- to late teens.
    b. late teens and early twenties.
    c. mid- to late twenties.
    d. early thirties.

11. Which of the following adults is likely to experience loneliness? (p. 374)
    a. Meg, a married mother of two who plays cards with a small group of friends twice a month
    b. Joel, a recent college graduate who just started a new job but continues to live with his college roommates
    c. Denzel, a recently divorced father who stays in close contact with his ex-wife and child
    d. Brenda, a college student who still lives at home with her parents

12. Most well-educated, career-oriented women expect a(n) (p. 376)
    a. egalitarian marriage.
    b. traditional marriage.
    c. reverse-role marriage.
    d. same-sex marriage.

13. In partner abuse, women are more often targets of (p. 378)
    a. threats with knives.
    b. slapping.
    c. kicking.
    d. choking.

14. The arrival of a baby results in little marital strain (p. 379)
    a. in supportive marriages.
    b. in troubled marriages.
    c. when women take primary responsibility for caregiving.
    d. in young couples who are just launching their careers.

15. More people seek family therapy during the period when their children are ___________ than at any other time in the family life cycle. (p. 380)
    a. young adults
    b. infants
    c. adolescents
    d. starting elementary school

16. Frequently cited advantages of singlehood are (p. 382)
    a. freedom and mobility.
    b. exciting social and sex lives.
    c. greater sense of financial security.
    d. reduced loneliness.

17. Voluntarily childless adults (p. 383)
    a. are just as content with their lives as parents who have warm relationships with their children.
    b. are less content with their lives than parents who have warm relationships with their children.
    c. generally find that their marriages become increasingly unhappy over time.
    d. almost never change their minds about having children later in life.

18. The voluntarily childless usually (p. 383)
    a. are high school dropouts.
    b. are college-educated and have prestigious occupations.
    c. come from large families with many siblings.
    d. are not deeply committed to a career.

19. A factor that increases the chances of divorce is (p. 383)
    a. older age at marriage.
    b. high religious involvement.
    c. high SES.
    d. having parents who divorced.

20. In a study of racial bias in the labor market, researchers found that (p. 387)
    a. résumés with white-sounding names evoked more callbacks than résumés with black-sounding names.
    b. as a result of affirmative action, individuals with black-sounding names received more callbacks than individuals with white-sounding names, regardless of the quality of their résumé.
    c. individuals with high-quality résumés received more callbacks than individuals with low-quality résumés, regardless of whether their names sounded white or black.
    d. individuals with black-sounding names received more callbacks for low-paying jobs, while individuals with white-sounding names received more callbacks for skilled and managerial jobs.

POWERPOINT SLIDES

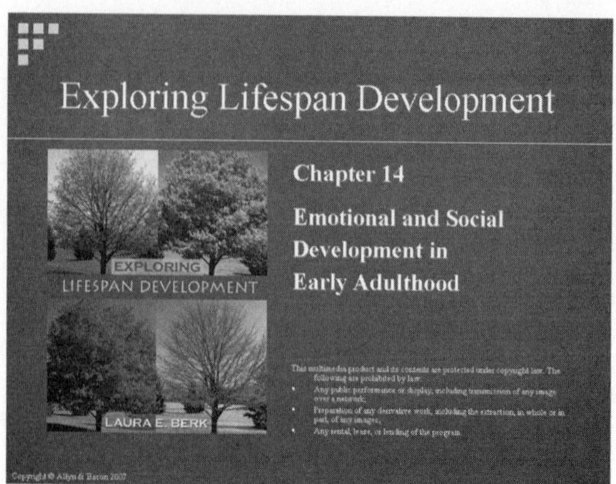

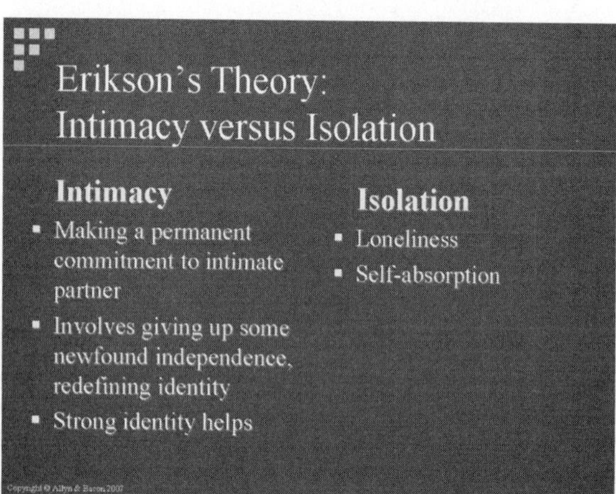

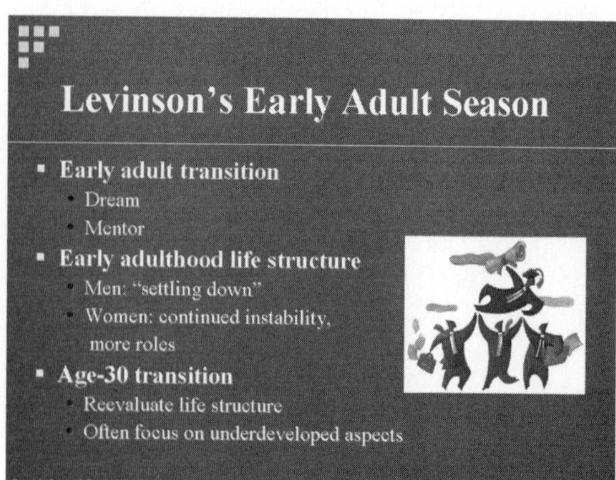

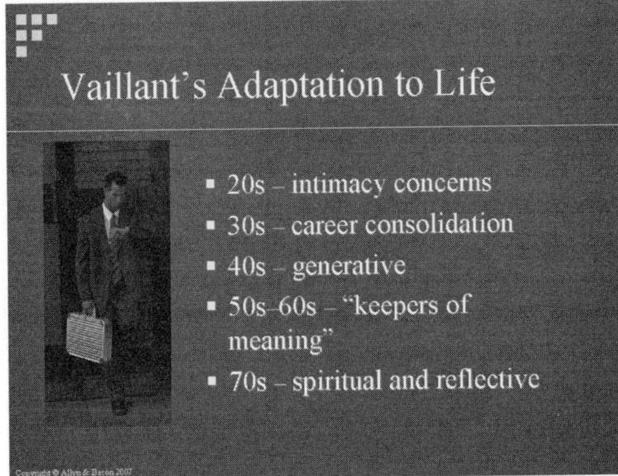
Vaillant's Adaptation to Life
20s – intimacy concerns
30s – career consolidation
40s – generative
50s-60s – "keepers of meaning"
70s – spiritual and reflective
Copyright © Allyn & Bacon 2007

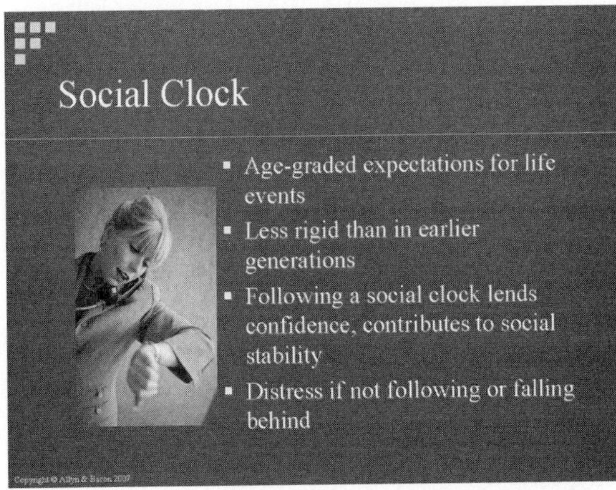
Social Clock
Age-graded expectations for life events
Less rigid than in earlier generations
Following a social clock lends confidence, contributes to social stability
Distress if not following or falling behind
Copyright © Allyn & Bacon 2007

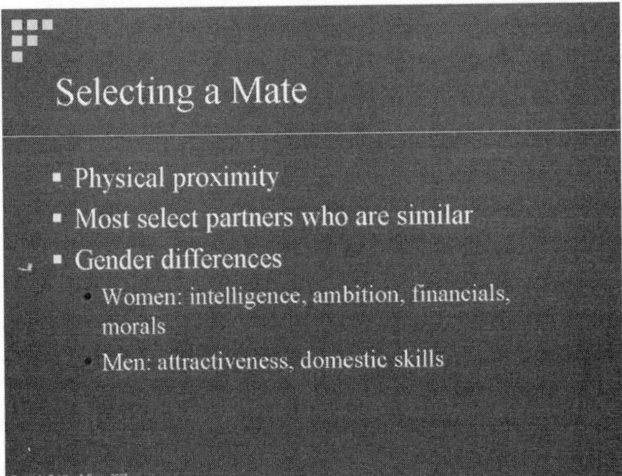
Selecting a Mate
Physical proximity
Most select partners who are similar
Gender differences
Women: intelligence, ambition, financials, morals
Men: attractiveness, domestic skills
Copyright © Allyn & Bacon 2007

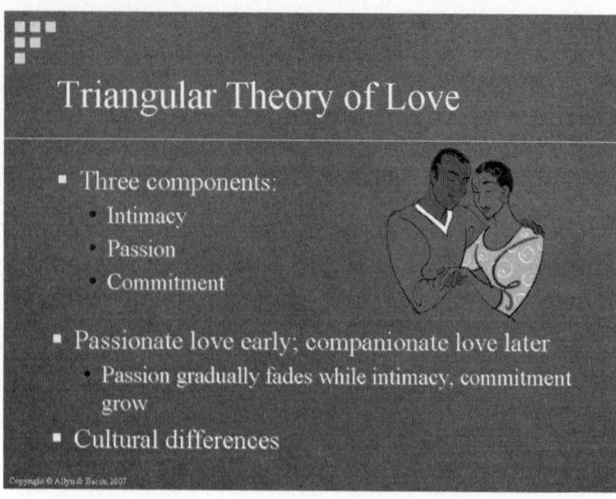

Childhood Attachment and Adult Romantic Relationships

Attachment History	Working Model	Adult Relationships
Secure	Comfortable with intimacy; unafraid of abandonment	Trust, happiness, friendship
Avoidant	Stress independence, mistrust, anxiety about closeness	Jealousy, emotional distance, little physical pleasure
Resistant	Seek quick love, complete merging	Jealousy, desperation, emotional highs & lows

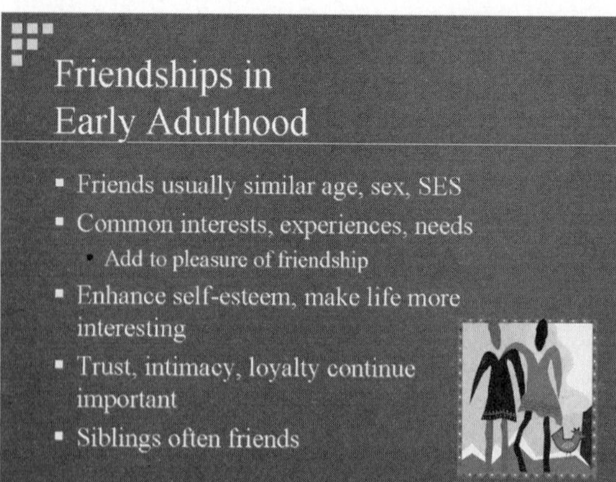

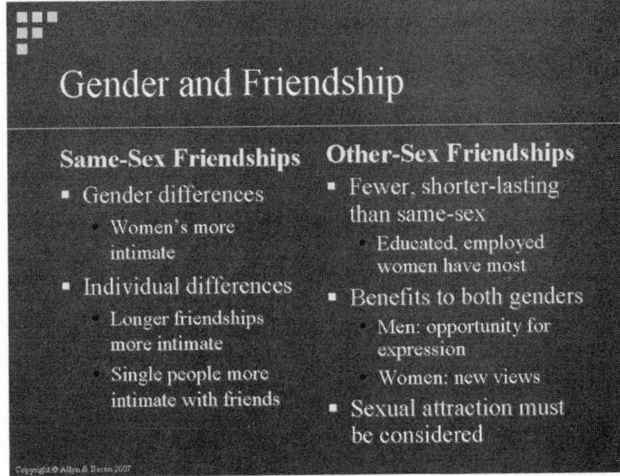
Gender and Friendship
Same-Sex Friendships
Gender differences
Women's more intimate
Individual differences
Longer friendships more intimate
Single people more intimate with friends
Other-Sex Friendships
Fewer, shorter-lasting than same-sex
Educated, employed women have most
Benefits to both genders
Men: opportunity for expression
Women: new views
Sexual attraction must be considered

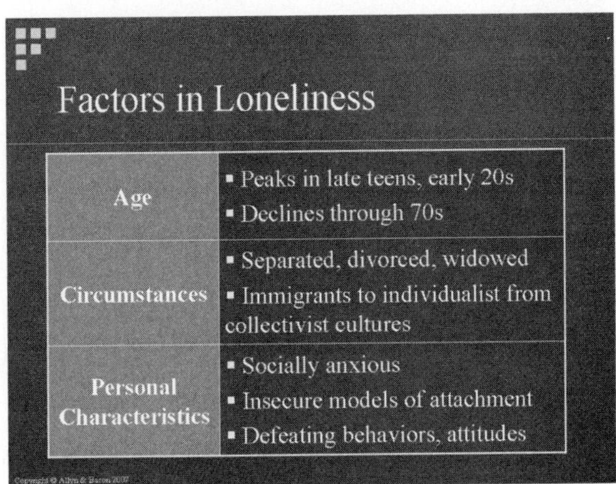
Factors in Loneliness
Age
Peaks in late teens, early 20s
Declines through 70s
Circumstances
Separated, divorced, widowed
Immigrants to individualist from collectivist cultures
Personal Characteristics
Socially anxious
Insecure models of attachment
Defeating behaviors, attitudes

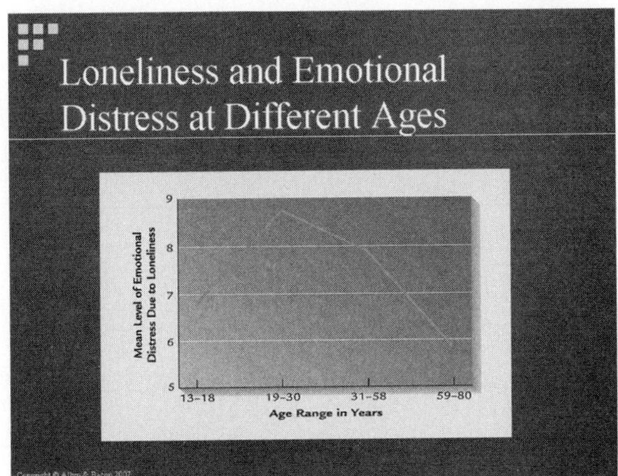
Loneliness and Emotional Distress at Different Ages
Mean Level of Emotional Distress Due to Loneliness
9
8
7
6
5
13–18
19–30
31–58
59–80
Age Range in Years

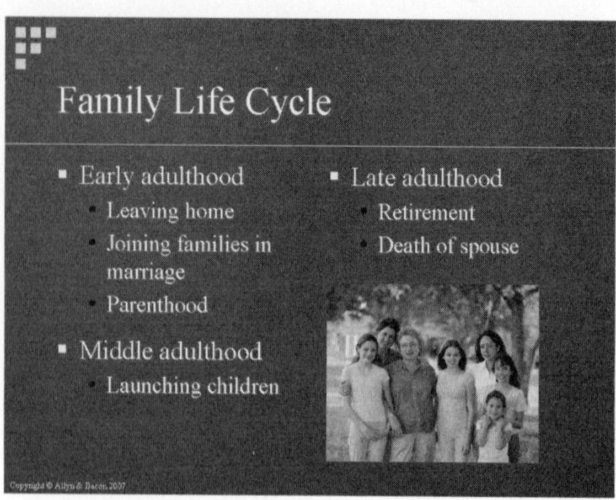
Family Life Cycle
Early adulthood
Leaving home
Joining families in marriage
Parenthood
Middle adulthood
Launching children
Late adulthood
Retirement
Death of spouse

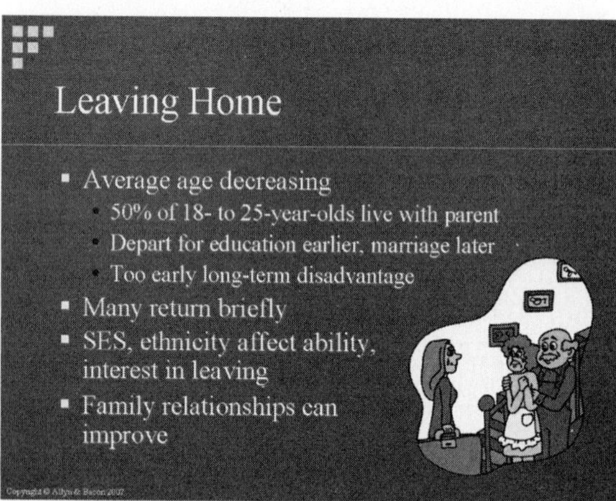
Leaving Home
Average age decreasing
50% of 18- to 25-year-olds live with parent
Depart for education earlier, marriage later
Too early long-term disadvantage
Many return briefly
SES, ethnicity affect ability, interest in leaving
Family relationships can improve

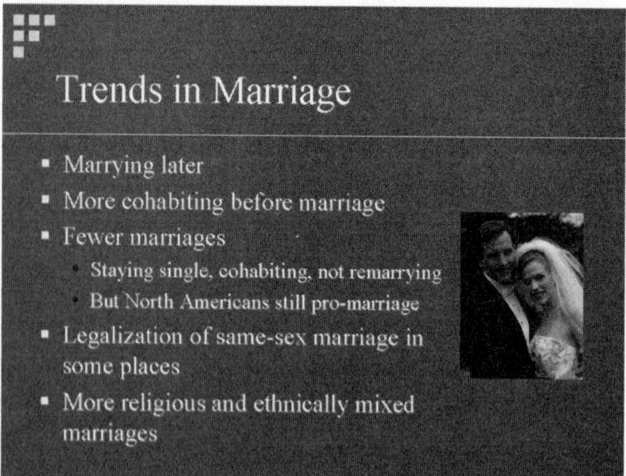
Trends in Marriage
Marrying later
More cohabiting before marriage
Fewer marriages
Staying single, cohabiting, not remarrying
But North Americans still pro-marriage
Legalization of same-sex marriage in some places
More religious and ethnically mixed marriages

Traditional and Egalitarian Marriages
Traditional
Clear division of roles
Woman: cares for husband, children, home
Man: head of household, economic support
Egalitarian
Partners relate as equals
Share authority
Balance attention to jobs, children, home, spouse

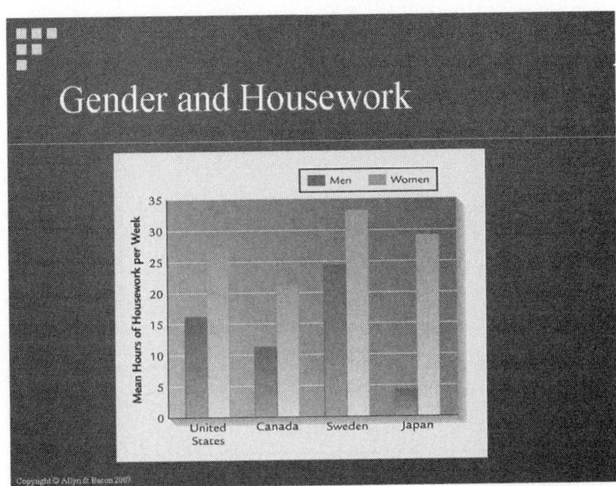
Gender and Housework
Men
Women
Mean Hours of Housework per Week
35
30
25
20
15
10
5
0
United States
Canada
Sweden
Japan

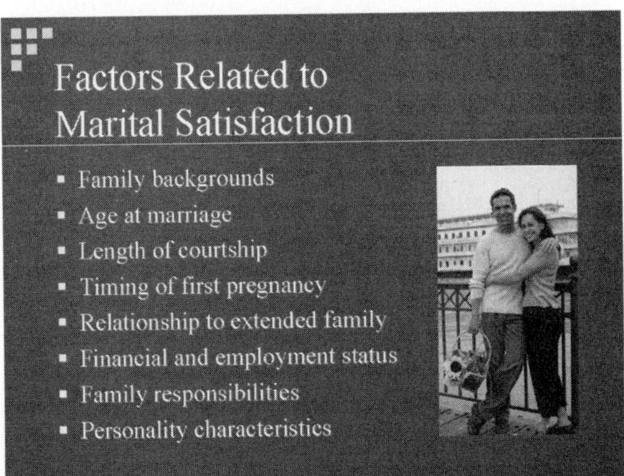
Factors Related to Marital Satisfaction
Family backgrounds
Age at marriage
Length of courtship
Timing of first pregnancy
Relationship to extended family
Financial and employment status
Family responsibilities
Personality characteristics

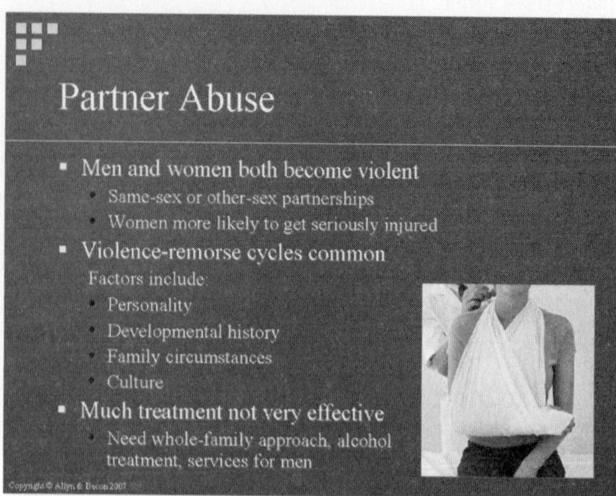
Partner Abuse
Men and women both become violent
Same-sex or other-sex partnerships
Women more likely to get seriously injured
Violence-remorse cycles common
Factors include:
Personality
Developmental history
Family circumstances
Culture
Much treatment not very effective
Need whole-family approach, alcohol treatment, services for men

Assaults Against Women by Intimate Partners
Switzerland
New Zealand
United States
Canada
South Korea
Ethiopia
Peru
0 10 20 30 40 50 70
Percentage Reporting Ever Having Experienced Partner Assault

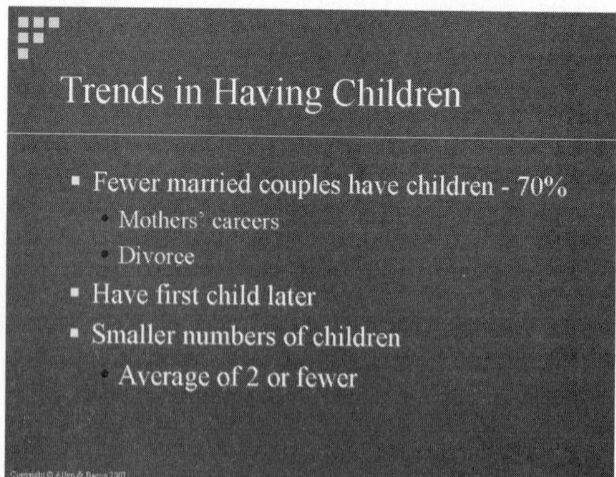
Trends in Having Children
Fewer married couples have children - 70%
Mothers' careers
Divorce
Have first child later
Smaller numbers of children
Average of 2 or fewer

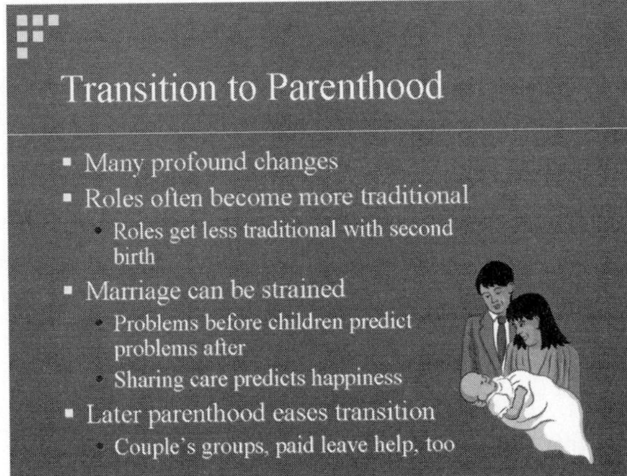
Transition to Parenthood
Many profound changes
Roles often become more traditional
Roles get less traditional with second birth
Marriage can be strained
Problems before children predict problems after
Sharing care predicts happiness
Later parenthood eases transition
Couple's groups, paid leave help, too
Copyright © Allyn & Bacon 2007

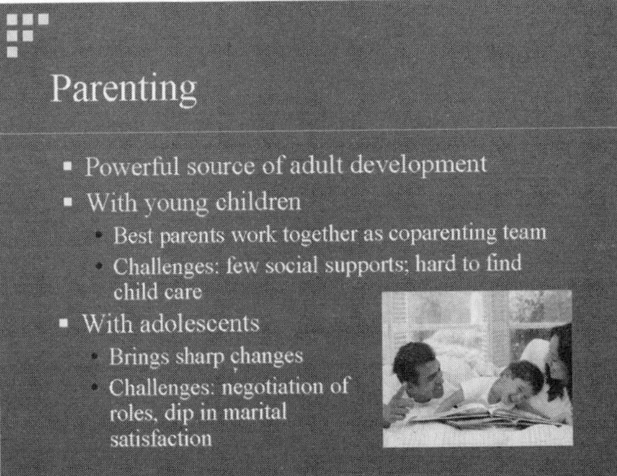
Parenting
Powerful source of adult development
With young children
Best parents work together as coparenting team
Challenges: few social supports; hard to find child care
With adolescents
Brings sharp changes
Challenges: negotiation of roles, dip in marital satisfaction
Copyright © Allyn & Bacon 2007

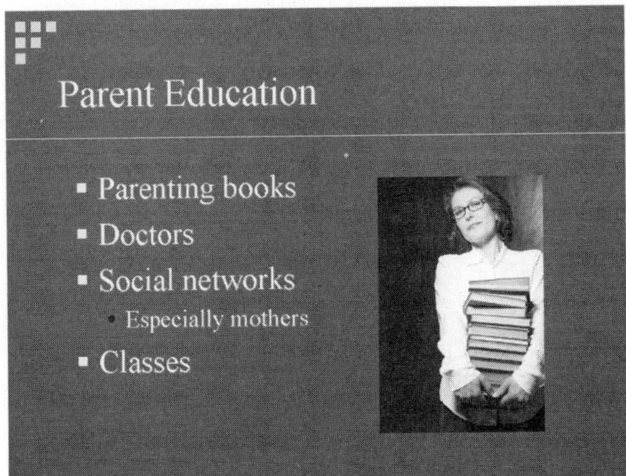
Parent Education
Parenting books
Doctors
Social networks
Especially mothers
Classes
Copyright © Allyn & Bacon 2007

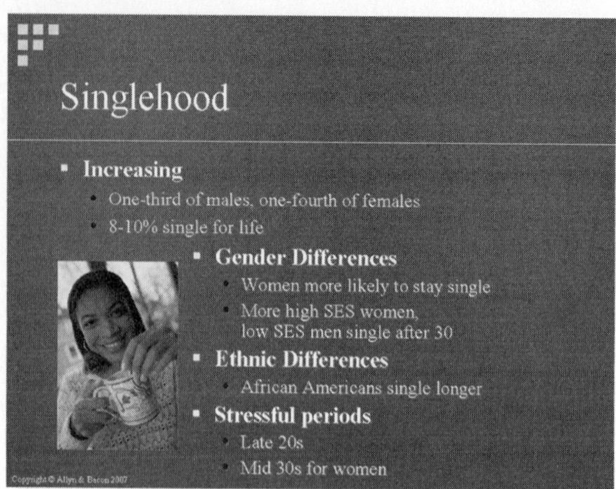
Singlehood
Increasing
One-third of males, one-fourth of females
8-10% single for life
Gender Differences
Women more likely to stay single
More high SES women, low SES men single after 30
Ethnic Differences
African Americans single longer
Stressful periods
Late 20s
Mid 30s for women

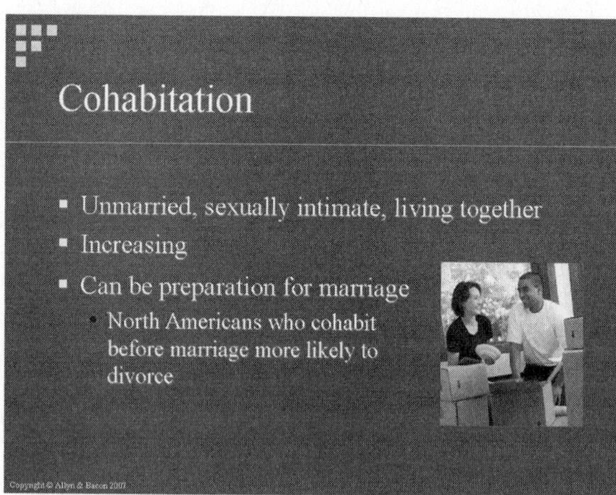
Cohabitation
Unmarried, sexually intimate, living together
Increasing
Can be preparation for marriage
North Americans who cohabit before marriage more likely to divorce

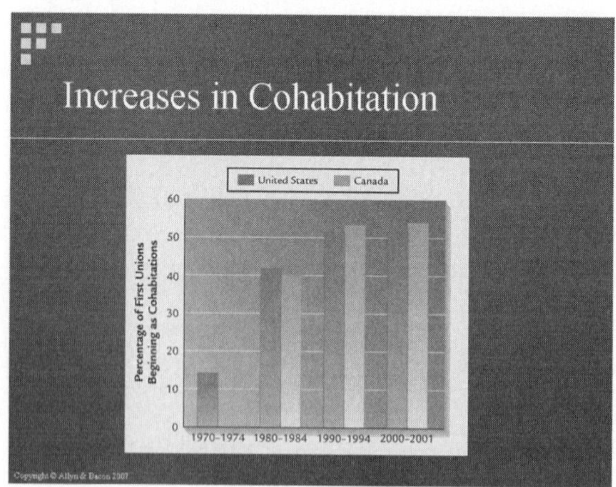
Increases in Cohabitation
United States
Canada
Percentage of First Unions Beginning as Cohabitations
0
10
20
30
40
50
60
1970–1974
1980–1984
1990–1994
2000–2001

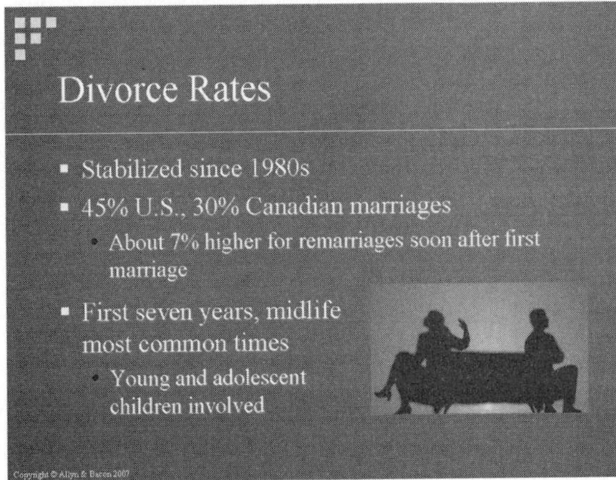
Divorce Rates
Stabilized since 1980s
45% U.S., 30% Canadian marriages
About 7% higher for remarriages soon after first marriage
First seven years, midlife most common times
Young and adolescent children involved
Copyright © Allyn & Bacon 2007

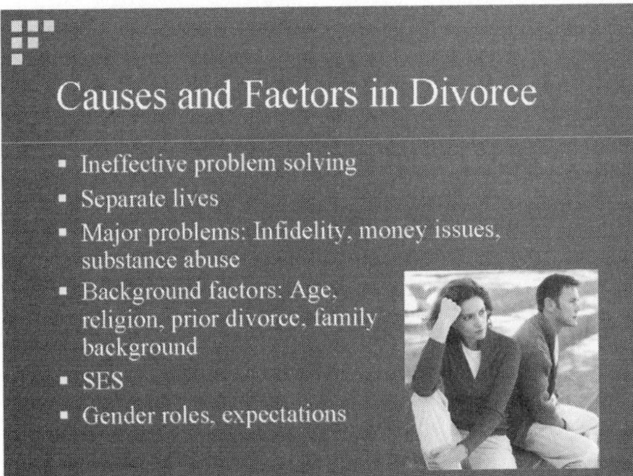
Causes and Factors in Divorce
Ineffective problem solving
Separate lives
Major problems: Infidelity, money issues, substance abuse
Background factors: Age, religion, prior divorce, family background
SES
Gender roles, expectations
Copyright © Allyn & Bacon 2007

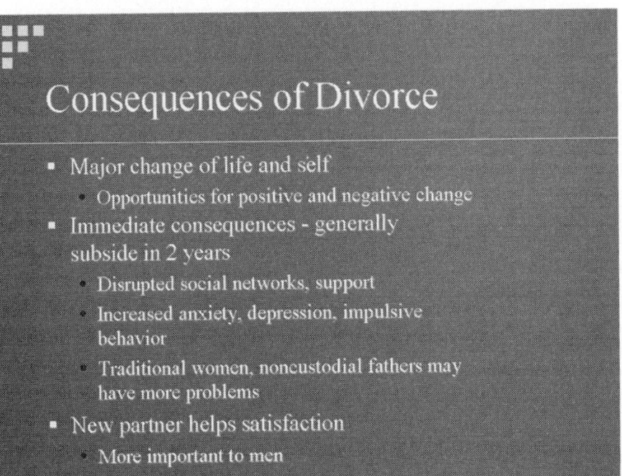
Consequences of Divorce
Major change of life and self
Opportunities for positive and negative change
Immediate consequences - generally subside in 2 years
Disrupted social networks, support
Increased anxiety, depression, impulsive behavior
Traditional women, noncustodial fathers may have more problems
New partner helps satisfaction
More important to men
Copyright © Allyn & Bacon 2007

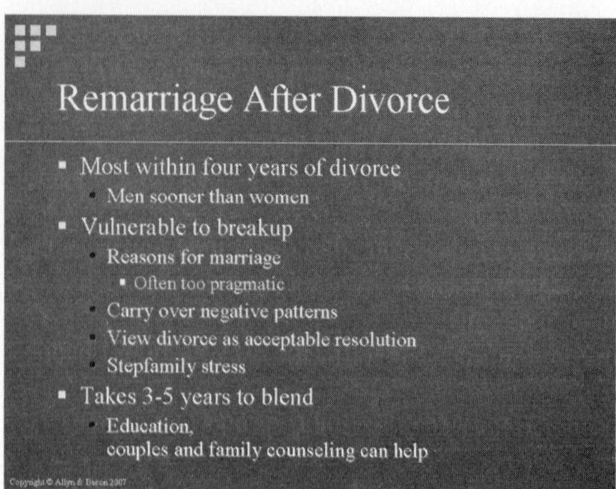
Remarriage After Divorce
Most within four years of divorce
Men sooner than women
Vulnerable to breakup
Reasons for marriage
Often too pragmatic
Carry over negative patterns
View divorce as acceptable resolution
Stepfamily stress
Takes 3-5 years to blend
Education,
couples and family counseling can help

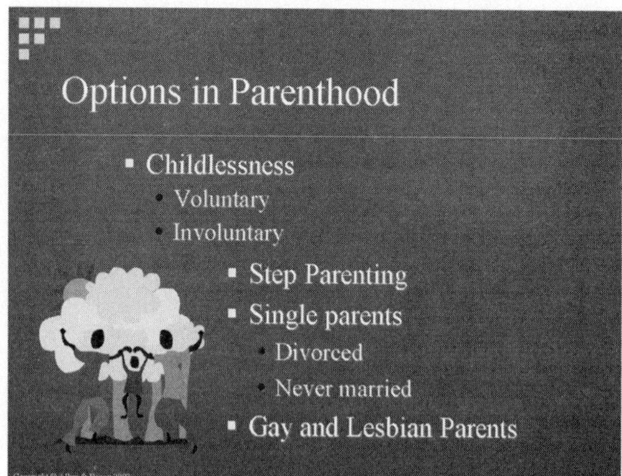
Options in Parenthood
Childlessness
Voluntary
Involuntary
Step Parenting
Single parents
Divorced
Never married
Gay and Lesbian Parents

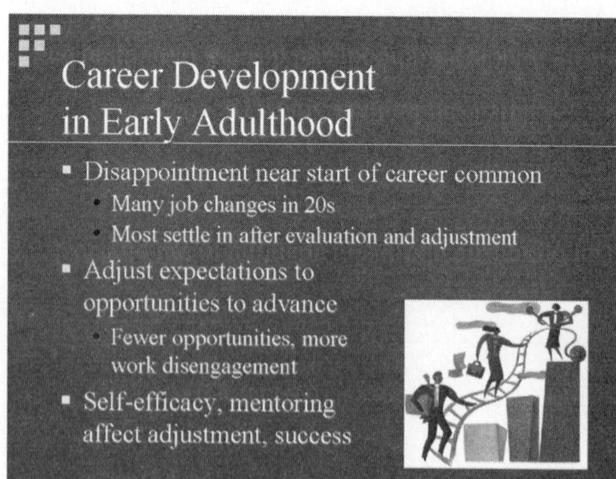
Career Development in Early Adulthood
Disappointment near start of career common
Many job changes in 20s
Most settle in after evaluation and adjustment
Adjust expectations to opportunities to advance
Fewer opportunities, more work disengagement
Self-efficacy, mentoring affect adjustment, success

Challenges to Women's Career Development

- Discontinuous employment
  - Leave for child-rearing, family care
  - Hinders advancement
- Concentration low-paying, low-advancement jobs
  - Contributes to salary gap
- Low self-efficacy for male-dominated fields
- Gender stereotyping
- Few mentors

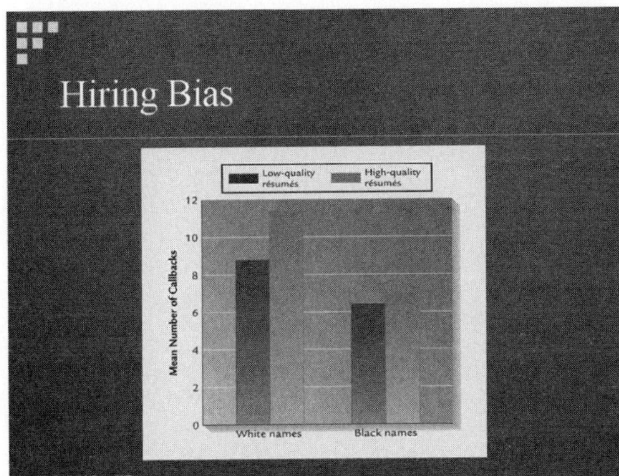

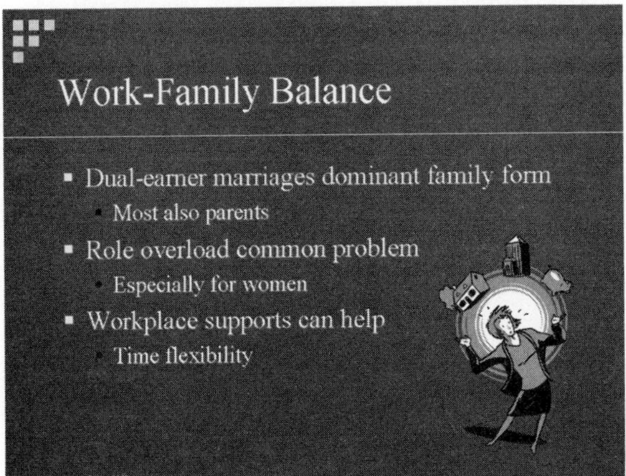

CHAPTER 15
PHYSICAL AND COGNITIVE DEVELOPMENT IN MIDDLE ADULTHOOD

CHAPTER-AT-A-GLANCE

Chapter Outline	Instruction Ideas	Supplements
Physical Development **Physical Changes pp. 395–400** Vision • Hearing • Skin • Muscle–Fat Makeup • Skeleton • Reproductive System	Learning Objectives 15.1–15.2 Learning Activities 15.1–15.2 Ask Yourself p. 399	Transparency 175 Test Bank Items 1–40 Videos: *Exploring Lifespan Development in Action* and *A Window on Lifespan Development* Please contact your Allyn and Bacon publisher's representative for a wide range of video offerings available to adopters.
Health and Fitness pp. 401–404 Sexuality • Illness and Disability • Hostility and Anger	Learning Objectives 15.3–15.5 Learning Activity 15.1	Transparency 176 Test Bank Items 41–64
Adapting to the Challenges of Midlife pp. 404–406 Stress Management • Exercise • An Optimistic Outlook • Gender and Aging: A Double Standard	Learning Objectives 15.6–15.7 Lecture Enhancement 15.1 Learning Activity 15.3 Ask Yourself p. 406	Test Bank Items 65–79
Cognitive Development **Changes in Mental Abilities pp. 407-409** Cohort Effects • Crystallized and Fluid Intelligence	Learning Objectives 15.8–15.9 Lecture Enhancement 15.2 Learning Activity 15.4	Transparency 178 Test Bank Items 80–100
Information Processing pp. 409–412 Speed of Processing • Attention • Memory • Practical Problem Solving and Expertise • Creativity	Learning Objectives 15.10–15.11 Lecture Enhancement 15.3 Learning Activities 15.4, 15.6 Ask Yourself p. 412	Test Bank Items 101–111
Vocational Life and Cognitive Development p. 412	Learning Objective 15.12 Learning Activity 15.5	Test Bank Item 112
Adult Learners: Becoming a College Student in Midlife pp. 412–413 Characteristics of Returning Students • Supporting Returning Students	Learning Objective 15.13 Lecture Enhancement 15.4 Learning Activities 15.7–15.8 Ask Yourself p. 413	Test Bank Items 113–118

BRIEF CHAPTER SUMMARY

Physical development in midlife continues the gradual changes under way in early adulthood. Age-related deterioration in vision, hearing, and the condition of the skin becomes more apparent. Weight gain coupled with loss of lean body mass is a concern for both men and women, as is a loss of bone mass. Dietary changes and weight-bearing exercise can offset these effects of aging.

The climacteric, or decline in fertility, occurs gradually over a 10-year period for women, concluding with menopause—the end of menstruation and of reproductive capacity. Doctors may prescribe hormone therapy to reduce the discomforts of menopause and to protect women from other impairments due to estrogen loss, but research also shows some potential risks of this therapy. The wide variation in physical symptoms and attitudes indicates that menopause is not merely a hormonal event but is also affected by societal beliefs and practices. Men also experience a climacteric, but the change is less dramatic, limited to a decrease in quantity of semen and sperm after age 40.

Frequency and intensity of sexual activity tends to decline in middle adulthood, although it continues to be an important component of married couples' lives. Cancer and cardiovascular disease are the leading causes of death in middle age. Unintentional injuries continue to be a major health threat, although they occur at a lower rate than in young adulthood, largely because of a decline in motor vehicle collisions. When age-related bone loss is severe, a disabling condition called osteoporosis develops. In both men and women, hostility and anger predict heart disease.

Stress management in middle adulthood can limit the age-related rise in illness and, when disease strikes, reduce its severity. Heredity, diet, exercise, social support, coping strategies, and hardiness contribute to middle-aged adults' ability to cope with stress. Negative stereotypes of aging lead many middle-aged adults to fear physical changes. These unfavorable stereotypes are more likely to be applied to women than to men, yielding a double standard, which may be declining as a result of societal changes.

Although declines in cognitive development occur in some areas, most middle-aged people display cognitive competencies, especially in familiar contexts, and some attain outstanding accomplishment. Consistent with the lifespan perspective, cognitive change in middle adulthood is viewed as multidimensional, multidirectional, and plastic. Crystallized intelligence (which depends on accumulated knowledge and experience) increases steadily through middle adulthood, while fluid intelligence (which depends on basic information-processing skills) begins to decline in the twenties. Research shows that using intellectual skills seems to affect the degree to which they are maintained.

Speed of cognitive processing slows with age, making it harder for middle-aged people to divide their attention, focus on relevant stimuli, and switch from one task to another as the situation demands. With age, the amount of information people can retain in working memory diminishes, but general factual knowledge, procedural knowledge, and knowledge related to one's occupation either remain unchanged or increase into midlife. Middle-aged adults in all walks of life often become good at practical problem solving, largely as a result of development of expertise, and creativity in midlife becomes more deliberately thoughtful.

At all ages and in different cultures, a reciprocal relationship exists between vocational life and cognitive development. Stimulating, complex work and flexible, abstract, autonomous thinking support each other. Often motivated by life transitions, adults are returning to undergraduate and graduate study in record numbers. The majority of adult learners are women, who often experience role overload. Social supports for returning students can make the difference between continuing in school and dropping out.

LEARNING OBJECTIVES

After reading this chapter, you should be able to:

15.1 Describe physical changes of middle adulthood, paying special attention to vision, hearing, the skin, muscle–fat makeup, and the skeleton. (pp. 395–397)

15.2 Summarize reproductive changes in middle adulthood, paying special attention to the symptoms of menopause, the benefits and risks of hormone therapy, and women's psychological reactions to menopause. (pp. 397–400)

15.3 Discuss sexuality in middle adulthood and its association with psychological well-being. (p. 401)

15.4 Discuss cancer, cardiovascular disease, and osteoporosis, noting sex differences, risk factors, and interventions. (pp. 401–403)

15.5 Explain how hostility and anger affect health. (pp. 403–404)

15.6 Discuss the benefits of stress management, exercise, and an optimistic outlook in adapting to the physical challenges of midlife. (pp. 404–406)

15.7 Explain the double standard of aging. (p. 406)

15.8 Describe cohort effects on intelligence revealed by Schaie's Seattle Longitudinal Study. (p. 407)

15.9 Describe changes in crystallized and fluid intelligence during middle adulthood, and discuss individual and group differences in intellectual development. (pp. 407–409)

15.10 Describe changes in information processing in midlife, paying special attention to speed of processing, attention, and memory. (pp. 409–411)

15.11 Discuss the development of practical problem solving, expertise, and creativity in middle adulthood. (pp. 411–412)

15.12 Describe the relationship between vocational life and cognitive development. (p. 412)

15.13 Discuss the challenges of adult learners, ways to support returning students, and benefits of earning a degree in midlife. (pp. 412–413)

LECTURE OUTLINE

Physical Development

I. PHYSICAL CHANGES (pp. 395–400)
  A. Vision (p. 396)
    1. By the forties, the lens of the eye enlarges; around age 60, the lens loses its capacity to adjust to objects at varying distances entirely, a condition called **presbyopia** ("old eyes").
    2. Presbyopia, combined with weakening of the muscle that enables the eye to *accommodate* (adjust its focus), leads to farsightedness, making it difficult to read small print without corrective lenses—or, for nearsighted people, bifocals.
    3. Changes in the lens and vitreous:
      a. A decline in the ability to see in dim light occurs as the size of the pupil shrinks and the lens yellows.
      b. After age 40, the *vitreous* (transparent gelatin-like substance that fills the eye) develops opaque areas, reducing the amount of light that reaches the retina.
      c. These changes cause light to scatter within the eye, increasing sensitivity to glare.
      d. Yellowing of the lens and increasing density of the vitreous limit color discrimination, especially at the green–blue–violet end of the spectrum.
    4. Neural changes in the visual system include gradual loss of *rods* and *cones* (light- and color-receptor cells) in the retina and of neurons in the optic nerve, contributing to visual declines.
    5. **Glaucoma**, a disease in which poor fluid drainage leads to a buildup of pressure within the eye, damaging the optic nerve, affects nearly 2 percent of people over age 40 and is a leading cause of blindness.
  B. Hearing (pp. 396–397)
    1. About 14 percent of North Americans between ages 45 and 64 suffer from hearing loss, often as a result of age-related hearing impairments called **presbycusis** ("old hearing").
    2. With aging, inner-ear structures that transform mechanical sound waves into neural impulses deteriorate through natural cell death or reduced blood supply caused by atherosclerosis, and processing of neural messages in the auditory cortex also declines.
    3. Around age 50, a noticeable hearing loss at high frequencies occurs, gradually extending to all frequencies and eventually leading to difficulty in making out human speech.

4. African tribal peoples display little age-related hearing loss, suggesting that factors other than biological aging are involved.
5. Men's hearing declines earlier and more rapidly than women's, a difference associated with cigarette smoking, intense noise in some male-dominated occupations, and underlying conditions such as high blood pressure, cerebrovascular disease, or strokes.

C. Skin (p. 397)
 1. With aging, the *epidermis* (the skin's outer protective layer) becomes less firmly attached to the *dermis* (the middle supportive layer), fibers in the dermis thin, and fat in the *hypodermis* (the inner fatty layer) diminishes, leading the skin to wrinkle and loosen.
 2. In the thirties and forties, lines develop on the forehead, and the skin loses elasticity and begins to sag; after age 50, "age spots" (collections of pigment under the skin) increase, and blood vessels in the skin become more visible as the fatty layer thins.
 3. Sun exposure hastens wrinkling and spotting, and women's skin ages more quickly than that of men, partly because the dermis is thinner in women.

D. Muscle–Fat Makeup (p. 397)
 1. Both men and women tend to gain weight in middle age and often experience an increase in body fat and a loss of lean body mass (muscle and bone).
 2. Muscle mass declines gradually in the forties and fifties, largely through atrophy of fast-twitch fibers, responsible for speed and explosive strength.
 3. Prevention of excessive weight gain and loss of muscle power:
    a. With age, people must gradually reduce caloric intake to adjust for the age-related decline in basal metabolic rate.
    b. A low-fat diet involving increased consumption of vegetables, fruits, and grains has been associated with weight loss and sustained weight maintenance in longitudinal studies.
    c. Weight-bearing exercise can help offset both excess weight and muscle loss.

E. Skeleton (p. 397)
 1. As new cells accumulate on their outer layers, the bones broaden, but their mineral content declines, making them more porous and leading to a gradual but substantial loss in bone mass starting in the late thirties and accelerating in the fifties, especially among women.
 2. Women start with a lower reserve of bone minerals than men and, after menopause, lose the favorable impact of estrogen on bone mineral absorption.
 3. Loss of bone strength causes the disks in the spinal column to collapse, so that height drops by as much as an inch by age 60, and more thereafter.
 4. A healthy lifestyle, including weight-bearing exercise, adequate calcium and vitamin D, and avoidance of smoking and heavy alcohol consumption, can slow bone loss in postmenopausal women by 30 to 50 percent.
 5. The weakened bones fracture more easily and heal more slowly; when bone loss is very great, it leads to a debilitating disorder called *osteoporosis.*

F. Reproductive System (p. 397)
 1. The **climacteric**, the midlife transition in which fertility declines, brings an end to reproductive capacity in women and leads to diminished fertility in men.
 2. Reproductive Changes in Women (pp. 397–398)
    a. The production of estrogen drops over a 10-year period until the climacteric concludes with **menopause**, the end of menstruation and reproductive capacity, which occurs between the late thirties and the late fifties among North American, European, and East Asian women.
    b. Effects of the drop in estrogen following menopause:
       (1) It causes the reproductive organs to shrink in size, the genitals to be less easily stimulated, and the vagina to lubricate more slowly during arousal.
       (2) It contributes to decreased elasticity of the skin, loss of bone mass, and loss of estrogen's protection against accumulation of plaque on the walls of the arteries.
       (3) About 35 to 40 percent of women report difficulties in sexual functioning following menopause, and many report increased irritability and less satisfying sleep, although no physiological link has been identified.

   (4) The period surrounding menopause is often accompanied by emotional and physical symptoms, including mood fluctuations and hot flashes, affecting about 75 percent of women in Western industrialized nations.
   (5) Women with a history of depression or other risk factors are more likely to experience depressive episodes during the climacteric, but no link has been shown between menopause and depression in the general population.
  c. Asian women report fewer menopausal complaints than North American, European, African, and Middle Eastern women, perhaps because Asian diets are low in fat and high in soy-based foods (a rich source of plant estrogen).

3. Hormone Therapy (pp. 398–399)
  a. **Hormone therapy**—low daily doses of estrogen—may be prescribed to reduce the physical discomforts of menopause.
   (1) *Estrogen replacement therapy (ERT),* or estrogen alone, is prescribed for women who have had hysterectomies (surgical removal of the uterus).
   (2) *Hormone replacement therapy (HRT),* consisting of estrogen plus progesterone, is prescribed for other women because the combination reduces the risk of cancer of the endometrium (lining of the uterus), a serious side effect of hormone therapy.
  b. Benefits and risks of ERT and HRT:
   (1) Hormone therapy counteracts hot flashes and vaginal dryness; it may add to the effectiveness of antidepressant medication for women with depression; and it offers some protection against bone deterioration and colon cancer.
   (2) Studies have shown increased risk of breast cancer and blood clots with ERT; a slightly increased risk of heart attacks, stroke, blood clots, and breast cancer with HRT; and a slightly elevated risk of mild cognitive declines and nearly double the risk of Alzheimer's disease and other dementias, although hormone therapy that is begun much earlier may actually reduce the risk of Alzheimer's.
   (3) Research is needed to determine whether the cardiovascular risks of hormone therapy apply to early postmenopausal women.
   (4) Because hormone therapy provides the most reliable relief from menopausal symptoms, some experts argue that prescribing it to low-risk women on a short-term basis (no longer than five years) is justified.

4. Women's Psychological Reactions to Menopause (p. 399)
  a. Wide variation in physical symptoms and attitudes toward menopause indicates that it is not just a hormonal event but is also affected by cultural beliefs and practices.
  b. Negative reactions:
   (1) Women who wanted marriage and family but did not attain these goals may find menopause traumatic, representing the end of their childbearing years.
   (2) Physical symptoms and loss of a youthful appearance can make menopause a difficult time.
  c. Positive reactions:
   (1) Many women find menopause to be little or no trouble, and some are thankful to be freed from worry about birth control.
   (2) Highly educated, career-oriented Caucasian-American women with fulfilling lives outside the home usually have more positive attitudes toward menopause than those with less education.
   (3) African-American and Mexican-American women, who tend to regard menopause as normal and even welcome, experience less irritability and moodiness than Caucasian Americans.

5. Reproductive Changes in Men (p. 399)
  a. Men also experience a climacteric, but it is not a counterpart to menopause: Sperm production continues throughout life, although quantities of semen and sperm decrease after age 40.
  b. Testosterone production declines gradually with age, but the change is minimal in healthy men who remain sexually active.

c. Erectile dysfunction and its treatment:
    (1) The inability to attain an erection when desired becomes more common in midlife.
    (2) Drugs that increase blood flow to the penis, such as Viagra, offer temporary relief from erectile dysfunction.
    (3) Publicity surrounding these drugs has prompted open discussion of men's sexuality and encouraged more men to seek help.
    (4) Other medical factors that contribute to impotence include disorders of the nervous, circulatory, and endocrine systems; anxiety and depression; pelvic injury; and loss of interest in one's sexual partner.

II. HEALTH AND FITNESS (pp. 401–404)
  A. Sexuality (p. 401)
    1. Frequency of sexual activity among married couples tends to decline slightly in middle adulthood, but stability is more typical than dramatic change.
    2. Intensity of sexual response declines in midlife because of physical changes of the climacteric.
    3. The majority of married people over age 50 say that sex is an important component of their relationship, and most find ways to overcome difficulties with sexual functioning.
  B. Illness and Disability (pp. 401–402)
    1. Causes of death in middle age:
      a. The leading causes of death in middle age are cancer and cardiovascular disease.
      b. The rate of unintentional injuries is lower than in early adulthood, but falls leading to bone fractures and death nearly double from early to middle adulthood.
      c. The United States exceeds Canada in death rates from all major causes, largely because of more severe poverty and lack of universal health insurance.
      d. Personality traits that magnify stress, especially hostility and anger, are serious threats to health in midlife.
    2. Cancer (p. 402)
      a. From early to middle adulthood, the death rate due to cancer multiplies tenfold, accounting for about one-third of all midlife deaths in the United States and one-half in Canada.
      b. The incidence of many types of cancer is currently leveling off or declining, but for many decades, cancer mortality rose, largely because of a dramatic increase in lung cancer due to cigarette smoking.
      c. Today, 50 percent fewer men smoke than in the 1950s, but lung cancer has increased in women, many of whom took up smoking after World War II.
      d. Cancer occurs when a cell's genetic program is disrupted, leading to uncontrolled growth and spread of abnormal cells that crowd out normal tissues and organs.
      e. Cancer-linked mutations can be either *germline* (due to an inherited predisposition) or *somatic* (occurring in a single cell, which then multiplies).
      f. According to one theory, error in DNA duplication increases with age, either spontaneously or because of the release of free radicals or breakdown of the immune system, sometimes initiated or intensified by environmental toxins.
      g. Men are generally more vulnerable than women to cancers that affect both sexes, as a result of genetic makeup, greater exposure to cancer-causing agents, and a tendency to delay going to the doctor.
      h. Cancer death rates increase sharply as SES decreases, especially among low-income ethnic minorities.
      i. Overall, a complex interaction of heredity, biological aging, and environment contributes to cancer, with environmental factors (such as alcohol consumption and overweight) heightening the risk posed by genetic factors.
      j. Breast cancer is the leading malignancy for women, prostate cancer for men; lung cancer ranks second for both sexes, followed closely by colon and rectal cancer.
    3. Cardiovascular Disease (pp. 402–403)
      a. Cardiovascular disease causes about 25 percent of the deaths of middle-aged Americans and Canadians each year.

   b. Indicators of cardiovascular disease, including high blood pressure, high blood cholesterol, and atherosclerosis, are often "silent killers" that cause no symptoms until they finally take the form of a heart attack, arrhythmia (irregular heartbeat), or angina pectoris (chest pain that reveals an oxygen-deprived heart).
   c. Treatments include coronary bypass surgery, medication, pacemakers to regulate heart rhythm, and angioplasty to allow blood to flow freely through the arteries.
   d. Heart disease is often viewed as a male problem, so doctors may overlook symptoms in women, especially African-American women, who are at greater risk for heart disease than Caucasian-American women.
4. Osteoporosis (p. 403)
   a. Severe age-related bone loss leads to **osteoporosis**, which affects more than 25 million Americans and 1.4 million Canadians and that greatly magnifies the risk of bone fractures.
   b. Risk factors include age, heredity, body type, ethnicity, and lifestyle.
   c. Major bone fractures, such as a hip fracture, lead to death within a year for 10 to 20 percent of patients, with a higher rate for men, who are less likely than women to have received interventions aimed at preserving bone density.
   d. Treatments include a diet enriched with calcium and vitamin D, weight-bearing exercise, and bone-strengthening medications.
   e. Early prevention efforts should include maximizing peak bone density by increasing calcium and vitamin D intake and engaging in regular exercise in childhood, adolescence, and early adulthood.

C. Hostility and Anger (pp. 403–404)
1. Researchers found that in 35- to 59-year-old men, the **Type A behavior pattern**—extreme competitiveness, ambition, impatience, hostility, angry outbursts, and a sense of time pressure—was associated with a greater risk of developing heart disease, but some later studies have failed to confirm these results.
2. Among the "Type A" behaviors, the "toxic" ingredient is most likely hostility, especially *expressed hostility*, which is associated with a rise in heart rate, blood pressure, and stress hormones, and consistently predicts heart disease and other health problems in both men and women.

III. ADAPTING TO THE CHALLENGES OF MIDLIFE (pp. 404–406)

A. Stress Management (pp. 404–405)
1. In middle adulthood, stress management can help limit the age-related rise in illness and, when disease strikes, can reduce its severity.
2. Techniques for reducing stress include reevaluating the situation, focusing on events one can control, viewing life as fluid, considering alternatives, setting reasonable goals for oneself, exercising regularly, mastering relaxation techniques, using constructive approaches to anger reduction, and seeking social support.
3. Two general strategies for coping with stress are *problem-centered coping* and *emotion-centered coping.*
   a. Problem-centered coping is useful in situations that are changeable; it involves identifying the difficulty and deciding what to do about it.
   b. Emotion-centered coping is internal and private; it is helpful for controlling distress when little can be done to change a situation.
   c. Adults who reduce stress effectively move flexibly between problem-centered and emotion-centered techniques, while ineffective coping is largely emotion-centered.
4. Learning to be assertive rather than hostile and to negotiate rather than explode interrupts the intense physiological response that intervenes between psychological stress and illness.
5. People tend to cope with stress more effectively as they move from early to middle adulthood, perhaps because they become more realistic about their ability to change situations and more skilled at anticipating stressful events and taking steps to avoid them.
6. For people who have difficulty handling midlife challenges, community programs addressing typical concerns of this age group can be helpful in reducing stress.

B. Exercise (p. 405)
   1. More than half of North American middle-aged adults are sedentary, and half of those who begin an exercise program discontinue it within the first six months; even most of those who are active do not exercise at levels that lead to health benefits.
   2. *Self-efficacy*—belief in one's ability to succeed—is vital in adopting, maintaining, and exerting oneself in an exercise regimen, which in turn can lead to a gain in self-efficacy and to a rise in physical self-esteem.
   3. Availability of attractive, safe exercise environments and frequent opportunities to observe others using them promote physical activity.
      a. Low-SES adults often mention inconvenient access to facilities, expense, and unsafe neighborhoods as barriers to exercise—important reasons that activity level declines sharply with SES.
      b. Interventions aimed at increasing physical activity among low-SES adults must address the availability of affordable facilities and safe neighborhoods, in addition to lifestyle and motivational factors.

C. An Optimistic Outlook (p. 406)
   1. **Hardiness** refers to a set of personal qualities—control, commitment, and challenge—that make some individuals better able than others to cope adaptively with stress resulting from inevitable changes.
      a. Hardy individuals regard most experiences as *controllable.*
      b. They display a *committed* approach to daily activities.
      c. They view change as a *challenge*—a normal part of life and a chance for personal growth.
   2. High-hardy individuals are likely to use active, problem-centered coping strategies in situations they can control, whereas low-hardy people more often use emotion-centered and avoidant coping strategies.

D. Gender and Aging: A Double Standard (p. 406)
   1. Negative stereotypes of aging are more likely to be applied to women than to men, yielding a double standard whereby many women in midlife are seen as less attractive and as having more negative characteristics than middle-aged men.
   2. The ideal of a sexually attractive woman—smooth skin, good muscle tone, lustrous hair—may be at the heart of the double standard of aging, and social forces exaggerate this view.
   3. The double standard appears to be declining, with more people viewing middle age as a potentially upbeat, satisfying time for both genders.

Cognitive Development

IV. CHANGES IN MENTAL ABILITIES (pp. 407–409)

A. Cohort Effects (p. 407)
   1. Research using intelligence tests sheds light on the widely held belief that intelligence inevitably declines in middle and late adulthood as the brain deteriorates.
   2. Although many early cross-sectional studies showed a peak in performance at age 35 followed by a steep drop into old age, longitudinal research on college students and soldiers, starting in the 1920s and retesting participants in middle adulthood, revealed an age-related increase in performance.
   3. To explain this contradiction, K. Warner Schaie's Seattle Longitudinal Study used a sequential design, combining longitudinal and cross-sectional approaches.
      a. In 1956, people ranging in age from 22 to 70 were tested cross-sectionally.
      b. Longitudinal follow-ups were conducted at regular intervals, and new samples were added, yielding a total of 5,000 participants, five cross-sectional comparisons, and longitudinal data spanning 35 years.
      c. Although findings on five mental abilities showed the typical cross-sectional drop after the mid-thirties, longitudinal trends for those abilities revealed modest gains in midlife, sustained into the fifties and the early sixties, after which performance decreased gradually.
      d. *Cohort effects* are largely responsible for this difference, as each new generation experienced better health and education than the one before it.

B. Crystallized and Fluid Intelligence (pp. 407–409)
   1. **Crystallized intelligence**, which is heavily influenced by culture, refers to skills that depend on accumulated knowledge and experience, good judgment, and mastery of social conventions—measured on intelligence tests by performance on vocabulary, general information, verbal comprehension, and logical reasoning.
   2. **Fluid intelligence**, which is influenced less by culture than by learning unique to the individual, depends more heavily on basic information-processing skills—ability to detect relationships among visual stimuli, speed of analyzing information, and capacity of working memory—measured on intelligence tests by items involving spatial visualization, digit span, letter–number sequencing, and symbol search.
   3. In many cross-sectional studies, crystallized intelligence increases steadily though middle adulthood, while fluid intelligence begins to decline in the twenties.
   4. Schaie's Seattle Longitudinal Study (pp. 408–409)
      a. Schaie found that five factors that gained in early and middle adulthood—verbal ability, inductive reasoning, verbal memory, spatial orientation, and numeric ability—include both crystallized and fluid skills.
      b. His findings confirmed that middle-aged adults are intellectually "in their prime"—not "over the hill."
      c. A sixth ability, *perceptual speed,* is a fluid skill that decreased from the twenties to the late eighties—a pattern that fits with research indicating that cognitive processing slows with age.
      d. Late in life, fluid factors show greater decrements than crystallized factors—trends that have been confirmed in short-term longitudinal follow-ups of individuals varying widely in age.
      e. Some theorists believe that a general slowing of central nervous system functioning underlies most age-related declines in cognitive performance.
      f. Gains followed by stability in crystallized abilities, despite an earlier decline in fluid intelligence, can be explained by the fact that the decrease in basic processing may not be great enough to affect many well-practiced performances until later in life.
      g. Adults can often compensate for cognitive limitations by drawing on their cognitive strengths or by accommodating—shifting to activities that depend less on cognitive efficiency and more on accumulated knowledge.

V. INFORMATION PROCESSING (pp. 409–412)
   A. Speed of Processing (p. 409)
      1. On both simple reaction-time tasks (pushing a button in response to a light) and complex ones (pushing a left-hand button to a blue light, a right-hand button to a yellow light), response time increases steadily from the early twenties into the nineties.
      2. Researchers agree that changes in the brain cause this age-related slowing of cognitive processing, but disagree on the precise explanation.
         a. The **neural network view** states that as neurons in the brain die, breaks in neural networks occur, and the brain adapts by forming bypasses—new synaptic connections that go around the breaks but are less efficient.
         b. The **information-loss view** suggests that older adults experience greater loss of information as it moves through the cognitive system, so the whole system must slow down to inspect and interpret the information, with particularly negative effects on complex tasks.
      3. Processing speed predicts adults' performance on many tests of complex abilities.
         a. The slower their reaction time, the lower their scores on memory, reasoning, and problem-solving tasks, with particularly strong relationships for fluid-ability items.
         b. Correlations between processing speed and other cognitive performances strengthen with age, suggesting that processing speed is a core ability that contributes broadly to declines in cognitive functioning.
         c. In everyday activities, knowledge and experience can often compensate for impairments in processing speed, especially on verbal items.

B. Attention (pp. 409–410)
   1. Studies of attention focus on how much information adults can take into their mental systems at once; the extent to which they can attend selectively, ignoring irrelevant information; and the ease with which they can switch their attention from one task to another.
   2. Sustaining two complex tasks at once becomes more challenging with age, as does the ability to focus on relevant information and to switch back and forth between different mental operations, perhaps because the slowdown in information processing limits the amount of information a person can attend to at once.
   3. As adults get older, *inhibition*—resistance to interference from irrelevant information—becomes harder, leading to a decline in performance on *continuous performance tasks,* which can cause older adults to appear distractible in everyday life.
   4. People who are highly experienced in attending to critical information and performing several tasks at once, such as air traffic controllers and pilots, are able to compensate for these changes and, as a result, show smaller age-related attentional declines.
   5. Practice can improve older adults' ability to divide attention between two tasks, selectively focus on relevant information, and switch back and forth between mental operations.

C. Memory (pp. 410–411)
   1. From the twenties into the sixties, the amount of information people can retain in working memory diminishes, largely because of a decline in use of memory strategies on these tasks.
   2. Older individuals rehearse less than younger individuals, reflecting their slower rate of thinking.
   3. Older people are also less likely to use organization and elaboration, memory strategies that involve linking incoming information with already stored information; they find it harder to retrieve information from long-term memory that would help them recall.
   4. Changes in task design, such as slowing the pace at which information is presented, can help older people compensate for age-related declines in working memory.
   5. Research suggests that aging has little impact on metacognition and middle-aged people often use metacognitive knowledge to maximize performance.

D. Practical Problem Solving and Expertise (p. 411)
   1. Gains in *expertise* support middle-aged adults' continued cognitive growth in **practical problem solving**—analyzing how to achieve goals in real-world situations involving a high degree of uncertainty.
   2. Expertise is seen in individuals in all types of work, not just in those who are highly educated or work in high-status professions.
   3. Age-related advantages are also evident in solutions to everyday problems, where middle-aged and older adults choose better strategies than young adults because of their greater emphasis on using logical analysis to solve a practical problem.

E. Creativity (pp. 411–412)
   1. Creative accomplishment tends to peak in the late thirties or early forties and then decline.
   2. The *quality* of creativity may change with advancing age in several ways.
      a. Creative works produced after age 40 in literature and the arts often appear more deliberately thoughtful than the spontaneous, intensely emotional works of younger people.
      b. With age, many creators shift from generating unusual products to creating works that sum up or integrate their extensive knowledge and experience.
      c. Creativity in middle adulthood often reflects a shift from an egocentric concern with self-expression to more altruistic goals.

VI. VOCATIONAL LIFE AND COGNITIVE DEVELOPMENT (p. 412)

A. Because of negative stereotypes of age-related problem-solving and decision-making skills, older employees may be given less challenging work.

B. Learning on the job generalizes to other realms of life, promoting cognitive flexibility, which is also likely to be passed on to the next generation.

C. The impact of a challenging job on cognitive growth is as great for people in their fifties and early sixties as for younger adults, with consistent findings across different generations and widely varying life experiences, reflecting the plasticity of development.

D. Because cognitive flexibility is responsive to vocational experience into middle adulthood and perhaps beyond, more jobs should be designed to promote intellectual stimulation and challenge.

VII. ADULT LEARNERS: BECOMING A STUDENT IN MIDLIFE (pp. 412–413)
   A. Characteristics of Returning Students (p. 413)
      1. During the past 25 years, students over age 25 in North American colleges and universities increased from 28 to 40 percent of total enrollment, with an especially sharp rise in those over age 35.
      2. About 60 percent of adult learners are women, who may experience anxiety related to negative aging and gender stereotypes.
      3. Role demands outside of school can create high psychological stress for many returning women, leading many to progress more slowly than men of similar age.
      4. Role overload is the most common reason for middle-age women not completing their degrees.
   B. Supporting Returning Students (pp. 413)
      1. Social supports for returning students can make the difference between continuing in school and dropping out.
         a. Encouragement and help from family and friends are crucial.
         b. Institutional services available to returning students should include personal relationships with faculty, peer networks, conveniently scheduled evening and Saturday classes, online courses, and financial aid for part-time students.
      2. Nontraditional students rarely require assistance in defining career goals but often seek help in choosing the most appropriate courses and in exploring jobs related to their talents.
      3. Low-income students often need special assistance, such as academic tutoring, sessions in confidence building and assertiveness, and, in the case of ethnic minorities, help adjusting to styles of learning that are at odds with their cultural background.
      4. When support systems are in place, most returning students gain in self-efficacy and do well academically.
      5. Education can transform development by providing new life options, financial rewards, and higher self-esteem—often powerfully reshaping the life course.

LECTURE ENHANCEMENTS

LECTURE ENHANCEMENT 15.1
Long-Term Effects of Optimism and Pessimism on Physical and Mental Health (p. 406)

Time: 5–10 minutes

Objective: To examine the long-term effects of optimism and pessimism on physical and mental health.

As noted in the text, an optimistic outlook affects how people cope with stress and, in turn, reduces risk of illness and mortality. To examine the relationship of optimism and pessimism in early adulthood to health status in middle and late adulthood, Maruta and colleagues (2003) recruited 447 participants who were self-referred to the Mayo Clinic between 1962 and 1965. At the time of treatment, participants completed the Minnesota Multiphasic Personality Inventory (MMPI), which is commonly used to identify psychiatric conditions. The MMPI also contains a scale that measures optimism and pessimism. Thirty years later, participants were asked to complete the Short-Form-36 (SF-36), a self-report questionnaire that assesses overall health and quality of life. The SF-36 asks individuals about physical functioning, role limitations resulting from physical problems, bodily pain, general health perception, vitality, social functioning, role limitations resulting from emotional problems, and mental health.

Findings indicated that participants who scored high in optimism in the 1960s were in better physical and mental health than pessimists 30 years later. Compared to pessimists, optimists reported fewer health-related limitations, fewer problems with work or daily activities, and less pain. Optimists also indicated that they had more energy, were more involved in social activities, and felt more peaceful, happy, and calm than their pessimistic counterparts.

In small groups, ask students to list characteristics of optimistic adults. What role does hardiness play in an optimistic outlook? Why are optimists generally more healthy and well-adjusted than pessimists?

Maruta, T., Colligan, R. C., Malinchoc, M., & Offord, K. P. (2003). Optimism-pessimism assessed in the 1960s and self-reported health status 30 years later. *Mayo Clinic Proceedings, 77,* 748–753.

LECTURE ENHANCEMENT 15.2
The Relationship Between Age, Hormones, and Cognitive Functioning in Middle-Aged and Elderly Men (pp. 407–409)

Time: 10–15 minutes

Objective: To investigate the link between age, hormones, and cognitive functioning in middle-aged and elderly men.

To investigate the relationship between age, hormones, and cognitive functioning, Fonda and colleagues (2005) recruited 981 middle-aged and elderly men who were participating in the Massachusetts Male Aging Study. Participants completed standardized assessments of working memory, processing speed, and spatial ability. In the working memory task, participants listened to sequences of numbers and were then asked to repeat the numbers backward. To measure processing speed, participants reviewed numbered boxes with corresponding symbols. Next, they had 90 seconds to insert the same symbols in empty, numbered boxes. In the spatial ability task, participants were presented with a figure and then had to identify the same figure after it was rotated and/or drawn backward.

Participants provided two nonfasting blood samples, which were used to analyze testosterone and other hormone concentrations. Because educational level, health conditions, and depression affect cognitive functioning, the researchers also collected demographic and health information and administered a standardized depression scale.

Findings revealed that age differences predicted differences in cognitive functioning. Compared to middle-aged men, elderly men scored lower on tasks that measured working memory, processing speed, and spatial ability. Although some studies have found a link between hormone levels and cognition (higher levels of testosterone, for example, have been linked to higher levels of cognitive functioning), this study was unable to support such findings after controlling for demographic variables, educational level, and overall health. Thus, after controlling for hormone levels, overall health, education, and depression, age was the strongest predictor of cognitive change from middle to late adulthood.

In small groups, have students list strategies that can help middle-aged and older adults compensate for declines in certain aspects of intellectual functioning, such as decrements in processing speed, attention, and memory.

Fonda, S. J., Bertrand, R., O'Donnell, A., Longcope, C., & McKinlay, J. B. (2005). Age, hormones, and cognitive functioning among middle-aged and elderly men: Cross-sectional evidence from the Massachusetts Male Aging Study. *Journal of Gerontology: MEDICAL SCIENCES, 60,* 385–390.

LECTURE ENHANCEMENT 15.3
Age-Related Changes in Self-Perceptions of Creativity (pp. 411–412)

Time: 10–15 minutes

Objective: To highlight age-related changes in self-perceptions of creativity in a sample of current or retired visual artists.

The text notes that creativity tends to peak in the late thirties or early forties and then declines. However, considerable variation exists across individuals and disciplines. To examine age-related changes in self-perceptions of creativity, Reed (2005) recruited 21 adults between the ages of 53 and 75. The participants were visual artists or retired visual artists. To assess self-perceptions about creativity and aging, participants were asked the following questions:

1. How many years have you been working as an artist?
2. Do you rely on selling your artwork to make a living?
3. When did you decide to become an artist?
4. Did you recognize that you had a certain ability when you were younger?
5. Can you describe your motivations for making art?
6. Do you feel that you are more creative, as creative, or less creative than when you first began making art?

7. Can you elaborate on the differences that you see in your process of working between the way you work now and the way you approached your work 20 years ago?
8. Are there differences in your working habits, the way you carry out your inspirations, and your drive to complete work between now and then (20 years ago)?
9. How much of what you are doing now relies on the experience of working in your area for many years?

Findings indicated that older visual artists believed that creativity increases or remains stable with age. These individuals also believed that experience helps maintain or enhance creativity over time. For example, one participant mentioned technical experience versus artistic design. As one ages, he or she gains experience in the technical aspects of creating art. Once artists have mastered the techniques, they are free to spend more time on creative design. Compared to younger artists, older artists spent more time creating art for leisure or personal use. This was not surprising, given that younger artists were more likely to rely on art sales to make a living. Therefore, the motivations for creating art were different for older and younger participants.

Another important finding was the older participants were more likely to compensate for changes in ability. For example, some artists modified their work to accommodate changes in speed or productivity. Instead of spending 10 hours a day working on their art, they spent 6 or 8 hours a day and accepted that it would take longer to complete a project. Because age brings about changes in flexibility and strength, some artists had to find outside help for certain aspects of their work. One 69-year-old participant mentioned that glass cutting was now painful. Instead of abandoning glasswork, he found someone to help with that task. Thus, older participants accepted age-related changes in ability, while finding alternative ways to produce creative and personally satisfying artwork.

Ask students to reflect on these findings. Specifically, how might self-perceptions of creativity promote creative work in middle adulthood and beyond? Using research from previous chapters, what do we know about the relationship between self-perceptions and actual behavior?

Reed, I. C. (2005). Creativity: Self-perceptions over time. *International Journal of Aging & Human Development, 60,* 1–18.

LECTURE ENHANCEMENT 15.4
Returning Students' Perspectives About College Education (pp. 412–413)

Time: 10–15 minutes

Objective: To highlight returning students' perceptions about college education.

As noted in the text, adults are returning to undergraduate and graduate study in record numbers. But what are their perceptions of the college experience? To find out, Chao and Good (2004) recruited 43 nontraditional undergraduate students between ages 26 and 62 years. The researchers conducted one-hour interviews with each participant and focused on his or her perspectives about college education, including career development, life transition, financial investment, support systems, and motivation.

Results indicated that hopefulness was a major theme among the participants. For example, most indicated that they were optimistic about their decision to return to college and expected positive outcomes. As a result, they were willing to adjust and manage other important roles, such as work, family, and interpersonal relationships. The participants also indicated that they felt excitement and a sense of self-fulfillment about their decision to return to college. Another important finding was that these nontraditional students integrated their college education into their career development—they believed that their college degree would advance their career opportunities. Because they were hopeful and motivated to succeed in their new role, the participants were not overly anxious about the financial investment of college.

The results also highlighted the importance of social support. Participants indicated that their decision to return to college was strongly influenced by friends and family. As a result of their new student role, many had to negotiate work and family responsibilities. One woman noted, "My husband encouraged me to earn a college degree, since he knew I was stuck with my work. Then we negotiated on sharing our responsibilities of taking care of the kids." Other participants dealt with midlife changes by returning to school: "I had a tumultuous marriage before I came back to school. After divorce, I noticed that I really wanted to do something new. I wanted a new life, new job, and new self. To reach the new experiences. I thought college education would be the first step."

Taken together, the results suggest that returning students are hopeful and have positive expectations about the college experience. They are aware of changing roles and responsibilities and seem willing and prepared to deal with the challenges. As noted in the text, although role overload can occur with returning students, many express high motivation to work through these difficulties, referring to the excitement of learning, to the fulfillment academic success brings, and to their sense of hopefulness that a college education will improve both their work and family lives.

The text describes the characteristics and challenges of returning students. How can colleges and universities support the unique needs of returning students?

Chao, R., & Good, G. E. (2004). Nontraditional students' perspectives on college education: A qualitative study. *Journal of College Counseling, 7,* 5–12.

LEARNING ACTIVITIES

LEARNING ACTIVITY 15.1
True or False: Physical Development in Middle Adulthood (pp. 395–406)

Present the following exercise to students as a quiz or in-class activity:

Directions: Read each of the following statements and indicate whether it is *True* (T) or *False* (F).

Statements:

_____ 1. Glaucoma affects nearly 15 percent of people over age 40.
_____ 2. Women's hearing declines earlier and at a faster rate than men's.
_____ 3. In middle age, weight gain and loss of muscle power are inevitable.
_____ 4. EEG and other physiological measures reveal that menopause is linked to changes in quantity and quality of sleep.
_____ 5. In one study, HRT slightly elevated the risk of mild cognitive declines and nearly doubled the risk of Alzheimer's disease and other dementias.
_____ 6. In middle adulthood, the best predictor of sexual frequency is good health.
_____ 7. Cancer and cardiovascular disease are the leading causes of death in middle age.
_____ 8. Because osteoporosis is considered a "woman's disease," men are far less likely to be screened and treated for it.
_____ 9. Research pinpoints hostility as the toxic ingredient of the Type A behavior pattern.
_____ 10. Low-hardy individuals are likely to use active-problem-centered coping strategies in situations they can control.

Answers:

1. F
2. F
3. F
4. F
5. T
6. F
7. T
8. T
9. T
10. F

LEARNING ACTIVITY 15.2
Creating a Pamphlet on Physical Changes in Middle Adulthood (pp. 395–406)

Many people have negative or inaccurate perceptions of physical development in middle adulthood. For example, young people tend to believe that menopause is a traumatic event for middle-aged women. Ask students to pretend that a local health department has asked them to create a pamphlet on physical changes in middle adulthood. Using research in the text as a guide, have students list the information they would include in the pamphlet. For instance, what physical changes often accompany middle adulthood? How do these changes differ for men and women? How can middle-aged adults maintain good health? What positive changes occur in middle adulthood?

LEARNING ACTIVITY 15.3
Media Advertisements and the Double Standard of Aging (p. 406)

Ask students to bring to class several copies of newspaper or magazine advertisements that include middle-aged adults. In small groups, have students answer the following questions: Is there evidence of a double standard of aging? What products do older men and women advertise? What personal characteristics do males and females seem to display? Is one sex represented more favorably in the advertisement? Do students think advertisers should portray middle-aged adults as more androgynous? Why or why not?

LEARNING ACTIVITY 15.4
Matching: Cognitive Development in Middle Adulthood (pp. 407–411)

Present the following exercise as an in-class activity or quiz:

Directions: Match each of the following terms with its correct description.

Terms:

1. Crystallized intelligence
2. Fluid intelligence
3. Neural network view
4. Information-loss view
5. Practical problem solving
6. Expertise

Descriptions:

A. Requires people to size up real-world situations and analyze how best to achieve goals that have a high degree of uncertainty.
B. As neurons in the brain die, breaks in mental networks occur. The brain adapts by forming bypasses.
C. An extensive, highly organized, and integrated knowledge base that can be used to support a high level of performance.
D. Skills that depend on accumulated knowledge and experience, good judgment, and mastery of social conventions.
E. Depends on basic information-processing skills—the ability to detect relationships among visual stimuli, the speed with which we can analyze information, and the capacity of workingmemory.
F. Suggests that older adults experience greater loss of information as it moves through the cognitive system.

Answers:

1. D
2. E
3. B
4. F
5. A
6. C

LEARNING ACTIVITY 15.5
Creating a Resume for Middle-Aged Workers (p. 412)

Ask students to pretend they have been hired by a local employment agency. Due to recent layoffs, a large number of middle-aged adults have lost their jobs. Many companies are reluctant to hire these individuals, fearing they will not be as productive as younger adults. Using research on cognitive development and vocational life, have students create a generic resume that highlights the many strengths and skills of middle-aged workers. How will companies likely benefit from the experiences and skills of older employees?

LEARNING ACTIVITY 15.6
Age-Related Differences in Practical Problem Solving (p. 411)

Have students present the following dilemma to a young adult and a middle-aged adult (a parent, aunt or uncle, family friend):

What would you do if you had a landlord who refused to make some expensive repairs you want done because he or she thinks they are too costly?

1. Try to make the repairs yourself.
2. Try to understand your landlord's view and decide whether they are necessary repairs.
3. Try to get someone to settle the dispute between you and your landlord.
4. Accept the situation and don't dwell on it.

Students should record their answers and indicate the approximate age of the respondents. Compile students' findings into a handout for class discussion. Were there age-related differences in the answers to the dilemma? For instance, were older adults more likely to select response (2)? Were students surprised by any of the findings? Explain.

LEARNING ACTIVITY 15.7
Exploring the Characteristics and Challenges of Nontraditional/Returning Students (pp. 412–413)

In small groups, ask students to list characteristics of returning students, including challenges they often face. Are there different perceptions about traditional-age and returning students? How can colleges and universities support nontraditional and returning students? If you have any returning students in your class, ask them to reflect on their experiences. Have they felt supported by the college and university? Explain.

LEARNING ACTIVITY 15.8
Campus Supports for Returning Students (pp. 412–413)

Social supports for returning students can make the difference between continuing in school and dropping out. Ask students to find out what social supports are offered for returning students on their campus. For example, are there specialized orientation programs and literature available for these students? Are classes scheduled in ways that help students balance career and family responsibilities (for example, evening and Saturday classes, online classes, off-campus classes)? What financial aid resources are available for part-time students? Are there on-campus child-care services?

ASK YOURSELF . . .

REVIEW: Describe cultural influences on the experience of menopause. (pp. 399, 400)

Highly educated, career-oriented Caucasian-American women with fulfilling lives outside the home usually have more positive attitudes toward menopause than do women with less education. Research also suggests that African-American and Mexican-American women hold generally favorable views of menopause. African-American women experience less irritability and moodiness than Caucasian Americans and tend to regard menopause as normal, inevitable, and even welcome. Similarly, Mexican-American women who have not yet adopted the language—and perhaps certain beliefs—of the larger society tend to have especially positive values toward menopause.

Research in non-Western cultures reveals that middle-aged women's social status also affects the experience of menopause. In societies where older women are respected and the mother-in-law and grandmother roles bring new privileges and responsibilities, complaints about menopausal symptoms are rare. Perhaps partly for this reason, women in Asian nations seldom report discomforts, and when they do, their symptoms usually differ from those of Western women. For example, although they rarely complain of hot flashes, a small number of Japanese women do report shoulder stiffness, back pain, headaches, and fatigue. Neither Japanese women nor their doctors consider menopause to be a significant marker of female middle age. Rather, midlife is the time when a Japanese woman attains peak respect and responsibility, typically involving household management, attending to grandchildren, caring for dependent parents-in-law, and working part-time.

Many rural Mayan women of the Yucatán, who marry as teenagers and have many children, are eager for childbearing to end and welcome menopause, describing it with phrases such as "being happy" and "free like a young girl again." None report hot flashes or other symptoms of discomfort. In contrast, like North Americans, rural Greek women use birth control to limit family size, and most report hot flashes and sweating at menopause. However, they regard these as temporary discomforts that will stop on their own, not as medical symptoms requiring treatment.

APPLY: At age 42, Stan began to wear bifocals, and over the next 10 years, he required an adjustment to his corrective lenses almost every year. What physical changes account for Stan's repeated need for new eyewear? (p. 396)

Stan's vision is going through a set of normative changes. By the forties, difficulty reading small print is common, due to growth in size of the lens combined with weakening of the muscle that enables the eye to *accommodate* (adjust its focus) to nearby objects. As new fibers appear on the surface of the lens, they compress older fibers toward the center, creating a thicker, denser, less pliable structure that eventually cannot be transformed at all. Gradually, around age 60, the lens loses its capacity to adjust to objects at varying distances entirely, a condition called *presbyopia* (literally, "old eyes"). As the lens enlarges, the eye rapidly becomes more farsighted between ages 40 and 60. Corrective lenses—or, for nearsighted people, bifocals—ease reading problems.

REFLECT: In view of the benefits and risks of hormone therapy, what factors would you consider, or advise others to consider, before taking such medication? (pp. 398–399)

This is an open-ended question with no right or wrong answer.

REVIEW: Cite evidence that biological aging, individual heredity, and environmental factors contribute to osteoporosis. (p. 403)

When age-related bone loss is severe, a condition called *osteoporosis* develops. A major factor related to osteoporosis is the decline in estrogen associated with menopause. In middle and late adulthood, women lose about 50 percent of their bone mass, about half of it in the 10 years following menopause. In men, the age-related decrease in testosterone, though much more gradual than women's estrogen loss, also contributes to bone loss.

Heredity also plays an important role. A family history of osteoporosis increases risk, and identical twins are more likely than fraternal twins to share the disorder. People with thin, small-framed bodies are more likely to be affected because they typically attain a lower peak bone mass in adolescence. In contrast, higher bone density makes African Americans less susceptible than Asian Americans, Caucasians, and Hispanics. An unhealthy lifestyle also contributes: A calcium-deficient diet and lack of physical activity both reduce bone mass, as do cigarette smoking and alcohol consumption, which interfere with the replacement of bone cells.

APPLY: During a routine physical exam, Dr. Furrow gave 55-year-old Bill a battery of tests for cardiovascular disease but did not assess his bone density. In contrast, when 60-year-old Cara complained of chest pains, Dr. Furrow opted to "wait and see" before initiating further testing. What might account for Dr. Furrow's different approaches to Cara and Bill? (pp. 402–403)

Because men account for over 70 percent of cases of cardiovascular disease in middle adulthood, doctors often view cardiovascular disease as a "male problem." Consequently, they frequently overlook women's symptoms, which tend to be milder, more often taking the form of angina than a full-blown heart attack. In one study, researchers had male and female actors present identical symptoms of angina to a sample of over 700 doctors. The doctors were far less likely to suspect heart problems in women. And among victims of full-blown heart attacks, women are less likely than men to be offered costly, invasive treatment, such as angioplasty or bypass surgery.

In contrast, because osteoporosis usually develops earlier in women than in men, it has become known as a "women's disease." Men are far less likely to be screened and treated for it. This means that, compared with women, men with hip fractures tend to be older and to lack a history of interventions aimed at preserving bone density, which are less likely to be initiated for men than for women.

In both cases, these findings help explain why Dr. Furrow took a different approach to Cara than to Bill.

REFLECT: Which midlife health problem is of greatest personal concern to you? What steps can you take now to help prevent it? (pp. 401–406)

This is an open-ended question with no right or wrong answer.

REVIEW: How does slowing of cognitive processing affect attention and memory in midlife? What can older adults do to compensate for these declines? (pp. 409–411)

Sustaining two complex tasks at once becomes more challenging with age, along with an age-related decrement in the ability to switch back and forth between mental operations. These declines in attention are probably due to a slowdown in information processing, which limits the amount of information a person can attend to at once.

Cognitive inhibition—resistance to interference from irrelevant information—also becomes harder as adults get older. In everyday life, inhibitory difficulties can cause older adults to appear distractible—inappropriately captured by a thought or feature of the environment and diverted from the task at hand.

Similarly, when given lists of words or digits or meaningful prose passages to learn, middle-aged and older adults recall less than young adults. This change is largely due to a decline in use of memory strategies on these tasks. Older individuals rehearse less than younger individuals—a difference believed to be due to a slower rate of thinking. Older people cannot repeat new information to themselves as quickly as younger people, and they are less likely to use memory strategies of organization and elaboration, or may use these strategies less effectively. Older adults find it harder to retrieve information from long-term memory that would help them use these techniques. Greater difficulty focusing on relevant as opposed to irrelevant information seems to be involved: As irrelevant stimuli take up space in working memory, less space is available for the memory task at hand.

Practice can improve the ability to divide attention between two tasks, switch back and forth between mental operations, and selectively focus on relevant information. When older adults receive training in these skills, their performance improves as much as that of younger adults, although training does not close the gap between age groups. Likewise, on memory tasks in which a word list has a strong category-based structure, older adults organize as well as younger adults do. And when instructed to organize or elaborate, middle-aged and older people willingly do so, and their performance improves. Also, tasks can be designed to help older people compensate for age-related declines in working memory—for example, by slowing the pace at which information is presented. Finally, middle-aged people can draw on their accumulated *metacognitive knowledge* about how to maximize their own performance. Aging appears to have little impact on metacognition.

APPLY: Asked about hiring older sales personnel, a department store manager replied, "They are my best employees!" Why does this manager find older employees desirable, despite the age-related decline in speed of processing? (p. 411)

Although processing speed may decline for older workers, practical problem solving and expertise reach their height in midlife, leading to highly efficient and effective approaches to solving problems. And expertise is not just the province of the highly educated and those who rise to the top of administrative ladders. Although physical skills (strength and dexterity) decline with age, job knowledge and practice increase. As a result, compared to younger adults with similar years of experience, middle-aged sales personnel can be expected to perform more competently, serving customers in especially adept, attentive ways.

REFLECT: Describe the expert and/or creative performance of a middle-aged adult whom you know well. (pp. 411–412)

This is an open-ended question with no right or wrong answer.

REVIEW: In view of the impact of vocational and educational experiences on midlife cognitive development, evaluate the saying "You can't teach an old dog new tricks." (pp. 412–413)

Research has shown that while cognitively flexible employees seek work that offers challenge and autonomy, the relationship between vocational life and cognition is reciprocal: Engaging in complex work can lead to gains in cognitive flexibility, as well. Findings of large-scale studies carried out in Japan and Poland revealed that stimulating, nonroutine jobs help explain the relationship between SES and flexible abstract thinking. Furthermore, learning on the job generalizes to other realms of life. People who do intellectually demanding work also seek out stimulating leisure pursuits, which in turn foster cognitive flexibility. And research shows that the impact of a challenging job on cognitive growth is not limited to young adults. People in their fifties and sixties gain as much as do those in their twenties and thirties.

Adults are returning to undergraduate and graduate study in record numbers. Most adults who return to college reap great personal benefits and do well academically. Ultimately, returning to school can powerfully reshape the life course in middle adulthood. Flexible thinking, academic achievement, and altered life paths indicate that "old dogs" can, indeed, learn "new tricks."

APPLY: Marcella completed one year of college, in her twenties. Now, at age 42, she has returned to earn a degree. Plan a set of experiences for Marcella's first semester that will increase her chances of success. (pp. 412–413)

As Marcella reenters college, she will benefit if she has the social support of her friends and family. Before school starts, Marcella should discuss her plans with friends and family so they are prepared to encourage her in her efforts. She should also seek their assistance in finding uninterrupted time to study. For example, another family member might take over doing the laundry or another household chore on a regular basis.

Before school starts, Marcella should check to see what institutional services are available for returning students. For example, she might look into the availability of evening and weekend classes that would fit her schedule more conveniently than day classes. She might also investigate financial aid for part-time students or consider going to school part-time, which could increase her chances for success. Marcella should set up appointments at the campus for testing to identify her academic strengths and weaknesses and should meet with her academic advisor and with other students to expand her perspective.

Once school starts, Marcella should take the time to develop personal relationships with faculty and other students. She might attend academic tutoring sessions and sessions in confidence-building and assertiveness if her school provides them. In addition, she should continue to seek social support from friends and family as she strives to meet the varying role demands both within and outside of the educational setting.

REFLECT: Interview a nontraditional student in one of your classes about the personal challenges and rewards of working toward a degree at a later age. What services does your institution offer to support returning students? (pp. 412–413)

This is an open-ended question with no right or wrong answer.

SUGGESTED STUDENT READINGS

Brim, O. G., Kessler, R. C., & Ryff, C. D. (Eds.). (2005). *How healthy are we? A national study of well-being at midlife.* Chicago, IL: University of Chicago Press. Using results from the Midlife in the United States Study (MIDUS), which included over 7,000 adults between the ages of 25 and 74, this book examines physical health, psychological well-being, and quality of life in middle-aged Americans. Findings represent adults from diverse economic, geographic, and ethnic backgrounds.

Jarvis, P. (2004). *Adult education and lifelong learning: Theory and practice.* New York: Taylor & Francis. Examines current theories of adult learning and education, such as characteristics of adult learners, adult learning needs and opportunities, and distance education.

Levine, S. B. (2005). *Inventing the rest of our lives: Women in the second adulthood.* New York: Penguin. Presents a thorough and optimistic overview of middle adulthood for women, including physical changes, self-discovery, modifications in marital and family roles, and unique career opportunities.

TRANSPARENCIES

T-175 Percentage of Menopausal Women in Different Regions of the World Reporting Hot Flashes
Figure 15.1 (p. 398)

T-176 Leading Causes of Death Between 45 and 64 Years of Age in the United States and Canada
Figure 15.2 (p. 401)

T-178 Longitudinal Trends in Six Mental Abilities, from the Seattle Longitudinal Study
Figure 15.3 (p. 408)

MEDIA MATERIALS

EXPLORING LIFESPAN DEVELOPMENT IN ACTION

Middle Adulthood

Physical development in midlife is a continuation of the gradual changes already underway in early adulthood. Although middle-aged adults become increasingly conscious of aging, they can take many steps to promote physical vigor and good health. Janet, a dancer and dance teacher for over 40 years, discusses the aging process and her strategies for maintaining health and physical fitness.

Middle age often brings advances in emotional and social development. Midlife transition may involve vocational readjustments. Judy, mayor of a midwestern town, discusses how she entered a political career in midlife and learned to deal with the stresses of a campaign. Judy also reflects on her thoughts and feelings about breaking the "glass ceiling" as the first elected female mayor of her town. Last, she shares her feelings about her approaching sixtieth birthday.

For some adults, midlife involves adjustment to major changes. Herm and Fran each reflect on the end of their previous marriages and on the factors that account for the success of their marriage to each other. Both Herm and Fran talk about their positive attitude toward midlife as they prepare for and anticipate retirement.

Finally, Dale describes some of the challenges that she and her brother have faced in taking care of their mother, who has Alzheimer's disease. Dale talks about the difficulties of balancing caretaking with other life and family responsibilities, as well as the emotional toll of watching her mother's disease progress.

A WINDOW ON LIFESPAN DEVELOPMENT

Remaining Mentally and Physically Active in Midlife: Miss Janet, Age 59

Miss Janet, a dancer, copes with the challenges of aging by seeking new learning opportunities, staying active, and eating well.

Divorce and Remarriage in Midlife: Herm and Fran

Herm and Fran reflect on their experiences with divorce. Herm views his divorce as a learning experience and is enjoying his marriage to Fran. Fran had a very difficult time with her divorce. Now, in her marriage to Herm, she is more comfortable and feels she can be herself.

VIDEOTAPES AND DVDs

Aging (1993, RMI Media Productions, 30 min.). This program examines the aging process, theories of aging, changes associated with aging, and health issues common to aging. The emphasis is on maintaining one's health in later years, including ways that individuals can help improve the quality of life for their aging family members and friends.

Cancer (2003, RMI Media Productions, 30 min.). This program presents an overview of cancer, with a focus on the importance of early diagnosis, various treatment modalities, cancer research, and the role of support groups and other complementary therapies as part of cancer treatment. In addition to medical information, the program offers insight into the personal and emotional aspect of living with cancer.

Cardiovascular Disease (1993, RMI Media Productions, 30 min.). This program provides an overview of the cardiovascular system and the major cardiovascular diseases, including hypertension, atherosclerosis, heart attack, and stroke. The emphasis is on lifestyle factors that increase the risk of cardiovascular disease.

Development: Journey of a Lifetime (2004, Insight Media; CD-ROM). This multimedia program looks at human development across the lifespan, from infancy to old age. Using animation, self-tests, and other activities, the program explores the physiology of the human body, including an overview of the reproductive system.

Diet and Health: Cancer, Immunology, and AIDS (1996, RMI Media Productions, 30 min.). This program examines the effects of nutrition on the immune system. It includes interviews with a man who is HIV positive and a woman who has had breast cancer.

Diet and Health: Cardiovascular Disease (Revised) (2005, RMI Media Productions, 30 min.). This program uses the stories of three very different individuals to illustrate the effects of nutrition, lifestyle, and heredity on cardiovascular disease. It presents profiles of a woman who had heart surgery in her early forties, a 68-year-old woman with high blood pressure, and a man who had heart surgery in his late sixties.

Discovering Psychology: Maturing and Aging (2001, Annenberg Media, 30 min.; Part 18 of a 26-part series). This program focuses on the physical and psychological changes that are part of aging and at how society responds to aging. Part of the updated edition of Annenberg Media's Discovering Psychology series, the program, narrated by Stanford University professor and author Philip Zimbardo, highlights major new developments in the field.

Eye Exam (Films Media Group, 19 min.). This program uses a quiz format to explain a number of conditions that affect sight, including myopia, hyperopia, presbyopia, cataracts, glaucoma, diabetic retinopathy, and macular degeneration. It makes the point that regular eye exams are the best protection against gradual loss of vision.

Factors in Healthy Aging (1991, Films Media Group/Dartmouth-Hitchcock Medical Center, 28 min.). This program, part of the series The Doctor Is In, uses the results of a half-century study of Harvard graduates over their lifetimes to illustrate the predictors of healthy aging. The program also follows several elderly people as they go through a typical day and talk about their routines and their health. Topics include the impact of diet, smoking, drinking, family history, and personality.

Growing Old in a New Age: How the Body Ages (1993, Annenberg Media, 60 min.; Part 2 of a 13-part series). This program describes the physical changes of aging and explains some of the steps individuals can take to prevent physical deterioration.

Growing Old in a New Age: The Myths and Realities of Aging (1993, Annenberg Media, 60 min.; Part 1 of a 13-part series). This program looks at some of the common myths surrounding aging and compares them with today's realities. Elders and experts discuss how we learn about aging and how knowledge can help us get beyond prevalent myths.

Middle Adulthood: Physical Development (2000, Magna Systems, 28 min.). This program begins with a comprehensive look at the physiological changes that take place as men and women move beyond age 40. Topics include the impact of lifestyle choices on one's overall health and well-being, along with insights into why people find it so difficult to make changes in diet and exercise at this stage of life. The program explores changes in the male and female reproductive system, including a discussion of sexuality and menopause as it is experienced by both men and women.

Physical Activity: Fitness Basics (1996, RMI Media Productions, 30 min.). This program illustrates how physical activities can improve health by examining the nutrition and exercise routines of one woman—a mother who exercises at home—and three men: one who is enrolled in a college physical education class, one who has an exercise facility at his workplace, and one who walks the malls for exercise.

Running Out of Time: Time Pressure, Overtime, and Overwork (1994, Films Media Group, 57 min.). This program, hosted by NPR's Scott Simon, explores the societal impact of time pressure as people attempt to schedule more and more activity into their lives at the expense of leisure time. The program contrasts conditions in the United States today with the lives of people in other countries and in other periods of history. It includes interviews with a postal worker and a single mother of two children, as well as AFL-CIO economist John Zalusky and Karen Nussbaum, head of the Women's Bureau at the Department of Labor.

Sight (1990, Films Media Group, 23 min.). This program describes how the brain and the eye work together to enable us to see. It includes a discussion of visual problems and of research on artificial vision.

Stress (2003, RMI Media Productions, 30 min.). This program looks at various causes and effects of stress on the individual, including the effects on the body's systems. It explores some ways that people cope with stress in their lives and introduces several stress reduction techniques, including journaling.

Stress, Health, and Coping (2001, RMI Media Productions, 30 min.). This program tells the story of a breast cancer survivor who makes use of successful coping strategies to help her maintain good health in stressful situations.

The Study of Attention (1996, Films Media Group, 43 min.). This program examines the concepts of selective attention, divided attention, and visual attention. It uses real-life examples of situations where attention is particularly important, such as the work of air traffic controllers.

Thriving in Midlife (2003, RMI Media Productions, 30 min.). This program focuses on the physical signs of aging seen in middle adulthood, including changes in skin elasticity, muscle tone, hair color, eyesight, and hearing. The program looks at how both genetic inheritance and lifestyle choices influence the rate at which these declines occur. It also explores ways in which adults in midlife compensate for the physiological declines of aging. A discussion of midlife health concerns examines the use of hormone replacement therapy by women going through menopause, the prevalence of osteoporosis, and the effects on men of diminishing levels of testosterone.

Weight Control: Treatment and Health Effects (1996, RMI Media Productions, 30 min.). This program describes the health effects of body composition and risk for disease. It includes a profile of a man with an "apple" shape and looks at effective and ineffective treatments for obesity through the story of a woman who has experienced gastric bypass surgery. Finally, it examines eating disorders through profiles of a mother and daughter who both received treatment for bulimia.

Women at Midlife (1996, Films Media Group/Dartmouth-Hitchcock Medical Center, 29 min.). This program, part of the series The Doctor Is In, discusses physical changes, illnesses, and treatments relevant to women at midlife, including menopause, heart disease, cancer, stroke, osteoporosis, and hormone replacement therapy. Featuring Dr. Eileen Hoffman, author of *Our Health, Our Lives,* the program emphasizes women's transition from a focus on childbearing and child rearing to an emphasis is on preventing chronic diseases that can impair their health and enjoyment of their later years.

TEST BANK

MULTIPLE CHOICE

1) Middle age begins around age __________ and ends around age __________.

   A) 40; 65
   B) 45; 60
   C) 50; 75
   D) 60; 80

   Answer: A
   Page Ref: 395
   Skill: Factual
   Objective: 15.1

2) Middle age is hard to define because
   A) most people in their forties and fifties do not consider themselves to be middle-aged.
   B) there is consistency in the family life cycle during this period, despite basic inconsistencies in physical abilities.
   C) it is a contemporary phenomenon, basically nonexistent before the twentieth century.
   D) adults delay child rearing into their later years, and so are just beginning the aspects of the life cycle that are traditionally associated with early adulthood.

Answer: C
Page Ref: 395
Skill: Factual
Objective: 15.1

3) Getting a fatal disease, being too ill to maintain independence, and losing mental capacities are all
   A) typical experiences of middle-aged adults.
   B) prominent concerns of middle-aged adults.
   C) unlikely to occur during the middle adulthood years.
   D) formerly common problems of middle adulthood that have been pushed back to the seventies or later, thanks to medical advances.

Answer: B
Page Ref: 395
Skill: Factual
Objective: 15.1

4) Growth of the lenses in Jim's eyes, combined with the weakening of the muscle that enables them to adjust their focus, will result in which outcome?
   A) Jim will have difficulty discriminating colors.
   B) Jim will have problems driving at night.
   C) Jim will be very sensitive to the light.
   D) Jim will have difficulty reading small print.

Answer: D
Page Ref: 396
Skill: Applied
Objective: 15.1

5) Presbyopia is
   A) the inability of the lens to adjust to objects at varying distances.
   B) a limited ability to see in dim light.
   C) yellowing of the lens.
   D) a disease in which pressure builds up within the eye due to poor fluid drainage.

Answer: A
Page Ref: 396
Skill: Factual
Objective: 15.1

6) Which of the following contributes to the problems of those in middle adulthood who cannot see clearly in dim light?
   A) broadening of the pupil
   B) changes in the lens and vitreous that cause light to scatter within the eye
   C) thinning of the lens
   D) development of opaque areas in the vitreous

Answer: D
Page Ref: 396
Skill: Conceptual
Objective: 15.1

7) Increased scattering of light within the eye, due to changes in the lens and vitreous, causes
   A) reduced sensitivity to bright lights.
   B) difficulty adjusting to different distances.
   C) increased sensitivity to glare.
   D) serious eye disorders and blindness.
   Answer: C
   Page Ref: 396
   Skill: Factual
   Objective: 15.1

8) Which of the following is an example of a neural change in vision?
   A) presbyopia
   B) glaucoma
   C) loss of rods and cones
   D) yellowing of the lens
   Answer: C
   Page Ref: 396
   Skill: Factual
   Objective: 15.1

9) Juanita cannot feel the buildup of pressure in her eye due to poor fluid drainage. This pressure, left untreated, can damage her optic nerve and is a leading cause of blindness. Juanita has
   A) presbyopia.
   B) glaucoma.
   C) presbycusis.
   D) myopia.
   Answer: B
   Page Ref: 396
   Skill: Applied
   Objective: 15.1

10) Floyd complains that his hearing isn't as sharp, and refers to his condition as "old hearing." The technical term for Floyd's condition is
   A) presbyopia.
   B) presbycusis.
   C) prelingual hearing loss.
   D) sensorineural hearing loss.
   Answer: B
   Page Ref: 396
   Skill: Factual
   Objective: 15.1

11) The first sign of hearing loss in middle age is typically
   A) a sharp hearing loss at high frequencies.
   B) problems making yourself understood.
   C) hearing ghostly knocks and whistles.
   D) difficulty in understanding other people.
   Answer: A
   Page Ref: 396
   Skill: Factual
   Objective: 15.1

12) Which of the following provides evidence that severe hearing problems are caused by factors other than biological aging?
    A) Most people in middle adulthood hear reasonably well across a wide frequency range.
    B) The first hearing loss experienced by most people occurs at high frequencies.
    C) Most people begin to experience hearing loss at around 50 years of age.
    D) Human speech is more difficult to make out after about age 60.

Answer: A
Page Ref: 396
Skill: Conceptual
Objective: 15.1

13) Cigarette smoking, occupational noise, higher blood pressure, and cerebrovascular disease are all thought to be
    A) factors contributing to middle-aged hearing loss in industrialized societies.
    B) reasons why men's hearing declines earlier and more rapidly than women's.
    C) individuals from upper-SES backgrounds show greater hearing losses than their lower-SES counterparts.
    D) unrelated to hearing and vision losses among older individuals.

Answer: B
Page Ref: 397
Skill: Factual
Objective: 15.1

14) In which skin layer are new skin cells constantly produced?
    A) epidermis
    B) protodermis
    C) dermis
    D) hypodermis

Answer: A
Page Ref: 397
Skill: Factual
Objective: 15.1

15) The aging process causes fat in the __________ to diminish, resulting in skin that becomes more wrinkled and loose.
    A) epidermis
    B) protodermis
    C) dermis
    D) hypodermis

Answer: D
Page Ref: 397
Skill: Factual
Objective: 15.1

16) Alana (age 20) wants to avoid premature aging of her skin. Which preventive measure will have the greatest impact on her skin?
    A) using proper skin protection or avoiding the sun
    B) avoiding harsh soaps
    C) yearly checkups by a dermatologist
    D) weekly sessions at a tanning booth

Answer: A
Page Ref: 397
Skill: Applied
Objective: 15.1

17) Women's skin ages more quickly because
A) the dermis is not as thick as that of men.
B) of hormonal changes caused by menopause.
C) the use of makeup impairs the skin's ability to retain elasticity.
D) the weight changes brought about by childbearing reduce elasticity.
Answer: A
Page Ref: 397
Skill: Factual
Objective: 15.1

18) One area where fat DECREASES during middle adulthood is
A) the abdomen.
B) beneath the skin of the arms and legs.
C) on the back.
D) on the face.
Answer: B
Page Ref: 397
Skill: Factual
Objective: 15.1

19) Theresa is a woman entering her fifties. She can anticipate an accumulation of fat in which area(s) of her body?
A) face and legs
B) upper abdomen
C) waist and upper arms
D) back and hips
Answer: C
Page Ref: 397
Skill: Applied
Objective: 15.1

20) Muscle mass declines during middle adulthood, primarily due to
A) atrophy of slow-twitch fibers.
B) changes in exercise and diet.
C) atrophy of fast-twitch fibers.
D) increased metabolism.
Answer: C
Page Ref: 397
Skill: Factual
Objective: 15.1

21) Mrs. Chang wants to avoid the characteristic weight gain of middle adulthood. She should
A) maintain a low-fat diet, with a gradual reduction in caloric intake.
B) eat a high-carbohydrate, low-protein diet.
C) be aware that this is a highly unrealistic goal.
D) maintain a high-fat diet and exercise at least once a week.
Answer: A
Page Ref: 397
Skill: Applied
Objective: 15.1

22) What type of exercise should Mrs. Chang consider during middle adulthood to offset excess weight and muscle loss?
   A) endurance training that focuses on heart rate
   B) weight-bearing exercise that includes resistance training
   C) any kind of activity that does NOT result in a buildup of sweat
   D) stretching exercises that work on flexibility

Answer: B
Page Ref: 397
Skill: Applied
Objective: 15.1

23) Explain how an individual's height can drop by as much as 1 inch by age 60.
   A) Bones become more porous, resulting in a weakened structure that becomes compacted under a typical individual's weight.
   B) Muscle strength is reduced, creating problems in standing erect for many individuals.
   C) Loss of bone strength causes the disks in the spinal column to collapse.
   D) Tendons and cartilage in the knee collapse, resulting in decreased leg length.

Answer: C
Page Ref: 397
Skill: Conceptual
Objective: 15.1

24) Sixty-year-old Mrs. Banning wants to slow her bone loss. She should
   A) engage in weight-bearing exercise.
   B) consume at least three alcoholic beverages per day.
   C) ensure that her diet includes adequate amounts of beta-carotene and soy products.
   D) avoid going outside during the peak sunlight hours of 11 a.m. to 3 p.m.

Answer: A
Page Ref: 397
Skill: Applied
Objective: 15.1

25) Mr. and Mrs. Riediger are undergoing reproductive transitions. Mrs. Riediger is no longer able to have children, while Mr. Riediger's fertility has diminished. They are BOTH undergoing
   A) menopause.
   B) spermarche.
   C) menarche.
   D) the climacteric.

Answer: D
Page Ref: 397
Skill: Applied
Objective: 15.2

26) When Marona was in her twenties, she experienced a very regular, 28-day menstrual cycle. Now that she is in her late forties, what can she anticipate?
   A) The length of her cycle may decrease to around 23 days and become more irregular.
   B) Her cycle will remain regular, but will increase in length to around 33 days.
   C) Her cycle will increase in length gradually over time until it stops altogether.
   D) No change in length or regularity will occur, but it will stop suddenly when she reaches menopause.

Answer: A
Page Ref: 397
Skill: Applied
Objective: 15.2

27) Lillian's menstrual periods have stopped and she is no longer able to bear children. She has experienced
A) menarche.
B) menopause.
C) menses.
D) menstruation.
Answer: B
Page Ref: 397–398
Skill: Applied
Objective: 15.2

28) Menopause may impact a woman's sex life because
A) she is likely to feel depressed and unattractive.
B) her mate will see her differently.
C) her body isn't producing enough sexually stimulating hormones.
D) her genitals are less easily stimulated and her vagina lubricates more slowly during arousal.
Answer: D
Page Ref: 398
Skill: Factual
Objective: 15.2

29) Which of the following statements about menopause is correct?
A) Women who experience menopause are at a decreased risk for atherosclerosis, as decreases in estrogen lead to subsequent decreases in plaque buildup on artery walls.
B) Hot flashes tend to happen at night, resulting in the sleep problems often reported by menopausal women.
C) Decreased estrogen results in increases in bone mass, making bones too heavy and resulting in osteoporosis.
D) Studies show no association between menopause and depression, so symptoms of depression merit serious evaluation and treatment.
Answer: D
Page Ref: 398
Skill: Factual
Objective: 15.2

30) As she approaches menopause, Glinda wonders if there are any lifestyle changes she can make to minimize potential hot flashes. She should know that
A) there are no known preventive measures for avoiding hot flashes.
B) there is no clinical evidence to support the existence of hot flashes, which are primarily described as problematic by women with depression or other emotional illnesses.
C) a diet low in fat and high in soy-based foods may help.
D) hot flashes are only experienced by 25 percent of the population, so chances are she won't experience them very often, if at all.
Answer: C
Page Ref: 398
Skill: Applied
Objective: 15.2

31) Marlene, who had a hysterectomy, is undergoing menopause. Her doctor will probably recommend
A) hormone replacement therapy (HRT).
B) surgical removal of the ovaries (SRO).
C) estrogen replacement therapy (ERT).
D) postmenopausal surgery (PMS).
Answer: C
Page Ref: 398
Skill: Applied
Objective: 15.2

32) Hormone replacement therapy is UNLIKELY to
   A) counteract hot flashes.
   B) provide some protection against bone deterioration and colon cancer.
   C) reduce the incidence of Alzheimer's if begun during menopausal age.
   D) reduce the risk of breast cancer and blood clots.

Answer: D
Page Ref: 398
Skill: Conceptual
Objective: 15.2

33) Many of Dr. Kittenbrink's patients experiencing menopause want to undergo hormone therapy for relief from menopausal symptoms. Because she is a responsible physician, Dr. Kittenbrink is likely to
   A) prescribe it to low-risk patients for no longer than five years.
   B) prescribe it to all her patients until they no longer have any menopausal symptoms.
   C) only prescribe it for women who are experiencing severe physical discomfort due to menopause.
   D) avoid hormone therapy due to the dangerous side effects and recommend a healthy diet, increased physical activity, and meditation instead.

Answer: A
Page Ref: 398–399
Skill: Applied
Objective: 15.2

34) Which of these women is most likely to experience a positive attitude toward menopause and have fewer negative symptoms?
   A) Marcie, who always wanted children but never had any
   B) Bonita, who never finished high school and has four children
   C) Shawna, a successful lawyer with a busy private practice
   D) Lisa, who has always taken pride in her physical appearance

Answer: C
Page Ref: 399
Skill: Applied
Objective: 15.2

35) Which group of women is most likely to experience a negative attitude toward menopause and have more negative symptoms?
   A) African-American women
   B) Mexican-American women
   C) highly educated women
   D) Caucasian-American women

Answer: D
Page Ref: 399
Skill: Applied
Objective: 15.2

36) Men produce less semen and sperm after age 40,
   A) and eventually stop producing sperm altogether around age 70.
   B) and consequently are less interested in sex.
   C) but continue to produce sperm throughout life.
   D) with a resulting reduction in testes size.

Answer: C
Page Ref: 399
Skill: Factual
Objective: 15.2

37) Which statement about testosterone production is true?
   A) Frequent sexual activity diminishes any remaining levels of testosterone during middle adulthood.
   B) Healthy men who engage in sexual activity experience minimal change in testosterone production.
   C) Testosterone levels rise steadily throughout adulthood.
   D) Testosterone levels remain stable throughout adulthood.

Answer: B
Page Ref: 399
Skill: Conceptual
Objective: 15.2

38) Martha and Brian have been very happy with the sexual aspect of their 30-year marriage. As Brian experiences climacteric, knowing which fact below will probably ensure their continued happiness?
   A) Brian will need more stimulation to achieve and maintain an erection.
   B) Brian will be able to father children for the rest of his life.
   C) Brian's sex drive will decrease drastically over the next five years.
   D) Brian will be at risk for an extramarital affair.

Answer: A
Page Ref: 401
Skill: Applied
Objective: 15.2

39) In addition to midlife physical changes, __________ can be caused by disorders of the nervous, circulatory, and endocrine systems; anxiety and depression; and pelvic injury.
   A) atherosclerosis
   B) osteoporosis
   C) hot flashes
   D) male impotence

Answer: D
Page Ref: 399
Skill: Factual
Objective: 15.2

40) Cross-cultural research reveals that women are LESS likely to experience menopause as difficult, unpleasant, or uncomfortable if it
   A) is treated medically.
   B) leads to improved social status.
   C) occurs earlier in their lives.
   D) is associated with other health problems.

Answer: B
Page Ref: 400
Skill: Conceptual
Objective: Box CI: Menopause as a Biocultural Event

41) Which statement about health and fitness during midlife is correct?
   A) Men are more likely than women to suffer from nonfatal, limiting health problems.
   B) Women are more likely than men to suffer from fatal illnesses.
   C) Understanding of health in middle and late adulthood is limited by insufficient research on women and minorities.
   D) Sexuality is typically excluded as a positive indicator of health.

Answer: C
Page Ref: 401
Skill: Factual
Objective: 15.3

42) The best predictor for how much sex a couple has in middle age is
   A) how many children they have had.
   B) how happily married they are.
   C) the physical health of the woman.
   D) the physical health of the man.

Answer: B

Page Ref: 401
Skill: Factual
Objective: 15.3

43) As Mr. and Mrs. Golloher reach midlife, they are likely to experience which of the following with regards to their sexual activity?
   A) Mr. Golloher is likely to show a marked decline in interest, while Mrs. Golloher will have a greater sex drive but decreased sexual response.
   B) The frequency of sexual activity will increase as their children leave the home, but quality will decline.
   C) Both frequency of activity and intensity of response will decline, but spontaneity will increase.
   D) They will replace sexual activity with behaviors such as cuddling, holding hands, and talking.

Answer: C

Page Ref: 401
Skill: Applied
Objective: 15.3

44) Which statement reflects an INCORRECT stereotype or belief about middle-aged adults?
   A) Falls resulting in bone fractures and death increase substantially from early to middle adulthood.
   B) Older adults' driving skills decline and result in a greater number of motor vehicle collisions.
   C) Men are more vulnerable than women to most health problems.
   D) Cancer is a leading cause of death among middle-aged women.

Answer: B

Page Ref: 401
Skill: Factual
Objective: 15.4

45) Which type of cancer has decreased in men, but increased in women?
   A) skin cancer
   B) prostate cancer
   C) breast cancer
   D) lung cancer

Answer: D

Page Ref: 402
Skill: Factual
Objective: 15.4

46) An illness that occurs when a cell's normal genetic programming is disrupted, causing uncontrolled growth and crowding out of normal cells, is called
   A) atherosclerosis.
   B) stroke.
   C) climacteric.
   D) cancer.

Answer: D

Page Ref: 402
Skill: Factual
Objective: 15.4

47) One reason men are more vulnerable to cancer than women is their
   A) bulkier physical builds.
   B) attitude of invincibility coupled with a fear of dying.
   C) higher rates of sedentary occupations.
   D) tendency to delay going to the doctor.
Answer: D
Page Ref: 402
Skill: Conceptual
Objective: 15.4

48) Mr. Lavery is a low-SES male in his fifties, which puts him at a greater risk for __________ cancer.
   A) lung and stomach
   B) breast
   C) prostate
   D) skin
Answer: A
Page Ref: 402
Skill: Applied
Objective: 15.4

49) Mrs. Nagra has a BRCA2 mutation. What does this diagnosis tell Mrs. Nagra about her chances of developing breast cancer?
   A) She has already developed cancerous cells.
   B) Her risk for developing breast cancer can be eliminated if she eats a healthy diet and avoids tobacco and alcohol products.
   C) She has less than a 25 percent risk of actually developing breast cancer.
   D) She is especially likely to develop breast cancer before age 30.
Answer: D
Page Ref: 402
Skill: Applied
Objective: 15.4

50) Mrs. Ng has just had an operation to remove a cancerous lump in her breast. The medical community considers her to be
   A) cured of cancer.
   B) cured of cancer if she remains free of the disease for a year.
   C) cured of cancer if she remains free of the disease for five years.
   D) a high risk for cancer reoccurrence.
Answer: C
Page Ref: 402
Skill: Applied
Objective: 15.4

51) One hundred North American middle-aged adults died last year. If the adults are statistically average, how many of those deaths were caused by cardiovascular disease?
   A) 50
   B) 47
   C) 33
   D) 25
Answer: D
Page Ref: 402
Skill: Conceptual
Objective: 15.4

52) Peter's doctor has just diagnosed him with cardiovascular disease. Because Peter had no symptoms, he is unlikely to have been experiencing __________ at the time of his diagnosis.

A) a heart attack
B) atherosclerosis
C) high blood pressure
D) high blood cholesterol

Answer: A
Page Ref: 402
Skill: Factual
Objective: 15.4

53) A heart attack occurs when an artery that supplies blood to part of __________ is blocked.

A) the brain
B) the heart
C) the lungs
D) the liver

Answer: B
Page Ref: 402
Skill: Factual
Objective: 15.4

54) Mr. Kher has an irregular heartbeat. This condition causes him to feel faint, and is dangerous because it can allow clots to form in the heart's chambers. Mr. Kher has

A) osteoporosis.
B) atherosclerosis.
C) arrhythmia.
D) arterial thrombosis.

Answer: C
Page Ref: 402
Skill: Applied
Objective: 15.4

55) Mr. Caffrey is experiencing indigestion-like pain, which increases to a crushing chest pain. The emergency room doctors diagnose him with an oxygen-deprived heart and inform him that he is experiencing

A) a heart attack.
B) atherosclerosis.
C) a stroke.
D) angina pectoris.

Answer: D
Page Ref: 402
Skill: Applied
Objective: 15.4

56) Mrs. Gobodo is an African American experiencing symptoms of angina. She

A) may face a double gender-racial bias from doctors who may not recognize or treat her symptoms appropriately.
B) has a higher risk of heart attack than her husband.
C) belongs to a group with the highest rate of heart attacks, followed by Asian women.
D) probably has heartburn or acid reflux syndrome and has misdiagnosed her own symptoms.

Answer: A
Page Ref: 403
Skill: Applied
Objective: 15.4

57) Mrs. Kishel's bones have become more porous over the years, reducing her bone density levels and putting her at risk for fractures. Mrs. Kishel has which condition?
   A) atherosclerosis
   B) osteoporosis
   C) coronary thrombosis
   D) ulnar halitosis
   Answer: B
   Page Ref: 403
   Skill: Applied
   Objective: 15.4

58) Mrs. McWhirter is going through menopause and wonders how this relates to development of osteoporosis. She should know that
   A) once she begins menopause, osteoporosis-related bone loss will end.
   B) half of her bone mass loss will occur in the first 10 years after menopause.
   C) most of her bone mass will be lost during her menopausal years.
   D) the greater her menopausal symptoms, the greater her bone loss will be.
   Answer: B
   Page Ref: 403
   Skill: Applied
   Objective: 15.4

59) Which person has the LEAST risk of developing osteoporosis?
   A) Myra, who smokes
   B) Nyra, who exercises very little
   C) Kyra, who has a thin, small-framed body
   D) Lyra, who is African American
   Answer: D
   Page Ref: 403
   Skill: Applied
   Objective: 15.4

60) Mrs. Lacayo's doctor has recommended that she engage in weight-bearing exercise, maintain a calcium- and vitamin D-rich diet, and take bone-strengthening medications. This recommendation is consistent with the treatment plan for
   A) osteoporosis.
   B) atherosclerosis.
   C) uterine cancer.
   D) angina pectoris.
   Answer: A
   Page Ref: 403
   Skill: Conceptual
   Objective: 15.4

61) Pauline gets to work early and leaves late, works through lunch, and stays up late doing more work at home. She is very competitive and determined to be vice-president within five years. She loses her temper easily and always seems angry. Her behavior pattern would best be described as
   A) passive-aggressive.
   B) Type A.
   C) Type B.
   D) hyperactive.
   Answer: B
   Page Ref: 404
   Skill: Applied
   Objective: 15.5

62) Which component of Type A behavior, when isolated, consistently predicts heart disease and other health problems?
    A) hostility
    B) extreme competitiveness
    C) ambition
    D) impatience
Answer: A
Page Ref: 404
Skill: Factual
Objective: 15.5

63) Frequent and angry outbursts; rude, disagreeable behavior; and critical and condescending nonverbal cues during social interactions are all aspects of
    A) mental illness.
    B) insensitivity.
    C) competitiveness.
    D) expressed hostility.
Answer: D
Page Ref: 404
Skill: Conceptual
Objective: 15.5

64) The best way for people with a Type A behavior pattern to reduce their risk of heart attack is to
    A) develop more effective ways of handling stress.
    B) learn not to express the hostility they feel.
    C) force themselves to take an extended vacation.
    D) take one aspirin tablet every other day.
Answer: A
Page Ref: 404
Skill: Factual
Objective: 15.5

65) During middle adulthood, __________ can limit the rise in age-related illnesses and reduce the severity of disease.
    A) regular medical checkups
    B) effective stress management
    C) vitamin supplements
    D) holistic medicine
Answer: B
Page Ref: 404
Skill: Factual
Objective: 15.6

66) Sharon decided that she was unhappy at work. She realized that the primary cause was frustration with an irresponsible co-worker. She met with the individual, came up with strategies to help the young woman meet her responsibilities, and subsequently enjoyed her job more. Sharon used
    A) Stress Identification Therapy (SIT).
    B) an emotion-centered coping strategy.
    C) a problem-centered coping strategy.
    D) an indirect method of stress management.
Answer: C
Page Ref: 404
Skill: Applied
Objective: 15.6

67) __________ are internal, private, and aimed at controlling distress when there is little one can do about a situation.
   A) Stress Identification Therapies (SIT)
   B) Emotion-centered coping strategies
   C) Problem-centered coping strategies
   D) Indirect methods of stress management
Answer: B
Page Ref: 404
Skill: Factual
Objective: 15.6

68) Which of the following is a characteristic of an effective coping strategy for dealing with stress?
   A) a mixture of problem- and emotion-centered techniques
   B) impulsiveness
   C) avoidance
   D) aggression
Answer: A
Page Ref: 404
Skill: Conceptual
Objective: 15.6

69) People are better at coping effectively with stress during middle adulthood, and they are
   A) more susceptible to the physical symptoms of stress than those at younger stages of development.
   B) less able to anticipate and avoid stressful events. Consequently, they have more practice dealing with stress, which causes the subsequent improvement in effectiveness.
   C) more skilled at anticipating and avoiding stressful situations.
   D) more likely to use emotion-centered than problem-centered coping.
Answer: C
Page Ref: 405
Skill: Factual
Objective: 15.6

70) Eileen is the new aerobics instructor for a class aimed at mid-lifers. She is excited to have 20 adults show up for her first class. Eileen should know that
   A) 10 of her students will drop out within the first six months.
   B) most of them will probably end up in better shape than she is.
   C) her high expectations for this group should be revised in order to avoid any physical stress-related heart attacks during class.
   D) the majority of her students are probably Type A personalities.
Answer: A
Page Ref: 405
Skill: Applied
Objective: 15.6

71) An important psychological factor that helps people begin and maintain a regular exercise program is
   A) a sense of competitiveness.
   B) a sense of self-efficacy.
   C) a Type A behavior pattern.
   D) a Type B behavior pattern.
Answer: B
Page Ref: 405
Skill: Factual
Objective: 15.6

72) Which person would be better suited to a home-based exercise program that is planned by a consultant?
   A) Jennifer, who leads a very stressful lifestyle
   B) Jacob, who is overweight
   C) Jaina, who is normal-weight
   D) Jacen, who loves to exercise

Answer: B

Page Ref: 405

Skill: Applied

Objective: 15.6

73) Mrs. Olinghouse lives in a low-SES neighborhood and would like to begin exercising. She is LEAST likely to cite __________ as a major barrier to her goal.
   A) health problems
   B) motivation
   C) safety
   D) access to exercise facilities

Answer: B

Page Ref: 405

Skill: Applied

Objective: 15.6

74) When Nani's supervisor relocated, she was forced to assume the directorship of her division. Although the division was fraught with internal problems, Nani was committed to doing a good job, so she signed up for personnel and budget management workshops to make her a better administrator. No matter how difficult things got, Nani always looked at the situation as a challenge, rather than as a problem. After a year, the division was running better than ever. Because of the combination of traits exhibited, Nani could be characterized as displaying
   A) a Type A behavior pattern.
   B) a Type B behavior pattern.
   C) fluidity.
   D) hardiness.

Answer: D

Page Ref: 406

Skill: Applied

Objective: 15.6

75) An individual with a high level of hardiness is likely to use which type of coping strategy?
   A) Stress Identification Therapy (SIT)
   B) an emotion-centered coping strategy
   C) a problem-centered coping strategy
   D) excessive eating, drinking, or drug use

Answer: C

Page Ref: 406

Skill: Factual

Objective: 15.6

76) Cody just found out he received a negative appraisal from his boss at work. If Cody is a low-hardy individual, which of these responses is he most likely to take?
   A) discussing the issue with his boss
   B) writing a response for his job file
   C) getting drunk to forget about it
   D) planning how to improve himself

Answer: C

Page Ref: 406

Skill: Applied

Objective: 15.6

77) Erica is a middle-aged woman who feels confident, versatile, and able to resolve many of life's problems. She is likely to be rated by others as __________ than a man of the same age.
   A) conveying a stronger sense of leadership
   B) less attractive but more competent
   C) more trustworthy and productive
   D) less attractive with more negative characteristics
   Answer: D
   Page Ref: 406
   Skill: Applied
   Objective: 15.7

78) When people are judging the appearance, maturity, and power of young and middle-aged people from their photographs, which person is likely to give the LOWEST rating?
   A) a man judging an older woman
   B) a man judging a younger woman
   C) a woman judging an older man
   D) a woman judging a younger man
   Answer: A
   Page Ref: 406
   Skill: Applied
   Objective: 15.7

79) The ideal of a woman characterized as __________ represents the heart of the double standard of aging.
   A) passive and submissive
   B) young and sexually attractive
   C) indecisive and dependent
   D) assertive and competent
   Answer: B
   Page Ref: 406
   Skill: Factual
   Objective: 15.7

80) Past research results showed a pattern of intelligence declines in middle and late adulthood. Which of the following statements explains this pattern?
   A) Cohort effects, where younger generations benefited from improved health and education, created the appearance of age-related intelligence declines.
   B) Increased cognitive declines and incidence of Alzheimer's disease in older generations are responsible for the research findings.
   C) Age-related intelligence declines are a standard part of the aging process, as proven with past research.
   D) The dramatic decreases in intelligence in late adulthood skewed the results, making nonexistent patterns appear during middle adulthood as well.
   Answer: A
   Page Ref: 407
   Skill: Factual
   Objective: 15.8

81) Mai Song prefers meeting with clients face-to-face, rather than by phone or written correspondence. Although her knowledge and experience in the field make her well-respected, it is her ability to successfully maneuver social situations and her interactions with clients that have made her successful. Mai Song has developed __________ intelligence.
   A) crystallized
   B) fluid
   C) cohort
   D) stored
   Answer: A
   Page Ref: 407
   Skill: Applied
   Objective: 15.8

82) Which of these tasks most clearly makes use of crystallized intelligence?
   A) learning to speak a new language
   B) finding hidden figures in a drawing
   C) using the right words to express an idea
   D) creating unusual, challenging artwork
   Answer: C
   Page Ref: 407
   Skill: Applied
   Objective: 15.8

83) The ability to analyze information quickly and detect patterns in new information is called __________ intelligence.
   A) crystallized
   B) creative
   C) emotional
   D) fluid
   Answer: D
   Page Ref: 407
   Skill: Factual
   Objective: 15.8

84) Which of these tasks most clearly makes use of fluid intelligence?
   A) using the right word to express an idea
   B) rapidly processing new information
   C) deciding how to deal with a problem
   D) winning the company spelling bee
   Answer: B
   Page Ref: 407
   Skill: Applied
   Objective: 15.8

85) Which type of intelligence increases steadily throughout adulthood?
   A) fluid intelligence
   B) crystallized intelligence
   C) short-term memory
   D) long-term memory
   Answer: B
   Page Ref: 408
   Skill: Factual
   Objective: 15.8

86) Trends in both crystallized and fluid mental abilities reported from the Seattle Longitudinal Study show that, intellectually, middle-aged adults
   A) show steady increases in perceptual speed.
   B) typically overestimate their intellectual abilities, often with embarrassing results.
   C) are "in their prime," rather than "over the hill."
   D) show sharp decrements in ability starting around age 40.
   Answer: C
   Page Ref: 408
   Skill: Factual
   Objective: 15.8

87) Eighty-year-old Gladys has taken various tests of intelligence every ten years for the last five decades. Based on information in your text, what changes would you anticipate for Gladys?
A) Her verbal ability scores will show little decline.
B) Her spatial orientation scores will show little decline.
C) Gladys's inductive reasoning skills will show marked decline.
D) Gladys's verbal memory scores will show marked decreases.
Answer: A
Page Ref: 408
Skill: Applied
Objective: 15.8

88) Many researchers believe that most or all cognitive changes in adulthood are based on
A) research that is flawed by poor designs.
B) environmental influences such as pollution.
C) society's bias against people who are older.
D) a general slowing of the central nervous system.
Answer: D
Page Ref: 408
Skill: Factual
Objective: 15.8

89) Basic information-processing skills decline throughout adulthood, but overall cognitive functioning remains quite steady. The author suggests that this apparent contradiction can be reconciled by noting that
A) adults use stronger abilities to compensate for weaker ones.
B) basic information-processing skills don't affect most abilities.
C) declines occur, but only for highly practiced, automatic skills.
D) cognitive declines are masked by social bias against older people.
Answer: A
Page Ref: 409
Skill: Factual
Objective: 15.8

90) James, age 20; Dylan, age 40; and Brandon, age 60 are all given simple reaction time tests. Based on research cited in your text, we can anticipate that
A) Brandon will have the slowest reaction times, but only about 1 second slower than James'.
B) James will have the fastest reaction times, beating Dylan and Brandon by nearly 10 seconds on each task.
C) Dylan will have the fastest reaction times, beating James by 2-3 seconds and Brandon by nearly 5 seconds.
D) Brandon will have the slowest reaction times, nearly 3 seconds slower than Dylan and 6 seconds slower than James.
Answer: A
Page Ref: 409
Skill: Applied
Objective: 15.9

91) The viewpoint that the general slowing of cognitive processes is due to breaks in the connections in the brain, which must then be bypassed, is called the __________ view.
A) neural network
B) information-loss
C) interconnectionist
D) path construction
Answer: A
Page Ref: 409
Skill: Factual
Objective: 15.9

92) The viewpoint that the general slowing of cognitive processes is due to an increase in the rate at which information degrades as it is transferred within the brain is called the __________ view.
   A) neural network
   B) information-loss
   C) over-copying
   D) signal breakdown
   Answer: B
   Page Ref: 409
   Skill: Factual
   Objective: 15.9

93) As an older person's neural processing slows down, the person will often minimize the effects this has by
   A) concentrating more on new, unfamiliar tasks.
   B) pushing to complete tasks as quickly as possible.
   C) using experience to plan further ahead in a task.
   D) withdrawing and doing fewer and fewer activities.
   Answer: C
   Page Ref: 409
   Skill: Conceptual
   Objective: 15.9

94) Bridget is used to multitasking. As she grows older, she will find
   A) it easier to do two things at one time.
   B) that she tends to switch back and forth more quickly between the tasks.
   C) that she slows down, but is able to coordinate the tasks better.
   D) it harder to do two things at one time.
   Answer: D
   Page Ref: 409
   Skill: Applied
   Objective: 15.9

95) Riley works in a large business where he has to juggle many activities simultaneously. As he has gotten older, he has increasing difficulty concentrating on his work, due to the many interruptions he must endure. Riley is demonstrating age-related declines in
   A) code-switching.
   B) cognitive inhibition.
   C) attentional persistence.
   D) perseverance processing.
   Answer: B
   Page Ref: 410
   Skill: Applied
   Objective: 15.9

96) Fifty-five year-old Heartley wants to improve her ability to divide her attention between two tasks, focus on relevant information, and switch between mental operations. What can you recommend to help her achieve her goal?
   A) Play card games like *concentration* to improve her focus.
   B) Begin hormone therapy.
   C) Begin language therapy.
   D) Receive training and practice in these skills.
   Answer: D
   Page Ref: 410
   Skill: Applied
   Objective: 15.9

97) As Clarissa gets older, which type of memory activity will be the LEAST likely to suffer?
A) matching names with faces of people she has met
B) memorization of digits such as phone numbers
C) memorization of list items
D) memorization of prose
Answer: D
Page Ref: 410
Skill: Applied
Objective: 15.9

98) Sixty-two-year-old Hudson is given a list of words to memorize that includes *trout* and *flounder*. Hudson will
A) rehearse the words more, and rely on categorization to help the memorization process.
B) rehearse the words less, and will not immediately access the category of "fish."
C) immediately organize the words based on categories.
D) elaborate the words more by associating each word with a specific characteristic.
Answer: B
Page Ref: 410
Skill: Applied
Objective: 15.9

99) A college class is given two assignments: a pressured, classroom-like condition and a self-paced condition. Which of the following is likely to occur?
A) Middle-aged students will refuse to do the pressured condition.
B) Middle-aged students will outperform younger students in both conditions.
C) Middle-aged students will show performance declines only in the pressured condition.
D) Middle-aged students will show performance declines only in the self-paced condition.
Answer: C
Page Ref: 410
Skill: Applied
Objective: 15.9

100) Melina has trouble remembering where she parks her car. Subsequently, she parks in the same area of the parking garage every day at work. She is using
A) metacognitive knowledge.
B) general knowledge.
C) procedural knowledge.
D) common sense.
Answer: A
Page Ref: 410
Skill: Applied
Objective: 15.9

101) Washington Middle School was known for its poor test scores, large numbers of violent incidents, and a teaching force comprised mostly of long-term substitutes. Roberta was hired as the new principal and immediately launched an action plan to address these issues. Within two years she had recruited highly qualified teachers, reduced disruptive behaviors, and raised test scores substantially. Roberta, like many middle-aged adults, shows increased cognitive abilities with respect to
A) general processing speed.
B) practical problem solving.
C) fluid intelligence.
D) overall reaction times.
Answer: B
Page Ref: 411
Skill: Applied
Objective: 15.10

102) The term "__________" refers to an extensive, highly organized, and integrated knowledge base that can be used to support a high level of performance.
A) experience
B) knowledge
C) expertise
D) intuition
Answer: C
Page Ref: 411
Skill: Factual
Objective: 15.10

103) Which person is most likely to have reached the height of expertise in any particular area?
A) Tom, a 15-year-old
B) Tonika, a 24-year-old
C) Tennyson, a 55-year-old
D) Ted, a 75-year-old
Answer: C
Page Ref: 411
Skill: Applied
Objective: 15.10

104) Expertise tends to develop
A) in those who are highly educated.
B) in those at the top of career ladders.
C) in those from high-SES backgrounds.
D) at all levels in any field of endeavor.
Answer: D
Page Ref: 411
Skill: Factual
Objective: 15.10

105) You must choose which of three candidates to hire for a job: a young adult, a middle-aged adult, and an older adult. They all have similar training, experience, and pay expectations. Research suggests that which of these will be the most effective employee?
A) the middle-aged adult
B) the younger adult
C) the older adult
D) There is no way to tell.
Answer: A
Page Ref: 411
Skill: Applied
Objective: 15.10

106) Compared to younger individuals, when solving an everyday problem, middle-aged adults will
A) select better strategies.
B) make decisions based on emotion.
C) solve it through institutional guessing.
D) consult with other people.
Answer: A
Page Ref: 411
Skill: Conceptual
Objective: 15.10

107) Cynthia is a writer who feels that her work steadily improved during her forties and fifties. She is most likely to explain this as the result of
   A) extensive planning and molding of her stories.
   B) a positive career change.
   C) intense competition with other artists her age.
   D) carefully balancing work and family.
   Answer: A
   Page Ref: 412
   Skill: Applied
   Objective: 15.10

108) George is a famous Hollywood actor. During his early adulthood years, he prioritized work that would bring him recognition and money. Now, in his fifties, he wants to focus on making movies that can positively influence the way people think and act. George's transition
   A) reflects an egocentrism of early adulthood, despite his age.
   B) reflects a typical change in the quality of creativity during middle adulthood.
   C) will probably result in more poetic works or unusual products.
   D) will reflect less creative works than his earlier years.
   Answer: B
   Page Ref: 412
   Skill: Applied
   Objective: 15.10

109) The relationship between a person's ability to think flexibly and hold a job that requires complex cognitive skills can best be summarized by saying that
   A) flexible thinking makes a person select a complex job.
   B) having a complex job makes a person think flexibly.
   C) each of these factors has an influence on the other one.
   D) there is no relationship between these two factors.
   Answer: C
   Page Ref: 412
   Skill: Factual
   Objective: 15.11

110) Zack has a stimulating, nonroutine job that is intellectually demanding. During his leisure time, Zack is likely to
   A) seek out stimulating leisure pursuits, which also foster cognitive flexibility.
   B) prefer nonstimulating leisure pursuits, like watching television, which allows him to "rest his brain."
   C) gravitate toward physically demanding, and slightly dangerous, leisure pursuits like rock climbing or dirt biking.
   D) select pursuits in which he supervises younger people, such as youth group minister or counselor.
   Answer: A
   Page Ref: 412
   Skill: Applied
   Objective: 15.11

111) Why are parents who are flexible, abstract thinkers likely to have children with similar traits?
   A) Flexibility and abstract thought are genetic traits.
   B) They tend to have more children than concrete thinkers, increasing the probability that their offspring will inherit the same traits.
   C) Flexible thinkers from high-SES backgrounds can provide proper nutrition for their children, which is essential for brain development necessary for abstract thought.
   D) They tend to value self-direction for themselves and their children and are likely to pass their cognitive preferences on.
   Answer: D
   Page Ref: 412
   Skill: Factual
   Objective: 15.11

112) The impact of a challenging job on cognitive growth is greatest for
   A) individuals of any age.
   B) people in their twenties and thirties.
   C) those in administrative or supervisory positions.
   D) people living in Japan or Poland.
Answer: A
Page Ref: 412
Skill: Factual
Objective: 15.12

113) Dr. Hung teaches a course for older adults who are either entering college for the first time or returning after a long hiatus. The purpose of the course is to help them acclimate to the demands of college coursework in the 21st century. If Dr. Hung's students are statistically average, then the majority of them are
   A) men.
   B) women.
   C) older workers who were laid off due to age discrimination.
   D) ethnic minorities.
Answer: B
Page Ref: 413
Skill: Applied
Objective: 15.13

114) Which person is likely to feel the most anxious about going to college?
   A) Mary Ann, an 18-year-old college freshman
   B) Thurston, a 55-year-old returning male student
   C) Ginger, a 45-year-old returning female student
   D) Skipper, a 20-year-old college junior
Answer: C
Page Ref: 413
Skill: Applied
Objective: 15.13

115) Why do mature-age women who return to school take longer to finish their degrees?
   A) Many attend college for personal fulfillment, so they are not under a "time clock" to finish the degree.
   B) Multiple demands on their time interfere with course work.
   C) They are often unable to decide upon a degree, so end up taking additional courses as they switch majors.
   D) Because of the discrimination they experience from male professors, they often drop courses and then take them again later with different, more supportive instructors.
Answer: B
Page Ref: 413
Skill: Conceptual
Objective: 15.13

116) The most important factor in the success of an adult college student is
   A) receiving social support.
   B) a high intelligence level.
   C) taking a full course load.
   D) studying at regular times.
Answer: A
Page Ref: 413
Skill: Factual
Objective: 15.13

117) Nontraditional students report a strong desire for help in
A) settling on career goals.
B) finding high-quality daycare.
C) academic advising and finding jobs appropriate to their talents.
D) effective time management strategies.
Answer: C
Page Ref: 413
Skill: Factual
Objective: 15.13

118) Which student would possibly need help adjusting to styles of learning that are at odds with her cultural background?
A) Trisha, a single mother of two
B) Mae Ling, a Native Hawaiian student
C) Emily, a third-generation college student
D) Julia, a foreign exchange student from England
Answer: B
Page Ref: 413
Skill: Applied
Objective: 15.13

ESSAY

119) Discuss differences in the hearing loss between men and women.
Answer: Men's hearing declines earlier and at a faster rate than women's, a difference associated with cigarette smoking, exposure to intense noise in some male-dominated occupations, and (at older ages) high blood pressure and cerebrovascular disease, or strokes that damage brain tissue. Most middle-aged and elderly people with hearing difficulties benefit from sound amplification with hearing aids.
Page Ref: 396

120) Describe the symptoms most often associated with menopause.
Answer: Following menopause, estrogen declines further, causing the reproductive organs to shrink in size, the genitals to be less easily stimulated, and the vagina to lubricate more slowly during arousal. As a result, complaints about sexual functioning increase, with about 35 to 40 percent of women reporting difficulties, especially among those with health problems or whose partners have sexual performance difficulties. The drop in estrogen also contributes to decreased elasticity of the skin and loss of bone mass. And estrogen's ability to help protect against accumulation of plaque on the walls of the arteries, boosting "good cholesterol," is lost.

The period leading up to and following menopause is often accompanied by emotional and physical symptoms, including mood fluctuations and *hot flashes*—periodic sensations of warmth accompanied by a rise in body temperature and redness in the face, neck, and chest, followed by sweating. Hot flashes—which may occur during the day and also, as *night sweats*, during sleep—affect about 75 percent of women in Western industrialized nations.

Although menopausal women tend to report increased irritability and less satisfying sleep, research using EEG and other physiological measures finds no links between menopause and changes in quantity or quality of sleep. Also, many studies reveal no association between menopause and depression in the general population. Rather, women who have a previous history of depression, are physically inactive, or have financial difficulties are more likely to experience depressive episodes during the climacteric.
Page Ref: 397–398

121) Explain the combined gender-racial bias that can dangerously impact African-American women with heart disease.

Answer: Because men account for over 70 percent of cases in middle adulthood, doctors often view a heart condition as a "male problem." Consequently, they tend to overlook women's symptoms, which tend to be milder, more often taking the form of angina than a full-blown heart attack. In one study, researchers had male and female actors present identical symptoms of angina to a sample of over 700 doctors. The doctors were far less likely to suspect heart problems in women, especially African-American women, who are at greater risk for heart disease than are Caucasian-American women. This combined gender-racial bias greatly reduced the extent to which African-American women were referred for a standard follow-up test.

Page Ref: 403

122) Discuss the gender differences related to osteoporosis, and mortality rates associated with the disease.

Answer: In middle and late adulthood, women lose about 50 percent of their bone mass, about half of it in the first 10 years following menopause. In men, the age related decrease in testosterone—though much more gradual than estrogen loss in women—contributes to bone loss because the body converts some to estrogen.

When major bone fractures (such as the hip) occur, 10 to 20 percent of patients die within a year. Because osteoporosis usually develops earlier in women than in men, it has become known as a "women's disease," and men are far less likely to be screened and treated. Compared with women, men with hip fractures tend to be older and to lack a history of interventions aimed at preserving bone density. Probably for these reasons, the one-year mortality rate after hip fracture is nearly twice as great for men as for women.

Page Ref: 403

123) What type of exercise format would be appropriate for an individual beginning to exercise in midlife who is normal weight and leads a highly stressful life? Justify your answer.

Answer: Group exercise classes are most appropriate. Normal-weight adults are more likely to stick with group classes than are overweight adults, who may strain to keep up with the pace of the class and feel embarrassed in front of others. Further, adults with highly stressful lives are more likely to persist in group classes, offering a regular schedule and the face-to-face support of others, than in a home-based program.

Page Ref: 405

124) Describe how the quality of creativity changes from early to middle adulthood.

Answer: The quality of creativity may change with advancing age in at least three ways.

First, youthful creativity in literature and the arts is often spontaneous and intensely emotional, while creative works produced after age 40 often appear more deliberately thoughtful. Perhaps for this reason, poets produce their most frequently cited works at younger ages than do authors of fiction and nonfiction. Poetry depends more on language play and "hot" expression of feelings, whereas story- and book-length works require extensive planning and molding.

Second, with age, many creators shift from generating unusual products to combining extensive knowledge and experience into unique ways of thinking. Creative works by older adults more often sum up or integrate ideas. Mature academics typically devote less energy to new discoveries in favor of writing memoirs, histories of their field, and other reflective works.

Finally, creativity in middle adulthood frequently reflects a transition from a largely egocentric concern with self-expression to more altruistic goals. As the middle-aged person overcomes the youthful illusion that life is eternal, the desire to contribute to humanity and enrich the lives of others increases.

Page Ref: 411–412

125) Central State College wants to provide supports for mature adults who are returning to school. What recommendations could you make, based upon information in your text?

Answer: Orientation for family members on how to provide supports at home. Adult students need family members and friends who encourage their efforts and help them find time for uninterrupted study.

Institutional services for returning students are also essential. Personal relationships with faculty, peer networks enabling adults to get to know one another, conveniently scheduled evening and Saturday classes, online courses, and financial aid for part-time students increase the chances of academic success.

Academic advising and professional internship opportunities responsive to their needs are vital. Low-income students often need special assistance, such as academic tutoring, sessions in confidence building and assertiveness, and—in the case of ethnic minorities—help adjusting to styles of learning that are at odds with their cultural background.

Page Ref: 413

STUDY QUESTIONS

Physical Development

Physical Changes

Vision

1. Describe the condition known as *presbyopia,* and explain how changes in the structures of the eye contribute to this condition. (p. 396)

____

____

____

2. Cite declines in visual functioning that are associated with yellowing of the lens, shrinking of the pupil, and increasing density of the vitreous. (p. 396)

____

____

____

3. Describe neural changes in the visual system that occur in midlife. (p. 396)

____

____

____

4. Middle-aged adults are at increased risk for ______________—a disease in which pressure builds up within the eye due to poor fluid drainage, causing damage to the optic nerve. (p. 396)

Hearing

1. Most adult-onset hearing impairments are age-related, declines called ______________, meaning "old hearing." (p. 396)

2. Cite two physical changes that lead to age-related hearing loss. (p. 396)

   A. ____

   B. ____

3. (Men's / Women's) hearing tends to decline earlier. Explain your answer. (p. 397)

____

____

Skin

1. Name and describe the three layers that make up our skin, explaining how each changes with age. (p. 397)

   A. ____

   Changes: ____

   B. ____

   Changes: ____

   C. ____

   Changes: ____

2. Describe changes in the skin at the following ages: (p. 397)

   Thirties: ____

   Forties: ____

   Fifties: ____

Muscle–Fat Makeup

1. Briefly summarize changes in body fat and muscle mass in middle adulthood. (p. 397)

____

____

____

2. Describe sex differences in fat distribution during middle adulthood. (p. 397)

   Men: ____

   Women: ____

3. Explain how weight gain and muscle loss can be prevented. (p. 397)

____

____

____

Skeleton

1. What change leads to substantial reduction in bone density during adulthood? (p. 397)

____

2. Why are women especially susceptible to loss in bone mass in middle adulthood? (p. 397)

____

____

3. Cite one health problem associated with weakened bones. (p. 397)

____

4. Cite factors that can slow bone loss in postmenopausal women by 30 to 50 percent. (p. 397)

____

____

Reproductive System

1. The midlife transition in which fertility declines is called the ______________. (p. 397)
2. In women, the climacteric concludes with ______________—the end of menstruation and reproductive capacity. This occurs, on average, in the ______________ among North American, European, and East Asian women. (p. 397)
3. Summarize gradual changes that precede menopause, as well as the physical changes that occur after menopause. (pp. 397–398)

   Changes preceding menopause: ____

   ____

   ____

   Changes after menopause: ____

   ____

   ____

4. True or False: Research reveals that menopause is not linked to changes in the quantity or quality of sleep. (p. 398)
5. Describe characteristics of women who are likely to experience depressive episodes during climacteric. (p. 398)

   ____

   ____

6. Describe two types of hormone therapy. (p. 398)

   A. ____

   ____

   B. ____

   ____

7. Briefly summarize the benefits and risks associated with hormone therapy. (p. 398)

   Benefits: ____

   ____

   Risks: ____

   ____

8. Describe factors that affect women's psychological reactions to menopause. (p. 399)

   ____

   ____

   ____

9. Provide an example of ethnic differences in the way women experience and view menopause. (p. 399)

10. True or False: Men lose their reproductive capacity during midlife and can no longer father children. (p. 399)

11. Summarize reproductive changes in middle-aged men. (p. 399)

Cultural Influences: Menopause as a Biocultural Event

1. Summarize the differing views of menopause held by individuals in Western industrialized nations compared to their non-Western counterparts. (p. 400)

   Western:

   Non-Western:

2. True or False: Japanese women and doctors, like their North American counterparts, consider menopause to be a significant marker of female middle age. (p. 400)

3. Compare Mayan and Greek perspectives on menopause, noting similarities and differences. (p. 400)

   Similarities:

   Differences:

Health and Fitness

Sexuality

1. Frequency of sexual activity declines (dramatically / slightly) in middle adulthood. (p. 401)

2. What is the best predictor of sexual frequency in midlife? (p. 401)

3. How does the intensity of sexual response change during middle adulthood? (p. 401)

4. True or False: The majority of people over age 50 say that sex is an important component of their relationship. (p. 401)

Illness and Disability

1. List the two leading causes of death in midlife. (p. 401)

   A. ______________________________

   B. ______________________________

2. Overall, middle-aged (men / women) are more vulnerable to most health problems. (p. 401)
3. In the last 15 years, the incidence of lung cancer dropped in (men / women), but it has increased in (men / women). (p. 402)
4. Describe two types of mutations that contribute to cancer. (p. 402)

   A. ______________________________

   B. ______________________________

5. True or False: Cancer death rates increase sharply as SES decreases and are especially high among low-income ethnic minorities. (p. 402)
6. Provide an example of the complex interaction of heredity, biological aging, and environment on cancer. (p. 402)

   ____

   ____

   ____

7. Name the three most common types of cancer among men and women. (p. 402)

   Men: ______________________________

   Women: ______________________________

8. Describe two ways to reduce cancer illness and cancer death. (p. 402)

   A. ______________________________

   B. ______________________________

9. List three indicators of cardiovascular disease that are known as "silent killers" because they often have no symptoms. (p. 402)

   A. ______________________________

   B. ______________________________

   C. ______________________________

10. List three symptoms of cardiovascular disease. (p. 402)

    A. ______________________________

    ____

    B. ______________________________

    ____

    C. ______________________________

    ____

11. List four ways to reduce the risk of having a heart attack. (p. 402)

    A. ______________________________

    B. ______________________________

    C. ______________________________

    D. ______________________________

12. Accurate diagnosis of cardiovascular disease is of special concern to (women / men), since doctors frequently overlook their symptoms. (pp. 402–403)

13. When age-related bone loss is severe, a condition called ______________ develops. (p. 403)

14. True or False: Osteoporosis affects the majority of people of both sexes over age 70. (p. 403)

15. Summarize the symptoms of osteoporosis. (p. 403)

16. List biological and environmental risk factors associated with osteoporosis. (p. 403)

    Biological: ______________________________

    Environmental: ______________________________

17. True or False: Men are far less likely than women to be screened and treated for osteoporosis. Explain your answer. (p. 403)

18. List several interventions for treating osteoporosis. (p. 403)

Hostility and Anger

1. Describe characteristics of the *Type A behavior pattern.* (pp. 403–404)

2. What is the "toxic" ingredient of the Type A behavior pattern? (p. 404)

3. Explain the link between expressed hostility and health problems. (p. 404)

4. True or False: Suppressing anger is a healthier way of dealing with negative feelings than expressing anger. (p. 404)

Adapting to the Challenges of Midlife

Stress Management

1. Identify five strategies for managing stress. (p. 404)

   A. ______

   B. ______

   C. ______

   D. ______

   E. ______

2. Distinguish between *problem-centered* and *emotion-centered* coping. (p. 404)

   Problem-centered: ______

   Emotion-centered: ______

3. What approach to coping is most effective for reducing stress? (p. 404)

   ______

4. Cite several constructive approaches to anger reduction. (p. 405)

   ______

5. Summarize changes in coping with stress from early to middle adulthood. (p. 405)

   ______

Exercise

1. Of those who begin an exercise program in midlife, ____ percent discontinue within the first six months. Among those who stay active, fewer than ____ percent exercise at levels that lead to health benefits. (p. 405)
2. Define *self-efficacy,* and describe the link between self-efficacy and exercise. (p. 405)

   Definition: ______

   Link to exercise: ______

3. Identify characteristics of beginning exercisers that best fit group versus home-based exercise programs. (p. 405)

   Group: ______

   Home-based: ______

4. List barriers to exercise often mentioned by low-SES adults. (p. 405)

____

____

An Optimistic Outlook

1. ______________ refers to a set of three personal qualities that help people cope with stress adaptively, thereby reducing its impact on illness and mortality. List and describe the three qualities that make up this trait. (p. 406)

   A. ____

   ____

   B. ____

   ____

   C. ____

   ____

2. Summarize the coping strategies of high-hardy and low-hardy individuals. (p. 406)

   High-hardy: ____

   ____

   Low-hardy: ____

   ____

3. Cite five factors that act as stress-resistant resources. (p. 406)

   A. ____

   B. ____

   C. ____

   D. ____

   E. ____

Gender and Aging: A Double Standard

1. Unfavorable stereotypes about aging are more often applied to (women / men), who are rated as less attractive and as having more negative characteristics. (p. 406)

2. What factor is at the heart of the double standard of aging? (p. 406)

   ____

3. New evidence suggests that the double standard of aging is (increasing / declining). (p. 406)

Cognitive Development

Changes in Mental Abilities

Cohort Effects

1. Schaie examined adult development of intellectual abilities using a ________________ design, which combines cross-sectional and longitudinal approaches. Describe differences in Schaie's longitudinal and cross-sectional findings. What accounts for this difference? (p. 407)

   Cross-sectional: ____

   ____

   Longitudinal: ____

   ____

   Difference: ____

   ____

Crystallized and Fluid Intelligence

1. Differentiate between *crystallized* and *fluid intelligence.* (pp. 407–408)

   Crystallized: ____

   ____

   Fluid: ____

   ____

2. (Crystallized / Fluid) intelligence increases steadily throughout middle adulthood, whereas (crystallized / fluid) intelligence begins to decline in the twenties. (p. 408)

3. Using findings from Schaie's Seattle Longitudinal Study, list five crystallized and fluid skills that continue to show gains in midlife and one fluid skill that declines steadily from the twenties to the late eighties. (p. 408)

   Crystallized:

   A. ____

   B. ____

   C. ____

   D. ____

   E. ____

   Fluid:

   F. ____

4. List three reasons why middle-aged adults show stability in crystallized abilities despite a much earlier decline in fluid intelligence. (pp. 408–409)

   A. ____

   B. ____

   C. ____

Information Processing

Speed of Processing

1. True or False: Response time on both simple and complex reaction time tasks remains stable across early and middle adulthood. (p. 409)
2. Provide two explanations for age-related declines in speed of processing. (p. 409)

   A. ______________________________

   ____

   B. ______________________________

   ____
3. How does processing speed affect adults' performance on many complex tasks? (p. 409)

   ____

   ____

   ____
4. True or False: Knowledge and experience help older adults compensate for declines in processing speed. (p. 409)

Attention

1. Studies of attention focus on the following three changes: (p. 409)

   A. ______________________________

   B. ______________________________

   C. ______________________________
2. Explain how declines in attention might be related to a slowdown in information processing during midlife. (p. 410)

   ____

   ____

   ____
3. Describe changes in inhibition in middle adulthood. (p. 410)

   ____

   ____
4. True or False: Practice and experience with attentional skills can help midlifers compensate for age-related declines. (p. 410)

Memory

1. From early to middle adulthood, the amount of information people can retain in working memory (increases / diminishes). What explains this change? (p. 410)

   ____

   ____

2. Memory strategies, such as organization and elaboration, are applied (less / more) often and (less / more) effectively with age. What explains these changes? (p. 410)

____

____

____

3. How can memory tasks be designed to help older people compensate for age-related declines in working memory? (p. 410)

____

____

____

4. Middle-aged people who have trouble recalling something often drawn on decades of accumulated ________________ about how to maximize performance. (pp. 410–411)

Practical Problem Solving and Expertise

1. What is *practical problem solving*? (p. 411)

____

____

2. Expertise (peaks / declines) in midlife. (p. 411)
3. True or False: Advances in expertise are found only among highly educated individuals in administrative occupations. (p. 411)
4. Briefly describe advances in practical problem solving during middle adulthood. (p. 411)

____

____

____

Creativity

1. Summarize three ways that creativity changes with age. (p. 412)

A. ____

____

B. ____

____

C. ____

____

Vocational Life and Cognitive Development

1. Summarize the relationship between vocational life and cognition. (p. 412)

____

____

____

2. Cross-cultural findings (support / refute) the notion that complex work leads to gains in cognitive flexibility. (p. 412)

3. True or False: The impact of challenging work on cognition is greater in early adulthood than in middle adulthood. (p. 412)

Adult Learners: Becoming a Student in Midlife

1. List several reasons why middle-aged adults may decide to enroll in undergraduate and graduate programs. (p. 412)

____

____

____

Characteristics of Returning Students

1. (Men / Women) represent the majority of adult learners. (p. 413)

2. Describe common feelings of women during their first-year reentry as a student. What factors influence these feelings? (p. 413)

   A. _______________

   ____

   B. _______________

   ____

3. What challenges do middle-aged women who return to college face? (p. 413)

____

____

____

4. What is the most common reason women do not complete their degree in middle adulthood? (p. 413)

____

Supporting Returning Students

1. List social supports and institutional services that facilitate adult reentry into college. (p. 413)

   Social supports: _______________

   ____

   Institutional services: _______________

   ____

2. Summarize the benefits of adult reentry to college. (p. 413)

____

____

____

PUZZLE 15.1

Across

3. A disease in which pressure builds up within the eye due to poor fluid drainage, damaging the optic nerve
6. ______ problem solving: requires people to size up real-world situations and analyze how best to achieve goals that have a high degree of uncertainty
7. ______ intelligence: skills that largely depend on basic information-processing skills
10. Treatment in which a woman takes daily doses of estrogen, sometimes combined with progesterone, during the climacteric and after menopause
11. ______ - ______ view: attributes age-related slowing of cognitive processing to greater loss of information as it moves through the system
12. ______ network view: attributes age-related slowing of cognitive processing to breaks in neural networks as neurons die
13. Behavior pattern consisting of competitiveness, ambition, impatience, angry outbursts, and time pressure
14. Set of three personal qualities—commitment, control, and challenge—that help people cope with stress adaptively

Down

1. Condition associated with severe age-related bone
2. Age-related hearing impairments that involve a sharp loss of hearing at high frequencies, gradually extending to all frequencies loss
4. Midlife transition in which fertility declines
5. Condition of aging in which the eye loses its capacity to accommodate entirely to nearby objects
8. ______ intelligence: skills that depend largely on accumulated knowledge and experience, good judgment, and mastery of social conventions
9. The end of menstruation and, therefore, reproductive capacity in women

CROSSWORD PUZZLE SOLUTION

PUZZLE 15.1

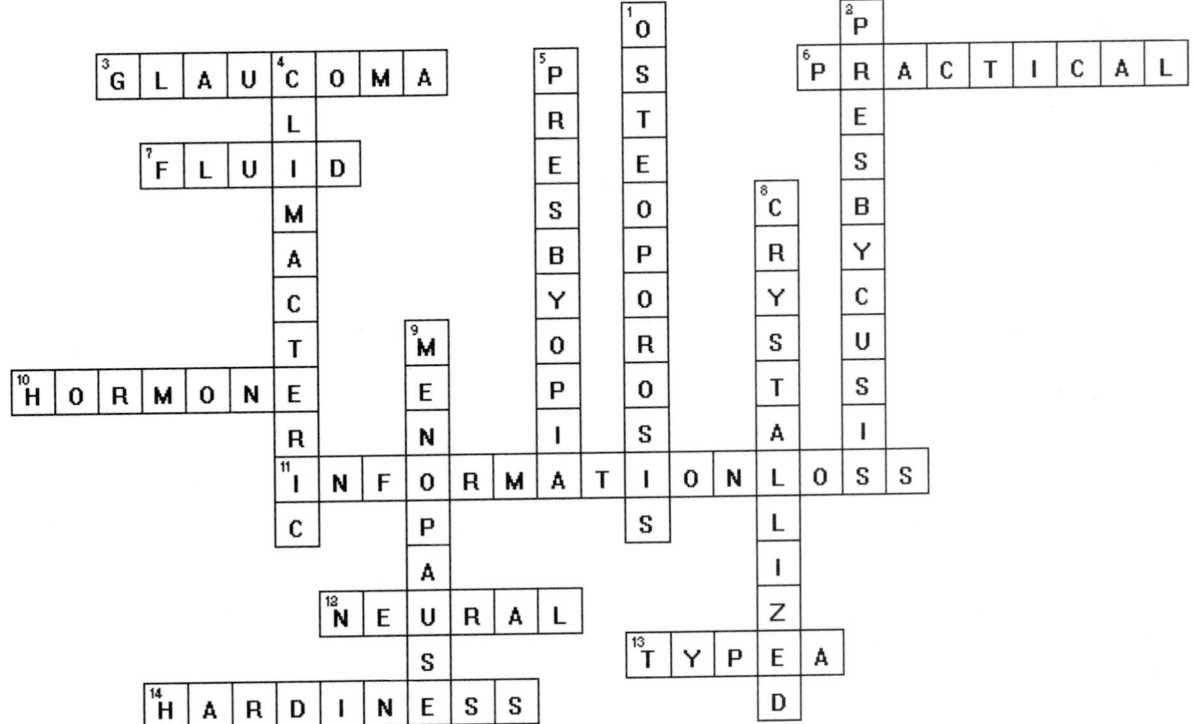

PRACTICE TEST #1

1. Middle age is loosely defined as taking place between ages (p. 395)
   a. 20 and 35.
   b. 30 and 45.
   c. 40 and 65.
   d. 50 and 75.

2. Throughout adulthood, the size of the pupil shrinks and the lens (p. 396)
   a. yellows.
   b. expands.
   c. thins.
   d. dissolves.

3. Middle-aged adults are at increased risk of __________, a disease in which poor fluid drainage causes a buildup of pressure within the eye, damaging the optic nerve. (p. 396)
   a. glaucoma
   b. presbycusis
   c. presbyopia
   d. climacteric

4. Men's hearing declines (p. 397)
   a. less rapidly than women's.
   b. more rapidly than women's.
   c. at the same rate as women's.
   d. while women's hearing does not decline.

5. Reduction in bone mass during midlife (p. 397)
   a. is caused by increased mineral content.
   b. is more substantial in men than in women.
   c. causes bones to fracture more easily and heal more slowly.
   d. cannot be slowed, even with lifestyle changes such as increased calcium intake.

6. What percentage of individuals affected with cancer are cured? (p. 402)
   a. 10 percent
   b. 20 percent
   c. 40 percent
   d. 60 percent

7. Which indicator of cardiovascular disease is referred to as a "silent killer"? (p. 402)
   a. atherosclerosis—a buildup of plaque in the coronary arteries
   b. a heart attack—blockage of normal blood supply to an area of the heart
   c. arrhythmia—an irregular heartbeat
   d. angina pectoris—indigestion-like or crushing chest pain

8. To treat osteoporosis, doctors recommend a diet enriched with vitamin D and (p. 403)
   a. calcium.
   b. magnesium.
   c. iron.
   d. vitamin C.

9. Expressed hostility (p. 404)
   a. predicts heart disease and other health problems only in men.
   b. is the toxic ingredient in the Type A behavior pattern that predicts heart disease and other health problems.
   c. poses fewer health risks than does suppressed hostility.
   d. elevates heart rate and blood pressure, but reduces levels of stress hormones in the body.

10. Sharon decided that she was unhappy at work. She realized that the primary cause was frustration with an irresponsible co-worker. She met with this individual, came up with strategies to help the young woman meet her responsibilities, and subsequently derived more enjoyment from her job. Sharon used (p. 404)
    a. avoidant coping.
    b. problem-centered coping.
    c. emotion-centered coping.
    d. behavior-focused coping.

11. When a person has a sense of control over life events, a commitment to important activities, and a tendency to view change as a challenge rather than a disappointment, this person is said to display (p. 406)
    a. fluid intelligence.
    b. Type A behavior pattern.
    c. resilience.
    d. hardiness.

12. Hardy individuals (p. 406)
    a. seldom view stressful situations as controllable.
    b. fail to find interest and meaning in daily activities.
    c. more often use emotion-centered coping strategies.
    d. view challenge as a chance for personal growth.

13. The double standard of aging refers to the notion that (p. 406)
    a. middle-aged men become less committed to occupational status and physical fitness, yet they are viewed by the larger culture as powerful and driven.
    b. middle-aged women often feel assertive and confident, yet they are viewed by the larger culture as being less attractive and as having more negative traits than middle-aged men.
    c. middle-aged women gain in positive judgments of appearance, maturity, and power, whereas middle-aged men show a decline in such ratings.
    d. middle-aged adults of both sexes prefer younger sexual partners.

14. Many cross-sectional studies show that _______________ increases steadily through middle adulthood, whereas _______________ begins to decline in the twenties. (p. 408)
    a. crystallized intelligence, fluid intelligence
    b. fluid intelligence, general intelligence
    c. problem-solving intelligence, crystallized intelligence
    d. fluid intelligence, crystallized intelligence

15. Studies of attention during midlife indicate that (pp. 409–410)
    a. cognitive inhibition—the ability to resist interference from irrelevant information—improves during middle adulthood.
    b. it becomes more difficult to engage in two complex activities at the same time.
    c. decrements in attention are caused by sensory impairments, such as diminished vision and hearing.
    d. practice with attention-related tasks does little to improve these skills.

16. With respect to memory in middle adulthood, (p. 410)
    a. the amount of information people can retain in working memory declines.
    b. adults more often use memory strategies of rehearsal, organization, and elaboration.
    c. recall is better in highly structured than in self-paced conditions.
    d. adults have difficulty compensating for memory limitations.

17. Declines in working memory in midlife largely result from (p. 410)
    a. changes in the structure of the brain.
    b. declines in metacognitive knowledge.
    c. decreased motivation to learn and remember new information.
    d. infrequent and ineffective use of memory strategies.

18. During middle adulthood, creativity (p. 412)
    a. becomes less deliberately thoughtful.
    b. is focused more on generating unusual products and less on combining knowledge and experience.
    c. shifts from an egocentric concern with self-expression to more altruistic goals.
    d. is more spontaneous and intensely emotional.

19. Research on the relationship between vocational life and cognitive development shows that (p. 412)
    a. the impact of challenging work on cognitive growth is greatest for young adults.
    b. people in their fifties and early sixties show as many cognitive gains from complex work as do individuals in their twenties and thirties.
    c. the relationship between challenging work and continued cognitive development is only evident in cultures similar to the United States.
    d. cognition has a unidirectional influence on vocational life—that is, cognitive ability affects vocational choice, but vocational life does not affect cognitive development.

20. Adults who return to college for undergraduate and graduate study are most likely to be (p. 413)
    a. women.
    b. under the age of 35.
    c. divorced, single parents.
    d. free of other career and family obligations.

PRACTICE TEST #2

1. Adult-onset hearing loss (pp. 396–397)
    a. is greater among women than men.
    b. is most often caused by a hereditary condition.
    c. is typically first noticeable by a hearing loss at low frequencies.
    d. is minimal in most middle-aged adults, suggesting that severe hearing problems are caused by factors other than biological aging.

2. As we age, (p. 397)
    a. fibers in the dermis thicken.
    b. the epidermis becomes less firmly attached to the dermis.
    c. fat in the hypodermis increases.
    d. skin becomes much more elastic.

3. Which of the following is true of fat distribution in middle adulthood? (p. 397)
    a. Women accumulate more on the back and upper abdomen.
    b. Men accumulate more around the waist and upper arms.
    c. The rise in fat largely affects the torso as fat levels decline on the limbs.
    d. Men and women both tend to lose fat during middle age.

4. With age, people must gradually reduce caloric intake to adjust for the age-related decline in (p. 397)
    a. presbyopia.
    b. basal metabolic rate.
    c. hormone therapy.
    d. bone mass.

5. The period leading up to and following menopause is often accompanied by (p. 398)
    a. rapid declines in body temperature.
    b. excessive sleep.
    c. a sharp rise in estrogen levels.
    d. mood fluctuations.

6. Hormone therapy (p. 398)
   a. works poorly in counteracting hot flashes and vaginal drying.
   b. is linked to a mild increase in heart attacks, stroke, and blood clots.
   c. is associated with increased depression.
   d. enhances cognitive functioning in 65- to 79-year-old women.

7. The leading causes of death in middle adulthood are (p. 401)
   a. suicide and homicide.
   b. motor vehicle accidents and cancer.
   c. AIDS and heart disease.
   d. heart disease and cancer.

8. Cancer-causing mutations that are due to an inherited predisposition are called (p. 402)
   a. somatic.
   b. BRCA1.
   c. germline.
   d. BRCA2.

9. Mary, a 65-year-old woman, does not exercise regularly, has smoked on and off for thirty years, and is deficient in her vitamin D and calcium intake. As a result, Mary has suffered several minor bone fractures in recent years. Mary most likely has (p. 403)
   a. climacteric.
   b. osteoporosis.
   c. cardiovascular disease.
   d. lung cancer.

10. Which of the following is as vital to adoption and maintenance of an exercise program in midlife as it is to career progress? (p. 405)
   a. intelligence
   b. capacity to cope with stress
   c. self-control
   d. self-efficacy

11. Which group of beginning exercisers is most likely to benefit from a home-based program? (p. 405)
   a. normal-weight individuals
   b. overweight individuals
   c. adults with highly stressful lives
   d. middle-aged women

12. The heart of the double standard of aging may be related to the ideal woman being represented as (p. 406)
   a. passive and submissive.
   b. young and sexually attractive.
   c. indecisive and dependent.
   d. assertive and competent.

13. Which of these tasks most clearly makes use of crystallized intelligence? (p. 407)
   a. in response to a green light, pressing a button as fast as possible
   b. finding hidden figures in a drawing
   c. articulate expression of ideas and information
   d. creating novel pieces of art work

14. According to the neural network view, what causes age-related slowing of cognitive processing? (p. 409)
   a. Neurons continue to increase in size, resulting in crowding and slowing.
   b. Neurons die, resulting in the formation of less efficient connections.
   c. The neural network is adversely affected by changes in the balance of neurotransmitters.
   d. Information loss increases as it moves along the neural network.

15. Researchers who believe that, with age, the entire information processing system slows down to inspect and interpret information espouse the (p. 409)
    a. information-loss view.
    b. theory of successful intelligence.
    c. neural network view.
    d. reaction-time view.

16. As Shamiya gets older, which type of memory task will probably be the most difficult for her? (p. 410)
    a. Recalling meaningful prose
    b. Recalling word lists with a strong category-based structure
    c. Recalling lists of unrelated words or numbers
    d. Recalling information related to her occupation

17. Expertise tends to develop (p. 411)
    a. in those who are highly educated.
    b. in those who reach the top of career ladders.
    c. in those from middle- and high-SES backgrounds, regardless of their own education and occupational status.
    d. among individuals from all fields of endeavor, from food service to upper-level administration.

18. Creative accomplishment tends to peak in the (p. 412)
    a. early thirties.
    b. late thirties or early forties.
    c. late forties or early fifties.
    d. late fifties or early sixties.

19. What percentage of returning student adults are women? (p. 413)
    a. 20 percent
    b. 40 percent
    c. 60 percent
    d. 80 percent

20. The most important factor in the success of returning students is (p. 413)
    a. social support.
    b. high intellectual ability.
    c. full-time attendance.
    d. studying at regular times.

POWERPOINT SLIDES

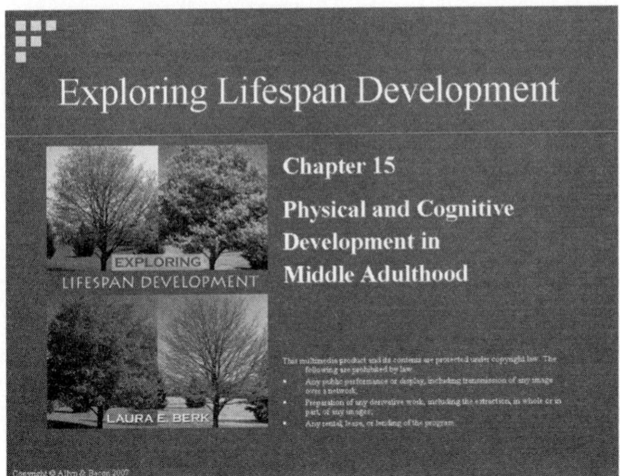

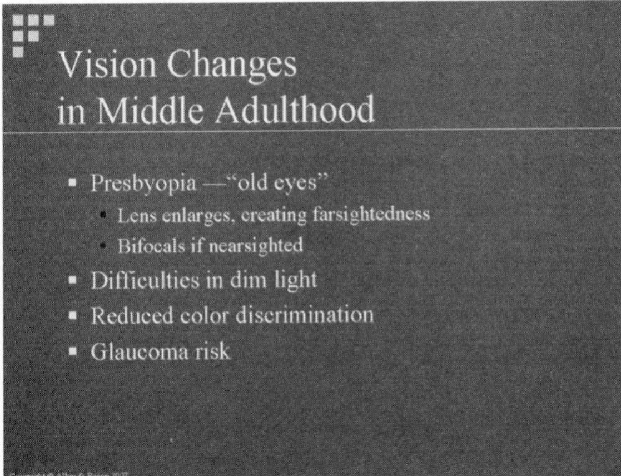

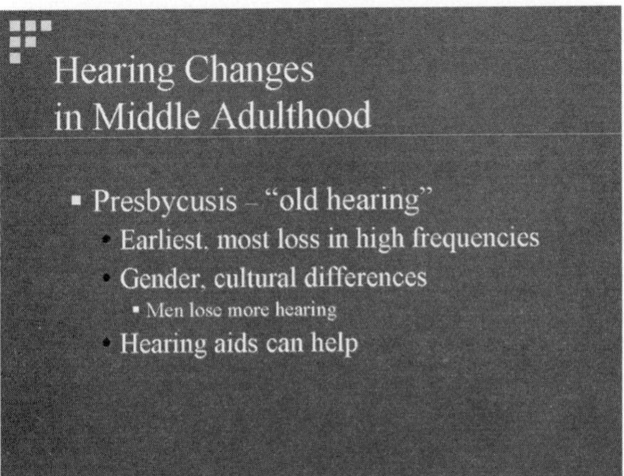

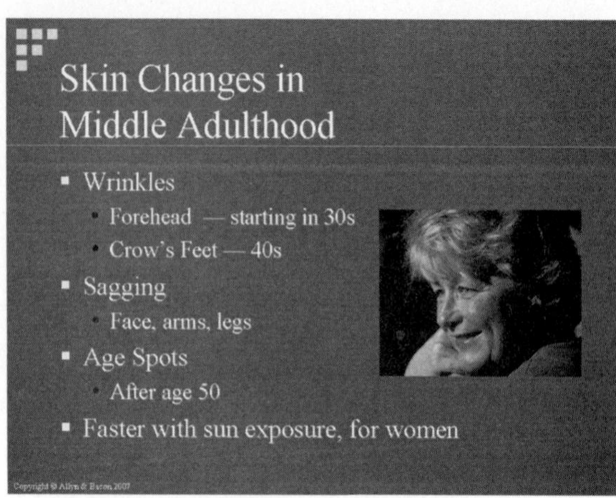
Skin Changes in Middle Adulthood
Wrinkles
Forehead — starting in 30s
Crow's Feet — 40s
Sagging
Face, arms, legs
Age Spots
After age 50
Faster with sun exposure, for women

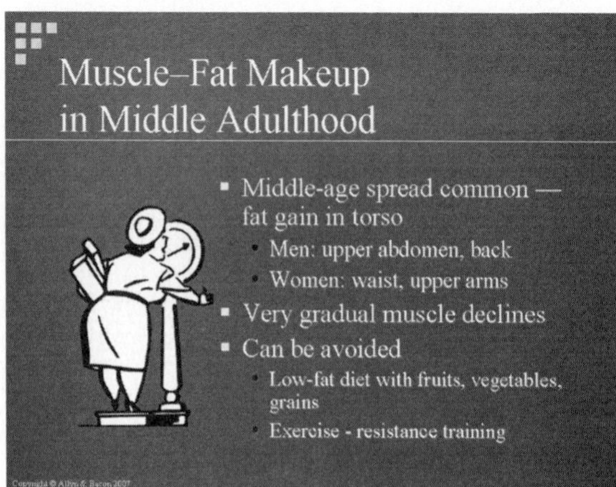
Muscle–Fat Makeup in Middle Adulthood
Middle-age spread common — fat gain in torso
Men: upper abdomen, back
Women: waist, upper arms
Very gradual muscle declines
Can be avoided
Low-fat diet with fruits, vegetables, grains
Exercise - resistance training

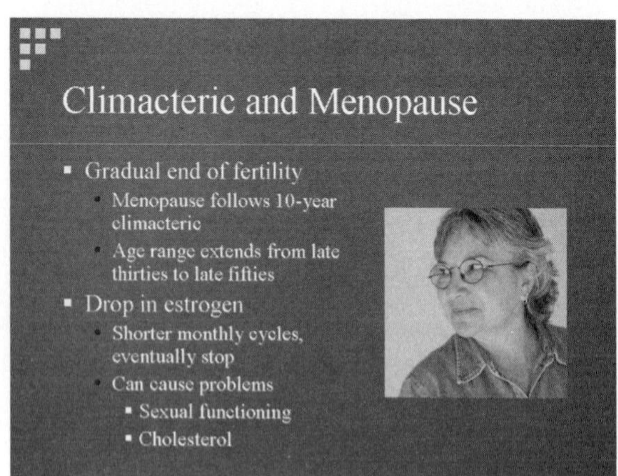
Climacteric and Menopause
Gradual end of fertility
Menopause follows 10-year climacteric
Age range extends from late thirties to late fifties
Drop in estrogen
Shorter monthly cycles, eventually stop
Can cause problems
Sexual functioning
Cholesterol

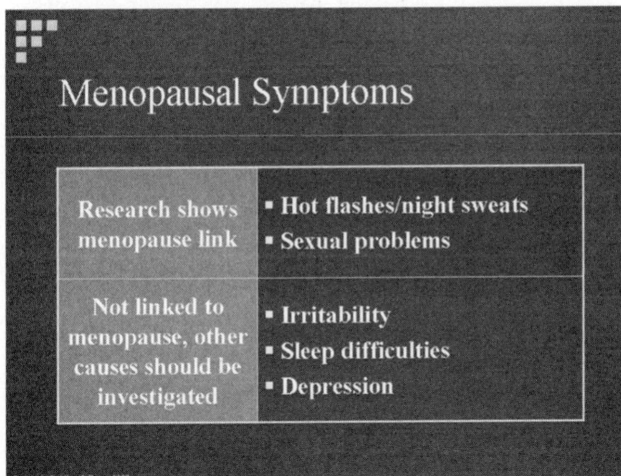
Menopausal Symptoms
Research shows menopause link
Hot flashes/night sweats
Sexual problems
Not linked to menopause, other causes should be investigated
Irritability
Sleep difficulties
Depression

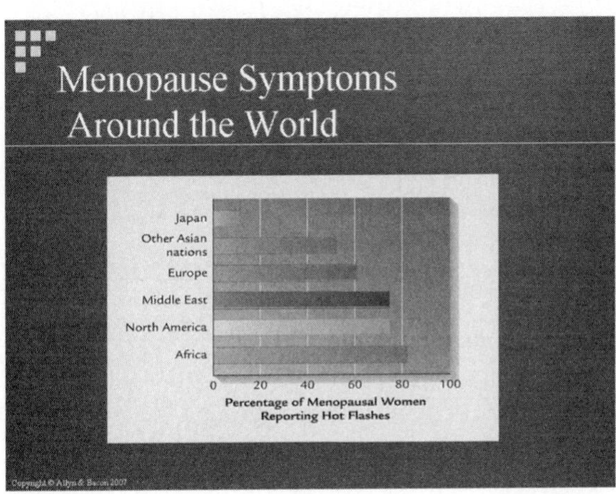
Menopause Symptoms Around the World
Japan
Other Asian nations
Europe
Middle East
North America
Africa
0
20
40
60
80
100
Percentage of Menopausal Women Reporting Hot Flashes

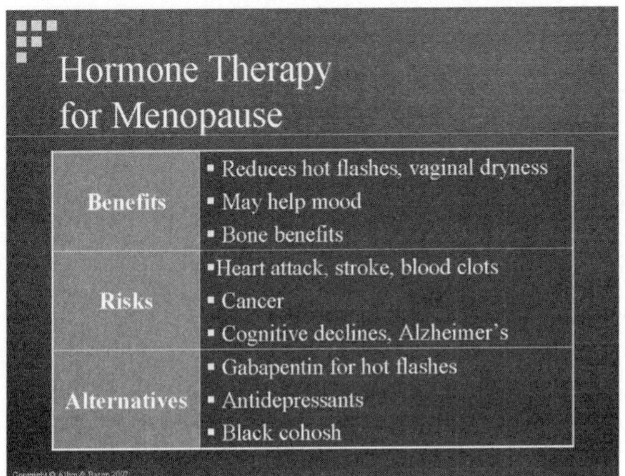
Hormone Therapy for Menopause
Benefits
Reduces hot flashes, vaginal dryness
May help mood
Bone benefits
Risks
Heart attack, stroke, blood clots
Cancer
Cognitive declines, Alzheimer's
Alternatives
Gabapentin for hot flashes
Antidepressants
Black cohosh

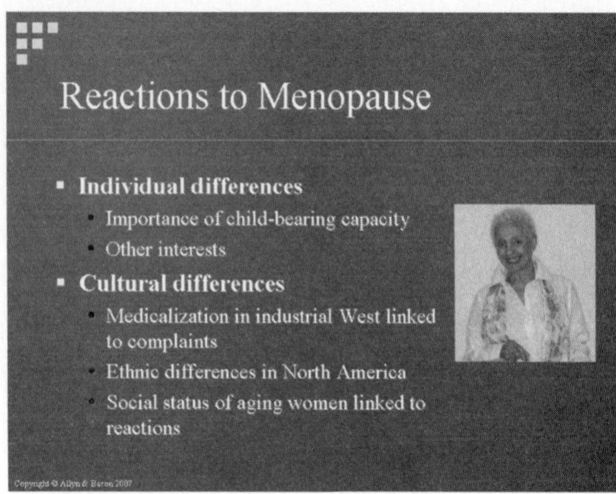
Reactions to Menopause
Individual differences
Importance of child-bearing capacity
Other interests
Cultural differences
Medicalization in industrial West linked to complaints
Ethnic differences in North America
Social status of aging women linked to reactions
Copyright © Allyn & Bacon 2007

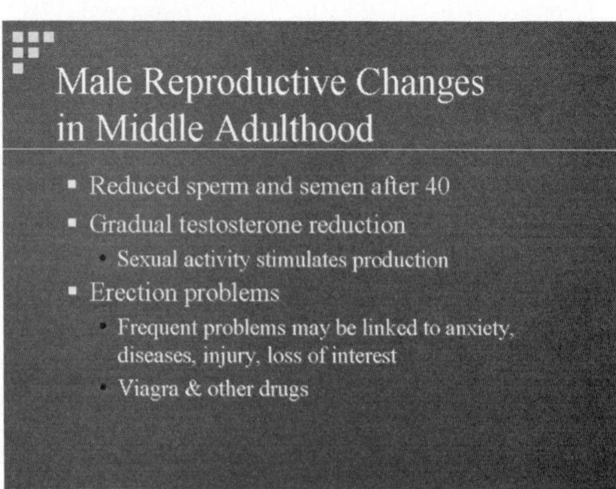
Male Reproductive Changes in Middle Adulthood
Reduced sperm and semen after 40
Gradual testosterone reduction
Sexual activity stimulates production
Erection problems
Frequent problems may be linked to anxiety, diseases, injury, loss of interest
Viagra & other drugs
Copyright © Allyn & Bacon 2007

Health in Middle Age
Over 80% rate as good or excellent
Decline from early adulthood
More chronic diseases than in early adulthood
Copyright © Allyn & Bacon 2007

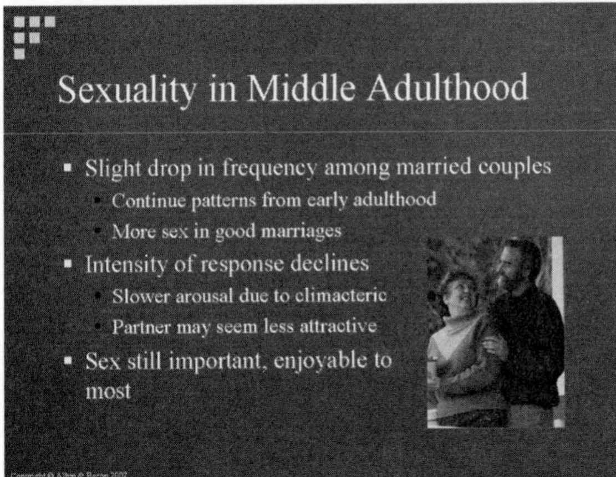
Sexuality in Middle Adulthood
Slight drop in frequency among married couples
Continue patterns from early adulthood
More sex in good marriages
Intensity of response declines
Slower arousal due to climacteric
Partner may seem less attractive
Sex still important, enjoyable to most
Copyright © Allyn & Bacon 2007

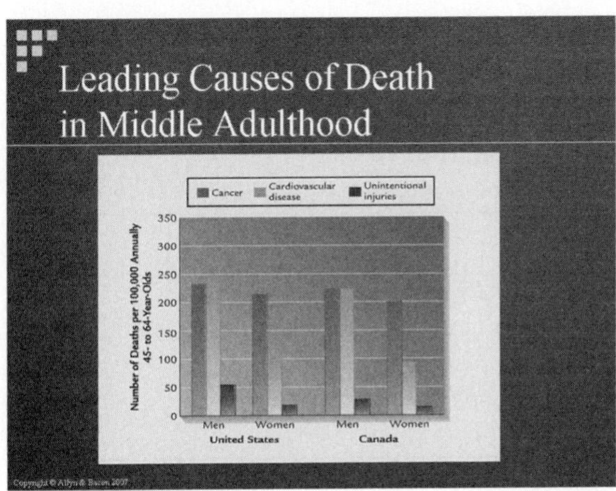
Leading Causes of Death in Middle Adulthood
Cancer
Cardiovascular disease
Unintentional injuries
Number of Deaths per 100,000 Annually 45- to 64-Year-Olds
350
300
250
200
150
100
50
0
Men
Women
Men
Women
United States
Canada
Copyright © Allyn & Bacon 2007

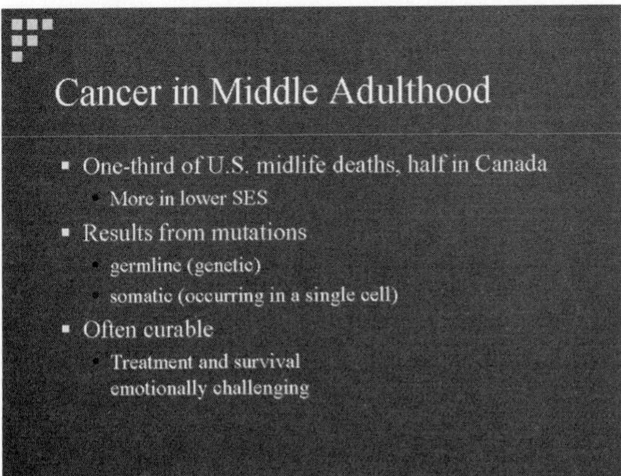
Cancer in Middle Adulthood
One-third of U.S. midlife deaths, half in Canada
More in lower SES
Results from mutations
germline (genetic)
somatic (occurring in a single cell)
Often curable
Treatment and survival emotionally challenging
Copyright © Allyn & Bacon 2007

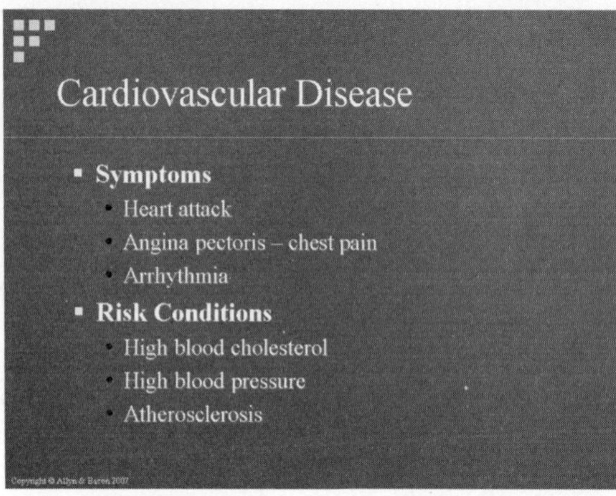
Cardiovascular Disease
Symptoms
Heart attack
Angina pectoris – chest pain
Arrhythmia
Risk Conditions
High blood cholesterol
High blood pressure
Atherosclerosis

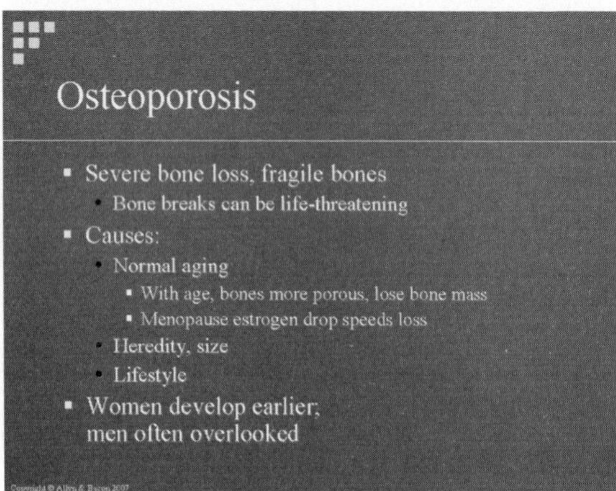
Osteoporosis
Severe bone loss, fragile bones
Bone breaks can be life-threatening
Causes:
Normal aging
With age, bones more porous, lose bone mass
Menopause estrogen drop speeds loss
Heredity, size
Lifestyle
Women develop earlier;
men often overlooked

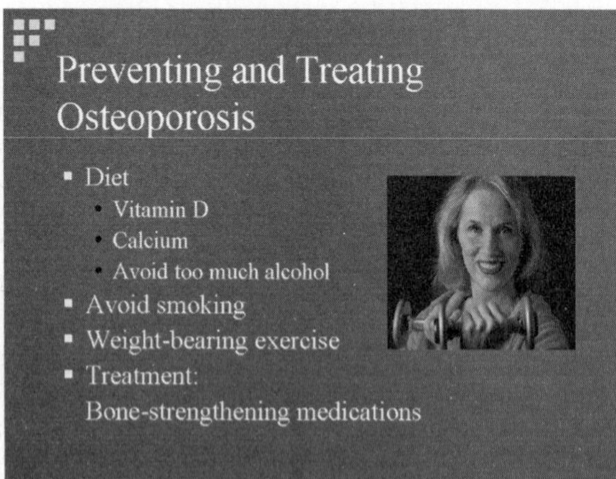
Preventing and Treating Osteoporosis
Diet
Vitamin D
Calcium
Avoid too much alcohol
Avoid smoking
Weight-bearing exercise
Treatment:
Bone-strengthening medications

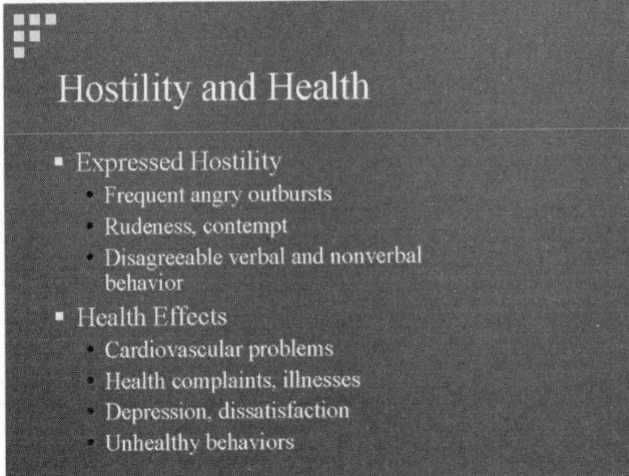
Hostility and Health
Expressed Hostility
Frequent angry outbursts
Rudeness, contempt
Disagreeable verbal and nonverbal behavior
Health Effects
Cardiovascular problems
Health complaints, illnesses
Depression, dissatisfaction
Unhealthy behaviors
Copyright © Allyn & Bacon 2007

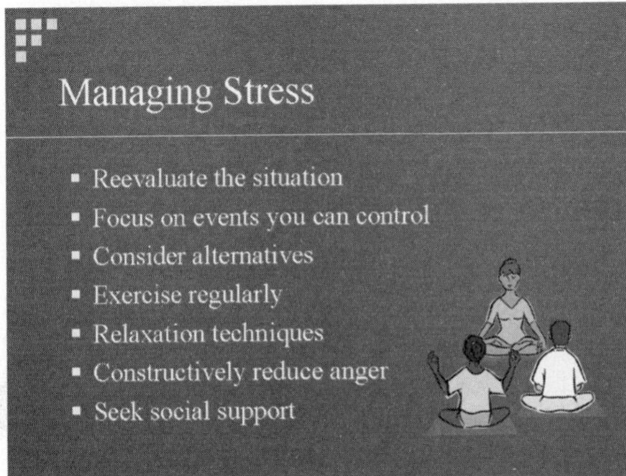
Managing Stress
Reevaluate the situation
Focus on events you can control
Consider alternatives
Exercise regularly
Relaxation techniques
Constructively reduce anger
Seek social support
Copyright © Allyn & Bacon 2007

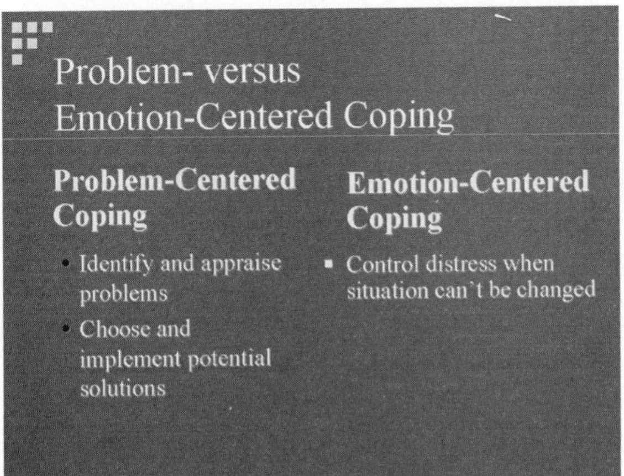
Problem- versus Emotion-Centered Coping
Problem-Centered Coping
Identify and appraise problems
Choose and implement potential solutions
Emotion-Centered Coping
Control distress when situation can't be changed
Copyright © Allyn & Bacon 2007

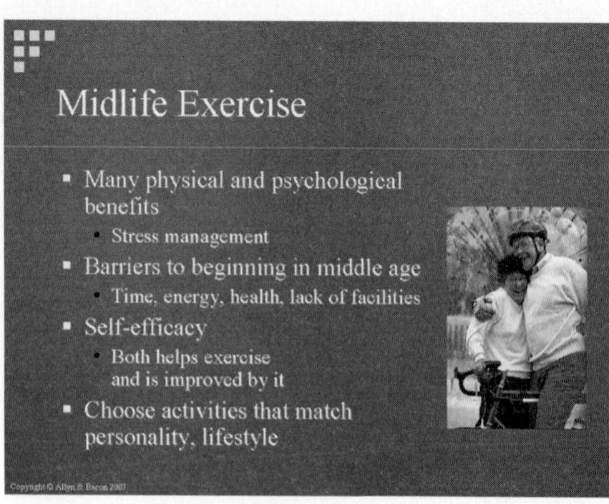
Midlife Exercise
Many physical and psychological benefits
Stress management
Barriers to beginning in middle age
Time, energy, health, lack of facilities
Self-efficacy
Both helps exercise and is improved by it
Choose activities that match personality, lifestyle
Copyright © Allyn & Bacon 2007

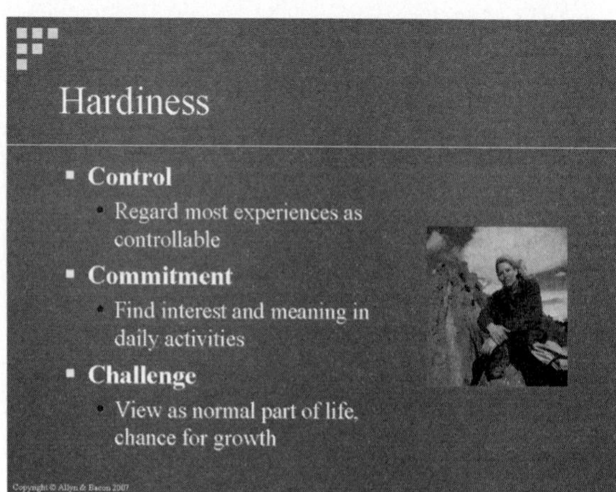
Hardiness
Control
Regard most experiences as controllable
Commitment
Find interest and meaning in daily activities
Challenge
View as normal part of life, chance for growth
Copyright © Allyn & Bacon 2007

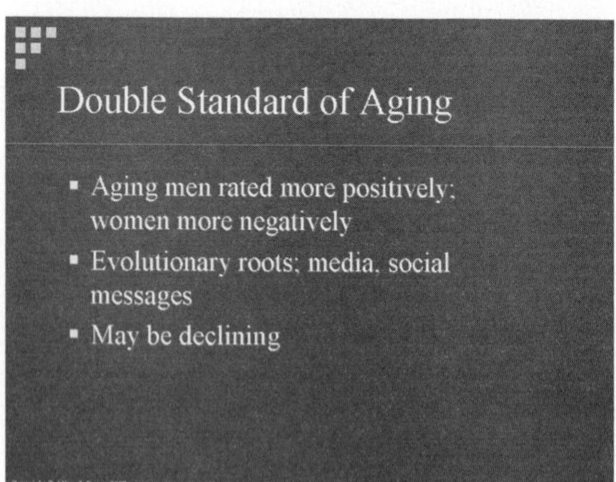
Double Standard of Aging
Aging men rated more positively; women more negatively
Evolutionary roots; media, social messages
May be declining
Copyright © Allyn & Bacon 2007

Fluid and Crystallized Intelligence

Fluid

- Depends on basic information processing skills:
  - Detecting relationships among stimuli
  - Analytical speed
  - Working memory

Crystallized

- Skills that depend on:
  - Accumulated knowledge
  - Experience
  - Good judgment
  - Mastery of social conventions
- Valued by person's culture

Age-Related Slowing of Information Processing

Neural Network View

- Neurons in brain die, breaking neural connections
- Brain forms new connections
- New connections are less efficient

Information-Loss View

- Information lost at each step through cognitive system
- Whole system slows down to inspect, interpret information

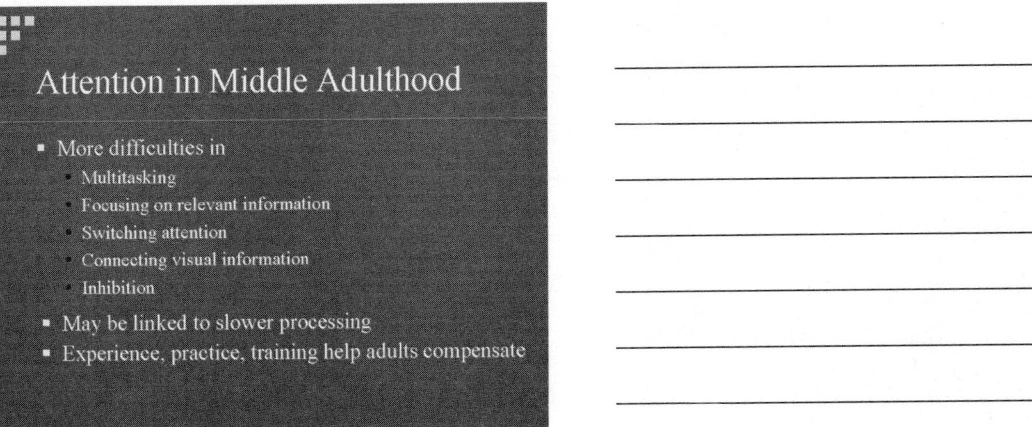

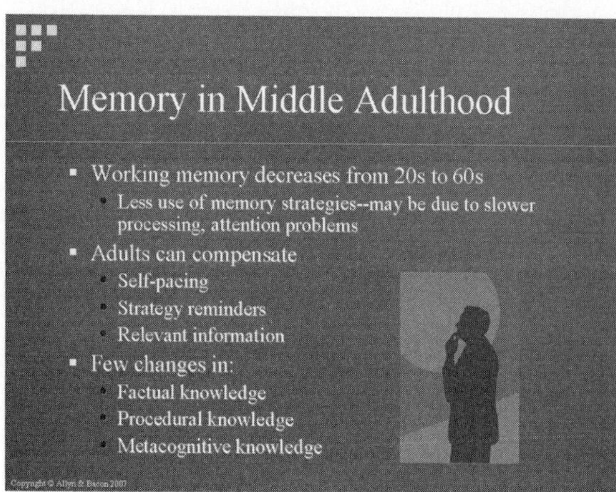
Memory in Middle Adulthood
Working memory decreases from 20s to 60s
Less use of memory strategies--may be due to slower processing, attention problems
Adults can compensate
Self-pacing
Strategy reminders
Relevant information
Few changes in:
Factual knowledge
Procedural knowledge
Metacognitive knowledge
Copyright © Allyn & Bacon 2007

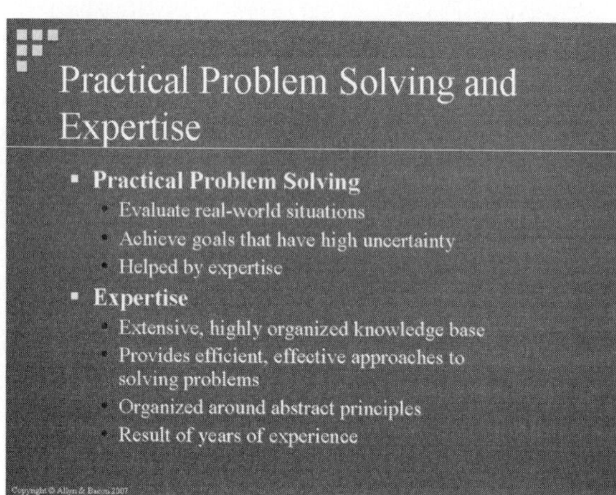
Practical Problem Solving and Expertise
Practical Problem Solving
Evaluate real-world situations
Achieve goals that have high uncertainty
Helped by expertise
Expertise
Extensive, highly organized knowledge base
Provides efficient, effective approaches to solving problems
Organized around abstract principles
Result of years of experience
Copyright © Allyn & Bacon 2007

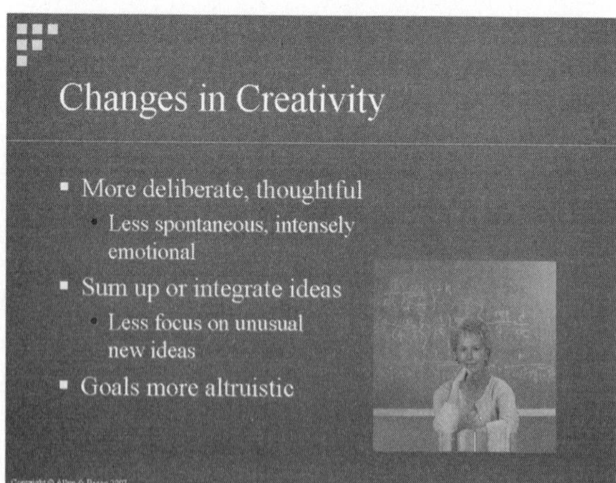
Changes in Creativity
More deliberate, thoughtful
Less spontaneous, intensely emotional
Sum up or integrate ideas
Less focus on unusual new ideas
Goals more altruistic
Copyright © Allyn & Bacon 2007

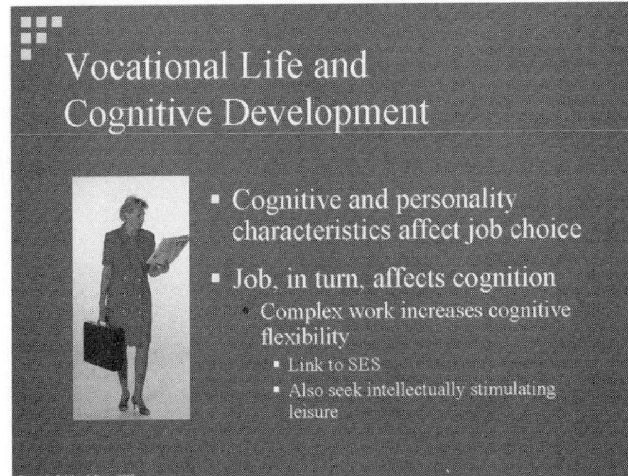
Vocational Life and Cognitive Development
Cognitive and personality characteristics affect job choice
Job, in turn, affects cognition
Complex work increases cognitive flexibility
Link to SES
Also seek intellectually stimulating leisure

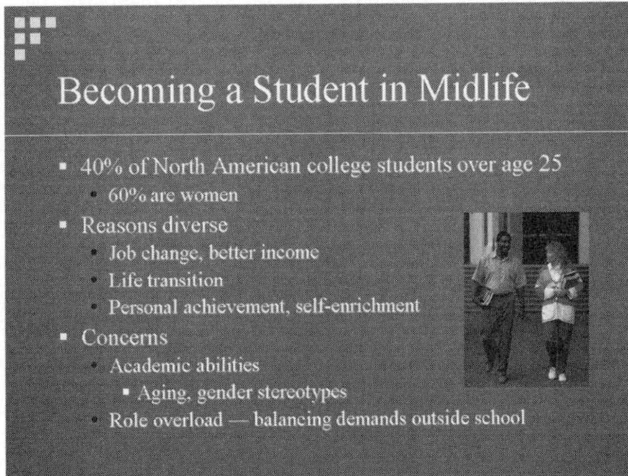
Becoming a Student in Midlife
40% of North American college students over age 25
60% are women
Reasons diverse
Job change, better income
Life transition
Personal achievement, self-enrichment
Concerns
Academic abilities
Aging, gender stereotypes
Role overload — balancing demands outside school

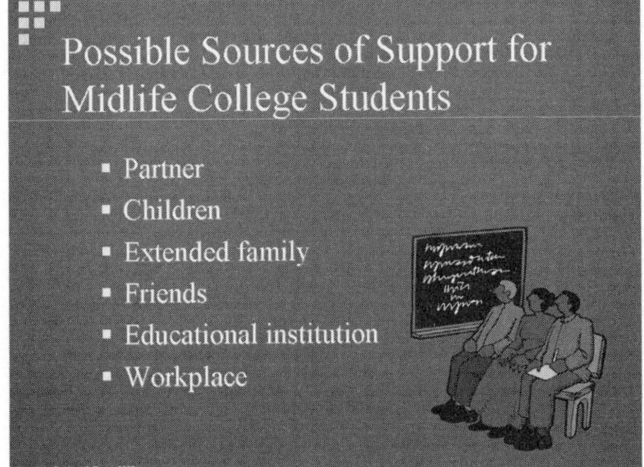
Possible Sources of Support for Midlife College Students
Partner
Children
Extended family
Friends
Educational institution
Workplace

CHAPTER 16
EMOTIONAL AND SOCIAL DEVELOPMENT IN MIDDLE ADULTHOOD

CHAPTER-AT-A-GLANCE

Chapter Outline	Instruction Ideas	Supplements
Erikson's Theory: Generativity versus Stagnation pp. 417–418	Learning Objective 16.1 Learning Activities 16.1–16.2	Test Bank Items 1–11 Videos: *Exploring Lifespan Development in Action* and *A Window on Lifespan Development* Please contact your Allyn and Bacon publisher's representative for a wide range of video offerings available to adopters.
Other Theories of Psychosocial Development in Midlife pp. 419–421 Levinson's Seasons of Life • Vaillant's Adaptation to Life • Is There a Midlife Crisis?	Learning Objectives 16.2–16.3 Learning Activities 16.1, 16.2 Ask Yourself p. 421	Test Bank Items 12–30 Transparency 180
Stability and Change in Self-Concept and Personality pp. 422–425 Possible Selves • Self-Acceptance, Autonomy, and Environmental Mastery • Coping Strategies • Gender Identity • Individual Differences in Personality Traits	Learning Objectives 16.4–16.6 Learning Activity 16.3 Ask Yourself p. 425	Test Bank Items 31–56
Relationships at Midlife pp. 425–433 Marriage and Divorce • Changing Parent–Child Relationships • Grandparenthood • Middle-Aged Children and Their Aging Parents • Siblings • Friendships	Learning Objectives 16.7–16.8 Lecture Enhancements 16.1–16.3 Learning Activities 16.4–16.5 Ask Yourself p. 433	Test Bank Items 37–89 Transparency 183
Vocational Life pp. 433–436 Job Satisfaction • Career Development • Planning for Retirement	Learning Objectives 16.9–16.10 Lecture Enhancement 16.4 Learning Activities 16.6–16.7 Ask Yourself p. 436	Test Bank Items 90–103

BRIEF CHAPTER SUMMARY

Generativity begins in early adulthood but expands greatly as middle-aged adults face Erikson's psychological conflict of midlife: generativity versus stagnation. Highly generative people find fulfillment as they make contributions to society through parenthood, other family relationships, the workplace, volunteer activities, and many forms of productivity and creativity. From Levinson's perspective, middle-aged adults go through a transition in which they reassess their relation to themselves and the world. At midlife, adults must give up certain youthful qualities, find age-appropriate ways to express other qualities, and accept being older. Rebuilding the life structure depends on supportive social contexts. Vaillant added that middle-aged adults become guardians of their culture, and the most successful and best adjusted enter a calmer, quieter time of life. Few people experience a midlife crisis, although most must adapt to important events, which often lead to new understandings and goals.

Midlife changes in self-concept and personality reflect growing awareness of a finite lifespan, longer life experience, and generative concerns. But certain aspects of personality remain stable, revealing that individual differences established during earlier phases persist. Possible selves become fewer and more realistic. Midlifers also become more introspective, and self-acceptance, autonomy, environmental mastery, and coping strategies improve. Both men and women become more androgynous in middle adulthood—a change that results from a complex combination of social roles and life conditions. Despite changes in the organization of personality, basic, underlying personality traits change little during midlife and beyond.

Because of a declining birthrate and longer life expectancy, the midlife phase of the family life cycle, called "launching children and moving on," has greatly lengthened over the past century. The changes of midlife prompt many adults to focus on improving their marriages, but when divorce occurs, midlifers seem to adapt more easily than do younger people. Gains in practical problem solving and effective coping strategies may reduce the stressful impact of divorce. Most middle-aged parents adjust well to departure of children, especially if the parents have a strong work orientation and if parent–child contact and affection are sustained. When family relationships are positive, grandparenthood is an important means of fulfilling personal and societal needs. A growing number of North American children live apart from their parents in households headed by grandparents, a situation that can create great emotional and financial strain.

A longer life expectancy means that adult children and their parents are increasingly likely to grow old together. The burden of caring for aging parents can be great. Many middle-aged adults become "sandwiched" between the needs of aging parents and financially dependent children. Although middle-aged adults often become more appreciative of their parents' strengths and generosity, caring for chronically ill or disabled parents is highly stressful. Sibling contact and support generally declines from early to middle adulthood, although many siblings feel closer, often in response to major life events, such as parental illness. Friendships become fewer and more selective in midlife and they serve as current sources of pleasure and satisfaction.

Work continues to be a salient aspect of identity and self-esteem in middle adulthood. More so than in earlier or later years, people attempt to increase the personal meaning and self-direction of their vocational lives. Job satisfaction has both psychological and economic significance. Overall job satisfaction improves during midlife, but burnout has become a greater problem in recent years, especially in the helping professions. Vocational development is less available to older workers, and many women and ethnic minorities leave the corporate world to escape the "glass ceiling" limiting their advancement. Still, radical career changes are rare in middle adulthood. Unemployment is especially difficult for middle-aged individuals, and retirement is an important change that is often stressful, making effective planning important for positive adjustment.

LEARNING OBJECTIVES

After reading this chapter, you should be able to:

16.1 Describe Erikson's stage of generativity versus stagnation, noting major personality changes of middle adulthood and related research findings. (pp. 417–418)

16.2 Discuss Levinson's and Vaillant's views of psychosocial development in middle adulthood, noting gender similarities and differences. (pp. 419–421)

16.3 Summarize research on whether or not most middle-aged adults experience a midlife crisis. (p. 421)

16.4 Describe stability and change in self-concept and personality in middle adulthood. (pp. 421–424)

16.5 Describe changes in gender identity in midlife. (p. 424)

16.6 Discuss stability and change in the "big five" personality traits in adulthood. (pp. 424–425)

16.7 Describe the middle adulthood phase of the family life cycle, including relationships with a marriage partner, adult children, grandchildren, and aging parents. (pp. 425–432)

16.8 Describe midlife sibling relationships and friendships. (pp. 432–433)

16.9 Discuss job satisfaction and career development in middle adulthood, paying special attention to gender differences and experiences of ethnic minorities. (pp. 433–435)

16.10 Discuss the importance of planning for retirement, noting various issues that middle-aged adults should address. (pp. 435–436)

LECTURE OUTLINE

I. ERIKSON'S THEORY: GENERATIVITY VERSUS STAGNATION (pp. 417–418)
- A. Generativity:
  1. Erikson's psychological conflict of midlife is called **generativity versus stagnation**.
     - a. Generativity—reaching out to others in ways that give to and guide the next generation—begins in early adulthood and expands greatly in midlife as commitment extends to family, community, and society.
     - b. Generative adults combine the need for self-expression with the need for communion, integrating personal goals with the welfare of the larger social world.
     - c. Erikson chose the term *generativity* to encompass everything generated that can outlive the self and ensure society's continuity and improvement—children, ideas, products, and works of art.
     - d. Parenting is a major means of realizing generativity, but adults can also be generative through other family relationships, workplace and volunteer relationships, and other forms of productivity and creativity.
     - e. Generativity brings together personal desires and cultural demands.
       - (1) Middle-aged adults feel a need to make a contribution that will survive their death.
       - (2) Society imposes a social clock for generativity in midlife, requiring adults to take responsibility for the next generation as parents, teachers, mentors, leaders, and coordinators.
       - (3) According to Erikson, a major motivator of generative action is a culture's "belief in the species"—the conviction that life is good and worthwhile, even in the face of human destructiveness and deprivation.
- B. Stagnation:
  1. The negative outcome of midlife is *stagnation,* which occurs when people, after attaining certain life goals (such as marriage, children, and career success), become self-centered and self-indulgent.
  2. Adults with a sense of stagnation express their self-absorption through lack of interest in young people; a focus on what they can get from others rather than what they can give; and little interest in being productive at work, developing their talents, or bettering the world.
- C. Generativity increases in midlife.
- D. Characteristics of highly generative people:
  1. They appear especially well-adjusted—low in anxiety and depression, high in self-acceptance and life satisfaction, and more likely to have successful marriages and close friends.
  2. They are more open to differing viewpoints; possess leadership qualities; desire more from work than financial rewards; and care greatly about the welfare of their children, their partner, their aging parents, and the wider society.

3. Throughout adulthood, people's descriptions of their current selves show considerable stability, although, with age, they become fewer in number and more modest and concrete.
4. Because the future is no longer holds limitless opportunities, adults preserve mental health by adjusting their hopes and fears.

B. Self-Acceptance, Autonomy, and Environmental Mastery (p. 422)
   1. Middle-aged adults tend to offer more complex, integrated descriptions of themselves than do younger and older individuals.
   2. In research on well-educated adults from the late teens into the seventies, three traits increased from early to middle adulthood and then leveled off:
      a. *Self-acceptance:* Middle-aged people acknowledge and accept both their good and bad qualities.
      b. *Autonomy:* Middle-aged adults see themselves as less concerned about others' expectations and more focused on self-chosen standards.
      c. *Environmental mastery:* Middle-aged people see themselves as capable of managing a complex array of tasks easily and effectively.
   3. Midlife's gains in expertise and practical problem solving make this a time of increased comfort with the self, independence, assertiveness, commitment to personal values, psychological well-being, and life satisfaction.

C. Coping Strategies (pp. 422–424)
   1. Midlife brings an increase in effective coping strategies, including a greater ability to draw flexibly on both problem-centered and emotion-centered strategies.
   2. In one study, *cognitive-affective complexity*—the ability to blend personal strengths and weaknesses into an organized self-description, which increases in middle age—predicted good coping strategies.

D. Gender Identity (p. 424)
   1. Many studies report an increase in "masculine" traits in women and "feminine" traits in men across middle age, in various Western and non-Western cultures, consistent with Levinson's view that gender identity in midlife becomes more androgynous.
   2. Biological explanations for greater androgyny in midlife:
      a. **Parental imperative theory**, an evolutionary view, holds that identification with traditional gender roles is maintained during the active parenting years to help ensure the survival of children, but that after children reach adulthood, parents are free to express the "other-gender" side of their personalities.
      b. The decline in sex hormones associated with aging may contribute to androgyny in later life.
   3. Criticisms of biological explanations:
      a. In longitudinal research, college-educated women in the labor force became more independent by their early forties, regardless of whether they had children, while those who were homemakers did not.
      b. Androgyny is not associated with menopause—a finding at odds with a hormonal explanation.
   4. Androgyny in adulthood is associated with advanced moral reasoning and psychosocial maturity.
   5. Conversely, people who do not integrate the masculine and feminine sides of their personalities tend to have mental health problems, perhaps because they are unable to adapt flexibly to the challenges of aging.

E. Individual Differences in Personality Traits (pp. 424–425)
   1. The hundreds of personality traits on which individuals differ have been organized into five basic factors, called the **"big five" personality traits**: neuroticism, extroversion, openness to experience, agreeableness, and conscientiousness.
      a. In longitudinal and cross-sectional studies, agreeableness and conscientiousness increase from the teens through middle age; neuroticism declines; and extroversion and openness to experience are stable or may decrease slightly.
      b. In a reanalysis of longitudinal studies including more than 50,000 participants, personality-trait stability increased in early and middle adulthood and peaked during the fifties.
   2. Adults change in overall organization and integration of personality, but they do so on a foundation of basic, enduring dispositions that support a coherent sense of self while adapting to changing life circumstances.

IV. RELATIONSHIPS AT MIDLIFE (pp. 425–433)

A. The vast majority of middle-aged people live in families, most with a spouse, and tend to have a larger number of close relationships during midlife than at any other period.

B. Middle adulthood is the phase of "launching children and moving on."

1. For adults who have devoted themselves entirely to their children, the end of active parenting can trigger feelings of emptiness and regret (the "empty nest").
2. For many people, however, middle adulthood is a liberating time, offering a sense of completion and an opportunity to strengthen existing ties and build new ones.

C. Because of a declining birthrate and longer life expectancy, contemporary parents often launch children long before retirement, and then seek other rewarding activities.

D. Marriage and Divorce (p. 426)

1. Marital satisfaction is a strong predictor of psychological well-being in midlife.
2. Although most divorces occur within 5 to 10 years of marriage, about 10 percent take place after 20 years or more.
3. A survey of more than 13,000 Americans revealed that following divorce, middle-aged men and women reported less decline in psychological well-being than their younger counterparts, perhaps because of midlife gains in practical problem solving and effective coping strategies that reduce the stressful impact of divorce.
4. For many women, marital breakup severely reduces standard of living and is a strong contributor to the **feminization of poverty**—a trend in which women who support themselves or their families have become the majority of the adult population living in poverty, regardless of age and ethnic group.
5. Adjustment to divorce:
   a. Middle-aged women who weather divorce successfully tend to become more tolerant, comfortable with uncertainty, nonconforming, and self-reliant in personality.
   b. Little is known about long-term adjustment following divorce among middle-aged men, perhaps because most enter new relationships and remarry within a short time.

E. Changing Parent–Child Relationships (pp. 426–427)

1. Most middle-aged parents adjust well to the launching phase of the family life cycle, while only a minority have difficulty.
   a. Parents who have developed gratifying alternative activities, especially those who have a strong work orientation, typically welcome their children's adult status.
   b. Whether or not they reside with parents, adolescent and young adult children who are "off-time" in development can prompt parental strain.
   c. Wide variations exist in the social clock for launching children, and many young people from low-SES homes and with cultural traditions of extended-family living do not leave home early.
   d. Departure of children is a relatively minor event when parent-child contract and affection are sustained.
2. Relationships with married children:
   a. When children marry, parents face additional challenges in enlarging the family network to include in-laws.
   b. Once young adults strike out on their own, members of the middle generation, especially mothers, usually take on the role of **kinkeeper**, gathering the family for celebrations and making sure everyone stays in touch.

F. Grandparenthood (pp. 427–428)

1. Despite stereotypes of grandparents as elderly, on average, American adults become grandparents in their mid- to late forties, Canadian adults in their late forties to early fifties.
2. Longer life expectancy means that adults spend as much as one-third of their lifespan in the grandparent role.

3. Meanings of Grandparenthood (p. 427)
   a. It allows people to be perceived as valued elders.
   b. It gives them immortality through descendants.
   c. It offers an opportunity to pass family history and values to a new generation.
   d. It provides opportunities for indulgence—having fun with children without major child-rearing responsibilities.
4. Grandparent–Grandchild Relationships (pp. 427–428)
   a. Typically, relationships are closer between grandparents and grandchildren of the same sex, especially between maternal grandmothers and granddaughters.
   b. Relationships also depend on whether grandparents live far from young grandchildren, and on SES and ethnicity, with grandparents often performing essential activities in low-income families, or those with single parents or going through family transitions.
   c. In some cultures, grandparents are absorbed into an extended-family household and become actively involved in child rearing.
   d. When family relationships are positive, grandparenthood provides an important means of fulfilling personal and societal needs in midlife and beyond.
   e. A rising number of North American children live apart from their parents in grandparent-headed households.
   f. Grandparents who take full responsibility for young children experience considerable emotional and financial strain, and need much more assistance from community and government agencies than is currently available.
   g. After divorce, grandparents on the custodial parent's side have more frequent contact with grandchildren.

G. Middle-Aged Children and Their Aging Parents (pp. 428–433)
1. The percentage of North American middle-aged people with living parents has risen from 10 percent in 1900 to 50 percent in 2000.
2. Frequency and Quality of Contact (pp. 428–430)
   a. About two-thirds of older adults in the United States and Canada live close to at least one of their children, with high frequency of contact through visits and telephone calls.
   b. In middle age, adults tend to reassess relationships with their parents, just as they rethink other close ties, especially in the case of mother–daughter relationships, which tend to be closer than other parent–child ties.
   c. In the non-Western world (for example, in China, Japan, and Korea), older adults most often live with their married children, but this pattern is changing.
   d. Help exchanged between adult children and their aging parents reflects both past and current family circumstances, but even when parent–child relationships have been emotionally distant, adult children offer more support as their parents age, out of a sense of altruism and family duty.
3. Caring for Aging Parents (pp. 430–432)
   a. The term **sandwich generation** is widely used to refer to the idea that middle-aged adults must care for multiple generations above and below them at the same time.
      (1) About 20 percent of midlifers in the United States and Canada are involved in caring for an aging parent with a chronic illness or disability.
      (2) African-American and Hispanic adults give aging parents more financial help and direct care than Caucasian-American adults do.
      (3) Middle-aged adults who care for elderly parents often are also helping young-adult children and grandchildren—obligations that, along with work and community responsibilities, can lead them to feel "sandwiched" between older and younger generations.
   b. In all ethnic groups, responsibility for providing care to aging parents falls more on daughters than on sons.
      (1) About 50 percent of North American women caregivers are employed; another 10 to 30 percent quit their jobs to provide care.
      (2) In later middle age, the sex difference in parental caregiving declines, perhaps because men reduce their vocational commitments and also may feel less need to conform to a "masculine" gender role.

   c. Parental caregiving can lead to role overload (conflict among employment, spouse, parent, and elder care roles), high job absenteeism, exhaustion, inability to concentrate, feelings of hostility, anxiety about aging, and high rates of depression—especially in cultures where adult children feel an especially strong sense of obligation to care for aging parents.
   d. Unlike Denmark, Sweden, and Japan, where a government-sponsored home helper system eases the burden of parental care, in the United States and Canada, in-home care by a nonfamily caregiver is too costly for most families, as is formal care (such as nursing homes)—which, in any case, most people want to avoid.

H. Siblings (p. 432)
   1. Sibling contact and support decline from early to middle adulthood, rebounding only after age 70 for siblings living near one another.
   2. However, many siblings feel closer in midlife, often in response to major life events such as launching and marriage of children, a parent's serious illness, or the death of a parent.
   3. Sister–sister relationships are closer than sister–brother and brother–brother ties, a difference apparent in many industrialized nations.
   4. In industrialized nations, sibling relationships are voluntary; in village societies, they are generally involuntary and basic to family functioning.

I. Friendships (pp. 432–433)
   1. Women in midlife report a greater number of close friends than men do, but for both sexes, number of friends declines with age, probably because people become less willing to invest in nonfamily ties unless they are very rewarding.
   2. By midlife, family relationships and friendships support different aspects of psychological well-being.
      a. Family ties protect against serious threats and losses, offering security within a long-term time frame.
      b. Friendships serve as current sources of pleasure and satisfaction.
   3. Middle-aged couples may combine the best of family and friendship; research indicates that viewing a spouse as a best friend contributes greatly to marital happiness.

V. VOCATIONAL LIFE (pp. 433–436)

A. Changes for older workers:
   1. The post–World War II baby boom and the elimination of mandatory retirement age in most industrialized nations will mean a rise in the number of older workers over the next few decades.
   2. Transition to the status of older worker is hindered by negative stereotypes of aging and, for women, by gender discrimination.

B. Job Satisfaction (pp. 433–434)
   1. Job satisfaction increases in midlife at all occupational levels, from executives to hourly workers.
      a. This trend is weaker for women than for men, perhaps because of limited opportunities for advancement, and for blue-collar workers, who have less control over their work lives.
      b. Intrinsic satisfaction—happiness with the work itself—shows a strong age-related gain, while extrinsic satisfaction—contentment with supervision, pay, and promotions—changes very little.
      c. Key characteristics that predict job well-being include involvement in decision making, reasonable workloads, and good physical working conditions.
   2. Emotional engagement with work is usually psychologically healthy but can also lead to **burnout**—a condition in which long-term job stress leads to mental exhaustion, a sense of loss of personal control, and feelings of reduced accomplishment.
      a. Burnout occurs more often in the helping professions, which place high emotional demands on employees.
      b. Burnout is especially likely to occur in unsupportive work environments, where work assignments exceed time available to complete them and encouragement and feedback from supervisors are scarce.
      c. Burnout is a greater problem in North America than in Western Europe, perhaps because of North Americans' greater achievement orientation.

C. Career Development (pp. 434–435)
   1. Job Training (p. 434)
      a. Training and on-the-job career counseling are less available to older workers, and older employees may be less likely to take advantage of available opportunities, for several reasons.
         (1) Older workers may be more focused on security needs than on learning and challenge.
         (2) Older employees depend more on coworker and supervisor encouragement for career development but are less likely to have supportive supervisors.
         (3) Negative stereotypes of aging reduce older workers' confidence that they can renew and expand their skills.
      b. Workplace characteristics:
         (1) Older workers sometimes receive more routine tasks than younger workers, making them less motivated to engage in career-relevant learning.
         (2) Age-balanced work groups (with more than one person in each age range) foster on-the-job learning because communication is a source of support as well as a means of acquiring job-relevant information.
   2. Gender and Ethnicity: The Glass Ceiling (pp. 434–435)
      a. Women and ethnic minorities face a **glass ceiling**, or invisible barrier to advancement up the corporate ladder, which becomes more pronounced over time, for several reasons.
         (1) Women and members of ethnic minorities have less access to mentors, role models, and informal networks that serve as training routes.
         (2) Because of stereotyped doubts about women's career commitment and ability to become strong managers, large companies spend less money on formal training programs for their female employees.
         (3) Women who demonstrate qualities linked to leadership and advancement—assertiveness, confidence, forcefulness, and ambition—are evaluated more negatively than men with these traits, which deviate from traditional gender expectations for women.
      b. Largely because of lack of advancement opportunities, female middle managers are more likely than men to quit their jobs in large corporations, often going into business for themselves.
         (1) More than half of all start-up businesses in the United States are owned and operated by women.
         (2) Among these entrepreneurs, 72 percent achieve or exceed their expansion and earnings goals.

D. Planning for Retirement (pp. 435–436)
   1. Because of government-sponsored retirement benefits—which began in Canada in 1927 and in the United States in 1935—retirement is no longer a privilege reserved for the wealthy.
      a. In 1900, about 70 percent of North American men age 65 and over were in the labor force, but by 1970 the figure was only 27 percent, and it is now only 9 percent in Canada and 18 percent in the United States.
      b. In both countries, the federal governments pay social security to the majority of the aged, and others are covered by employer-based private pension plans.
   2. The average age of retirement declined during the past two decades, to 62 in Canada and the United States and between 60 and 63 in other Western nations.
   3. Retirement planning is important because retirement brings the loss of both income and status, but nearly half of middle-aged people engage in no concrete retirement planning—both financial planning and planning for the satisfying use of leisure time, as well as decisions about whether to relocate.
   4. Enhancing adjustment to retirement among the economically disadvantaged depends on access to better health care, vocational training, and jobs at early ages.

LECTURE ENHANCEMENTS

LECTURE ENHANCEMENT 16.1
Is Marriage Linked to Affluence? (p. 426)

Time: 5–10 minutes

Objective: To examine the relationship between marriage and affluence in a sample of young and middle-aged adults.

The text notes that middle-aged households are well off economically compared with other age groups. There is also evidence to suggest that marriage increases the likelihood of becoming affluent. To further examine the relationship between marriage and affluence, Hirschl, Altobelli, and Rank (2003) used data from the Panel Study of Income Dynamics (PSID), which included a longitudinal sample of 4,800 American households. The families were followed for 25 years, and roughly 18,000 individuals participated in the study. The participants were divided into two age groups: 25–45 and 45–65.

To determine the likelihood of affluence over time, the researchers used household demographics (which included marital status) and income to create life tables. The life tables were updated every year. Participants who lived in households with combined incomes of at least 10 times over the poverty level were considered affluent. For example, in 2000, the poverty level for a two-person household was $11,239. To be considered affluent, a two-person household would have to earn at least $112,390. The researchers were then able to compare affluence in married and nonmarried adults (divorced, widowed, and never married) over time.

Results indicated that married adults were far more likely than their unmarried counterparts to achieve affluence. This finding was particularly strong for older participants and participants who were married for long periods of time. Specifically, 33 percent of the married 25- to 45-year-olds achieved at least one year of affluence, while 42 percent of the married couples between ages of 45 and 65 encountered a year or more of affluence. A mere 16 percent of the unmarried 25- to 45-year-olds and 18 percent of the 45- to 65-year-olds experienced a year or more of affluence throughout the study. Findings also revealed that marriage had greater economic benefits for women than for men. This makes sense given that women tend to earn less than men across the lifespan.

Hirschl, T., Altobelli, J., & Rank, M. R. (2003). Does marriage increase the odds of affluence? Exploring the life course probabilities. *Journal of Marriage and Family, 65,* 927–938.

LECTURE ENHANCEMENT 16.2
More on Women's Reactions to Adult Children Leaving the Family Home (pp. 426–427)

Time: 10–15 minutes

Objective: To extend existing research on women's reactions to the launching phase of the family life cycle.

The text notes that most middle-aged parents adjust well to the launching phase of the family life cycle. To extend existing research on the effects of children leaving and returning to the family home, Dennerstein, Dudley, and Guthrie (2002) recruited 438 women between the ages of 45 and 55 years. The study lasted nine years, with researchers administering questionnaires and conducting interviews annually. The researchers were primarily interested in worries about children moving out of the family home, household composition (spouse or partner, children, parents, in-laws, other adults), feelings toward one's spouse or partner (if one existed), and whether anyone had moved in or out of the house since the last interview. Based on information gathered through the interviews and questionnaires, the researchers were able to calculate total well-being, positive and negative mood, and number of bothersome symptoms associated with changing household composition.

Findings revealed that adult children leaving the family home did not adversely affect women's quality of life. Specifically, the majority of the participants did not report an increase in depression, bothersome symptoms, or negative feelings toward their partner or spouse following their child's departure from the home. For participants who did not express worries about their children moving out of the family home, overall mood and well-being increased after the child departed. Findings also showed that adult children moving back into the family home did not have a significant effect on women's quality of life, although some women reported a decrease in sexual activity with their spouse or partner. Therefore, the belief that the "empty nest" is a time of crisis for many mothers is not supported. The authors note that over the last century, social changes have contributed to changing roles for women. In the past, women were expected to devote most of their time to marriage and family. When their children left home, it was often a difficult time. Today, women are more likely to look forward to the launching phase and adjust favorably to their child's departure. In addition, because more children are returning to the family home after their initial departure, many women expect the launching phase to be delayed and are not negatively affected by the "revolving door."

Ask students reflect on their own experiences leaving the family home. How did their parents react to the departure? How did students feel about leaving home? For students who still reside with their parents, how do they think their parents will adjust to their leaving? What factors lead to favorable adaptation to the launching phase of the family life cycle?

Dennerstein, L., Dudley, E., & Guthrie, J. (2002). Empty nest or revolving door? A prospective study of women's quality of life in midlife during the phase of children leaving and re-entering the home. *Psychological Medicine, 32,* 545–550.

LECTURE ENHANCEMENT 16.3
More on Grandparent–Grandchild Relationships (pp. 427–428)

Time: 15–20 minutes

Objective: To examine factors related to relationship quality between grandparents and grandchildren.

As discussed in the text, grandparent–grandchild relationships often play an important role in children's development. Some grandparents are caregivers of grandchildren, serve as mentors, or provide financial support. However, grandparent involvement is influenced by a number of factors, such as geographic proximity, age of child and grandparent, gender of child and grandparent, number of grandchildren, and the nature of family relationships (how well the grandparent gets along with his or her own child).

To further examine the nature of grandparent–grandchild relationships, Mueller and Elder (2003) used longitudinal data from the Iowa Youth and Families Project and Iowa Single Parent Project. Participants included 655 grandparents and 546 target grandchildren, who were seniors in high school at the time. The primary goals of this study were to investigate (1) factors that contribute to various patterns of grandparent–grandchild involvement, (2) characteristics of the grandchild and grandparent, and (3) how relationships with other family members affect the grandparent–grandchild relationship. Researchers used telephone interviews and mail questionnaires to gather background information (such as age and health status, educational background, employment, and sources of income), to assess the quality of the grandparent–grandchild relationship (perceptions of quality, closeness, relative closeness, and relative contact between grandparents and grand children), and to assess the quality of the grandparent-parent relationship (closeness, affection, and tension between grandparents and parents). On the basis of this information, researchers identified five types of grandparents:

1. *Influential.* Grandparents who were highly involved in their grandchildren's lives and who acted as a source of parent-like authority and discipline.
2. *Supportive.* Grandparents who were highly involved in their grandchildren's lives but did not function as a parent-like authority figure.
3. *Authority-oriented.* Grandparents who perceived themselves to be a primary source of parent-like authority and discipline for their grandchildren.
4. *Passive.* Grandparents who were moderately involved with their grandchildren but did not take on a parent-like authority or disciplinarian role.
5. *Detached.* Grandparents who had little contact with their grandchildren and did not act as a source of authority or discipline.

The researchers also gathered information on grandparent perceptions of grandchild characteristics by asking them to identity positive and negative traits (for example, the grandchild "is usually happy," "is usually sad," "has a short temper," "is a caring person").

Results indicated that grandchild traits were highly predictive of relationships with grandparents. Happy, caring grandchildren were more likely to be close to their grandparents than grandchildren who were perceived as having a number of negative traits. Relative closeness was also found to be important. For instance, grandparents who reported being closer to *this* grandchild (the target grandchild) than to *other* grandchildren (grandchildren from another set of parents) were nearly twice as likely to be involved in that grandchild's life than grandparents who reported being closer to *other* grandchildren. One especially noteworthy finding was that influential, supportive, and authority-oriented grandparents were particularly close to their grandchildren; they were relatively closer in geographic proximity and saw their grandchildren more often than other grandparents. Finally, more involved grandparents tended to have positive relationships with their own child (the parent of the grandchild). This finding is certainly not surprising; mothers and fathers who have strained relationships with their own parents are less likely to encourage grandparent involvement than are parents with positive family ties.

Ask students to reflect on factors that contribute to their own sense of closeness to or distance from their grandparents. How are those factors related to the findings of this study?

Mueller, M. M., & Elder, G. H. (2003). Family contingencies across generations: Grandparent–grandchild relationships in holistic perspective. *Journal of Marriage and Family, 65,* 404–417.

LECTURE ENHANCEMENT 16.4
Are There Generational Differences in the Effects of Home and Work Spillover? (pp. 422, 424)

Time: 10–15 minutes

Objective: To examine generational differences in the effects of home and work spillover in young adults, middle-aged adults, and elders.

To determine generational differences in home and work spillover, Long Dilworth and Kingsbury (2005) recruited 2,737 participants and grouped them into three categories: generation Xers (adults under the age of 33), baby boomers (adults between the ages of 33 and 51), and matures (adults over the age of 51). The researchers collected the following information:

1. Demographic variables included race/ethnicity, household income, educational attainment, total hours of work each week, number of adults and children living in the home, and number of adults and/or children requiring caregiving assistance.
2. To determine home-to-job spillover, participants were asked how often their personal or family life kept them from completing work on time, from doing a good job at work, from taking on extra work, or from being able to concentrate at work.
3. To determine job-to-home spillover, participants were asked how often they did not have time for themselves or their family because of work, how often they could not complete duties at home because of work, and how often they experienced a negative mood because of work.
4. Participants were asked to report how much time they spent on household tasks, child care, and/or elder care on both work and nonwork days. They were also asked how many days they had been late to work because of home responsibilities and how many days of work they had missed because of home responsibilities.
5. To determine satisfaction with one's job and family life, participants were asked, "All in all, how satisfied are you with your job?" "All in all, how satisfied are you with your life?" Participants answered these questions using a four-point Likert scale (1 = extremely satisfied and 4 = not too satisfied).

Results indicated that baby boomers experienced more negative spillover than younger or older participants. That is, home-to-work and work-to-home spillover led to greater life dissatisfaction in baby boomers than in generation Xers or matures. One of the most significant stressors for baby boomers was missing work because of family concerns. Baby boomers also spent more time on household duties and child care than generation Xer's or matures.

Interestingly, although matures spent more time caring for elders than baby boomers or the generation X group, this time did not contribute to negative spillover effects. Matures also took less time off work for caregiving duties than the other two groups. Of the three groups, matures reported the highest levels of both job and life satisfaction. It is important to note that the mature group included adults as young as age 51, which is considered middle age. Therefore, a large number of midlifers were included in the mature group. Thus, these findings are consistent with research in the text—both job and life satisfaction tend to increase in middle adulthood.

Long Dilworth, J. E., & Kingsbury, N. (2005). Home-to-job spillover for generation X, boomers, and matures: A comparison. *Journal of Family and Economic Issues, 26,* 267–281.

LEARNING ACTIVITIES

LEARNING ACTIVITY 16.1
True or False: Theories of Psychosocial Adjustment in Midlife (pp. 417–421)

Present the following exercise to students as a quiz or in-class activity.

Directions: Read each of the following statements and indicate whether it is *True* (T) or *False* (F).

_____ 1. Adults can be generative as parents and in other family relationships, as mentors in the workplace, in volunteer endeavors, and through many forms of productivity and creativity.
_____ 2. Adults with a sense of generativity cannot contribute to society's welfare because they place their own comfort and security above challenge and sacrifice.
_____ 3. Having children seems to foster women's generative development more than men's.
_____ 4. During the midlife transition, some people make drastic revisions in family and occupational components of the life structure.
_____ 5. Despite the double standard of aging, equal numbers of men and women express concern about appearing less attractive as they grow older.
_____ 6. Middle age brings about greater rigidity in masculine and feminine parts of the self.
_____ 7. In societies around the world, older people are guardians of traditions, laws, and cultural values.
_____ 8. Research shows that the majority of adults experience a midlife crisis.
_____ 9. Sharp disruption and agitation in midlife are the exception, not the rule.
_____ 10. Midlifers who experience a crisis typically have had early adulthoods in which gender roles, family pressures, or low income and poverty severely limited their ability to fulfill personal needs and goals, at home or in the wider world.

Answers:

1. T
2. F
3. F
4. T
5. F
6. F
7. T
8. F
9. T
10. T

LEARNING ACTIVITY 16.2
Panel Discussion of Volunteer Service (pp. 419–420)

According to Levinson, adults in midlife desire to be creative through endeavors that advance human welfare. Middle-aged adults want to leave a legacy for future generations. One way the image of a legacy can be satisfied is through volunteer service. To highlight the meanings and importance of volunteer service, invite a panel of middle-aged community volunteers to your class. Social service agencies within the community can be a source of recruitment for panel members.

Ask students to prepare some questions for panel members. For instance: What are your volunteer activities? Why do you volunteer? How long have you been doing volunteer work? How do others benefit from your volunteer activities? Do you feel you have made a difference in others' lives through your volunteer services? Can volunteering make a broader difference in our society and in our world? What lessons have you learned though your volunteerism? Have you had any experiences that especially stand out?

An alternative activity is to invite panel members who represent different age groups—young adults, middle-aged adults, and elders. The questions listed above may provide interesting insight into the meanings and importance of volunteering across the lifespan.

LEARNING ACTIVITY 16.3
The "Big Five" Personality Test (pp. 424–425)

After discussing individual differences in personality traits, have students visit the website, *http://www.outofservice.com/bigfive/* and complete the "big five" personality test. Once students have taken the test, instruct them to briefly summarize the results. What did students' scores reveal about their personality? Do they agree with the results? Why or why not? Which characteristics are likely to change from early to middle adulthood? Which characteristics are likely to remain stable?

LEARNING ACTIVITY 16.4
Exploring Meanings of Grandparenthood (p. 427–428)

Ask students to pose the following question to a grandparent or to a friend's grandparent: What does it mean to be a grandparent? Students should record responses and bring them to class for discussion. Did responses reflect gratifications listed on page 427 of the text? Did any responses reflect negative stereotypes of aging (for example, being a grandparent means you're old)? How might lifetime experiences contribute to perceptions of grandparenthood?

LEARNING ACTIVITY 16.5
Linking Physical and Cognitive Milestones to Relations at Midlife (pp. 425–433)

In Chapter 1 of the text, students learned that physical, cognitive, and social development overlap and interact throughout the lifespan. Ask students to review Chapter 15 and consider the various physical and cognitive milestones of middle adulthood. Next, ask students to think of as many examples as they can of physical and cognitive changes that may influence and contribute to relationships with adult children, aging parents, siblings, and friends. For example, how might responses to physical changes in middle adulthood carry over into relations with family and friends? How might hardiness influence one's relationships at midlife? What characteristics of a Type A behavior pattern might negatively impact one's relationships at midlife?

LEARNING ACTIVITY 16.6
Job Satisfaction Interview (pp. 433–434)

Ask students to interview a middle-aged adult (parent, a friend's parent, employer, or acquaintance) about his or her current occupation and job satisfaction. Students may want to combine this activity with Learning Activity 16.4. The following questions can help guide the interview:

1. What is your current occupation?
2. How would you describe your current level of job satisfaction?
3. How does your current level of job satisfaction compare to earlier years? If the interviewee mentions a discrepancy between past and current job satisfaction, ask what factors have contributed to this difference.
4. Do you perceive job satisfaction as increasing, decreasing, or remaining essentially the same from early to middle adulthood? Explain.
5. What working conditions contribute to job satisfaction? How about dissatisfaction?
6. What are your career aspirations and how have they changed since early adulthood?

Have students bring their interviews to class for small group discussion. How did the interviewees describe their current level of job satisfaction? Did they indicate that job satisfaction has increased in midlife? Were there gender differences in job satisfaction? Did responses from blue-collar workers differ from those of white-collar workers? Explain. What did the interviewees mention as positive working conditions? How about negative working conditions? Have their career aspirations changed? Were there any responses that might suggest burnout? If so, explain. Finally, how did responses compare to research presented in the text?

LEARNING ACTIVITY 16.7
Creating a Brochure on Retirement Planning (pp. 435–436)

Tell students to pretend that a local employment agency has asked them to prepare a brochure on retirement planning. Have students list information that should be included in the brochure. For example, why is retirement planning important? What are some characteristics of high-quality retirement preparation programs? How can employers help with retirement planning?

ASK YOURSELF . . .

REVIEW: What personal and cultural forces motivate generativity? Why does it increase and contribute vitally to favorable adjustment in midlife? (pp. 417–418)

On the personal side, middle-aged adults feel a need to be needed—to attain symbolic immortality by making a contribution that will survive their death. On the cultural side, society imposes a social clock for generativity in midlife, requiring adults to take responsibility for the next generation through their roles as parents, teachers, mentors, leaders, and coordinators. According to Erikson, a culture's "belief in the species"—the conviction that life is good and worthwhile, even in the face of human destructiveness and deprivation—is also a major motivator of generative action.

Highly generative people appear especially well-adjusted—low in anxiety and depression, high in self-acceptance and life satisfaction, and more likely to have successful marriages and close friends. They are more open to differing viewpoints, possess leadership qualities, desire more from work than financial rewards, and care greatly about the welfare of their children, their partner, their aging parents, and the wider society. Generativity is also associated with more effective child rearing—higher valuing of trust, open communication, transmission of values to children, and an authoritative parenting style.

APPLY: After years of experiencing little personal growth at work, 42-year-old Mel looked for a new job and received an attractive offer in another city. Although he felt torn between leaving close friends and pursuing a long-awaited career opportunity, after several weeks of soul searching, he took the new job. Was Mel's dilemma a midlife crisis? Why or why not? (p. 421)

Mel's decision to seek and take a new job does not represent a midlife crisis. It could better be described as a "turning point" or midlife transition, in which Mel was responding to the realization that from now on, more time lay behind than ahead of him, making the remaining years increasingly precious. During his period of questioning and ultimately deciding to change his career situation, Mel did not seem to go through the type of inner turmoil, agitation, or self-disruption that would characterize a midlife crisis. Rather, through personal assessment and reevaluation of what was important to him, he developed the confidence and insight that he needed to make what a change that, to some observers, might appear radical.

REFLECT: Think of a middle-aged adult whom you admire. Describe the various ways that individual expresses generativity. (pp. 417–418)

This is an open-ended question with no right or wrong answer.

REVIEW: Summarize personality changes at midlife. How can these changes be reconciled with increasing stability of the "big five" personality traits, peaking in the fifties? (pp. 424–425)

An evolving mix of competencies and experiences leads to changes in certain personality traits in middle adulthood. Middle-aged adults tend to offer more complex, integrated descriptions of themselves than do either younger or older individuals. And many have reshaped contexts to suit their personal needs and values. Midlife brings gains in expertise and practical problem solving that may support the confidence, initiative, and decisiveness characteristic of this period. Overall, midlife is a time of increased comfort with the self, independence, assertiveness, commitment to personal values, psychological well-being, and life satisfaction. It brings an increase in effective coping strategies, with a greater tendency to identify the positive side of difficult situations and to draw flexibly on both problem-centered and emotion-centered strategies for dealing with challenges.

Many studies report an increase in "masculine" traits in women and "feminine" traits in men across middle age: Women become more confident, self-sufficient, and forceful; men more emotionally sensitive, caring, considerate, and dependent.

In terms of the "big five" personality traits—neuroticism, extroversion, openness to experience, agreeableness, and conscientiousness—cross-sectional studies of Canadian and American men and women reveal that agreeableness and conscientiousness increase from the teenage years through middle age, while neuroticism declines, and extroversion and openness to experience either do not change or decrease slightly. These changes reflect "settling down" and greater maturity. To reconcile the high stability in personality traits with the significant changes in personality that occur, it is helpful to think of adults as changing in overall organization and integration of personality, but doing so on a foundation of basic, enduring dispositions that supports a coherent sense of self as people adapt to changing life circumstances.

APPLY: Jeff, age 46, suggested to his wife, Julia, that they set aside time once a year to discuss their relationship—both positive aspects and ways to improve. Julia reacted with surprise—Jeff had never before expressed interest in working on their marriage. What developments at midlife probably fostered this new concern? (p. 424)

Jeff's new interest in talking with Julia about their marriage reflects the tendency for men to increase in "feminine" traits across middle age. In general, gender identity in midlife becomes more androgynous—a mixture of "masculine" and "feminine" characteristics. According to one evolutionary view, parental imperative theory, parents—particularly fathers—become free to express the "other-gender" side of their personalities once their children have reached adulthood, when it is less important for them to identify with traditional gender roles. Also among men, the need to enrich a marital relationship after children have departed, along with reduced opportunities for career advancement, may awaken emotionally sensitive traits. In adulthood, androgyny is associated with advanced moral reasoning and with the ability to adapt flexibly to the challenges of aging.

REFLECT: List your hoped-for and feared possible selves. Then ask your family members in the early and middle adulthood periods to do the same. Are their reports consistent with age-related research findings? Explain. (p. 422)

This is an open-ended question with no right or wrong answer.

REVIEW: How do age, sex, proximity, and culture affect grandparent–grandchild ties? (pp. 427–428, 429)

Typically, relationships are closer between grandparents and grandchildren of the same sex, especially between maternal grandmothers and granddaughters. Grandmothers also report higher satisfaction with the grandparent role than grandfathers, perhaps because grandmothers more often participate in recreational, religious, and family activities with grandchildren, and also because the grandparent role is a vital means through which middle-aged women satisfy their kinkeeping function.

Grandparents who live far from young grandchildren usually have more distant relationships with them, with little contact except on holidays, birthdays, and other formal occasions. But despite high family mobility in Western industrialized nations, most grandparents live close enough to at least one grandchild to make regular visits possible. And as grandchildren get older, distance has less impact. Relationships between grandparents and their daughter-in-law or son-in-law strongly affect the closeness of grandparent–grandchild ties.

In low-income families, grandparents are more likely to perform essential activities, providing financial and caregiving assistance. For children experiencing the stress of family transition, bonds with grandparents can be especially important.

Finally, in some cultures, grandparents are absorbed into an extended-family household and become actively involved in child rearing. For example, when a Chinese, Korean, or Mexican-American maternal grandmother is a homemaker, she is the preferred caregiver while parents of young children are at work. And, in a recent development, a rising number of North American children live apart from their parents in grandparent-headed households—an arrangement that can create considerable emotional and financial stress.

APPLY: Raylene and her brother Walter live in the same city as their aging mother, Elsie. When Elsie could no longer live independently, Raylene took primary responsibility for her care. What factors probably contributed to Raylene's involvement in caregiving and Walter's lesser role? (pp. 428, 430–432)

About 20 percent of midlife adults in the United States and Canada are involved in caring for an aging parent with a chronic illness or disability. And in all ethnic groups, responsibility for providing care to aging parents falls more on daughters than on sons—especially when the elderly parent has no spouse. Elsie, like most aging parents, may also have had a preference for a same-sex caregiver. Daughters also feel a stronger sense of obligation to care for aging parents than do sons. The care that sons and daughters provide tends to be divided along gender-role lines. Raylene is providing more hands-on care, such as cooking, feeding, and bathing. Walter is more likely to visit Elsie frequently, run errands, assist with household repairs, and take care of her finances.

REFLECT: Ask a middle-aged couple you know well to describe the number and quality of their friendships today compared to their friendships of early adulthood. Does their report match research findings? Explain. (pp. 432–433)

This is an open-ended question with no right or wrong answer.

REVIEW: What factors lead job satisfaction to increase with age? (pp. 433–434)

A broader time perspective probably contributes to the rise in job satisfaction during middle adulthood. For example, older people are better able to distinguish big problems from trivial ones. Key characteristics that predict job well-being include involvement in decision making, reasonable workloads, and good physical working conditions. Older people may have greater access to jobs that are attractive in these ways. Finally, having fewer alternative positions into which they can move, older workers generally reduce their career aspirations. As the perceived gap between actual and possible achievements declines, work involvement generally increases.

APPLY: An executive wonders how his large corporation can foster advancement of women and ethnic minorities to upper management positions. What strategies would you recommend? (pp. 434–435)

Management is both an art and a skill that must be taught. Executives can help women and minorities break through the "glass ceiling" by providing improved access to mentors, role models, and informal networks that serve as training routes. Executives also must be equitable when they make decisions about spending money on formal training programs. Finally, for some women, the best approach to the glass ceiling is to go around it—often by quitting a job with a large corporation and going into business for themselves.

SUGGESTED STUDENT READINGS

de St. Aubin, E., McAdams, D. P., & Tae-Chang, K. (Eds.). (2003). *The generative society: Caring for future generations.* Washington, DC: American Psychological Association. A multidisciplinary approach to understanding generativity, this book examines the developmental significance of generative behavior in middle adulthood. Other topics include Erikson's theory of generativity, cross-cultural differences in generativity, and the role of volunteerism.

Fingerman, K. L. (2002). *Mothers and their adult daughters: Mixed emotions, enduring bonds.* Amherst, NY: Prometheus Books. A thorough and insightful look at mother-daughter relationships in middle and late adulthood, this book addresses the bond between mothers and daughters, including the challenges they face in maintaining the relationship.

Hayslip, B., & Patrick, J. H. (Eds.). (2005). *Diversity among custodial grandparents.* New York: Springer. Using up-to-date research from leading experts, this book examines the diverse experiences of grandparents raising grandchildren, including role satisfaction in traditional and custodial grandparents, gender and ethnic differences in custodial grandparents, and caregiving interventions and support.

Hedge, J. W., Borman, W. C., & Lammlein, S. E. (2006). *The aging workforce: Realities, myths, and implications for organizations.* Washington, DC: American Psychological Association. Examines the strengths, weaknesses, expertise, and unique needs of workers over the age of 60. The authors also address myths and stereotypes about the aging workforce, age discrimination, and strategies for attracting and retaining older workers.

Kuttner, R. & Trotter, S. (2002). *Family reunion: Reconnecting parents and children in adulthood.* Tampa, FL: Free Press. Emphasizing a lifespan perspective, this book explores the dynamic relationship between adult children and their parents, including how to negotiate changes in a positive way.

TRANSPARENCIES

T-180 **Age-Related Changes in Self-Rated Generativity, Awareness of Aging, Identity Security, and Sense of Competence**
Figure 16.1 (p. 420)

T-183 **Percentage of American and Canadian 45- to 54-Year-Olds Providing Care to an Aging Parent**
Figure 16.3 (p. 431)

MEDIA MATERIALS

EXPLORING LIFESPAN DEVELOPMENT IN ACTION

Middle Adulthood

Physical development in midlife is a continuation of the gradual changes already underway in early adulthood. Although middle-aged adults become increasingly conscious of aging, they can take many steps to promote physical vigor and good health. Janet, a dancer and dance teacher for over 40 years, discusses the aging process and her strategies for maintaining health and physical fitness.

Middle age often brings advances in emotional and social development. Midlife transition may involve vocational readjustments. Judy, mayor of a midwestern town, discusses how she entered a political career in midlife and learned to deal with the stresses of a campaign. Judy also reflects on her thoughts and feelings about breaking the "glass ceiling" as the first elected female mayor of her town. Last, she shares her feelings about her approaching sixtieth birthday.

For some adults, midlife involves adjustment to major changes. Herm and Fran each reflect on the end of their previous marriages and on the factors that account for the success of their marriage to each other. Both Herm and Fran talk about their positive attitude toward midlife as they prepare for and anticipate retirement.

Finally, Dale describes some of the challenges that she and her brother have faced in taking care of their mother, who has Alzheimer's disease. Dale talks about the difficulties of balancing caretaking with other life and family responsibilities, as well as the emotional toll of watching her mother's disease progress.

A WINDOW ON LIFESPAN DEVELOPMENT

Remaining Mentally and Physically Active in Midlife: Miss Janet, Age 59
Miss Janet, a dancer, copes with the challenges of aging by seeking new learning opportunities, staying active, and eating well.

Generativity Without Children: Stephanie and Susan
Stephanie and Susan are twin sisters who explain that singlehood and childlessness have not created a void in their lives. As teachers, they have worked with hundreds of children and regard their students as extended family.

Divorce and Remarriage in Midlife: Herm and Fran
Herm and Fran reflect on their experiences with divorce. Herm views his divorce as a learning experience and is enjoying his marriage to Fran. Fran had a very difficult time with her divorce. Now, in her marriage to Herm, she is more comfortable and feels she can be herself.

Elder Caregiving: Dale, Age 47
Dale discusses the challenges she and her brother face in caring for their mother, who has Alzheimer's disease. Dale describes the changes in her mother as the disease progresses, and her efforts to balance care for her mother with her other family responsibilities.

VIDEOTAPES AND DVDs

And Thou Shalt Honor (2003, Aquarius Health Care Media; Part 1, 52 min., Part 2, 64 min.). This two-part documentary program examines the various aspects of extended-family caregiving from a warm, caring perspective.

Caring for Your Parents (1993, Films Media Group, 19 min.). This program deals with the challenges of caring for one's parents while also raising a family and maintaining a career. It examines typical stressors, role reversals, feelings of helplessness, and criteria for choosing among the available care options.

Family Caregivers (1992, Films Media Group/Dartmouth-Hitchcock Medical Center, 30 min.). This program, part of the series The Doctor Is In, looks at the stresses of extended-family caregiving for both caregivers and their families, and offers some ideas for dealing with these challenges. It includes interviews with Maggie Strong, author of *Mainstay,* a book about caregiving, and researchers Leonard Kaye and Jeffrey Applegate, who talk about their research on men as caregivers.

Low-Income Resistance (1994, UNL Video Services, 60 min.). This program examines the effects of low income and limited resources on women, which are greater than the impact on men, and looks at how women resist stereotypes and economic barriers.

Middle Adulthood: Intimate Relationships and the Sandwich Generation (2000, Magna Systems, 28 min.). This program examines current research on intimate relationships, with a focus on how middle-aged adults adapt and change during the years when many couples become "empty nesters." It includes a discussion of the phenomenon of gender convergence in middle age, as many people come to feel less tightly bound to traditional gender roles. Also included is an overview of the issues confronted by middle adults who must assume greater responsibility for their aging parents while still actively caring for their children.

Middle Adulthood: Midlife Crisis? (2000, Magna Systems, 28 min.). This program examines the experience often described as a "midlife crisis"—how it is defined, who tends to experience it, life circumstances that may promote it, and its role in individuals' lives. The program presents opposing theories about whether a true "midlife crisis" occurs or whether the challenges of midlife are simply analogous to those of other stages of the lifespan.

The Sandwich Generation: Caring for Both Children and Parents (1994, Films Media Group, 28 min.). In this special adaptation of a Phil Donahue program, Hugh Downs talks with senior citizens who do not want their children to have to care for them but see no other options. He also talks with adult children who explore a range of feelings about caring for their parents.

Sex and Gender (1991, RMI Media Productions, 30 min.). This program examines the effects of gender on the lives of three women spanning several generations. It shows the impact on individuals of society's unequal treatment based on gender.

TEST BANK

MULTIPLE CHOICE

1) In Erikson's theory of adult development, the major psychological conflict of midlife is called
   A) intimacy versus confusion.
   B) autonomy versus shame and doubt.
   C) controversy versus stability.
   D) generativity versus stagnation.
   Answer: D
   Page Ref: 417
   Skill: Factual
   Objective: 16.1

2) Which of the following best describes the term *generativity*?
   A) everything generated that can outlive the self and ensure society's continuity and improvement
   B) anything involving reproduction and parenting
   C) any product resulting from the need for self-expression
   D) eternity
   Answer: A
   Page Ref: 417
   Skill: Factual
   Objective: 16.1

3) Which of the following is a product of generativity?
   A) volunteer work with Habitat for Humanity
   B) a close personal friendship with someone you work with
   C) a sense of dissatisfaction with the world as it currently is
   D) a strong, fulfilling marriage
   Answer: A
   Page Ref: 417
   Skill: Applied
   Objective: 16.1

4) At age 43, Darryl is a successful lawyer who gets a lot of satisfaction from guiding young lawyers starting out in the firm, coaching his daughter's basketball team, and being camp leader for his son's Boy Scout troop. According to Erikson, he has most clearly developed a sense of
   A) intimacy.
   B) generativity.
   C) autonomy.
   D) integrity.
   Answer: B
   Page Ref: 417
   Skill: Applied
   Objective: 16.1

5) According to Erikson, generativity is motivated by
   A) a desire to be remembered by one's good works.
   B) the need to protect one's children from danger, violence, and evil.
   C) a "belief in the species" that promotes an optimistic world view, despite destructiveness and deprivation.
   D) the sense that one's days are numbered and the sense of quiet desperation that ensues.

Answer: C
Page Ref: 418
Skill: Factual
Objective: 16.1

6) The negative outcome, or lack of a sense of generativity, of Erikson's midlife stage is __________ which focuses on self-indulgence.
   A) insecurity
   B) autonomy
   C) generativity
   D) stagnation

Answer: D
Page Ref: 418
Skill: Factual
Objective: 16.1

7) Although Inez has a stable marriage, three successful grown children, and a good job, she is very self-centered and self-indulgent. She has little involvement with her children or their families, other than to remind them what gifts she wants for her birthday or Mother's Day. She "puts in her hours" at work, but is indifferent to how she could improve her productivity or that of her office. Erikson would say that Inez
   A) has developed a strong sense of stagnation.
   B) is typical of those in middle adulthood.
   C) is going through a midlife crisis.
   D) is a pain in the neck.

Answer: A
Page Ref: 418
Skill: Applied
Objective: 16.1

8) Arlen is highly generative. As a result, he is likely to
   A) be high in self-acceptance.
   B) lack leadership qualities.
   C) exhibit depression.
   D) have high anxiety.

Answer: A
Page Ref: 418
Skill: Applied
Objective: 16.1

9) Because Arlen is highly generative, he is also UNLIKELY to
   A) use authoritative parenting.
   B) be close-minded about differing viewpoints.
   C) use open communication.
   D) value trust.

Answer: B
Page Ref: 418
Skill: Applied
Objective: 16.1

10) Which person is likely to experience the greatest increase in generativity?
A) a man who has no children
B) a man who has children
C) a woman who has children
D) a woman who has no children
Answer: B
Page Ref: 418
Skill: Conceptual
Objective: 16.1

11) Sha'da is African American and Porsche is Caucasian American. Based on information in your text, we can conclude that
A) Porsche will display more generativity than Sha'da if she belongs to a church group.
B) Sha'da will more often display generativity through her involvement in religious groups and will offer more social support to others.
C) Sha'da and Porsche will display similar levels of generativity in midlife, but Sha'da will display higher levels when they reach their seventies.
D) their generativity will be lower than other midlifers who are Asian American or Native American.
Answer: B
Page Ref: 418
Skill: Applied
Objective: 16.1

12) In Levinson's theory of adult development, the period when people evaluate how successful they have been in meeting their early goals and focus on how best to modify their lives to have a meaningful future is called the
A) midlife transition.
B) middle-age spread.
C) life pivot point.
D) sense of generativity.
Answer: A
Page Ref: 419
Skill: Factual
Objective: 16.2

13) Esteban is trying to repair his relationship with his long-estranged parents. According to Levinson, he is engaged in which developmental task?
A) young–old
B) destruction–creation
C) masculinity–femininity
D) engagement–separateness
Answer: B
Page Ref: 419
Skill: Applied
Objective: 16.2

14) Fifty-year-old Brielle really likes the look of short skirts and low-slung pants, but has decided that her wardrobe needs to reflect a more mature style. She has also decided that her crow's feet reflect years of laughter and should be considered a sign of a happy life, rather than a sign of aging. On the other hand, she has decided to take up rollerblading as a way to spend time with her teenage son. According to Levinson, Brielle is engaged in which developmental task?
A) young–old
B) destruction–creation
C) masculinity–femininity
D) engagement–separateness
Answer: A
Page Ref: 419
Skill: Applied
Objective: 16.2

15) Marisal devoted herself to raising her two daughters during early adulthood. She is now becoming more involved in work and her community. According to Levinson, she is engaged in which developmental task?
A) young–old
B) destruction–creation
C) masculinity–femininity
D) engagement–separateness
Answer: D
Page Ref: 419
Skill: Applied
Objective: 16.2

16) Mr. and Mrs. Li's adult children have noticed gradual changes in their parents' personalities over the last decade. Mr. Li has become more empathic and caring; Mrs. Li has become more autonomous and assertive. According to Levinson, the Lis are engaged in which developmental task?
A) young–old
B) destruction–creation
C) masculinity–femininity
D) engagement–separateness
Answer: C
Page Ref: 419
Skill: Applied
Objective: 16.2

17) Basing your response on research cited in your text, which person is likely to be the MOST sensitive to physical aging over the midlife years?
A) Fitima, a college-educated female
B) Andrew, a male who never attended college
C) Ayanna, a female who never attended college
D) Tyler, a college-educated male
Answer: B
Page Ref: 419–420
Skill: Applied
Objective: 16.2

18) According to Levinson, middle-aged adults often feel a desire to __________ in order to advance human welfare and leave a legacy for future generations.
   A) reconcile masculine and feminine parts of the self
   B) find age-appropriate ways to express personal qualities
   C) counter destructive forces
   D) balance their engagement with the external world and separateness
   Answer: C
   Page Ref: 420
   Skill: Factual
   Objective: 16.2

19) During midlife, people's gender roles tend to become
   A) more masculine.
   B) more feminine.
   C) more gender-typed.
   D) more androgynous.
   Answer: D
   Page Ref: 420
   Skill: Factual
   Objective: 16.2

20) Which person is more likely to pursue a satisfying life structure successfully?
   A) Parker, a blue-collar worker
   B) Peter, who lives in poverty
   C) Patsanne, a corporate executive who works only the hours she wants to
   D) Penny, who is unemployed
   Answer: C
   Page Ref: 420
   Skill: Applied
   Objective: 16.2

21) According to Vaillant, the primary responsibility for the functioning of society falls on people who are
   A) young adults.
   B) elderly adults.
   C) midlife adults.
   D) politically motivated.
   Answer: C
   Page Ref: 420
   Skill: Factual
   Objective: 16.2

22) In societies around the world, older people become
   A) a liability, as costs associated with aging diminish resources for the entire population.
   B) more dissatisfied with what they perceive to be the failures of their generation.
   C) impatient with the lack of positive changes that have occurred over their lifetime.
   D) a stabilizing force that holds in check the rapid change sparked by younger adults.
   Answer: D
   Page Ref: 420–421
   Skill: Factual
   Objective: 16.2

23) Victor, who has just turned 45, is going through a period of great stress. He is filled with self-doubt and begins some major life-restructuring as a result. Victor is exhibiting behaviors consistent with
   A) neuroticism.
   B) conscientiousness.
   C) the young-old developmental task.
   D) a midlife crisis.

Answer: D
Page Ref: 421
Skill: Applied
Objective: 16.3

24) Which statement is true?
   A) Levinson's work showed little evidence of a midlife crisis in most people's lives.
   B) Vaillant's work showed little evidence of a midlife crisis in most people's lives.
   C) According to Vaillant, men are more likely to experience a midlife crisis.
   D) Typical change related to inner turmoil happens suddenly during middle adulthood.

Answer: B
Page Ref: 421
Skill: Conceptual
Objective: 16.3

25) Marita, in her early fifties, is making some life changes. These changes are most likely motivated by
   A) the age of her husband, and whether he is also instigating life changes.
   B) whether she has a college degree.
   C) a reduction in parenting responsibilities, freeing her to confront personal issues.
   D) the quality of her social network.

Answer: C
Page Ref: 421
Skill: Applied
Objective: 16.3

26) In his mid-forties, Edgar felt enormous turmoil, dissatisfaction, and unhappiness with his life. He decided to quit his job, leave his family, and start a new life on a communal farm in Colorado. Research on midlife crisis indicates that Edgar is
   A) very unusual for middle-aged adults.
   B) typical of most people in midlife.
   C) typical of men, but totally unlike most women.
   D) much less satisfied with the results of his new life.

Answer: A
Page Ref: 421
Skill: Applied
Objective: 16.3

27) The majority of adults who report experiencing a midlife crisis report all of the following EXCEPT
   A) changes attributed to challenging life events.
   B) a much looser definition of *midlife crisis* than that of researchers.
   C) major depression or anxiety attacks.
   D) a very wide age range in which the crisis occurred.

Answer: C
Page Ref: 421
Skill: Conceptual
Objective: 16.3

28) Sina, who has a Ph.D. in archaeology, dreamed of spending her life among archaeological ruins and discovering lost artifacts. In fact, she has spent the majority of her career as a university professor, in order to give her family the stability she thinks they need. When looking back on the last two decades of her life, she wishes she had made different career choices. Sina is experiencing
   A) life regrets.
   B) a midlife crisis.
   C) Levinson's young-old task.
   D) openness to experience.
   Answer: A
   Page Ref: 421
   Skill: Applied
   Objective: 16.3

29) Sankaran turned down a highly lucrative job in the private sector that required extensive travel to take a position at a local college, in order to spend more time with his family. Which of the following outcomes would be predictive of Sankaran's long-term greater life satisfaction?
   A) Sankaran quits his college position and takes the more lucrative job which, eventually causes his wife to divorce him, allowing little time for him to see his children.
   B) Sankaran constantly reminds his family of the sacrifice he made for them, and they act appropriately appreciative every time he does this.
   C) Sankaran identifies benefits associated with his college job, but still strongly regrets his career choice.
   D) Sankaran accepts that his college position is not completely satisfying, but identifies the benefits to his relationship with his family as being worth the sacrifice.
   Answer: D
   Page Ref: 421
   Skill: Applied
   Objective: 16.3

30) Most people in midlife
   A) who experience some sort of crisis typically come from higher-SES backgrounds, with the flexibility to relocate, change careers, or even stop working altogether.
   B) experience some life reflection, but most do not implement any kind of life change.
   C) engage in major life alterations, but since the outcomes are usually positive these life changes are not considered to reflect a "crisis."
   D) make changes that are best described as "turning points" rather than drastic alterations of their lives.
   Answer: D
   Page Ref: 421
   Skill: Factual
   Objective: 16.3

31) Shamika hopes that she will continue to be healthy in the future, and will be able to retire early enough to enjoy her grandchildren. She worries about her husband's health and hopes she will not have to face widowhood. Shamika is considering her
   A) future model.
   B) possible self.
   C) internal map.
   D) generalized goal.
   Answer: B
   Page Ref: 422
   Skill: Applied
   Objective: 16.4

32) Possible selves are the __________ dimension of self-concept.
   A) positive
   B) negative
   C) temporal
   D) most inaccurate
   Answer: C
   Page Ref: 422
   Skill: Factual
   Objective: 16.4

33) As a young adult, Christian wanted to be a great athlete and a very successful businessman. As he enters middle adulthood, he will probably
   A) strive harder to make his current self match his possible self.
   B) become depressed that he didn't achieve his goals.
   C) focus less on the business success and more on the athleticism in an attempt to regain his youth.
   D) concentrate more on enhancing personal relationships and being competent at work.
   Answer: D
   Page Ref: 422
   Skill: Applied
   Objective: 16.4

34) As Alberto progresses from early to late adulthood, we can anticipate that his self-acceptance, autonomy, and environmental mastery will
   A) increase throughout his lifespan.
   B) decrease from early to middle adulthood.
   C) increase from early to middle adulthood and then level off.
   D) decrease from early to middle adulthood and then increase in old age.
   Answer: C
   Page Ref: 422
   Skill: Applied
   Objective: 16.4

35) As Oksana reaches middle adulthood, she acknowledges and accepts both her good and bad traits. She feels positively about herself and her life. Oksana is displaying
   A) self-acceptance.
   B) resignation.
   C) autonomy.
   D) environmental mastery.
   Answer: A
   Page Ref: 422
   Skill: Applied
   Objective: 16.4

36) Middle-aged people see themselves as more __________, that is, less concerned about expectations and evaluations of others and more concerned with following self-chosen standards.
   A) self-accepting
   B) self-regulating
   C) insecure
   D) autonomous
   Answer: D
   Page Ref: 422
   Skill: Factual
   Objective: 16.4

37) Kascey knows that she is able to manage a wide array of tasks easily and effectively, which is what makes her such a good administrator. Kascey is displaying
    A) environmental mastery.
    B) autonomy.
    C) self-acceptance.
    D) a life interpretation.
Answer: A
Page Ref: 422
Skill: Applied
Objective: 16.4

38) Research on the quality of life in middle age has found that this period can generally be described as
    A) a time of crisis.
    B) the prime of life.
    C) filled with insecurity.
    D) a period of rapid change.
Answer: B
Page Ref: 422
Skill: Factual
Objective: 16.4

39) Lucas is a middle-aged accountant. When frustrated by coworkers, he is LEAST likely to
    A) deny how upsetting their behavior is to him.
    B) anticipate and plan ways to handle future discomforts.
    C) postpone responding to their actions in order to evaluate alternatives to handling the situation.
    D) use humor to express his ideas and feelings without offending others.
Answer: A
Page Ref: 422
Skill: Applied
Objective: 16.4

40) Shakira, an office supervisor, is well liked and respected by those who work for her. She can find the "silver lining" to a stressful situation, anticipates and plans for possible problems, and uses humor to express ideas and feelings. Shakira is probably
    A) a middle-aged individual.
    B) not effective as a supervisor, even though she is well liked.
    C) using emotion-centered strategies for coping with stress.
    D) a young adult.
Answer: A
Page Ref: 424
Skill: Applied
Objective: 16.5

41) Maura, age 56, engages in a daily exercise regimen. As a result, she is likely to
    A) be more afraid of losing an active lifestyle as she gets older.
    B) worry more about age-related physical deterioration than less active individuals her age.
    C) have reduced feelings of vulnerability to illness that typically increase with age.
    D) have more physical injuries than other adults her age.
Answer: C
Page Ref: 423
Skill: Applied
Objective: Box B&E: What Factors Promote Psychological Well-Being

42) Deb becomes so engaged in a professional writing activity that she loses all track of time. She is experiencing
   A) the early onset of senility.
   B) ADD.
   C) preoccupation.
   D) flow.
   Answer: D
   Page Ref: 423
   Skill: Applied
   Objective: Box B&E: What Factors Promote Psychological Well-Being

43) Virginia places occupational prestige and a high income over the importance of friends in her life. On a test of psychological well-being, she is likely to
   A) score highly in the "well-adjusted" category.
   B) describe herself as "unhappy."
   C) describe herself as "extremely happy."
   D) show evidence of a highly stressful life.
   Answer: B
   Page Ref: 423
   Skill: Applied
   Objective: Box B&E: What Factors Promote Psychological Well-Being

44) Gayle is a 46-year-old married doctor who exercises daily. Which factor is the most powerful predictor of Gayle's mental health in midlife?
   A) being married
   B) being in good health
   C) the financial security associated with being a doctor
   D) the ability to multitask that is required of a doctor
   Answer: A
   Page Ref: 423
   Skill: Applied
   Objective: Box B&E: What Factors Promote Psychological Well-Being

45) Research showing that gender identity becomes more androgynous in midlife
   A) exists both in Western industrialized nations and village societies.
   B) has not been conducted in other cultures.
   C) is not consistent among nonindustrialized nations.
   D) is based solely upon work done with Mayan villagers in Guatemala.
   Answer: A
   Page Ref: 424
   Skill: Factual
   Objective: 16.5

46) Which of the following statements is inconsistent with the parental imperative theory?
   A) Traditional gender role identity is maintained during active parenting years to help ensure survival of the children.
   B) After children leave the home, parents are free to express the "other-gender" side of their personalities.
   C) Children's departure from the home is related to men's openness to the "feminine" side of their personalities.
   D) Both warmth and assertiveness are necessary to rear children effectively.
   Answer: D
   Page Ref: 424
   Skill: Conceptual
   Objective: 16.5

47) Abigail has just been appointed director of the research and development division of her company. Because she is a college-educated woman who has attained high status at work, research indicates that she will probably gain in __________ by her early forties.

A) submissiveness
B) independence
C) passivity
D) guardedness

Answer: B
Page Ref: 424
Skill: Applied
Objective: 16.5

48) An alternative to parental imperative theory suggests that men become more androgynous in midlife because

A) self-reliance and assertiveness are vital for coping with reduced career advancement opportunities.
B) of a need to enrich a marital relationship after children have departed.
C) a high number become widowers, requiring them to modify gender-role behaviors in order to compete for a steadily declining number of middle-aged women.
D) their wives get fed up with male assertiveness and threaten to leave if they don't change.

Answer: B
Page Ref: 424
Skill: Factual
Objective: 16.5

49) Androgyny in middle adulthood is associated with

A) decreased self-acceptance and autonomy.
B) greater environmental mastery and neuroticism.
C) advanced moral reasoning and psychosocial maturity.
D) fewer life regrets and more possible selves.

Answer: C
Page Ref: 424
Skill: Factual
Objective: 16.5

50) Marjorie worries constantly about the trouble her children might get into. She complains that they go out of their way to make her life miserable and that she doesn't know how to deal with her life. Marjorie is at one extreme of which of these "big five" personality traits?

A) agreeableness
B) extroversion
C) conscientiousness
D) neuroticism

Answer: D
Page Ref: 424
Skill: Applied
Objective: 16.5

51) Pavel enjoys parties, the bigger and louder the better. He is talkative, emotionally reactive to others, and tends to be bored and depressed if he is alone for too long. Pavel best exemplifies which of these "big five" personality traits?

A) extroversion
B) neuroticism
C) agreeableness
D) conscientiousness

Answer: A
Page Ref: 425
Skill: Applied
Objective: 16.6

52) Sonja is very imaginative and creative. She enjoys tasting new foods, meeting new people, thinking new ideas. Sonja best exemplifies which of these "big five" personality traits?
A) conscientiousness
B) openness to experience
C) agreeableness
D) extroversion
Answer: B
Page Ref: 425
Skill: Applied
Objective: 16.6

53) Warren is generous, kind, and good-natured. He always has good words to say about his friends and tries to find the best qualities in everyone he meets. Warren best exemplifies which of these "big five" personality traits?
A) extroversion
B) conscientiousness
C) agreeableness
D) neuroticism
Answer: C
Page Ref: 425
Skill: Applied
Objective: 16.6

54) Donna is highly organized, punctual, and reliable. Her friends and coworkers know she can always be counted on to meet her deadlines and keep her promises. Donna best exemplifies which of these "big five" personality traits?
A) neuroticism
B) agreeableness
C) extroversion
D) conscientiousness
Answer: D
Page Ref: 425
Skill: Applied
Objective: 16.6

55) Prit can be characterized by the "big five" personality trait of agreeableness. He
A) can anticipate that this trait will increase through middle age.
B) can anticipate that this trait will decrease through middle age.
C) will probably also become more open and extroverted as he reaches middle adulthood.
D) will probably become less conscientious as he ages.
Answer: A
Page Ref: 425
Skill: Applied
Objective: 16.6

56) Cross-cultural research of the "big five" personality traits has led researchers to conclude that
A) adult personality change is genetically influenced.
B) individual differences in the traits are small but highly unstable.
C) the stability of the personality traits is inconsistent across time.
D) they are not consistent across cultures.
Answer: A
Page Ref: 425
Skill: Factual
Objective: 16.6

57) Because they have ties to older and younger generations in their families and have well-established friendships, people in midlife tend to __________ than at any other period of their lives.
   A) experience more relationship-related stress
   B) have less time to engage in leisurely pursuits
   C) have a larger number of close relationships
   D) have a harder time balancing work responsibilities
   Answer: C
   Page Ref: 426
   Skill: Factual
   Objective: 16.7

58) __________ is the more current term for the phase formerly known as the "empty nest."
   A) "Launching children and moving on"
   B) "The beginning of independence"
   C) "Liberation and advancement"
   D) "Expanding horizons"
   Answer: A
   Page Ref: 426
   Skill: Factual
   Objective: 16.7

59) Midlifers are able to adapt more easily to __________ than younger people, resulting in less decline in psychological well-being when it does occur.
   A) changing gender roles
   B) divorce
   C) job layoffs
   D) remarriage
   Answer: B
   Page Ref: 426
   Skill: Factual
   Objective: 16.7

60) The __________ refers to a trend in which women who support themselves or their families have become the majority of the adult poverty population.
   A) marriage-divorce-poverty phase
   B) female poverty cycle
   C) gender equity movement
   D) feminization of poverty
   Answer: D
   Page Ref: 426
   Skill: Factual
   Objective: 16.7

61) The author of your text suggests that __________ could reduce the United States gender gap in poverty, which is currently higher than other industrialized nations.
   A) stronger public policies that safeguard families
   B) federally mandated premarital counseling
   C) stricter divorce laws
   D) stronger alimony laws
   Answer: A
   Page Ref: 426
   Skill: Conceptual
   Objective: 16.7

62) Cherita has just divorced after 23 years of marriage. When asked what she considers important in a healthy relationship, she is likely to place
   A) greater weight on passionate love.
   B) greater weight on equal friendship.
   C) less emphasis on romance.
   D) more emphasis on financial security.

Answer: B
Page Ref: 426
Skill: Applied
Objective: 16.7

63) Current information on how middle-aged men adjust to divorce shows that
   A) they are generally happier after divorce than before.
   B) they adjust poorly and typically show anger and depression.
   C) how well they adjust depends on the reasons for the divorce.
   D) there is little research on them, because most remarry very quickly.

Answer: D
Page Ref: 426
Skill: Factual
Objective: 16.7

64) Your friend's children will be growing up and leaving home in the next five years or so, and your friend is concerned about how satisfying life can be after they are gone. According to the book, the best advice you can give for ensuring increased life happiness after they leave is for her to
   A) develop a strong work orientation.
   B) spend as much time with them as possible now.
   C) keep them in the family unit as long as possible.
   D) separate completely from them after they go.

Answer: A
Page Ref: 427
Skill: Applied
Objective: 16.7

65) Which of these factors can create parental strain as parents and children approach the launching phase?
   A) a child who is off the social clock
   B) a strong focus on the children
   C) a strong orientation toward work
   D) difficulties in raising the children

Answer: A
Page Ref: 427
Skill: Factual
Objective: 16.7

66) Mr. and Mrs. Gallassetti live in Italy with their 23-year-old son. Based upon cultural norms, we can anticipate that
   A) he will probably not move out until he marries.
   B) their son is significantly off the social clock.
   C) their parent–child relationship is probably strained.
   D) his parents are eager for his departure.

Answer: A
Page Ref: 427
Skill: Applied
Objective: 16.7

67) Research on early child-rearing styles and parents' relations with adult children shows that
   A) permissive parents maintain the strongest ties with their children after launching them off.
   B) children whose parents were authoritarian tend to keep in closer contact with their parents.
   C) warm and supportive parents will have closer relationships with their grown children.
   D) there is no relationship between parenting styles and adult relationships.

Answer: C
Page Ref: 427
Skill: Factual
Objective: 16.7

68) Maile has become the person in her family who brings everyone together for family celebrations. She spends considerable time and energy ensuring that family members stay in touch. Maile is her family's
   A) social secretary.
   B) family guardian.
   C) kinkeeper.
   D) arranger.

Answer: C
Page Ref: 427
Skill: Applied
Objective: 16.7

69) Sharon and Robin love being grandparents and delight in the ability to have fun with the grandchildren without the major responsibilities of child-rearing. Which aspect of grandparenthood does this refer to?
   A) valued elder
   B) immortality through descendants
   C) reinvolvement with personal past
   D) indulgence

Answer: D
Page Ref: 427
Skill: Applied
Objective: 16.7

70) The closest grandparent relationships are typically those between
   A) grandmothers and granddaughters.
   B) grandmothers and grandsons.
   C) grandfathers and granddaughters.
   D) grandfathers and grandsons.

Answer: A
Page Ref: 428
Skill: Factual
Objective: 16.7

71) Which of the following is most likely to promote a close bond between an older grandchild and grandparent?
   A) whether they live near each other
   B) the extent to which the grandchild believes the grandparent values contact
   C) the relationship between the child's parent and grandparent
   D) the health of the grandparent

Answer: B
Page Ref: 428
Skill: Factual
Objective: 16.7

72) In which family would you expect the grandparent role to be more structured, diverse, and engaged in higher-quality activities?
   A) the Jacksons, upper-SES grandparents who live 600 miles from their grandchildren
   B) the Johnsons, who live 30 minutes from their married daughter and her children
   C) the Jeffreys, a lower-SES family whose single daughter and her children live with them
   D) the Jetsons, who live within 30 minutes of all five of their married children and their 15 grandchildren

Answer: C
Page Ref: 428
Skill: Applied
Objective: 16.7

73) In many ethnic subcultures, including Chinese and Mexican-American families, the role of the grandparent is
   A) seen as interfering with the parents' authority.
   B) primarily one of storyteller and entertainer.
   C) focused on passing down cultural traditions.
   D) central to the grandchild's caregiving.

Answer: D
Page Ref: 428
Skill: Factual
Objective: 16.7

74) In __________, children live with grandparents but apart from parents.
   A) skipped-generation families
   B) most cases of adult drug abuse
   C) many states with strong grandparent visitation rights laws
   D) many countries other than the United States

Answer: A
Page Ref: 429
Skill: Factual
Objective: Box SI: Grandparents Rearing Grandchildren

75) Mr. and Mrs. X are unemployed and caring for their two grandchildren. This is particularly stressful for them, as they live in poverty and Mr. X is a diabetic who uses a wheelchair and requires frequent medical attention. Mr. and Mrs. X's situation is more common among which ethnic group?
   A) Native Americans
   B) Caucasian Americans
   C) Asian Americans
   D) African Americans

Answer: A
Page Ref: 429
Skill: Conceptual
Objective: Box SI: Grandparents Rearing Grandchildren

76) Help is more likely to be exchanged between adult children and their aging parents when
   A) both parents are still living and married.
   B) the parents are in generally good health.
   C) they have a positive relationship history.
   D) there are a large number of grandchildren.

Answer: C
Page Ref: 430
Skill: Factual
Objective: 16.7

77) Middle-aged adults who balance the needs of aging parents and financially dependent children are called
   A) Real Troopers.
   B) kinkeepers.
   C) economically challenged.
   D) the sandwich generation.

Answer: D

Page Ref: 430
Skill: Factual
Objective: 16.7

78) Eighty-year-old Shirley requires more personal care than her husband can provide. If they are representative of most families, the person who will most likely step in to help is
   A) her daughter.
   B) her son.
   C) their neighbor.
   D) her doctor.

Answer: A

Page Ref: 430
Skill: Applied
Objective: 16.7

79) One of the reasons that caring for a chronically ill parent is different, and often more stressful, than caring for a young child is that
   A) parents are often unaware that they need care, so they display frustration with the adult son or daughter's attempts to help.
   B) the need for parental care arises suddenly, with little time for preparation.
   C) the grandchild–grandparent conflicts that result from living in the same home force adults to make choices between their children or their parents.
   D) the duration of caregiving is usually for a fixed amount of time, leading caregivers to try and maintain work, family, and social obligations, rather than cutting back on their responsibilities like they would if the caregiving were for an undetermined period.

Answer: B

Page Ref: 431
Skill: Factual
Objective: 16.7

80) Which type of relationship between an adult child and an elderly parent tends to produce the greatest stress?
   A) living separately and having little contact
   B) living separately and having frequent contact
   C) living together with an elderly parent who is ill
   D) living together with an elderly parent who is well

Answer: C

Page Ref: 431
Skill: Factual
Objective: 16.7

81) Role overload, high job absenteeism, exhaustion, inability to concentrate, and high rates of depression are typical of
   A) parental caregivers.
   B) parents who live with their children.
   C) grandparents who live with children and grandchildren.
   D) young children whose grandparents live with them.

Answer: A

Page Ref: 431
Skill: Factual
Objective: 16.7

82) The factor that is most effective in reducing the stress of caring for an elderly parent is
   A) having enough space to keep the parent at home.
   B) governmental subsidies to help with the finances.
   C) gratitude from the parent for the help that is provided.
   D) social support from family, friends, and neighbors.

Answer: D
Page Ref: 431
Skill: Factual
Objective:

83) Teresa is considering quitting her job in order to take care of her aging father. Based on information in your text, what should you tell her?
   A) She should quit work as soon as she is able to, as the longer her father is without care, the more his condition may worsen.
   B) The United States has a government-sponsored home helper system to ease the burden of parental care, so she should not have to quit her job.
   C) A nursing home is an easily affordable solution and can provide better quality care than she can.
   D) She should avoid quitting work as long as possible, as the social isolation and loss of financial resources will add to her stress.

Answer: D
Page Ref: 431
Skill: Applied
Objective: 16.7

84) Sibling relationships typically
   A) improve during middle adulthood for African Americans and Mexican Americans, and hold constant for all other ethnic groups.
   B) improve during middle adulthood.
   C) decline between early and middle adulthood.
   D) fluctuate significantly, depending on the gender of the siblings and the health of the parents.

Answer: C
Page Ref: 432
Skill: Factual
Objective: 16.8

85) Which event tends to cause an increase in sibling ties during middle adulthood?
   A) the birth of children
   B) beginning a new job
   C) the birth of grandchildren
   D) parental illness

Answer: D
Page Ref: 432
Skill: Factual
Objective: 16.8

86) In industrialized nations, __________ tend to be emotionally closest during middle adulthood.
   A) sister–sister bonds
   B) sister–brother bonds
   C) brother–brother bonds
   D) siblings who did not get along as children

Answer: A
Page Ref: 432
Skill: Factual
Objective: 16.8

87) Compared to adult men, adult women report
A) a greater number of close friends.
B) less satisfaction with their friendships.
C) more friendships as they get older.
D) a greater willingness to break off a friendship.
Answer: A
Page Ref: 432
Skill: Factual
Objective: 16.8

88) Which statement about friendships during midlife is true?
A) The number of friendships increases with age.
B) People are more willing to invest in nonfamily ties.
C) Older adults try harder to get along with friends.
D) Older adults work harder to initiate new friendships.
Answer: C
Page Ref: 433
Skill: Conceptual
Objective: 16.8

89) Compared with younger people, how do middle-aged adults deal with problems in their friendships?
A) They are more likely to stop being friends with the person.
B) They are more likely to ignore the problem and keep going.
C) They are likely to work harder to preserve the friendship.
D) They are likely to feel personally threatened by the problem.
Answer: C
Page Ref: 433
Skill: Conceptual
Objective: 16.8

90) As employees grow older, what generally happens to their overall job satisfaction?
A) It shows no change.
B) It decreases slightly.
C) It decreases substantially.
D) It increases steadily.
Answer: D
Page Ref: 433
Skill: Factual
Objective: 16.9

91) Which of the following adults would probably have the highest job satisfaction?
A) a 45-year-old woman
B) a 40-year-old blue-collar worker
C) a 25-year-old teacher
D) a 50-year-old male executive
Answer: D
Page Ref: 433
Skill: Applied
Objective: 16.9

92) Which aspect of a worker's job satisfaction changes the most during adulthood?
   A) intrinsic satisfaction
   B) extrinsic satisfaction
   C) borderline satisfaction
   D) corporate satisfaction
   Answer: A
   Page Ref: 433
   Skill: Factual
   Objective: 16.9

93) Dorinda has been experiencing job stress for several years. As a result, she is emotionally exhausted and feels a loss of personal control and accomplishment. Dorinda is experiencing
   A) depression.
   B) a midlife crisis.
   C) burnout.
   D) a life regret.
   Answer: C
   Page Ref: 434
   Skill: Applied
   Objective: 16.9

94) As workers get older, their opportunities for training and vocational development tend to
   A) increase steadily.
   B) decrease somewhat.
   C) increase slightly.
   D) remain constant.
   Answer: B
   Page Ref: 434
   Skill: Factual
   Objective: 16.9

95) Jarrett has been working in his field for over three decades, but has not received any type of professional development for the last five years. Which of the following statements is probably accurate?
   A) Jarrett's skills are so advanced that he doesn't need additional training.
   B) The younger workers in Jarrett's company are in greater need of vocational training than he is, so they receive priority for the limited professional development funds.
   C) Jarrett's supervisor has negative stereotypes about older workers, so she doesn't think additional training would be helpful for him.
   D) Jarrett is unwilling to receive additional training because the trainers are all younger than he is.
   Answer: C
   Page Ref: 434
   Skill: Applied
   Objective: 16.9

96) Which person is most likely to encounter a glass ceiling?
   A) a Caucasian-American man
   B) a Caucasian-American woman
   C) an African-American man
   D) an African-American woman
   Answer: D
   Page Ref: 434
   Skill: Conceptual
   Objective: 16.9

97) Which of these factors is most likely to contribute to the glass ceiling that prevents many women and ethnic minorities from reaching the top levels of their profession?
A) They are often given more difficult assignments than white men.
B) There aren't many women and minority mentors and role models.
C) Companies have to do more on-the-job training for these people.
D) They are generally less effective as managers and supervisors.
Answer: B
Page Ref: 434
Skill: Factual
Objective: 16.9

98) When women demonstrate qualities such as assertiveness, confidence, and ambition,
A) they encounter prejudice because they deviate from traditional gender roles.
B) the glass ceiling is typically lifted.
C) the glass ceiling disappears completely.
D) they are generally given positions that reflect the value of those qualities.
Answer: A
Page Ref: 434–435
Skill: Factual
Objective: 16.9

99) Olivia, a female middle manager, and Octavio, a male middle manager, are both frustrated with the lack of advancement opportunities in their company. Which of the following can you predict?
A) Octavio is probably a better manager.
B) Olivia is more likely than Octavio to receive any future promotions.
C) Olivia is more likely than Octavio to quit her job and start her own business.
D) Olivia will probably leave her job to devote more time to her family.
Answer: C
Page Ref: 435
Skill: Applied
Objective: 16.9

100) The average age of retirement has decreased in North America due to
A) a longer lifespan and greater physical health of older adults.
B) an increase in post-retirement options for older adults.
C) government-sponsored retirement benefits.
D) pressure from corporations to hire younger, less expensive workers to replace older employees.
Answer: C
Page Ref: 435
Skill: Factual
Objective: 16.10

101) Retirement can be stressful because it leads to a loss of two important work-related rewards,
A) income and benefits.
B) interaction with others and a steady income.
C) income and status.
D) intrinsic and extrinsic satisfaction.
Answer: C
Page Ref: 435
Skill: Factual
Objective: 16.10

102) Which of these is most necessary for a retired person to be happy and well-adjusted after retirement?
   A) good health insurance
   B) a long working career
   C) moving to a new city
   D) planning for an active life
   Answer: D
   Page Ref: 435
   Skill: Factual
   Objective: 16.10

103) People with lower educational achievements and who earned less while working tend to approach retirement with
   A) more preparation for how they will live after working.
   B) little preparation, though they need it more than others.
   C) little preparation because they do not need it as much.
   D) the same preparation as higher-paid and educated workers.
   Answer: B
   Page Ref: 435–436
   Skill: Factual
   Objective: 16.10

ESSAY

104) What is meant by generativity? Describe three examples of ways you or people you know well have expressed generativity in middle adulthood. Explain why each is an example of generativity.
   Answer: Generativity involves reaching out to others in ways that give to and guide the next generation. Generativity is under way in early adulthood, typically through childbearing and child rearing and establishing a niche in the occupational world. But it expands greatly in midlife, when commitment extends beyond oneself to a larger group-family, community, or society. The generative adult combines his or her need for self-expression with a need for communion, integrating personal goals with the welfare of the larger social environment. The result is the capacity to care for others in a broader way than in previous stages.

   Erikson selected the term *generativity* to encompass everything generated that can outlive the self and ensure society's continuity and improvement: children, ideas, products, and works of art. Although parenting is a major means of realizing generativity, it is not the only means: adults can also be generative in other family relationships, as mentors in the workplace, in volunteer endeavors, and through many forms of productivity and creativity. Accept reasonable responses for the three examples.
   Page Ref: 417–418

105) Discuss possible reasons, *aside from the parental imperative theory*, that could explain why men and women become more androgynous in middle adulthood.
   Answer: Besides reduced parenting responsibilities, other demands and experiences of midlife may prompt a more androgynous orientation. For example, among men, a need to enrich a marital relationship after children have departed, along with reduced opportunities for career advancement, may awaken emotionally sensitive traits. Compared with men, women are far more likely to face economic and social disadvantages. A greater number remain divorced, are widowed, and encounter discrimination in the workplace. Self-reliance and assertiveness are vital for coping with these circumstances.
   Page Ref: 424

106) Which of the "big five" personality traits do you think best describes you? Give a brief description of the trait and personal characteristics to justify your answer.

Answer: Brief descriptions of the traits are below. Accept reasonable answers for their justification.

Neuroticism: Individuals who are high on this trait are worrying, temperamental, self-pitying, self-conscious, emotional, and vulnerable. Individuals who are low are calm, even-tempered, self-content, comfortable, unemotional, and hardy.

Extroversion: Individuals who are high on this trait are affectionate, talkative, active, fun-loving, and passionate. Individuals who are low are reserved, quiet, passive, sober, and emotionally unreactive.

Openness to experience: Individuals who are high on this trait are imaginative, creative, original, curious, and liberal. Individuals who are low are down-to-earth, uncreative, conventional, uncurious, and conservative.

Agreeableness: Individuals who are high on this trait are soft-hearted, trusting, generous, acquiescent, lenient, and good-natured. Individuals who are low are ruthless, suspicious, stingy, antagonistic, critical, and irritable.

Conscientiousness: Individuals who are high on this trait are conscientious, hardworking, well-organized, punctual, ambitious, and persevering. Individuals who are low are negligent, lazy, disorganized, late, aimless, and nonpersistent.

Page Ref: 425

107) Discuss the changes in the mother–daughter relationship from early through middle adulthood.

Answer: Mother–daughter relationships tend to be closer than other parent–child ties. As the tensions of the adolescent years ease, many young-adult daughters and mothers build rewarding, intimate bonds. As daughters move into middle age, their descriptions of the mother–daughter bond become more complex, reflecting both positive and negative aspects—a change that may stem from daughters' more mature perspective and from growing relationship tensions. Although middle-aged daughters love their aging mothers and desire their approval, they face many competing demands on their time and energy.

Page Ref: 430

108) Explain why women and ethnic minorities face a glass ceiling.

Answer: Women and ethnic minorities face a glass ceiling, or invisible barrier to advancement up the corporate ladder. Management is an art and skill that must be taught. Yet women and members of ethnic minorities have less access to mentors, role models, and informal networks that serve as training routes. And because of stereotyped doubts about women's career commitment and ability to become strong managers, large companies spend less money on formal training programs for their female employees. Furthermore, women who demonstrate qualities linked to leadership and advancement—such as assertiveness, confidence, forcefulness, and ambition—encounter prejudice because they deviate from traditional gender roles.

Page Ref: 434

STUDY QUESTIONS

Erikson's Theory: Generativity versus Stagnation

1. Define *generativity,* and cite characteristics of generative adults. (p. 417)

   A. ____

   ____

   B. ____

   ____

2. In addition to parenting, list four ways adults can be generative. (p. 417)

   A. ______________________ B. ______________________

   C. ______________________ D. ______________________

3. Explain how generativity brings together personal desires and cultural demands. (pp. 417–418)

   Personal desires: ______________________

   Cultural demands: ______________________

4. Cite characteristics of adults who develop a sense of stagnation. (p. 418)

   ____

   ____

5. Having children seems to foster generative development more in (men / women). (p. 418)

Other Theories of Psychosocial Development in Midlife

Levinson's Seasons of Life

1. According to Levinson, what four developmental tasks do midlifers confront in order to reassess their relation to themselves and to the external world? (p. 419)

   A. ______________________

   B. ______________________

   C. ______________________

   D. ______________________

2. True or False: Because of the double standard of aging, women are more likely than men to perceive themselves as younger than their chronological age. (p. 419)

3. True or False: Middle-aged men almost never express concern about appearing less attractive as they grow older. (p. 419)

4. How does confronting one's own mortality and the actual or impending death of agemates influence awareness in middle adulthood? (p. 420)

   ____

   ____

5. List four ways the desire for a legacy can be satisfied in midlife. (p. 420)

   A. ______________________ B. ______________________

   C. ______________________ D. ______________________

6. Explain how men and women reconcile masculine and feminine parts of the self in middle age. (p. 420)

   Men: ______________________

   ____

   Women: ______________________

   ____

7. True or False: Midlife requires that men and women with highly active, successful careers reduce their concern with ambition and achievement and focus on themselves. (p. 420)

8. What social contexts support rebuilding the life structure in middle adulthood? (p. 420)

____

____

____

9. How do opportunities for advancement ease the transition to middle adulthood? (p. 420)

____

Vaillant's Adaptation to Life

1. According to Vaillant, adults in their late forties and early fifties become _______________. (p. 420)
2. What personal changes occur as people approach the end of middle age? (p. 421)

____

____

Is There a Midlife Crisis?

1. What is a *midlife crisis*? (p. 421)

____

2. How do men and women differ in their responses to midlife? (p. 421)

Men: _______________

____

Women: _______________

____

3. True or False: Sharp disruption and agitation are common in middle adulthood. (p. 421)
4. What are some characteristics of adults who experience a midlife crisis? (p. 421)

____

____

Stability and Change in Self-Concept and Personality

Possible Selves

1. What are *possible selves,* and how do they change with age? (p. 422)

A. _______________

B. _______________

2. How do possible selves differ from self-concept? (p. 422)

____

____

3. True or False: Throughout adulthood, people's descriptions of their current selves tend to fluctuate drastically. (p. 422)

Self-Acceptance, Autonomy, and Environmental Mastery

1. Explain why self-acceptance, autonomy, and environmental mastery tend to increase from early to middle adulthood among well-educated adults. (p. 422)

   A. ______________________________

   B. ______________________________

   C. ______________________________

2. Cite two cognitive changes that probably support the confidence, initiative, and decisiveness of middle adulthood. (p. 422)

   A. ____________________ B. ____________________

Biology and Environment: What Factors Promote Psychological Well-Being in Midlife?

1. Explain how exercise promotes well-being in midlife. (p. 423)

   ____

   ____

2. What is *flow,* and why does it increase in middle adulthood? (p. 423)

   A. ______________________________

   ____

   B. ______________________________

   ____

3. In a longitudinal study of 90 men, ____________ and ____________ in early adulthood were among the best predictors of well-being in middle adulthood. (p. 423)

4. True or False: Friendships are more effective than a good marriage in boosting psychological well-being in midlife. (p. 423)

5. True or False: Women are generally happier today than in the past. Explain your answer. (p. 423)

   ____

   ____

Coping Strategies

1. Midlife brings a(n) (increase / decrease) in effective coping strategies. (p. 422)

2. What is *cognitive-affective* complexity, and how might it contribute to effective coping in middle adulthood? (pp. 422, 424)

   A. ______________________________

   ____

   B. ______________________________

   ____

Gender Identity

1. Gender identity becomes (more / less) androgynous in midlife. Explain your answer. (p. 424)

____

____

____

2. How does *parental imperative theory* explain androgyny in later life? (p. 424)

____

____

____

3. Besides reduced parenting responsibilities, what other demands and experiences promote a more androgynous orientation in midlife? (p. 424)

____

____

Individual Differences in Personality Traits

1. List the *"big five" personality traits.* (pp. 424–425)

   A. ____________________ B. ____________________

   C. ____________________ D. ____________________

   E. ____________________

2. Which "big five" personality traits show modest declines in midlife? Which ones increase? (p. 425)

   Declines: ______________________________________

   Increases: ______________________________________

3. True or False: An individual who scores high or low at one age in the "big five" personality traits is likely to do the same from 3 to 30 years later. (p. 425)

4. How can there be high stability in personality traits, yet significant changes in certain aspects of personality? (p. 425)

____

____

____

Relationships at Midlife

1. Why is the middle adulthood phase of the family life cycle often referred to as "launching children and moving on"? (p. 426)

____

____

Marriage and Divorce

1. True or False: Middle-aged adults are more likely than younger or older adults to experience financial difficulty. (p. 426)

2. True or False: Midlifers seem to adapt more easily to divorce than younger people. (p. 426)
3. Marital breakup is a strong contributor to the *feminization of poverty.* Explain what this means. (p. 426)

____

____

____

4. List outcomes for middle-aged women who weather divorce successfully. (p. 426)

____

____

____

Changing Parent–Child Relationships

1. True or False: Even when their children are "off-time" in development of independence and accomplishment, middle-aged adults adjust well. (p. 427)
2. Describe how the parental role changes in midlife. (p. 427)

____

____

____

3. When children marry, parents face additional challenges in enlarging the family network to include in-laws. Explain why. (p. 427)

____

____

4. Once young adults strike out on their own, members of the middle generation, especially mothers, usually take on the role of ______________, gathering the family for celebrations and making sure everyone stays in touch. (p. 427)

Grandparenthood

1. On average, American adults become grandparents in their ____________, Canadian adults in their ____________. (p. 427)
2. List four commonly mentioned gratifications of grandparenthood. (p. 427)

   A. ____

   B. ____

   C. ____

   D. ____

3. How does the grandchild's age affect grandparent–grandchild relationships? (pp. 427–428)

____

____

____

____

4. Typically, (same-sex / opposite-sex) grandparents and grandchildren are closer, especially ________________ ________________ (p. 428)

5. As grandchildren get older, distance has a (greater / lesser) impact on grandparent–grandchild relationships. (p. 428)

6. Explain how SES and ethnicity influence grandparent–grandchild ties. (p. 428)

   SES: ________________

   ____

   Ethnicity: ________________

   ____

7. True or False: Involvement in care of grandchildren is high among Chinese, Korean, Mexican-American, and Canadian-Aboriginal grandparents. (p. 428)

Social Issues: Grandparents Rearing Grandchildren: The Skipped-Generation Family

1. What are *skipped-generation families*? (p. 429)

   ____

2. Cite several reasons that grandparents step in and rear grandchildren. (p. 429)

   ____

   ____

3. Describe challenges grandparents encounter when they raise grandchildren. (p. 429)

   ____

   ____

   ____

Middle-Aged Children and Their Aging Parents

1. True or False: Mother–daughter relationships tend to be closer than other parent–child ties. (p. 430)
2. True or False: In the non-Western world, older adults often live with their married children. (p. 430)
3. Why are today's middle-aged adults called the *sandwich generation*? (p. 430)

   ____

4. Why are women more often caregivers of aging parents? (p. 430)

   ____

   ____

5. Cite contributions that men make to caring for aging parents. (p. 431)

   ____

   ____

6. Explain why caring for a chronically ill or disabled parent is highly stressful. (p. 431)

____

____

7. What emotional and physical health consequences are associated with parental caregiving? (pp. 431–432)

____

____

8. List four ways to relieve the stress of caring for an aging parent. (p. 432)

   A. _______________

   B. _______________

   C. _______________

   D. _______________

Siblings

1. Sibling contact and support (increase / decline) from early to middle adulthood, yet siblings often feel (closer / less close) during this time of life. (p. 432)
2. True or False: As siblings get older, good relationships often strengthen and poor relationships often worsen. (p. 432)
3. Provide an illustration of differences in sibling relationships between village and industrialized societies. (p. 432)

____

____

____

Friendships

1. Briefly describe sex differences in middle-aged friendships. (p. 432)

   Men: _______________

   ____

   Women: _______________

   ____

2. Number of friends (increases / declines) with age. (p. 433)
3. Explain how family relationships and friendships support different aspects of psychological well-being. (p. 433)

   Family: _______________

   ____

   Friendships: _______________

   ____

Vocational Life

1. Work (does / does not) continue to be a salient aspect of identity and self-esteem in middle adulthood. (p. 433)
2. What two factors will contribute to the dramatic rise in the number of older workers during the next few decades? (p. 433)

   A. ______________________________

   B. ______________________________

Job Satisfaction

1. Research shows that job satisfaction (increases / decreases) in midlife at all occupational levels. (p. 433)
2. Describe one aspect of job satisfaction that rises with age and one that remains stable. (p. 433)

   Rises: ______________________________

   Remains stable: ______________________________
3. Under what conditions does *burnout* occur, and why is it a serious occupational hazard? (p. 434)

   A. ______________________________

   B. ______________________________
4. How can employers prevent burnout? (p. 434)

   ____

Career Development

1. True or False: Research suggests that training and on-the-job career counseling are more available to older workers. (p. 434)
2. List personal and workplace characteristics that influence employees' willingness to engage in job training and updating. (p. 434)

   A. ______________________________

   ____

   B. ______________________________

   ____
3. How do age-balanced work groups foster on-the-job learning? (p. 434)

   ____
4. Cite workplace factors that contribute to a *glass ceiling* for women and ethnic minorities. (p. 434)

   ____

   ____

   ____

   ____

5. More than ________ of all start-up businesses in the United States are owned and operated by women. How successful are these businesses? (p. 435)

____

____

Planning for Retirement

1. True or False: Most workers report looking forward to retirement. (p. 435)
2. What are some benefits of retirement planning? (p. 435)

____

____

3. Less educated people with lower lifetime earnings are (most / least) likely to attend retirement preparation programs. (p. 435)
4. True or False: Financial planning is more important than planning for an active life in promoting happiness after retirement. (p. 435)

PUZZLE 16.1 TERM REVIEW

Across

2. ______ imperative theory claims that traditional gender roles are maintained during the active parenting years to help ensure the survival of children
3. ______ selves: future-oriented representations of what one hopes to become and is afraid of becoming
5. Role assumed by members of the middle generation who take responsibility for gathering the family for celebrations and making sure everyone stays in touch
6. Generativity versus ______ : Erikson's psychological conflict of midlife
8. Middle-aged adults who are squeezed between the needs of aging parents and financially dependent children are known as the ______ generation
9. Glass ______ : invisible barrier to advancement up the corporate ladder faced by women and ethnic minorities
10. The ______ crisis refers to inner turmoil, self-doubt, and major restructuring of personality during the transition to middle adulthood

Down

1. ______ of poverty: trend in which women who support themselves or their families have become the majority of the adult poverty population
4. Condition in which long-term job stress leads to emotional exhaustion, a sense of loss of personal control, and feelings of reduced accomplishment
6. ______-generation family: children live with grandparents but apart from parents
7. ______ ______ personality traits: five basic factors into which hundreds of personality traits have been organized: neuroticism, extroversion, openness to experience, agreeableness, and conscientiousness (2 words)

CROSSWORD PUZZLE SOLUTION

PUZZLE 16.1

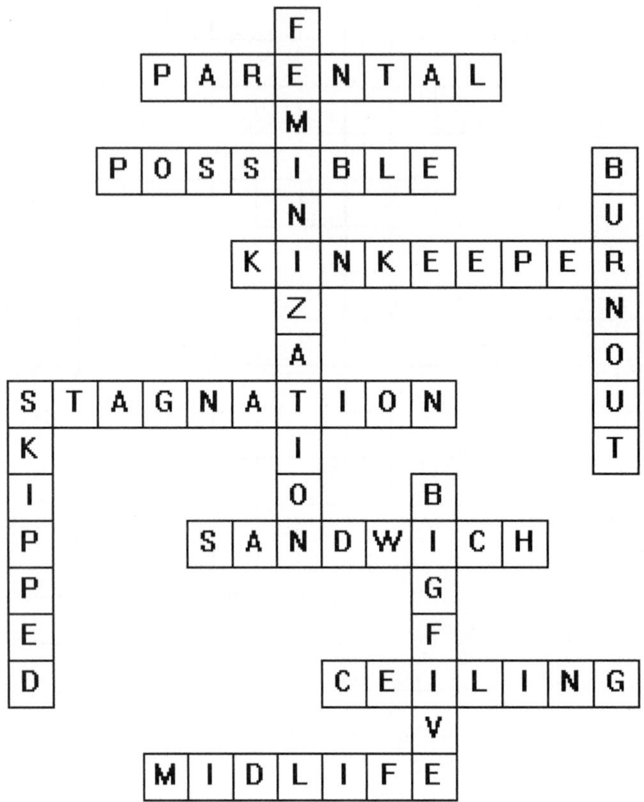

PRACTICE TEST #1

1. In midlife, generativity expands greatly when (p. 417)
   a. individuals become more self-centered and self-indulgent.
   b. midlifers finally place their own comfort above sacrifice.
   c. a focus on what one can get from others replaces a focus on what one can give.
   d. commitment extends beyond oneself to a larger group.

2. According to Erikson, a culture's ________________ is a major motivator of generative action. (p. 418)
   a. attitude toward peace
   b. belief in the species
   c. sense of security
   d. set of support systems

3. In middle adulthood, some individuals choose to participate in activities that advance human welfare. Which of Levinson's developmental tasks are these individuals attempting to reconcile? (p. 419)
   a. masculinity–femininity
   b. young–old
   c. engagement–separateness
   d. destruction–creation

4. As people approach the end of middle age, they tend to focus on (p. 421)
   a. shorter-term, career-oriented goals.
   b. personal, physical goals.
   c. longer-term, less personal goals.
   d. specific, household goals.

5. Levinson reported that during the transition to middle adulthood, most men and women in his samples experienced (p. 421)
   a. substantial inner turmoil.
   b. slow, steady changes.
   c. smooth acceptance of aging.
   d. personal and financial gratification.

6. Sharp disruption and agitation during the midlife transition (p. 421)
   a. are common experiences among adults.
   b. are more the exception than the rule.
   c. ultimately result in favorable adjustment.
   d. are more common in men than in women.

7. At lunch, Louisa tells a colleague, "I'm thinking about changing jobs. I feel like I'm doing the same thing day after day. Or maybe I can save some money and start a small business in a few years. I've always wanted to do that, and if I don't do it soon, it will never happen." Louisa is discussing (p. 422)
   a. possible selves.
   b. emotion-centered coping.
   c. environmental mastery.
   d. self-acceptance.

8. Research on well-educated adults ranging in age from the late teens into the seventies, the following three traits increased from early to middle adulthood and then leveled off: (p. 422)
   a. self-acceptance, self-concept, and possible selves
   b. self-acceptance, autonomy, and possible selves
   c. self-concept, patience, and autonomy
   d. self-acceptance, autonomy, and environmental mastery

9. Midlife brings an increase in the use of effective coping strategies. For example, middle-aged people are more likely to (p. 422)
   a. not care very much about problems.
   b. take immediate action to resolve problems.
   c. look for the positive side of a difficult situation.
   d. avoid using humor to express their feelings about problems.

10. Studies of gender identity in midlife reveal (p. 424)
   a. an increase in "masculine" traits in women.
   b. an increase in "feminine" traits in women.
   c. an increase in "masculine" traits in men.
   d. no increase in either "masculine" or "feminine" traits in men.

11. Studies of men and women show that from the teenage years through middle age, (p. 425)
   a. agreeableness and conscientiousness increase.
   b. extroversion and agreeableness increase.
   c. neuroticism and openness to experience increase.
   d. neuroticism and agreeableness do not change.

12. When people in midlife divorce, they usually (p. 426)
   a. have more difficulty adapting than young adults.
   b. adapt in much the same way as young adults.
   c. adapt more easily than young adults.
   d. direct their anger toward their children.

13. In inner cities, welfare recipients, regardless of age and ethnicity, often include a large number of single mothers. This trend is an example of (p. 426)
   a. the parental imperative theory.
   b. the feminization of poverty.
   c. environmental mastery.
   d. feminine midlife crises.

14. Once young adults strike out on their own, members of the middle generation, especially mothers, often take on the kinkeeper role, which involves (p. 427)
   a. supporting their adult children financially.
   b. providing child care for their grandchildren.
   c. moving to a new residence closer to a grown child, usually a daughter.
   d. gathering the family for celebrations and making sure everyone stays in touch.

15. Most people experience grandparenthood as a (p. 427)
   a. burdensome reminder of old age.
   b. significant milestone.
   c. time to reflect on past mistakes.
   d. period of resurgence in youthful energy.

16. Which pair typically has the closest relationship? (p. 428)
   a. maternal grandmother and granddaughter
   b. paternal grandfather and grandson
   c. maternal grandfather and granddaughter
   d. paternal grandmother and grandson

17. In skipped-generation families, grandparents most often step in to raise grandchildren because of (p. 429)
   a. parental physical illness.
   b. parental emotional illness.
   c. child abuse and neglect.
   d. parents' substance-abuse problems.

18. When an aging person's spouse cannot provide care, the relative who is most likely to do so is (p. 430)
    a. an adult son.
    b. a younger sibling.
    c. an adult daughter.
    d. an adult granddaughter.

19. Research shows that in midlife, and at all occupational levels, job satisfaction (p. 433)
    a. increases.
    b. decreases.
    c. remains unchanged.
    d. increases at a higher rate for women than for men.

20. Willingness to engage in job training and updating in midlife is influenced by (p. 434)
    a. co-worker and supervisor encouragement.
    b. participation in work groups that include younger people.
    c. simplified work tasks.
    d. negative stereotypes of aging.

PRACTICE TEST #2

1. Adults with a sense of stagnation (p. 418)
    a. are well-adjusted and report a high level of life satisfaction.
    b. possess leadership qualities and are open to differing viewpoints.
    c. cannot contribute to the welfare of society because they place their own comfort and security above challenge and sacrifice.
    d. view themselves as role models and sources of wisdom for their children.

2. According to Levinson, middle adulthood begins with a transitional period that spans the ages from (p. 419)
    a. 30 to 35.
    b. 35 to 40.
    c. 40 to 45.
    d. 45 to 50.

3. Rebuilding the life structure during middle adulthood depends on (p. 420)
    a. supportive social contexts.
    b. dramatic revision of family and occupational commitments.
    c. success in confronting the double standard of aging.
    d. strengthening of gender-typed characteristics.

4. As a young adult, Christian dreamed of being a great athlete and a very successful businessman. At age 40, as a high-paid administrator for a large corporation, he has largely attained one of those goals. As he enters middle adulthood, Christian will probably (p. 422)
    a. strive harder to make his current self match his early dreams.
    b. become depressed because he has not achieved all of his goals.
    c. focus less on his business success and more on athletic pursuits in an attempt to recapture his youth.
    d. concentrate more on nurturing personal relationships and on performing competently at work.

5. As individuals reach adulthood with less time left to make life changes, their __________ plays a significant role in their well-being. (p. 421)
    a. tendency toward experiencing a midlife crisis
    b. interpretation of life regrets
    c. lack of possible selves
    d. declining sense of autonomy

6. According to parental imperative theory, identification with traditional gender roles is maintained during active parenting years to help ensure (p. 424)
   a. that mothers will remain with children if fathers do not.
   b. that children receive warmth from their mothers and discipline from their fathers.
   c. that children develop androgynous traits.
   d. the survival of children.

7. Neuroticism, extroversion, and openness to experience (p. 425)
   a. show a sharp increase from early to middle adulthood.
   b. are common among well-adjusted adults.
   c. show modest declines or remain unchanged from the teenage years through middle age.
   d. are often transformed into agreeableness and conscientiousness in midlife.

8. Studies show that 9 out of 10 middle-aged North Americans (p. 426)
   a. live with families, usually with a spouse.
   b. live alone after their children are grown.
   c. are or will eventually be divorced.
   d. come from families that have experienced divorce.

9. Although most divorces occur within 5 to 10 years of marriage, ___ percent take place after 20 years or more. (p. 426)
   a. 5
   b. 7
   c. 10
   d. 15

10. In the southern European countries of Greece, Italy, and Spain, middle-aged parents (p. 427)
    a. do not experience the "launching children" phase of the family life cycle.
    b. encourage their children to leave home during the teenage years.
    c. actively delay their children's departure from the home.
    d. have more conflict-ridden relationships with adult children than northern Europeans.

11. When parent–child contact and affection are sustained, (p. 427)
    a. departure of children from the home is a relatively mild event.
    b. mothers and fathers are able to maintain parental authority.
    c. parents' life satisfaction declines.
    d. adult children must struggle to become independent and accomplished.

12. Marcia's ability to keep her family of grown children together by holding bimonthly parties and get-togethers at her home shows that she has (p. 427)
    a. mastered her femininity.
    b. become more androgynous.
    c. adopted the parental imperative theory.
    d. taken on the role of kinkeeper.

13. From 1900 to the present, the percentage of North American middle-aged people with living parents has (p. 428)
    a. risen from 10 percent to 20 percent.
    b. risen from 10 percent to 25 percent.
    c. risen from 10 percent to 50 percent.
    d. fallen from 10 percent to 5 percent.

14. Compared with adult children who assist in the care of aging parents while maintaining a separate residence, those who live with an ill or disabled parent (p. 431)
    a. experience more stress.
    b. are more well-adjusted.
    c. have less role overload.
    d. rarely find rewards in parental caregiving.

15. In the United States and Canada, in-home care of an ill, elder parent by a nonfamily caregiver is (p. 431)
    a. readily available and government supported.
    b. generally not an option because of its high cost.
    c. patterned after the Swedish home helper system.
    d. rarely used because it does not relieve stress on the family caregiver.

16. During middle adulthood, many siblings (p. 432)
    a. spend more time together than they did in early adulthood.
    b. report strained relations.
    c. feel closer than they did in early adulthood.
    d. provide each other with more support than at any other time of life.

17. The aspect of job satisfaction that shows the greatest age-related gain in midlife is (p. 433)
    a. contentment with supervision.
    b. satisfaction with opportunities for promotion.
    c. satisfaction with pay.
    d. happiness with the work itself.

18. Burnout occurs more often in (p. 434)
    a. young workers.
    b. helping professions.
    c. high-income professions.
    d. men.

19. Women face a glass ceiling in their careers because (p. 434)
    a. they are less effective managers than men.
    b. modern businesses realize that the best managers display "masculine" traits.
    c. they have less access to mentors, role models, and informal networks than men.
    d. they are less committed to their careers than men.

20. Even though it is essential for better retirement and adjustment, nearly ______ of middle-aged people engage in no concrete retirement planning (p. 435)
    a. one-fourth
    b. one-third
    c. half
    d. two-thirds

POWERPOINT SLIDES

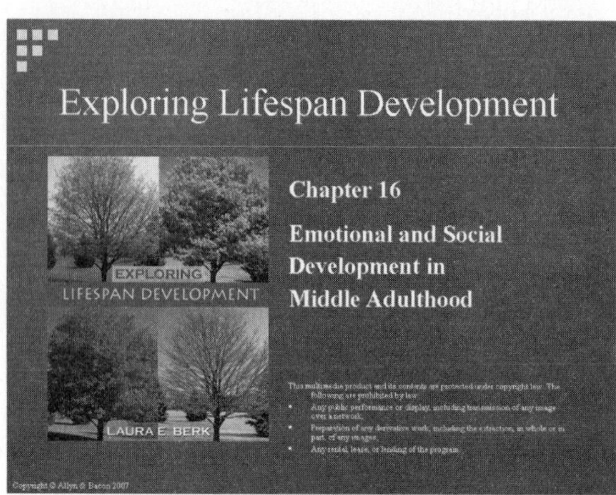

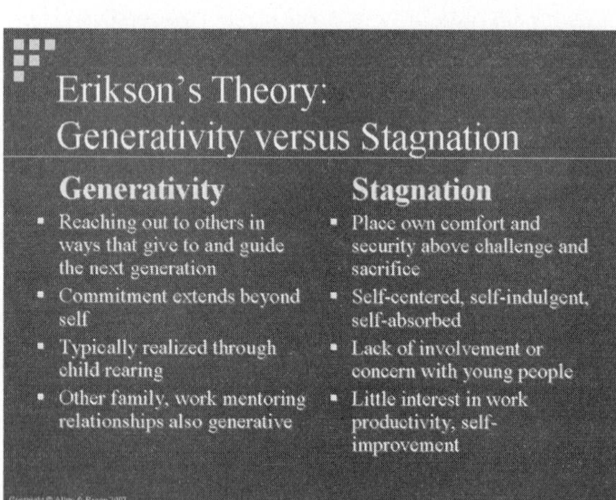

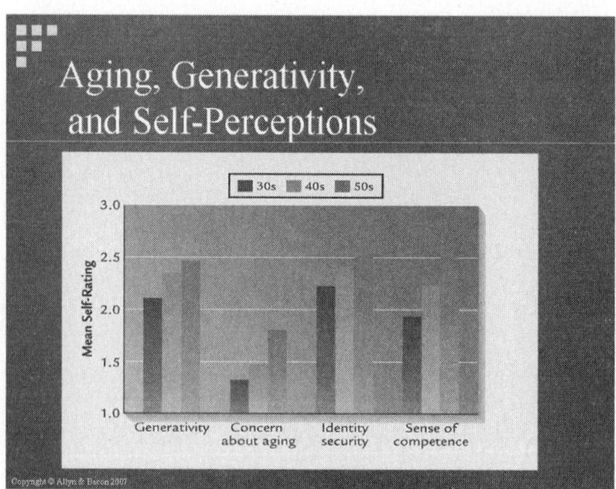

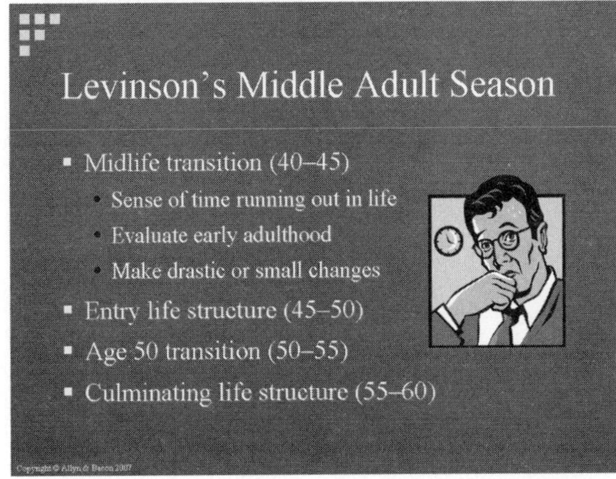

Levinson's Four Tasks of Middle Adulthood

Young–Old	Find new ways of being both young and old
Destruction–Creation	Acknowledge past destructiveness, try to create products of value
Masculinity–Femininity	Balance masculine and feminine parts of self
Engagement–Separateness	Balance involvement with external world and separateness from it

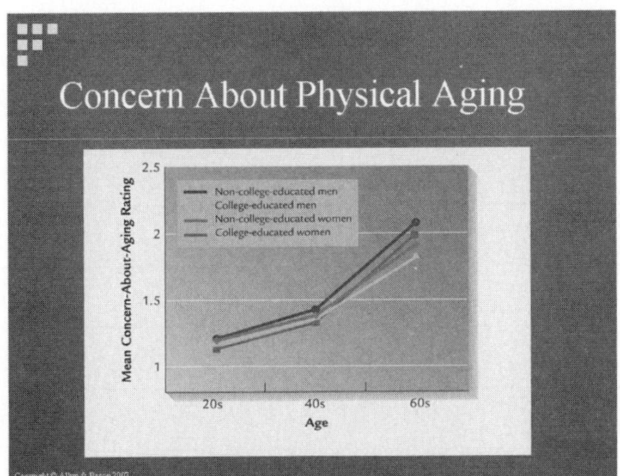

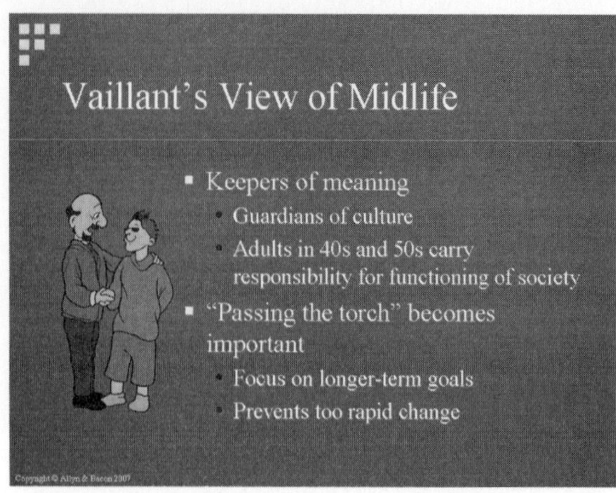
Vaillant's View of Midlife
Keepers of meaning
Guardians of culture
Adults in 40s and 50s carry responsibility for functioning of society
"Passing the torch" becomes important
Focus on longer-term goals
Prevents too rapid change

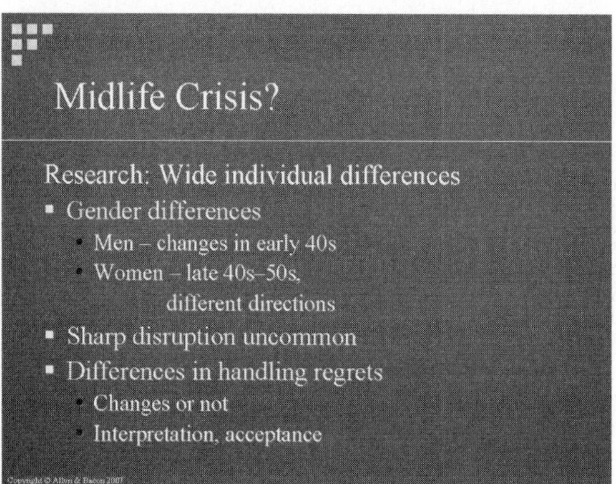
Midlife Crisis?
Research: Wide individual differences
Gender differences
Men – changes in early 40s
Women – late 40s–50s, different directions
Sharp disruption uncommon
Differences in handling regrets
Changes or not
Interpretation, acceptance

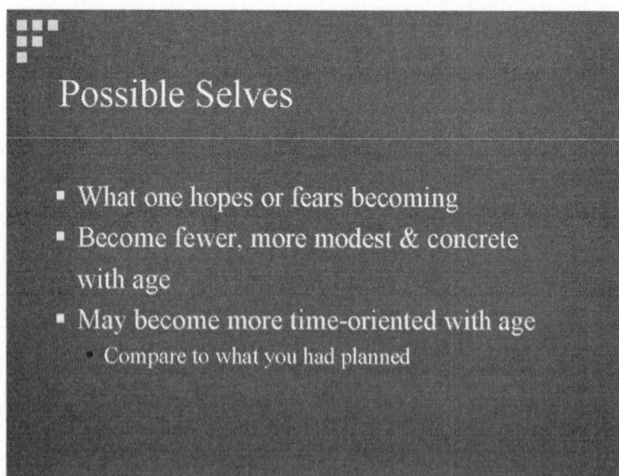
Possible Selves
What one hopes or fears becoming
Become fewer, more modest & concrete with age
May become more time-oriented with age
Compare to what you had planned

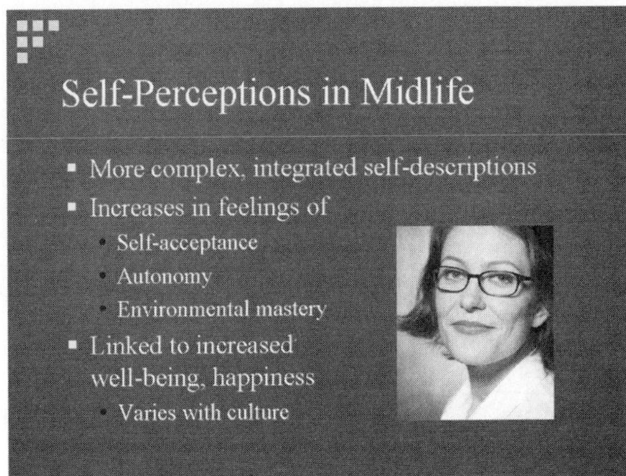
Self-Perceptions in Midlife
More complex, integrated self-descriptions
Increases in feelings of
Self-acceptance
Autonomy
Environmental mastery
Linked to increased well-being, happiness
Varies with culture
Copyright © Allyn & Bacon 2007

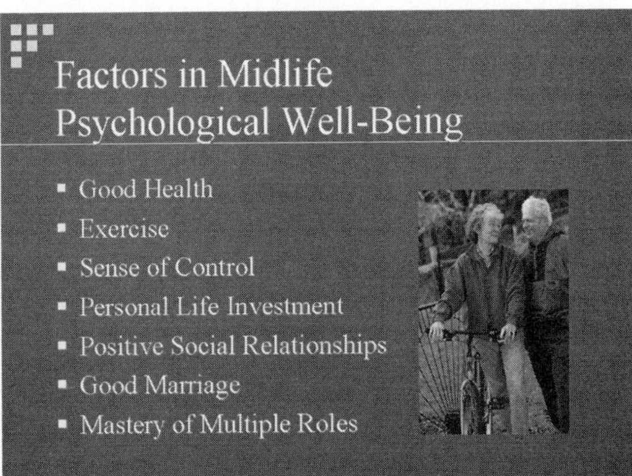
Factors in Midlife Psychological Well-Being
Good Health
Exercise
Sense of Control
Personal Life Investment
Positive Social Relationships
Good Marriage
Mastery of Multiple Roles
Copyright © Allyn & Bacon 2007

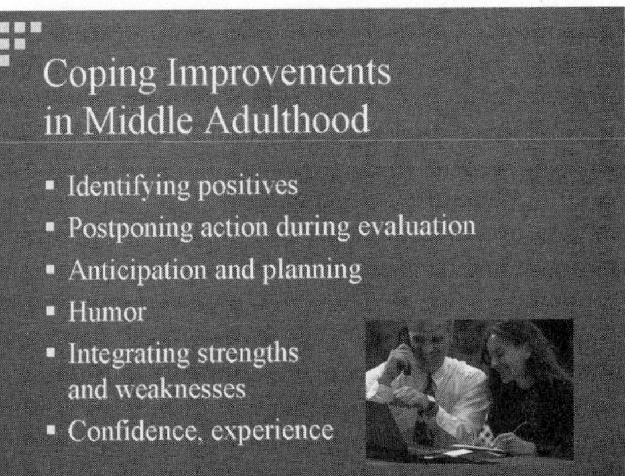
Coping Improvements in Middle Adulthood
Identifying positives
Postponing action during evaluation
Anticipation and planning
Humor
Integrating strengths and weaknesses
Confidence, experience
Copyright © Allyn & Bacon 2007

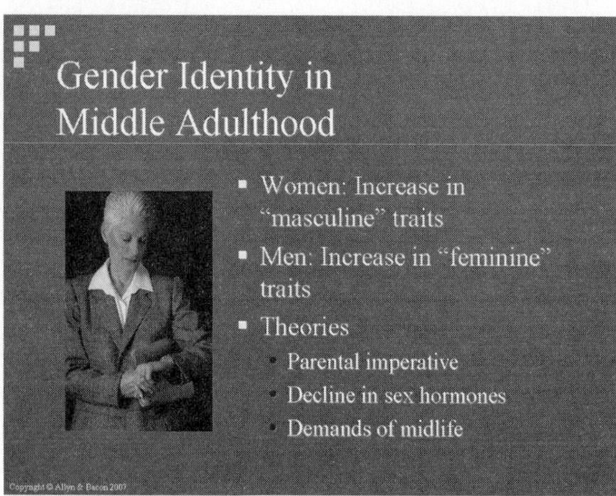
Gender Identity in Middle Adulthood
Women: Increase in "masculine" traits
Men: Increase in "feminine" traits
Theories
Parental imperative
Decline in sex hormones
Demands of midlife
Copyright © Allyn & Bacon 2007

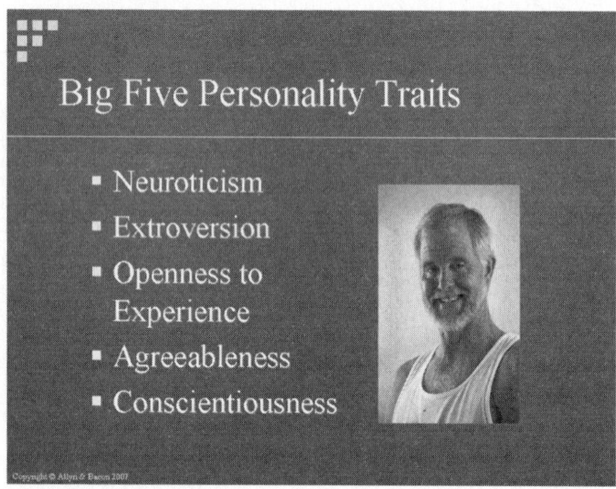
Big Five Personality Traits
Neuroticism
Extroversion
Openness to Experience
Agreeableness
Conscientiousness
Copyright © Allyn & Bacon 2007

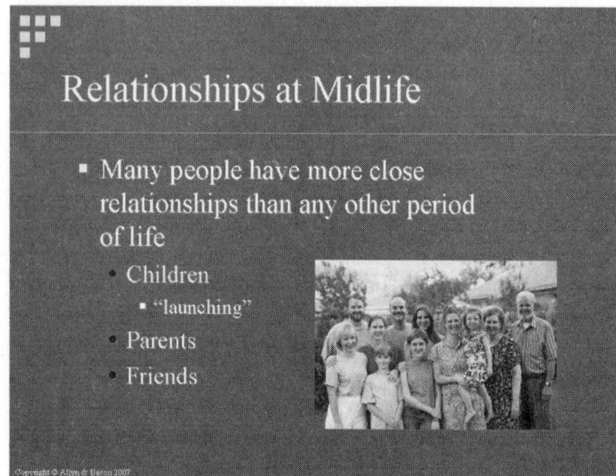
Relationships at Midlife
Many people have more close relationships than any other period of life
Children
"launching"
Parents
Friends
Copyright © Allyn & Bacon 2007

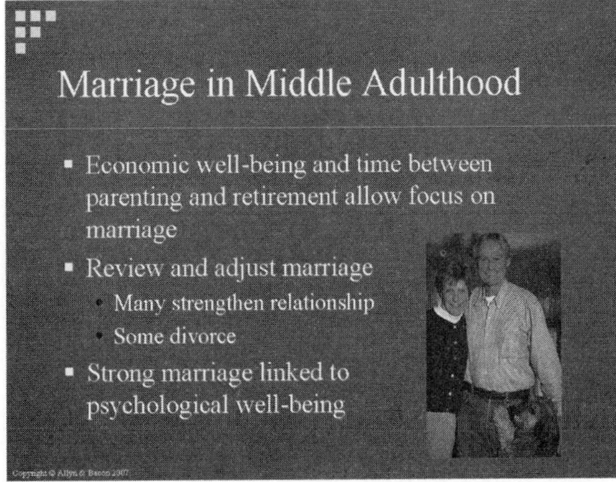

Divorce in Midlife

- Midlifers adjust more easily than young adults
  - Practical problem solving
  - Effective coping strategies
- Feminization of poverty

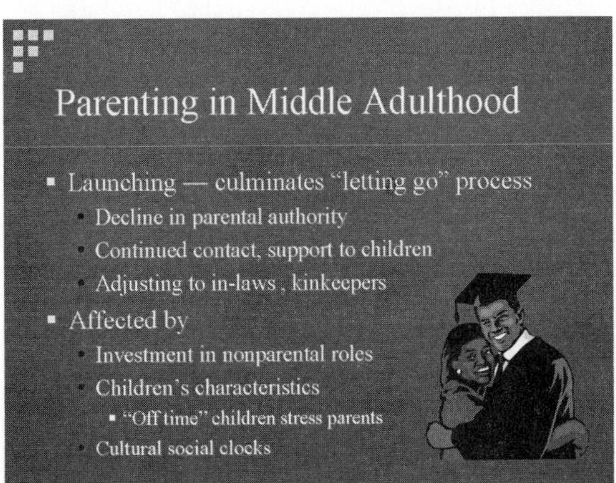

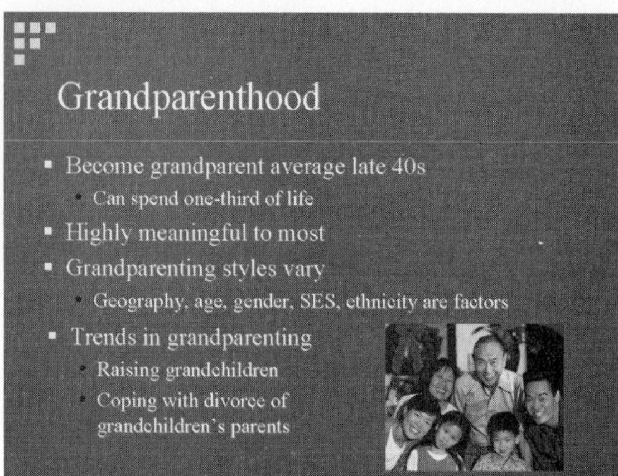
Grandparenthood
Become grandparent average late 40s
Can spend one-third of life
Highly meaningful to most
Grandparenting styles vary
Geography, age, gender, SES, ethnicity are factors
Trends in grandparenting
Raising grandchildren
Coping with divorce of grandchildren's parents

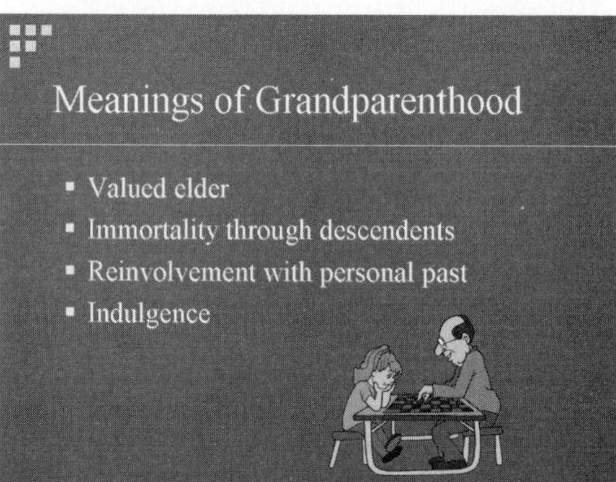
Meanings of Grandparenthood
Valued elder
Immortality through descendents
Reinvolvement with personal past
Indulgence

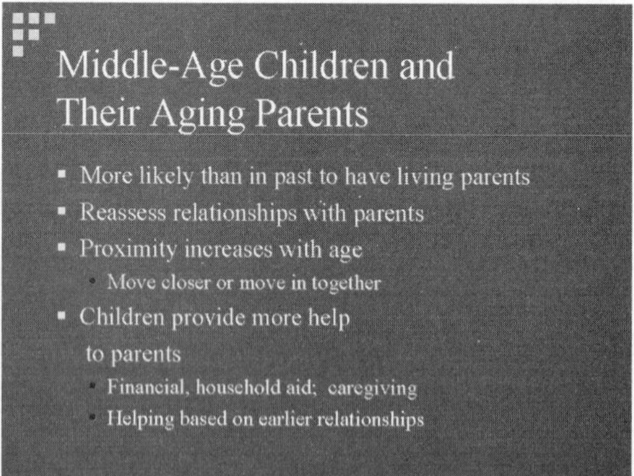
Middle-Age Children and Their Aging Parents
More likely than in past to have living parents
Reassess relationships with parents
Proximity increases with age
Move closer or move in together
Children provide more help to parents
Financial, household aid; caregiving
Helping based on earlier relationships

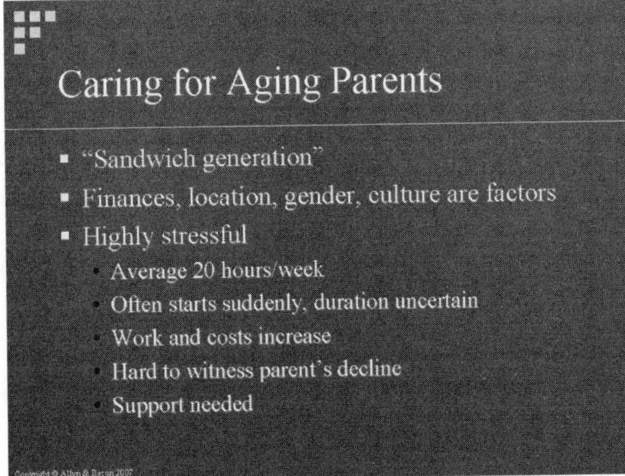
Caring for Aging Parents
"Sandwich generation"
Finances, location, gender, culture are factors
Highly stressful
Average 20 hours/week
Often starts suddenly, duration uncertain
Work and costs increase
Hard to witness parent's decline
Support needed

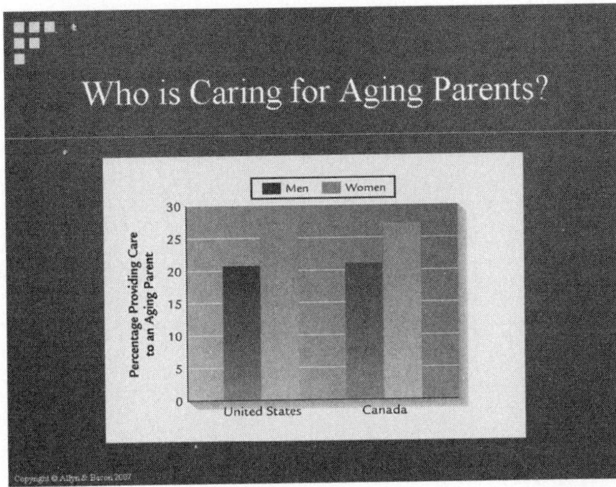
Who is Caring for Aging Parents?
Men
Women
Percentage Providing Care to an Aging Parent
30
25
20
15
10
5
0
United States
Canada

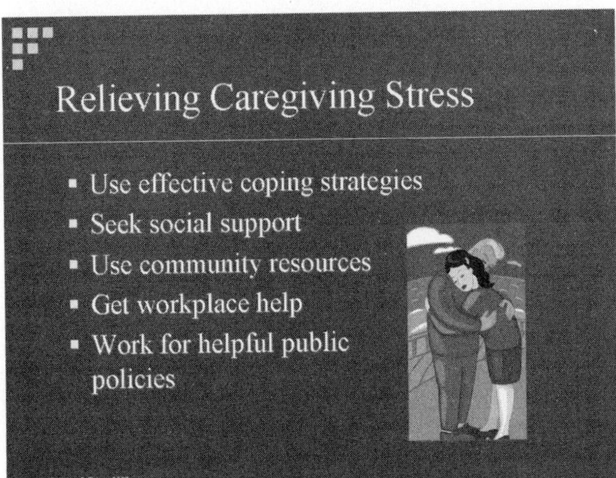
Relieving Caregiving Stress
Use effective coping strategies
Seek social support
Use community resources
Get workplace help
Work for helpful public policies

Siblings in Middle Adulthood
Contact and support decline during middle adulthood
Demands of diverse roles
Still, often feel closer
Share similar events
Affected by
Earlier relations
Culture
Copyright © Allyn & Bacon 2007

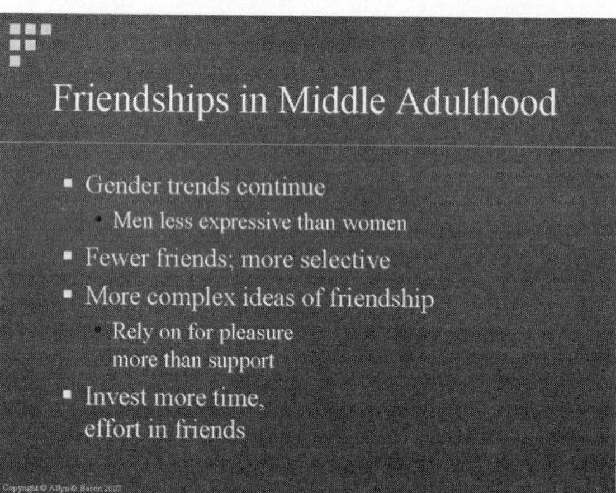
Friendships in Middle Adulthood
Gender trends continue
Men less expressive than women
Fewer friends; more selective
More complex ideas of friendship
Rely on for pleasure more than support
Invest more time, effort in friends
Copyright © Allyn & Bacon 2007

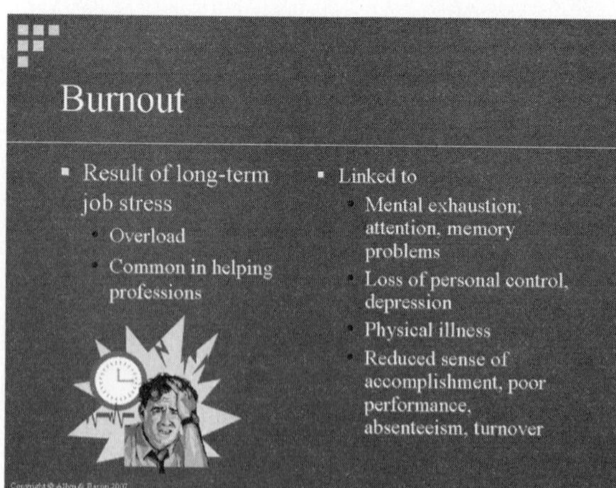
Burnout
Result of long-term job stress
Overload
Common in helping professions
Linked to
Mental exhaustion; attention, memory problems
Loss of personal control, depression
Physical illness
Reduced sense of accomplishment, poor performance, absenteeism, turnover
Copyright © Allyn & Bacon 2007

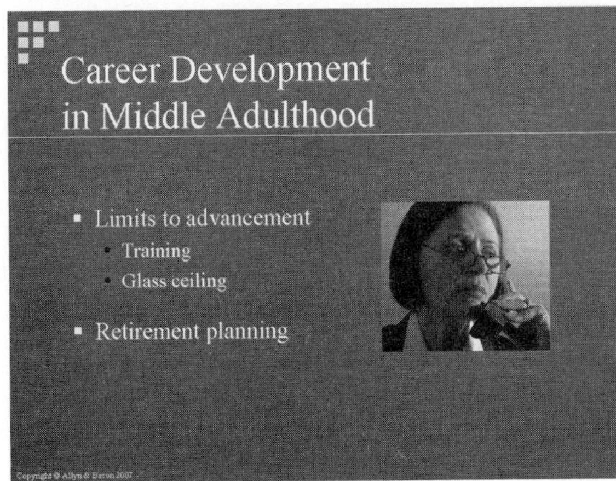
Career Development
in Middle Adulthood
Limits to advancement
Training
Glass ceiling
Retirement planning

Influences on
Interest in Job Training
Personal
Desire to change
Growth v. security needs
Coworkers, supervisor
Stereotypes
Self-efficacy
Job
Challenging tasks
Co-workers, teams

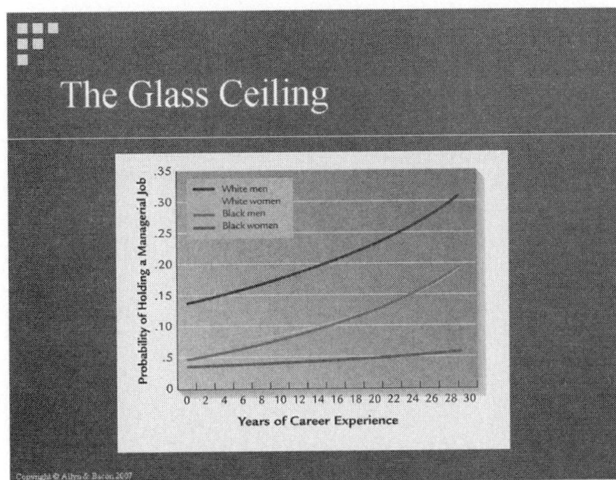
The Glass Ceiling
Probability of Holding a Managerial Job
White men
White women
Black men
Black women
Years of Career Experience

CHAPTER 17
PHYSICAL AND COGNITIVE DEVELOPMENT IN LATE ADULTHOOD

CHAPTER-AT-A-GLANCE

Chapter Outline	Instruction Ideas	Supplements
Physical Development **Life Expectancy pp. 441–443** Variations in Life Expectancy • Life Expectancy in Late Adulthood • Maximum Lifespan	Learning Objective 17.1 Learning Activity 17.1	Transparency 184 Test Bank Items 1–14 Videos: *Exploring Lifespan Development in Action* and *A Window on Lifespan Development* Please contact your Allyn and Bacon publisher's representative for a wide range of video offerings available to adopters.
Physical Changes pp. 443–450 Nervous System • Sensory Systems • Cardiovascular and Respiratory Systems • Immune System • Sleep • Physical Appearance and Mobility • Adapting to Physical Changes of Late Adulthood	Learning Objectives 17.2–17.6 Lecture Enhancement 17.1 Learning Activities 17.1–17.4 Ask Yourself p. 450	Transparencies 186, 187 Test Bank Items 15–41
Health, Fitness, and Disability pp. 450–460 Nutrition and Exercise • Sexuality • Physical Disabilities • Mental Disabilities • Health Care	Learning Objectives 17.7–7.10 Lecture Enhancement 17.2 Learning Activities 17.5–17.6 Ask Yourself p. 460	Transparencies 189, 190 Test Bank Items 42–89
Cognitive Development **Memory pp. 461–463** Deliberate versus Automatic Memory • Associative Memory • Remote Memory • Prospective Memory	Learning Objectives 17.11 Learning Activity 17.7	Transparency 192 Test Bank Items 90–101
Language Processing p. 463	Learning Objective 17.12 Lecture Enhancement 17.3	Test Bank Items 102–105
Problem Solving pp. 463–464	Learning Objective 17.13	Test Bank Items 106–108
Wisdom pp. 464–465	Learning Objective 17.14	Test Bank Items 109–111
Factors Related to Cognitive Change p. 465	Learning Objective 17.15	Test Bank Items 112–116
Cognitive Interventions pp. 465–466	Learning Objective 17.16 Learning Activity 17.7	Test Bank Item 117
Lifelong Learning pp. 466–467	Learning Objective 17.17 Lecture Enhancement 17.4 Learning Activities 17.8–17.9 Ask Yourself p. 467	Test Bank Items 118–121

BRIEF CHAPTER SUMMARY

Vastly different rates of aging are apparent in late adulthood. A complex array of genetic and environmental factors combine to determine longevity. Dramatic gains in average life expectancy—the number of years that an individual born in a particular year can expect to live—provide powerful support for the multiplicity of factors that slow biological aging, including improved nutrition, medical treatment, sanitation, and safety. Although most North Americans over age 65 can live independently, some need assistance with activities of daily living or, more commonly, with instrumental activities of daily living, such as shopping and paying bills.

The programmed effects of specific genes as well as the random cellular events believed to underlie biological aging make physical declines more apparent in late adulthood. Although aging of the nervous system affects a range of complex thoughts and activities, research reveals that the brain can respond adaptively to some of these age-related cognitive declines. Changes in sensory functioning become increasingly noticeable in late life: Older adults see and hear less well, and taste, smell, and touch sensitivity may also decline. Hearing impairments are far more common than visual impairments and affect many more men than women.

Aging of the cardiovascular and respiratory systems becomes more apparent in late adulthood. As at earlier ages, not smoking, reducing dietary fat, avoiding environmental pollutants, and exercising can slow the effects of aging on these systems. A less competent immune system can increase the elderly person's risk for a variety of illnesses, including infectious diseases, cardiovascular disease, certain forms of cancer, and a variety of autoimmune disorders.

As people age, they have more difficulty falling asleep, staying asleep, and sleeping deeply. Outward signs of aging, such as white hair, wrinkled and sagging skin, age spots, and decreases in height and weight, become more noticeable in late adulthood. Problem-centered coping strategies yield improved physical functioning in the elderly, and assistive technology is increasingly available to help older people cope with physical declines.

Physical and mental health are intimately related in late life. The physical changes of late life lead to an increased need for certain nutrients, and exercise continues to be a powerful health intervention. Although sexual desire and frequency of sexual activity decline in older people, longitudinal evidence indicates that most healthy older married couples report continued, regular sexual enjoyment. Illness and disability climb as the end of the lifespan approaches. Cardiovascular disease, cancer, and stroke claim many lives, while arthritis and adult-onset diabetes increase substantially. At age 65 and older, the death rate from unintentional injuries is at an all-time high.

When cell death and structural and chemical abnormalities are profound, serious deterioration of mental and motor functions occurs. Alzheimer's disease, the most common form of dementia, can be either familial (which runs in families) or sporadic (where there is no obvious family history). With no cure available, family interventions ensure the best adjustment possible for the Alzheimer's victim, spouse, and other relatives. Careful diagnosis is crucial because other disorders can be misidentified as dementia. Family members provide most long-term care, especially among ethnic minorities. Individual differences in cognitive functioning are greater in late adulthood than at any other time of life. As older adults take in information more slowly and find it harder to apply strategies, inhibit irrelevant information, and retrieve knowledge from long-term memory, the chance of memory failure increases. Research shows that language and memory skills are closely related. Although language comprehension changes very little in late life, retrieving words from long-term memory and planning what to say become more difficult. Finally, traditional problem solving, in the absence of real-life context, declines.

Cultures around the world assume that age and wisdom go together. Older adults with the cognitive, reflective, and emotional qualities that make up wisdom tend to be better educated and physically healthier and to forge more positive relations with others. As in middle adulthood, a mentally active life—above average education, stimulating leisure pursuits, community participation, and a flexible personality—predicts maintenance of mental abilities into advanced old age. And interventions that train the elderly in cognitive strategies can partially reverse age-related declines in mental ability. Elders who participate in continuing education through university courses, community offerings, and programs such as Elderhostel, are enriched by new knowledge, new friends, a broader perspective on the world, and an image of themselves as more competent.

LEARNING OBJECTIVES

After reading this chapter, you should be able to:

17.1 Distinguish between chronological age and functional age, and discuss variations in life expectancy over the past century. (pp. 441–443)

17.2 Describe changes in the nervous system during late adulthood. (pp. 443–445)

17.3 Summarize changes in sensory functioning during late adulthood, including vision, hearing, taste, smell, and touch. (pp. 445–447)

17.4 Describe cardiovascular, respiratory, and immune system changes in late adulthood. (p. 447)

17.5 Discuss sleep difficulties in late adulthood. (p. 447)

17.6 Summarize changes in physical appearance and mobility, including elders' adaptation to the physical changes of late adulthood, and reactions to stereotypes of aging. (pp. 448–450)

17.7 Discuss health and fitness in late life, paying special attention to nutrition, exercise, and sexuality. (pp. 450–452)

17.8 Discuss common physical disabilities in late adulthood, including arthritis, adult-onset diabetes, and unintentional injuries. (pp. 452–455)

17.9 Describe mental disabilities common in late adulthood, including Alzheimer's disease, cerebrovascular dementia, and misdiagnosed and reversible dementia. (pp. 455–459)

17.10 Discuss health care issues that affect senior citizens. (pp. 459–460)

17.11 Summarize memory changes in late life, including implicit, associative, remote, and prospective memories. (pp. 460–463)

17.12 Describe changes in language processing in late adulthood. (p. 463)

17.13 Summarize changes in problem solving during late adulthood. (p. 463–464)

17.14 Discuss the capacities that contribute to wisdom, noting how it is affected by age and life experience. (pp. 464–465)

17.15 Cite factors related to cognitive change in late adulthood. (p. 465)

17.16 Explain how cognitive interventions help older adults sustain their mental abilities. (p. 465–466)

17.17 Describe types of continuing education and benefits of participation in such programs in late life. (pp. 466–467)

LECTURE OUTLINE

Physical Development

I. LIFE EXPECTANCY (pp. 441–443)
   A. Chronological age is an imperfect indicator of **functional age,** which refers to the actual competence and performance of an older adult.
   B. **Average life expectancy** is the number of years that an individual born in a particular year can expect to live.
      1. In 2004, this figure reached 77.9 in the United States and 80.1 in Canada.
      2. Steady declines in infant mortality are a major contributor to longer life expectancy, as are lower death rates among adults resulting from advances in medical treatment.

C. Variations in Life Expectancy (pp. 442–443)
  1. Women tend to live 4 to 7 years longer than men, although this gap has narrowed in industrialized nations.
  2. SES, ethnicity, and nationality also influence life expectancy because of higher rates of infant mortality, unintentional injuries, life-threatening disease, poverty-linked stress, and, in the United States, violent death in low-SES minority groups.
  3. **Active lifespan** refers to the number of years of vigorous, healthy life an individual born in a particular year can expect.
    a. Japan ranks first, Canada twelfth, and the United States a disappointing twenty-fourth.
    b. In developing nations with widespread poverty, malnutrition, disease, and armed conflict, active lifespan hovers around 50 years.

D. Life Expectancy in Late Adulthood (p. 443)
  1. The number of people age 65 and older has risen dramatically in the industrialized world.
  2. People reaching age 65 in the early twenty-first century can look forward, on the average, to 18 more years of life in the United States and 19 more in Canada.
  3. Although women continue to outnumber men with advancing age, these gender discrepancies in life expectancy decline as people get older, and the gender gap disappears after age 100.
  4. Around age 85, a **life expectancy crossover** occurs, in that surviving members of low-SES ethnic minority groups live longer than members of the white majority.
  5. Researchers speculate that only the sturdiest males and members of these low-SES groups survive into very old age.
  6. The need for assistance:
    a. Although most Americans age 65 and older are capable of living independent, productive lives, after age 70, about 10 percent have difficulty carrying out **activities of daily living (ADLs)**—basic self-care tasks required to live on one's own, such as bathing, dressing, getting in and out of bed or a chair, or eating.
    b. About 20 percent cannot carry out **instrumental activities of daily living (IADLs)**—tasks necessary to conduct the business of daily life and also requiring some cognitive competence, such as telephoning, shopping, food preparation, housekeeping, and paying bills.
    c. The proportion of elders with these limitations rises sharply with age.
  7. Genetic and environmental factors jointly affect aging.
    a. Identical twins typically die within 3 years of each other.
    b. People with long-lived ancestors tend to survive longer and to be physically healthier in old age.
    c. However, evidence from twin studies suggests that as we get older, the contribution of heredity to length of life decreases in favor of environmental factors, such as a healthy diet, normal body weight, regular exercise, an optimistic outlook, low psychological stress, social support, and little or no use of tobacco, alcohol, or drugs.

E. Maximum Lifespan (p. 443)
  1. **Maximum lifespan** refers to the genetic limit to length of life for a person free of external risk factors.
  2. For most people, maximum lifespan varies between 70 and 110, with 85 about average.
  3. The oldest verified age to which an individual has lived is 122 years.
  4. Researchers disagree on whether these figures represent the upper bound of human longevity.
  5. Most experts agree that only after reducing high rates of preventable illness and disability among low-SES individuals and wiping out age-related diseases should we invest in lengthening the maximum lifespan.

II. PHYSICAL CHANGES (pp. 443–450)

A. Nervous System (pp. 443–445)
  1. Aging of the central nervous system affects a wide range of complex thoughts and activities.
  2. Although brain weight declines throughout adulthood, the loss becomes greater after age 60 and may be as much as 5 to 10 percent by age 80, due to death of neurons and enlargement of ventricles (spaces) within the brain.

3. Neuron loss occurs throughout the cerebral cortex but at varying rates in different regions of the brain.
    a. The front lobes and the corpus callosum tend to show greater shrinkage than the parietal and temporal lobes, while the occipital lobes change very little.
    b. Glial cells, which myelinate neural fibers, decrease as well, contributing to diminished efficiency of the central nervous system.
4. However, the brain can overcome some of these declines.
    a. In several studies, growth of neural fibers in the brains of older adults unaffected by illness occurred at the same rate as in middle-aged people.
    b. Aging neurons established new synapses after other neurons had degenerated, and the aging cerebral cortex can, to some degree, generate new neurons.
5. The autonomic nervous system, involved in many life support functions, also performs less well in old age.
    a. Reduced tolerance for temperature extremes puts elderly people at risk during heat waves and cold spells.
    b. The autonomic nervous system also releases higher levels of stress hormones into the bloodstream than it did earlier, perhaps in an effort to arouse body tissues that have become less responsive to these hormones over the years—a change that may contribute to decreased immunity and to sleep problems in older adults.

B. Sensory Systems (pp. 445–447)
1. Vision (pp. 445–446)
    a. Structural changes in the eye make it harder to focus on nearby objects, see in dim light, and perceive color.
    b. The cornea (clear covering of the eye) becomes more translucent and scatters light, which blurs images and increases sensitivity to glare.
    c. The lens continues to yellow, leading to further impairment in color discrimination.
    d. From middle to old age, cloudy areas in the lens called **cataracts** increase, resulting in foggy vision and (without surgery) eventual blindness.
        (1) The number of individuals with cataracts increases tenfold from middle to late adulthood, affecting 25 percent of people in their seventies and 50 percent of those in their eighties.
        (2) Removal of the lens and replacement with an artificial lens implant or corrective eyewear are very successful in restoring vision.
    e. Impaired eyesight in late adulthood largely results from a reduction in light reaching the retina, caused by yellowing of the lens, shrinking of the pupil, and clouding of the vitreous.
        (1) Dark adaptation—moving from a brightly lit to a dim environment—is harder.
        (2) Depth perception is less reliable, since binocular vision (the brain's ability to combine images received from both eyes) declines.
        (3) Visual acuity (fineness of discrimination) worsens, with a sharp drop after age 70.
    f. When blood flow to the macula, or central region of the retina, is restricted due to hardening of small blood vessels, older adults may develop a condition called **macular degeneration**, the leading cause of blindness in older adults, in which central vision blurs and gradually is lost.
        (1) If diagnosed early, macular degeneration can sometimes be treated with laser therapy.
        (2) Protective factors include a diet rich in green, leafy vegetables, which are sources of vitamins A, C, and E and carotenoids (yellow and red plant pigments); these are believed to protect cells in the macula from free-radical damage.
        (3) Vitamin pills, however, show no consistent benefits in preventing this condition.
    g. When vision loss is extensive, it can affect leisure pursuits and lead to isolation.
2. Hearing (p. 446)
    a. Hearing declines in late adulthood as a result of reduced blood supply and natural cell death in the inner ear and stiffening of membranes (such as the eardrum).
    b. Decrements are greatest at high frequencies, but detection of soft sounds diminishes throughout the frequency range, and responsiveness to startling noises also lessens in old age.
    c. Although hearing loss has less impact on self-care than vision loss, it affects safety and enjoyment of life.

d. Of all hearing difficulties, the age-related decline in speech perception has the greatest impact on life satisfaction; by attending to facial expressions, gestures, and lip movements, older adults can use vision to help interpret the spoken word.
e. As with vision, most elders do not suffer from hearing loss great enough to disrupt their daily lives.

3. Taste and Smell (p. 446)
   a. Reduced sensitivity to the four basic tastes—sweet, salty, sour, and bitter—is evident in many adults after age 60—a change that may be largely due to environmental factors such as smoking, dentures, medications, and environmental pollutants.
   b. When taste is harder to detect, food is less enjoyable, increasing the likelihood of deficiencies in the elderly person's diet.
   c. Besides enhancing enjoyment of food, smell also has a self-protective function, and an aging person who has difficulty detecting rancid food, gas fumes, or smoke may be in a life-threatening situation.
   d. A decrease in the number of smell receptors after age 60 undoubtedly contributes to declines in odor sensitivity.
   e. Researchers believe that odor perception becomes distorted in late adulthood, prompting complaints that "food no longer smells and tastes right."
4. Touch (pp. 446–447)
   a. Touch sensitivity is especially crucial for certain adults, including the severely visually impaired, who must read in Braille, and people who make fine judgments about texture in their occupations or leisure pursuits.
   b. Findings indicate that aging brings a sharp decline of sensitivity on the hands, particularly the fingertips, and a lesser decline on the arms and lips.
   c. Decreased touch sensitivity may be due to loss of touch receptors in certain regions of the skin and slowing of blood circulation to the extremities, affecting nearly all adults after age 70.

C. Cardiovascular and Respiratory Systems (p. 447)
1. Signs of aging of the cardiovascular and respiratory systems begin in early and middle adulthood but are not likely to be apparent until late adulthood.
2. Changes in the cardiovascular system:
   a. The heart muscle becomes more rigid.
   b. Some of its cells die while others enlarge, leading the walls of the left ventricle (the largest heart chamber, from which blood is pumped to the body) to thicken.
   c. Artery walls stiffen and accumulate some plaque (cholesterol and fats) due to normal aging (much more in those with atherosclerosis).
   d. The heart muscle becomes less responsive to signals from pacemaker cells within the heart, which initiate each contraction.
3. As a combined result of these changes, the heart pumps with less force, maximum heart rate decreases, and blood flow throughout the circulatory system slows, so that sufficient oxygen may not be delivered to body tissues during high physical activity.
4. Changes in the respiratory system:
   a. Lung tissue loses its elasticity, so the lungs fill and empty less efficiently, compounding the effects of reduced oxygenation of the heart.
   b. As the blood absorbs less oxygen and gives off less carbon dioxide, older people increase their breathing rate more and feel more out of breath while exercising.
5. Cardiovascular and respiratory deficiencies are more extreme in lifelong smokers and in those who have failed to reduce dietary fat or have had many years of exposure to environmental pollutants.

D. Immune System (p. 447)
1. As the immune system ages, T cells, which attack antigens (foreign substances) directly, become less effective.
2. The immune system is more likely to malfunction by turning against normal body tissues in an **autoimmune response**.
3. A less competent immune system can increase the elderly person's risk for a variety of illnesses, including infectious diseases (such as the flu), cardiovascular disease, certain forms of cancer, and a variety of autoimmune disorders, such as rheumatoid arthritis and diabetes.

4. Older adults vary greatly in immunity.
5. The strength of the aging person's immune system seems to be a sign of overall physical vigor.

E. Sleep (p. 447)
1. Older adults require about the same total sleep time as younger adults—around 7 hours per night.
2. As people age, they have more difficulty falling asleep, staying asleep, and sleeping deeply, and the timing of sleep tends to change, toward earlier bedtime and earlier morning awakening.
3. Changes in brain structures controlling sleep and higher levels of stress hormones in the bloodstream, which have an alerting effect on the central nervous system, are believed to be responsible.
4. Older adults often express concern about sleep difficulties, and worries about sleep can make matters worse by interfering with sleep.
5. There are many ways to foster restful sleep.
   a. Explaining that even very healthy older adults have trouble sleeping lets people know that age-related change in the sleep–waking pattern is normal.
   b. Use of prescription sedatives (more commonly prescribed to older than to younger adults) can be helpful in relieving temporary insomnia.
   c. Long-term medication is not advised because it can increase the frequency and severity of sleep apnea and may induce rebound insomnia after the drug is discontinued.

F. Physical Appearance and Mobility (p. 448)
1. Outward signs of growing older include changes in the skin, hair, facial structure, and body build.
2. Creasing and sagging of the skin extends into old age.
   a. Oil glands that lubricate the skin become less active, leading to dryness and roughness.
   b. "Age spots" increase; in some elderly individuals, the arms, backs of the hands, and face may be dotted with these pigmented marks.
   c. Moles and other small skin growths may also appear.
   d. Blood vessels can now be seen beneath the now more transparent skin, which has largely lost its layer of fatty support.
   e. The face is especially likely to show these effects because it is frequently exposed to the sun, which accelerates aging.
3. Other facial changes occur:
   a. The nose and ears broaden as new cells are deposited on the outer layer of the skeleton.
   b. Teeth may be yellowed, cracked, and chipped, and gums may recede.
   c. As hair follicles under the skin's surface die, hair on the head thins in both sexes, and the scalp may be visible.
   d. In men with hereditary pattern baldness, follicles do not die but, instead, begin to produce fine, downy hair.
4. Body build changes as well.
   a. Height continues to decline, especially in women, as loss of bone mineral content leads to further collapse of the spinal column.
   b. Weight generally drops after age 60 because of loss of lean body mass (bone density and muscle), which is heavier than the fat deposits accumulating on the torso.
5. Several factors affect mobility.
   a. Muscle strength generally declines at a faster rate in late adulthood than it did in middle age.
   b. Bone strength deteriorates, as do flexibility and strength of the tendons and ligaments (which connect muscle to bone) and the joints.
6. Careful planning of an exercise program can also enhance joint flexibility and range of movement.

G. Adapting to Physical Changes of Late Adulthood (pp. 448–450)
1. Great diversity exists in older adults' adaptation to the physical changes of aging.
2. Some older adults take advantage of an enormous industry designed to stave off the appearance of old age, including cosmetics, wigs, and plastic surgery.
3. The most obvious, outward signs of aging—graying hair, facial wrinkles, and baldness—bear no relationship to cognitive and motor functioning or to longevity.
4. In contrast, neurological, sensory, cardiovascular, respiratory, immune-system, and skeletal and muscular health strongly predict cognitive and motor performance and both quality and length of later life.

5. Effective Coping Strategies (p. 448)
    a. Employing problem-centered and emotion-centered coping, older adults can prevent and compensate for age-related declines through diet, exercise, environmental adjustments, and an active, stimulating lifestyle, thereby feeling a sense of personal control over their fates.
    b. In contrast, those who view age-related change as inevitable and uncontrollable tend to respond passively and to report more physical and psychological symptoms.
6. Assistive Technology (pp. 448–449)
    a. A rapidly expanding **assistive technology**, or array of devices that permit people with disabilities to improve their functioning, is available to help older people cope with physical declines.
    b. Elders with disabilities who use assistive devices require fewer hours of personal caregiving, as seen in countries such as Sweden that cover the cost of many such devices, helping older adults to remain as independent as possible.
7. Overcoming Stereotypes of Aging (pp. 449–450)
    a. Stereotypes of late adulthood, which view "deterioration as inevitable" are widespread in Western nations.
    b. As elders encounter negative views, they experience "stereotype threat," which results in diminished performance on tasks related to the stereotype.
    c. In cultures where the elderly are treated with deference and respect, an aging appearance may be a source of pride, signifying success in living to a ripe maturity, and elderly status is often cause for celebration.

III. HEALTH, FITNESS, AND DISABILITY (pp. 450–460)
  A. Health is central to psychological well-being in late life.
    1. When researchers ask the elderly about their possible selves, the number of hoped-for physical selves declines and the number of feared physical selves increases with age.
    2. Older adults are generally optimistic about their health.
    3. With respect to protecting their health, older adults' sense of self-efficacy is as high as that of young adults and higher than that of middle-aged people.
    4. The more optimistic elders are about their capacity to cope with physical challenges, the better they are at overcoming threats to health, which in turn promotes further optimism and health-enhancing behaviors.
    5. SES and ethnic variations in health diminish in late adulthood.
        a. Before age 85, SES continues to predict physical functioning, with African-American and Hispanic elderly (one-fifth of whom live in poverty) at greater risk for certain health problems.
        b. The majority of Native-American and Canadian-Aboriginal older adults are poor, and chronic health conditions are so widespread that in the United States, the federal government grants Native Americans special health benefits starting as early as age 45—reflecting a much harder and shorter lifespan.
        c. Low-SES elders are less likely to seek medical treatment than their high-SES counterparts and are less likely to comply with their doctor's directions because they are less likely to believe they can control their health and that treatment will work.
    6. Health-related sex differences extend into late adulthood, with men more prone to fatal diseases and women to non-life-threatening disabling conditions.
        a. By very old age (85 and beyond), women are more impaired than men because only the sturdiest men have survived.
        b. With fewer physical limitations, older men are better able to remain independent and engage in exercise, hobbies, and involvement in the social world, all of which promote better health.
    7. As life expectancy extends, we want the average period of diminished vigor before death to decrease—a public health goal called the **compression of morbidity**.
  B. Nutrition and Exercise (p. 451)
    1. Physical changes of late life lead to an increased need for certain nutrients.
        a. Calcium and vitamin D protect the bones.
        b. Zinc and vitamins B6, C, and E protect the immune system.
        c. Vitamins A, C, and E prevent free radicals.

2. Impairments associated with aging increase the risk of dietary deficiencies.
   a. Declines in physical activity, in the senses of taste and smell, and the ease of chewing due to deteriorating teeth, reduce the quantity and quality of food eaten.
   b. The aging digestive system also has greater difficulty absorbing certain nutrients, such as protein, calcium, and vitamin D.
3. Effective interventions:
   a. Older adults who take vitamin-mineral supplements show an enhanced immune response and a 50 percent drop in days of infectious illness.
   b. Sedentary healthy older adults up to age 80 who began endurance training have shown gains in vital capacity comparable to those of much younger individuals.
   c. Weight-bearing exercise begun in late adulthood promotes muscle size and strength.
4. It is never too late to benefit from good nutrition and physical exercise, but lack of awareness of the health benefits of exercise, and the expected discomforts from physical activity, are a barrier to getting older men and women to take up a fitness routine.

C. Sexuality (p. 451–452)
   1. Although virtually all cross-sectional studies report a decline in sexual desire and frequency of sexual activity in older people, this trend may be exaggerated by cohort effects.
   2. Too often, intercourse is used as the only measure of sexual activity—a circumstance that promotes a narrow view of pleasurable sex, which includes more than intercourse itself.
   3. Both older men and women report that the male partner is usually the one who ceases to interact sexually, because men may withdraw from all erotic activity when they find that erections are harder to achieve and that more time must elapse between them.
   4. Disabilities that disrupt blood flow to the penis—most often disorders of the autonomic nervous system, cardiovascular disease, and diabetes—are responsible for dampening sexuality in older men.
   5. Cigarette smoking, excessive alcohol intake, and a variety of prescription medications also lead to diminished sexual performance.
   6. Among women, poor health and absence of a partner are major factors that reduce sexual activity.
   7. Educational programs that dispel myths and foster a view of sex as extending throughout adulthood promote positive sexual attitudes.

D. Physical Disabilities (pp. 452–455)
   1. Illness and disability climb as the end of the lifespan approaches.
      a. Cardiovascular disease and cancer increase dramatically from mid- to late life and remain the leading causes of death.
      b. Respiratory diseases also rise sharply.
      c. A weakened immune system makes older adults susceptible to infectious diseases such as *pneumonia.*
      d. *Stroke,* the fourth most common killer among the aged, is caused by hemorrhage or blockage of blood flow in the brain and is a major cause of disability in late adulthood and, after age 75, of death.
      e. Osteoporosis continues to rise in late adulthood, and *arthritis* causes physical limitations for many elders.
      f. *Adult-onset diabetes* and *unintentional injuries* also multiply in late adulthood.
   2. Many experts distinguish between conditions that are a product of aging and those that are *related to age* but are not *entirely caused by aging.*
      a. **Primary aging** (another term for *biological aging*) refers to genetically influenced declines that affect all human beings and occur even in the context of overall good health.
      b. **Secondary aging** refers to declines due to hereditary defects and negative environmental influences such as poor diet, lack of exercise, disease, substance abuse, environmental pollution, and psychological stress.
      c. Another concept, **frailty**, refers to weakened functioning of diverse organs and body systems, which profoundly interferes with everyday competence and leaves older adults highly vulnerable to infection, weather extremes, or injury.
      d. Although primary aging contributes to frailty, secondary aging plays a larger role.

3. Arthritis (pp. 453–454)
    a. A condition of inflamed, painful, stiff, and sometimes swollen joints and muscles, arthritis becomes more common in late adulthood.
    b. The most common type, **osteoarthritis**, is known as "wear-and-tear arthritis" or "degenerative joint disease," and is one of the few age-related disabilities where years of use makes a difference.
        (1) Although a genetic proneness seems to exist, the disease usually does not appear until the forties and fifties.
        (2) In frequently used joints, cartilage on the ends of the bones, which reduces friction during movement, gradually deteriorates.
        (3) Almost all older adults show some degree of osteoarthritis on X-rays, although wide individual differences in severity exist.
    c. Unlike osteoarthritis, which is limited to certain joints, **rheumatoid arthritis** involves the whole body.
        (1) An autoimmune response leads to inflammation of connective tissue, particularly the membranes that line the joints, leading to overall stiffness, inflammation, and aching.
        (2) Tissue in the cartilage tends to grow, damaging surrounding ligaments, muscles, and bones and causing deformed joints and often serious loss of mobility.
        (3) Sometimes other organs, such as the heart and lungs, are affected.
    d. Disability due to arthritis affects 43 percent of U.S. and 34 percent of Canadian men over age 65 and rises modestly with age.
    e. Among women, the incidence is 50 percent among 65- to 84-year-olds and 70 percent among those over age 85.
        (1) The reason for the sex difference is unclear.
        (2) Although rheumatoid arthritis can strike at any age, it rises after age 60, possibly due to a late-appearing genetic defect in the immune system.
        (3) Early treatment with new, powerful anti-inflammatory medications helps slow its course.
    f. Managing arthritis requires a balance of rest when the disease flares, pain relief, and physical activity involving gentle stretching of all muscles to maintain mobility, as well as weight loss in obese people.
    g. With proper analgesic medication, joint protection, and lifestyle changes, many people with either form of the illness can lead long, productive lives.
    h. If hip or knee joints are badly damaged or deformed, they can be surgically rebuilt or replaced with plastic or metal devices.
4. Diabetes (p. 454)
    a. Insulin, produced by the pancreas, keeps the blood concentration of glucose within set limits by stimulating muscle and fat cells to absorb it.
    b. When this balance system fails, either because not enough insulin is produced or body cells become insensitive to it, *adult-onset diabetes* (*diabetes mellitus*) occurs.
    c. Over time, abnormally high blood glucose damages the blood vessels, increasing the risk of stroke, heart attack, circulatory problems in the legs, and injury to the eyes, kidneys, and nerves.
    d. From middle to late adulthood, the incidence of adult-onset diabetes doubles; it affects 10 percent of the elderly in the United States.
    e. Diabetes runs in families, suggesting that heredity is involved, and the risk is greatly increased by inactivity and abdominal fat deposits.
    f. Higher rates of adult-onset diabetes are found among African-American, Mexican-American, Native-American, and Canadian-Aboriginal minorities for both genetic and environmental reasons, including high-fat diets and obesity associated with poverty.
    g. Treating adult-onset diabetes requires lifestyle changes, including a carefully controlled diet, regular exercise, and weight loss.
5. Unintentional Injuries (pp. 454–455)
    a. At age 65 and older, the death rate from unintentional injuries is at an all-time high, largely due to motor vehicle collisions and falls.

b. Motor Vehicle Accidents (p. 454)
   (1) Older adults have higher rates of traffic violations, accidents, and fatalities per mile driven of any age group with the exception of drivers under age 25.
   (2) The high rate of injury persists, even though many elders, especially women, limit their driving after noticing that their ability to drive safely is slipping.
   (3) The greater elders' visual processing difficulties, the higher their rate of moving violations and crashes.
   (4) The elderly are less likely to drive quickly and recklessly but more likely to fail to heed signs, give right-of-way, and turn appropriately.
   (5) They often try to compensate for their difficulties by being more cautious, but slowed reaction time and indecisiveness can pose hazards as well.
   (6) Giving up driving results in loss of freedom, control over one's life, and self-esteem, so elders usually try to drive as long as possible.
   (7) The elderly account for more than 30 percent of all pedestrian deaths, often occurring when crossing signals do not allow them enough time to cross a street.

c. Falls (p. 454–455)
   (1) About 30 percent of adults over age 65 and 40 percent over age 80 have experienced a fall within the last year.
   (2) Because of weakened bones and decline in ability to break a fall, about 10 percent of falls result in serious injury.
   (3) Among the most common is hip fracture, which increases twentyfold from age 65 to 85 and is associated with a 10 to 20 percent increase in mortality.
   (4) Of those who survive hip fractures, half never regain the ability to walk without assistance.
   (5) Falling can also impair health indirectly, by promoting fear of falling, leading older adults to avoid activities because they are afraid of falling again, thereby limiting mobility and social contact.
   (6) Although an active lifestyle may expose the elderly to more events and situations that can cause a fall, the health benefits of activity far outweigh the risk of serious injury due to falling.

E. Mental Disabilities (pp. 455–459)
   1. **Dementia** refers to a set of disorders occurring almost entirely in old age in which many aspects of thought and behavior are so impaired that everyday activities are disrupted.
      a. Dementia rises sharply with age, striking adults of both sexes about equally and affecting about 1 percent of people in their sixties.
      b. In Canada, the United States, and other Western nations, the rate increases steadily with age, rising sharply after age 75 until it reaches about 50 percent for those age 85 and older.
      c. Although dementia rates are similar across SES and most ethnic groups, African Americans are at higher risk.
      d. About a dozen types of dementia have been identified, most of them irreversible and incurable.
      e. A few forms, such as Parkinson's disease, involve deterioration in subcortical brain regions (primitive structures below the cortex), but in most dementia cases, damage occurs only to the cerebral cortex, as is seen in Alzheimer's disease and cerebrovascular dementia—the two forms of *cortical dementia.*
   2. Alzheimer's Disease (pp. 455–459)
      a. Alzheimer's disease is the most common form of dementia, accounting for 60 percent of all cases and affecting 8 to 10 percent of people over age 65 and nearly 45 percent of those over age 80.
      b. Each year, about 5 percent of all deaths among the elderly involve Alzheimer's.
      c. Symptoms and Course of the Disease (p. 455)
         (1) The earliest symptoms are often severe memory problems—forgetting names, dates, appointments, familiar routes of travel, or the need to turn off the kitchen stove.
         (2) At first, recent memory is most impaired, but as serious disorientation sets in, recall of distant events and such basic facts as time, date, and place evaporates.

(3) Faulty judgment puts the affected person in danger.
(4) Personality changes develop, including loss of spontaneity and sparkle, anxiety in response to uncertainties created by mental problems, aggressive outbursts, reduced initiative, and social withdrawal.
(5) Depression often appears in the early phase of Alzheimer's and other forms of dementia and worsens.
(6) As the disease progresses, skilled and purposeful movements disintegrate.
(7) The course of Alzheimer's varies greatly, from a few years to as long as 15 years, with an average life expectancy of about 4½ years for a 70-year-old man with the disease and about 8 years for a 70-year-old woman.

d. Brain Deterioration (p. 455–456)
(1) A diagnosis of Alzheimer's disease is made through exclusion, after ruling out other causes of dementia by a physical examination and psychological testing—an approach that is more than 90 percent accurate.
(2) Doctors can only be certain that a person has Alzheimer's by inspecting the brain after death for a set of abnormalities that either cause or result from the disease.
(3) However, brain-imaging techniques (MRI and PET), which yield three-dimensional pictures of brain volume and activity, predict whether elders who do not yet show symptoms will receive an after-death confirmation of Alzheimer's.
(4) Two major structural changes in the brain occur in Alzheimer's disease: neurofibrillary tangles and amyloid plaques.
(5) Inside neurons, **neurofibrillary tangles** appear—bundles of twisted threads that are the product of collapsed neural structures.
(6) Outside neurons, **amyloid plaques**—dense deposits of a deteriorated protein called *amyloid,* surrounded by clumps of dead nerve and glial cells—develop.
(7) Although some neurofibrillary tangles and amyloid plaques are present in the brains of normal middle-aged and older people and increase with age, they are far more abundant in Alzheimer's victims.
(8) New findings suggest that a major culprit in the disease may be abnormal breakdown of amyloid and that plaques reflect the brain's effort to eject the harmful amyloid from the nerve cells.
(9) In both Alzheimer's and Parkinson's disease, disruptions occur in a key neuronal structure responsible for chopping up and disposing of abnormal protein so that damaged proteins build to toxic levels, causing cell damage and death.
(10) Levels of *neurotransmitters* also decline as neurons die and brain volume shrinks.
(11) A drop in serotonin, one of these neurotransmitters, may contribute to sleep disturbances, aggressive outbursts, and depression.

e. Risk Factors (pp. 456–457)
(1) Alzheimer's disease comes in two types: *familial,* which runs in families, and *sporadic,* which has no obvious family history.
(2) Familial Alzheimer's generally has early onset (before age 65) and progresses more rapidly than later-appearing, sporadic Alzheimer's.
(3) Researchers have identified genes on chromosomes 1, 14, and 21 that are linked to familial Alzheimer's.
(4) Heredity also plays a role in sporadic Alzheimer's through spontaneous mutations, leading to an abnormal gene on chromosome 19 that results in excess levels of a blood protein that carries cholesterol through the body, affecting the expression of a gene involved in regulating insulin—creating an increased risk of Alzheimer's in elders with diabetes.
(5) Many victims of sporadic Alzheimer's show no family history or currently known genetic marker.
(6) Evidence is increasing for the role of other factors, including excess dietary fat, cardiovascular disease, and stroke, as well as diabetes.
(7) Head injury may also increase risk by accelerating deterioration of amyloid.
(8) A high-fat diet appears to be risky, leading to higher blood levels of "bad" cholesterol (low-density lipoproteins), which are associated with a higher incidence of Alzheimer's.

f. Protective Factors (p. 457)
   (1) Hormone therapy was previously thought to offer protection against Alzheimer's to women, but rigorously designed research has yielded contrary findings.
   (2) A "Mediterranean diet" emphasizing fish, unsaturated fat (olive oil), and moderate consumption of red wine is linked to a 60 percent reduced incidence of Alzheimer's disease and to a reduction in cerebrovascular dementia.
   (3) Education and an active lifestyle seem beneficial as well; education may promote more synaptic connections, which act as a *cognitive reserve* that is protective against mental disability, though not in the presence of the ApoE4 gene associated with hereditary Alzheimer's.

g. Helping Alzheimer's Victims and Their Caregivers (p. 457)
   (1) With no cure available, family interventions ensure the best adjustment possible for the Alzheimer's victim, spouse, and other relatives.
   (2) Avoiding dramatic changes in living conditions—such as moving to a new location, rearranging furniture, or modifying daily routines—is important to help the patient, whose cognitive world is gradually disintegrating, feel as secure as possible.

3. Cerebrovascular Dementia (p. 457)
   a. In **cerebrovascular dementia**, a series of strokes leaves areas of dead brain cells, producing step-by-step degeneration of mental ability, with each step occurring abruptly after a stroke.
   b. Cerebrovascular dementia appears to be the combined result of genetic and environmental forces.
      (1) A hereditary tendency toward cerebrovascular dementia appears to be indirect, through high blood pressure, cardiovascular disease, and diabetes, each of which increases the risk of stroke.
      (2) Environmental influences, including cigarette smoking, heavy alcohol use, high salt intake, a diet very low in animal protein, obesity, inactivity, and psychological stress, also heighten stroke risk.
   c. Because of their susceptibility to cardiovascular disease, more men than women have cerebrovascular dementia by their late sixties, while women are not at great risk until after age 75.
   d. Prevention is the only effective way to stop the disease; its incidence has dropped in the last two decades largely as a result of a decline in heart disease and more effective stroke prevention methods.

4. Misdiagnosed and Reversible Dementia (p. 459)
   a. Depression is the disorder most often misdiagnosed as dementia.
   b. The depressed (but not demented) older adult is likely to exaggerate his or her mental difficulties, whereas the demented person minimizes them and is not fully aware of cognitive declines.
   c. Depression rises with age, often in response to physical illness and pain, and can lead to cognitive deterioration.
   d. The elderly, however, are unlikely to seek mental health services, increasing the chances that depression will deepen and be confused with dementia.
   e. As people age, they are increasingly likely to be taking drugs whose side effects may resemble dementia.
   f. Some diseases can cause temporary memory loss and mental symptoms, especially among the elderly, who often become confused and withdrawn when ill.
   g. Environmental changes and social isolation can trigger mental declines, but when supportive ties are restored, cognitive functioning usually bounces back.

F. Health Care (p. 459)
   1. Cost of Health Care for the Elderly (p. 459)
      a. Adults age 65 and older, who make up 12 percent of the North American population, account for 30 percent of government health care expenditures in the United States and 44 percent in Canada.
      b. The cost of government-sponsored health insurance for the elderly, or Medicare, will double by 2025 and nearly triple by 2050 as the baby boom generation ages.

c. Because U.S. Medicare funds only about half of older adults' medical needs, American elders spend nearly five times the percentage of their annual incomes on health care compared with Canadian elders—19 versus 4 percent.

2. Long-Term Care (pp. 459–460)
   a. Advancing age is strongly associated with use of long-term care services, especially nursing homes.
   b. Among disorders of aging, dementia, especially Alzheimer's disease, most often leads to nursing home placement, followed by arthritis, hip fracture, and stroke.
   c. Greater use of nursing homes is also prompted by loss of informal caregiving support through widowhood (which mostly affects women) and aging of adult children and other relatives.
   d. Overall, only 5 percent of Americans and 8 percent of Canadians age 65 and older are institutionalized, about half the rate in other industrialized nations that provide more generous public financing of institutional care.
   e. In Canada and in the United States, only when elders are destitute does the government cover all costs of nursing home care.
   f. Nursing home use also varies across ethnic groups, with Caucasian Americans nearly twice as likely as African Americans to be institutionalized.
      (1) Large, close-knit extended families mean that over 70 percent of African-American older adults do not live alone.
      (2) Asian, Hispanic, Native-American, and Canadian-Aboriginal elders also use nursing homes less often than Caucasian Americans because of a cultural emphasis on families' caregiving responsibility.
   g. Overall, families provide at least 60 to 80 percent of all long-term care for older adults in Australia, Canada, New Zealand, the United States, and Western Europe.
   h. To reduce institutionalized care of the elderly, some experts have advocated alternatives, such as publicly funded in-home help for family caregivers and *assisted living,* a homelike housing arrangement providing more help than can be provided at home but less than is typical of nursing homes.
   i. Assisted living is a cost-effective alternative to nursing homes that prevents unnecessary institutionalization and can enhance residents' autonomy, social life, community involvement, and life satisfaction.

Cognitive Development

I. Overview:
   A. Research reveals large individual differences in cognitive functioning among the elderly—greater than at any other time of life.
   B. According to one view, elders who sustain high levels of functioning engage in **selective optimization with compensation**.
      1. They narrow their goals, selecting personally valued activities as a way of optimizing returns from their diminishing energy.
      2. They also come up with new ways of compensating for cognitive losses.

II. MEMORY (pp. 461–463)
   A. Deliberate versus Automatic Memory (p. 461)
      1. Because older adults take in less about a stimulus and its context, they sometimes cannot distinguish an experienced event from one they imagined, and they may have difficulty remembering the source of information.
      2. Compared to recall, recognition memory suffers far less in late adulthood because it is fairly automatic, demanding little mental effort, and because a multitude of environmental supports for remembering are present.
      3. **Implicit memory**, or memory without conscious awareness, is another automatic form of memory, with smaller age differences than in explicit, or deliberate, memory.
      4. Memory that depends on familiarity rather than on conscious use of strategies is largely spared in old age.

B. Associative Memory (p. 462)
   1. Memory deficits can be described in terms of a general, age-related decline in binding information into complex memories, which is called an **associative memory deficit**—difficulty creating and retrieving links between pieces of information.
   2. Providing older adults with repeated presentations of information to be learned and more memory cues improves their associative memory.

C. Remote Memory (p. 462)
   1. Although older people often say that their **remote memory**, or very long-term recall, is clearer than their memory for recent events, research does not support this conclusion.
   2. Older people recall personally meaningful events through *autobiographical memory,* as well as recent events, more frequently than intermediate events, with recent events mentioned most often.
   3. Older adults recall recent personal experiences more readily than remote ones as a result of interference produced by years of additional experience.

D. Prospective Memory (pp. 462–463)
   Prospective memory refers to remembering to engage in planned actions at an appropriate time in the future.
   1. The amount of mental effort required determines whether older adults have trouble with prospective memory.
   2. In the laboratory, older adults do better on *event-based* than on *time-based* prospective memory tasks.
   3. Elders compensate for their reduced-capacity working memories and the challenges of dividing attention between what they are doing now and what they must do in the future.

III. LANGUAGE PROCESSING (p. 463)

A. Like implicit memory, language comprehension changes little in late life as long as conversational partners do not speak too quickly and elders are given enough time to process written text accurately.

B. Two aspects of language production do show age-related losses, probably as a result of age-related limits on working memory.
   1. They may have difficulty retrieving words from long-term memory.
   2. They may have more difficulty planning what to say and how to say it.

C. As with memory, older adults develop compensatory techniques for their language production problems.
   1. They simplify their grammatical structures so they can devote more effort to retrieving words and organizing their thoughts.
   2. Sacrificing efficiency for greater clarity, elders use more sentences to convey meaning.

IV. PROBLEM SOLVING (p. 463–464)

A. Aging brings both deterioration and adaptive changes in problem solving.

B. Traditional problem solving, which lacks a real-life context, declines in late adulthood.

C. The problematic situations the elderly encounter are often different from those experienced at earlier ages.
   1. Being retired, most do not have to deal with problems in the workplace.
   2. The social problems they confront at home may be reduced because their children are typically grown and living on their own, and their marriages have endured long enough to have fewer difficulties.
   3. Major concerns involve managing activities of daily living, such as preparing nutritious meals, handling finances, and attending to health concerns.

D. As long as they perceive problems as under their control, elders are active and effective in solving them.
   1. Findings indicate that older adults make quicker decisions about whether they are ill and seek medical care sooner than younger people, who are more likely to adopt a "wait and see" approach to health problems, even serious ones.
   2. This tendency to act decisively when faced with health risks is particularly adaptive in old age.
   3. Older adults often consult others for advice about everyday problems, and couples more often collaborate in problem solving, jointly compensating for moments of cognitive difficulty.

V. WISDOM (pp. 464–465)
   A. A wealth of life experience enhances the verbal messages and problem solving of the elderly.
   B. Life experience also underlies another capacity believed to reach its height in old age: **wisdom**, which is described as breadth and depth of practical knowledge, ability to reflect on that knowledge in ways that make life more bearable and worthwhile, emotional maturity, and an integrative form of creativity.
   C. Cultures around the world assume that age and wisdom go together.
      1. In village and tribal societies, the most important social positions, such as chieftain and shaman (religious leader), are reserved for the old.
      2. In industrialized nations, older adults are chief executive officers of large corporations, high-level religious leaders, members of legislatures, and supreme court justices.
      3. According to an evolutionary view, the genetic program of our species grants health, fitness, and strength to the young, while culture tames this youthful advantage in physical power with the insights of the old, thereby ensuring balance and interdependence among generations.
   D. In one study on development of wisdom, in which adults from age 20 to 89 responded to uncertain real-life situations and responses were rated for five ingredients of wisdom, a very small number of adults—some young, some middle aged, and some old—made the wisest choices.
      1. People in human-service careers, where they received extensive training and practice in grappling with human problems, were well-represented among the wise.
      2. Other high-scorers held leadership positions.
   E. Compared with their agemates, elders with the qualities that make up wisdom have greater psychological well-being, better physical health, and more positive relations with others, and are more open to experience.

VI. FACTORS RELATED TO COGNITIVE CHANGE (p. 465)
   A. A mentally active life—above-average education, stimulating leisure pursuits, community participation, and a flexible personality—predicts maintenance of mental activities into advanced old age.
   B. Health status powerfully predicts older adults' intellectual performance.
      1. Chronic conditions such as vision and hearing impairments, cardiovascular disease, osteoporosis, and arthritis, are associated with cognitive declines.
      2. However, this relationship may be exaggerated by the fact that brighter adults are more likely to engage in health-protecting behaviors, which postpone the onset of serious disease.
   C. Retirement also affects cognitive change, both positively and negatively.
      1. When people leave routine jobs for stimulating leisure activities, outcomes are favorable.
      2. In contrast, retiring from a highly complex job without developing challenging substitutes accelerates intellectual declines.
   D. After age 75 cognitive decrements are related to distance to death rather than chronological age.
      1. **Terminal decline** refers to a steady, marked decrease in cognitive functioning prior to death.
      2. Researchers are not certain if it is limited to a few aspects of intelligence or if it affects all aspects, signifying general deterioration.
      3. Findings vary greatly in estimated length of terminal decline, with some reporting that it lasts only 1 to 3 years, others report that it extends for as much as 14 years, with an average of 4 to 5 years.
      4. All we know for sure is that an extended, steep falloff in cognitive functioning is a sign of loss of vitality and impending death.

VII. COGNITIVE INTERVENTIONS (p. 465–466)
   A. The Adult Development and Enrichment Project (ADEPT) is the most extensive cognitive intervention program conducted to date.
      1. By using participants in the Seattle Longitudinal Study, researchers could do what no other investigation had yet done: assess the effects of cognitive training on long-term development.
      2. Intervention began with adults over age 64, some of whom had maintained their scores on two mental abilities (inductive reasoning and spatial orientation) over the previous 14 years and others of whom had shown declines.
      3. After just five one-hour training sessions in relevant cognitive skills, two-thirds of the participants improved their performance.
      4. Gains for decliners were dramatic: Forty percent returned to the level at which they had been functioning 14 years earlier.

5. A follow-up 7 years later revealed that although the scores of trained adults dropped somewhat, they were still doing better than untrained controls.
6. "Booster" training at this time led to further gains, although these were not as large as the earlier gains.

B. In another large-scale intervention study, ACTIVE (Advanced Cognitive Training for Independent and Vital Elderly), trained elders similarly showed an immediate advantage in trained skills—speed of processing, memory, or reasoning—over controls that was still evident at one- and two-year follow-ups.

VIII. LIFELONG LEARNING (pp. 466–467)

A. Elderhostel programs (in Canada, called Routes to Learning) hosted by local educational institutions combine stimulating one- to three-week courses taught by experts with recreational pursuits.
B. Educational programs similar to Elderhostel have sprung up in North America and elsewhere, including Osher Lifelong Learning Institutes on college campuses around the United States.
C. Community senior centers often provide inexpensive offerings related to everyday living, which attract more low-SES people than programs like Elderhostel.
D. Elders say they learn interesting facts and come to understand new ideas in many disciplines, while also making new friends and developing a broader perspective on the world.
E. Elders who participate in educational programs also come to see themselves differently.
   1. They abandon ingrained stereotypes of aging when they realize adults in their seventies and eighties can still engage in complex learning.
   2. In Elderhostel courses, elders who previously had the least education report learning the most.

LECTURE ENHANCEMENTS

LECTURE ENHANCEMENT 17.1
Is Loneliness Bad for the Heart? (p. 447)

Time: 10–15 minutes

Objective: To investigate the relationship between loneliness, lack of emotional support, and the likelihood of having a heart condition in late adulthood.

Research shows that social isolation contributes to a variety of adverse health outcomes, including heart disease. To further examine the relationship between loneliness, lack of emotional support, and the likelihood of having a heart condition in late adulthood, Sorkin, Rook, and Lu (2003) recruited 180 adults between the ages of 58 and 90 years. Sixty-four percent of the participants were widowed, divorced, or single. The researchers collected the following information:

1. Participants provided demographic information, including age, sex, ethnicity, educational attainment, marital status, income, and the presence of any chronic conditions.
2. Participants completed a brief, 10-item loneliness scale.
3. To identify the presence or absence of emotional support, participants were asked to name people who provided them with emotional support and to identify the type of support they received.
4. To identify the presence or absence of companionship, participants were asked to name people with whom they could chat on the phone, visit, or have fun.
5. All participants received a thorough medical examination. Physicians recorded the presence of any heart condition or heart abnormality and completed a battery of blood tests.
6. Participants answered questions about lifestyle, including diet, exercise, and smoking and drinking habits.
7. Participants completed a standardized depression scale and were asked to keep a two-week diary of mood. For example: Today I felt ________ (hopeless, tense, depressed, satisfied, optimistic, confident). Participants were asked to rate each mood using a 5-point Likert scale (1 = not at all; 5 = all of the time).

Results indicated that loneliness was associated with the presence of a heart condition, even after controlling for age and other chronic health problems. Specifically, participants who lacked emotional support and companionship were more likely to be lonely and were more likely to have a heart condition than participants who had emotional support and companionship. Another important finding was that access to emotional support, not the number of people who provided emotional support, was strongly related to heart condition status. Thus, having a strong bond with at least one other person seemed to reduce feelings of loneliness and the likelihood of having a heart condition. These findings support previous research on the importance of social support for diverse aspects of health and well-being across the lifespan.

In small groups, ask students to list additional benefits of social support in early, middle, and late adulthood.

Sorkin, D., Rook, K. S., & Lu, J. L. (2003). Loneliness, lack of emotional support, lack of companionship, and the likelihood of having a heart condition in an elderly sample. *Annals of Behavioral Medicine, 24,* 290–298.

LECTURE ENHANCEMENT 17.2
Does Cigarette Smoking Place Elders at Risk for Cognitive Decline? (p. 459)

Time: 5–10 minutes

Objective: To examine the relationship between cigarette smoking and cognitive decline in elders.

The text notes that environmental influences, including cigarette smoking, heavy alcohol use, obesity, and psychological stress, are linked to cognitive decline and dementia in late adulthood. To further examine the relationship between cigarette smoking and cognitive decline in elders, Ott and colleagues (2004) collected data on 11,003 adults aged 65 and over who were already participating in four different European studies. The researchers had access to all relevant demographic and health information collected for the other studies.

At baseline, the researchers used the Mini-Mental State Examination (MMSE) to screen for dementia. The MMSE measures orientation to time and place, recognition and recall memory, language ability, attention, and the ability to follow simple verbal and written commands. The researchers also collected information on smoking habits, using the following categories: current smoker, former smoker, and never smoked. The researchers then computed "pack years" for current and former smokers—the number of years smoked multiplied by the average number of daily cigarettes. After approximately 2.3 years, participants were again screened for dementia using the MMSE.

Results indicated that cognitive decline was greater for current smokers than for former and never smokers. Participants with higher "pack years" experienced greater cognitive decline than participants with lower "pack years," suggesting that dosage plays a role in the relationship between cigarette smoking and cognitive decline in the elderly. These findings remained strong even after controlling for age, sex, education, and medical and family history. Not surprisingly, participants who had never smoked experienced the lowest rates of cognitive decline over the course of the study.

Pose the following question to students: Based on these findings, should tobacco companies be forced to place a warning label on cigarettes stating that smoking is linked to cognitive decline and possibly Alzheimer's disease? Why or why not?

Ott, A., Andersen, K., Dewey, M. E., Letenneur, L., Brayne, C., Copeland, J. R., Dartiques, J. F., Kragh-Sorensen, P., Lobo, A., Martinez-Lage, J. M., Stijnen, T., Hofman, A., & Launer, L. J. (2004). Effect of smoking on global cognitive functioning in nondemented elderly. *Neurology, 62,* 920–924.

LECTURE ENHANCEMENT 17.3
The Relationship Between Literacy and Cognition in Late Adulthood (p. 463)

Time: 10–15 minutes

Objective: To examine the relationship between literacy and cognition in a sample of elders.

Research shows that literacy is correlated with general intelligence. However, few studies have investigated the relationship between literacy and specific cognitive abilities. To extend existing research on the relationship between literacy and cognition in late adulthood, Barnes and colleagues (2004) recruited 664 adults aged 65 and older and administered the following assessments:

1. The North American Adult Reading Test (NAART) was used to measure literacy. Participants were asked to pronounce a list of words with irregular spellings (for example, *debt* and *synecdoche*).
2. The Mini-Mental State Examination (MMSE) was used to determine overall cognitive ability. The MMSE measures orientation to time and place, recognition and recall memory, language ability, attention, and the ability to follow simple verbal and written commands.
3. Participants completed three executive functioning tasks. (Executive functioning allows individuals to plan and carry out goal-directed activities and is related to attention.) In one task, participants were asked to draw a continuous line that alternated between numbers and letters randomly arranged on a page. In a second task, called the Stroop Interference Test, participants were presented with a list of color words that were printed in different colors of ink. Participants were asked to name the color of ink but not to read the word (for example, the word *green* printed in red ink). In the third task, participants were asked to fill in blank squares using a key of numbers and nonsense symbols.
4. Participants completed a verbal memory and verbal fluency task. In the verbal memory task, participants memorized a list of words and verbally recalled them after a 20-minute delay. In the verbal fluency task, participants named as many animals as they could in one minute.
5. The researchers collected demographic and health information, including educational attainment, cigarette and alcohol use, depressive symptoms, and the presence of any medical conditions that might affect cognitive test performance.

Results showed a strong relationship between literacy scores and all measures of cognitive ability. That is, elders with high literacy scores scored better on the cognitive tasks than elders with low literacy scores. This finding remained strong even after controlling for education. Therefore, in this study, literacy was more predictive of cognitive ability than educational attainment. The authors note that these findings may have important implications for cognitive interventions: Interventions focusing on improving literacy may help prevent cognitive decline in elders.

Barnes, D. E., Tager, I. B., Satarino, W. A., & Yaffe, K. (2004). The relationship between literacy and cognition in well-educated elders. *Journal of Gerontology, 59A,* 390–395.

LECTURE ENHANCEMENT 17.4
More on Lifelong Learning: Characteristics of High-Quality Programs (pp. 466–467)

Time: 5–10 minutes

Objective: To highlight characteristics of high-quality continuing education programs.

As noted in the text, elderly participants in continuing education report a rich array of benefits, including learning interesting facts, understanding new ideas in many disciplines, making new friends, and developing a broader perspective on the world. You can supplement the text discussion of high-quality continuing education programs with the following recommendations, which are associated with cognitive aging (Knox, 2003):

1. Instruction should be responsive to diverse learning characteristics. As in the college years, elders have various skills, backgrounds, and learning experiences that affect how they learn and process information. Successful programs should be sensitive to these differences.
2. Because older adults do not process information as effectively as younger adults, program goals and objectives must be clear and well-organized.
3. Active engagement in learning activities is critical for achieving mastery. Elders not only need more time to learn new material (compared to younger adults), they also need frequent opportunities for active participation. For example, small group work, presentations, question-and-answer periods, and creative learning activities can help older adults master new material.

4. Like college students and younger adults, elders should be provided with frequent evaluative feedback to indicate progress and guide inquiry. Specific suggestions for improvement and an overview of strengths should be included in evaluations.

5. Elders need lots of support as they learn and apply new material. Visuals, memory aids, modifications in instructional pace, challenging activities, and vivid examples can help older adults absorb, retain, and recall instructional material.

Using research presented in Lecture Enhancement 17.1, how might continuing education programs reduce loneliness and increase companionship opportunities in elders? Why is social support and companionship especially important in late adulthood?

Knox, A. B. (2003). Building on abilities. *The Journal of Continuing Education in the Health Professions, 23,* 141–145.

LEARNING ACTIVITIES

LEARNING ACTIVITY 17.1
Matching: Physical Development in Late Adulthood (pp. 441–450)

Present the following exercise as an in-class activity or quiz:

Directions: Match each of the following terms with its correct definition.

Terms:

1. Functional age
2. Average life expectancy
3. Active lifespan
4. Life expectancy crossover
5. Activities of daily living (ADLs)
6. Instrumental activities of daily living (IADLs)
7. Maximum lifespan
8. Cataracts
9. Macular degeneration
10. Autoimmune response
11. Assistive technology

Definitions:

A. Basic self-care tasks required to live on one's own, such as bathing, dressing, getting in and out of bed or a chair, or eating
B. The immune system is more likely to malfunction by turning against normal body tissues
C. The array of devices that permit people with disabilities to improve their functioning
D. When surviving members of low-SES ethnic minority groups live longer than members of the white majority
E. Cloudy areas in the lens, resulting in foggy vision and (without surgery) eventual blindness
F. Tasks necessary to conduct the business of daily life and that require some cognitive competence, such as telephoning, shopping, food preparation, housekeeping, and paying bills
G. The number of years that an individual born in a particular year can expect to live
H. Unlike chronological age, this refers to actual competence and performance
I. When light-sensitive cells in the macula break down, central vision blurs and gradually is lost
J. The genetic limit to length of life for a person free of external risk factors
K. The number of years of vigorous, healthy life an individual born in a particular year can expect

Answers:

1. H
2. G
3. K
4. D
5. A
6. F
7. J
8. E
9. I
10. B
11. C

LEARNING ACTIVITY 17.2
Researching the Life of a Centenarian (p. 444)

Ask students to visit the website *http://www.hcoa.org/centenarians/centenarians.htm,* which presents a wealth of information about centenarians. Have students select one centenarian and summarize his or her life achievements. What significant events occurred in the centenarian's life? Using examples to support your answer, what characteristics of the centenarian's life history probably contributed to a long and healthy life?

LEARNING ACTIVITY 17.3
Compensating for Age-Related Declines in the Five Senses (pp. 445–447)

Have students review age-related declines in each of the five senses: vision, hearing, taste, smell, and touch. Next, ask students to list environmental modifications that can help compensate for these declines. Examples include "talking books," books and magazines written in large print, closed-caption television, and telephones that light up as well as ring. After students have made a list of existing modifications, have them brainstorm with a partner some original ideas/modifications. Encourage students to share their ideas with the class.

LEARNING ACTIVITY 17.4
Conducting an Interview on Physical Changes in Late Adulthood (pp. 443–450)

Ask students to interview a grandparent, a friend's grandparent, or another elder about physical changes in late adulthood. For example, what changes have been most noticeable? Have there been any positive changes? Has sleep or diet changed since middle adulthood? How has the individual adapted to these physical changes? Next, students should compare the answers with research in the text. Did the elder mention physical changes that are common in late adulthood? In the student's opinion, has the elder adapted favorably to the physical changes? Why or why not? Were students surprised by any of the answers? If so, explain.

LEARNING ACTIVITY 17.5
Designing an Exercise Program for Older Adults (p. 451)

As discussed in the text, exercise continues to be a powerful health intervention in late adulthood. Instruct students to design an exercise program for older adults. What types of exercise will be included, and why? Which exercises might require modification based on elders' current level of physical health? How will students recruit participants? For example, will they collaborate with community agencies? Why should elders participate in this program? That is, what benefits can they hope to achieve?

LEARNING ACTIVITY 17.6
Identifying Mental Disabilities in Late Adulthood (pp. 455–459)

In small groups, present students with the following vignette:

> Norman has noticed some changes in his wife, Peg, over the past 6 or 8 months. She seems more forgetful and moody and got lost driving to church twice in one month. Peg no longer wants to visit with friends and family and is unable to explain changes in her behavior. She is prone to crying spells, and although he tries, Norman doesn't seem to be able to comfort his wife. Norman has decided to take Peg to their family physician to find out if her symptoms have a medical explanation.

How should the physician go about determining if Peg has Alzheimer's disease, cerebrovascular dementia, or depression? That is, what techniques are used to diagnose each of the disorders? If Peg has Alzheimer's, how will her physician rule out cerebrovascular dementia and depression? Finally, have students create a list of recommendations that will help Norman care for Peg if her diagnosis is Alzheimer's disease.

LEARNING ACTIVITY 17.7
True or False: Cognitive Development in Late Adulthood (pp. 460–465)

Present the following exercise to students as a quiz or in-class activity:

Directions: Read each of the following statements and indicate whether it is *True* (T) or *False* (F).

Statements:

_____ 1. Research reveals only slight individual differences in cognitive functioning in late adulthood.
_____ 2. Elders often have difficulty remembering the source of information.
_____ 3. Age differences in implicit memory are much smaller than in explicit, or deliberate, memory.
_____ 4. In old age, remote memory is clearer than memory for recent events.
_____ 5. In the laboratory, older adults do better on time-based than on event-based prospective memory tasks.
_____ 6. Language comprehension changes very little in late life as long as conversational partners do not speak very quickly and elders are given time to process written text accurately.
_____ 7. Sacrificing efficiency for greater clarity, elders use more sentences to convey their message.
_____ 8. As long as they perceive their problems as under their control and as important, elders are active and effective in solving them.
_____ 9. Few cultures around the world assume that age and wisdom go together.
_____ 10. A wide range of chronic conditions, including vision and hearing impairments, cardiovascular disease, osteoporosis, and arthritis, are strongly associated with cognitive declines.

Answers:

1. F
2. T
3. T
4. F
5. F
6. T
7. T
8. T
9. F
10. T

LEARNING ACTIVITY 17.8
Discovering Opportunities for Lifelong Learning in Your Community (pp. 466–467)

Ask students to gather information about lifelong learning in your community. Elderhostel programs, college courses designed for older adults, travel groups, book discussions at public libraries, exercise classes for elders, and field trips offered by community centers are just a handful of programs available in many communities. These programs often have brochures, fliers, or course descriptions available that describe the content of the activities. Local newspapers and newsletters published for older adults are also a good source of information about community events. Once students have gathered some information, ask them to share their findings with the class.

LEARNING ACTIVITY 17.9
Creating a Pamphlet on Physical and Cognitive Development in Late Adulthood

Tell students to pretend they have been asked by a local senior center to create a pamphlet on physical and cognitive development in late adulthood. Students should highlight physical and cognitive changes that commonly occur in late life, including the many strengths and contributions that elders possess. What can elders do to enhance their quality of life? For example, how can good nutrition, exercise, and participation in cognitively stimulating activities promote favorable health and psychological well-being? What activities or behaviors should elders avoid, and why?

ASK YOURSELF . . .

REVIEW: Cite examples of how older adults can compensate for age-related physical declines. (pp. 448–450)

Older adults can prevent and compensate for age-related changes through diet, exercise, environmental adjustments, and an active, stimulating lifestyle, all of which give them a sense of personal control over their fates. This prompts additional positive coping and improved physical functioning.

A rapidly expanding assistive technology—an array of devices that permit people with disabilities to improve their functioning—is available to help older people cope with physical declines. Computers are the greatest source of these innovative products. People with sensory impairments, for example, can use special software to enlarge text or have it read aloud. Phones that can be dialed and answered by voice commands help elders who have difficulty pushing buttons or getting across a room to answer the phone. Some medicine bottles now feature a tiny computer chip called a "smart cap" that beeps on a programmed schedule to remind the older person to take a dose of medication. And architects are now designing "smart homes" with a variety of features that promote safety and mobility. For instance, sensors in floors can activate room lights when an older person gets up at night to use the bathroom, thereby preventing injuries. Another remarkable device is a harness attached to a track in the ceiling, which carries people with reduced mobility from room to room. Although these devices are currently too expensive for most elders, future housing may be designed to facilitate their use.

Overcoming widespread stereotypes of late adulthood that view "deterioration as inevitable" is vital for helping people adapt favorably to late-life physical changes. In cultures where the elderly are treated with deference and respect, an aging appearance can be a source of pride rather than an unwelcome reminder of physical decline.

APPLY: "The best way to adjust to this is to learn to like it," thought 65-year-old Herman, inspecting his thinning hair in the mirror. "I remember reading that bald older men are regarded as leaders." What type of coping is Herman using, and why is it effective? (p. 448)

Herman is using an *emotion-centered coping strategy* to adapt to his thinning hair. Emotion-centered coping is internal and is aimed at controlling distress when there is little that we can do about a situation. Because Herman cannot stop the thinning of his hair, his strategy is effective. Herman's identity is less bound up with his appearance than with his ability to remain actively engaged in his surroundings. He values being a leader more than having thick hair. Herman is approaching aging with a positive outlook and with peace of mind. He is not trying to hold on to a youthful identity but, instead, is accepting the physical aspects of aging that cannot be changed.

REFLECT: While watching TV during the coming week, keep a log of portrayals of older adults in programs and commercials. Were elders underrepresented? How many images were positive? How many negative? Compare your observations with research findings. (p. 449–450)

This is an open-ended question with no right or wrong answer.

REVIEW: Cite evidence that both genetic and environmental factors contribute to Alzheimer's disease and cerebrovascular dementia. (pp. 455–457)

Alzheimer's disease comes in two types: *familial,* which runs in families, and *sporadic,* which has no obvious family history. Researchers have identified genes on chromosomes 1, 14, and 21 that are linked to familial Alzheimer's. In each case, the abnormal gene is dominant; if it is present in only one of the pair of genes inherited from parents, the person will develop early-onset Alzheimer's.

Heredity also plays a role in sporadic Alzheimer's, through spontaneous mutations. People with this form of the disease often have an abnormal gene on chromosome 19, which results in excess levels of ApoE4, a blood protein that carries cholesterol throughout the body. Researchers believe that a high blood concentration of ApoE4 affects the expression of a gene involved in regulating insulin. Deficient insulin and resulting glucose buildup in the bloodstream are linked to brain damage and to abnormally high buildup of amyloid in brain tissue. For this reason, elders with diabetes have a 65 percent increased risk of developing Alzheimer's disease.

The high incidence of Alzheimer's and other forms of dementia among African-American elderly illustrates the complexity of potential causes. Because incidence is much higher among African Americans than among Yoruba village dwellers of Nigeria, some investigators speculate that intermarriage with Caucasians heightened genetic risk among African Americans and that environmental factors, such as a high-fat diet, have also played a role.

Heredity affects cerebrovascular dementia indirectly, through high blood pressure, cardiovascular disease, and diabetes, each of which increases the risk of stroke. But a combination of genetic and environmental factors is involved, because the risk of stroke is also heightened by many environmental influences, including cigarette smoking, heavy alcohol use, high salt intake, very low dietary protein, obesity, inactivity, and psychological stress. Head injury, which accelerates deterioration of amyloid, may also increase the risk of developing Alzheimer's, especially among people with the ApoE4 gene.

APPLY: Marissa complained to a counselor that at age 68, her husband, Wendell, no longer initiated sex or cuddled her. Why might Wendell have ceased to interact sexually? What interventions—both medical and educational—could be helpful to Marissa and Wendell? (pp. 451–452)

Marissa and Wendell's situation is typical in that it is usually the male partner who ceases to interact sexually in later life. In cultures that emphasize an erection as necessary for being sexual, a man may withdraw from all erotic activity when he finds that erections are harder to achieve and more time must elapse between them. Wendell may think of intercourse as the only measure of his sexuality. Education can help him understand that sexuality involves more than the sex act itself—feeling sensual, enjoying close companionship, and being loved and wanted.

Disabilities that disrupt blood flow to the penis—most often, disorders of the autonomic nervous system, cardiovascular disease, and diabetes—are responsible for dampening sexuality in older men. Medical interventions that treat an underlying conditions such as disorders of the autonomic nervous system, cardiovascular disease, and diabetes may be helpful to Marissa and Wendell. Cigarette smoking, excessive alcohol intake, and some prescription medications also lead to diminished sexual performance. Educational programs that provide information about normal age-related changes in sexual functioning should enhance Marissa and Wendell's sexual interactions.

REFLECT: What care and living arrangements have been made for elders needing assistance in your family? How did culture, personal values, financial means, health, and other factors influence those decisions? (pp. 459–460)

This is an open-ended question with no right or wrong answer.

REVIEW: Describe cognitive functions that are maintained or improve in late adulthood. What aspects of aging contribute to them? (pp. 460–465)

Cognitive abilities that depend on extensive life experience rather than on processing efficiency are sustained or increased in old age. *Recognition memory*—a fairly automatic type of memory that demands little mental effort—suffers far less in late adulthood than does recall because a multitude of environmental supports for remembering are present. *Implicit memory,* or memory without conscious awareness, is another form of automatic memory that shows little change with age. These types of memory do not place heavy demands on working memory, which is more limited in old age. And although age-related declines in *prospective memory* (remembering to engage in planned future actions) are seen in the laboratory, these difficulties do not appear in real life, where adults are highly motivated to remember future events and are good at setting up reminders for themselves.

Language comprehension changes very little in late life as long as conversational partners do not speak too quickly. As with implicit memory, we recollect what we have heard or read without conscious awareness, so age-related limits on working memory do not affect language comprehension. Older adults do experience more word-retrieval failures and a greater frequency of "tip-of-the-tongue" states than younger people, but they also resolve these at a higher rate than younger people.

Life experience enables older adults to act quickly and decisively in solving problems of daily living, especially problems related to health. Finally, a capacity that is believed to reach its height in old age is *wisdom*—a combination of breadth and depth of practical knowledge; ability to reflect on and apply that knowledge in ways that make life more bearable and worthwhile; emotional maturity, including the ability to listen, evaluate, and give advice; and altruistic creativity that contributes to humanity and enriches others' lives—what one group of researchers summed up as "expertise in the conduct and meaning of life."

A mentally active life, including above-average education, stimulating leisure pursuits, community participation, and a flexible personality, together with a positive health status, predicts maintenance of mental abilities into advanced old age. Retirement can also affect cognitive change positively, as happens when people leave routine jobs for stimulating leisure activities. Finally, lifelong learning through participation in continuing education programs is yet another means of helping older adults maintain and improve their cognitive abilities.

APPLY: Estelle complained that she had recently forgotten two of her regular biweekly hair appointments and sometimes had trouble finding the right words to convey her thoughts. What cognitive changes account for Estelle's difficulties? What can she do to compensate? (pp. 462–463)

Estelle is experiencing difficulties with prospective memory and with retrieving words from long-term memory. Age-related memory declines affect tasks like these, which require deliberate processing. Prospective memory refers to remembering to engage in planned activities in the future. Studies show that older adults do better on prospective memory tasks that are *event-based* (with an event as a cue for remembering to do something) rather than *time-based,* with no such cue. Therefore, to compensate for declines in prospective memory, Estelle should set up reminders, such as a note tacked up in a prominent location, to help her remember appointments. To enhance word retrieval, Estelle can try simplifying the grammatical structures she uses so she can devote more effort to retrieving words and organizing her thoughts.

REFLECT: Interview an older adult in your family, asking about ways the individual engages in selective optimization with compensation to make the most of declining cognitive resources. Describe several examples. (p. 461)

This is an open-ended question with no right or wrong answer.

SUGGESTED STUDENT READINGS

Achenbaum, W. A. (2005). *Older Americans, vital communities: A bold vision for societal aging.* Baltimore, MD: Johns Hopkins University Press. In an ecological approach to understanding the health, vitality, and productivity of today's elders, the author describes how increases in life expectancy have transformed America's aging society.

Ballenger, J. F. (2006). *Self, senility, and Alzheimer's disease in modern America: A history.* Baltimore, MD: Johns Hopkins University Press. Based on current research in psychiatry and gerontology, this book provides an extensive overview of Alzheimer's disease, including health concerns, neurological changes, cultural perceptions about cognitive decline, and treatment options.

Cabeza, R., Nyberg, L., & Park, D. (Eds.). (2005). *Cognitive neuroscience of aging: Linking cognitive and cerebral aging.* New York: Oxford University Press. A collection of chapters examining the effects of aging on cognition. Topics include age-related changes in neural activity, the effects of aging on memory and perception, recent advances in the field of neurology, and the benefits of cognitive training.

Ellis, N. (2004). *If I live to be 100: Lessons from the Centenarians*. New York: Three Rivers Press. Based on extensive research and a year of interviews, this book highlights the extraordinary lives of centenarians, including their unique life experiences and secrets to living a long, healthy life.

TRANSPARENCIES

T-184 **Active Lifespan in Twenty-Five Nations**
Figure 17.1 (p. 442)

T-186 **Rates of Visual and Hearing Impairments among American Men and Women by Age (Part One)**
Figure 17.2 (p. 445)

T-187 **Rates of Visual and Hearing Impairments among American Men and Women by Age (Part Two)**
Figure 17.2 (p. 445)

T-189 **Leading Causes of Death Among People Age 65 and Older in the United States and Canada**
Figure 17.3 (p. 453)

T-190 **Increase with Age in Nursing Home Care in the United States and Canada**
Figure 17.4 (p. 459)

T-192 **Distribution of Older Adults' Autobiographical Memories by Reported Age at Time of the Event**
Figure 17.5 (p. 462)

MEDIA MATERIALS

EXPLORING LIFESPAN DEVELOPMENT IN ACTION

Late Adulthood

This part of the Observation Program begins by illustrating the most obvious physical changes of late adulthood, along with variations in physical aging. Several factors that promote longevity are reviewed. A visit to the Senior Center in Normal, Illinois, depicts many services that support development and well-being late in life—health checks; a government-subsidized hot lunch program; educational workshops and lectures that teach elders to understand, recognize, and prevent health problems; exercise classes; pleasurable leisure pursuits; and the opportunity to form warm friendships.

Attention, memory, and verbal expression difficulties are common concerns of older adults. However, as the Writers Group at Westminster Village, a life-care community, reveals, elders who actively use their minds sustain complex cognitive skills. Members share the fruits of their creative efforts and comment on why they like to write. George and Dorothy, married for 56 years, reside in their own home and lead an active and rewarding life. George comes up with an innovative solution to an everyday problem and describes how he volunteers at a nearby nursing home.

Jeanne and Charles, recently retired, defy the stereotype of retirement as stressful. Good health, continued involvement in professional activities and leisure pursuits, and the pleasures of grandparenthood helped make the transition a welcome one.

Alexander talks about how volunteering has helped him meet new people, stay active, and continue learning well after retirement. He also discusses how he has been able to compensate for age-related physical changes in order to continue doing the things he used to when he was younger, such as take care of his lawn.

Rabbi Gordon exemplifies the increasingly blurred distinction between work and retirement. Since retiring 25 years ago, he has had a dozen careers and has just taken a full-time position. He explains why he returned to the pulpit at this time in his life and what it means to him. Next, Rabbi Gordon and his 16-year-old granddaughter Rachel discuss their relationship and what it has meant to live in the same city for the first time in each of their lives. Finally, Rabbi Gordon speaks about the role of the community in making the elder years more rewarding.

Onie, age 107, describes her good memory, love of learning, and appreciation for the good things in her life, including having had the ability to see until age 100. She talks about her desire to travel, her positive outlook for the future, and the sense of purpose she feels every day.

A WINDOW ON LIFESPAN DEVELOPMENT

Creativity in Late Life: An Older Adults Writers' Group
Members tell how they became interested in writing and what motivates them to put their thoughts onto paper. Some members read samples of their work.

Challenges of Advanced Age and Retirement: Rabbi Gordon, Age 89
Rabbi Gordon describes his many post-retirement careers and the way that challenging work fulfills him. He also comments on the importance of community response to the many needs of elders.

Coping with Widowhood: Anna Mae, Age 82
Anna Mae's life changed drastically with the death of her husband and her own stroke. But with the help of neighbors and her two sons, she hopes to stay in her own house as long as possible.

Finding Enjoyment in Retirement and Grandparenthood: Jeanne and Charles
Jeanne and Charles find retirement a happy relief from their previously hectic schedules. Both stay active in professional and volunteer activities. They enjoy tennis, time with friends, and bonding with their grandchildren.

Retirement and Volunteering: Alexander, Age 90, Marguerite, Age 82, Eleanor, Age 82, and Doris, Age 87
Four retirees describe the personal and social benefits they have experienced as a result of doing volunteer work after retirement, including meeting new people, feeling useful, and staying active.

Centenarian Perspectives: Onie, Age 107
Onie talks about her good memory, her desire to go on learning, her love of travel, and her appreciation for the good life she has had. She notes that she was fortunate to have her sight for 100 of her 107 years. Typical of centenarians, she expresses a positive view of life and of the future.

VIDEOTAPES AND DVDs

Age Happens (2000, Aquarius Health Care Media, 28 min.). This program focuses on the psychological and physiological aspects of aging. It looks at factors that help older people maintain their health and functional independence.

Aging (1993, RMI Media Productions, 30 min.). This program examines the aging process, theories of aging, changes associated with aging, and health issues common to aging. The emphasis is on maintaining one's health in later years, including ways that individuals can help improve the quality of life for their aging family members and friends.

The Aging Mind (1998, Aquarius Health Care Media, 28 min.). This program explains how to determine when memory loss is simply the result of age and when it might result from depression, vitamin deficiency, or Alzheimer's disease. Experts differentiate between normal and pathological aging, making the point that poor health is not a natural result of growing older.

The Aging Process (1991, Films Media Group, 19 min.). This program explains theories of aging and looks at some habits that affect both longevity and the quality of life, including exercise, regular medical checkups, proper diet, moderate drinking, and no smoking.

Aging Well (1994, Films Media Group, 18 min.). This program describes some of the medical advances and lifestyle changes that are continuing to boost life expectancy rates. It explores the effects of aging on mental skills and the emotional issues of aging through profiles of two senior women, a 76-year-old and a 65-year-old, who typify the "new" senior citizens of the late twentieth century.

Alzheimer's Disease: How Families Cope (1997, Films Media Group/Dartmouth-Hitchcock Medical Center, 29 min.). In this program, part of the series The Doctor Is In, families who are caregivers provide practical information on how to care for a loved one with Alzheimer's disease in the home. It looks at the important decisions facing caregivers, such as the choice between using outside day care and in-home health aides. Two Alzheimer's specialists describe the stages of the disease and talk about how caregivers can modify its effects on both the patient and the caregiving family.

BPH: Aging and the Enlarged Prostate (2000, Films Media Group, 23 min.). This program provides information about benign prostatic hyperplasia, a condition that most men will eventually experience but that is often ignored until severe urinary discomfort develops. The program covers the symptoms of BPH, current drug and surgical interventions, and future treatment options, with an emphasis on the importance of an annual prostate exam for men over 50.

The Family Guide to Alzheimer's Disease (2005, Aquarius Health Care Media/LifeView Resources; 5-part series). This five-part series, hosted by TV talk show host Leeza Gibbons, looks at what a diagnosis of Alzheimer's disease means for both sufferers and their caregivers. The series is designed to help families understand what to expect, to deal effectively with the challenges of Alzheimer's, and to improve the quality of life for patient and caregivers alike.

Fitness and Nutrition: How to Improve Life as You Age (2003, Aquarius Health Care Media/Grand Rapids Community College, 27 min.). This program offers information and advice for how people can improve their lives as they age through proper fitness and good nutrition.

Growing Old in a New Age: How the Body Ages (1993, Annenberg Media/University of Hawaii Center on Aging, 60 min.). This program, Part 2 of the 13-part series, looks at the physical changes of aging and explains how to prevent physical deterioration.

Growing Old in a New Age: Illness and Disability (1993, Annenberg Media/University of Hawaii Center on Aging, 60 min.). In this program, Part 10 of a 13-part series, older adults talk about how the challenges of coping with chronic illness. The program also looks at decisions about institutionalized care and at the cost of long-term care.

Growing Old in a New Age: Love, Intimacy and Sexuality (1993, Annenberg Media/University of Hawaii Center on Aging, 60 min.). This program, Part 4 of a 13-part series, focuses on the role of love and affection in late-adult life. Older adults talk about their continuing need for companionship, intimacy, love, and sex.

Growing Old in a New Age: Maximizing Physical Potential of Older Adults (1993, Annenberg Media/University of Hawaii Center on Aging, 60 min.). In this program, Part 3 of a 13-part series, older adults talk about lifestyle choices that have enabled them to remain active and healthy.

Life Cycle: Adulthood and Aging (1996, RMI Media Productions, 30 min.). This program uses three profiles to discuss the influences of nutrition and lifestyle on aging. A 30-year-old couple makes lifestyle choices that differ from those of their parents. A 70-year-old woman who has had coronary bypass surgery is seen as a member of the Dancing Grannies traveling aerobic troupe. Finally, a 90-year-old couple display health and vitality.

Life Expectancy: Geography as Destiny (2004, Films Media Group, 31 min.). This program looks at the wide variations in life expectancy statistics around the world, with a focus on economic and cultural factors influencing lifespans in the United States, Japan, Russia, and the developing nation of Sierra Leone, which—because of a high infant mortality rate—has the world's lowest life expectancy. The program demonstrates links between obesity and rising mortality rates, as well as negative effects of other types of social change.

New Views on Alzheimer's (1994, Films Media Group, 28 min.). This specially adapted Phil Donahue program features interviews with four members of the Sisters of Notre Dame who are participants in a study of Alzheimer's disease involving 550 elderly Catholic nuns. David Snowdon, who oversees the study, explains why these women are still functioning at such high levels even at advanced ages.

Nutrition for Independent Elders (2002, Concept Media, 25 min.). This program focuses on seniors who are relatively healthy and are community-based. It highlights diseases with an underlying nutritional origin and examines some physiological changes of aging that can have negative effects on nutrition. The program provides information about the nutrients and fiber needed by elderly people, including a description of the Food Guide Pyramid and the Tufts 70+ Pyramid, as well as a brief discussion of supplements.

Nutritional Risks and Challenges (2002, Concept Media, 24 min.). This program focuses on some of the major nutritional challenges facing elders, especially those who are ill or at risk of malnutrition. It looks at contributing factors, assessment tools, and possible interventions, as well as the role of the interdisciplinary team.

100-Something (1999, Films Media Group, 47 min.). In this program, doctors from Harvard Medical School's New England Centenarian Study and the University of Georgia's study of extreme longevity look for a correlation between lifespan and the genetic, physical, psychological, and cognitive dimensions of aging. People who have reached age 100 also provide personal insights into the factors that they believe account for their longevity, including faith, exercise, good nutrition, sexuality, and continuation of their involvement in daily routines and meaningful work.

Preventing Falls (2002, Concept Media, 24 min.). This program explores the common causes of falls among elderly people—dehydration, medications, urinary problems, impaired visual function, and poor balance and gait—and looks at some interventions that can minimize the risk. The program emphasizes that many falls are preventable and that fall reduction plans are the responsibility of everyone caring for the elderly, whether at home or in a health-care institution.

Sleeping Well (1996, Films Media Group/Dartmouth-Hitchcock Medical Center, 28 min.). This program, part of the series The Doctor Is In, covers the widespread problems of sleeplessness, including insomnia, sleep apnea, narcolepsy, and restless legs. The program offers tips on how to fall asleep, as well as the specific problems of sleep difficulties caused by shift work and jet lag.

Substance Abuse in the Elderly (2000, Aquarius Health Care Media, 28 min.). This program, part of the series The Doctor Is In, interviews experts and profiles several older Americans who are dealing with alcohol and prescription drug misuse. The program also shows some innovative substance-abuse programs that have been created specifically for the elderly.

To Be Old, Black, and Poor (1993, Films Media Group, 52 min.). This program documents the day-to-day experiences of poor, black, elderly people in the United States through the story of six months in the lives of Leonard and Sarah Bass, as they struggle to survive against difficult odds.

TEST BANK

MULTIPLE CHOICE

1) According to your text, late adulthood is best viewed as
   A) a break from earlier periods and a time of decreasing potential.
   B) an extension of earlier periods and a time of continued potential.
   C) very different from earlier periods due to the decline, rather than the growth, of skills.
   D) technically a part of middle adulthood, but delineated separately by researchers because of beliefs held by the general population.

   Answer: B
   Page Ref: 441
   Skill: Factual
   Objective: 17.1

2) The term psychologists use for a person's actual competence and performance in dealing with life's challenges is __________ age.
   A) chronological
   B) biological
   C) functional
   D) internal

   Answer: C
   Page Ref: 441
   Skill: Factual
   Objective: 17.1

23) After age 70, an elder's capacity to respond appropriately to other people declines because he or she is less able to
   A) hear at high frequencies.
   B) detect the content and emotionally expressive features of conversation.
   C) distinguish simple tone patterns, particularly lower frequencies and at a softer level.
   D) hear startling noises.
   Answer: B
   Page Ref: 446
   Skill: Factual
   Objective: 17.3

24) An elderly person who has a problem with hearing loss can deal with this loss most effectively by
   A) acting as though there has been no change in hearing.
   B) closing his or her eyes to minimize visual distractions.
   C) seeking out quieter environments for conversations.
   D) avoiding unnatural solutions such as hearing aids.
   Answer: C
   Page Ref: 446
   Skill: Applied
   Objective: 17.3

25) Smoking, dentures, medication, and environmental pollutants can affect taste perception, but __________ can help make food more attractive to older adults.
   A) social gatherings at mealtimes
   B) artistic arrangements
   C) culinary counseling
   D) flavor additives
   Answer: D
   Page Ref: 446
   Skill: Factual
   Objective: 17.3

26) If impaired, which sensory loss would impact an elder's ability to detect rancid food and the presence of a fire?
   A) taste
   B) smell
   C) vision
   D) touch
   Answer: B
   Page Ref: 446
   Skill: Factual
   Objective: 17.3

27) A reduction in the sense of touch affects primarily what portion of the body?
   A) the face
   B) the arms
   C) the fingertips
   D) the feet
   Answer: C
   Page Ref: 446
   Skill: Factual
   Objective: 17.3

28) The primary effect of the normal age-related changes in the functioning of the heart is
   A) a faster, more effective heartbeat.
   B) softer, thinner artery walls.
   C) higher heart rates during exercise.
   D) slower blood flow through the body.

Answer: D
Page Ref: 447
Skill: Factual
Objective: 17.4

29) The amount of air that can be forced in to and out of a person's lungs decreases throughout adulthood primarily because
   A) the lung tissue becomes less elastic.
   B) the lungs grow smaller as their cells die.
   C) the blood cannot absorb as much oxygen.
   D) the rib cage can no longer expand as much.

Answer: A
Page Ref: 447
Skill: Factual
Objective: 17.4

30) Marchelle's immune system has begun to turn against normal body tissues, which is referred to as
   A) selective optimization with compensation.
   B) primary aging.
   C) an autoimmune response.
   D) compression of morbidity.

Answer: C
Page Ref: 447
Skill: Conceptual
Objective: 17.4

31) Ninety-year-old Barbara wants her doctor to predict her odds of surviving over the next two years. Her doctor
   A) should tell her that there is no way to do this.
   B) could run tests on her heart and lung capacity, which are the strongest indicators of longevity.
   C) should recommend that she eat a low-fat diet, take vitamin supplements, and abstain from exercise and walking in her neighborhood to avoid life-threatening falls.
   D) can determine whether she has high T cell activity, which is a strong predictor.

Answer: D
Page Ref: 447
Skill: Factual
Objective: 17.4

32) Elijah is 80 years old. He is UNLIKELY to have difficulty with which sleep-related activity?
   A) falling asleep
   B) staying asleep
   C) sleeping deeply
   D) waking up early

Answer: D
Page Ref: 447
Skill: Applied
Objective: 17.5

33) Elderly people who have trouble sleeping can reduce their difficulties by
   A) realizing they are normal and not worrying.
   B) taking sleeping pills on a regular basis.
   C) taking frequent short naps during the day.
   D) cutting back on their exercise level.
   Answer: A
   Page Ref: 447
   Skill: Factual
   Objective: 17.5

34) Which of the following is a likely age-related change in the appearance of elderly adults?
   A) The skin gains a layer of fatty support.
   B) Teeth become yellowed, cracked, or chipped and gums recede.
   C) The nose and ears become more narrow and pinched.
   D) Hair on the head thins in women but not in men.
   Answer: B
   Page Ref: 448
   Skill: Factual
   Objective: 17.6

35) Weight changes after age 60 typically involve
   A) less fat accumulated on the torso.
   B) weight gain due to decreased activity.
   C) weight loss due to less lean body mass.
   D) weight gain from fat accumulations.
   Answer: C
   Page Ref: 448
   Skill: Factual
   Objective: 17.6

36) Eighty-six-year-old Anne has lost much of her muscle strength and has lost flexibility and strength in her tendons and ligaments. As a result, which of the following will be most difficult for her?
   A) sitting up straight
   B) taking a shower
   C) tying her shoes
   D) rising from a chair
   Answer: D
   Page Ref: 448
   Skill: Applied
   Objective: 17.6

37) Which of the following signs of aging is linked to longevity?
   A) sensory functioning
   B) graying hair
   C) facial wrinkles
   D) baldness
   Answer: A
   Page Ref: 448
   Skill: Factual
   Objective: 17.6

38) Elderly people tend to report more physical and psychological problems with aging if they
   A) see it as inevitable and uncontrollable.
   B) fight aging with exercise and diet.
   C) use cosmetics and surgery to look young.
   D) see aging as a time of social importance.

Answer: A
Page Ref: 448
Skill: Factual
Objective: 17.6

39) Mrs. Kovak's medications all have "smart caps" on them that beep to remind her to take her medicine and track the times and number of pills she takes. The "smart cap" is an example of
   A) implicit memory.
   B) selective optimization with compensation.
   C) assistive technology.
   D) a "crutch" used by many elders that reduces their independence and hastens the onset of Alzheimer's by reducing cognitive functioning.

Answer: C
Page Ref: 448–449
Skill: Factual
Objective: 17.6

40) Voice-command telephones and sensor-activated room lights are examples of
   A) assistive technology usually covered in the United States and Canada under government-sponsored health-care programs.
   B) assistive technology usually covered in Sweden under government-sponsored health-care programs, but not the United States or Canada.
   C) assistive technology that may become available for purchase in the near future.
   D) assistive technology that will soon be available in all new housing.

Answer: B
Page Ref: 449
Skill: Conceptual
Objective: 17.6

41) The check-out clerk assumes Mrs. Banerje cannot hear due to her advanced age and speaks very loudly to her. Which of the following scenarios depicts stereotype threat?
   A) Mrs. Banerje does not realize the clerk is yelling. She pays the clerk and then leaves the store.
   B) Mrs. Banerje becomes flustered and has trouble counting out her money and then cannot remember where she parked her car when she leaves the store.
   C) Mrs. Banerje is appreciative of the clerk's consideration for her hearing loss.
   D) Mrs. Banerje is embarrassed by the clerk's behavior and speaks to the store manager. She suggests the store conduct a discrimination awareness training to avoid alienating other customers.

Answer: B
Page Ref: 449
Skill: Applied
Objective: 17.6

42) The main reason low-SES ethnic minority elders are less likely to follow a doctor's instructions is that
   A) they do not trust their doctors, most of whom are white.
   B) they do not wish to prolong their lives.
   C) they do not believe they can control their health through their own actions.
   D) they are healthier overall than other people.

Answer: C
Page Ref: 450
Skill: Factual
Objective: 17.7

43) How do men and women compare in their physical health after age 85?
  A) Women have fewer health problems overall.
  B) Men have more nonfatal conditions than do women.
  C) Women have more fatal diseases than do men.
  D) Men are less likely to be impaired than are women.
Answer: D
Page Ref: 450
Skill: Factual
Objective: 17.7

44) The public health goal of reducing the average period of diminished vigor before death as life expectancy extends is called
  A) compression of morbidity.
  B) reduction of complaints.
  C) anticipation of mortality.
  D) living until you die.
Answer: A
Page Ref: 450
Skill: Factual
Objective: 17.7

45) Mr. Prieto is an elder who does not eat as much as he used to. Which of the following statements is relevant to this situation?
  A) Elders should reduce their caloric intake significantly in their later years, as the body requires less fuel to maintain a healthy status.
  B) Declines in taste and smell often reduce the quantity and quality of food eaten.
  C) As long as he is taking vitamin supplements, he should remain physically and cognitively healthy.
  D) Mr. Prieto probably leaves a very active lifestyle.
Answer: B
Page Ref: 451
Skill: Applied
Objective: 17.7

46) Your elderly neighbor is wondering whether she should take daily vitamin-mineral supplements to improve her health. What should you tell her?
  A) This is a good idea, as research has shown these supplements improve cardiovascular health and memory loss.
  B) These supplements are not necessary if you are eating well.
  C) These supplements are only useful for very active people.
  D) These supplements have benefits for enhanced immune response and a significant drop in days of infectious illness.
Answer: D
Page Ref: 451
Skill: Applied
Objective: 17.7

47) A friend of yours, who is generally healthy at age 80, is considering beginning an exercise program that involves vigorous walking. What advice should you give?
  A) This is a very good idea and can provide real benefits.
  B) Exercise this late in life is dangerous and not helpful.
  C) Exercise is good, but it should not be weight-bearing.
  D) Your friend should only do this if male, because there are risks for females.
Answer: A
Page Ref: 451
Skill: Applied
Objective: 17.7

48) A major barrier to getting older men and women to take up a fitness routine is
A) the fact that "taking it easy" is the best treatment for many chronic diseases.
B) few exercise classes are available that are appropriate for this age group.
C) lack of transportation to and from exercise classes.
D) lack of awareness of benefits and discomforts expected from physical activity.
Answer: D
Page Ref: 451
Skill: Factual
Objective: 17.7

49) Reports of a decline in sexual desire and activity among older people
A) are inaccurate, as elders with more leisure time on their hands are able to commit more time to sexual activity.
B) may be exaggerated by cohort effects, as newer generations of elders will probably be more sexually active.
C) reflect one of the few stereotypes about elders that is true.
D) are based upon a very small sample of individuals over the age of 90.
Answer: B
Page Ref: 452
Skill: Factual
Objective: 17.7

50) If an elderly couple stops having sexual activity, which partner typically initiates this cessation?
A) both of them equally
B) the woman
C) the man
D) neither; elderly couples never stop having sex
Answer: C
Page Ref: 452
Skill: Factual
Objective: 17.7

51) What are the sex differences in death rates from cardiovascular disease and cancer?
A) Women have higher death rates for both cardiovascular disease and cancer than men.
B) Men have higher death rates for cardiovascular disease and women have higher death rates from cancer.
C) There are no sex differences in the death rates from these two diseases.
D) Men have higher death rates for both cardiovascular disease and cancer than women.
Answer: D
Page Ref: 452
Skill: Factual
Objective: 17.7

52) Why does the death rate due to pneumonia increase so sharply during late adulthood?
A) Pneumonia is much more deadly today than it was several decades ago.
B) Because many lung inflammations are classified as pneumonia, it erroneously appears that pneumonia kills more people than it actually does.
C) As the immune systems of elders weaken over time, they eventually encounter an infection that they cannot fight.
D) The death rate is calculated as a percentage, and because so few people live until late adulthood, the percentages killed by certain diseases calculate higher.
Answer: C
Page Ref: 452
Skill: Factual
Objective: 17.8

53) Mrs. Schmida has just experienced a blockage of blood flow to her brain. This condition is known as __________ and is the fourth most common killer of older adults.
   A) stroke
   B) pneumonia
   C) a heart attack
   D) Alzheimer's
   Answer: A
   Page Ref: 452
   Skill: Applied
   Objective: 17.8

54) Which of these is the best example of primary aging?
   A) farsightedness from a stiffening lens
   B) lung cancer from smoking cigarettes
   C) weight gain from a sedentary lifestyle
   D) high blood pressure from prolonged stress
   Answer: A
   Page Ref: 452
   Skill: Conceptual
   Objective: 17.8

55) Which of these is the best example of secondary aging?
   A) decrease in the maximum heart rate
   B) farsightedness from a stiffening lens
   C) heart disease from smoking cigarettes
   D) lack of menstruation after menopause
   Answer: C
   Page Ref: 452
   Skill: Conceptual
   Objective: 17.8

56) Arthritis, diabetes, and unintentional injuries are all major sources of __________, in which an individual's weakened functioning interferes with everyday competence and leaves the older person vulnerable.
   A) primary aging
   B) frailty
   C) secondary aging
   D) terminal decline
   Answer: B
   Page Ref: 453
   Skill: Factual
   Objective: 17.8

57) Mr. Hiroshi is experiencing painful, stiff, and swollen joints and muscles. His doctor informs him that the cartilage on the ends of his bones is deteriorating due to decades of wear and tear. Mr. Hiroshi has
   A) osteoarthritis.
   B) rheumatoid arthritis.
   C) osteoporosis.
   D) diabetes.
   Answer: A
   Page Ref: 453
   Skill: Applied
   Objective: 17.8

58) At age 72, your friend has just been told by the doctor that he shows signs of osteoarthritis. You can tell your friend that

A) he should increase the calcium in his diet.
B) this is a normal condition in older adults.
C) it is caused by an autoimmune reaction.
D) it is caused by a lack of exercise in his life.

Answer: B
Page Ref: 453
Skill: Applied
Objective: 17.8

59) Mrs. Shanteau is experiencing inflammation in most of her joints, resulting in stiffness, inflammation, and aching. Her doctor informs her that the swelling is due to an autoimmune response that causes the tissue in the cartilage to grow, which will damage surrounding ligaments, muscles, and bones. Mrs. Shanteau should be aware that her condition can result in

A) minimal discomfort that can usually be treated with over-the-counter pain medications.
B) incontinence, dementia, and possible heart failure.
C) some discomfort, which can usually be relieved if she loses between 5 and 10 pounds.
D) deformed joints that frequently impact mobility, and a possibility that her heart and lungs can be affected as well.

Answer: D
Page Ref: 453
Skill: Applied
Objective: 17.8

60) Which condition is associated with an elevated risk for Alzheimer's disease?

A) osteoarthritis
B) rheumatoid arthritis
C) diabetes
D) hip fractures

Answer: C
Page Ref: 454
Skill: Factual
Objective: 17.8

61) Higher rates of adult-onset diabetes are associated with which of the following environmental factors?

A) an illness of the pancreas
B) inactivity and obesity
C) insufficient nutrition
D) a late-appearing genetic defect in the immune system

Answer: B
Page Ref: 454
Skill: Factual
Objective: 17.8

62) Which statement about elderly drivers and motor vehicle accidents is true?
   A) Because of personal worries about visual processing deficits, elders tend to drive less and therefore have the lowest rates of traffic violations, accidents, and fatalities per mile driven than any other age group.
   B) Elders have higher rates of traffic violations, accidents, and fatalities per mile driven than any other age group.
   C) Elders have higher rates of traffic violations, accidents, and fatalities per mile driven than any age group EXCEPT drivers under age 25.
   D) Because so few elders drive after the age of 75, there is little data available on their motor vehicle accident rate.

Answer: C
Page Ref: 454
Skill: Factual
Objective: 17.8

63) The most powerful factor in the high rate of automobile accidents in which elders are involved is
   A) driving too quickly and recklessly.
   B) hearing loss.
   C) driving too slowly as a precautionary measure for slower reflexes.
   D) an increase in visual processing difficulties.

Answer: D
Page Ref: 454
Skill: Factual
Objective: 17.8

64) Falls among the elderly are caused in many cases by
   A) declines in vision, hearing, and mobility.
   B) weakened bones.
   C) difficulty breaking a fall.
   D) osteoporosis, which compacts the spinal column and severely limits mobility.

Answer: A
Page Ref: 454–455
Skill: Factual
Objective: 17.8

65) Which of these is a common indirect effect on an elderly person who has had a fall?
   A) an increase in their health insurance rates
   B) a fear of falling that limits their mobility and social activity
   C) a general softening of bones near the site of the injury
   D) anger at the friends and family who let them fall

Answer: B
Page Ref: 455
Skill: Factual
Objective: 17.8

66) A set of disorders that occurs almost exclusively in old age and in which many aspects of thought and behavior are so impaired that everyday activities are disrupted is referred to as
   A) Alzheimer's disease.
   B) frailty.
   C) dementia.
   D) epilepsy.

Answer: C
Page Ref: 455
Skill: Factual
Objective: 17.9

67) A form of dementia that involves deterioration in subcortical brain regions is
   A) Alzheimer's disease.
   B) cerebrovascular dementia.
   C) reversible dementia.
   D) Parkinson's disease.
   Answer: D
   Page Ref: 455
   Skill: Factual
   Objective: 17.9

68) Alzheimer's disease and cerebrovascular dementia are both types of
   A) cardiovascular disease.
   B) cortical dementia.
   C) angioplastic illness.
   D) cerebral hypertrophy.
   Answer: B
   Page Ref: 455
   Skill: Factual
   Objective: 17.9

69) Mrs. LaMarche has been diagnosed with a form of dementia. She is experiencing the gradual loss of many aspects of thought and behavior due to structural and chemical brain deterioration. Mrs. LaMarche has
   A) cerebrovascular dementia.
   B) Parkinson's disease.
   C) Alzheimer's disease.
   D) retrograde amnesia.
   Answer: C
   Page Ref: 455
   Skill: Applied
   Objective: 17.9

70) The earliest symptoms of Alzheimer's disease are generally
   A) personality changes.
   B) lack of motor control.
   C) inability to recognize loved ones.
   D) severe memory lapses.
   Answer: D
   Page Ref: 455
   Skill: Factual
   Objective: 17.9

71) After psychological symptoms, such as memory loss and depression, Alzheimer's disease generally progresses to
   A) a lack of motor control.
   B) difficulty digesting food.
   C) extreme sensitivity to cold.
   D) inability to see or to hear.
   Answer: A
   Page Ref: 455
   Skill: Factual
   Objective: 17.9

72) A definitive diagnosis of Alzheimer's disease is made by
A) administering a blood test.
B) examining the brain after death.
C) measuring the person's memory.
D) taking an X-ray image of the brain.
Answer: B
Page Ref: 456
Skill: Factual
Objective: 17.9

73) The brain of a person with Alzheimer's is likely to
A) have fewer neurofibrillary tangles and amyloid plaques than people without Alzheimer's.
B) overcompensate for the breakdown and disposal of abnormal proteins, leaving too few remaining.
C) have more neurofibrillary tangles and amyloid plaques than people without Alzheimer's.
D) have higher levels of neurotransmitters.
Answer: C
Page Ref: 456
Skill: Factual
Objective: 17.9

74) __________ is the most commonly known risk factor for sporadic Alzheimer's, present in 50 percent of the cases.
A) The abnormal ApoE4 gene
B) The presence of amyloid plaques
C) Occurrence of a head injury prior to age 15
D) An extremely low level of aluminum in the bloodstream
Answer: A
Page Ref: 456
Skill: Factual
Objective: 17.9

75) Of the characteristics below, which one has little evidence to link it to Alzheimer's disease?
A) head injury
B) excess dietary fat
C) smoking
D) cardiovascular disease
Answer: C
Page Ref: 456
Skill: Factual
Objective: 17.9

76) Which of these factors seems to REDUCE an individual's risk of contracting Alzheimer's disease?
A) the blood protein ApoE4
B) a "Mediterranean diet"
C) having Down syndrome
D) low educational attainment
Answer: B
Page Ref: 457
Skill: Factual
Objective: 17.9

77) The relationship between Alzheimer's disease and education can best be summarized by saying that
A) many years of higher education increases the risk of Alzheimer's.
B) highly educated people tend to live healthier lifestyles all around.
C) education increases brain growth, producing a cognitive reserve.
D) education teaches techniques for avoiding Alzheimer's disease.
Answer: C
Page Ref: 457
Skill: Factual
Objective: 17.9

78) Mr. Omosigho has experienced a series of strokes that have left areas of dead brain cells, causing step-by-step degeneration of his mental ability. Mr. Omosigho is experiencing
A) familial Alzheimer's.
B) sporadic Alzheimer's.
C) atherosclerosis.
D) cerebrovascular dementia.
Answer: D
Page Ref: 457
Skill: Applied
Objective: 17.9

79) A decline in heart disease and more effective stroke prevention methods have resulted in
A) a decrease in the incidence of cerebrovascular dementia.
B) an increase in the incidence of cerebrovascular dementia.
C) an decrease in the incidence of cerebrovascular dementia in Japan only.
D) no change in the incidence of cerebrovascular dementia, as it is directly influenced by heredity and not lifestyle.
Answer: A
Page Ref: 457
Skill: Factual
Objective: 17.9

80) Depressed older adults are likely to __________ their mental difficulties, whereas the demented person will often __________ them.
A) minimize; exaggerate
B) exaggerate; minimize
C) be unaware of; imagine
D) make up; imagine
Answer: B
Page Ref: 459
Skill: Factual
Objective: 17.9

81) It is important that doctors monitor the side effects of the medications they prescribe for elderly people because
A) they often need much larger doses of a drug to get the same effect.
B) elderly people often request medications they do not really need.
C) these medications may produce symptoms similar to dementia.
D) no one really knows the side effects the drugs might produce.
Answer: C
Page Ref: 459
Skill: Factual
Objective: 17.9

82) Interventions that work best for Alzheimer patient's caregivers
 A) should begin early in the caregiving process.
 B) begin after the caregiver has had about six months of experience caring for the patient.
 C) are effective if the caregiver has a strong system of family supports.
 D) are more effective if the patient has familial rather than sporadic Alzheimer's.
Answer: A
Page Ref: 458
Skill: Factual
Objective: Box SI: Interventions for Caregivers of Elders with Dementia

83) Your neighbor is exhausted from caring for her elderly husband who has Alzheimer's. She confides that she is considering the methods below to cope with his constant questioning, agitation, and memory problems. Which of the following would be LEAST effective?
 A) distracting rather than scolding when the person asks the same question over and over
 B) responding patiently with reminders and lists when the person blames others for memory problems
 C) introducing pleasant activities that relieve agitation
 D) being nonresponsive (silent) when the person asks an inappropriate question
Answer: D
Page Ref: 458
Skill: Applied
Objective: Box SI: Interventions for Caregivers of Elders with Dementia

84) Caregivers for people with Alzheimer's usually say that __________ is/are the type of assistance they most desire.
 A) respite
 B) caregiving skills
 C) coping strategies
 D) knowledge
Answer: A
Page Ref: 458
Skill: Factual
Objective: Box SI: Interventions for Caregivers of Elders with Dementia

85) According to REACH information, which caregiver of a person with Alzheimer's will benefit MOST from intervention programs?
 A) a man
 B) a spouse
 C) a higher-SES caregiver
 D) a friend
Answer: B
Page Ref: 458
Skill: Factual
Objective: Box SI: Interventions for Caregivers of Elders with Dementia

86) Which elder is most likely to enter a nursing home?
 A) Mr. Holzman, who has dementia
 B) Mrs. Nairon, who has cancer
 C) Mr. Overholser, who had a heart attack
 D) Mrs. Pegel, who fractured her hip
Answer: A
Page Ref: 459
Skill: Applied
Objective: 17.10

87) Which person is MOST likely to be placed in a nursing home?
  A) Neva, an 83-year-old African American
  B) Natasha, an 80-year-old Caucasian American
  C) Nyree, a 90-year-old Japanese great-grandmother
  D) Nyung, a 95-year-old Asian American

Answer: B
Page Ref: 460
Skill: Applied
Objective: 17.10

88) In Western nations, at least 60 to 80 percent of all long-term care for older adults is provided by
  A) government assistance.
  B) nursing homes.
  C) family members.
  D) charitable organizations.

Answer: C
Page Ref: 460
Skill: Factual
Objective: 17.10

89) Mr. and Mrs. Archuleta have no severe medical needs but have difficulty keeping up with such "life maintenance" issues as cooking and cleaning. They moved into a housing situation that was very homelike, but had staff that provided extra supports. This is an example of
  A) a nursing home.
  B) assisted living.
  C) institutionalization.
  D) hospice care.

Answer: B
Page Ref: 460
Skill: Applied
Objective: 17.10

90) Mental abilities that decline at an earlier age typically depend on __________ intelligence, while those that are sustained until later in life depend on __________ intelligence.
  A) crystallized; fluid
  B) fluid; crystallized
  C) cognitive; emotional
  D) emotional; cognitive

Answer: B
Page Ref: 460
Skill: Factual
Objective: 17.11

91) When older adults engage in selective optimization with compensation, they
  A) select only activities that are personally valued to optimize their energy and also develop ways to compensate for losses.
  B) tend to show gains in fluid intelligence.
  C) show losses in crystallized intelligence only.
  D) attend to only certain parts of a conversation (selective optimization) and then try to fill in the missing pieces later (compensation).

Answer: A
Page Ref: 461
Skill: Factual
Objective: 17.11

92) An important reason older adults remember less about the things they have experienced is that they
   A) are not as interested in the world around them.
   B) process information more slowly and incompletely.
   C) frequently suffer from cognitive dementia.
   D) have a great deal of trouble with recognition memory.
Answer: B
Page Ref: 461
Skill: Factual
Objective: 17.11

93) __________ memory is a fairly automatic type of memory that demands little mental effort, so performance does not change much in old age.
   A) Explicit
   B) Recognition
   C) Recall
   D) Automatic
Answer: B
Page Ref: 461
Skill: Factual
Objective: 17.11

94) Mrs. Gaffney sees her neighbor in the supermarket and recognizes her immediately. This recognition takes place without conscious awareness or intent. Mrs. Gaffney's experience is an example of __________ memory.
   A) recall
   B) prospective
   C) remote
   D) implicit
Answer: D
Page Ref: 461
Skill: Applied
Objective: 17.11

95) Which sort of memory shows the smallest decline as people grow older?
   A) implicit memory
   B) recall memory
   C) prospective memory
   D) remote memory
Answer: A
Page Ref: 461
Skill: Factual
Objective: 17.11

96) When 70-year-old Mrs. Heinen realizes that she frequently recognizes faces, but cannot remember names or information about the person, she is exhibiting
   A) associative memory deficit.
   B) a loss in implicit memory.
   C) difficulty with remote memory.
   D) prospective memory deficits.
Answer: A
Page Ref: 462
Skill: Applied
Objective: 17.11

97) Mr. Hackebeil's grandchildren love to hear him talk about the things that he did growing up, and how different the typical lifestyle was back then. When he remembers events from his childhood, he is exhibiting __________ memory.
   A) implicit
   B) remote
   C) recall
   D) prospective
   Answer: B
   Page Ref: 462
   Skill: Applied
   Objective: 17.11

98) Why do older adults recall youthful events more readily than in their mid-adulthood lives?
   A) Those events occurred during a period of rapid life change and identity development, and were probably novel experiences of personal significance.
   B) Declines in fluid intelligence make information retrieval of events in mid-life more difficult.
   C) Deficits in recall memory make it harder for people to describe experiences.
   D) The memories of earlier life events have been recalled more, so the neural pathways to and from those memories are more easily traveled, thus leading to ease of recall.
   Answer: A
   Page Ref: 462
   Skill: Factual
   Objective: 17.11

99) Which of these is the best example of prospective memory?
   A) remembering your second-grade teacher's name
   B) remembering the capitals of all 50 states of the United States
   C) remembering to go to a dentist appointment next week
   D) remembering the name of a movie you saw recently
   Answer: C
   Page Ref: 462
   Skill: Conceptual
   Objective: 17.11

100) Which of the following is an example of an event-based memory task?
   A) taking medicine when an alarm goes off
   B) taking medicine every 12 hours
   C) setting an alarm to remind you to take medicine
   D) remembering a special event, like high school graduation
   Answer: A
   Page Ref: 463
   Skill: Conceptual
   Objective: 17.11

101) Laboratory studies of prospective memory typically show greater declines in old age than do real-life studies, primarily because
   A) laboratories are often stressful places for older adults.
   B) elderly people make no attempt to perform well in laboratories.
   C) the lab tasks are focused more on recall than on recognition.
   D) older people set up systems to remind themselves in real life.
   Answer: D
   Page Ref: 463
   Skill: Factual
   Objective: 17.11

102) Language comprehension changes very little in late life
  A) until the late 80s, when skills drop quickly.
  B) as long as conversational partners speak slowly and elders are given enough time to process written text.
  C) for people who speak more than one language, as the dual processing stimulates additional neural regeneration.
  D) as long as individuals spend at least two hours per day communicating with others.

Answer: B
Page Ref: 463
Skill: Factual
Objective: 17.12

103) The major reason older adults tend to use more pronouns and vague references and to speak more slowly than younger adults is that they
  A) have a harder time understanding spoken language.
  B) are showing the earliest symptoms of dementia.
  C) have difficulty retrieving words from long-term memory.
  D) are beginning to lose muscle control over their mouths.

Answer: C
Page Ref: 463
Skill: Factual
Objective: 17.12

104) A common technique used by many elders to compensate for their difficulties in producing language is to
  A) speak more loudly and forcefully.
  B) avoid talking as much as possible.
  C) convey information through sign language.
  D) use simpler grammatical structures.

Answer: D
Page Ref: 463
Skill: Factual
Objective: 17.12

105) Which of the following statements about language production and age is accurate?
  A) Elders show a greater frequency of tip-of-the-tongue states, but they resolve them at a higher rate than do younger people.
  B) Elders show a lower frequency of tip-of-the-tongue states, indicating minimal loss in language production skills.
  C) Elders' speech contains fewer pronouns and unclear references, showing an age-related communicative competence.
  D) Elders tend to use more complex grammatical structures, as their listening partner is usually another elder who has greater powers of auditory retention than does a younger person.

Answer: A
Page Ref: 463
Skill: Factual
Objective: 17.12

106) Mr. and Mrs. Isabor are an elderly couple living at home. One-third to one-half of their typical day will be spent
  A) relating to their children.
  B) managing IADLs.
  C) working out marital difficulties.
  D) dealing with situations that arise in the course of their volunteer work.

Answer: B
Page Ref: 463
Skill: Applied
Objective: 17.13

107) What type of problem is an elder most likely to actively try to solve?
A) interpersonal conflicts
B) problems in the workplace
C) conflicts with grown children
D) daily living issues that they feel are under their control
Answer: D
Page Ref: 463
Skill: Conceptual
Objective: 17.13

108) Which of these cognitive abilities shows improvement as adults grow older?
A) traditional problem solving
B) health problem solving
C) practical problem solving
D) linguistic problem solving
Answer: B
Page Ref: 464
Skill: Factual
Objective: 17.13

109) Broad practical knowledge, the ability to use it practically to make life bearable and meaningful, emotional maturity, and altruistic creativity are important dimensions of
A) fluid intelligence.
B) crystallized intelligence.
C) wisdom.
D) generativity.
Answer: C
Page Ref: 464
Skill: Factual
Objective: 17.14

110) According to your text, wisdom can be summed up as
A) a cumulative benefit of age.
B) expertise in the conduct and meaning of life.
C) an intrinsic characteristic that develops with age.
D) general familiarity with human problems.
Answer: B
Page Ref: 464
Skill: Factual
Objective: 17.14

111) In an uncertain, real-life test of wisdom—such as what to do if a friend is considering suicide—which person is MOST likely to display wisdom?
A) a person who had few adversities in his or her life
B) a male
C) a younger person
D) someone whose career involved human service
Answer: D
Page Ref: 464
Skill: Conceptual
Objective: 17.14

112) The relationship between chronic health conditions and poor intellectual performance in late adulthood may be
A) the best method of predicting intellectual decline.
B) exaggerated by the fact that brighter adults are more likely to engage in health-protective behaviors.
C) underestimated by most researchers.
D) overlooked by many doctors who deal with aging.
Answer: B
Page Ref: 465
Skill: Factual
Objective: 17.15

113) Marla is retiring from a job as a receptionist. If she wants to retain positive intellectual abilities, she needs to
A) find leisure activities that are similar in nature to the job she left.
B) maintain a relaxed, unstructured life.
C) develop stimulating leisure activities.
D) maintain open communication with family and friends.
Answer: C
Page Ref: 465
Skill: Applied
Objective: 17.15

114) At age 78, Mr. Janek's scores on cognitive tasks have become increasingly unstable, indicating cognitive declines. These declines
A) are an indication of distance to death.
B) are related to chronological age.
C) are an early warning sign of diabetes.
D) signify possible depression.
Answer: A
Page Ref: 465
Skill: Applied
Objective: 17.15

115) Before he died, Jaime's family noticed a marked decrease in his cognitive functioning. He spent less time talking and reading, and more time staring off into space or out the window. Jaime's behavior is indicative of
A) increased morbidity.
B) the cognitive slope.
C) mental despair.
D) terminal decline.
Answer: D
Page Ref: 465
Skill: Applied
Objective: 17.15

116) In an older adult, an extended, steep decline in cognitive functioning is a sign of
A) impending death.
B) an infectious disease.
C) atherosclerosis.
D) cortical dementia.
Answer: A
Page Ref: 465
Skill: Factual
Objective: 17.15

117) Cognitive intervention
   A) doesn't affect cognitive abilities as much as it makes older people try harder to remember things and stay focused.
   B) has shown strong gains for those who had shown cognitive functioning declines over time periods as long as 14 years.
   C) is only helpful with those who have shown no declines in cognitive functioning yet.
   D) has not been proven through objective research.

Answer: B
Page Ref: 465
Skill: Factual
Objective: 17.16

118) Your elderly relative is concerned that she seems to be losing some of her cognitive abilities. What is the best advice you can give her?
   A) Don't worry about it, this is normal for people your age.
   B) There must be a physical cause, such as a brain tumor.
   C) Keep your mind active and learn cognitive coping strategies.
   D) There is nothing you can do; this is a sign of Alzheimer's disease.

Answer: C
Page Ref: 465–466
Skill: Applied
Objective: 17.17

119) Mr. and Mrs. Taber are taking a course through the University of the Third Age. From this information, we can infer that the Tabers
   A) are unaware of the many scams targeting older adults.
   B) do not live in the United States.
   C) are deeply religious.
   D) are active, well-educated, and financially well-off.

Answer: D
Page Ref: 467
Skill: Applied
Objective: 17.17

120) You have been asked to help coordinate a two-week university program for elders. Which of the following pieces of advice should you follow?
   A) Relate new material to what elders have already learned by drawing on their experiences and giving many vivid examples.
   B) Get a lot of young instructors that the elders can relate to.
   C) Present information at a fairly rapid pace, because of elders' advanced cognitive processing skills.
   D) Charge tuition to increase attendance; elders are more likely to attend the entire two weeks if they've had to pay for it in advance.

Answer: A
Page Ref: 466,467
Skill: Applied
Objective: 17.17

121) Which of the following statements about continuing education for seniors is accurate?
   A) Community senior centers experience little demand for course offerings for low-SES elders.
   B) Continuing education opportunities help elders overcome their own ingrained stereotypes of aging.
   C) Government-sponsored programs often partially cover Elderhostel costs for seniors.
   D) Higher-educated participants in Elderhostel courses report learning the most from their experiences.

Answer: B
Page Ref: 467
Skill: Factual
Objective: 17.17

ESSAY

122) Describe factors that influence life expectancy.

Answer: Life expectancy is a joint function of heredity and environment. On average, women can look forward to 4 to 7 more years of life than men—a difference found in almost all cultures. The protective value of the female's extra X chromosome is believed to be responsible. Yet since the early 1970s, the gender gap in life expectancy has narrowed in industrialized nations. Because men are at higher risk for disease and early death, they reap somewhat larger generational gains from positive lifestyle changes and new medical discoveries.

Life expectancy varies substantially with SES, ethnicity, and nationality. As education and income increase, so does length of life. And a U.S. white child born in the year 2004 is likely to live 5 to 7 years longer than an African-American child and 4 to 5 years longer than a Native-American child. Similarly, in regions of Canada with an Aboriginal population greater than 20 percent, average life expectancy is 5 to 15 years below that for the nation as a whole. Accounting for these differences are higher rates of infant mortality, unintentional injuries, life-threatening disease, poverty-linked stress, and (in the United States) violent death in low-SES minority groups.

Page Ref: 442

123) An elderly relative has trouble falling asleep at night and wonders if he should take prescription sleeping aids. What advice can you give him?

Answer: Older adults require around 7 hours of sleep per night. Yet as they age, people have more difficulty falling asleep, staying asleep, and sleeping deeply. Students may suggest any of the following to foster restful sleep: establishing a consistent bedtime and waking time; exercising regularly; using the bedroom only for sleep (not for eating, reading, or watching TV); reassuring him that age-related changes in sleeping patterns are normal. Cautions about sleeping aids: These drugs can help relieve insomnia temporarily, but long-term use can worsen the situation by inducing rebound insomnia after the drug is discontinued.

Page Ref: 447

124) How do physical appearance and mobility change in late adulthood? What can elders do to limit declines in mobility?

Answer: Creasing and sagging of the skin extends into old age. In addition, the skin becomes dry and rough, "age spots" increase, and moles and other small skin growths may appear. Blood vessels can be seen beneath the more transparent skin, which has largely lost its layer of fatty support.

The face is especially likely to show these effects because it is frequently exposed to the sun, which accelerates aging. The nose and ears broaden as new cells are deposited on the outer layer of the skeleton. Teeth may be yellowed, cracked, and chipped, and gums may recede. As hair follicles die, hair on the head thins in both sexes.

Body build changes as well. Height continues to decline, especially in women, as loss of bone mineral content leads to further collapse of the spinal column. Weight generally drops after age 60 due to additional loss in lean body mass (bone density and muscle), which is heavier than the fat deposits accumulating on the torso.

Several factors affect mobility. The first is muscle strength, which generally declines at a faster rate in late adulthood than it did in middle age. Second, bone strength deteriorates, as does flexibility and strength of the joints and the tendons and ligaments. **Prevention**: Careful planning of an exercise program can minimize declines in strength, joint flexibility, and range of movement.

Page Ref: 448

125) Your text discussed how assistive technology can help elderly people maintain their independence. Pick a typical room in an average house, and add assistive technology to make it "ideal" for an older person. Discuss what you would do.

Answer: Accept reasonable responses. Possible ideas for rooms could include sensors in floors that activate lights; harnesses to help those with reduced mobility move from room to room; ramps entering the house and lowered doorknobs and light switches for those in wheelchairs; rails in bathrooms to help get in and out of showers, etc.

Page Ref: 448–449

126) Discuss nutritional problems and considerations for older adults.

Answer: The physical changes of late life lead to an increased need for certain nutrients—calcium and vitamin D to protect the bones; zinc and vitamins B6, C, and E to protect the immune system; and vitamins A, C, and E to prevent free radicals. Yet declines in physical activity, in the senses of taste and smell, and in ease of chewing can reduce the quantity and quality of food eaten. Furthermore, the aging digestive system has greater difficulty absorbing certain nutrients, such as protein, calcium, and vitamin D. And older adults who live alone may have problems shopping or cooking and may feel less like eating by themselves. Together, these physical and environmental conditions increase the risk of dietary deficiencies, which affect 10 to 25 percent of North American elders. In several studies, a daily vitamin-mineral tablet resulted in an enhanced immune response and a 50 percent drop in days of infectious illness.

Page Ref: 451

127) Your grandfather complains that his arthritis is acting up and preventing him from doing many of his favorite activities. What are some options you could recommend for managing his condition? Would the options differ based on the type of arthritis he has?

Answer: Managing arthritis requires a balance of rest when the disease flares, pain relief, and physical activity involving gentle stretching of all muscles to maintain mobility. Water-based exercise classes can provide such benefits. With proper analgesic medication, joint protection, and lifestyle changes, many people with either form of the illness lead long, productive lives. If hip or knee joints are badly damaged or deformed, they can be surgically rebuilt or replaced with plastic or metal devices.

Page Ref: 453

128) Discuss how comparisons of African-American and Yoruban incidences of Alzheimer's contribute to theories of joint genetic and environmental factors.

Answer: The high incidence of Alzheimer's and other forms of dementia among African-American elderly illustrates the complexity of potential causes. Compared with African Americans, Yoruba village dwellers of Nigeria show a much lower Alzheimer's incidence and no association between the ApoE4 gene and the disease. Some investigators speculate that intermarriage with Caucasians heightened genetic risk among African Americans and that environmental factors translated that risk into reality. Whereas the Yoruba of Nigeria eat a low-fat diet, the African-American diet is high in fat. Eating fatty foods may increase the chances that the ApoE4 gene will lead to Alzheimer's. The more fat consumed and the higher the blood level of "bad" cholesterol (low-density lipoproteins), the greater the incidence of Alzheimer's.

Page Ref: 456–457

129) Explain how difficulties with working memory impact recall for older adults.

Answer: As older adults take in information more slowly and find it harder to apply strategies, inhibit irrelevant information, and retrieve relevant knowledge from long-term memory, the chances of memory failure increase. A reduced capacity to hold material in working memory while operating on it means that memory problems are especially evident on complex tasks.

Because their working memories hold less at once, older adults attend poorly to context—where something happened and who else was there. When we try to remember something, context serves as an important retrieval cue.

These memory difficulties mean that elders sometimes cannot distinguish an experienced event from one they imagined. They also have difficulty remembering the source of information. Temporal memory—recall of the order in which events ocurred or how recently they happened—suffers as well.

Page Ref: 461–462

130) What are the similar characteristics among older adults who are considered to display wisdom?

Answer: Older adults with the cognitive and emotional qualities that make up wisdom are better educated and physically healthier, forge more positive relations with others, and score higher on the personality dimension of openness to experience. Wisdom is also a strong predictor of psychological well-being. Wise elders seem to flourish, even when faced with physical and cognitive challenges.

Page Ref: 464

131) Explain the benefits of continuing education for elders.

Answer: Elderly continuing education participants report a rich array of benefits. These include learning interesting facts, understanding new ideas in many disciplines, making new friends, and developing a broader perspective on the world. Furthermore, seniors come to see themselves differently. Many arrive with ingrained stereotypes of aging, which they abandon when they realize that adults in their seventies and eighties, including themselves, can still engage in complex learning. In Elderhostel courses, participants with the least education report learning the most, an argument for recruiting less economically privileged people into these programs.

Page Ref: 466–467

STUDY QUESTIONS

Physical Development

1. ____________________ *age* refers to actual competence and performance of an older adult. (p. 441)
2. True or False: Researchers have identified a single biological measure that predicts rate of aging. (p. 442)

Life Expectancy

1. What is *average life expectancy?* (p. 442)

____

____

2. In 2004, average life expectancy reached age ______ in the United States and age _____ in Canada. (p. 442)

Variations in Life Expectancy

1. On average, (men / women) can expect to live 4 to 7 years longer than their other-sex counterparts—a difference found in almost all cultures. What accounts for this gender gap in life expectancy? (p. 442)

____

____

____

2. List factors that contribute to SES and ethnic differences in life expectancy. (p. 442)

____

____

____

3. Define *active lifespan,* and indicate how the United States and Canada rank internationally in their measure. (p. 442)

A. ____

____

B. ____

____

Life Expectancy in Late Adulthood

1. The number of people age 65 and older has (risen / declined) dramatically in the industrialized world. (p. 443)
2. Summarize sex differences in life expectancy in late adulthood. (p. 443)

____

____

____

3. True or False: With advancing age, gender and SES differences in life expectancy increase. (p. 443)
4. Describe the *life expectancy crossover.* (p. 443)

____

____

____

5. After age 70, about 10 percent of adults have difficulty carrying out ____________________, basic self-care tasks required to live on one's own. About 20 percent cannot carry out ____________________ ____________________, tasks necessary to conduct the business of daily life and that require some cognitive competence. (p. 443)
6. Summarize evidence that heredity affects longevity. (p. 443)

____

____

____

7. True or False: Twin studies suggest that once people pass age 75 to 80, the contribution of heredity to length of life decreases, while environmental factors play an increasingly large role. (p. 443)

A Lifespan Vista: What Can We Learn About Aging from Centenarians?

1. True or False: Recent increases in the number of centenarians in the industrialized world are expected to accelerate in the years to come. (p. 444)
2. Centenarians are more likely to be (men / women). (p. 444)
3. True or False: Less than 20 percent of centenarians have physical and mental impairments that interfere with independent functioning. (p. 444)
4. True or False: Longevity runs in centenarians' families. p. 444)
5. Describe the health, personality, and activities of robust centenarians. (p. 444)

   Health: ____

   ____

   Personality: ____

   ____

   Activities: ____

   ____

Maximum Lifespan

1. Define *maximum lifespan,* and cite current estimates of it. (p. 443)

   Definition: ______________________________

   ____

   Estimates: ______________________________

   ____

2. Summarize both sides of the controversy on whether current figures for maximum lifespan represent the upper bound of human longevity or whether lifespan can be extended even further. (p. 443)

   Represents upper bound: ______________________________

   ____

   Can be extended further: ______________________________

   ____

Physical Changes

Nervous System

1. True or False: Death of neurons and enlargement of ventricles cause brain weight to decrease throughout adulthood. (pp. 443, 445)
2. Describe neuron loss in different regions of the cerebral cortex in late adulthood. (p. 445)

   ____

   ____

   ____

3. True or False: In healthy older adults, growth of neural fibers takes place at the same rate as in middle-aged adults. (p. 445)
4. Cite two changes in autonomic nervous system functioning in old age. (p. 445)

   A. ______________________________

   B. ______________________________

Sensory Systems

1. What are *cataracts,* and how do they affect vision? (p. 445)

   Definition: ______________________________

   ____

   Impact on vision: ______________________________

   ____

2. Cite two factors that largely account for visual impairments in late adulthood. (p. 445)

   A. ______________________________

   B. ______________________________

3. Depth perception and visual acuity (improve / remain stable / decline) in late life. (p. 445)

4. When light-sensitive cells in the central region of the retina break down, older adults may develop ______________ ________________, in which central vision blurs and is gradually lost. (pp. 445–446)

5. True or False: Cataracts are the leading cause of blindness in older adults. (p. 446)

6. Describe the consequences of severe vision loss in late adulthood. (p. 446)

____

____

7. List changes in the ear that cause hearing to decline in late adulthood. (p. 446)

____

____

____

8. Hearing decrements in late life are greatest at (high / low) frequencies. List two additional hearing declines. (p. 446)

   A. ____

   B. ____

9. What hearing difficulty has the greatest impact on life satisfaction? (p. 446)

____

10. Most older adults (do / do not) suffer hearing loss that is great enough to disrupt their daily lives. (p. 446)

11. List several ways in which older adults can compensate for hearing loss. (p. 446)

____

____

12. True or False: Age-related reductions in taste sensitivity are caused by changes in the number and distribution of taste buds. (p. 446)

13. List several factors that contribute to declines in taste sensitivity. (p. 446)

____

____

____

14. Summarize changes in smell during late adulthood. (p. 446)

____

____

____

15. Older adults experience a sharper decline in touch sensitivity on their (arms and lips / hands). (p. 446)

16. What two factors likely account for age-related declines in touch sensitivity? (pp. 446–447)

   A. ____

   B. ____

Cardiovascular and Respiratory Systems

1. List five ways the heart muscle changes with advancing age. (p. 447)

   A. ______________________________

   B. ______________________________

   C. ______________________________

   D. ______________________________

   E. ______________________________

2. What changes in the cardiovascular and respiratory systems lead to reduced oxygen supply to body tissues? (p. 447)

   ____

   ____

   ____

Immune System

1. What is an *autoimmune response*? What are some consequences of a less competent immune system? p. 447)

   Definition: ______________________________

   ____

   Consequences: ______________________________

   ____

2. List an immune indicator that predicts survival in very old people. (p. 447)

   ____

Sleep

1. True or False: Older adults require two to three more hours of total sleep time per night than younger adults. (p. 447)

2. Describe sleep difficulties common in older adults, and cite two factors that are largely responsible for these problems. (p. 447)

   Sleep difficulties: ______________________________

   ____

   Factors responsible: ______________________________

   ____

3. Describe ways to foster restful sleep in late adulthood. (p. 447)

   ____

   ____

   ____

Physical Appearance and Mobility

1. Describe changes in the skin in late adulthood. (p. 448)

____

____

2. True or False: The face is especially likely to show signs of aging because it is frequently exposed to the sun. (p. 448)

3. Describe facial changes that occur in late adulthood. (p. 448)

____

____

4. True or False: Both height and weight tend to decline in late adulthood. (p. 448)

5. List three age-related changes that affect mobility. (p. 448)

   A. ____

   B. ____

   C. ____

Adapting to the Physical Changes of Late Adulthood

1. True or False: Outward signs of aging, such as graying hair, facial wrinkles, and baldness, are closely related to sensory, cognitive, and motor functioning, as well as longevity. (p. 448)

2. Explain how problem-centered coping strategies help older adults adjust to the physical changes of late life. (p. 448)

____

____

____

3. Define *assistive technology,* and provide several examples of devices that help older adults cope with physical declines. (pp. 448–449)

   Definition: ____

____

   Examples: ____

____

4. Like gender stereotypes, aging stereotypes often operate ________________. Explain what this means. (p. 449)

____

____

5. How do stereotypes of aging affect older adults' functioning and self-esteem? (pp. 449–450)

____

____

____

6. Summarize cross-cultural evidence from Inuit and Japanese populations suggesting that positive cultural views of aging contribute to better mental and physical health in the elderly. (p. 450)

Health, Fitness, and Disability

1. The majority of older adults rate their health (favorably / unfavorably). (p. 450)
2. Explain how physical and mental health are intimately related in late life. (p. 450)

3. Summarize SES and ethnic variations in physical functioning during late life, noting reasons for these differences. (p. 450)

   SES:

   Ethnic variations:

4. True or False: Beyond age 85, women are more impaired than men and are less able to remain independent. (p. 450)
5. Define *compression of morbidity,* noting recent trends. (p. 450)

6. Describe evidence indicating that compression of morbidity can be greatly extended. (pp. 450–451)

Nutrition and Exercise

1. Briefly describe the physical and environmental conditions that lead to increased risk of dietary deficiencies in late life. (p. 451)

2. True or False: In several studies, a daily vitamin-mineral tablet resulted in an enhanced immune response and a 50 percent drop in days of infectious illness. (p. 451)
3. True or False: Endurance training and weight-bearing exercise are too strenuous for older adults and present more health risks than benefits. (p. 451)

4. Explain how exercise benefits the brain and cognition in late adulthood. (p. 451)

____

____

____

5. List several barriers to initiation of an exercise program in late life. (p. 451)

____

____

____

Sexuality

1. Virtually all cross-sectional studies report (maintenance / decline) in sexual desire and frequency of sexual activity in old age. Why might this finding be exaggerated? (pp. 451–452)

____

____

2. True or False: Most healthy married couples report diminished sexual enjoyment in late adulthood. (p. 452)
3. (Men / Women) are more likely to withdraw from sexual activity in late life. Explain your answer. (p. 452)

____

____

____

Physical Disabilities

1. List the four leading causes of death in late adulthood. (p. 452)

   A. ____

   B. ____

   C. ____

   D. ____

2. Distinguish between *primary* and *secondary aging.* (p. 452)

   Primary: ____

   Secondary: ____

3. Define *frailty,* and list factors that contribute to it. (p. 453)

   Definition: ____

   ____

   ____

   Contributing factors: ____

   ____

   ____

4. Contrast two forms of arthritis that increase in late life—*osteoarthritis* and *rheumatoid arthritis.* (p. 453)

   Osteoarthritis: ______________________________

   ____

   Rheumatoid arthritis: ______________________________

   ____

5. Describe sex differences in disability due to arthritis. (p. 453)

   Men: ______________________________

   ____

   Women: ______________________________

   ____

6. How can older adults manage arthritis? (pp. 453–454)

   ____

   ____

7. What factors are associated with a risk of developing adult-onset diabetes? (p. 454)

   ____

   ____

8. What treatments are used to control adult-onset diabetes? (p. 454)

   ____

   ____

9. The death rate from unintentional injuries is highest during (adolescence and young adulthood / late adulthood). (p. 454)

10. True or False: Older adults have the lowest rates of traffic violations, accidents, and fatalities of any age group. (p. 454)

11. List three factors that contribute to driving difficulties in older adults. (p. 454)

    A. ______________________________

    B. ______________________________

    C. ______________________________

12. True or False: The elderly account for more than 30 percent of all pedestrian deaths. (p. 454)

13. What is the leading type of unintentional injury among the elderly? (p. 454)

    ____

14. List factors that place older adults at increased risk for falling. (p. 455)

    ____

    ____

15. How does falling indirectly impair health? (p. 455)

    ____

Mental Disabilities

1. Define *dementia.* (p. 455)

____

____

2. Dementia (declines / rises) sharply with age, striking men and women (disproportionately / equally). (p. 455)

3. The most common form of dementia is ______________, in which structural and chemical brain deterioration is associated with gradual loss of many aspects of thought and behavior. (p. 455)

4. What is usually the first symptom of Alzheimer's disease? (p. 455)

____

5. List personality changes associated with Alzheimer's disease. (p. 455)

____

____

6. List three symptoms other than memory loss and personality changes that are associated with the progression of Alzheimer's disease. (p. 455)

   A. ____

   B. ____

   C. ____

7. Explain how Alzheimer's disease is diagnosed. (pp. 455–456)

____

____

8. Describe two major structural changes in the cerebral cortex associated with Alzheimer's disease. (p. 456)

   A. ____

   ____

   B. ____

   ____

9. At one time, researchers thought that plaques contributed to neuronal damage of Alzheimer's. What does new evidence suggest? (p. 456)

____

____

____

10. Explain how declining levels of neurotransmitters contribute to many primary symptoms of Alzheimer's disease. (p. 456)

____

____

____

11. Describe the two types of Alzheimer's disease. (p. 456)

    Familial: ______________________________

    ____

    Sporadic: ______________________________

    ____

12. Other than genetic abnormalities, cite biological and environmental risk factors for sporadic Alzheimer's disease. (p. 456)

    Biological: ______________________________

    ____

    Environmental: ______________________________

    ____

13. True or False: Among the Yoruba of Nigeria, the ApoE4 gene is not associated with Alzheimer's. Explain your answer. (pp. 456–457)

14. List four factors that protect against Alzheimer's disease. (p. 457)

    A. ______________________________

    B. ______________________________

    C. ______________________________

    D. ______________________________

15. True or False: Alzheimer's is a curable disease. (p. 457)

16. Describe interventions that help to ensure the best possible adjustment for Alzheimer's victims and their families. (pp. 457)

    ____

    ____

    ____

17. Describe *cerebrovascular dementia.* (p. 457)

    ____

    ____

18. Summarize genetic and environmental influences on cerebrovascular dementia. (p. 457)

    Genetic: ______________________________

    ____

    Environmental: ______________________________

    ____

19. True or False: Most cases of cerebrovascular dementia are caused by atherosclerosis. (p. 457)

20. Name the disorder that is most often misdiagnosed as dementia, and explain at least one difference between adults with this disorder and those with dementia. (p. 459)

    Disorder: ______________________________

    Difference: ______________________________

21. In addition to the disorder named above, cite three factors that can lead to reversible symptoms of dementia. (p. 459)

    A. ____

    B. ____

    C. ____

Social Issues: Interventions for Caregivers of Elders with Dementia

1. Explain how Alzheimer's disease affects caregivers. (p. 458)

   ____

   ____

   ____

2. List and briefly describe caregiver needs that are addressed by effective interventions. (p. 458)

   A. ____

   B. ____

   C. ____

   D. ____

3. Briefly summarize research on "active" intervention programs, including which caregivers benefit the most. (p. 458)

Health Care

1. True or False: The cost of government-sponsored health insurance for the elderly is expected to double by the year 2025 and triple by the year 2050. (p. 459)

2. True or False: In the United States, Medicare funds 100 percent of older adults' medical expenses. (p. 459)

3. Which disorders of aging most often lead to nursing home placement? (p. 459)

   ____

   ____

4. True or False: Older adults in the Untied States and Canada are less likely to be institutionalized than elders in other industrialized nations. Explain your answer. (p. 459)

   ____

   ____

5. (Caucasian / African) Americans are more likely to be placed in nursing homes. Why is this so? (p. 460)

   ____

   ____

6. Describe two recommendations for reducing institutionalized care for the elderly and its associated costs. (p. 460)

   A. ____

   B. ____

7. Briefly summarize ways to improve the quality of nursing home services. (p. 460)

Cognitive Development

1. True or False: Individual differences in cognitive functioning are greater during late adulthood than at any other time of life. (p. 460)

2. Explain how older adults can use *selective optimization with compensation* to sustain high levels of cognitive functioning in late life. (p. 461)

Memory

Deliberate versus Automatic Memory

1. Describe the link between working memory declines and ability to use context cues to aid recall. (p. 461)

2. (Recall / Recognition) memory shows fewer declines in late adulthood. (p. 461)

3. What is *implicit memory*? (p. 461)

4. Age differences are greater for (implicit / deliberate) memory. Explain your answer. (p. 461)

Associative Memory

1. What are *associative memory deficits*? (p. 462)

2. True or False: Older adults maintain the ability to recognize single pieces of information but have difficulty with tasks that require them to form associations between multiple pieces of information. (p. 462)

3. List a strategy for improving associative memory in late adulthood. (p. 462)

Remote Memory

1. True or False: Research shows that memory for recent events is clearer than memory for remote events in late life. (p. 462)

2. Explain why older adults recall their adolescent and early adulthood experiences more easily than their midlife experiences. (p. 462)

____

____

Prospective Memory

1. What is *prospective memory*? (p. 462)

____

____

2. Older adults do better on (event-based / time-based) prospective memory tasks. Explain your answer. (p. 462)

____

____

3. Explain why prospective memory difficulties in the laboratory setting do not always appear in real-life contexts. (p. 463)

____

____

Language Processing

1. What factors help older adults maintain their language comprehension skills? (p. 463)

____

____

2. Describe two aspects of language production that show age-related declines, and note factors that contribute to these changes. (p. 463)

   A. ____

   B. ____

   Factors that contribute to changes: ____

   ____

3. List two ways that older adults often compensate for difficulties with language production. (p. 463)

   A. ____

   B. ____

Problem Solving

1. (Traditional / Real-life) problem solving declines in old age. Explain why. (p. 463)

____

2. What types of everyday problems are of concern to most older adults? (p. 463)

____

____

3. Summarize adaptive problem-solving strategies used by older adults to solve problems of daily living. (pp. 463–464)

___

___

___

4. Older adults are (quicker / slower) than younger adults to make decisions about seeking health care. (p. 463)
5. True or False: Older couples are less likely than younger couples to collaborate in everyday problem solving. (p. 464)

Wisdom

1. Define *wisdom,* noting characteristics often used to describe this quality. (p. 464)

   A. ___

   ___

   B. ___

   ___

2. True or False: Cultures around the world assume that age and wisdom go together. Explain your answer. (p. 464)

   ___

   ___

3. True or False: Research shows that age is more important than life experience in the development of wisdom. (pp. 464–465)
4. In addition to age and life experience, what other factor contributes to late-life wisdom? (p. 465)

   ___

5. True or False: Wisdom is a strong predictor of psychological well-being, and wise elders seem to flourish, even when faced with physical and cognitive challenges. (p. 465)

Factors Related to Cognitive Change

1. List four factors that predict maintenance of mental abilities in late life. (p. 465)

   A. ___

   B. ___

   C. ___

   D. ___

2. Explain how retirement can affect cognitive change both positively and negatively. (p. 465)

   Positively: ___

   ___

   Negatively: ___

   ___

3. Define *terminal decline,* and note its average length. (p. 465)

   Definition: ______________________________

   Average length: ______________________________

Cognitive Interventions

1. For most of late adulthood, cognitive declines are (rapid / gradual). (p. 466)
2. Summarize findings from the Adult Development and Enrichment Project (ADEPT) and from the Advanced Cognitive Training for Independent and Vital Elderly (ACTIVE). (pp. 466–467)

   ADEPT: ______________________________

   ____

   ACTIVE: ______________________________

   ____

Lifelong Learning

1. Elders' participation in continuing education has (increased / declined) over the past few decades. (p. 467)
2. Describe characteristics of Elderhostel programs, noting opportunities that they offer. (pp. 467–468)

   ____

   ____

3. Describe the University of the Third Age and similar programs offered in Europe and Australia. (p. 468)

   ____

   ____

4. Summarize three ways to increase the effectiveness of instruction for older adults. (p. 468)

   A. ______________________________

   B. ______________________________

   C. ______________________________

5. List five benefits of elders' participation in continuing education programs for the elderly. (p. 468)

   A. ______________________________

   B. ______________________________

   C. ______________________________

   D. ______________________________

   E. ______________________________

PUZZLE 17.1

Across

2. _____ lifespan: the number of years of vigorous, healthy life that an individual born in a particular year can expect
3. __________ lifespan: genetic limit to length of life for a person free of external risk factors
9. Bundles of twisted threads that are the product of collapsed neural structures are called __________ tangles.
10. Life expectancy __________ : age-related reversal in life expectancy of sectors of the population
11. Cloudy areas in the lens of the eye that result in foggy vision and (without surgery) eventually blindness
12. __________ life expectancy: the number of years that a person born in a particular year can expect to live
13. __________ degeneration is a blurring and eventual loss of central vision due to a break-down of light sensitive cells in the center of the retina

Down

1. Form of arthritis characterized by deteriorating cartilage on the ends of bones of frequently used joints
4. Set of disorders occurring almost entirely in old age; many aspects of thought and behavior are so impaired that everyday activities are disrupted
5. __________ dementia: a series of strokes leaves areas of dead brain cells, producing degeneration of mental abilities
6. __________ disease is the most common form of dementia in which structural and chemical deterioration in the brain is associated with gradual loss of many aspects of thought and behavior.
7. __________ response: abnormal response of the immune system in which it turns against normal body tissues
8. __________ plaques: dense deposits of a deteriorated protein surrounded by clumps of dead neurons

PUZZLE 17.2

Across

3. Type of memory deficit that involves difficulty creating or retrieving links between pieces of information
5. Memory without conscious awareness is called __________ memory
7. __________ activities of daily living: tasks necessary to conduct the business of daily life and that require some cognitive competence, such as telephoning, shopping, housekeeping, and paying bills
9. __________ of daily living: basic self-care tasks required to live on one's own, such as dressing, bathing, or eating
10. __________ age: actual competence and performance of an older adult
11. __________ memory involves remembering to engage in planned actions at an appropriate time in the future
12. __________ aging: declines due to hereditary defects and environmental influences
14. __________: form of cognition that combines breadth and depth of practical knowledge, ability to reflect on that knowledge in ways that make life more bearable and worthwhile, emotional maturity, and creative integration of experience and knowledge into new ways of thinking and acting

Down

2. Compression of __________: public health goal of reducing the average period of diminished vigor before death as life expectancy extends
4. Selective __________ with compensation: strategies that permit older adults to sustain high levels of functioning
6. __________ involves weakened functioning of diverse organs and body systems, which profoundly interfere with everyday competence, leaving the older adult highly vulnerable to infection, temperature changes, or injury
8. __________ decline is a steady, marked decrease in cognitive functioning prior to death
11. __________ aging: genetically influenced age-related declines in functioning of organs and systems that affect all members of our species and take place in the context of overall good health
13. __________ memory: recall of events that happened long ago

CROSSWORD PUZZLE SOLUTIONS

PUZZLE 17.1

PUZZLE 17.2

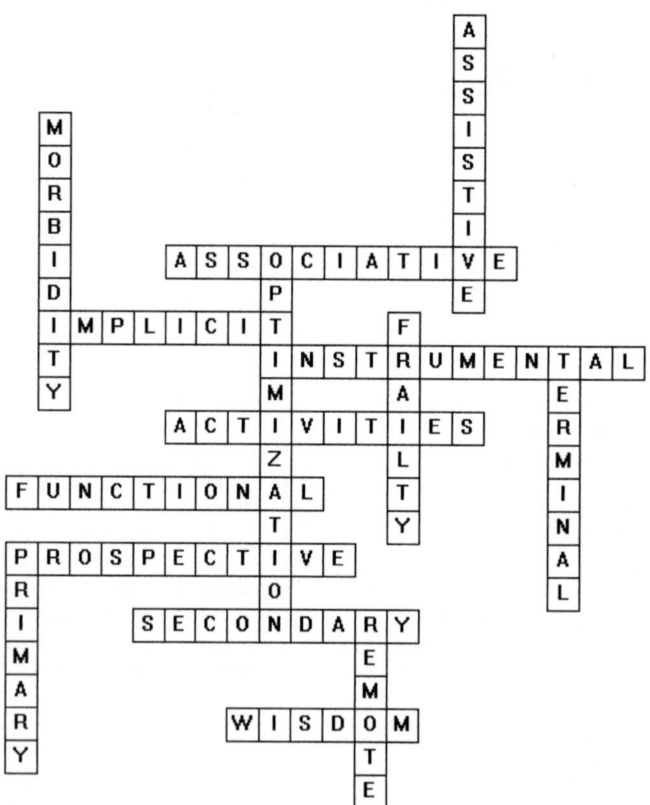

PRACTICE TEST #1

1. Today, average life expectancy in North America is approximately (p. 442)
   a. 40 to 45 years.
   b. 55 to 60 years.
   c. 75 to 80 years.
   d. 95 to 100 years.

2. When researchers estimate the active lifespan, the country that ranks first is (p. 442)
   a. the United States.
   b. Canada.
   c. Japan.
   d. Sweden.

3. Which of the following statements is true of the brain in late adulthood? (pp. 443, 445)
   a. Brain weight can decline by as much as 5 to 10 percent by age 80.
   b. Neuron loss occurs only in the temporal lobe of the cerebral cortex.
   c. The brain is incapable of overcoming late adulthood declines.
   d. Glial cells increase in size and number throughout late adulthood.

4. Which of the following statements is true of eyesight in late adulthood? (pp. 445–446)
   a. Macular degeneration is the leading cause of blindness among older adults.
   b. Cataracts are cloudy areas in the lens of the eye that cannot be repaired and usually lead to blindness.
   c. Dark adaptation usually becomes easier in late adulthood.
   d. More than three-fourths of people age 85 and older experience visual impairment severe enough to interfere with daily living.

5. Ellen is worried about developing cataracts or macular degeneration. To reduce her risk of developing these conditions, she can (p. 446)
   a. spend fewer hours working at the computer.
   b. wear glasses for reading.
   c. take a daily multivitamin pill.
   d. eat a diet rich in green, leafy vegetables.

6. Age-related declines in hearing (p. 446)
   a. are greatest at low frequencies.
   b. have the greatest impact on life satisfaction when speech perception declines.
   c. are severe enough to disrupt the daily lives of nearly all elders.
   d. have a greater impact on self-care than does vision loss.

7. Aging of the cardiovascular system causes the (p. 447)
   a. heart muscle to become less rigid, so it pumps less efficiently.
   b. cells within the heart to shrink and multiply.
   c. artery walls to stiffen and accumulate some plaque.
   d. heart muscle to become more responsive to signals from pacemaker cells.

8. Older adults need about 7 hours of sleep per night, which is about __________ younger adults require. (p. 447)
   a. the same amount as
   b. twice as much as younger adults
   c. an hour more than younger adults
   d. an hour less than

9. Declines in mobility in late adulthood are the result of (p. 448)
   a. diminished muscle strength.
   b. visual declines associated with depth perception and acuity.
   c. changes in body structure, particularly height and weight.
   d. age-related changes in the structure of the middle ear, which affect balance.

10. Research demonstrates that over the past two decades, compression of morbidity has occurred in developed countries due largely to (p. 450)
    a. a decrease in rates of obesity and sedentary lifestyles.
    b. a reduction in the number of major surgical procedures performed.
    c. medical advances and improved socioeconomic conditions.
    d. an increase in the age at which the average person retires.

11. The leading cause of death among individuals age 65 and older is (p. 453)
    a. respiratory disease, such as pneumonia.
    b. cardiovascular disease.
    c. cancer.
    d. unintentional injury.

12. The most common type of arthritis afflicting older adults is (p. 453)
    a. osteoarthritis.
    b. rheumatoid arthritis.
    c. diabetic arthritis.
    d. Alzheimer's arthritis.

13. Diabetes (p. 454)
    a. is not hereditary but results only from environmental factors such as obesity and lack of exercise.
    b. is a disease of the bones that usually develops after age 60.
    c. affects people of all ages.
    d. always requires daily medication; it cannot be treated with diet.

14. Older adults are particularly susceptible to motor vehicle injury because they (p. 454)
    a. tend to drive at much higher speeds than younger adults.
    b. are likely to have visual impairments and slower reaction time than younger people.
    c. are less cautious than younger drivers.
    d. are more decisive than younger drivers, but often in a reckless way.

15. Among the earliest symptoms of Alzheimer's disease is (p. 455)
    a. the disintegration of skilled, purposeful movements.
    b. severe loss of memory for such items as names, dates, appointments, familiar routes of travel, and everyday safety precautions.
    c. disruption of sleep by delusions and imaginary fears.
    d. loss of the ability to comprehend and produce speech.

16. Which of the following statements about Alzheimer's disease is true? (p. 455)
    a. It can result in coma and, eventually, death.
    b. It affects only the mind and emotions, not the physical aspects of life.
    c. Memory problems usually present themselves at the end stages of the disease.
    d. The disease follows the same course in nearly all individuals.

17. The disorder most often misdiagnosed as dementia is (p. 459)
    a. depression.
    b. Alzheimer's disease.
    c. diabetes.
    d. arthritis.

18. Which of the following statements about memory in late adulthood is true? (p. 463)
    a. Recognition suffers more than recall.
    b. Associative memory deficit is usually not a problem.
    c. Problems with prospective memory are more evident in the laboratory than in real life.
    d. Remote memory is usually much clearer than memory for recent events.

19. The Adult Development and Enrichment Project (ADEPT) was an intervention program that (pp. 465–466)
    a. contributed to improved memory and problem-solving abilities among elderly participants.
    b. hastened the rate of terminal decline among elderly participants.
    c. provided better strategies for overcoming the physical declines of aging.
    d. was designed to assist caregivers of older adults with Alzheimer's disease.

20. Which of the following language processing skills changes very little in late life? (p. 463)
    a. retrieving words from long-term memory
    b. understanding the meaning of spoken words
    c. planning what to say
    d. planning how to say something

PRACTICE TEST #2

1. A North American baby born in 1900 had an average life expectancy of just under 50 years. In 2004, this figure reached ___________ in the United States and _________ in Canada (p. 442)
    a. 57.9; 59.9
    b. 67.9; 65.9
    c. 77.9; 80.1
    d. 87.9; 92.2

2. The likely reason that women live 4 to 7 years longer than men, on average, is that women have (p. 442)
    a. less stressful lives.
    b. better access to health care.
    c. more supportive social relationships.
    d. the protective value of their extra X chromosome.

3. Declines in brain weight throughout adulthood largely result from (pp. 443, 445)
    a. shrinkage of the ventricles within the brain.
    b. death of neurons.
    c. myelination of neural fibers.
    d. increased incidence of stroke.

4. The leading cause of blindness among older adults is (p. 446)
    a. glaucoma.
    b. cataracts.
    c. macular degeneration.
    d. neural death in the visual cortex of the brain.

5. Aging of the immune system (p. 447)
    a. leads to increased production and responsiveness of T-cells.
    b. results in profound loss of function for most older adults.
    c. shows little variation from one person to the next.
    d. is related to increased malfunction, so that the immune system is more likely to turn against normal body tissues.

6. Among the best ways to foster restful sleep is (p. 447)
    a. to use long-term medication.
    b. to try to stay in bed for longer periods of time.
    c. to establish a consistent bedtime and waking time.
    d. to take naps during the daytime.

7. Creasing and sagging of the skin and the appearance of age spots all extend into old age. The face is especially likely to show these effects because it is (p. 448)
   a. frequently exposed to the sun.
   b. the area that is most elevated in relation to the heart.
   c. in constant motion.
   d. damaged by lotions, shaving cream, and other products.

8. Older adults who use __________ coping strategies adapt more favorably to the everyday challenges of aging and show improved physical functioning. (p. 448)
   a. problem-centered
   b. cognition-centered
   c. emotion-centered
   d. avoidant

9. Older adults are generally __________ about their own health. (p. 450)
   a. optimistic
   b. pessimistic
   c. indifferent
   d. uninformed

10. By very old age (85 and beyond), women are more impaired than men because (p. 450)
    a. women are more prone to fatal diseases.
    b. men are more prone to non-life-threatening disabling conditions.
    c. only the sturdiest men have survived.
    d. men have longer life expectancies.

11. Your elderly grandparent is wondering whether to take a daily vitamin–mineral nutritional supplement. What useful information should you offer? (p. 451)
    a. There is no evidence that vitamin–mineral supplements offer health benefits.
    b. Vitamin–mineral supplements are only advantageous to older adults who are sedentary.
    c. Daily vitamin–mineral supplements are probably unnecessary as older adults require fewer nutrients and have fewer dietary deficiencies.
    d. Daily vitamin–mineral supplements have been linked to an enhanced immune response and a 50 percent drop in days of infectious illness.

12. Which of these is the best example of primary aging? (p. 452)
    a. Farsightedness resulting from stiffening of the lens of the eye
    b. Lung cancer caused by smoking cigarettes
    c. Weight gain resulting from a sedentary lifestyle
    d. High blood pressure resulting from prolonged stress in the workplace

13. Although __________ contributes to frailty, researchers agree that __________ plays a larger role, through genetic disorders, unhealthy lifestyle, and chronic disease. (p. 453)
    a. secondary aging; primary aging
    b. primary aging; secondary aging
    c. functional aging; biological aging
    d. biological aging; functional aging

14. Dementia (p. 455)
    a. is usually, though not always, irreversible and incurable, depending on the type.
    b. never affects the subcortical regions of the brain.
    c. causes deterioration in quality of life, but is not, in itself, a cause of death.
    d. can occur at any age, not just in the elderly.

15. Sporadic Alzheimer's disease (p. 456)
    a. tends to run in families.
    b. is linked to genes on chromosomes 1, 14, and 21.
    c. is associated with an abnormal gene on chromosome 19, resulting in excess levels of ApoE4.
    d. has an earlier onset and a more rapid progression than does familial Alzheimer's disease.

16. Of the following individuals, the most likely to be placed in a nursing home is (p. 460)
    a. a Caucasian American with Alzheimer's disease.
    b. an African American with cardiovascular disease.
    c. a Native American with cancer.
    d. an Asian elder with a hip fracture.

17. Research on memory capacity in late adulthood shows that (p. 461)
    a. age-related memory declines are greatest for automatic activities, whereas memory for tasks requiring deliberate processing does not change much in old age.
    b. recognition memory suffers less in late adulthood than does recall memory.
    c. older adults recall remote personal experiences more easily than recent ones.
    d. older adults perform better on time-based than event-based prospective memory tasks.

18. Which of the following statements about problem solving in old age is true? (p. 463)
    a. Older adults solve everyday problems more effectively than complex hypothetical problems.
    b. Problems encountered in late adulthood are nearly identical to those encountered earlier in life.
    c. Because older adults view most problems as beyond their control, they seldom use adaptive coping strategies.
    d. Compared to younger married couples, older married couples are less likely to collaborate in everyday problem solving.

19. Wisdom (p. 465)
    a. is directly related to age and is seen at high levels in virtually all older adults.
    b. is more common in early and middle adulthood than in late adulthood.
    c. is closely linked to life experiences, particularly exposure to and success in overcoming adversity.
    d. shows no relationship to life satisfaction.

20. Elderhostel, Routes to Learning, and similar programs (p. 466)
    a. combine educational programs and recreational activities.
    b. provide direct instruction in compensatory strategies to help elders address cognitive processing declines.
    c. are only beneficial for active, wealthy, well-educated older adults.
    d. are specially designed to meet the needs of elders with little education and few economic resources.

POWERPOINT SLIDES

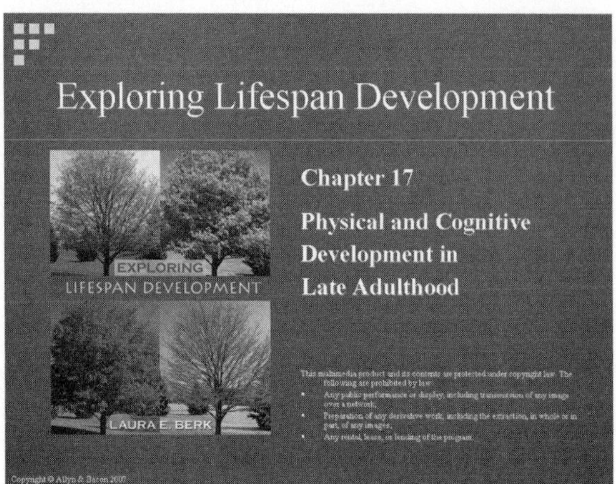

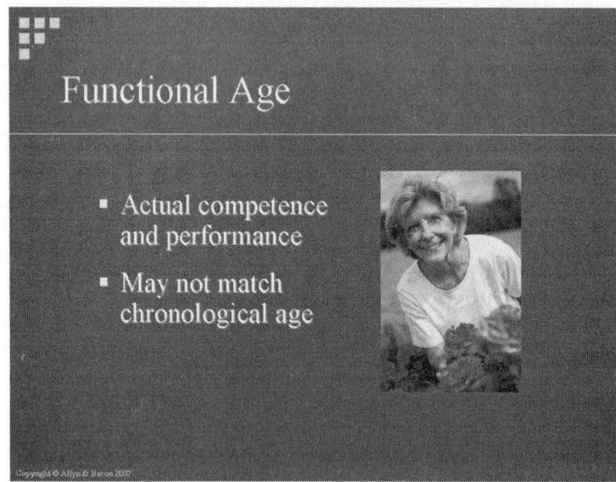

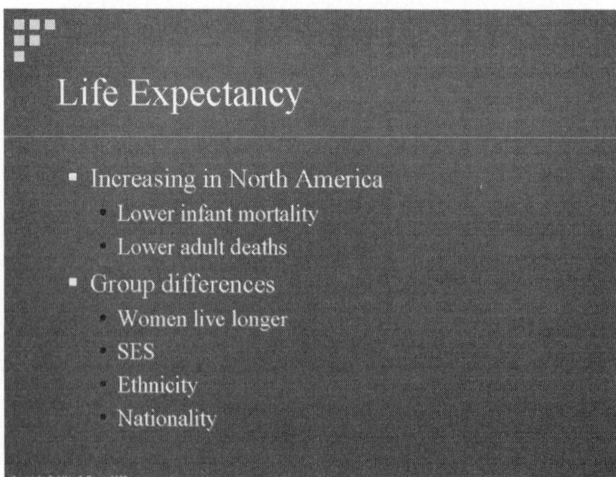

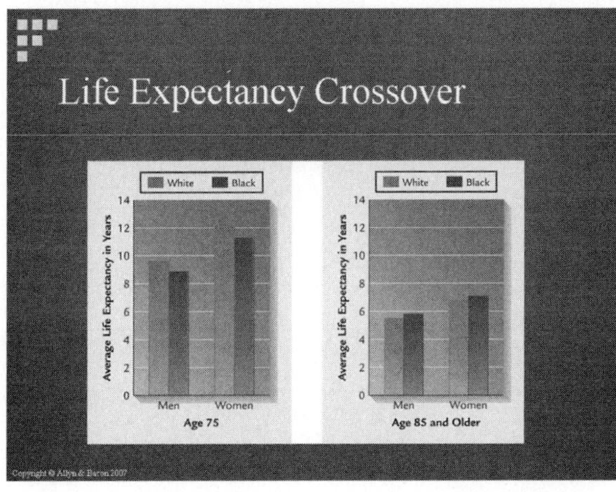
Life Expectancy Crossover
White
Black
Average Life Expectancy in Years
14
12
10
8
6
4
2
0
Men
Women
Age 75
Age 85 and Older
Copyright © Allyn & Bacon 2007

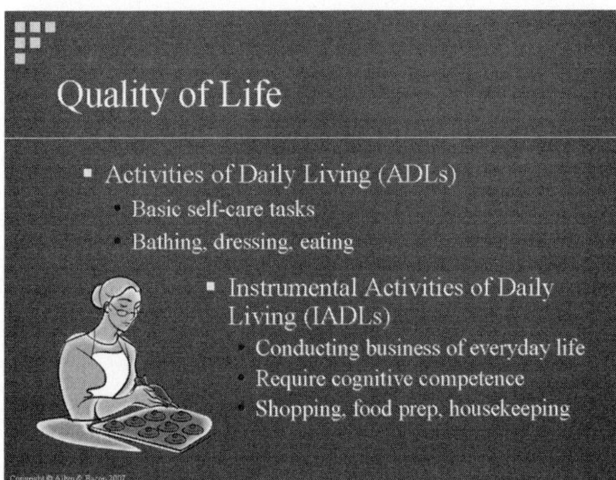
Quality of Life
Activities of Daily Living (ADLs)
Basic self-care tasks
Bathing, dressing, eating
Instrumental Activities of Daily Living (IADLs)
Conducting business of everyday life
Require cognitive competence
Shopping, food prep, housekeeping
Copyright © Allyn & Bacon 2007

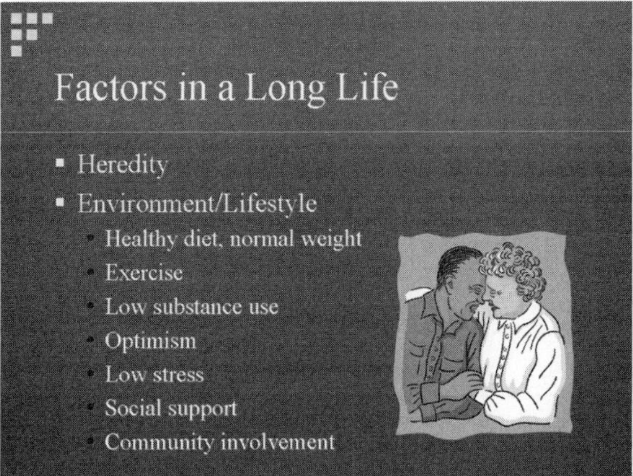
Factors in a Long Life
Heredity
Environment/Lifestyle
Healthy diet, normal weight
Exercise
Low substance use
Optimism
Low stress
Social support
Community involvement
Copyright © Allyn & Bacon 2007

Aging and the Nervous System

- Loss of brain weight accelerates after 60
- Neurons lost in frontal lobes, corpus callosum, cerebellum (balance), glial cells
- Autonomic nervous system less efficient
- Brain can compensate
  - New fibers, neurons
  - New connections
  - Use more parts of brain

Visual Impairments and Aging

- Lower visual acuity
- Poor dark adaptation, sensitivity to glare
- Decreased color, depth perception
- Cataracts
- Macular degeneration

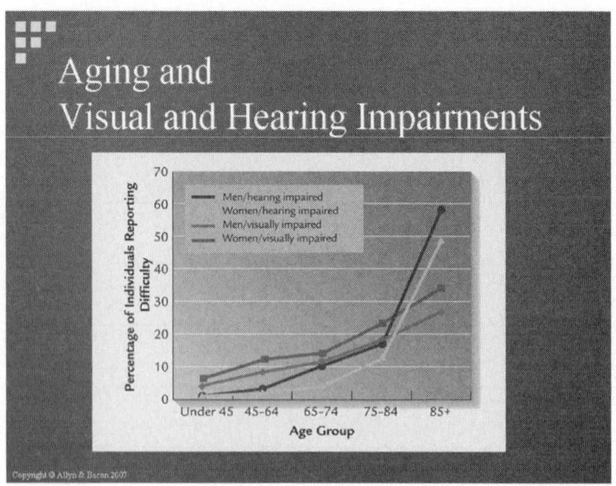

Effects of Sensory Changes

Vision problems	▪ **Changes in leisure activities** ▪ **Possible problems in daily activities**
Hearing loss	▪ **Social isolation** ▪ **Lower safety and enjoyment**
Decreased taste and smell	▪ **Nutritional, safety risks**
Less sensitive touch	▪ **Difficulties with leisure, daily activities**

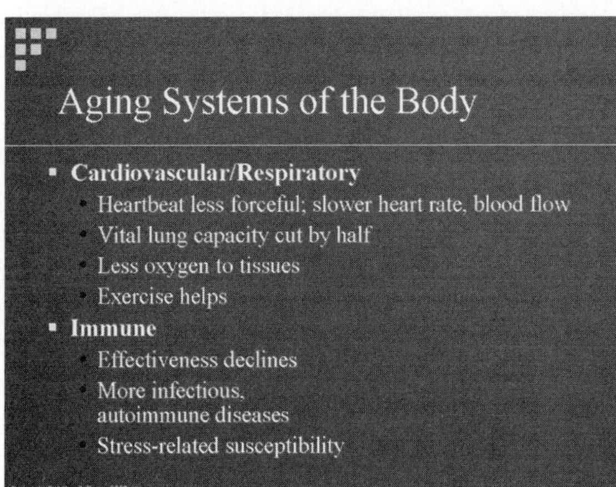

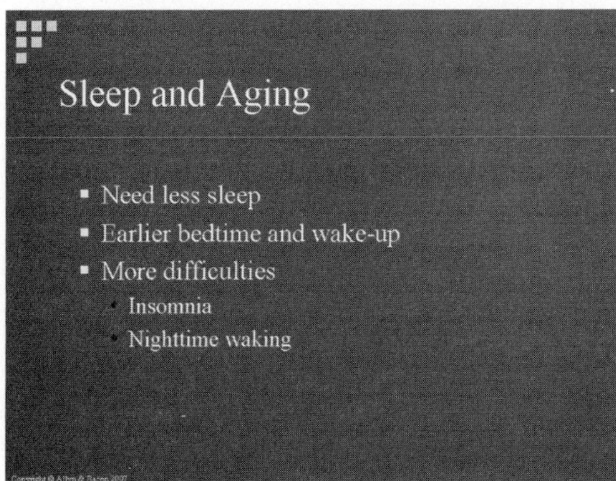

Physical Appearance and Mobility

- Skin thinner, rougher wrinkled, spotted
- Ears, nose, teeth, and hair change
- Lose height and weight after 60
- Muscle strength declines
- Bone strength drops
- Less flexibility

Adapting to Physical Changes of Aging

- Appearance versus functioning
- Effective coping strategies
  - Prevention, compensation
  - Problem-centered coping
- Assistive technology
- Overcoming stereotypes of aging

Factors in Good Health
and Aging
Optimism
Self-efficacy
SES
Ethnicity
Sex
Nutrition
Exercise
Copyright © Allyn & Bacon 2007

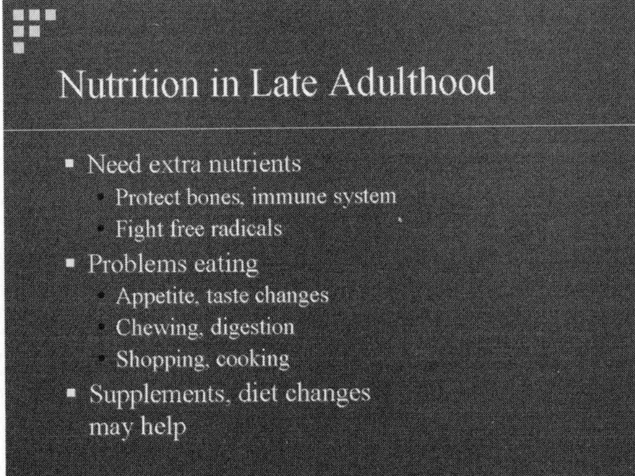
Nutrition in Late Adulthood
Need extra nutrients
Protect bones, immune system
Fight free radicals
Problems eating
Appetite, taste changes
Chewing, digestion
Shopping, cooking
Supplements, diet changes
may help
Copyright © Allyn & Bacon 2007

Exercise in Late Adulthood
Continued exercise best, but never too late
to start
Benefits
Physical capacities
Brain function
Self-esteem
Barriers
Unaware of benefits
Discomforts
Copyright © Allyn & Bacon 2007

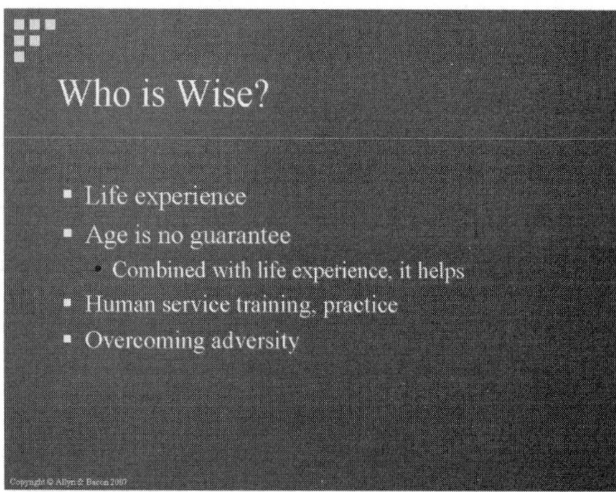
Who is Wise?
Life experience
Age is no guarantee
Combined with life experience, it helps
Human service training, practice
Overcoming adversity
Copyright © Allyn & Bacon 2007

Factors Related to Cognitive Change
Mentally active life
Education, stimulating leisure, social participation, flexibility
Health
Retirement
Distance to death
Terminal decline
Cognitive interventions
ADEPT, ACTIVE
Copyright © Allyn & Bacon 2007

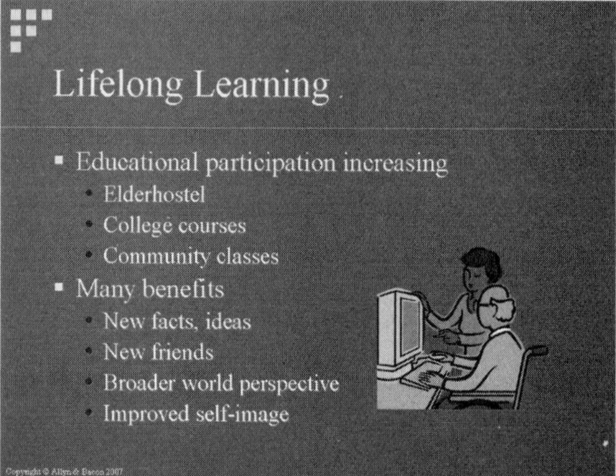
Lifelong Learning
Educational participation increasing
Elderhostel
College courses
Community classes
Many benefits
New facts, ideas
New friends
Broader world perspective
Improved self-image
Copyright © Allyn & Bacon 2007

CHAPTER 18
EMOTIONAL AND SOCIAL DEVELOPMENT IN LATE ADULTHOOD

CHAPTER-AT-A-GLANCE

Chapter Outline	Instruction Ideas	Supplements
Erikson's Theory: Ego Integrity versus Despair p. 471	Learning Objective 18.1	Test Bank Items 1–2 Videos: *Exploring Lifespan Development in Action* and *A Window on Lifespan Development* Please contact your Allyn and Bacon publisher's representative for a wide range of video offerings available to adopters.
Other Theories of Psychosocial Development in Late Adulthood pp. 471–473 Peck's Tasks of Ego Integrity and Joan Erikson's Gerotranscendence • Labouvie-Vief's Emotional Expertise • Reminiscence and Life Review	Learning Objectives 18.2–18.3 Learning Activity 18.1	Test Bank Items 3–22
Stability and Change in Self-Concept and Personality pp. 473–475 Secure and Multifaceted Self-Concept • Resilience: Agreeableness, Sociability, and Acceptance of Change • Spirituality and Religiosity	Learning Objectives 18.4–18.5 Lecture Enhancements 18.1–18.2 Learning Activities 18.2–18.3	Test Bank Items 23–31
Individual Differences in Psychological Well-Being pp. 475–478 Control versus Dependency • Health • Negative Life Changes • Social Support and Social Interaction	Learning Objectives 18.6–18.7 Ask Yourself p. 478	Test Bank Items 32–45
A Changing Social World pp. 478–483 Social Theories of Aging • Social Contexts of Aging: Communities, Neighborhoods, and Housing	Learning Objectives 18.8–18.9 Learning Activity 18.4 Ask Yourself p. 483	Test Bank Items 46–66 Transparency 193
Relationships in Late Adulthood pp. 483–490 Marriage • Gay and Lesbian Partnerships • Divorce, Remarriage, and Cohabitation • Widowhood • Never-Married, Childless Older Adults • Siblings • Friendships • Relationships with Adult Children • Elder Maltreatment	Learning Objectives 18.10–18.12 Learning Activities 18.5–18.6 Ask Yourself p. 490	Test Bank Items 67–99 Transparency 195
Retirement and Leisure pp. 490–492 The Decision to Retire • Adjustment to Retirement • Leisure Activities	Learning Objective 18.13 Lecture Enhancement 18.3 Learning Activity 18.7	Test Bank Items 100–104 Transparency 196
Successful Aging pp. 492–493	Learning Objective 18.14 Lecture Enhancement 18.4 Learning Activities 18.8–18.9 Ask Yourself p. 493	Test Bank Items 105–109

BRIEF CHAPTER SUMMARY

The final psychological conflict of Erikson's theory, ego integrity versus despair, involves coming to terms with one's life. Adults who arrive at a sense of integrity feel whole, complete, and satisfied with their achievements, whereas despair occurs when elders feel they have made many wrong decisions. In Peck's theory, ego integrity requires that older adults move beyond their life's work, their bodies, and their separate identities. Joan Erikson, widow of Erik Erikson, believes that older people can arrive at a psychosocial stage she calls gerotranscendence—a cosmic, transcendent perspective directed beyond the self. Labouvie-Vief addresses the development of adults' reasoning about emotion, pointing out that older adults develop affect optimization, the ability to maximize positive emotion and dampen negative emotion. Although researchers do not yet have a full understanding of why older people reminisce more than younger people do, current theory and research indicate that reflecting on the past can be positive and adaptive.

Older adults have accumulated a lifetime of self-knowledge, leading to more secure and complex conceptions of themselves than at earlier ages. During late adulthood, shifts in three personality traits take place. Agreeableness and acceptance of change tend to rise, while sociability dips slightly. Although declining health and transportation difficulties reduce organized religious participation in advanced old age, informal religious activities remain prominent in the lives of today's elders.

In patterns of behavior called the dependency–support script and independence–ignore script, older adults' dependency behaviors are attended to immediately, while their independent behaviors are ignored, encouraging elders to become more dependent than they need or want to be. Physical declines and chronic disease can be highly stressful, leading to a sense of loss of personal control—a major factor in adult mental health. In late adulthood, social support continues to play a powerful role in reducing stress, thereby promoting physical health and psychological well-being.

In late adulthood, extroverts continue to interact with a wider range of people than introverts and people with poor social skills. Disengagement theory, activity theory, continuity theory, and socioemotional selectivity theory offer varying explanations for the decline in amount of social interaction in late adulthood. The physical and social contexts in which elders live affect their social experiences and, consequently, their development and adjustment. Seniors tend to prefer to live independently as long as possible, but different communities, neighborhoods, and housing arrangements (including congregate housing and life care communities) vary in the extent to which they enable aging residents to satisfy their social needs.

The social convoy is an influential model of changes in our social networks as we move through life. Marital satisfaction rises from middle to late adulthood as perceptions of fairness in the relationship increase, couples engage in joint leisure activities, and communication becomes more positive. Most gay and lesbian elders also report happy, highly fulfilling relationships. Couples who divorce in late adulthood constitute a very small proportion of all divorces in any given year. Compared to divorced younger adults, divorced elders find it harder to separate their identity from that of their former spouse, and they suffer more from a sense of personal failure. Wide variation in adaptation to widowhood exists, with age, social support, and personality making a difference. Today, more older adults who enter a new relationship choose to cohabit rather than remarrying.

Siblings, friends, and adult children provide important sources of emotional support and companionship to elders. Although the majority of older adults enjoy positive relationships with family members, friends, and professional caregivers, some suffer maltreatment at the hands of these individuals.

Financial and health status, opportunities to pursue meaningful activities, and societal factors (such as early retirement benefits) affect the decision to retire. Retirement also varies with gender and ethnicity. Most elders adjust well to retirement. Involvement in satisfying leisure activities is related to better physical and mental health and reduced mortality. Successful aging, which involves maximizing gains and minimizing losses, is best viewed as a process rather than a list of specific accomplishments. Social contexts that permit elders to manage life changes effectively foster successful aging.

LEARNING OBJECTIVES

After reading this chapter, you should be able to:

18.1 Describe Erikson's stage of ego integrity versus despair. (p. 471)

18.2 Discuss Peck's tasks of ego integrity, Joan Erikson's gerotranscendence, and Labouvie-Vief's emotional expertise. (pp. 471–473)

18.3 Describe the functions of reminiscence and life review in older adults' lives. (p. 473)

18.4 Summarize stable and changing aspects of self-concept and personality in late adulthood. (pp. 473–474)

18.5 Discuss spirituality and religiosity in late adulthood, and trace the development of faith. (pp. 474–475)

18.6 Discuss individual differences in psychological well-being as older adults respond to increased dependency, declining health, and negative life changes. (pp. 475–476, 477))

18.7 Summarize the role of social support and social interaction in promoting physical health and psychological well-being in late adulthood. (pp. 476, 478)

18.8 Describe social theories of aging, including disengagement theory, activity theory, socioemotional selectivity theory, and continuity theory. (pp. 478–480, 481)

18.9 Explain how communities, neighborhoods, and housing arrangements affect elders' social lives and adjustment. (pp. 480, 482–483)

18.10 Describe changes in social relationships in late adulthood, including marriage, gay and lesbian partnerships, divorce, remarriage, and widowhood, and discuss never-married, childless older adults. (pp. 483–486)

18.11 Explain how sibling relationships, friendships, and relationships with adult children change in late life. (pp. 486–488)

18.12 Discuss elder maltreatment, including risk factors and strategies for prevention. (pp. 488–490)

18.13 Discuss the decision to retire, adjustment to retirement, and involvement in leisure activities. (pp. 490–492)

18.14 Discuss the meaning of successful aging. (pp. 492–493)

LECTURE OUTLINE

I. ERIKSON'S THEORY: EGO INTEGRITY VERSUS DESPAIR (p. 471)
   A. The final psychological conflict of Erikson's theory, **ego integrity versus despair**, involves coming to terms with one's life.
   B. Ego Integrity
      1. Adults who arrive at a sense of integrity feel whole, complete, and satisfied with their achievements.
      2. They have adapted to the mix of triumphs and disappointments that are an inevitable part of relationships and other life experiences.
      3. The capacity to view one's life in the larger context of all humanity contributes to the serenity and contentment that accompany integrity.
   C. Despair
      1. Despair occurs when elders feel they have made many wrong decisions, yet time is too short to find an alternate route to integrity.
      2. The despairing person finds it hard to accept that death is near and is overwhelmed with bitterness, defeat, and hopelessness.
      3. These feelings are often expressed as anger and contempt for others, which disguise contempt for oneself.

II. OTHER THEORIES OF PSYCHOSOCIAL DEVELOPMENT IN LATE ADULTHOOD (pp. 471–473)
   A. Peck's Tasks of Ego Integrity and Joan Erikson's Gerotranscendence (p. 472)
      1. According to Peck, Erikson's conflict of ego integrity versus despair comprises three distinct tasks:
         a. *Ego differentiation versus work-role preoccupation:* After retirement, people who have invested heavily in their careers must find other ways of affirming their self-worth—through family, friendship, and community roles that are as satisfying as work life.
         b. *Body transcendence versus body preoccupation:* Older adults must *transcend* physical limitations by emphasizing the compensating rewards of cognitive, emotional, and social powers.
         c. *Ego transcendence versus ego preoccupation:*
            (1) Elderly people must find a way to face the reality of death constructively, by investing in a future that goes beyond their own lifespan.
            (2) Attaining ego integrity requires a continuing effort to make life more secure, meaningful, and gratifying for those who will go on after one dies.
      2. Peck's concept of ego integrity requires that older adults move beyond their life's work, their bodies, and their separate identities.
      3. Recent evidence suggests that *body transcendence* and *ego transcendence* increase in very old age as people move beyond fear of death.
      4. Erikson's widow, Joan Erikson, believes that these attainments represent further development beyond ego integrity, to an additional psychosocial stage that she calls **gerotranscendence**—a cosmic and transcendent perspective directed forward and outward, beyond the self.
      5. She believed that success in attaining gerotranscendence is seen in heightened inner calm and contentment, with additional time spent in quiet reflection.
      6. More research is needed to confirm the existence of a distinct, transcendent late-life stage.
   B. Labouvie-Vief's Emotional Expertise (pp. 472–473)
      1. Elders improve in **affect optimization**, the ability to maximize positive emotions and dampen negative emotions, which contributes to their remarkable resilience.
      2. Despite physical declines, increased health problems, a restricted future, and death of loved ones, most elders sustain a sense of optimism.
      3. About 30 to 40 percent of elders also retain a considerable capacity for cognitive-emotional complexity—a combination that is related to especially effective emotional self-regulation.
      4. Older adults' emotional perceptiveness helps them separate interpretations from objective aspects of situations so that their coping strategies often include making sure they fully understand their own feelings before deciding on a course of action.
      5. A significant late-life psychosocial attainment is becoming expert at processing emotional information and regulating negative affect.
   C. Reminiscence and Life Review (p. 473)
      1. **Reminiscence** refers to telling stories about people and events from the past and reporting associated thoughts and feelings.
      2. Current theory and research indicate that reflecting on the past can be positive and adaptive.
      3. **Life review** is a form of reminiscence in which a person calls up, reflects on, and reconsiders past experiences, contemplating their meaning with the goal of achieving greater self-understanding.
      4. Older adults who participate in counselor-led life review report increased self-esteem, greater sense of purpose in life, improved life satisfaction, and reduced depression.
      5. When reminiscence is *self-focused,* engaged in to reduce boredom and revive bitter events, it is linked to adjustment problems, in contrast to the *other-focused* reminiscence of extroverted elders, which is directed at social goals, or *knowledge-based* reminiscence, in which older people draw on the past for effective problem-solving strategies and for teaching younger people.

III. STABILITY AND CHANGE IN SELF-CONCEPT AND PERSONALITY (pp. 473–475)
   A. Secure and Multifaceted Self-Concept (pp. 473–474)
      1. Older adults have accumulated a lifetime of self-knowledge, leading to more secure and complex conceptions of themselves than at earlier ages.
      2. Positive, multifaceted self-definitions are associated with psychological well-being.
      3. Most elders continue to mention some hoped-for selves in the areas of good health, personal characteristics, relationships, and social responsibility, and are active in pursuing them.

B. Resilience: Agreeableness, Sociability, and Acceptance of Change (p. 474)
   1. In open-ended interviews with elders in their sixties and again with the same elders in their eighties and nineties, researchers found that scores on adjectives that make up *agreeableness*—generous, acquiescent, and good-natured—were higher for the older than the younger group for over one-third of the sample.
   2. Agreeableness seems to characterize people who have come to terms with life despite its imperfections.
   3. Participants in the open-ended interview study showed a slight dip in *sociability* as they aged, perhaps reflecting a narrowing of social contacts, but those who were extroverted throughout life tended to remain so.
   4. A related development is greater *acceptance of change*—an attribute the elderly frequently mention as important to psychological well-being.
   5. The capacity to accept life's twists and turns, many of which are beyond one's control, is vital for positive functioning in late adulthood.

C. Spirituality and Religiosity (pp. 474–475)
   1. Older adults may develop a more mature sense of spirituality.
   2. Spirituality is not the same as religion, but for many people, religion provides beliefs, symbols, and rituals that guide their quest for meaning.
   3. Older adults attach great value to religious beliefs and behaviors, and North American elders generally become more religious or spiritual as they age, although about one-fourth become less religious.
   4. Faith and spirituality may advance to a higher level in late adulthood—away from prescribed beliefs to a more reflective approach that emphasizes links to others and is at ease with mystery and uncertainty.
   5. Involvement in both organized and informal religious activities is especially high among low-SES ethnic minority elders and among women, who are more likely than men to belong to religious congregations and engage in religious activities.
   6. Both organized and informal religious participation is associated with longer survival.

IV. INDIVIDUAL DIFFERENCES IN PSYCHOLOGICAL WELL-BEING (pp. 475–478)

A. Control versus Dependency (pp. 475–476)
   1. Two predictable, complementary behavior patterns can be seen in observations of people interacting with older adults in both private homes and institutions.
      a. In the **dependency–support script**, dependent behaviors are attended to immediately.
      b. In the **independence–ignore script**, independent behaviors are mostly ignored.
   2. Both scripts reinforce dependent behavior at the expense of independent behavior.
   3. Social interaction while assisting elders with physical care, household chores, and errands is often not meaningful and rewarding but, rather, demeaning and unpleasant.
   4. Whether assistance from others undermines well-being is a function of many factors, including the quality of help, the caregiver–elder relationship, and the social and cultural context in which helping occurs.
   5. Responding to stereotypes of the elderly as incapable, family members and other caregivers often act in ways that promote excessive dependency.
   6. Dependency in old age can be adaptive if it permits older people to conserve their strength by investing it in highly valued activities, using the strategy of selective optimization with compensation.

B. Health (p. 476)
   1. Health is a powerful predictor of psychological well-being in late adulthood.
   2. Physical declines and chronic disease can be highly stressful, leading to a sense of loss of personal control—a major factor in adult mental health.
   3. Physical illness resulting in disability is one of the strongest risk factors for late-life depression.
   4. Effective coping and a sense of self-efficacy are vitally important to elders in surmounting the physical impairment–depression relationship.
   5. Families and caregivers must grant elders autonomy by avoiding the dependency–support script.

C. Negative Life Changes (p. 476)
   1. Negative life changes may actually evoke less stress and depression for older people than younger adults, because many elders have learned to cope with hard times and have come to accept loss as part of human existence.
   2. However, when negative changes pile up, they test the coping skills of older adults.
   3. Elderly women, especially, say that others depend on them for emotional support, and they may find their social relations a source of stress, even in very old age.

D. Social Support and Social Interaction (pp. 476–478)
   1. In late adulthood, social support continues to reduce stress, thereby promoting physical health and psychological well-being.
   2. However, many older adults place such high value on independence that they do not want a great deal of support from people close to them unless they can reciprocate.
   3. Formal support as a complement to informal assistance not only helps relieve caregiving burdens but also spares elders from feeling overly dependent in their close relationships.
   4. Ethnic minority elders do not readily accept formal assistance but are more willing to do so when home helpers are connected to a familiar neighborhood organization, especially the church.
   5. For social support to promote well-being, elders need to assume personal control of it, consciously giving up primary control in some areas so that they can remain in control of other, highly valued pursuits.

V. A CHANGING SOCIAL WORLD (pp. 478–483)

A. Social Theories of Aging (pp. 478–480)
   1. Disengagement Theory (p. 478)
      a. According to **disengagement theory**, mutual withdrawal between elders and society takes place in anticipation of death.
      b. Older people decrease their activity levels and interact less frequently, becoming more preoccupied with their inner lives.
      c. However, not everyone disengages, and even when old people disengage, it may not be their preference but, rather, due to a failure of the social world to provide opportunities for engagement.
   2. Activity Theory (p. 478–479)
      a. **Activity theory** states that social barriers to engagement, not the desires of elders, cause declining rates of interaction.
      b. When elders lose certain roles, they try to find others in an effort to stay active and busy.
      c. Elders' life satisfaction depends on conditions that permit them to remain engaged in roles and relationships.
      d. Activity theory fails to acknowledge any psychological change in old age.
      e. When health status is controlled, elders who have larger social networks and engage in more activities are not necessarily happier.
      f. Quality, not quantity, of relationships predicts psychological well-being in old age.
   3. Continuity Theory (p. 479)
      a. According to **continuity theory**, most aging adults strive to maintain a personal system—an identity and a set of personality dispositions, interests, skills, and roles—that promotes life satisfaction by ensuring consistency between their past and anticipated future.
      b. Participation in familiar activities with familiar people provides repeated practice that helps preserve physical and cognitive functioning, fosters self-esteem and mastery, and affirms identity.
   4. Socioemotional Selectivity Theory (pp. 479–480)
      a. **Socioemotional selectivity theory** asserts that our social networks become more selective as we age.
      b. Social interaction does not decline suddenly in late age; rather, it extends lifelong selection processes.
      c. Physical and psychological aspects of aging lead to changes in the functions of social interaction.

        d. As physical fragility makes it more important to avoid stress, elders emphasize the emotion-regulating function of interaction, rather than other functions such as information seeking and future contact.
        e. Interacting mostly with relatives and friends makes it more likely that older adults' self-concepts and emotional equilibrium will be preserved.

B. Social Contexts of Aging: Communities, Neighborhoods, and Housing (pp. 480–483)
    1. Communities and Neighborhoods (pp. 480–481)
        a. Suburban elders have higher incomes and report better health than inner-city elders do.
        b. Inner-city elders, however, are better off in terms of transportation and proximity to social services, and are not as disadvantaged in health, income, and availability of services as those who live in small towns and rural areas.
        c. Small-town and rural elderly compensate for distance from family and social services by interacting more with neighbors and friends.
        d. Small communities have other features that foster gratifying relationships, including stability of residents, shared values and lifestyles, willingness to exchange social support, and frequent informal social visits.
    2. Housing Arrangements (pp. 481–483)
        a. Overwhelmingly, older adults want to stay in their own homes where they spent their adult lives.
        b. In the United States and Canada, fewer than 5 percent relocate to other communities.
        c. Ordinary Homes (pp. 481–482)
            (1) For the majority of elders, who are not physically impaired, staying in their own homes affords the greatest possible personal control—freedom to arrange space and schedule daily events as one chooses.
            (2) More elders in the United States, Canada, and other Western nations live on their own today than ever before, as a result of improved health and economic well-being.
            (3) Older adults of Southern, Central, and Eastern European descent, as well as African Americans, Asian Americans, Hispanics, and Native Americans, more often live with extended families.
            (4) During the past half-century, the number of unmarried, divorced, and widowed elders living alone has risen dramatically.
            (5) Over 40 percent of American and 38 percent of Canadian elders who live alone are poverty stricken—rates many times higher than for elderly couples.
        d. Residential Communities (pp. 482–483)
            (1) About 5 percent of North American senior citizens live in residential communities.
            (2) Housing developments for the aged, either single-dwelling or apartment complexes, differ from ordinary homes in that they have been modified to suit elders' capacities.
            (3) For elders who desire more assistance with daily living, **congregate housing** adds a variety of support services, including meals in a common dining room and watchful oversight of residents with physical and mental disabilities.
            (4) **Life care communities** offer a range of options, from independent or congregate housing to full nursing home care, guaranteeing that elders' changing needs will be met in one place as they age.
            (5) Studies of diverse residential communities for the aged reveal that they can have positive effects on physical and mental health.
            (6) Older adults who feel socially integrated into a setting are more likely to consider it their home, but those who do not are at high risk for loneliness and depression.
        e. Nursing Homes (p. 483)
            (1) The small percentage of North Americans age 65 and over who live in nursing homes experience the most extreme restriction of autonomy.
            (2) Potential social partners are abundant in nursing homes, but interaction is low, because residents have little personal control over social experiences.
            (3) Designing more homelike nursing homes could do much to increase residents' sense of security and control over their social experiences.

VI. RELATIONSHIPS IN LATE ADULTHOOD (pp. 483–490)

A. The **social convoy** is an influential model of changes in our social networks as we move through life.
   1. Ships in the inner circle represent people's closest relationships, such as spouse, best friend, parent, or child.
   2. Those less close but still important travel on the outside.
   3. With age, ships exchange places in the convoy, some drift away, and others join; but as long as the convoy continues to exist, the individual adapts positively.

B. Marriage (pp. 483–484)
   1. One in every 4 or 5 first marriages in North America is expected to last at least 50 years.
   2. Marital satisfaction rises from middle to late adulthood because of several changes in life circumstance and couples' communication:
      a. Late-life marriages involve fewer stressful responsibilities, such as rearing children and balancing family and career.
      b. Perceptions of fairness in the relationship increase as men participate more in household tasks after retirement.
      c. With extra time together, most couples engage in more joint leisure activities.
      d. Greater emotional understanding and emphasis on regulating emotion in relationships lead to more positive interactions among older couples.
   3. Even in unhappy marriages, elders are less likely to let their disagreements escalate into expressions of anger and resentment.
   4. When marital dissatisfaction exists, it often takes a greater toll on women than men.

C. Gay and Lesbian Partnerships (p. 484)
   1. Most elderly gays and lesbians in long-term partnerships report happy, highly fulfilling relationships, having sustained their relationships through a historical period of hostility and discrimination toward homosexuals.
   2. Due to a lack of social recognition of their partnerships, aging gays and lesbians are faced with health care systems unresponsive to their needs.
   3. Where gay and lesbian unions are not legally recognized, if one partner becomes frail or ill, the other may not be welcome in hospitals or nursing homes or be allowed to participate in health care decisions.

D. Divorce, Remarriage, and Cohabitation (pp. 484–485)
   1. Couples who divorce in late adulthood constitute less than 1 percent of all divorces in any given year.
   2. However, the divorce rate among people age 65 and older is increasing as new generations of elders become more accepting of marital breakup and because of higher divorce rates for second and subsequent marriages.
   3. The long-time married find it harder to separate their identity from that of their former spouse, and they suffer more from a sense of personal failure if they divorce.
   4. Self-criticism in divorced elders heightens guilt and depression because their self-worth depends more on past than future accomplishments.
   5. Remarriage rates are low in late adulthood and decline with age, although they are considerably higher among divorced than widowed elders.
   6. Compared with younger people who remarry, remarried elders tend to enter more stable relationships and to have much lower divorce rates.
   7. More older adults who enter a new relationship are choosing cohabitation, which results in more stable relationships in older people than in younger couples.

E. Widowhood (pp. 485–486)
   1. Widows make up one-third of the elderly population in the United States and Canada, because women live longer than men and are less likely to remarry.
   2. Ethnic minorities with high rates of poverty and chronic disease are more likely to be widowed.
   3. Widowed elders with outgoing personalities and high self-esteem try to preserve social relationships and often report that relatives and friends respond in kind.
   4. A strong sense of self-efficacy also predicts favorable adjustment.
   5. Widowed individuals must reorganize their lives, reconstructing an identity that is separate from the deceased spouse—a task that is harder for wives whose roles depended on their husbands' than for those who developed rewarding roles of their own.

6. Overall, however, men show more physical and mental health problems and greater risk of mortality after their wives die, because their wives usually maintained social connectedness, took care of household tasks, and coped with stressors for the couple.
7. Although availability of potential partners overwhelmingly favors widowers, sex differences in the experience of widowhood contribute to men's higher remarriage rate.

F. Never-Married, Childless Older Adults (p. 486)
   1. About 5 percent of older North Americans remain unmarried and childless throughout their lives.
   2. Most develop alternative meaningful relationships.
   3. Never-married elderly women report a level of life satisfaction equivalent to that of married elders and greater than that of divorcees and recently widowed elders.

G. Siblings (pp. 486–487)
   1. Nearly 80 percent of Americans over age 65 have at least one living sibling.
   2. Both men and women perceive bonds with sisters to be closer than bonds with brothers, and closer ties with sisters are associated with greater psychological well-being in elders.
   3. Elderly siblings in industrialized nations are more likely to socialize than to provide each other with direct assistance, but most elders say they would turn to a sibling for help in a crisis.
   4. Because siblings share a long and unique history, joint reminiscing about earlier times increases in late adulthood.

H. Friendships (pp. 487–488)
   1. As family responsibilities and vocational pressures lessen in late adulthood, friendships take on increasing importance.
   2. Intimacy and companionship are basic to meaningful elder friendships.
   3. Elderly women mention acceptance as a primary aspect of close friendship.
   4. Friendships link elderly people to the larger community.
   5. Friendships can help protect elders from the psychological consequences of loss.
   6. Elders report that the friends they feel closest to are fewer in number and live in the same community.
   7. The very old report more intergenerational friendships.
   8. Women are more likely to have intimate friends; men depend on their wives or sisters for warm, open communication.
   9. Older women have more **secondary friends**—people who are not intimates but with whom they spend time occasionally.

I. Relationships with Adult Children (pp. 488)
   1. About 80 percent of older adults in North America are parents of living children, most of whom are middle aged.
   2. Elders and their adult children are often in touch, even when they live far from each other.
   3. As people grow older, children usually continue to provide rich rewards, including love, companionship, and stimulation.
   4. Alternatively, conflict or unhappiness with adult children contributes to poor physical and mental health.
   5. Help from children most often takes the form of emotional support, rather than practical assistance; extensive support that cannot be returned is linked to poor psychological well-being.
   6. As social networks shrink in size, relationships with adult children become more important sources of family involvement.

J. Elder Maltreatment (pp. 488–490)
   1. Estimates indicate that about 4 to 6 percent of all elders are victims of maltreatment: 1.8 million in the United States and 280,000 in Canada.
   2. Elder maltreatment takes the following forms:
      a. *Physical abuse:* Intentional infliction of pain, discomfort, or injury
      b. *Physical neglect:* Intentional or unintentional failure to fulfill caregiving obligations
      c. *Psychological abuse:* Verbal assaults, humiliation, and intimidation
      d. *Sexual abuse*: Unwanted sexual contact of any kind
      e. *Financial abuse:* Illegal or improper exploitation of the elder's property or financial resources, through theft or use without the elder's consent
   3. The perpetrator is usually a person the older adult trusts and depends on for care and assistance.

4. Another form of neglect, described in the media as "granny dumping," has increased over the past several decades, and involves abandonment of elders with severe disabilities by family caregivers, usually at hospital emergency rooms.
5. Risk Factors (p. 489)
   a. Dependency of the Victim (p. 489): Very old and mentally and physically impaired elders are more vulnerable to maltreatment.
   b. Dependency of the Perpetrator (p. 489): Many abusers are dependent, emotionally or financially, on their victims.
   c. Psychological Disturbance and Stress of the Perpetrator (p. 489): Abusers are more likely than other caregivers to have psychological problems and to have alcohol or other drug problems.
   d. History of Family Violence (p. 489): Elder abuse is often part of a long history of family violence.
   e. Institutional Conditions (p. 489): Elder maltreatment is more likely to occur in nursing homes that are rundown and overcrowded and that have staff shortages, minimal staff supervision, high staff turnover, and few visitors.
6. Preventing Elder Maltreatment. (pp. 489–490)
   a. Once abuse is discovered, intervention involves immediate protection and provision of unmet needs for the elder and mental health services and social support for the spouse or caregiver.
   b. Prevention programs offer counseling, education, and respite services.
   c. Support groups help seniors identify abusive acts, practice appropriate responses, and form new relationships.
   d. Legal action is the best way to shield elders from abusers when the abuse is extreme, yet it seldom happens.
   e. Combating elder maltreatment also requires efforts at the level of the larger society.
   f. Countering negative stereotypes of aging reduces maltreatment by recognizing elders' dignity, individuality, and autonomy.

VII. RETIREMENT AND LEISURE (pp. 490–492)
   A. The Decision to Retire (pp. 490–491)
      1. Affordability of retirement is usually the first consideration in the decision to retire.
      2. Personal and workplace factors in addition to income influence the decision to retire.
         a. People in good health, for whom vocational life is central to self-esteem, and whose work environments are pleasant and stimulating, are likely to keep on working.
         b. People in declining health; who are engaged in routine, boring work; and who have compelling leisure interests often opt for retirement.
      3. Societal factors also affect retirement decisions.
         a. When many younger, less costly workers are available to replace older workers, industries are likely to offer incentives for people to retire.
         b. When concern increases about the burden on younger generations of a rising population of retirees, eligibility for retirement benefits may be postponed to a later age.
      4. In many Western nations, generous social security benefits make retirement feasible even for the economically disadvantaged, but many U.S. retirees, in contrast, experience falling living standards.
   B. Adjustment to Retirement (pp. 491–492)
      1. Because retirement involves giving up roles that are a vital part of identity and self-esteem, it is often thought of as a stressful process that contributes to declines in physical and mental health.
      2. A cause-and-effect relationship does not necessarily exist each time retirement and an unfavorable reaction are paired.
      3. Countless research findings indicate that most older adults adapt well to retirement.
      4. A sense of personal control over life events, including the decision to retire, is strongly linked to retirement satisfaction.
      5. Social support reduces stress associated with retirement.
      6. Marital happiness tends to rise after retirement, especially when a couple's relationship is positive.

C. Leisure Activities (p. 492)
   1. The best preparation for leisure in late life is to develop rewarding interests at a young age.
   2. Elders select leisure pursuits because they permit self-expression, new achievements, the rewards of helping others, or pleasurable social interactions.
   3. Older adults make a vital contribution to society through volunteer work.
   4. Younger, better educated, and financially secure elders with social interests are more likely to do volunteer work, and women do so more often than men.

VIII. SUCCESSFUL AGING (pp. 492–493)
   A. The term **successful aging** applies to people for whom growth, vitality, and striving may limit and, at times, overcome physical, cognitive, and social declines.
   B. Recent definitions focus on how people minimize losses while maximizing gains.
   C. The goals of successful agers include the following:
      1. Optimism and sense of self-efficacy in improving health and physical functioning
      2. Selective optimization with compensation to make the most of limited physical energies and cognitive resources
      3. Strengthening of self-concept, which promotes self-acceptance and pursuit of hoped-for possible selves
      4. Enhanced emotional understanding and emotional self-regulation
      5. Acceptance of change, which fosters life satisfaction
      6. A mature sense of spirituality, permitting anticipation of death with calm composure
      7. Personal control over domains of dependency and independence
      8. High-quality relationships, which offer social support and pleasurable companionship

LECTURE ENHANCEMENTS

LECTURE ENHANCEMENT 18.1
More on Possible Selves in Late Adulthood (pp. 473–474)

Time: 10–15 minutes

Objective: To examine hoped-for and feared images of the self in old age.

To extend existing research on possible selves in old age, Smith and Freund (2002) recruited 206 adults between ages 70 and 100 who were participants in the Berlin Aging Study. To determine if hoped-for and feared images of the self changed over time, the researchers conducted a four-year longitudinal study.

The researchers collected the following information at baseline and again four years later:

1. To assess hoped-for selves, participants were asked: Who would you like to become some day? What experiences would you like to have? What feelings would you like to have? What are your personal wishes and hopes?
2. To assess feared selves, participants were asked: What sort of person would you not like to become? What experiences would you not like to have? What images of yourself do you fear or dread?
3. To identify any major health concerns, participants were given physicals at baseline and at four-year follow-up. To assess subjective perspectives of health, participants were asked to rate their present health on a scale of 1 to 5 (1 = very poor; 5 = excellent).
4. Participants were asked about any major life events (for example, a change in residence, a death in the family, or a change in marital status) that may have contributed to their overall health and well-being over the course of the study. They were also asked to rate their overall life satisfaction.

Findings revealed that participants generated a variety of possible selves into very old age. Hoped-for selves were not limited to avoidance of undesirable outcomes, such as death, physical disability, or loss of a spouse. Instead, many participants indicated a desire for new experiences and positive contacts with friends and family. Not surprisingly, feared selves tended to focus on health and loss of significant others.

Results also indicated that possible selves changed over the course of the study. Some participants added new hoped-for selves and feared selves, whereas others let go of previously feared selves. For participants who focused more on hoped-for selves than feared selves, overall life satisfaction remained high over the course of the study. In contrast, life satisfaction was low in participants who predominantly focused on feared selves. Taken together, these findings show that even the oldest adults are future-oriented and that possible selves continue to be an important component of personality in late adulthood.

Ask students to review research on hardiness (Chapter 15, p. 406). How might the hoped-for selves and feared selves of hardy elders differ from those of other older adults? What implications might these differences have for health and well-being in late adulthood?

Smith, J., & Freund, A. M. (2002). The dynamics of possible selves in old age. *Journal of Gerontology, 57B,* P492–P500.

LECTURE ENHANCEMENT 18.2
More on Religious Involvement in Elders (pp. 474–475)

Time: 5–10 minutes

Objective: To examine the relationship between social support, religious involvement, and psychological distress in late adulthood.

The text points out that religious involvement has many benefits, including outcomes as diverse as increased physical and psychological well-being, more time spent exercising, and greater sense of closeness to family and friends. To examine the relationship between social support, religious involvement, and psychological distress in late adulthood, Dulin (2005) recruited 115 low-income adults between age 65 and 90.

Demographic information was collected at the beginning of the study. To assess religious involvement, participants were asked: (1) How many times have you been to church in the last three months? (2) On a scale of 1 to 6, how active are you in your faith? (3) On a scale of 1 to 6, how important is your spiritual activity? The Social Provisions Scale (SPS) was used to measure overall perceptions of social support. The SPS includes five subscales—attachment to others, social integration, reassurance of worth, reliable alliance (assurance that others can be counted on in times of stress), and guidance. The Negative Affect Scale (NAS) was used to measure psychological distress, including nervousness, irritability, and contempt.

Results indicated that social support served as a moderator between religious participation and psychological distress. Specifically, religious involvement was associated with lower levels of psychological distress only among participants who lacked social support. Psychological distress was highest in participants who both lacked social support and reported low levels of religious involvement.

Taken together, these findings suggest that religious involvement may be especially important for low-income elders who lack social support. Providing access to religious activities and services may be an effective approach to reducing distress in socially isolated elders.

Using results from this study and research in the text, ask students to discuss the importance of religious involvement in late adulthood. Why is religious participation especially high among low-SES elders?

Dulin, P. L. (2005). Social support as a moderator of the relationship between religious participation and psychological distress in a sample of community dwelling older adults. *Mental Health, Religion, & Culture, 8,* 81–86.

LECTURE ENHANCEMENT 18.3
Does Involvement in Leisure Activities Protect Elders from Dementia? (p. 492)

Time: 10–15 minutes

Objective: To examine the relationship between participation in leisure activities and reduced risk of dementia in late adulthood.

As discussed in the text, involvement in leisure activities is related to better physical and mental health and reduced mortality. But does leisure involvement protect elders from dementia? To find out, Verghese and colleagues (2003) recruited 469 adults between ages 75 and 85 who were already participating in the Bronx Aging Study. The researchers had access to all relevant demographic information and included only participants who did not show any signs of dementia at baseline (on the basis of thorough clinical and neuropsychological evaluations). Participants completed routine neuropsychological evaluations every 12 to 18 months, with the study continuing for 21 years.

In addition to regular neurological evaluations, the researchers collected information on a diverse range of leisure activities. Participants were asked to rate how often they participated in the following activities: reading books or newspapers, writing for pleasure, doing crossword puzzles, playing board games or cards, participating in organized group discussions, playing musical instruments, playing tennis or golf, swimming, bicycling, dancing, participating in group exercise, playing team games (such as bowling), walking for exercise, doing housework, and baby-sitting.

Findings indicated that participation in leisure activities was associated with reduced risk of dementia. Compared to elders who rarely participated in leisure activities, elders who were highly involved in leisure pursuits were far less likely to be diagnosed with dementia, regardless of age, sex, educational background, and baseline cognitive status. The relationship was especially strong for participants who were highly involved in cognitive leisure activities (for example, reading books, writing for pleasure, and involvement in organized group discussions). Thus, the findings support research presented in the text: Elders who participate in leisure activities tend to experience better physical and mental health than elders who do not engage in leisure pursuits.

Verghese, J., Lipton, R., Katz, M. J., Hall, C. B., Derby, C. A., Kuslansky, G., Ambrose, A. F., Sliwinski, M., & Buschke, H. (2003). Leisure activities and the risk of dementia in the elderly. *New England Journal of Medicine, 348*, 2508–2516.

LECTURE ENHANCEMENT 18.4
Elders' Perceptions of Successful Aging (pp. 492–493)

Time: 5–10 minutes

Objective: To examine elders' perceptions of successful aging.

The text notes that successful agers are people for whom growth, vitality, and striving limit, and at times, overcome physical, cognitive, and social declines. To examine diverse aspects of successful aging, Knight and Ricciardelli (2003) recruited and interviewed 60 adults between the ages of 70 and 101. Researchers began each interview by asking, "What do you think it means to age successfully?" Participants were then asked about health, physical activity, social interaction, happiness, life satisfaction, what they considered "old" to be, how they felt about their own age, and adaptation to life changes. Participants also provided relevant demographic information, including age, gender, marital status, educational background, and residential status.

Results indicated that health and activity were major themes in elders' views of successful aging. Being physically, socially, and mentally active was important to most participants. When asked how they felt about their current age, the majority were accepting of their age. Nearly 70 percent indicated that "old" is more of a mindset than a reflection of chronological age.

Findings also revealed that participants compensated for losses in old age. For example, when their physical capabilities deteriorated, elders allowed more time for daily or leisurely activities, such as gardening or shopping. Finally, religion was an important component of successful aging for some participants. Religious elders indicated that their beliefs and values helped them cope with losses and adjust favorably to old age.

Knight, T., & Ricciardelli, L. A. (2003). Successful aging: Perceptions of adults aged between 70 and 101 years. *International Journal of Aging and Human Development, 56,* 223–245.

LEARNING ACTIVITIES

LEARNING ACTIVITY 18.1
Matching: Theories of Psychosocial Development in Late Adulthood (pp. 471–473)

Present the following exercise as an in-class activity or quiz:

Directions: Match each of the following terms with its correct description.

Terms:

1. Ego integrity versus despair
2. Body transcendence
3. Ego transcendence
4. Gerotranscendence
5. Affect optimization
6. Reminiscence
7. Life review
8. Self-focused reminiscence
9. Other-focused reminiscence
10. Knowledge-based reminiscence

Descriptions:

A. Reminiscence that is used to reduce boredom and revive bitter events
B. The ability to maximize positive emotion and dampen negative emotion
C. The final psychological conflict of Erikson's theory, which involves coming to terms with one's life
D. Reminiscence that is directed at social goals, such as solidifying family and friendship ties and reliving relationships with lost loved ones
E. Orienting toward a larger, more distant future
F. Telling stories about people and events from the past and reporting associated thoughts and feelings
G. Focusing on psychological strengths
H. When a person calls up, reflects on, and reconsiders past experiences, contemplating their meaning with the goal of achieving greater self-understanding
I. An additional pychosocial stage—a cosmic and transcendent perspective directed forward and outward, beyond the self
J. When elders draw upon their past for effective problem-solving strategies and for teaching younger people

Answers:

1. C
2. G
3. E
4. I
5. B
6. F
7. H
8. A
9. D
10. J

LEARNING ACTIVITY 18.2
Assessing Self-Concept in Late Adulthood (pp. 473–474)

Ask students so pose the following question to a grandparent, a friend's grandparent, or another elder: "How would you describe yourself?" Students should record the answer and compare it with research in the text. For example, did the elder mention a broad spectrum of life domains, including hobbies, interests, social participation, family, health, and personality traits? Did the response include more positive than negative evaluations? Based on the answer, does the elder appear to have a multifaceted self-concept? Explain.

LEARNING ACTIVITY 18.3
Religion and Aging (pp. 474–475)

Ask students to visit the website *http://www.trinity.edu/~mkearl/ger-relg.html,* which presents results from a study examining how religiosity changes with age and proximity to death. Using information from the website, have students answer the following questions: Which age group reported the strongest religiosity? The weakest? Is this consistent with research presented in the text? Return to Chapter 1 (page 29) and review cohort effects. How might cohort effects influence respondents' reported religiosity? What events in the life cycle might account for changes in religiosity over time? Next, have students review the percent of "very happy" people by health status, gender, and religiosity. Based on the data, are strongly religious elders healthier and happier than their less religious agemates? Are there noticeable gender differences? Finally, click on Islamic, Hindu, and Buddhist Conceptions of Aging, which examines how different faiths view old age. Do trends in religiosity differ among Islamic, Hindu, and Buddhist elders? Explain.

LEARNING ACTIVITY 18.4
Housing Arrangements for Elders (pp. 481–483)

In small groups, have students respond to the following scenario:

You have been approached by a family who is concerned about Jack, an 84-year-old relative who currently resides in his own home. Jack's wife died a year ago, and the family is worried that independent living may not be the best option for him. Generate a list of issues that should be addressed before deciding where Jack should reside. For example, what health issues should be considered? What are the advantages and disadvantages of being moved out of his home? Under what circumstances would Jack likely benefit from congregate housing or a life care community? When would a nursing home placement be most beneficial? What are some drawbacks of living in a nursing home?

LEARNING ACTIVITY 18.5
True or False: Relationships in Late Adulthood (pp. 483–488)

Present the following exercise to students as a quiz or in-class activity:

Directions: Read each of the following statements and indicate whether it is *True* (T) or *False* (F).

Statements:

_____ 1. Compared to younger couples, elderly couples married for many years disagree less often and—when they do disagree—resolve their differences in more constructive ways.
_____ 2. The majority of gay and lesbian couples assume that family members will provide support in old age.
_____ 3. Rather than remarrying, today more older adults who enter a new relationship choose cohabitation.
_____ 4. Sex differences in the experience of widowhood contribute to women's higher remarriage rate.
_____ 5. Same-sex friendships in never-married elderly women's lives tend to be unusually close and often involve joint travel, periods of co-residence, and associations with one another's extended families.
_____ 6. Elderly siblings in industrialized nations are less likely to socialize than to provide each other with direct assistance.
_____ 7. Older adults report more favorable experiences with friends than with family members.
_____ 8. Quality rather than quantity of parent-child interaction affects older adults' life satisfaction.
_____ 9. Even moderate support from adult children, with opportunities to reciprocate, is associated with poor psychological well-being.
_____ 10. Elders are more likely to be abused by in-home caregivers than family members.

Answers:

1. T
2. F
3. T
4. F
5. T
6. F
7. T
8. T
9. F
10. F

LEARNING ACTIVITY 18.6
Friendships Throughout the Lifespan (pp. 487–488)

Spend some class time discussing the nature of friendships throughout the lifespan. For example, how do friendships change from childhood to adolescence to adulthood? What characteristics of friendship remain stable? What are some gender differences in friendship, and how do these differences change over time? Why is friendship so important at each phase of the life cycle?

LEARNING ACTIVITY 18.7
Inviting a Panel of Older Adults to Class for a Discussion of Retirement (pp. 490–492)

Invite several older adults to participate in a panel discussion of retirement. Students should prepare a brief list of questions for each member prior to the class discussion. You may want to provide panel members with the questions prior to their visit. Questions might include: What factors influenced your decision to retire? How have you adjusted to retirement? Describe your leisure pursuits now that you have retired. Are they different from your leisure pursuits when you were working? Have you found any new part-time work experiences? What are the advantages and disadvantages of retirement? Following the panel discussion, spend some class time comparing the answers with research in the text.

LEARNING ACTIVITY 18.8
Applying Ecological Systems Theory to Cognitive, Emotional, and Social Development in Late Adulthood (pp. 492–493)

In small groups, ask students to list factors that contribute to favorable cognitive (Chapter 17), emotional, and social development in late adulthood. Next, have students review ecological systems theory on pages 19–21. For each factor listed, students should indicate the level of environment to which it belongs. Encourage students to consider the role of third parties and bidirectional influences.

LEARNING ACTIVITY 18.9
Creating a Pamphlet on Successful Aging (pp. 492–493)

Tell students to pretend they have been approached by a local community organization to develop a pamphlet on successful aging. What information would students include in the pamphlet? For example, what does it mean to age successfully? Are perceptions of successful aging the same for everyone? Explain. What are some characteristics of successful agers? What resources and social supports do elders need to age successfully?

ASK YOURSELF . . .

REVIEW: Many elders adapt effectively to negative life changes. List personal and environmental factors that facilitate this generally positive outcome. (pp. 471–478)

Many personal and environmental factors can facilitate effective adaptation to negative life changes. They include a sense of ego differentiation rather than work-role preoccupation, body transcendence rather than body preoccupation, and ego transcendence rather than ego preoccupation. Elders who arrive at a sense of integrity feel whole, complete, and satisfied with their achievements. Although basic information-processing skills diminish in late adulthood, elders display a compensating emotional strength: They improve in affect optimization—the ability to maximize positive emotion and dampen negative emotion. Older adults' greater emotional perceptiveness helps them separate interpretations from objective aspects of situations, and this is reflected in their coping strategies, which often include making sure they understand their own feelings before choosing a course of action. They readily use emotion-centered coping strategies in negatively charged situations.

Reflecting on the past can be a positive, adaptive aspect of elders' lives when they engage in life review—calling up, reflecting on, and reconsidering past experiences with the goal of achieving greater self-understanding. Some older adults, especially those who score high in openness to experience, also engage in knowledge-based reminiscence, drawing on their past to find effective problem-solving strategies and to teach younger people—socially engaged, mentally stimulating forms of reminiscence that help make life rich and rewarding.

A flexible, optimistic approach to life, which fosters resilience in the face of adversity, is common in old age. On personality tests, a rise in agreeableness, especially among men, seems to characterize those who have come to terms with life despite its imperfections.

Elderly people frequently mention greater acceptance of change as an attribute that is important to their psychological well-being, as seen in effective coping with the loss of loved ones. The development of a more mature sense of spirituality—an inspirational sense of life's meaning—helps many elders accept declines and losses while still feeling whole and complete, and enables them to anticipate death with calm composure.

APPLY: At age 80, Miriam took a long time to get dressed. Joan, her home helper, suggested, "Wait until I arrive before dressing. Then I can help you and it won't take so long." What impact is Joan's approach likely to have on Miriam's personality? What alternative approach to helping Miriam would you recommend? (pp. 476, 478)

Excessive help that is not wanted or needed or that exaggerates weaknesses can undermine elders' mental health. It can also accelerate physical disability by preventing elders from making use of existing skills. Joan is using both the *dependency–support script* and the *independence-ignore script,* which reinforce dependent behavior at the expense of independent behavior, regardless of the older person's competencies. Miriam, like many elders, may fear becoming dependent on others. However, Joan's overresponsive dependency script is likely to promote passivity and incompetence in Miriam, who may become overly dependent on the help of others.

To promote Miriam's well-being, Joan should allow Miriam to choose those activities in which she would like help so that Miriam can conserve her energy for personally valued activities—for example, walking her dog and having lunch with friends. In this way, Miriam assumes control over her dependency. She is using a set of strategies called *selective optimization with compensation.* To optimize her energies, Miriam can choose to be dependent and to let Joan help her with dressing. This will compensate for Miriam's diminished energy for daily tasks and social activities. In this case, Miriam's dependency behavior is not a sign of helplessness but, rather, will likely grant her autonomy—a means for managing her own aging. By freeing energy for pursuits that are personally satisfying, Miriam can enhance her quality of life.

REVIEW: Cite features of neighborhoods and residential communities that enhance elders' life satisfaction. (pp. 480–483)

Positive aspects of smaller communities include stability of residents, shared values and lifestyles, willingness to exchange social support, and frequent social visits as people "drop in" on one another. Many suburban and rural communities have responded to elder residents' needs by developing transportation programs (such as special buses and vans) to take elders to health and social services, senior centers, and shopping centers. In addition, both urban and rural older adults report greater life satisfaction when many senior citizens reside in their neighborhood and are available as like-minded companions. Compared with older adults in urban areas, those in quiet neighborhoods in small and midsized communities are more satisfied with life, primarily because smaller communities have lower crime rates.

Studies of diverse residential communities designed for the elderly reveal that they can have positive effects on physical and mental health. A specially designed physical space and care on an as-needed basis helps elders overcome mobility limitations, thereby permitting greater social participation. And in societies where old age leads to reduced status, age-segregated living can be gratifying, opening up useful roles and leadership opportunities and providing an opportunity to set aside past disappointments or failures and to relate to peers on the basis of their current life together.

APPLY: Sam lives alone in the same home he has occupied for over 30 years. His adult children can't understand why he won't move across town to a modern apartment. Using continuity theory, explain why Sam prefers to stay where he is. (p. 479)

According to continuity theory, most aging adults strive to maintain a personal system—an identity and a set of personality dispositions, interests, roles, and skills that ensure consistency between their past and anticipated future. This striving for continuity is a way for older adults to minimize stress and disruption, using familiar skills and engaging in familiar activities with familiar people—preferences that provide a secure sense of routine and direction in life. Sam's desire to remain in the home he has occupied for more than 30 years reflects this interest in maintaining continuity and consistency in his personal identity, by staying in the place where he has lived much of his adult life. Sam is deeply attached to his home as the site of memorable life events. Staying there allows him to maintain independence, privacy, and a network of nearby friends and neighbors. For Sam, a move to a modern apartment might mean the loss of personal control, of an extensive social network, and of daily reminders of memories spanning the last 30 years, which help him preserve his personal history and maintain a coherent sense of his lifelong identity—an essential aspect of ego integrity.

APPLY: Vera, a nursing home resident, speaks to her adult children and to a close friend on the phone every day. In contrast, she seldom attends nursing home social events or interacts with her roommate. Using socioemotional selectivity theory, explain Vera's behavior. (pp. 479–480)

According to socioemotional selectivity theory, our social networks become more selective as we age. In old age, contacts with family and long-term friends are sustained until the eighties, when they diminish in favor of a few very close relationships. In contrast, contacts with acquaintances and willingness to form new social ties declines steadily. Vera may be reluctant to initiate new contacts because, in old age, the information-gathering and self-affirmation functions of social interaction become less significant. Because Vera has gathered a lifetime of information, there are fewer people with knowledge that she desires. In addition, she may feel that it is risky to approach people she does not know for self-affirmation.

Elders emphasize the emotion-regulating function of interaction. It is important for Vera to avoid stress and maintain emotional equilibrium. As a result, she may be highly motivated to select associates on an emotional basis, pursuing pleasant relationships and avoiding unpleasant ones. Interacting mostly with family and close friends makes it easier for Vera to preserve her self-concept and emotional equilibrium. Selectivity theory is helpful in explaining Vera's behavior as she makes careful choices about how to allocate her time and energy.

REVIEW: Why is adjustment to late-life divorce usually more difficult for women and adjustment to widowhood more difficult for men? (pp. 484–485)

Women suffer more than men from late-life divorce because they are more likely to spend their remaining years living alone. Also, the financial consequences of divorce are greater than for widowhood because many accumulated assets are lost in property settlements.

Overall, men show more physical and mental health problems following the death of a spouse. Most relied on their wives for social connectedness, household tasks, and coping with stressors. Also, because of gender-role expectations, men feel less free to express their emotions and to ask for help with meals, household tasks, and social relationships. Finally, men tend to be less involved in religious activities—a vital source of support and inner strength.

APPLY: At age 51, Mae lost her job and couldn't afford to pay rent. She moved in with her 78-year-old widowed mother, Beryl. Although Beryl welcomed Mae's companionship, Mae grew depressed and drank heavily. When Beryl complained about Mae's failure to look for work, Mae pushed and slapped her. Explain why this mother–daughter relationship led to elder abuse. (pp. 488–489)

Mae and Beryl have a relationship of mutual dependency: Beryl depends on Mae to relieve her loneliness, while Mae is financially dependent on Beryl. This financial dependency, which Mae experiences as powerlessness, has led to her aggressive, exploitative behavior. Mae's heavy drinking, depression, unemployment, and social isolation are factors that increase the likelihood that Mae will lash out when Beryl is demanding or irritating.

REFLECT: Select one member of your extended family whom you know well, and describe that person's social convoy, or cluster or close relationships providing safety and support. In what ways has the convoy changed over the past five to ten years? How well has the person adapted to those changes? Explain. (pp. 483–488)

This is an open-ended question with no right or wrong answer.

REVIEW: What psychological and contextual factors predict favorable adjustment to retirement? (pp. 490–492)

Among psychological factors, a sense of personal control over life events, including the decision to retire for internally motivated reasons (to do other things), is strongly linked to retirement satisfaction. Well-educated people in high-status careers typically adjust favorably, perhaps because the satisfactions derived from challenging, meaningful work readily transfer to nonwork pursuits.

Workplace factors—especially financial worries or being pressured into giving up one's job—predict stress following retirement. But many contemporary elders view retirement as a time of opportunity and development and describe themselves as socially involved—major determinants of retirement satisfaction.

Social support reduces stress associated with retirement. Besides friends, spouses are a vital source of support. The number of leisure activities couples enjoy together predicts retirement satisfaction. Marital happiness tends to rise after retirement, which grants husband and wife more time for companionship.

APPLY: Nate, happily married to Gladys, adjusted well to retirement. He also found that his marriage became even happier. How can a good marriage ease the transition to retirement? How can retirement enhance marital satisfaction? (p. 492)

Social support reduces stress associated with retirement. Gladys is a vital source of support in fostering Nate's retirement adjustment. Nate and Gladys now have more time for leisure activities, and the number of leisure activities couples enjoy together predicts their satisfaction with retirement.

Retirement has given Nate more time for companionship with Gladys. Consequently, Nate and Gladys's marriage has benefited from the freedom of Nate's retirement years, and their satisfaction in marriage has also promoted Nate's positive adjustment to retirement.

REFLECT: Think of someone you know who is aging successfully. What personal qualities led you to select that person? (pp. 492–493)

This is an open-ended question with no right or wrong answer.

SUGGESTED STUDENT READINGS

Eyetsemitan, F. E. & Gire, J. T. (2003). *Aging and adult development in the developing world: Applying western theories and concepts.* West Point, CT: Greenwood Publishing. A collection of chapters highlighting the influence of environmental contexts on the aging process. According to the authors, Western theories of aging may be inappropriate for understanding the experiences of elders in developing societies.

Podnieks, E., Lowenstein, A., & Kosberg, J. (2005). *Elder abuse*. New York: Haworth Press. A multidisciplinary approach to understanding elder abuse, this book presents up-to-date research on domestic violence in late adulthood, including risk factors, characteristics of abusers, cultural perceptions of elder abuse, and practical strategies for dealing with elder abuse.

Roose, S. P., & Sackeim, H. A. (2004). *Late-life depression*. New York: Oxford University Press. Presents a thorough overview of late-life depression. Topics include symptoms of late-life depression, diagnosis and treatment options, the relationship between depression and mortality, elder suicide, and bereavement.

Vaillant, G. E. (2002). *Aging well: Surprising guideposts to a happier life from the landmark Harvard Study of Adult Development.* Boston: Little Brown. Based on a longitudinal study of 824 participants followed from adolescence through old age, this book explores the multitude of factors contributing to resilience across the lifespan. Vaillant concludes that individual lifestyle choices play a greater role in successful aging than genetics, wealth, race, and gender.

TRANSPARENCIES

T-193 Age-Related Change in Number of Social Partners Varying in Closeness
Figure 18.1 (p. 480)

T-195 Age-Related Change in Aid Given or Received from a Sibling
Figure 18.2 (p. 487)

T-196 Factors That Influence the Decision to Retire
Figure 18.3 (p. 491)

MEDIA MATERIALS

EXPLORING LIFESPAN DEVELOPMENT IN ACTION

Late Adulthood

This part of the Observation Program begins by illustrating the most obvious physical changes of late adulthood, along with variations in physical aging. Several factors that promote longevity are reviewed. A visit to the Senior Center in Normal, Illinois, depicts many services that support development and well-being late in life—health checks; a government-subsidized hot lunch program; educational workshops and lectures that teach elders to understand, recognize, and prevent health problems; exercise classes; pleasurable leisure pursuits; and the opportunity to form warm friendships.

Attention, memory, and verbal expression difficulties are common concerns of older adults. However, as the Writers Group at Westminster Village, a life-care community, reveals, elders who actively use their minds sustain complex cognitive skills. Members share the fruits of their creative efforts and comment on why they like to write. George and Dorothy, married for 56 years, reside in their own home and lead an active and rewarding life. George comes up with an innovative solution to an everyday problem and describes how he volunteers at a nearby nursing home.

Jeanne and Charles, recently retired, defy the stereotype of retirement as stressful. Good health, continued involvement in professional activities and leisure pursuits, and the pleasures of grandparenthood helped make the transition a welcome one.

Alexander talks about how volunteering has helped him meet new people, stay active, and continue learning well after retirement. He also discusses how he has been able to compensate for age-related physical changes in order to continue doing the things he used to when he was younger, such as take care of his lawn.

Rabbi Gordon exemplifies the increasingly blurred distinction between work and retirement. Since retiring 25 years ago, he has had a dozen careers and has just taken a full-time position. He explains why he returned to the pulpit at this time in his life and what it means to him. Next, Rabbi Gordon and his 16-year-old granddaughter Rachel discuss their relationship and what it has meant to live in the same city for the first time in each of their lives. Finally, Rabbi Gordon speaks about the role of the community in making the elder years more rewarding.

Onie, age 107, describes her good memory, love of learning, and appreciation for the good things in her life, including having had the ability to see until age 100. She talks about her desire to travel, her positive outlook for the future, and the sense of purpose she feels every day.

A WINDOW ON LIFESPAN DEVELOPMENT

Challenges of Advanced Age and Retirement: Rabbi Gordon, Age 89

Rabbi Gordon describes his many post-retirement careers and the way that challenging work fulfills him. He also comments on the importance of community response to the many needs of elders.

Coping with Widowhood: Anna Mae, Age 82

Anna Mae's life changed drastically with the death of her husband and her own stroke. But with the help of neighbors and her two sons, she hopes to stay in her own house as long as possible.

Finding Enjoyment in Retirement and Grandparenthood: Jeanne and Charles

Jeanne and Charles find retirement a happy relief from their previously hectic schedules. Both stay active in professional and volunteer activities. They enjoy tennis, time with friends, and bonding with their grandchildren.

Retirement and Volunteering: Alexander, Age 90, Marguerite, Age 82, Eleanor, Age 82, and Doris, Age 87

Four retirees describe the personal and social benefits they have experienced as a result of doing volunteer work since retirement, including meeting new people and feeling useful.

VIDEOTAPES AND DVDs

Adult Development (1990, Insight Media, 30 min.). Experts discuss key developmental tasks such as moving away from home, becoming a parent, midlife change of careers, and retirement.

Aging and Saging (1998, Films Media Group, 24 min.). This program gives viewers a glimpse of a weekend Elder Circle at the Omega Institute, a large human potential center, where a discussion is moderated by two author/teachers, Rabbi Zalman Schachter-Shalomi and Ram Dass. The program examines the need to help the elderly redefine themselves as role models of healthy and graceful aging and to reincorporate them into society as a valuable resource.

Aging Successfully (1997, Davidson Films, 31 min.). In this program, developmental psychologists Paul and Margret Baltes talk about their SOC (selection–optimization–compensation) model of adaptive competence in old age. They discuss positive aging experiences and show how cognitive tests can be used to assess older people's mental capabilities.

Aging with Grace: A Discussion About Identity (1999, Terra Nova Films, 20 min.). In this program, several older adults talk about themselves and how their roles and sense of who they are have changed as they have aged.

As Time Goes By (1998, Fanlight Productions/Canadian Broadcasting Corporation, 24 min.). In this documentary, aging men and women, couples and singles, share their experiences with love, romance, and growing old. As they discuss the place of sexuality in their lives, what emerges is often in striking counterpoint to society's perceptions of sex among the aged.

Curtain Call (1996, Aquarius Health Care Media, 52 min.). A film producer and her elderly mother struggle with issues of aging and independent living. They strike compromises that respect the rights and needs of both generations.

Elder Abuse: America's Growing Crime (1999, Films Media Group, 16 min.). In this program, ABC news correspondents Diane Sawyer and Marti Emerald investigate several cases of elder abuse. They also look at the efforts of people and organizations who are working to stop abuse, including the network of social workers, bankers, lawyers, doctors, and police personnel who volunteer as members of the Fiduciary Abuse Specialist Team, seeking out evidence of financial abuse of senior citizens.

Elder Abuse: Five Case Studies (1992, Fanlight Productions/Jim Vanden Bosch, 40 min.). Through the candid accounts of sufferers, this program offers insights into the ambivalent feelings of older victims of physical or emotional abuse. The program looks at a variety of interventions that can be helpful in stopping abuse, including counseling, shelters, supportive services, and legal action.

Elder Issues: Elder Abuse (2002, Concept Media, 27 min.). This program focuses on the growing problem of elder abuse. It describes the various types of abuse and the typical characteristics of abusers, as well as the social, cultural, and medical barriers to getting help for mistreated elders. The program looks at approaches to preventing abuse and to assessing and treating abused elders. It also outlines the role of government agencies and other service providers in helping elders and their family caregivers prevent abuse before it occurs.

Erik H. Erikson: A Life's Work (1991, Davidson Films, 38 min.). This film uses archival materials and new footage to introduce each of the eight life-cycle stages described by Erik Erikson. The program combines biographical information about Erikson with his theoretical ideas to give students an understanding of the relationship between a theorist's own life experience and the work that is produced.

Growing Old in a New Age: Family and Intergenerational Relationships (1993, Annenberg Media/University of Hawaii Center on Aging, 60 min.). This program, Part 8 of a series, looks at older people in the roles of spouses and grandparents and examines the ways in which elders sustain family traditions and culture.

Growing Old in a New Age: Intellect, Personality, and Mental Health (1993, Annenberg Media/University of Hawaii Center on Aging, 60 min.). This program, Part 6 of a series, examines intellectual functioning and the nature of personality. It includes descriptions by gerontologists of longitudinal and cross-section designs used to study intellect and personality across the lifespan, and discussions with elders about mental health and stress-reduction techniques.

Growing Old in a New Age: Social Roles and Relationships in Old Age (1993, Annenberg Media/University of Hawaii Center on Aging, 60 min.). This program, Part 7 of a series, explores how the roles of family, friendship, work, and leisure in our lives change with age and examines some ways in which older adults cope with role losses resulting from retirement or death of a loved one, and go on to create new roles appropriate to later life.

Growing Old in a New Age: Work, Retirement, and Economic Status (1993, Annenberg Media/University of Hawaii Center on Aging, 60 min.). This program, Part 9 of a series, explores early retirement, job opportunities, and trends in the labor force for older adults. Retired elders talk about their involvement in community service and leisure activities. The program also deals with income sources after retirement.

I'm Pretty Old (1993, Fanlight Productions/James Vanden Bosch, 20 min.). In this program, several residents of a nursing home talk about aging and what it is like to live in a long-term care facility, where they have had to give up some of their independence because of physical limitations. The program provides valuable insights and reflections on aging.

In Their Own Words: Retirement and Options for Living (2002, Magna Systems, 29 min.). In this program, elders talk about their retirement planning and their expectations, and whether these were met. They portray various ways of living in retirement and demonstrate differences in adjustment to being retired. The program also examines housing options for seniors, with a discussion of the importance to older people of maintaining a sense of control.

In Their Own Words: The Social Convoy (2002, Magna Systems, 29 min.). This program focuses on the "social convoy"—the group of people who accompany each of us on our journey through life, providing a vital element of good adjustment and well-being at every developmental stage. Seniors talk about their marriages and the issues they have confronted through the years. They also discuss their relationships with their adult children and grandchildren and, finally, talk about the importance of their friendships—a crucial element of late-life happiness.

Late Life Depression: Depression in the Elderly (2004, Aquarius Health Care Media, 28 min.). In this program, three elderly people talk about how they have coped with major depression, which affects as many as one in five older Americans. The program offers advice to families on getting help for a depressed elderly family member.

Living Longer ... Aging Well (2000, Films Media Group, 29 min.). This program presents the stories of several elders who, despite America's inhospitable social climate for the elderly, are nevertheless aging with dignity and courage.

On Old Age: A Conversation with Joan Erikson at 90 (1995, Davidson Films, 38 min.), and *On Old Age II: A Conversation with Joan Erikson at 92* (1997, Davidson Films, 30 min.), In *On Old Age,* Joan Erikson, interviewed at age 90, reviews the Eight Stages of Life that she and her husband, Erik Erikson, developed. She explains that her own experience of aging has led her to rethink the characteristics of the Eighth Stage. In *On Old Age II,* filmed two years later, Erikson describes her proposed Ninth Stage and its associated conflicts.

Optimal Aging: Slowing Down the Clock (2000, Aquarius Health Care Media, 27 min.). In this program, series creator and host Gail Harris visits the Corsello Center of Complementary and Integrative Medicine in Manhattan to learn some approaches to use in achieving optimal aging, including diagnostic techniques, stress reduction methods, and dietary changes. In an interview, Dr. Serafina Corsello talks about the importance of taking good care of one's digestive system, and offers practical advice for going so.

The Personals: Improvisations on Romance in the Golden Years (1998, Fanlight Productions/Keiko Ibi, 37 min.). This film, winner of the Academy Award for Best Short Documentary in 1998, follows a group of senior citizens as they rehearse and perform an original play about their quest for dates through the personal ads. The material for the play is drawn from the comedy and drama of their own lives, and the film follows them into their homes to explore the joys and sorrows of growing old in America.

When Help Was There: Four Stories of Elder Abuse (2000, Fanlight Productions/Jim Vanden Bosch, for the Goldman Institute for Aging, 19 min.). This program illustrates the complex problem of elder abuse through four separate, ethnically diverse cases: a Hispanic mother threatened by her son, an African-American woman physically abused by her husband, an Asian couple forced out of their home by their son-in-law, and a Caucasian man defrauded of his possessions and savings by a "friend." The program also describes how each of these people was aided by a network of services.

When Your Parent Needs You: Caring for an Aging Parent (2002, Aquarius Health Care Media, 35 min.). This program features two specialists in caregiving and issues of aging: Beth Witrogen McLeod, author of *Caregiving: The Spiritual Journey of Love, Loss and Renewal,* which was nominated for a Pulitzer Prize, and Avrene L. Brandt, a clinical psychologist who is a consultant to the Greater Philadelphia Chapter of the Alzheimer's Association.

TEST BANK

MULTIPLE CHOICE

1) In Erikson's theory of development, ego integrity versus despair involves
   A) preparing for death.
   B) a final attempt to reconcile any unhappinesses in one's life.
   C) coming to terms with one's life.
   D) heavy depression and disability for most adults.
   Answer: C
   Page Ref: 471
   Skill: Factual
   Objective: 18.1

2) Mr. Solimani reached the last years of his life feeling whole, complete, and satisfied with his achievements. While he made some decisions in his life that didn't turn out as expected, he acknowledges that the path he eventually followed was necessary for fashioning his life course. Mr. Solimani has achieved
   A) a sense of integrity.
   B) finality.
   C) tolerance.
   D) a sense of disengagement.
   Answer: A
   Page Ref: 471
   Skill: Applied
   Objective: 18.1

3) Nate, Tess, Leo, and Ian are all in their eighties. Nate arrives at this stage of life feeling whole, complete, and satisfied with his achievements. Tess regrets several major decisions in her life. Leo remains bitter and angry over some lost movie deals that he feels would have made his retirement worry-free, and expresses a great deal of anger and contempt for those in the movie business. Ian does not generally remember what happens from one week to the next, and depends heavily on his friendships with Nate, Tess, and Leo. According to Erikson's theory, who has arrived at a sense of ego integrity?
   A) Nate
   B) Tess
   C) Leo
   D) Ian
   Answer: A
   Page Ref: 472
   Skill: Applied
   Objective: 18.2

4) Nate, Tess, Leo, and Ian are all in their eighties. Nate arrives at this stage of life feeling whole, complete, and satisfied with his achievements. Tess regrets several major decisions in her life, but generally feels that her life turned out positively. Leo remains bitter and angry over some lost movie deals that he feels would have made his retirement worry-free, and expresses a great deal of anger and contempt for those in the movie business. Ian does not generally remember what happens from one week to the next, and depends heavily on his friendships with Nate, Tess, and Leo. According to Erikson's theory, who displays symptoms of despair?
   A) Nate
   B) Tess
   C) Leo
   D) Ian
   Answer: C
   Page Ref: 472
   Skill: Applied
   Objective: 18.2

5) Which characteristic is associated with greater psychosocial maturity, measured in terms of striving for generativity and ego integrity in everyday behavior?
   A) gender
   B) SES
   C) marital status
   D) age
   Answer: D
   Page Ref: 472
   Skill: Factual
   Objective: 18.2

6) Seventy-year-old Jim expresses a great deal of anger and contempt for other people. According to Erikson, his behavior disguises a sense of
   A) mistrust.
   B) shame.
   C) self-contempt.
   D) doubt.
   Answer: C
   Page Ref: 472
   Skill: Applied
   Objective: 18.2

7) Janelle, who recently retired from a high-level managerial job, has no interest in anything outside of her former work and feels that she is worthless. According to Peck, Janelle needs to work on the task of
   A) body transcendence.
   B) ego transcendence.
   C) vocational denial.
   D) ego differentiation.
   Answer: D
   Page Ref: 472
   Skill: Applied
   Objective: 18.2

8) Chad, just turned 65, feels anxious about wrinkles, flab, and gray hair. He tries cosmetics and surgery to keep his youthful looks, but his lack of success makes him depressed. According to Peck, Chad needs to work on
   A) body transcendence.
   B) ego differentiation.
   C) ego transcendence.
   D) physiological denial.
   Answer: A
   Page Ref: 472
   Skill: Applied
   Objective: 18.2

9) Yin-sing, at age 80, can't face the idea that she will die and the world will go on. She has children and grandchildren, but is not interested in their lives or futures. According to Peck, Yin-sing needs to work on
   A) body transcendence.
   B) ego transcendence.
   C) ego differentiation.
   D) future differentiation.
   Answer: B
   Page Ref: 472
   Skill: Applied
   Objective: 18.2

10) Mrs. Balaguer states that she has accepted the changes brought about by aging, is not afraid of dying, has a clearer sense of the meaning of life, and has found new, positive spiritual gifts to explore. Mrs. Balaguer is probably
   A) very ill.
   B) experiencing terminal decline.
   C) just recovering from a near-death experience.
   D) in her eighties or nineties.
   Answer: D
   Page Ref: 472
   Skill: Applied
   Objective: 18.2

11) Mr. Jeyakumar exhibits a heightened inner contentment and spends a lot of time in quiet reflection. According to Joan Erikson, Mr. Jeyakumar is displaying characteristics of
   A) gerotranscendence.
   B) disengagement.
   C) continuity.
   D) reminiscence.
   Answer: A
   Page Ref: 472
   Skill: Applied
   Objective: 18.2

12) Mrs. Handerhan has arthritis. She has also lost two close friends who died within a month of each other. In spite of this, she sustains a sense of optimism and good psychological well-being, dampening her negative emotions and maximizing her positive feelings. Mrs. Handerhan
   A) probably has Alzheimer's.
   B) is exhibiting affect optimization.
   C) is displaying socioemotional selectivity.
   D) was probably raised by authoritarian parents.
   Answer: B
   Page Ref: 472
   Skill: Applied
   Objective: 18.2

13) Elderly Mr. Herrera is asked to describe how he felt during his first battle as a soldier during World War II. According to Labouvie-Vief's theory of emotional expertise, he is likely to describe his emotions
   A) very technically, with excessive extraneous detail about things like the types of guns and ammunition used.
   B) in a detached state, as if he were observing them from the outside as a news reporter.
   C) with vivid descriptions that integrate both subjective and objective aspects.
   D) by emphasizing how he *should* have felt rather than how he *did* feel.
   Answer: C
   Page Ref: 473
   Skill: Applied
   Objective: 18.2

14) When confronted with a difficult situation, 83-year-old Mr. Lawrencenko makes sure he understands his own feelings before deciding on a course of action. According to Labouvie-Vief, in a negatively charged situation, Mr. Lawrencenko is likely to
   A) use emotion-centered coping strategies.
   B) use humor to diffuse the situation.
   C) find a way to end the situation as quickly as possible, even if it requires a less effective outcome.
   D) try and understand the perspectives of any other involved parties.

Answer: A
Page Ref: 473
Skill: Applied
Objective: 18.2

15) Mrs. Mayor sits with her grandchildren and tells them stories about her childhood, and her thoughts and feelings about those memories. Mrs. Mayor is engaged in
   A) gerotranscendence.
   B) reminiscence.
   C) life review.
   D) affect optimization.

Answer: B
Page Ref: 473
Skill: Applied
Objective: 18.3

16) Which of the following statements is true regarding reminiscence?
   A) Brain scan results indicate that engaging in reminiscence triggers activity in normally dormant areas in elders' brains.
   B) The widespread image of a reminiscing elder is one of the less common positive stereotypes of aging.
   C) Reminiscing occurs because elders have nothing else to do.
   D) Research shows that engaging in reminiscence can be positive and adaptive for elders.

Answer: D
Page Ref: 473
Skill: Factual
Objective: 18.3

17) Mr. Naisby is recalling many of the past experiences of his life. He reflects on these experiences and contemplates their meaning in an attempt to understand himself better. Mr. Naisby is engaged in
   A) life review.
   B) retrospection.
   C) recall.
   D) recognition.

Answer: A
Page Ref: 473
Skill: Applied
Objective: 18.3

18) Mrs. Kameenui typically engages in reminiscence when she is bored. During these times, she focuses on bitter events and painful content from her past. She is engaged in __________ reminiscence and probably __________.
   A) self-focused; has reached ego integrity
   B) self-focused; has adjustment problems
   C) other-focused; will move through this phase into knowledge-based reminiscence
   D) knowledge-based; has a rich and rewarding life

Answer: B
Page Ref: 473
Skill: Applied
Objective: 18.3

19) Mr. Schwertman spends time reminiscing about his life when his now-grown children were very young. As a result, he works to maintain and solidify his relationship with them as adults. Mr. Schwertman is engaging in __________ reminiscence.
   A) other-focused
   B) self-focused
   C) knowledge-based
   D) life review

   Answer: A
   Page Ref: 473
   Skill: Applied
   Objective: 18.3

20) Mrs. Raymer-King is drawing on her past experiences to help her solve a current problem. She also uses her past experiences to teach and mentor the young people in her church. Mrs. Raymer-King is using __________ reminiscence.
   A) self-focused
   B) other-focused
   C) knowledge-based
   D) life review

   Answer: C
   Page Ref: 473
   Skill: Applied
   Objective: 18.3

21) Mrs. Raymer-King is drawing on her past experiences to help her solve a current problem. She also uses her past experiences to teach and mentor the young people in her church. Based on this information, you can infer that Mrs. Raymer-King probably
   A) has achieved gerotranscendence.
   B) has adjustment problems.
   C) scores high in openness to experience.
   D) has a happy, stable marriage.

   Answer: C
   Page Ref: 473
   Skill: Applied
   Objective: 18.3

22) Which person is LEAST likely to engage in reminiscence to teach others about the past?
   A) Mrs. Powers, an African-American elder
   B) Mr. Li, a Chinese elder
   C) Mr. Howard, an African-American elder
   D) Mr. Jones, a Caucasian elder

   Answer: D
   Page Ref: 473
   Skill: Applied
   Objective: 18.3

23) In old age, a person's self-concept tends to become
   A) more secure and complex.
   B) more vague and tentative.
   C) more idealistic and less realistic.
   D) more focused on relationships with others.

   Answer: A
   Page Ref: 473
   Skill: Factual
   Objective: 18.4

24) A key feature of integrity is
   A) self-acceptance.
   B) self-awareness.
   C) self-esteem.
   D) self-consciousness.
   Answer: A
   Page Ref: 474
   Skill: Factual
   Objective: 18.4

25) Mr. Vickers is an senior who has several possible selves. As he continues to age, which of the following will likely occur?
   A) He will eliminate any possible selves that he views as impossible to achieve.
   B) He will delete some possible selves and replace them with new ones.
   C) He will become saddened by the possible selves that will never come to be.
   D) He will find humor in the list of possible selves he once had for himself.
   Answer: B
   Page Ref: 474
   Skill: Applied
   Objective: 18.4

26) In long-term studies of personality traits, elders who seemed to have come to terms with life despite its imperfections showed an increase in
   A) conscientiousness.
   B) agreeableness.
   C) neuroticism.
   D) extroversion.
   Answer: B
   Page Ref: 474
   Skill: Factual
   Objective: 18.4

27) As Mrs. Kaneda gets older, her sociability dips slightly.Which of the following statements about this change is correct?
   A) This slight dip in sociability is atypical for seniors, signaling the possibility of terminal decline.
   B) This slight dip is possibly due to narrowed social opportunities as family members and friends die.
   C) Most seniors experience a large drop in sociability, so Mrs. Kaneda's slight dip indicates a higher-than-average level of extroversion.
   D) Mrs. Kaneda has probably been moved into a nursing home recently.
   Answer: B
   Page Ref: 474
   Skill: Applied
   Objective: 18.4

28) A group of British elders has become less religious as they age. If their feelings are consistent with research findings cited in your text, one reason for this change is
   A) a rise in spirituality, which subsequently makes them realize the human-imposed limits of religion.
   B) a loss of fear of death and dying.
   C) disappointment at the support they received from their religious institution during stressful times.
   D) an acceptance of the growing materialism of the world.
   Answer: C
   Page Ref: 474
   Skill: Conceptual
   Objective: 18.5

29) Which of the following people is LEAST likely to be involved in both organized and informal religious activities?
   A) Mr. C, a Caucasian male
   B) Mrs. A, an African-American female
   C) Mr. H, a Hispanic male
   D) Mrs. N, a Canadian-Aboriginal female

Answer: A
Page Ref: 475
Skill: Applied
Objective: 18.5

30) Which of the following people is MOST likely to report a collaboration with God to overcome life problems?
   A) Mr. C, a Caucasian male
   B) Mrs. A, an African-American female
   C) Mr. H, a Hispanic male
   D) Mrs. N, an Asian-American female

Answer: B
Page Ref: 475
Skill: Applied
Objective: 18.5

31) Women are more likely to engage in religious activities than men due to
   A) higher SES levels.
   B) lower incidence of widowhood.
   C) higher levels of stress associated with poverty, widowhood, and caregiving.
   D) a greater sense of responsibility to God.

Answer: C
Page Ref: 475
Skill: Conceptual
Objective: 18.5

32) May stops by her mother June's house twice a day to check on her. If June is having trouble getting dressed or making the bed, then May helps her and the two women chat while they work. However, if June has no trouble with tasks like making coffee or unloading the dishwasher, then May withdraws and attends to other jobs. May's behavior toward June during dressing and bed-making can be referred to as the
   A) dependency-support script.
   B) independence-ignore script.
   C) assisted-independence script.
   D) co-dependency-support script.

Answer: A
Page Ref: 475
Skill: Applied
Objective: 18.6

33) May stops by her mother June's house twice a day to check on her. If June is having trouble getting dressed or making the bed, then May helps her and the two women chat while they work. However, if June has no trouble with tasks like making coffee or unloading the dishwasher, then May withdraws and attends to other jobs. May's behavior toward June as she makes coffee or unloads the dishwasher can be referred to as the
   A) dependency-support script.
   B) independence-ignore script.
   C) assisted-independence script.
   D) codependency-support script.

Answer: B
Page Ref: 475
Skill: Applied
Objective: 18.6

34) May stops by her mother June's house twice a day to check on her. If June is having trouble getting dressed or making the bed, then May helps her and the two women chat while they work. However, if June has no trouble with tasks like making coffee or unloading the dishwasher, then May withdraws and attends to other jobs. June's satisfaction with her support relationship with May is probably due to the fact that
   A) she really does not need May's help.
   B) her daughter, rather than hired help, provides the support.
   C) May is able to see her twice a day.
   D) the support is not perceived as demeaning or unpleasant.
Answer: D
Page Ref: 476
Skill: Applied
Objective: 18.6

35) A classmate of yours is worried about his grandmother. She recently stated that when she could no longer care for herself, it would be time to die. Your classmate wonders if he should encourage her to be as independent as possible. Based on information in your text, you should tell him
   A) that he should definitely stop helping her with daily activities in order to prolong her life.
   B) some dependency is adaptive if it permits elders to conserve their strength for more highly valued activities.
   C) if she really feels that her life is over, her rights should be respected and she should be allowed to die when she is ready.
   D) forcing independence will only result in stubborn resistance and increased passivity and incompetence on her part.
Answer: B
Page Ref: 476
Skill: Applied
Objective: 18.6

36) Mrs. Cantagallo is suffering from rheumatoid arthritis, which has resulted in significant physical declines. According to your text, Mrs. Cantagallo
   A) can avoid feelings of hopelessness as long as she remains socially isolated from others who may treat her as an invalid.
   B) will probably not be moved to a nursing home as long as she maintains a positive outlook on life.
   C) may develop a sense of loss of personal control, putting her at risk for depression.
   D) may be a good candidate for newly developed arthroscopic procedures for rheumatoid arthritis sufferers.
Answer: C
Page Ref: 476
Skill: Applied
Objective: 18.6

37) One of the strongest risk factors for depression in late adulthood is
   A) widowhood.
   B) poor sleep patterns.
   C) financial problems.
   D) physical illness.
Answer: D
Page Ref: 476
Skill: Factual
Objective: 18.6

38) Negative life events evoke __________ in older adults than in younger individuals.
  A) more stress
  B) less stress
  C) more emotional reactions
  D) more excitement at the prospect of facing a challenge
Answer: B
Page Ref: 476
Skill: Factual
Objective: 18.6

39) Mrs. O'Malley is 85 years old and reports that her social relations are often a source of stress. For many elderly women like Mrs. O'Malley, this is because
  A) younger family members often create friction by falling into the dependency-support script.
  B) others depend on them for emotional support, which can be draining.
  C) busy lifestyles cause visits with family and friends to be rushed, making the elder feel like "an afterthought."
  D) squabbles intensify as family members sense the impending death of the elder and try to settle estate affairs.
Answer: B
Page Ref: 476
Skill: Applied
Objective: 18.6

40) Why do adult children typically express a deeper sense of obligation toward their aging parents than the parents expect from them?
  A) Many older adults do not want a great deal of support unless they can reciprocate.
  B) Many adult children underestimate the feelings of their parents.
  C) The dependency-support script is too difficult to revise.
  D) Their realization of their own physical frailties and approaching age during the middle adult years makes them more empathic toward their parents' personal situations.
Answer: A
Page Ref: 476
Skill: Factual
Objective: 18.7

41) __________ is an indirect self-destructive act that is common among elders who commit suicide.
  A) Asking other people to cause your own death
  B) Taking large doses of prescription medications
  C) Turning on the gas in a house with closed windows
  D) Refusing food or necessary medical treatments
Answer: D
Page Ref: 477
Skill: Factual
Objective: Box SI: Elder Suicide

42) The two types of events that prompt suicide in late life are
  A) institutionalization (particularly if they are still fairly independent) and terminal illness.
  B) institutionalization (only if they are terminally ill) and widowhood.
  C) loss of independence and recent widowhood.
  D) losses (such as retirement and widowhood) and chronic and terminal illness.
Answer: D
Page Ref: 477
Skill: Factual
Objective: Box SI: Elder Suicide

43) Ethnic minority elders are more likely to accept social support and assistance from church congregation members because
   A) they feel it is motivated by a desire for a more positive afterlife.
   B) they feel it is motivated by a sense of obligation.
   C) the warm atmosphere of religious organizations fosters a sense of social acceptance and belonging.
   D) they do not want to appear ungrateful and subsequently embarrass family members.
   Answer: C
   Page Ref: 476, 478
   Skill: Conceptual
   Objective: 18.7

44) In order for social support to foster well-being,
   A) friends and family must provide the support in as unobtrusive a manner as possible.
   B) friends and family should follow the dependency-support script.
   C) elders need to assume personal control of it.
   D) elders need to request it, rather than having it offered.
   Answer: C
   Page Ref: 478
   Skill: Factual
   Objective: 18.7

45) Mrs. Himmel is a senior with limited mobility. Which of the following is more likely to be associated with her positive outlook on life?
   A) her perceived social support from friends and family
   B) the amount of help family and friends provide
   C) the quality of the help that family and friends provide
   D) her family's perceptions of Mrs. Himmel's independence
   Answer: A
   Page Ref: 478
   Skill: Applied
   Objective: 18.7

46) One theory about why elders interact less with others than younger adults do says that they deliberately withdraw from society as they become more preoccupied with their inner lives in anticipation of death. This is called
   A) activity theory.
   B) socioemotional selectivity theory.
   C) continuity theory.
   D) disengagement theory.
   Answer: D
   Page Ref: 478
   Skill: Factual
   Objective: 18.8

47) In contrast to implications of the disengagement theory, elders actually
   A) disengage from unsatisfying contacts but maintain satisfying ones.
   B) disengage from social contacts more than researchers predict.
   C) increase the number of social contacts over the years.
   D) maintain the same number of social contacts as they had during their young adulthood.
   Answer: A
   Page Ref: 478
   Skill: Factual
   Objective: 18.8

58) What percentage of older adults in Western industrialized nations remain in or near the home where they spent the majority of their adult lives?
   A) 5 percent
   B) 45 percent
   C) 75 percent
   D) 90 percent
   Answer: D
   Page Ref: 481
   Skill: Factual
   Objective: 18.9

59) The primary reason why more elders in many Western nations live on their own today than ever before is
   A) the high cost of nursing homes.
   B) lack of assistance from their children.
   C) decreasing governmental support.
   D) improved health and finances.
   Answer: D
   Page Ref: 481
   Skill: Factual
   Objective: 18.9

60) Although increasing numbers of ethnic minority elders want to live on their own, __________ often prevent(s) them from doing so.
   A) pride
   B) cultural values
   C) their children
   D) poverty
   Answer: D
   Page Ref: 482
   Skill: Factual
   Objective: 18.9

61) Assuming that they are representative of national samples, which elder(s) is/are most at risk for living in poverty?
   A) Mr. Baarda, a male who lives alone
   B) Mrs. Lavigne, a widow who lives alone
   C) Mr. and Mrs. Pipkin, who live together
   D) Mr. Summar, who lives with his adult daughter and her family
   Answer: B
   Page Ref: 482
   Skill: Applied
   Objective: 18.9

62) Mrs. Sullaivani resides in a long-term care facility that provides a variety of support services, such as meals in a common dining room. Because she has mobility issues, the staff keep a particularly watchful oversight of her. Mrs. Sullaivani lives in
   A) a nursing home.
   B) a retirement village.
   C) congregate housing.
   D) a life care community.
   Answer: C
   Page Ref: 482
   Skill: Applied
   Objective: 18.9

63) Mr. and Mrs. D'Esposito live independently in a residential community, where they made a large initial payment and continue to pay monthly fees. As they age and their needs change, they can move into a range of housing alternatives within the same community. Mr. and Mrs. D'Esposito live in

A) a nursing home.
B) a retirement village.
C) congregate housing.
D) a life care community.

Answer: D
Page Ref: 482
Skill: Applied
Objective: 18.9

64) Living in an age-segregated community, surrounded by other elders, tends to be beneficial to elders who live in a society in which old age leads to

A) reduced status.
B) increased status.
C) special social roles.
D) greater physical decline.

Answer: A
Page Ref: 483
Skill: Factual
Objective: 18.9

65) An elder's autonomy is restricted most sharply if he or she is living in

A) his or her own home.
B) a nursing home.
C) congregate housing.
D) an adult child's home.

Answer: B
Page Ref: 483
Skill: Factual
Objective: 18.9

66) One reason social interaction is so low in nursing homes is that

A) there are not very many available social partners.
B) attendants do not provide enough assistance.
C) residents do not have control over their social experiences.
D) the institution does not get involved in social contact.

Answer: C
Page Ref: 483
Skill: Factual
Objective: 18.9

67) The __________ is a model of age-related changes in social networks, which views the individual within a cluster of relationships moving through life. Close ties are in the inner circle, less-close ties on the outside. With age, places are exchanged, new ones are added, and some are lost entirely.

A) lifelong peer group
B) social clock
C) social convoy
D) personal entourage

Answer: C
Page Ref: 483
Skill: Factual
Objective: 18.10

68) When marital satisfaction is measured throughout adulthood, the pattern found is that
A) satisfaction rises from middle to late adulthood.
B) satisfaction drops slowly throughout adulthood.
C) satisfaction peaks in middle adulthood, then falls.
D) it is lowest in middle adulthood, highest in young adulthood.
Answer: A
Page Ref: 483
Skill: Factual
Objective: 18.10

69) The increase in marital satisfaction in late adulthood is due in part to
A) increased perceptions of fairness as men contribute more to household tasks.
B) engagement in more individual leisure activities.
C) greater financial security.
D) the transition from the role of the provider to recipient of caregiving.
Answer: A
Page Ref: 484
Skill: Conceptual
Objective: 18.10

70) Which statement about late-life marital discord is correct?
A) Little is known about late-life marital dissatisfaction, as elderly couples are often unwilling to expend the energy to discuss negative aspects of their relationship.
B) Men tend to expend more energy trying to work on a troubled relationship.
C) Women often protect themselves from the energy drain of a troubling relationship by avoiding discussion.
D) When marital dissatisfaction exists, it often takes a greater toll on women than on men.
Answer: D
Page Ref: 484
Skill: Factual
Objective: 18.10

71) Gay men and lesbians less often assume that family members will provide support for them in old age,
A) because of imagined or real strain in family relationships when they told others about their homosexuality.
B) as they are often childless and so have nobody upon whom they can depend.
C) due to lifelong experiences of rejection and insensitivity, which cause them to be much more independent than the average elder.
D) knowing that their same-sex relationship greatly reduces their chances of being widowed and alone for long periods of time.
Answer: A
Page Ref: 484
Skill: Factual
Objective: 18.10

72) When asked about the reasons for divorce, elderly men typically mention
A) stress resulting from sexual dysfunction.
B) emotional distancing.
C) their partner's refusal to communicate.
D) lack of shared interests and activities.
Answer: D
Page Ref: 484
Skill: Factual
Objective: 18.10

73) Which reason explains why elders have more difficulty dealing with divorce than younger adults?
   A) The stigma of divorce is much harder to bear for those raised in earlier generations.
   B) It is harder to separate one's identity from that of the former spouse due to a relationship that has lasted their entire adult life.
   C) Relationships with others stay the same at a time when redefining identity is crucial.
   D) Financial consequences are severe due to the loss of assets in property settlements.

Answer: B
Page Ref: 484
Skill: Conceptual
Objective: 18.10

74) Saba, age 62, and Victor, age 68, have just married. If their relationship is typical of late-life remarriages, what can we anticipate?
   A) They will have a conflict-ridden marriage, as both have decades of habits and ways of doing things to which they are accustomed and are not necessarily willing to compromise on or relinquish.
   B) The marriage will last only a few years, as elders who marry late in life tend to have shorter lifespans.
   C) Their successful marriage will involve more maturity, patience, and a balance of practical and romantic concerns.
   D) Their relationship will be happy, but they will experience stressful relationships with their children.

Answer: C
Page Ref: 485
Skill: Applied
Objective: 18.10

75) Louetta and Stuart are elders who cohabit but do not plan to marry. Your text indicates that __________ probably contributed to their decision.
   A) concerns about financial consequences with respect to taxes, social security, or pension benefits
   B) a more modern view on sexual morality
   C) feelings of betraying former spouses who died
   D) Stuart's unwillingness to give up his new-found independence

Answer: A
Page Ref: 485
Skill: Applied
Objective: 18.10

76) Elder __________ with high rates of poverty and chronic disease are more likely to be widowed.
   A) men
   B) Caucasians
   C) ethnic minorities
   D) women

Answer: C
Page Ref: 485
Skill: Factual
Objective: 18.10

77) Which factor contributes to resilience after widowhood?
   A) having an introverted personality
   B) having children upon whom they can draw support
   C) continued social relationships that were important before the spouse's death
   D) a weak sense of self-efficacy in handling tasks of daily living

Answer: C
Page Ref: 485
Skill: Conceptual
Objective: 18.10

78) Men have a more difficult time adjusting to widowhood than women do because they
   A) have financial worries due to the loss of the wife's job or estate.
   B) tend to rely on their wives for social connectedness, household tasks, and coping with stress.
   C) have large numbers of emotionally satisfying ties outside of marriage.
   D) are resentful about performing essential household tasks that were handled by their deceased wives.

Answer: B
Page Ref: 485
Skill: Conceptual
Objective: 18.10

79) One possible reason that elderly women feel less need to remarry is that
   A) there are more widowed men than widowed women.
   B) their kinkeeper role and ability to form close friendships allows them to maintain satisfying relationships.
   C) they are often well-off financially due to estate and inheritances, and worry about ulterior motives of potential suitors.
   D) they relish the time alone after a lifetime of carrying the emotional weight of the marriage.

Answer: B
Page Ref: 485–486
Skill: Factual
Objective: 18.10

80) A friend's elderly uncle has just died, and he wonders how best to support his aunt during this stressful time. Based on information in your text, what would you recommend?
   A) Allow her some "emotional space" during the grieving period, and then provide support when she requests it.
   B) Provide social support and interaction beyond the grieving period, while helping her use coping strategies.
   C) Take care of as many of her responsibilities as possible, while not pushing her into independence too quickly.
   D) Let her know that he is there for her whenever she needs him.

Answer: B
Page Ref: 486
Skill: Applied
Objective: 18.10

81) Most elders who never married or had children report that
   A) they feel alone and isolated from other people.
   B) their closest ties are to people of the other sex.
   C) they have developed other meaningful relationships.
   D) their overall life satisfaction is lower than that of married elders.

Answer: C
Page Ref: 486
Skill: Factual
Objective: 18.10

82) Compared with divorced or recently widowed elders, the overall level of life satisfaction felt by elderly women who have never married is
   A) much lower.
   B) somewhat lower.
   C) about the same.
   D) higher.

Answer: D
Page Ref: 486
Skill: Factual
Objective: 18.10

83) Regardless of the sex of the elder being interviewed, older adults perceive
  A) sibling bonds to be stronger than those with adult children.
  B) bonds with brothers to be closer than bonds with sisters.
  C) bonds with sisters to be closer than bonds with brothers.
  D) bonds with sisters to be more difficult than bonds with brothers.

Answer: C
Page Ref: 487
Skill: Factual
Objective: 18.11

84) What type of interactions are elder siblings more likely to engage in?
  A) providing direct assistance to each other
  B) day-to-day living assistance
  C) financial and medical assistance
  D) socializing

Answer: D
Page Ref: 487
Skill: Factual
Objective: 18.11

85) Eighty-two-year-old Gonzalo has never been married, but his brother Antonio has been happily married for 60 years. What type of interactions will most likely increase as the brothers age?
  A) joint reminiscing about their long and unique history together
  B) Gonzalo's care for Antonio in times of illness
  C) coresidency, where Antonio moves into Gonzalo's home
  D) joint vacations where Gonzalo brings along a significant other

Answer: A
Page Ref: 487
Skill: Applied
Objective: 18.11

86) Mrs. Hockaday's physical restrictions do not allow her to go out very much. As a result, she may depend more on her friendships to
  A) take care of her basic care needs.
  B) entertain her.
  C) help her accept her physical limitations.
  D) keep her abreast of events in their community.

Answer: D
Page Ref: 487
Skill: Applied
Objective: 18.11

87) Seventy-five-year-old Mr. Griego's son asks him who his closest friends are. According to information in your text, he is most likely to cite
  A) Mr. Hernandez, a childhood friend who lives three states away.
  B) his son and the son's wife.
  C) Mr. Apodaca, who lives in the same community with him.
  D) his brother, who lives 1,200 miles away but with whom he converses on the telephone daily.

Answer: C
Page Ref: 487–488
Skill: Applied
Objective: 18.11

88) Many of 83-year-old Alex's friends have died. As a result, he is likely to
   A) experience depression.
   B) require more daily living assistance from family members.
   C) attend fewer community-sponsored events for elders.
   D) develop more intergenerational friendships.
   Answer: D
   Page Ref: 488
   Skill: Applied
   Objective: 18.11

89) Mrs. Harkreader and Mrs. St. Jacques meet for lunch occasionally and meet each other once a month to volunteer in a local Head Start program. Mrs. Harkreader and Mrs. St. Jacques are
   A) partial friends.
   B) fair-weather friends.
   C) joint friends.
   D) secondary friends.
   Answer: D
   Page Ref: 488
   Skill: Applied
   Objective: 18.11

90) The relationship between elders' psychological well-being and their contacts with their children is best described by saying that
   A) warm bonds improve mental health; conflict reduces it.
   B) almost any contact with children improves mental health.
   C) contact with children affects only elderly women, not men.
   D) contact with children has no effect on elders' mental health.
   Answer: A
   Page Ref: 488
   Skill: Conceptual
   Objective: 18.12

91) As Joy Ruth's parents age, she wants to provide a great deal of support for them. Her parents will probably want her help in the form of
   A) assistance with day-to-day living tasks.
   B) emotional support.
   C) financial assistance with living expenses.
   D) dealing with medical emergencies.
   Answer: B
   Page Ref: 488
   Skill: Applied
   Objective: 18.12

92) Mr. and Mrs. Lai's adult children want to provide support that will be psychologically beneficial to them. What type of support should they provide?
   A) extensive support with no need for reciprocation
   B) mild support with no need for reciprocation
   C) moderate support with opportunities to reciprocate
   D) mild support with expected reciprocation
   Answer: C
   Page Ref: 488
   Skill: Applied
   Objective: 18.12

93) The incidence of elder abuse is __________ because __________.
A) underestimated; most acts take place in private, and victims are often unable or unwilling to complain
B) underestimated; most social workers do not believe elders' claims of abuse or neglect
C) overestimated; normal accidents and injuries that result from physical aging are mistaken for signs of abuse
D) overestimated; elders make up stories of abuse to gain attention and sympathy
Answer: A
Page Ref: 489
Skill: Factual
Objective: 18.12

94) Richard often fails to bring food to his elderly mother, forgets to take her to necessary medical appointments, and leaves her for days at a time with no outside contact. Richard is engaged in which type of elder abuse?
A) physical neglect
B) physical abuse
C) psychological abuse
D) financial abuse
Answer: A
Page Ref: 489
Skill: Applied
Objective: 18.12

95) Mrs. Girgenti is experiencing psychological abuse. The abuser is most likely
A) a store clerk.
B) a family member.
C) one of her former co-workers.
D) a neighbor.
Answer: B
Page Ref: 489
Skill: Applied
Objective: 18.12

96) Satonaka has seen a large increase in "granny dumping" at her job. Satonaka probably works
A) in a nursing home.
B) at a homeless shelter.
C) at the police department.
D) in a hospital.
Answer: D
Page Ref: 489
Skill: Applied
Objective: 18.12

97) Elder abuse is more common if the elder's caregiver is
A) a sibling or other close relative of the elder.
B) an adult who is at least middle-aged or older.
C) emotionally or financially dependent on the elder.
D) working in a challenging, rewarding career.
Answer: C
Page Ref: 489
Skill: Factual
Objective: 18.12

98) One type of elder maltreatment that is very difficult to prevent is
   A) abuse by family members.
   B) abuse at a nursing home.
   C) abuse by a stranger.
   D) abuse by physicians.
Answer: A
Page Ref: 489–490
Skill: Factual
Objective: 18.12

99) Effective prevention programs for elder abuse contain
   A) counseling on independent living skills for elders.
   B) self-efficacy training for elders.
   C) respite services, such as elder day care and in-home help.
   D) legal action against potential abusers.
Answer: C
Page Ref: 490
Skill: Conceptual
Objective: 18.12

100) Before she retired, Mrs. Choi moved to a part-time position within her division that helped her transition between full-time career and retirement. This is an example of
   A) vocational transition.
   B) a bridge job.
   C) a transition job.
   D) supplemental income.
Answer: B
Page Ref: 490
Skill: Applied
Objective: 18.13

101) The first consideration in the decision of whether to retire is generally
   A) what kind of job a person is retiring from.
   B) whether there will be enough income.
   C) the kinds of activities that will be pursued.
   D) how close a person is to his or her children.
Answer: B
Page Ref: 490
Skill: Factual
Objective: 18.13

102) Which person is likely to retire first?
   A) Brandes, who is in good health
   B) Lumeka, who has few leisure interests
   C) Elvester, who works in a blue-collar job
   D) Lui, who is self-employed
Answer: C
Page Ref: 490
Skill: Applied
Objective: 18.13

103) A person who __________ is more likely to convey satisfaction with the decision to retire.
   A) finds it hard to give up a predictable schedule
   B) had a sense of personal control over the choice to stop working
   C) has difficulty leaving the social contacts of a work setting
   D) had to stop working due to physical ailments

Answer: B
Page Ref: 491
Skill: Factual
Objective: 18.13

104) The leisure activities pursued during retirement typically include
   A) more vigorous physical activities.
   B) new activities never pursued before.
   C) activities that earn extra money.
   D) things that have been lifelong interests.

Answer: D
Page Ref: 492
Skill: Factual
Objective: 18.13

105) Mr. Beesly-Halpert is a senior citizen who reports great awareness of and interest in public affairs. Which of the following is probably true?
   A) His political knowledge will show signs of decline.
   B) While interested in politics, he will rarely vote.
   C) His voting behavior is probably driven by a deep desire for a safer, more secure world for future generations.
   D) His voting behavior is probably driven by self-interest, particularly in the areas of health and safety.

Answer: C
Page Ref: 492
Skill: Applied
Objective: 18.14

106) Elders who work hard to maintain their vitality and are able to limit the age-related declines in physical, cognitive, and social functioning are said to demonstrate
   A) grace under pressure.
   B) generativity.
   C) ego integrity.
   D) successful aging.

Answer: D
Page Ref: 492
Skill: Factual
Objective: 18.14

107) Modern definitions of successful aging have shifted the focus AWAY from
   A) specific achievements and physical characteristics.
   B) the processes elders use to reach personally valued goals.
   C) accepting and learning to compensate for personal declines.
   D) the ways in which elders minimize losses and maximize gains.

Answer: A
Page Ref: 492–493
Skill: Factual
Objective: 18.14

108) Which factor outweighs the others with regards to predicting a happy, active old age?
A) use of effective coping strategies
B) family warmth in childhood
C) early physical health
D) longevity of family members
Answer: A
Page Ref: 493
Skill: Factual
Objective: 18.14

109) Your textbook author recommends future-oriented approaches to prepare for the increased aging of the population, including
A) increased capacity of nursing homes.
B) more emphasis on lifelong learning.
C) a decreased number of bridge jobs available.
D) more family involvement in the care of elders.
Answer: B
Page Ref: 493
Skill: Factual
Objective: 18.14

ESSAY

110) Imagine two elderly people. One attains ego integrity; the other experiences despair. What life events might contribute to each of these outcomes? How are these outcomes likely to be revealed in each elder's behavior?
Answer: Accept reasonable responses.
Page Ref: 493

111) Define reminiscence and describe the different types.
Answer: Reminiscence is the telling of stories about people and events from one's past and reporting associated thoughts and feelings. It takes different forms.

Life review occurs when a person calls up, reflects on, and reconsiders past experiences, contemplating their meaning with the goal of achieving greater self-understanding. According to Robert Butler, most older adults engage in life review as part of attaining ego integrity and accepting the end of life.

Although life review often prompts self-awareness and self-respect, many elders do not spend much time evaluating their pasts. Reminiscence that is *self-focused*, engaged in to revive and ruminate about bitter events is linked to adjustment problems.

In contrast, extroverted elders more often engage in *other-focused* reminiscence directed at social goals, such as solidifying family and friendship ties and reliving relationships with lost loved ones.

And at other times, older adults—especially those who score high in openness to experience—engage in *knowledge-based* reminiscence, drawing on their past for effective problem-solving strategies and for teaching younger people.

Page Ref: 473

112) Briefly describe age-related developments in the three personality characteristics associated with resilience.

Answer: *Agreeableness* (generous, acquiescent, and good-natured) scores increase during old age, especially among men, who initially score lower than women. Agreeableness seems to characterize people who have come to terms with life despite its imperfections.

Sociability dips slightly. Perhaps this reflects a narrowing of social contacts as people become more selective about relationships and as family members and friends die. Still, older adults who were extroverted throughout their lives tend to remain so-a personality trait associated with greater life satisfaction.

Acceptance of change shows age-related gains. This attribute is mentioned by the elderly as important to psychological well-being. Acceptance of change is evident in most elders' effective coping with the loss of loved ones, including death of a spouse, which they describe as the most stressful event they ever experienced. The capacity to accept life's twists and turns, many of which are beyond one's control, is vital for positive functioning in late adulthood.

Page Ref: 474

113) How does religious involvement benefit elders?

Answer: Among elders of all backgrounds, religious involvement has many benefits. These include outcomes as diverse as increased physical and psychological well-being, more time spent exercising, and greater sense of closeness to family and friends. In longitudinal research, both organized and informal religious participation predicted longer survival, after family background, health, social, and psychological factors known to affect mortality were controlled.

Page Ref: 474–475

114) Describe continuity theory and discuss some of the benefits of elders' reliance on continuity.

Answer: Continuity theory maintains that most aging adults strive to maintain a personal system—an identity and a set of personality dispositions, interests, roles, and skills—that promotes life satisfaction by ensuring consistency between their past and anticipated future.

Participation in familiar activities with familiar people provides repeated practice that helps preserve physical and cognitive functioning, fosters self-esteem and mastery, and affirms identity. Investing in long-standing, close relationships provides comfort, pleasure, and a network of social support. Finally, striving for continuity is essential for attaining Erikson's sense of ego integrity, which depends on preserving a sense of personal history.

Page Ref: 479

115) Explain why marital satisfaction is at its peak late in life.

Answer: First, late-life marriages involve fewer stressful responsibilities that can negatively affect relationships, such as rearing children and balancing demands of career and family.

Second, perceptions of fairness in the relationship increase as men participate more in household tasks after retirement.

Third, with extra time together, the majority of couples engage in more joint leisure activities. In interviews with a diverse sample of retired couples, women often stated that more time with their husbands enhanced marital closeness.

Finally, greater emotional understanding and emphasis on regulating emotion in relationships lead to more positive interactions between spouses. Compared to younger couples, elderly couples disagree less often and resolve their differences in more constructive ways.

Page Ref: 483,484

116) Describe the four functions of elder friendships.

Answer: *Intimacy and companionship.* Mutual interests, sense of belongingness, and opportunities to confide in another sustain these bonds over time.

Acceptance. Late-life friends shield one another from others' negative judgments about their abilities and worth as a person, which frequently stem from stereotypes of aging.

A link to the larger community. For elders who cannot go out as often, interactions between friends can keep them abreast of events in the wider world. Friends can also open up new experiences that older adults might not take part in alone.

Protection from the psychological consequences of loss. Older adults in declining health who remain in contact with friends through phone calls and visits show improved psychological well-being. Similarly, when close relatives die, friends offer compensating social supports.

Page Ref: 487–488

117) *For students who have not retired:* Think about your life after retirement. What do you think will pose the greatest challenge for you? What are you doing right now that will make your retirement easier or harder to adjust to? What might you change right now to help make your retirement easier?

For students who have retired: In what ways has your retirement been easy or difficult to adjust to? What has posed the greatest challenge? What do you wish you had done differently that might have eased the transition to retirement?

Answer: Accept reasonable answers.

Page Ref: 490–492

STUDY QUESTIONS

Erikson's Theory: Ego Integrity versus Despair

1. Cite characteristics of elders who arrive at a sense of integrity and those who experience despair. (p. 471)

Integrity: ______________________________

____

Despair: ______________________________

____

Other Theories of Psychosocial Development in Late Adulthood

Peck's Tasks of Ego Integrity and Joan Erikson's Gerotranscendence

1. Cite three tasks that Peck maintained must be resolved for integrity to develop. (p. 472)

____

____

____

2. Recent evidence suggests that body transcendence and ego transcendence (decrease / increase) in very old age. (p. 472)

3. Describe and evaluate Joan Erikson's psychosocial stage of *gerotranscendence*. (p. 472)

Description: ______________________________

____

Evaluation: ______________________________

____

Labouvie-Vief's Emotional Expertise

1. Describe *affect optimization.* (p. 472)

2. How do gains in affect optimization contribute to resilience in late adulthood? (pp. 472–473)

3. Explain how older adults' emotional perceptiveness influences their coping strategies. (p. 473)

4. True or False: A significant late-life psychosocial attainment is becoming expert at processing emotional information and regulating negative affect. (p. 473)

Reminiscence and Life Review

1. True or False: Older people *reminisce* to escape the realities of a shortened future and nearness of death. (p. 473)
2. Define *life review,* and explain why it is an important form of reminiscence. (p. 473)

   Definition:

   Explanation:

3. Besides life review, cite three other purposes of reminiscence. (p. 473)

Stability and Change in Self-Concept and Personality

Secure and Multifaceted Self-Concept

1. True or False: Older adults have accumulated a lifetime of self-knowledge, leading to more secure and complex conceptions of themselves than at earlier ages. (p. 473)
2. Explain how a firm, secure, and multifaceted self-concept relates to psychological well-being. (p. 474)

3. In what areas do elders continue to mention hoped-for selves? (p. 474)

4. How do elders reorganize their possible selves? (p. 474)

Resilience: Agreeableness, Sociability, and Acceptance of Change

1. Cite three shifts in personality characteristics that take place during late adulthood. (p. 474)

   A. ______________________________

   B. ______________________________

   C. ______________________________

2. When elders take personality tests, agreeableness rises—especially among (men / women). (p. 474)

Spirituality and Religiosity

1. Older adults attach (great / moderate / little) value to religious beliefs and behaviors. (p. 474)

2. North American elders generally become (less / more) religious or spiritual as they age—a trend that (is / is not) universal. Explain your answer. (p. 474)

   ____

   ____

   ____

3. Involvement in both organized and informal religious activities is especially high among ______________________________ elders. (p. 475)

4. (Men / Women) are more likely to be involved in religion. What might explain this trend? (p. 475)

   ____

   ____

   ____

5. Briefly summarize the benefits of religious involvement. (p. 475)

   ____

   ____

Individual Differences in Psychological Well-Being

Control versus Dependency

1. Describe two complementary behavior patterns people often use when interacting with older adults. (p. 475)

   A. ______________________________

   ____

   B. ______________________________

   ____

2. What factors determine whether elders will react positively or negatively to social contact and caregiving? (p. 476)

   ____

   ____

   ____

3. In (Western / non-Western) societies, many elders fear becoming dependent on others. (p. 476)

4. Why do family members or other caregivers often respond to elders in ways that promote excess dependency in old age? (p. 476)

Health

1. What late-life situation is among the strongest risk factors for depression? (p. 476)

2. Summarize the impact of physical health on psychological well-being in late adulthood. (p. 476)

3. True or False: People age 65 and older have the lowest suicide rate of any age group. (p. 476)
4. Cite factors that help elders surmount physical impairment. (p. 476)

Social Issues: Elder Suicide

1. Cite sex and age differences in elder suicide. What explains these trends? (p. 477)
   A.
   B.
   C.
2. What factors help prevent suicide among ethnic minority elders? (p. 477)

3. Failed suicides are much more (common / rare) in old age than in adolescence. (p. 477)
4. List two reasons why elder suicides tend to be underreported. (p. 477)
   A.
   B.
5. What two types of events often prompt suicide in late life? (p. 477)
   A.
   B.
6. List several warning signs of elder suicide. (p. 477)

7. Describe the most effective treatment for depressed, suicidal elders. (p. 477)

____

____

____

Negative Life Changes

1. True or False: Negative life changes are less stressful for elders than for younger people. (p. 476)
2. Briefly describe sex differences in elders' coping skills. (p. 476)

____

____

Social Support and Social Interaction

1. Summarize the benefits of social support in late adulthood. (p. 476)

____

____

____

2. Many older adults place a high value on (dependency / independence) and (do / do not) want a great deal of unreciprocated support from people close to them. (p. 476)
3. List two factors that make ethnic minority elders more likely to accept formal support. (pp. 476, 478)

   A. ____

   B. ____

4. True or False: Perceived social support is associated with a positive outlook in older adults with disabilities, whereas the amount of help from family and friends has little impact. Provide research to support your answer. (p. 478)

____

____

A Changing Social World

Social Theories of Aging

1. According to ____________________ theory, mutual withdrawal between elders and society takes place in anticipation of death. Why does this theory not adequately explain the reduced social activity of older people? (p. 478)

____

____

____

2. ____________________ theory states that social barriers to engagement, not the desires of elders, cause declining rates of interaction. (p. 478)
3. True or False: Consistent with *activity theory*, studies show that simply offering older adults opportunities for social contact leads to greater social activity. (p. 479)

4. ___________________ theory posits that most aging adults strive to maintain a personal system that ensures consistency between their past and anticipated future, which promotes life satisfaction. (p. 479)

5. Describe ways that reliance on continuity benefits older adults. (p. 479)

____

____

____

6. According to *socioemotional selectivity theory*, how do the functions of social interaction change from middle to late adulthood? (p. 479)

____

____

____

7. According to socioemotional selectivity theory, what explains changes in the function of social interaction in late adulthood? (p. 479)

____

____

____

8. How do older adults apply their emotional expertise to promote harmony in social interactions? (pp. 479–480)

____

____

____

Biology and Environment: Aging, Time Perception, and Social Goals

1. True or False: Socioemotional selectivity theory underscores that our time perspective plays a crucial role in the social goals we select and pursue. (p. 481)

2. How do the social perspectives of men with AIDS support socioemotional selectivity theory? (p. 481)

____

____

____

3. Mainland Chinese elders express a (stronger / weaker) desire for familiar social partners because they perceive their future as (more / less) limited. (p. 481)

4. True or False: The preference for close partners when time is short stems from a need for social support, not meaningful interactions. (p. 481)

Social Contexts of Aging: Communities, Neighborhoods, and Housing

1. True or False: About half of American and three-fourths of Canadian ethnic minority elders live in cities, compared to only one-third of Caucasians. (p. 480)

2. The majority of senior citizens reside in ___________________, where they moved earlier in their lives and usually remain after retirement. (p. 480)

3. How do suburban elders differ from inner-city elders? (p. 480)

   A. ______________________________

   B. ______________________________

4. What aspects of smaller communities foster gratifying relationships for older adults? (p. 480)

   ____

   ____

5. Presence of family members (is / is not) as crucial to older adults' well-being if they have neighbors and nearby friends who can provide support. (p. 480)

6. Older adults in Western industrialized nations want to (leave / stay in) the neighborhoods where they spent their adults lives. (p. 481)

7. List three factors that prompt elder relocations. (p. 481)

   A. ______________________________

   B. ______________________________

   C. ______________________________

8. Which setting affords the greatest possible personal control for the majority of elders? Under what conditions does this setting pose risks? (p. 481)

   A. ______________________________

   B. ______________________________

9. Although increasing numbers of ethnic minority elders want to live on their own, __________________ often prevents them from doing so. (p. 482)

10. During the past half-century, the number of unmarried, divorced, and widowed elders living alone has (declined / risen) rapidly. This trend (is / is not) evident in all segments of the elderly population. (p. 482)

11. Cite factors that contribute to rising poverty rates among elderly women. (p. 482)

    ____

    ____

12. Identify and define two types of residential communities available to North American seniors. (p. 482)

    A. ______________________________

    ____

    B. ______________________________

    ____

13. Discuss the positive effects of residential communities on physical and mental health. (p. 483)

    ____

    ____

    ____

14. What factors enhance older adults' life satisfaction in residential communities? (p. 483)

____

____

____

15. Which residential setting represents the most extreme restriction of autonomy? (p. 483)

____

16. How do North American nursing homes differ from European facilities? (p. 483)

____

____

Relationships in Late Adulthood

1. How does the *social convoy* support adaptation to old age? (p. 483)

____

____

Marriage

1. Provide four reasons why marital satisfaction increases from middle to late adulthood. (pp. 483–484)

   A. _______________

   B. _______________

   C. _______________

   D. _______________

2. When marital dissatisfaction is present, it takes a greater toll on (men / women), who tend to confront marital problems and try to solve them. (p. 484)

Gay and Lesbian Partnerships

1. True or False: Most elderly gays and lesbians in long-term partnerships report happy, highly fulfilling relationships. (p. 484)

2. What unique challenges do aging gays and lesbians face? (p. 484)

____

____

____

Divorce, Remarriage, and Cohabitation

1. What reasons do men and women give for initiating divorce in late life? (p. 484)

   Men: _______________

   Women: _______________

2. Following divorce, older adults find it (easier / harder) to separate their identity from that of their former spouse, and they suffer (more / less) from a sense of personal failure. (p. 484)

3. Why do women suffer more than men from late-life divorce? (p. 484)

____

____

4. List three reasons why late adulthood remarriages are more frequent after divorce than widowhood. (p. 485)

   A. ______________________________

   B. ______________________________

   C. ______________________________

5. True or False: Rather than remarrying, today many older adults who enter a new relationship choose cohabitation. What explains this trend? (p. 485)

____

____

____

Widowhood

1. True or False: Widows make up one-third of the elderly population in the United States and Canada. (p. 485)
2. True or False: Ethnic minorities with high rates of poverty and chronic disease are more likely to be widowed. (p. 485)
3. The greatest problem for recently widowed elders is ______________________________. (p. 485)
4. (Men / Women) find it more difficult to adjust to widowhood. Cite three reasons for this gender difference. (p. 485)

   A. ______________________________

   B. ______________________________

   C. ______________________________

5. True or False: Older widowers report the most depression and the slowest rate of improvement in the two years following the death of a spouse. Explain your answer. (p. 485)

____

____

____

6. True or False: Providing older widows and widowers with information and support in acquiring daily living skills promotes favorable adjustment. (p. 486)

Never-Married, Childless Older Adults

1. Cite examples of alternative, meaningful relationships formed by adults who remain single and childless throughout life. (p. 486)

____

____

2. In a large, nationally representative sample of Americans over age 70, childless (men / women) without marital partners were far more likely to feel lonely. (p. 486)

Siblings

1. Both men and women perceive bonds with (sisters / brothers) to be closer. (p. 487)
2. Under what circumstances are elders likely to turn to siblings for assistance? (p. 487)

   ____

3. Cite the benefits of joint reminiscing between siblings in late adulthood. (p. 487)

   ____

   ____

   ____

Friendships

1. List four functions of elder friendships. (p. 487)

   A. ____

   B. ____

   C. ____

   D. ____

2. True or False: Friendship formation continues throughout life. (p. 487)
3. Describe characteristics of older adult friendships. (p. 488)

   ____

   ____

   ____

4. What are *secondary friends,* and why are women more likely than men to have them? (p. 488)

   A. ____

   B. ____

Relationships with Adult Children

1. As with other ties, the (quality / quantity) of interactions between elders and their adult children affects older adults' life satisfaction. (p. 488)
2. Explain how warm bonds between elders and their adult children foster psychological well-being. (p. 488)

   ____

   ____

3. (Moderate / Extensive) support from adult children is psychologically beneficial to elders. (p. 488)
4. As social networks shrink in size, ______________________________ become more important sources of family involvement. (p. 488)

Elder Maltreatment

1. List and briefly describe five forms of elder maltreatment. (p. 489)

   A. ____

   ____

   B. ____

   ____

   C. ____

   ____

   D. ____

   ____

   E. ____

   ____

2. What forms of elder maltreatment occur most frequently? (p. 489)

   ____

   ____

3. Perpetrators of elder abuse usually (are / are not) family members. (p. 489)

4. Describe a type of neglect, which the media refers to as "granny dumping." (p. 489)

   ____

   ____

5. List five risk factors that increase the likelihood of elder abuse. (p. 489)

   A. ____

   B. ____

   C. ____

   D. ____

   E. ____

6. Why is preventing elder maltreatment by family members especially challenging? (p. 490)

   ____

   ____

7. Identify several components of elder maltreatment prevention programs. (p. 490)

   ____

   ____

   ____

8. True or False: Combating elder maltreatment requires efforts at the level of the larger society. Explain your answer. (p. 490)

   ____

   ____

Retirement and Leisure

1. What social changes have led to a blurring of the distinction between work and retirement? (p. 490)

The Decision to Retire

1. What is usually the first consideration in the decision to retire? List additional considerations. (p. 490)

   First:

   Additional:

2. Provide an illustration of how societal factors affect older adults' retirement decisions? (pp. 490–491)

3. How do retirement programs in many Western countries compare to programs in the United States? (p. 491)

   A.

   B.

Adjustment to Retirement

1. True or False: For most people, mental health is fairly stable from the pre- to postretirement years. (p. 491)
2. Cite workforce and psychological factors that predict retirement satisfaction. (p. 491)

   Workforce:

   Psychological:

3. How can retirement enhance marital satisfaction? How does marital satisfaction, in turn, influence adjustment to retirement? (p. 492)

   A.

   B.

Leisure Activities

1. What is the best preparation for leisure in late life? (p. 492)

2. List several benefits of involvement in leisure activities. (p. 492)

3. List four characteristics of elders who become involved in volunteer work. (p. 492)

   A. ____

   B. ____

   C. ____

   D. ____

4. Older adults report (less / more) awareness of public affairs and vote at a (lower / higher) rate than other adults. (p. 492)

Successful Aging

1. Define *successful aging,* and cite characteristics of successful agers. (p. 492)

   A. ____

   B. ____

   ____

2. Explain how views of successful aging have changed in recent years. (p. 493)

   ____

   ____

3. List eight ways that older adults realize their goals. (p. 493)

   A. ____

   B. ____

   C. ____

   D. ____

   E. ____

   F. ____

   G. ____

   H. ____

4. Cite societal contexts that permit elders to manage life changes effectively. (p. 493)

   ____

   ____

   ____

PUZZLE 18.1

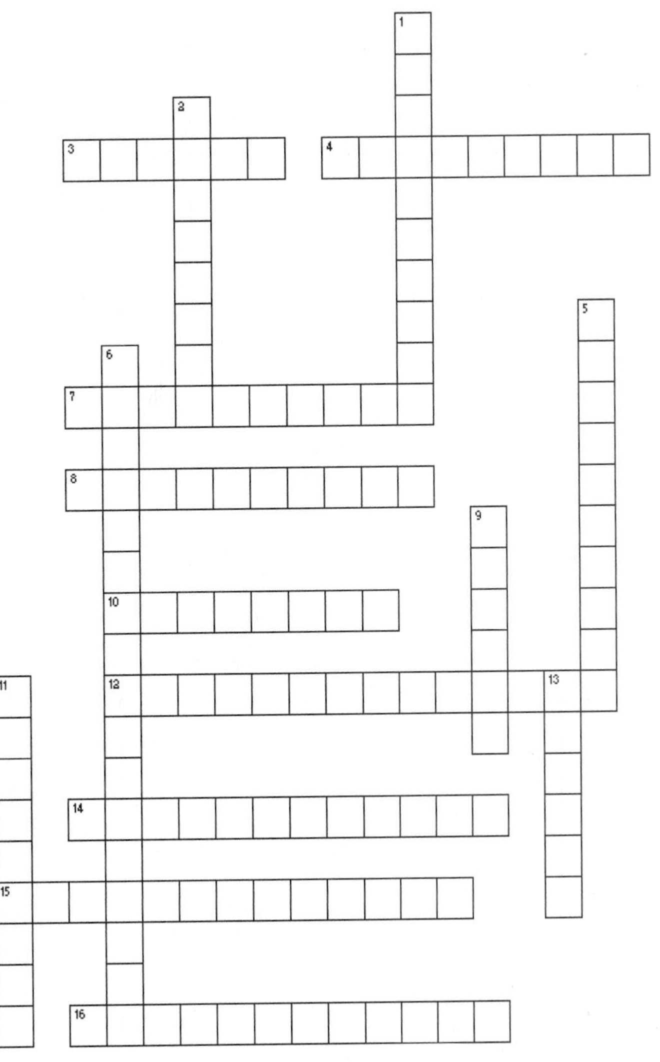

Across

3. Life __________: process of calling up, reflecting on, and reconsidering past experiences and contemplating the meaning with the goal of achieving greater self-understanding
4. Ego __________ versus despair: Erikson's psychological conflict of late adulthood
7. __________-support script: pattern of interaction in which elders' dependency behaviors are attended to immediately, thereby reinforcing those behaviors
8. __________ housing: housing for elderly that adds a variety of support services
10. According to __________ theory, declines in social interaction during late life are due to failure of the social environment to offer opportunities for social contact, not the desires of elders
12. __________ selectivity theory: declines in social interaction in late adulthood are due to physical and psychological changes, which lead elders to emphasize the emotion-regulating function of interaction
14. __________-ignore script: pattern of interaction in which elders' independent behaviors are largely ignored, leading them to occur less often
15. According to __________ theory, declines in social interaction during late adulthood are due to a mutual withdrawal between elders and society in anticipation of death
16. The process of telling stories about people and events from the past and reporting associated thoughts and feelings

Down

1. __________ theory states that social barriers to engagement, not the desires of elders, cause declining rates of interaction.
2. ________ ________ communities: housing for elderly that offers a range of options, from independent or congregate housing to full nursing home care (2 words)
5. __________ aging: gains are maximized and losses are minimized
6. A psychosocial stage proposed by Joan Erikson that represents development beyond ego integrity; when attained, there is a heightened inner calm, contentment, and additional time spent in reflection.
9. Social __________: views the individual within a cluster of relationships moving throughout life
11. __________ friends: people who are not intimates but with whom the individual spends time
13. __________ optimization: the ability to maximize positive emotion and dampen negative

CROSSWORD PUZZLE SOLUTION

PUZZLE 18.1

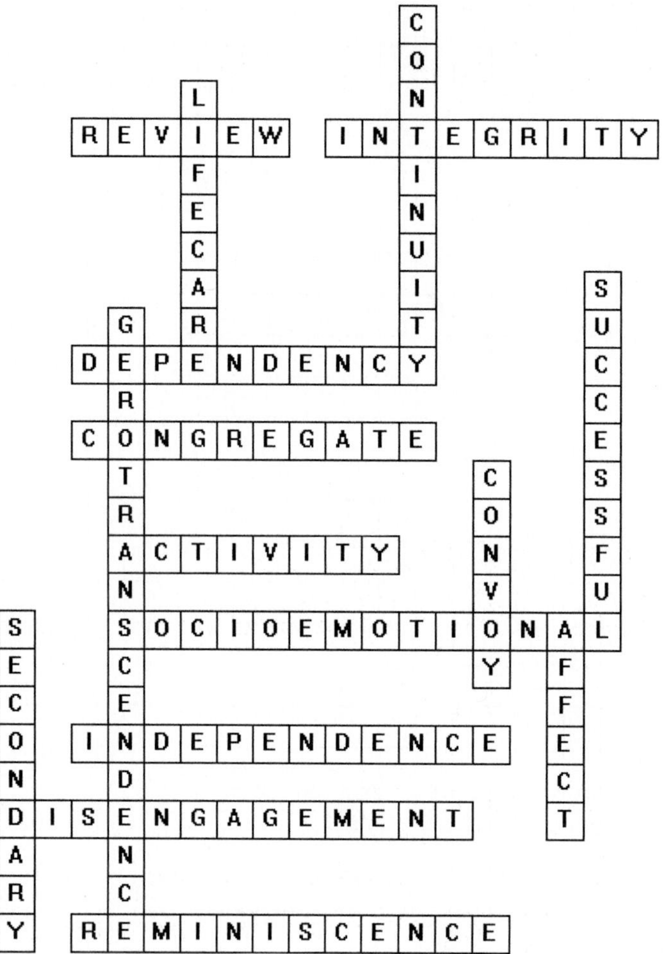

PRACTICE TEST #1

1. According to Erikson, adults who arrive at a sense of integrity (p. 471)
   a. feel they have made many wrong decisions throughout their lives.
   b. feel whole, complete, and satisfied with their achievements.
   c. feel contempt toward themselves and others.
   d. dealt with significant psychological problems early in life.

2. According to Labouvie-Vief, elders display a compensating emotional strength in their ability to maximize positive emotion and dampen negative emotion, or (p. 472)
   a. gerotranscendence.
   b. ego integrity.
   c. disengagement.
   d. affect optimization.

3. As 75-year-old Margaret tells her grandchildren of times long ago, when she was just a small child, she is engaging in (p. 473)
   a. reminiscence.
   b. disengagement.
   c. affect optimization.
   d. geotranscendence.

4. In old age, the majority of older adults (p. 474)
   a. fail to replace possible selves with new ones.
   b. characterize hoped-for selves as "declining" and "missing out on."
   c. continue to mention, but fail to pursue, hoped-for selves in areas of good health and social responsibility.
   d. continue to actively pursue hoped-for selves.

5. Longitudinal research suggests that religious involvement (p. 474)
   a. declines sharply in late adulthood.
   b. remains fairly stable throughout adulthood.
   c. is especially low among low-SES ethnic minority elders.
   d. has little impact on physical and psychological well-being.

6. As a result of negative changes, 82-year-old Jada is more likely to report __________ than her 85-year-old brother. (p. 476)
   a. a higher sense of psychological well-being
   b. a similar sense of psychological well-being
   c. a lower sense of psychological well-being
   d. higher self-esteem

7. According to __________, social barriers to engagement, not the desires of elders, cause declining rates of social interactions as people age. (p. 478)
   a. activity theory
   b. socioemotional selectivity theory
   c. continuity theory
   d. disengagement theory

8. Compared to younger adults, older adults place greater emphasis on (p. 479)
   a. seeking affirmation from social partners.
   b. information seeking and future contact as a basis for selecting social partners.
   c. the emotional-regulating function of their social interactions.
   d. increasing the size of their social networks.

9. Both urban and rural older adults report greater life satisfaction when __________ reside in their neighborhood (p. 480)
   a. many senior citizens
   b. many children
   c. few people
   d. many young adults

10. Although increasing numbers of ethnic minority elders want to live on their own, __________ often prevents them from doing so. (p. 482)
    a. pride
    b. cultural values
    c. their children
    d. poverty

11. From middle to late adulthood, marital satisfaction (p. 483)
    a. rises.
    b. remains stable.
    c. declines.
    d. has little impact on psychological well-being.

12. Elderly gay and lesbian couples in long-term partnerships typically (p. 484)
    a. have great difficulty achieving a sense of integrity.
    b. experience less hostility and discrimination than younger gay and lesbian couples.
    c. report happy, highly fulfilling relationships.
    d. turn to family members and friends instead of their partners for social support.

13. Couples who divorce in late adulthood constitute only about __________ of all divorces in a given year. (p. 484)
    a. 20 percent
    b. 10 percent
    c. 5 percent
    d. 1 percent

14. Compared with widowed women, divorced older women may be more motivated to remarry because of (p. 484)
    a. greater fear of living alone.
    b. more extreme economic circumstances.
    c. greater desire for companionship.
    d. greater interest in a male role model for their children.

15. Compared with younger adults, elders who must cope with the death of a spouse typically show (p. 485)
    a. the same type and intensity of reactions.
    b. a less intense but longer-lasting reaction.
    c. less resiliency in the face of loneliness.
    d. fewer lasting problems adjusting to the death.

16. The kind of assistance that elders most often receive from their adult children is (p. 488)
    a. emotional support.
    b. help with day-to-day living tasks.
    c. financial assistance.
    d. assistance with medical emergencies.

17. Which of the following is among the most frequently reported type of elder maltreatment? (p. 489)
    a. physical abuse
    b. financial abuse
    c. sexual abuse
    d. racial discrimination

18. Elder maltreatment is more likely to occur in nursing homes (p. 489)
    a. with many visitors.
    b. that have plentiful staff.
    c. that are overcrowded.
    d. with low staff turnover.

19. The first consideration in the decision to retire is usually (p. 490)
    a. relocation possibilities.
    b. affordability of retirement.
    c. accessibility to assisted living.
    d. physical health of the retiree.

20. Recent views of successful aging focus on the (p. 493)
    a. achievements of individuals with outstanding life accomplishments.
    b. processes people use to reach personally valued goals.
    c. social lives of successful and unsuccessful agers.
    d. identification of a single set of standards for aging well.

PRACTICE TEST #2

1. At age 80, Barbara can't face the idea that she will die and the world will go on. She has children and grandchildren but has little interest in their lives. According to Peck, Barbara needs to work on (p. 472)
    a. body transcendence.
    b. ego transcendence.
    c. ego differentiation.
    d. future differentiation.

2. Bruce, age 74, has lately been recalling events of his past, reflecting on and reconsidering experiences, and contemplating their meanings with the goal of achieving greater self-understanding. Bruce has been engaging in (p. 473)
    a. life review.
    b. affect optimization.
    c. ego transcendence.
    d. geotranscendence.

3. During late adulthood, self-concept becomes (pp. 473–474)
    a. more insecure.
    b. more complex and multifaceted.
    c. less self-accepting.
    d. simpler and more streamlined.

4. Compared with people of other age groups, elders have the (p. 476)
    a. lowest suicide rate.
    b. highest suicide rate.
    c. lowest rate of depression.
    d. lowest rate of suicide but highest rate of depression.

5. Women over age 75 are far more likely than men of the same age to (p. 476)
    a. have others depend on them for emotional support.
    b. be married.
    c. be healthy.
    d. have higher incomes.

6. Ethnic minority elders are more likely to accept agency-provided support services when they are (p. 476)
   a. connected to a familiar neighborhood organization, such as the church.
   b. arranged and paid for by their adult children.
   c. delivered by people they do not know.
   d. motivated by obligation rather than care and concern.

7. According to disengagement theory, declining rates of interaction in late adulthood are caused by (p. 478)
   a. social barriers to engagement.
   b. life-long selection processes.
   c. the desire of elders to reduce social interaction.
   d. mutual withdrawal between elders and society in anticipation of death.

8. Among ethnic minority older adults, about __________ percent of Americans and __________ percent of Canadians live in cities. (p. 480)
   a. 10; 40
   b. 25; 50
   c. 50; 75
   d. 75; 50

9. The majority of older adults in Western nations want to live (p. 481)
   a. in their own homes and neighborhoods, and 90 percent of them do.
   b. in their own homes and neighborhoods, but only 50 percent do.
   c. in a warmer climate like that found in Florida and Arizona.
   d. with their children or other family members.

10. Older Americans experience the most extreme restriction of autonomy if they live (p. 483)
    a. in a nursing home.
    b. at their own home.
    c. in congregate housing.
    d. in a life care community.

11. The influential model of changes in our social networks as we move through life is known as the (p. 483)
    a. socioemotional group.
    b. continuity group.
    c. social convoy.
    d. affect optimization convoy.

12. When marital dissatisfaction is present in late adulthood, it (p. 484)
    a. takes a greater toll on men than on women.
    b. takes a greater toll on women than on men.
    c. affects men and women similarly.
    d. often results in domestic violence.

13. When asked about the reasons for divorce, (p. 484)
    a. elderly men typically mention difficulty adjusting to spending more time with their spouse following retirement.
    b. elderly women typically mention boredom with the relationship and a desire to form new, more rewarding relationships.
    c. both elderly men and women mention interest in a younger partner.
    d. elderly men typically mention lack of shared interests and activities, while elderly women typically mention their partner's refusal to communicate and emotional distance.

14. The greatest problem for recently widowed elders is (p. 485)
    a. profound loneliness.
    b. poverty.
    c. declining physical health.
    d. housing.

15. In late adulthood, sibling relationships (p. 487)
    a. are closer with brothers.
    b. become more emotionally distant.
    c. more often involve direct assistance than socializing.
    d. involve increased levels of support when siblings live close to each other.

16. Older women, more often than older men, have friends who are not intimates but with whom they spend time occasionally, such as a group that meets for lunch. These friends are termed (p. 488)
    a. occasional friends.
    b. social friends.
    c. loose friends.
    d. secondary friends.

17. In relationships between elders and their adult children, which of the following is linked to positive psychological well-being? (p. 488)
    a. mild support, with expected reciprocation
    b. moderate support, with no opportunities to reciprocate
    c. moderate support, with opportunities to reciprocate
    d. extensive support, with no opportunities to reciprocate

18. Elder maltreatment is more common when caregivers (p. 489)
    a. are emotionally and financially independent.
    b. have a history of family violence.
    c. are not related to the victim.
    d. work in nursing homes, even those with good working conditions.

19. Involvement in leisure activities (p. 492)
    a. is related to better physical and mental health and reduced mortality.
    b. is related to better physical health, but has relatively little impact on mental health.
    c. does not change much over the course of late adulthood.
    d. most often develops suddenly, as new retirees gain free time.

20. Which of the following is true of volunteerism among older adults? (p. 492)
    a. Less-educated elders are more likely to volunteer.
    b. Older elders are more likely to volunteer than younger elders.
    c. Elder women are more likely to volunteer than elder men.
    d. Volunteer work usually begins in late adulthood.

POWERPOINT SLIDES

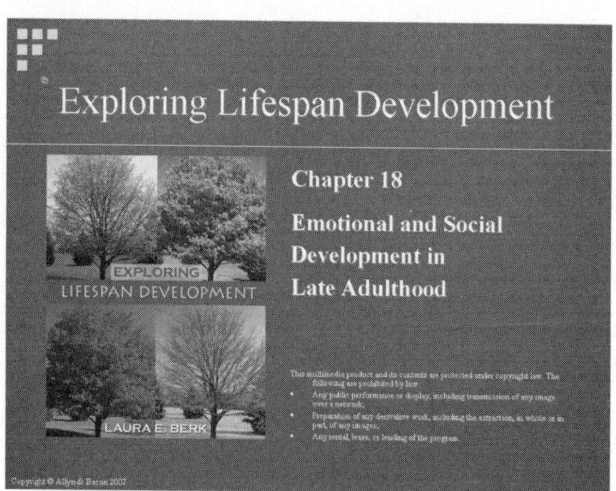

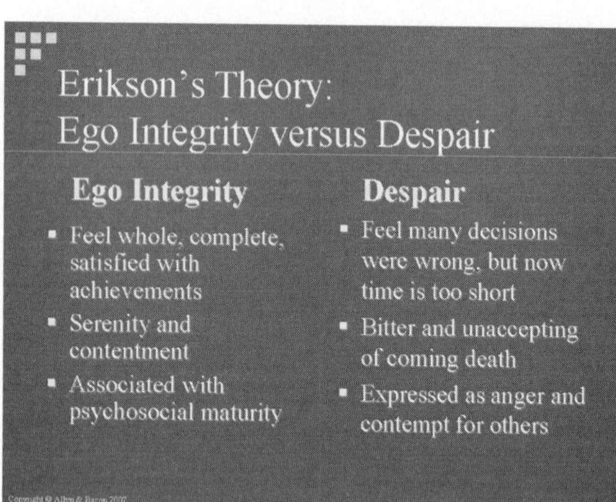

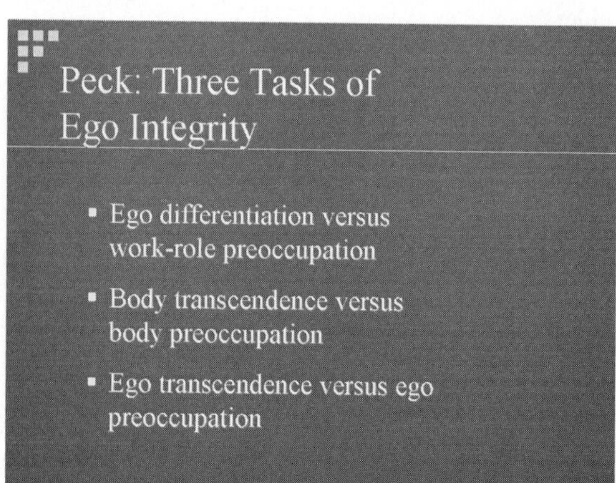

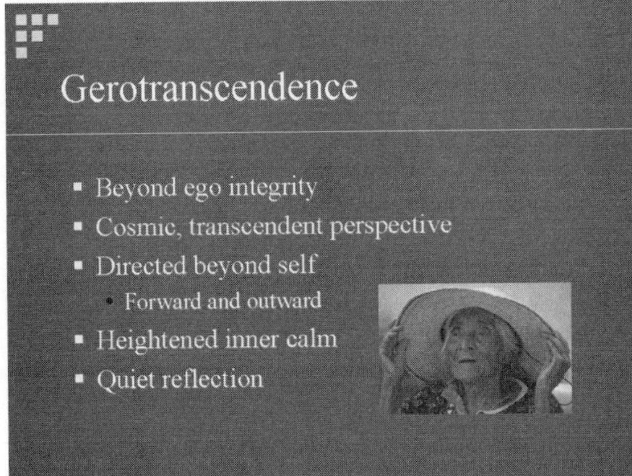

Emotional Expertise

- Cognitive-affective complexity
  - Declines for many
- Affect optimization improves
  - Maximize positive emotions, dampen negative ones
- More vivid emotional perceptions
  - Make sure of own emotions
  - Use emotion-centered coping

Reminiscence and Life Review

Reminiscence

- Telling stories about people, events, thoughts and feelings from past
  - **Self-focused**: can deepen despair
  - **Other-focused:** solidifies relationships
  - **Knowledge-based:** helps solve problems

Life Review

- Considering the meaning of past experiences
- A form of reminiscence
- For greater self-understanding
- Can help adjustment

Personality in Late Adulthood

- Secure, multifaceted self-concept
  - Allows self-acceptance
  - Continue to pursue possible selves
- Shifts in some characteristics
  - More agreeable
  - Less sociable
  - Greater acceptance of change

Spirituality and Religion in Late Adulthood

- Over 3/4 in U.S. say religion "very important"
- Over half attend services weekly
- Many become more religious or spiritual with age
  - Not all - about 1/4 get less religious
  - Cultural, SES, gender differences
- Physical, psychological benefits
  - Social engagement
  - Spiritual beliefs themselves

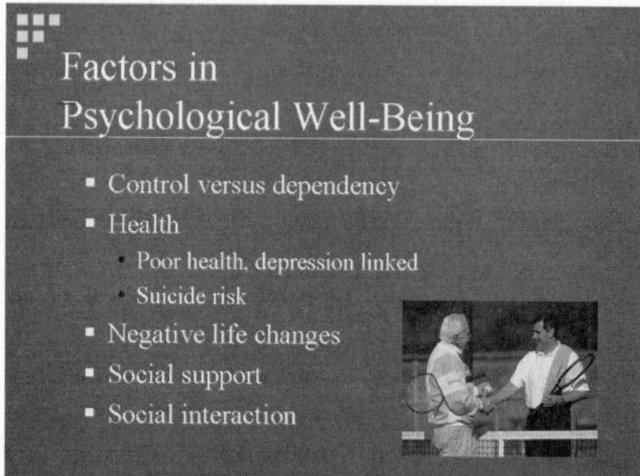

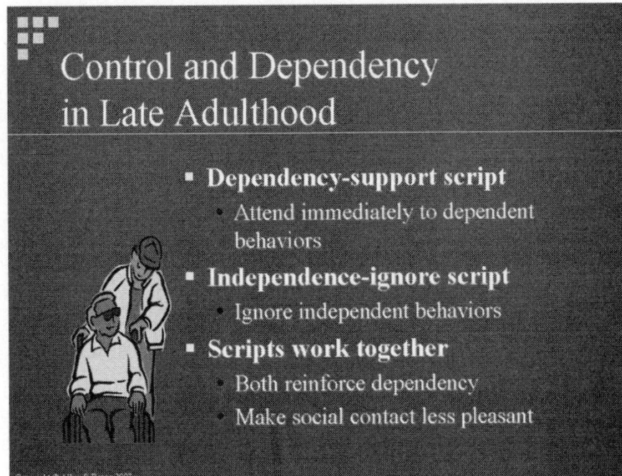

Elder Suicide

- Suicide increases over lifespan
  - Men more likely than women
  - Whites most likely
- Prompted by losses, terminal illnesses
  - Retirement, widowhood
- Indirect methods
  - Refusing food, medical treatment

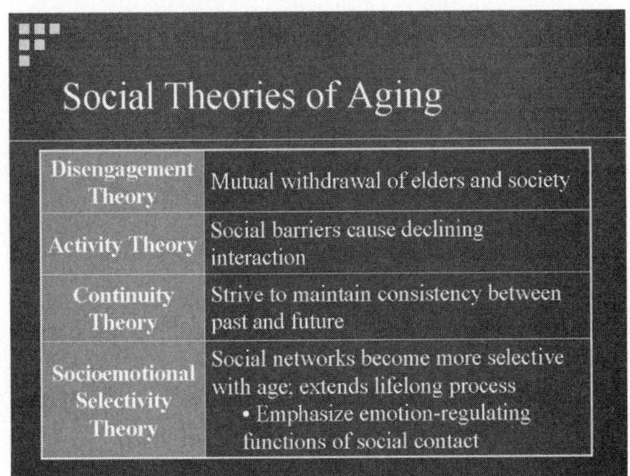

Disengagement Theory	Mutual withdrawal of elders and society
Activity Theory	Social barriers cause declining interaction
Continuity Theory	Strive to maintain consistency between past and future
Socioemotional Selectivity Theory	Social networks become more selective with age; extends lifelong process • Emphasize emotion-regulating functions of social contact

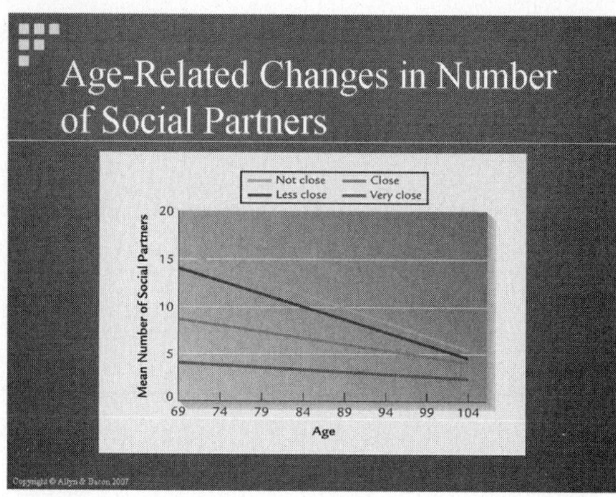
Age-Related Changes in Number of Social Partners
Not close
Close
Less close
Very close
Mean Number of Social Partners
20
15
10
5
0
69
74
79
84
89
94
99
104
Age
Copyright © Allyn & Bacon 2007

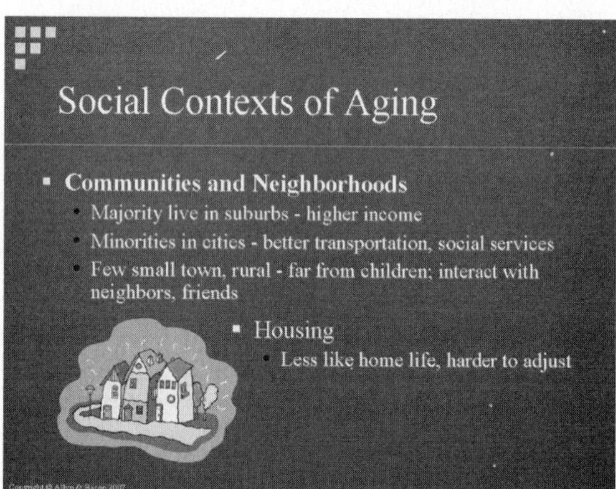
Social Contexts of Aging
Communities and Neighborhoods
Majority live in suburbs - higher income
Minorities in cities - better transportation, social services
Few small town, rural - far from children; interact with neighbors, friends
Housing
Less like home life, harder to adjust
Copyright © Allyn & Bacon 2007

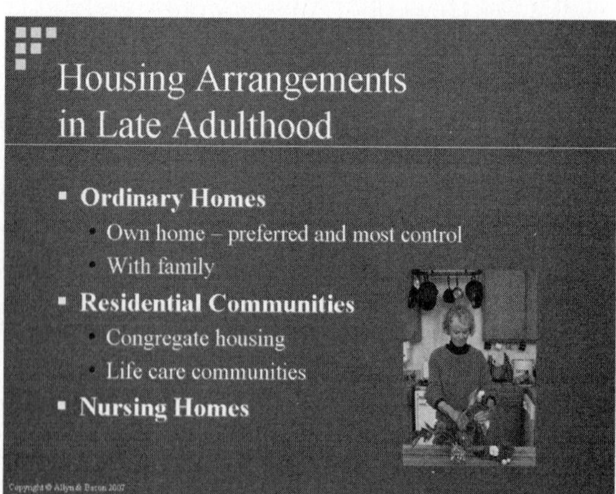
Housing Arrangements in Late Adulthood
Ordinary Homes
Own home – preferred and most control
With family
Residential Communities
Congregate housing
Life care communities
Nursing Homes
Copyright © Allyn & Bacon 2007

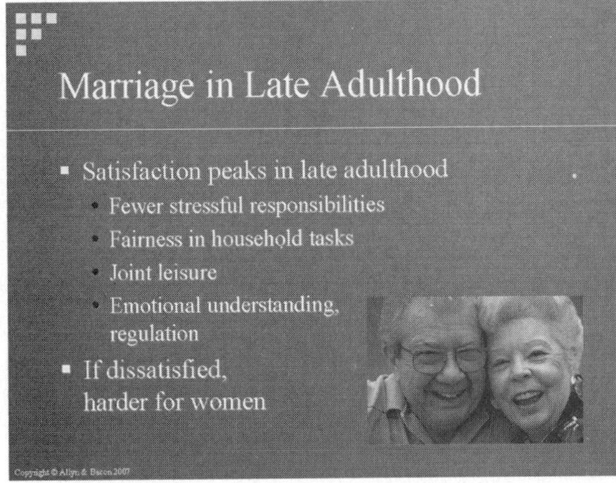
Marriage in Late Adulthood
Satisfaction peaks in late adulthood
Fewer stressful responsibilities
Fairness in household tasks
Joint leisure
Emotional understanding, regulation
If dissatisfied, harder for women
Copyright © Allyn & Bacon 2007

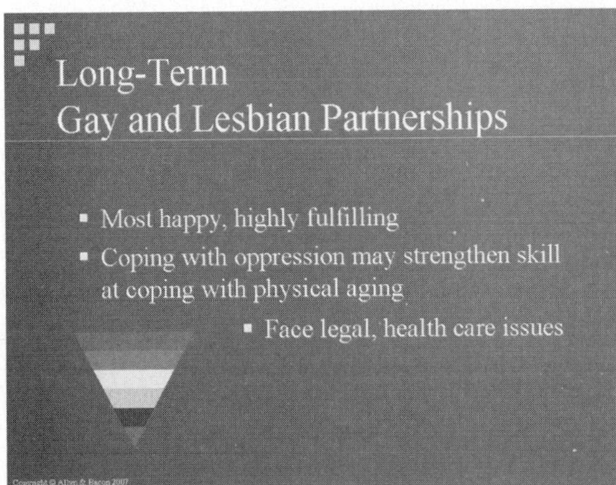
Long-Term Gay and Lesbian Partnerships
Most happy, highly fulfilling
Coping with oppression may strengthen skill at coping with physical aging
Face legal, health care issues
Copyright © Allyn & Bacon 2007

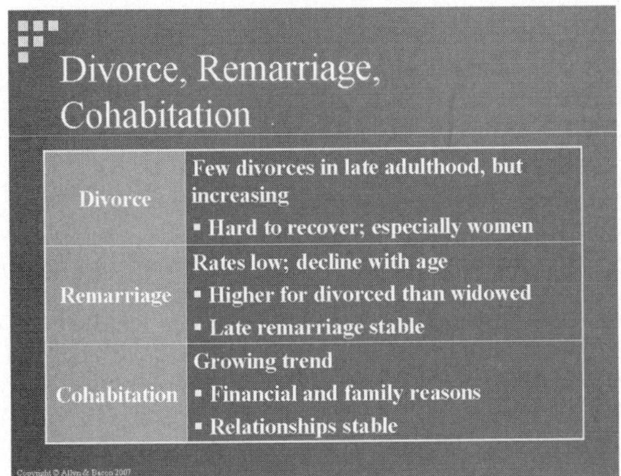
Divorce, Remarriage, Cohabitation
Divorce
Few divorces in late adulthood, but increasing
Hard to recover; especially women
Remarriage
Rates low; decline with age
Higher for divorced than widowed
Late remarriage stable
Cohabitation
Growing trend
Financial and family reasons
Relationships stable
Copyright © Allyn & Bacon 2007

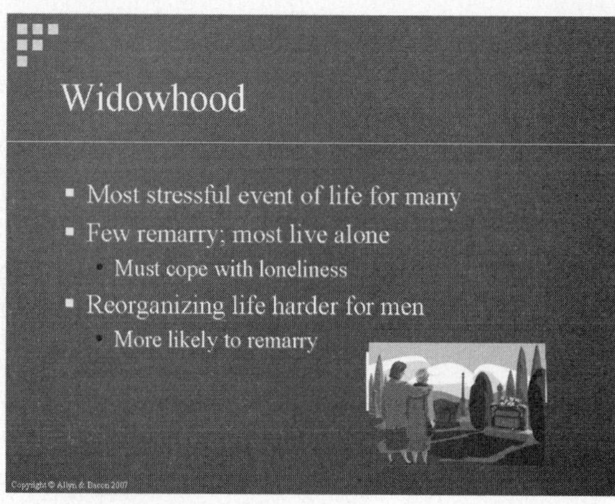
Widowhood
Most stressful event of life for many
Few remarry; most live alone
Must cope with loneliness
Reorganizing life harder for men
More likely to remarry

Possible Sources of Support for the Widowed
Family
Friends
Senior centers
Support groups
Religious activities
Volunteer activities

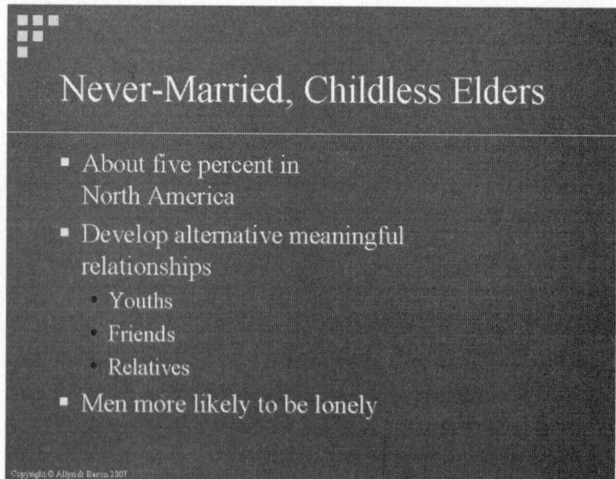
Never-Married, Childless Elders
About five percent in North America
Develop alternative meaningful relationships
Youths
Friends
Relatives
Men more likely to be lonely

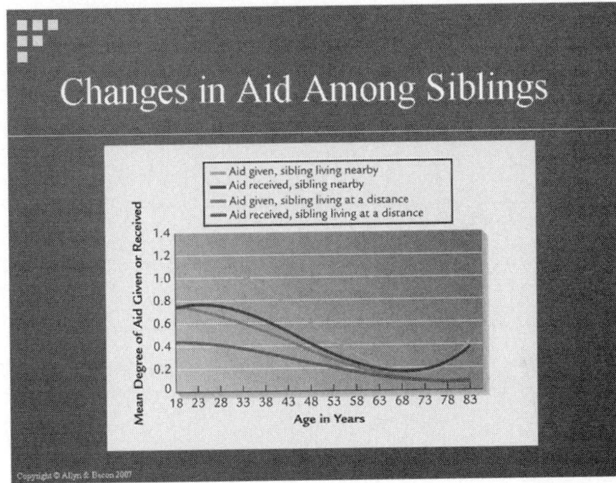
Changes in Aid Among Siblings
Aid given, sibling living nearby
Aid received, sibling nearby
Aid given, sibling living at a distance
Aid received, sibling living at a distance
Mean Degree of Aid Given or Received
1.4
1.2
1.0
0.8
0.6
0.4
0.2
0
18 23 28 33 38 43 48 53 58 63 68 73 78 83
Age in Years
Copyright © Allyn & Bacon 2007

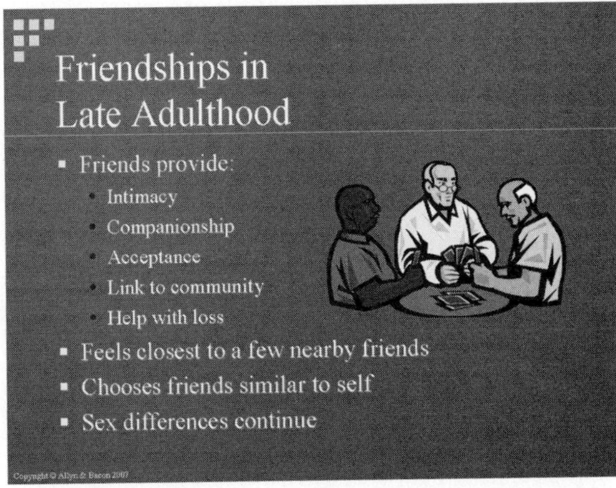
Friendships in Late Adulthood
Friends provide:
Intimacy
Companionship
Acceptance
Link to community
Help with loss
Feels closest to a few nearby friends
Chooses friends similar to self
Sex differences continue
Copyright © Allyn & Bacon 2007

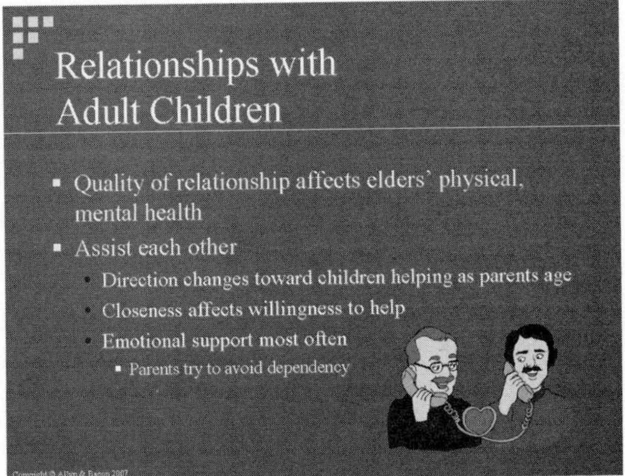
Relationships with Adult Children
Quality of relationship affects elders' physical, mental health
Assist each other
Direction changes toward children helping as parents age
Closeness affects willingness to help
Emotional support most often
Parents try to avoid dependency
Copyright © Allyn & Bacon 2007

Elder Maltreatment
Physical abuse
Physical neglect
Psychological abuse
Sexual abuse
Financial abuse
Copyright © Allyn & Bacon 2007

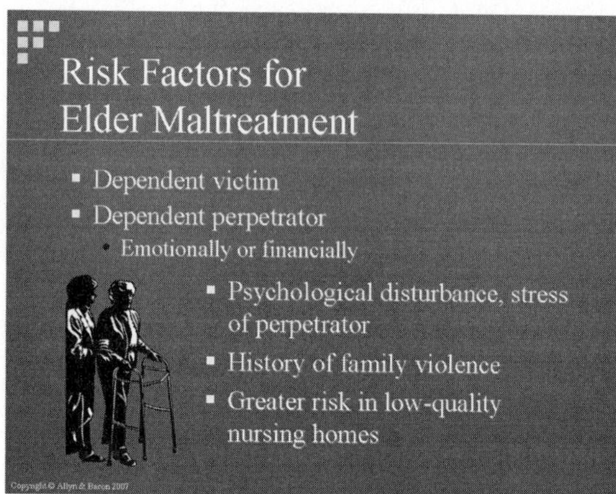
Risk Factors for Elder Maltreatment
Dependent victim
Dependent perpetrator
Emotionally or financially
Psychological disturbance, stress of perpetrator
History of family violence
Greater risk in low-quality nursing homes
Copyright © Allyn & Bacon 2007

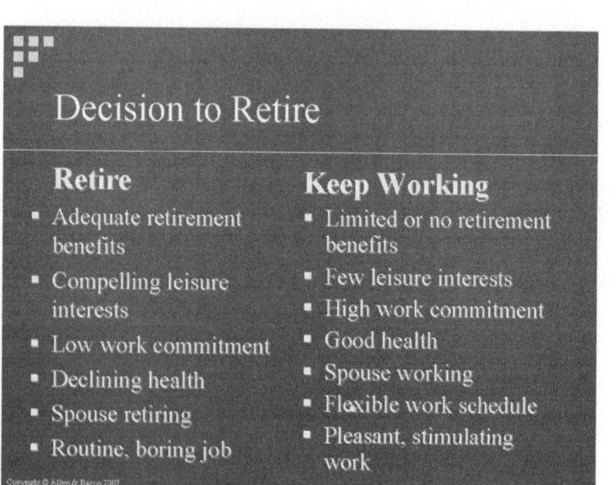
Decision to Retire
Retire
Adequate retirement benefits
Compelling leisure interests
Low work commitment
Declining health
Spouse retiring
Routine, boring job
Keep Working
Limited or no retirement benefits
Few leisure interests
High work commitment
Good health
Spouse working
Flexible work schedule
Pleasant, stimulating work
Copyright © Allyn & Bacon 2007

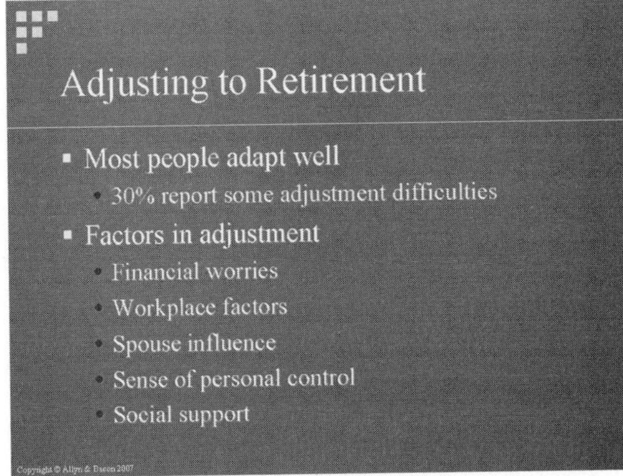
Adjusting to Retirement
Most people adapt well
30% report some adjustment difficulties
Factors in adjustment
Financial worries
Workplace factors
Spouse influence
Sense of personal control
Social support

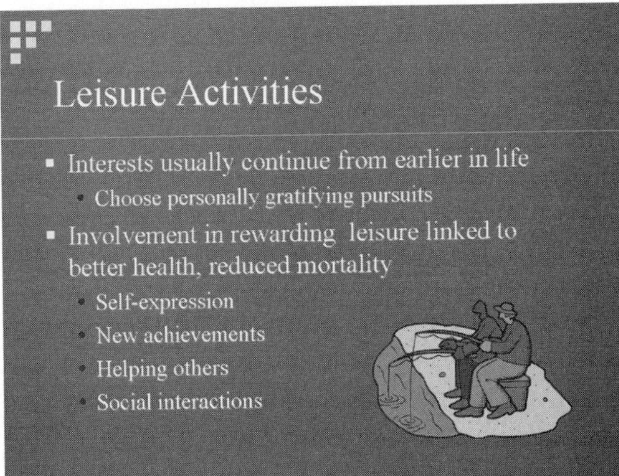
Leisure Activities
Interests usually continue from earlier in life
Choose personally gratifying pursuits
Involvement in rewarding leisure linked to better health, reduced mortality
Self-expression
New achievements
Helping others
Social interactions

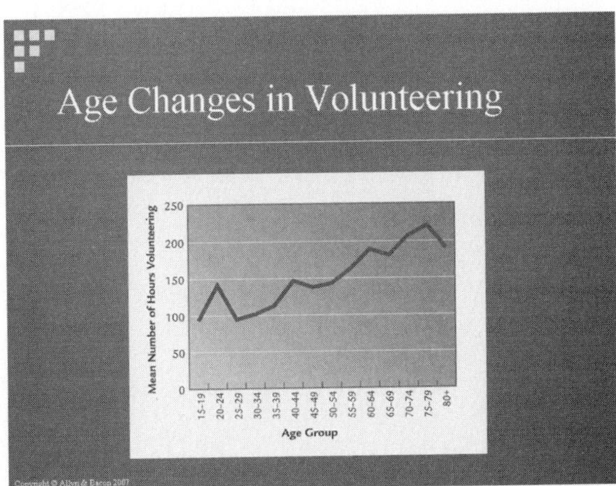
Age Changes in Volunteering
Mean Number of Hours Volunteering
250
200
150
100
50
0
15–19
20–24
25–29
30–34
35–39
40–44
45–49
50–54
55–59
60–64
65–69
70–74
75–79
80+
Age Group

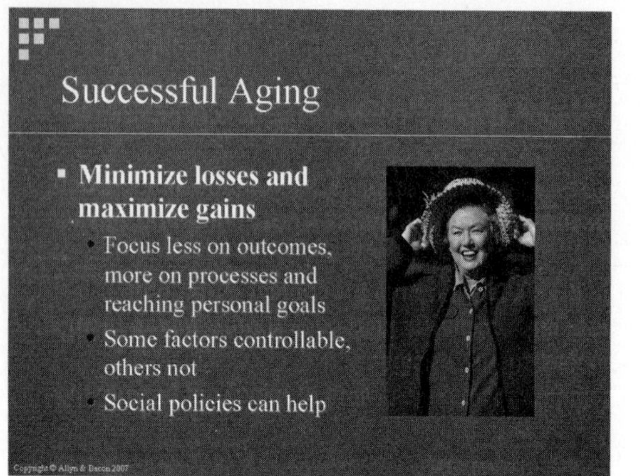
Successful Aging
Minimize losses and maximize gains
Focus less on outcomes, more on processes and reaching personal goals
Some factors controllable, others not
Social policies can help

CHAPTER 19
DEATH, DYING, AND BEREAVEMENT

CHAPTER-AT-A-GLANCE

Chapter Outline	Instruction Ideas	Supplements
How We Die pp. 499–501 Physical Changes • Defining Death • Death with Dignity	Learning Objective 19.1	Test Bank Items 1–13 Videos: *Exploring Lifespan Development in Action* and *A Window on Lifespan Development* Please contact your Allyn and Bacon publisher's representative for a wide range of video offerings available to adopters.
Attitudes Toward Death pp. 501–502	Learning Objective 19.2 Lecture Enhancement 19.1 Ask Yourself p. 502	Transparency 197 Test Bank Items 14–24
Thinking and Emotions of Dying People pp. 503–506 Do Stages of Dying Exist? • Contextual Influences on Adaptations to Dying	Learning Objectives 19.3–19.4 Learning Activities 19.1–19.2	Test Bank Items 25–51
A Place to Die pp. 506–508 Home • Hospital • The Hospice Approach	Learning Objective 19.5 Learning Activity 19.3 Ask Yourself p. 508	Test Bank Items52–66
The Right to Die pp. 509–512 Passive Euthanasia • Voluntary Active Euthanasia • Assisted Suicide	Learning Objective 19.6 Lecture Enhancement 19.2 Learning Activity 19.4 Ask Yourself p. 512	Test Bank Items 67–82 Transparency 199
Bereavement: Coping with the Death of a Loved One pp. 512–517 Grief Process • Personal and Situational Variations • Bereavement Interventions	Learning Objectives 19.7–19.8 Lecture Enhancement 19.3 Learning Activities 19.5–19.6	Test Bank Items 83–104
Death Education pp. 517–518	Learning Objective 19.9 Learning Activities 19.7–19.8 Ask Yourself p. 518	Test Bank Items 105–108

BRIEF CHAPTER SUMMARY

When asked how they would like to die, most people say they want death with dignity—either a quick, agony-free end during sleep or a clear-minded final few moments in which they can say farewell and review their lives. In reality, death is long and drawn out for three-fourths of people—many more than in times past, as a result of medical advances that have prolonged life.

In general, dying takes place in three phases: the agonal phase, clinical death, and mortality. In most industrialized nations, brain death is accepted as the definition of death, but thousands of patients who remain in a persistent vegetative state reveal that the brain-death standard does not always solve the dilemma of when to halt treatment for the incurably ill. Because most people will not experience an easy death, we can best ensure death with dignity by supporting dying patients through their physical and psychological distress, being candid about death's certainty, and helping them learn enough about their condition to make reasoned choices about treatment.

In early adulthood, many people brush aside thoughts of death, perhaps prompted by death anxiety or relative disinterest in death-related issues. Overall, fear of death declines with age, reaching its lowest level in late adulthood and in adults with deep faith in some form of higher being.

According to Kübler-Ross, dying people typically express five responses, which she initially proposed as "stages": denial, anger, bargaining, depression, and acceptance. Rather than stages, these five reactions are best viewed as coping strategies that anyone may call on in the face of threat. A host of contextual variables—nature of the disease; personality and coping style; family members' and health professionals' truthfulness and sensitivity; and spirituality, religion, and cultural background—affect the way people respond to their own dying and, therefore, the extent to which they attain an appropriate death.

Although the overwhelming majority of people want to die at home, caring for a dying patient is highly stressful. Hospital dying takes many forms, each affected by the physical state of the dying person, the hospital unit in which it takes place, and the goal and quality of care. Whether a person dies at home or in a hospital, the hospice approach strives to meet the dying person's physical, emotional, social, and spiritual needs by emphasizing quality of life over life-prolonging measures.

The same medical procedures that preserve life can prolong inevitable death, diminishing the quality of life and personal dignity. In the absence of national consensus on passive euthanasia, people can best ensure that their wishes will be followed by preparing an advance medical directive—a written statement of desired medical treatment should they become incurably ill. Although the practice has sparked heated controversy, public support for voluntary euthanasia is growing; slightly less public consensus exists for assisted suicide.

Although many theorists regard grieving as taking place in orderly phases of avoidance, confrontation, and restoration, in reality, people vary greatly in behavior and timing and often alternate between these reactions. Like dying, grieving is affected by many factors, including personality, coping style, and religious and cultural background. Circumstances surrounding the death—whether it is sudden and unanticipated or follows a prolonged illness—also shape mourners' responses. When a parent loses a child or a child loses a parent or sibling, grieving is generally very intense and prolonged. People who experience several deaths at once or in close succession are at risk for bereavement overload that may leave them emotionally overwhelmed and unable to resolve their grief.

Preparatory steps can be taken to help people of all ages cope with death more effectively. Today, instruction in death, dying, and bereavement can be found in colleges and universities; training programs for doctors, nurses, and helping professionals; adult education programs; and even a few elementary and secondary schools.

LEARNING OBJECTIVES

After reading this chapter, you should be able to:

19.1 Describe the physical changes of dying, along with their implications for defining death and the meaning of death with dignity. (pp. 499–501)

19.2 Discuss factors that influence attitudes toward death, including death anxiety. (pp. 501–502)

19.3 Describe and evaluate Kübler-Ross's theory, citing factors that influence dying patients' responses. (pp. 503–504)

19.4 List goals associated with an appropriate death, and summarize contextual factors that influence a person's adaptation to death. (pp. 504–506)

19.5 Evaluate the extent to which homes, hospitals, and the hospice approach meet the needs of dying people and their families. (pp. 506–508)

19.6 Discuss controversies surrounding euthanasia and assisted suicide. (pp. 509–512)

19.7 Describe bereavement and the phases of grieving, indicating factors that underlie individual variations in grief responses. (pp. 512–515)

19.8 Explain the concept of bereavement overload, and describe bereavement interventions. (pp. 515–517)

19.9 Explain how death education can help people cope with death more effectively. (pp. 517–518)

LECTURE OUTLINE

I. HOW WE DIE (pp. 499–501)
  A. Physical Changes (pp. 499–500)
    1. Death is long and drawn out for about three-fourths of people.
    2. Dying takes place in three phases.
      a. The **agonal phase** (from the Greek word *agon,* meaning "struggle") refers to gasps and muscle spasms during the moments in which the body can no longer sustain life.
      b. **Clinical death** is the short interval in which heartbeat, circulation, breathing, and brain functioning stop, but resuscitation is still possible.
      c. **Mortality** occurs when the individual passes into permanent death.
  B. Defining Death (p. 500)
    1. **Brain death**, defined as irreversible cessation of all activity in the brain and the brain stem (which controls reflexes), is used as the definition of death in most industrialized nations.
    2. When the cerebral cortex no longer registers electrical activity but the brain stem remains active, a person is said to be in a **persistent vegetative state**.
    3. In a few cases, patients have regained cortical responsiveness after being in a persistent vegetative state for months, but they usually recover only very limited functioning.
  C. Death with Dignity (pp. 500–501)
    1. The greatest dignity in death can be found in the integrity of the life that precedes it—an integrity we can foster by the way we communicate with and care for the dying person.
    2. The essential ingredients of a "good death" are present when we provide care, affection, and companionship for the dying person; the truth about diagnosis; and maximum personal control over this final phase of life.

II. ATTITUDES TOWARD DEATH (pp. 501–502)
  A. Compared with earlier generations, today more young people reach adulthood without having experienced the death of someone they know well.
  B. **Death anxiety** refers to fear and apprehension of death.
  C. Research findings reveal large individual and cultural variations in the fear-arousing aspects of death.
    1. Among Westerners, spirituality—a sense of life's meaning—seems to be more important than religious commitment in limiting death anxiety.
    2. Death anxiety is especially low among adults who have a deep faith in some form of higher force or being.
    3. Death anxiety declines with age, reaching its lowest level in late adulthood.
      a. Older adults are especially effective at regulating negative emotion, including anxiety.
      b. Elders also have had more time to develop *symbolic immortality*—the belief that one will live on through one's children, work, or personal influence.
    4. Regardless of age, in both Eastern and Western cultures, women appear more anxious about death than men do.
    5. Experiencing some anxiety about death is normal, but very intense death anxiety can undermine effective adjustment and, in adulthood, is related to mental health though not to physical health.

6. Death anxiety is rarely seen in children but is largely limited to adolescence and adulthood, except for children living in dangerous neighborhoods or war-torn areas where they are in constant danger, or for children who are terminally ill, especially those whose parents do not talk honestly with them about death.

III. THINKING AND EMOTIONS OF DYING PEOPLE (pp. 503–506)
  A. Do Stages of Dying Exist? (pp. 503–504)
    1. Kübler-Ross's Theory (p. 503)
      a. Elisabeth Kübler-Ross is credited with awakening society's sensitivity to the psychological needs of dying patients, although her theory of the stages of dying has been heavily criticized.
      b. From interviews with over 200 terminally ill people, Kübler-Ross devised a stage theory that describes a sequence of five typical responses to the prospect of death and the ordeal of dying.
        (1) *Denial:* On learning of the terminal illness, the person denies its seriousness to escape the prospect of death.
        (2) *Anger:* The realization that time is short promotes anger at having to die without being given a chance to do all one wants to do.
        (3) *Bargaining:* Realizing the inevitability of death, the terminally ill person attempts to bargain for extra time—a deal he or she may try to strike with family members, friends, doctors, nurses, or God.
        (4) *Depression:* When denial, anger, and bargaining fail to postpone the course of illness, the person becomes depressed about the impending loss of his or her life.
        (5) *Acceptance:* Most people who reach acceptance, a state of peace and quiet about upcoming death, do so only in the last weeks or days.
    2. Evaluation of Kübler-Ross's Theory (pp. 503–504)
      a. Kübler-Ross cautioned that her five "stages" should not be viewed as a fixed sequence and that not all people display each of them.
      b. Simplistic interpretation of her theory has sometimes led health professionals to try to push patients through this sequence or to dismiss a dying patient's legitimate complaints about treatment.
      c. These five reactions are best viewed as coping strategies that anyone may call on in the face of threat, rather than as stages.
      d. Kübler-Ross's list is much too limited, since dying people show many additional responses, including efforts to overcome the disease as well as efforts to "seize the day" and live in a fulfilling way in the remaining time.
      e. Perhaps the most serious drawback to Kübler-Ross's theory is that dying patients' thoughts and feelings are removed from the contexts that grant them meaning.
      f. People's adaptations to impending death can be understood only in relation to the multidimensional influences that have contributed to their life course.
  B. Contextual Influences on Adaptations to Dying (pp. 504–506)
    1. An **appropriate death** is one that makes sense in terms of the individual's pattern of living and values and, at the same time, preserves or restores significant relationships and is as free of suffering as possible.
    2. Most patients identify a "good death" as containing the following elements:
      a. Maintaining a sense of identity, or inner continuity with one's past
      b. Clarifying the meaning of one's life and death
      c. Maintaining and enhancing relationships
      d. Achieving a sense of control over the remaining time
      e. Confronting and preparing for death
    3. Biological, psychological, social, and cultural forces influence how people cope with dying and, therefore, the extent to which they attain these goals.
    4. Nature of the Disease (p. 504)
      a. The course of the illness and its symptoms affect the dying person's reactions.
      b. About one-third of cancer patients experience severe depression, which amplifies pain and is associated with poorer survival.

5. Personality and Coping Style (pp. 504–505)
    a. Understanding the way individuals view stressful life events and have coped with them in the past helps us appreciate the way they manage the dying process.
    b. Terminally ill patients may view dying as imprisonment, as a mandate to live ever more fully, as part of life's journey, or as an experience to be transformed so as to make it more bearable.
6. Family Members' and Health Professionals' Behavior (p. 505)
    a. A candid approach, in which everyone close to and caring for the dying person acknowledges the terminal illness, is best.
    b. Because some people find it hard to be candid about death, they pretend that the disease is not as bad as it is.
    c. Doctors who do want to inform patients of their prognosis may encounter resistance, especially within certain ethnic groups; in these cases, they must honor the patient's preference, reassessing it at regular intervals.
    d. Effective communication with the dying person is honest, fostering a trusting relationship, yet also oriented toward maintaining hope.
7. Spirituality, Religion, and Culture (pp. 505–506)
    a. A strong sense of spirituality reduces fear of death.
    b. Vast cultural differences in attitudes, guided by religious beliefs, also shape peoples' dying experiences.
    c. The idea that development is multidimensional and multidirectional—a vital assumption of the lifespan perspective—is as relevant to dying as to each earlier period of life.

IV. A PLACE TO DIE (pp. 506–508)
  A. Home (p. 506)
    1. About 80 to 90 percent of North Americans express a preference for dying at home, because the home offers an atmosphere of intimacy and loving care in which the terminally ill person is unlikely to feel abandoned.
    2. Only about one-fourth of Canadians and one-fifth of Americans experience home death, in part because of dramatic improvements in medicine, which means that dying people tend to be sicker or much older than in the past, and therefore extremely frail and difficult to care for at home.
    3. Adequate support for the caregiver is essential to make home death possible, and hospital-based equipment and technical support may need to be transported to the home.
    4. Family members of people who have died at home experience more psychological stress after the death than do family members whose loved one died elsewhere.
  B. Hospital (pp. 506–507)
    1. Hospital dying takes many forms, each one affected by the physical state of the dying person, the hospital unit in which it takes place, and the goal and quality of care.
    2. Sudden deaths, due to injury or critical illness, typically occur in emergency rooms, where medical personnel must evaluate the problem and act quickly, with little time for contact with family members.
    3. In intensive care units, which are focused on preventing death in patients whose condition can worsen quickly, privacy and communicating with the family are secondary to monitoring a patient's condition.
    4. Cancer patients, who account for most cases of prolonged dying, typically die in general or specialized cancer care hospital units.
    5. When hospitalized for a long time, these patients tend to reach out for help with physical and emotional needs, usually with mixed success because of a conflict of values between the hospital's goal of treating illness and the needs of the dying person.
  C. The Hospice Approach (pp. 507–508)
    1. In medieval times, a *hospice* was a place where travelers could find rest and shelter, while in the nineteenth and twentieth centuries, the word referred to homes for dying patients.
    2. Today, **hospice** is not a place but a comprehensive program of support services for terminally ill people and their families, with the goal of providing a caring community sensitive to the dying person's needs so that patients and family members can prepare for death in ways that are satisfying to them.

3. Quality of life is central to the hospice approach, which includes these main features:
    a. The patient and family are viewed as a unit of care.
    b. Emphasis is on meeting the patient's physical, emotional, social, and spiritual needs, including controlling pain, retaining dignity and self-worth, and feeling cared for and loved.
    c. Care is provided by an interdisciplinary team, including the patient's doctor, a nurse or nurse's aide, a chaplain, a counselor or social worker, and pharmacist.
    d. The patient is kept at home or in an inpatient setting with a homelike atmosphere where coordination of care is possible.
    e. Focus is on improving the quality of remaining life with **palliative**, or **comfort, care** designed to relieve pain and other symptoms, rather than to prolong life.
    f. In addition to regularly scheduled home-care visits, on-call services are available 24 hours a day, 7 days a week.
    g. Follow-up bereavement services are offered to families in the year after a death.
4. Central to the hospice approach is the idea that the dying person and his or her family should be offered choices that guarantee an appropriate death.
5. Because hospice care is a cost-effective alternative to expensive life-saving treatments, government health care benefits cover it in both the United States and Canada, making it affordable for most dying patients and their families.
6. Hospices also serve dying children—a tragedy so devastating that social support and bereavement intervention are vital.
7. As a long-range goal, hospice organizations are striving for broader acceptance of their patient- and family-centered approach—a philosophy with which the majority of North Americans are still unfamiliar, although most, when they learn of it, say it is the type of end-of-life care they want for themselves.
8. In developing countries, community-based teams that provide palliative care face many obstacles, including lack of funding, pain-relieving drugs, and professional and public education about hospice; these small "islands of excellence" are available to only a few families in the developing world.

V. THE RIGHT TO DIE (pp. 509–512)
  A. Highly publicized cases like those of Karen Ann Quinlan in the 1970s and, more recently, Terri Schiavo have brought right-to-die issues to the forefront of public attention.
  B. Today, all U.S. states and most Canadian provinces have laws that honor patients' wishes concerning withdrawal of treatment in cases of terminal illness or in cases of a persistent vegetative state.
  C. Neither the United States nor Canada has a uniform right-to-die policy, and heated controversy persists over how to handle the diverse circumstances in which patients and families make such requests.
  D. Passive Euthanasia (pp. 509–510)
    1. **Euthanasia** refers to the practice of ending the life of a person suffering from an incurable condition.
    2. In **passive euthanasia**, life-sustaining treatment is withheld or withdrawn, permitting a patient to die naturally.
        a. Broad public support exists for withholding life support when there is no hope of recovery.
        b. Passive euthanasia is widely practiced as part of ordinary medical procedure, in which doctors exercise professional judgment.
    3. People can best ensure that their wishes will be followed through an **advance medical directive**—a written statement of desired medical treatment should they become incurably ill.
    4. Two types of advance directives are recognized in most states: a living will and a durable power of attorney for health care.
        a. A **living will** specifies the treatments a person does or does not want in case of a terminal illness, coma, or other near-death situation.
        b. Sometimes living wills specify that comfort care be provided, which allows pain-relieving medication to be given even in cases where this may shorten life.
        c. Recognition of living wills is usually limited to patients who are terminally ill or are otherwise expected to die shortly.

   d. The **durable power of attorney for health care** authorizes appointment of another person (usually, though not always, a family member) to make health care decisions on one's behalf; it requires only a short signed and witnessed statement.
   e. The durable power of attorney for health care is more flexible than the living will because it permits a trusted spokesperson to confer with the doctor as medical circumstances arise.
   f. In gay and lesbian and other close relationships that are not sanctioned by law, it can ensure the partner's role in decision making and in advocating for the person's health care needs.
5. Fewer than 30 percent of Americans have executed either a living will or a durable power of attorney.
6. Some U.S. states and Canadian provinces permit appointment of a *health care proxy,* or substitute decision maker, if a patient has not provided an advance medical directive while competent.

E. Voluntary Active Euthanasia (pp. 510–511)
1. In **voluntary active euthanasia**, doctors or others act directly, at a patient's request, to end suffering before a natural end to life.
2. It is a criminal offense in most countries, including Canada and almost all U.S. states, but support for voluntary active euthanasia is growing.
3. Supporters believe that it represents the most compassionate option for terminally ill people in severe pain, while opponents stress the moral difference between "letting die" and "killing" and point out that, at times, even very sick patients recover.
4. Opponents also argue that involving doctors in taking the lives of suffering patients may impair people's trust in health professionals.
5. Some people fear that legalizing this practice could lead to a broadening of euthanasia and that, while initially limited to the terminally ill, it might be applied involuntarily to the frail, demented, or disabled—outcomes that most people find unacceptable and immoral.

F. Assisted Suicide (pp. 511–512)
1. In assisted suicide, physicians prescribe drugs so that terminally ill patients can end their own lives.
2. Assisting a suicide is illegal in Canada and in many but not all U.S. states but is legal in some Western European countries, including Belgium, Germany, the Netherlands, and Switzerland, and is tacitly accepted in many other countries.
3. In North America, Oregon is unique in having passed a law, the Death with Dignity Act, that explicitly allows physicians to prescribe drugs so terminally ill patients can end their lives.
4. Only 46 percent of Americans and 55 percent of Canadians approve of assisted suicide, and few terminally ill patients say that they would ask for it.
5. Public interest in assisted suicide was sparked in the 1990s by Dr. Jack Kevorkian, a proponent of euthanasia, who devised "suicide machines" that permitted terminally ill patients to self-administer lethal drugs and carbon monoxide.
   a. Kevorkian participated in more than 100 such deaths.
   b. Although juries have seldom returned guilty verdicts in cases involving doctor-assisted suicide, Kevorkian was convicted of second-degree murder in 1999 and sentenced to 10 to 25 years in prison.
6. Although public opinion consistently favors voluntary active euthanasia over assisted suicide, some experts believe that legalizing assisted suicide would be preferable, because in assisted suicide, the final act is solely the patient's, reducing the possibility of coercion that exists with voluntary active euthanasia.
7. Helping incurable, suffering patients who yearn for death is a profound moral and legal problem.

VI. BEREAVEMENT: COPING WITH THE DEATH OF A LOVED ONE (pp. 512–517)

A. **Bereavement** is the experience of losing a loved one by death.
B. We respond to loss with **grief**—intense physical and psychological distress.
C. **Mourning** is the culturally specified expression of the bereaved person's thoughts and feelings.
D. Grief Process (p. 513): Theorists have concluded that grieving usually takes place in three phases, each characterized by a different set of responses.
1. *Avoidance* (p. 513): On hearing the news, the survivor experiences shock followed by disbelief, which may last from hours to weeks; a numbed feeling serves as "emotional anesthesia" while the bereaved person begins to experience painful awareness of the loss.

2. *Confrontation* (p. 513): As the mourner begins to confront the reality of the loss, grief is experienced most intensely.
   a. The bereaved person may display a range of emotional reactions, including anxiety, sadness, protest, anger, helplessness, frustration, abandonment, and yearning for the loved one.
   b. The person may obsessively review the circumstances of death, asking how it might have been prevented, and searching for meaning in it.
   c. The person may be unable to concentrate, absentminded, and preoccupied with thoughts of the deceased.
   d. At times, self-destructive behaviors, such as taking drugs or driving too fast, occur.
3. *Restoration* (p. 513): As grief subsides, emotional energies increasingly shift toward life-restoring pursuits.
   a. According to a recent perspective, the **dual-process model of coping with loss**, effective coping requires people to alternate between dealing with the emotional consequences of loss and attending to life changes, which can have restorative, healing effects.
   b. On certain days, such as family celebrations or the anniversary of death, grief reactions may resurface and require attention, but they usually do not interfere with a healthy, positive approach to life.

E. Personal and Situational Variations (pp. 513–515)
1. Like dying, grieving is affected by many factors that make the duration of each phase and the reactions within it unique.
   a. Personality, coping style, and religious and cultural background are influential.
   b. Sex differences are also evident, with women better prepared to deal with grief because they express feelings and seek social support more readily.
   c. The quality of the mourner's relationship with the deceased is important.
   d. Circumstances surrounding the death—whether it is sudden and anticipated or follows a prolonged illness—also shape mourners' responses.
2. Sudden, Unanticipated versus Prolonged, Expected Deaths (pp. 513–514)
   a. Avoidance is especially pronounced after a sudden death because of extreme shock and disbelief.
   b. Shock and disbelief are usually minimal after prolonged dying because the bereaved person has had time to engage in **anticipatory grieving**—acknowledging the inevitability of the loss and preparing emotionally for it.
   c. Adjusting to a death is easier when the survivor understands the reasons for it, while sudden, unexpected deaths threaten basic assumptions about a just, benevolent, and controllable world.
   d. Suicide, particularly that of a young person, is especially hard to bear, and people grieving suicidal loss are more likely than survivors of other types of deaths to blame themselves for what happened.
3. Parents Grieving the Loss of a Child (p. 514)
   a. The death of a child, whether unexpected or foreseen, is the most difficult loss an adult can face.
   b. Children are extensions of parents' feelings about themselves—the focus of hopes and dreams, including the parents' sense of immortality.
   c. Since children depend on, admire, and appreciate their parents in a deeply gratifying way, they are an unmatched source of love.
   d. The unnaturalness of a child's death complicates it, because children are not supposed to die before their parents.
   e. If parents can reorganize the family system and reestablish a sense of life's meaning by investing in other children and activities, then the result can be firmer family commitments and personal growth.
4. Children and Adolescents Grieving the Loss of a Parent or Sibling (pp. 514–515)
   a. The loss of an attachment figure has long-term consequences for children.
   b. When a parent dies, children's basic sense of security and being cared for is threatened.
   c. Death of a sibling not only deprives children of a close emotional tie but also informs them, often for the first time, of their own vulnerability.

   d. Many children said they actively maintained mental contact with their dead parent or sibling, dreaming about and speaking to them regularly.
   e. These images seem to facilitate coping with loss and are sometimes reported by bereaved adults as well.
   f. Cognitive development contributes to the ability to grieve; young children need careful, repeated explanations assuring them that the parent did not want to die and was not angry at them.
   g. Keeping the truth from children isolates them and often leads to profound regrets.
   h. Grief-stricken school-age children are usually more willing than adolescents to confide in parents, who may keep their grieving from both adults and peers in an effort to appear "normal"—and, as a result, are more likely than younger children to become depressed or to escape into acting-out behavior.

5. Adults Grieving the Loss of an Intimate Partner (p. 515)
   a. Adaptation to widowhood varies greatly and is affected by age, social support, and personality.
   b. After a period of intense grieving, most widowed elders in Western nations fare well.
   c. Those who lose a partner in early or middle adulthood display more negative outcomes.
      (1) In addition to dealing with feelings of loss, young and middle-aged widows and widowers often must assume a greater role in comforting others, especially children.
      (2) They also may face the stresses of single parenthood.
   d. Death of an intimate partner in a gay or lesbian relationship presents unique challenges.
      (1) Families sometimes limit or bar a partner from participating in funeral services, disrupting the grieving process and leading to *disenfranchised grief*—a sense of loss without the opportunity to mourn publicly and benefit from others' support.
      (2) Fortunately, gay and lesbian communities provide helpful alternative support in the form of memorial services and other rituals.
6. Bereavement Overload (p. 515)
   a. When a person experiences several deaths in succession, *bereavement overload* can occur.
   b. Multiple losses deplete the coping resources of even well-adjusted people, leaving them emotionally overwhelmed and unable to resolve their grief.
   c. Because old age often brings the death of a spouse, siblings, and friends in close succession, elders are at risk for bereavement overload.
   d. Public tragedies such as random murders in schools, terrorist attacks, and natural disasters can also spark bereavement overload.
   e. Funerals and other bereavement rituals assist mourners of all ages in resolving grief with the help of family and friends.
   f. Bereaved individuals who have difficulty resuming interest in everyday activities benefit from special interventions designed to help them adjust to loss.

F. Bereavement Interventions (pp. 515–517)
   1. Social support is crucial during the aftermath of death, but it is often difficult to provide.
   2. Experts agree that sympathy and understanding are sufficient for most people to undertake the tasks necessary to recover from grief; listening patiently and "just being there" are among the best ways to help.
   3. Bereavement interventions typically help people to draw on their existing social network while providing extra social support.
   4. Self-help groups that bring together mourners who have experienced the same type of loss are highly effective in reducing stress.
   5. Interventions for children and adolescents following violent deaths must protect them from unnecessary reexposure, help parents and teachers deal with their own distress so they can effectively offer comfort, and be culturally sensitive.
   6. In some instances, grief therapy, or individual counseling with a specially trained professional, may be necessary, especially in cases of sudden, violent, and unexplainable deaths; the loss of a child; a death that the mourner feels he or she could have prevented; or an ambivalent or dependent relationship with the deceased.

VII. DEATH EDUCATION (pp. 517–518)

A. The death awareness movement that sparked increased sensitivity to the needs of dying patients has also led to the rise of death education in an effort to prepare people of all ages to cope with death more effectively.

B. Courses in death, dying, and bereavement are offered in colleges and universities, as part of professional training for medical and mental health professionals, in some adult education programs, and in a few elementary and secondary schools.

C. Death education at all levels has the following goals

1. Increasing students' understanding of the physical and psychological changes that accompany dying
2. Helping students learn how to cope with the death of a loved one
3. Preparing students to be informed consumers of medical and funeral services
4. Promoting understanding of social and ethical issues involving death

D. Educational format varies widely.

1. Some focus on conveying information.
2. Others are experiential and include many activities—role playing, discussions with the terminally ill, visits to mortuaries and cemeteries, and personal awareness exercises.
3. Research reveals that using a lecture style leads to gains in knowledge but often leaves students more uncomfortable about death than when they entered.
4. In contrast, experiential programs that help people confront their own mortality are less likely to heighten death anxiety and sometimes reduce it.

LECTURE ENHANCEMENTS

LECTURE ENHANCEMENT 19.1
The Relationship Between Self-Efficacy and Death Anxiety in Elders (pp. 501–502)

Time: 10–15 minutes

Objective: To examine the relationship between self-efficacy and death anxiety in elders.

As noted in the text, a variety of factors—including fear of no longer existing, loss of control, a painful death, being separated from loved ones, and the unknown—contribute to death anxiety. To examine the relationship between self-efficacy and death anxiety in elders, Fry (2003) recruited 288 adults between the ages of 65 and 87 years and collected the following information:

1. *Demographics.* Participants provided relevant demographic information, including age, gender, income, educational level, physical health status, and living arrangements. The majority were Caucasian.

2. *Fear of death.* Participants completed two subscales of the Multidimensional Fear of Death Scale (MFODS): Fear of Dying and Fear of the Unknown.

3. *Self-efficacy.* To assess overall self-efficacy, participants answered questions in eight domains: interpersonal, instrumental (the ability to manage instrumental activity effectively), emotional, social support, organizational (the ability to manage one's financial and business affairs), physical health, nutrition, and spiritual health.

4. *Physical health status.* Participants completed a checklist in which they identified current health conditions, illnesses, and perceptions of health.

5. *Social support.* Participants completed the Multidimensional Scale of Perceived Social Support (MSPSS), which measures three sources of support: family, friends, and significant others.

6. *Religiosity.* Participants were asked to rate the importance of religion, the importance of God, and the importance of private prayer in their everyday lives.

Results indicated that self-efficacy was related to death anxiety. Overall, participants with higher self-efficacy scores reported less death anxiety. This relationship remained strong even after controlling for demographic variables, physical health status, and social support. Findings also revealed that spiritual health and religiosity were strongly related to death anxiety. Elders who scored high on spiritual health and rated religion as an important aspect of their daily lives reported less death anxiety than participants who placed little or no value on spirituality and religion.

Results also revealed gender differences. For women, the stronger their self-efficacy in the interpersonal, social, and emotional domains, the lower their scores on the fear of death measures. For men, high self-efficacy in the instrumental, organizational, and physical health domains predicted low scores on the fear of death measures. Men and women may focus on different aspects of self-efficacy in old age, which may have important implications for how elders deal with their own demise.

Ask students to describe strategies for reducing death anxiety on the basis of this study's results and research in the text. Under what circumstances is death anxiety adaptive?

Fry, P. S. (2003). Perceived self-efficacy domains as predictors of fear of the unknown and fear of dying among older adults. *Psychology and Aging, 18,* 474–486.

LECTURE ENHANCEMENT 19.2
Factors Affecting the Desire for Euthanasia in the Terminally Ill (pp. 509–512)

Time: 10–15 minutes

Objective: To explore the desire for euthanasia in a sample of hospice patients with advanced, incurable cancer.

To examine the desire for euthanasia in the terminally ill, Mak and Elwyn (2005) recruited and interviewed six hospice patients with advanced, incurable cancer. Patients who were confused, unable to communicate, or emotionally distressed were excluded from the study. Participants were asked, "You mentioned earlier that you had desired help in ending your life. Can you tell me more?"

The interviews revealed five major themes in the desire for euthanasia:

1. *Reality of disease progression.* Participants understood that death was inevitable and that there was no hope for a cure. According to a 61-year-old woman, "This sort of disease ultimately leads to death. I have to walk the path."
2. *Perception of suffering for the self and significant others.* Participants were concerned not only about their own pain and suffering but about the impact of their illness on significant others. One participant commented, "For them to see me in pain is suffering. I fear the rushing around will make her [wife] ill."
3. *Anticipation of a future worse than death.* As they observed the dying process in other terminally ill patients, the participants feared the pain and helplessness that awaited them. They also believed that uncontrollable pain was inevitable. According to a 71-year-old patient with kidney cancer, "Someone with a tube sticking up the bottom, a tube sticking into the nostrils, another somewhere else. I mean, what for? Can you save them?" Another patient added, "It'll be extremely terrible . . . . The complications would give me so much pain and suffering. I anticipate the future would be like this. Very severe, very scary when I think about it."
4. *Desire for good quality of end-of-life care.* Participants indicated a desire to escape their pain and suffering and to relieve the perceived burden on relatives and significant others. One woman commented, "I just don't want to be in so much suffering . . . to endure these psychological effects."
5. *Holding environment.* Participants were appreciative of the care, connectedness, and respect they received from health care professionals, friends, and family. A 51-year-old man indicated, "Coming here [hospice] has helped me a lot, at least spiritually and in every other aspect. People comfort and reassure me, and so it doesn't feel so intolerable."

These findings suggest that the desire for euthanasia is a complex issue that is not limited to physical disintegration or suffering. Even patients who are satisfied with their end-of-life care and "holding environment" may desire physician-assisted death. In this study, the desire for euthanasia reflected cancer patients' understanding that death was inevitable, perceived effects of their illness on loved ones, and fears of the pain and helplessness that awaited them.

Considering these findings and research presented in the text, do students believe that voluntary active euthanasia should be legalized? Why or why not?

Mak, Y. W., & Elwyn, G. (2005). Voices of the terminally ill: Uncovering the meaning of desire for euthanasia. *Palliative Medicine, 19,* 344–350.

LECTURE ENHANCEMENT 19.3
Does Positive Parenting Protect Bereaved Children from Negative Mental Health Outcomes? (pp. 514–515)

Time: 5–10 minutes

Objective: To investigate the effects of positive parenting on mental health outcomes in parentally bereaved children.

Parentally bereaved children are at-risk for a diverse range of negative outcomes, including mental health problems, poor academic achievement, and low self-esteem. However, positive parenting (by the surviving parent or another caregiver) can help protect children from these adjustment difficulties. To further examine the effects of positive parenting on bereaved children, Haine and colleagues (2006) recruited 313 recently bereaved children and their current caregivers. Children were between the ages of 8 and 16 years. The researchers collected the following information at baseline and again 11 months later:

1. Children completed two measures of negative life events: the General Life Events Schedule for Children (GLESC) and the Parental Death Event List (PDEL). The researchers were not just interested in the effects of parental death; they also examined other life events, such as parental divorce, a change in residence, the birth of a sibling, or the death of another family member.
2. Both children and their caregivers completed questionnaires on positive parenting, caregiver warmth, and consistency of discipline. The researchers compared caregivers' perceptions of their parenting with those of their children.
3. To assess the presence and severity of child mental health problems, children and their caregivers completed a standardized depression inventory and an externalizing problems checklist that focused on noncompliance, hyperactivity, aggression, and impulsivity.

Results indicated that positive parenting—with high levels of caregiver warmth and consistent discipline—was associated with fewer child mental health problems over the course of the study. For children who experienced additional negative life events, such as a recent divorce or the death of another family member, positive parenting continued to protect against depression and externalizing problems. The impact of positive parenting on bereaved children's mental health was similar for both boys and girls.

Haine and colleagues (2006) note that these findings may have important implications for intervening with bereaved children and their families. Specifically, interventions that promote positive parenting may significantly reduce the likelihood of negative mental health outcomes in parentally bereaved children.

Haine, R. A., Wolchik, S. A., Sandler, I. N., Millsap, R. E., & Ayers, T. S. (2006). Positive parenting as a protective resource for parentally bereaved children. *Death Studies, 30,* 1–28.

LEARNING ACTIVITIES

LEARNING ACTIVITY 19.1
True or False: Thinking and Emotions of Dying People (pp. 503–506)

Present the following exercise to students as a quiz or in-class activity:

Directions: Read each of the following statements and indicate whether each is *True* (T) or *False* (F).

Statements:

_____ 1. On learning of a terminal illness, most people move in and out of denial.
_____ 2. Even when they realize the inevitability of death, few terminally ill people bargain for extra time.
_____ 3. Most people who reach acceptance do so only in the last few weeks or days.
_____ 4. Kübler-Ross maintains that her five stages should be viewed as a fixed sequence and that all people display each response.
_____ 5. According to recent theorists, a single strategy, such as acceptance, is not best for every dying patient.
_____ 6. Only about one-fifth of cancer patients experience severe depression.
_____ 7. A candid approach, in which everyone close to and caring for the dying person acknowledges the terminal illness, is best.
_____ 8. Even when doctors want to inform patients of their prognosis, they may encounter resistance, especially within certain ethnic groups.
_____ 9. Dying patients who feel they have much unfinished business to attend to experience little anxiety about impending death.
_____ 10. A strong sense of spirituality reduces fear of death.

Answers:

1. T
2. F
3. T
4. F
5. T
6. F
7. T
8. T
9. F
10. T

LEARNING ACTIVITY 19.2
Managing the Dying Process (pp. 503–506)

In small groups, ask students to jot down characteristics of adults who adapt favorably to stressful life events (see Chapters 13–18). Next, have students list characteristics of adults who struggle with stressful life events. How might personality and coping style affect one's reactions to the dying process? What role might life experiences play? Once students have completed the activity, ask them to share their reflections with the class.

6) Mrs. Beckett's body has succumbed to cancer. In the moments when her body can no longer sustain life, she gasps and experiences muscle spasms. She is experiencing

A) the agonal phase of death.
B) clinical death.
C) terminal death.
D) mortality.

Answer: A

Page Ref: 500
Skill: Applied
Objective: 19.1

7) Brianna was found unconscious in a swimming pool. Her heartbeat and breathing had stopped, and her dilated pupils indicated lack of oxygen to her brain. Yet, paramedics were able to revive her. Brianna was in the __________ phase of dying.

A) agonal
B) clinical death
C) mortality
D) miracle

Answer: B

Page Ref: 500
Skill: Applied
Objective: 19.1

8) When Mr. Beisswenger has a heart attack, his wife calls the paramedics. She is overwhelmed with grief when they arrive and tell her that they are unable to revive him. Mr. Beisswenger is in the __________ phase of death.

A) agonal
B) clinical death
C) mortality
D) terminal death

Answer: C

Page Ref: 500
Skill: Applied
Objective: 19.1

9) Loss of heartbeat and respiration

A) are not adequate criteria for signifying death, because resuscitation techniques frequently permit vital signs to be restored.
B) are generally what medical professionals use to classify a person as having officially died.
C) can signify death, if they last for at least 30 minutes without any resuscitation efforts occurring, and subsequent resuscitation efforts are fruitless.
D) signify death according to the American Medical Association definition, but are not an acceptable definition in Japan.

Answer: A

Page Ref: 500
Skill: Factual
Objective: 19.1

10) __________ is defined as irreversible cessation of all activity in the brain and the brain stem.

A) Clinical death
B) Mortality
C) Persistive vegetative state
D) Brain death

Answer: D

Page Ref: 500
Skill: Factual
Objective: 19.1

11) One way the Japanese government has addressed the conflicting issues of organ donation and religious beliefs is
    A) by allowing people who want to be organ donors to choose the standard of brain death, as long as their families do not object.
    B) to eliminate their national organ transplant program, as so few people volunteered to be organ donors.
    C) by supplementing organ transplant costs for Japanese citizens who have the procedures done in other countries.
    D) through a national media campaign advocating the responsibility of its citizens to provide for others, even after their deaths.

Answer: A
Page Ref: 500
Skill: Factual
Objective: 19.1

12) Mrs. Koppekin's doctor has determined that her brain stem continues to function but there is no electrical activity at all in her cortex. Mrs. Koppekin is
    A) brain dead.
    B) in a persistent vegetative state.
    C) experiencing imminent mortality.
    D) in a coma.

Answer: B
Page Ref: 500
Skill: Applied
Objective: 19.1

13) Although some insist that a definition of inactivity in the cerebral cortex is sufficient for a declaration of death, others disagree and argue that some patients were vegetative for months and regained consciousness. However,
    A) there are actually only two such documented cases.
    B) these patients usually had very limited functioning.
    C) there are no documented cases and the stories are being discounted as urban legends.
    D) these people usually demonstrated severe adjustment issues and the suicide rate among this group is extremely high.

Answer: B
Page Ref: 500
Skill: Factual
Objective: 19.1

14) Mrs. Halquist is dying. When communicating with her, one of the most important things her husband can do is to
    A) avoid discussing her impending death.
    B) lead her to believe that her health is better than it actually is.
    C) treat her with esteem and respect, and address her greatest concerns.
    D) let her know that he can make all of the important decisions regarding further treatment options.

Answer: C
Page Ref: 500
Skill: Applied
Objective: 19.2

15) Mrs. Hossen has terminal cancer. She will not be able to share the sentiments that bring closure to her most dear relationships unless
   A) her closest family members and friends first tell her what her life has meant to them.
   B) she has some sort of belief in an afterlife and is convinced that her post-death fate will be a positive one.
   C) she is told that she is dying, but that it will be a "gentle" death with relatively little pain.
   D) she is aware that she is dying and understands the likely circumstances of her death.

Answer: D
Page Ref: 501
Skill: Applied
Objective: 19.2

16) An important service doctors and other medical people can offer to dying people is to provide
   A) knowledge about their condition and their options.
   B) comfortable surroundings and no decisions to make.
   C) protection from too much clinical information.
   D) mood enhancers to keep them cheerful and optimistic.

Answer: A
Page Ref: 501
Skill: Factual
Objective: 19.2

17) Which of the following is an essential ingredient of a "good death"?
   A) provision of care, affection, and companionship to the dying person
   B) hiding the truth about the diagnosis from the dying person
   C) supporting the opportunity to die at home, even against doctor's orders
   D) giving the dying person minimal personal control over this phase of life

Answer: A
Page Ref: 501
Skill: Conceptual
Objective: 19.2

18) Which of the following contributes to a sense of uneasiness about death for many people in North America?
   A) early experiences with death before a child was emotionally prepared to deal with it
   B) a lack of spiritual fulfillment and questions about the afterlife
   C) the images of death seen in television shows, movies, and news reports
   D) the distance that most people have from death

Answer: D
Page Ref: 501
Skill: Factual
Objective: 19.2

19) Meredith feels fearful and apprehensive when she thinks about death. Meredith is experiencing
   A) morbidity.
   B) despair.
   C) isolation.
   D) death anxiety.

Answer: D
Page Ref: 501
Skill: Applied
Objective: 19.2

20) Among Westerners, which factor seems to have a greater impact on reducing death anxiety?
  A) a spiritual sense of life's meaning
  B) commitment to an organized religion
  C) the conviction that there is an afterlife
  D) good physical health for one's age
Answer: A
Page Ref: 502
Skill: Factual
Objective: 19.2

21) Death anxiety is LEAST common among people of which age group?
  A) adolescents
  B) elders
  C) middle-aged adults
  D) young adults
Answer: B
Page Ref: 502
Skill: Conceptual
Objective: 19.2

22) Mr. Honeywell really has no fear of death. He feels that a part of him will continue to live on through his children and through the engineering company that he built. Mr. Honeywell's beliefs reflect
  A) a form of denial of the inevitability of death.
  B) evidence that a person has accepted the inevitability of death.
  C) a personal fable.
  D) symbolic immortality.
Answer: D
Page Ref: 502
Skill: Applied
Objective: 19.2

23) Which group of people is most likely to experience death anxiety?
  A) elders
  B) people with close interpersonal ties
  C) women
  D) men
Answer: C
Page Ref: 502
Skill: Factual
Objective: 19.2

24) Which factor can cause increased death anxiety in children?
  A) having a terminal illness
  B) having a deep religious faith
  C) spirituality that focuses on a sense of life's meaning
  D) living in a safe neighborhood
Answer: A
Page Ref: 502
Skill: Factual
Objective: 19.2

25) Mrs. Polidoro has just learned that she has a terminal illness, but she refuses to acknowledge its seriousness. According to Kübler-Ross's theory of dying, Mrs. Polidoro is in the __________ stage.

A) anger
B) bargaining
C) depression
D) denial

Answer: D

Page Ref: 503
Skill: Applied
Objective: 19.3

26) The function of Kübler-Ross's __________ phase is self-protective, allowing the person to invest in rewarding activities and deal with the illness at his or her own pace.

A) denial
B) anger
C) bargaining
D) acceptance

Answer: A

Page Ref: 503
Skill: Factual
Objective: 19.3

27) Mr. Nkoyongo, who is dying, yells at his wife and daughter, telling them they cannot possibly understand his feelings because they get to keep on living. He also refuses phone calls from his friends. According to Kübler-Ross, Mr. Nkoyongo is in the __________ stage.

A) anger
B) denial
C) bargaining
D) depression

Answer: A

Page Ref: 503
Skill: Applied
Objective: 19.3

28) Mr. Nkoyongo, who is dying, yells at his wife and daughter, telling them they cannot possibly understand his feelings because they get to keep on living. He also refuses phone calls from his friends. According to Kübler-Ross, how should Mr. Nkoyongo's wife and daughter react to his outbursts?

A) Try to move him quickly into the next stage of death.
B) Try to reason with him, and get him to appreciate the time that he has left rather than spending it in such a negative state.
C) Recognize that the underlying cause for his behavior is the unfairness of death, and tolerate his outbursts.
D) Ignore him and his behavior until he treats them with more respect.

Answer: C

Page Ref: 503
Skill: Applied
Objective: 19.3

29) Shayna, a fine singer who learned she had a terminal illness, prayed to God, "Just let me get through this, Lord, and I'll never sing anything again but gospel music." According to Kübler-Ross, she is in which stage of the dying process?
A) denial
B) bargaining
C) anger
D) depression
Answer: B
Page Ref: 503
Skill: Applied
Objective: 19.3

30) Mrs. Datta, who has cancer, pleads with her doctor to keep her alive long enough to see her son graduate from college. Her doctor's best response would be to
A) be honest and tell her that is just not possible.
B) agree to do everything he can to keep her alive.
C) listen sympathetically.
D) refer her to someone more capable of handling her emotional needs.
Answer: C
Page Ref: 503
Skill: Applied
Objective: 19.3

31) One of the problems with medical treatment for the dying that emphasizes aggressive treatment rather than comfort care is that it promotes which of the stages of dying in Kübler-Ross's theory?
A) bargaining
B) denial
C) depression
D) morbidity
Answer: C
Page Ref: 503
Skill: Factual
Objective: 19.3

32) Most people who reach Kübler-Ross's acceptance stage
A) usually use emotion-centered coping strategies.
B) have a deep religious faith.
C) do so only in the last weeks or days of life.
D) have illnesses that cause them a great deal of physical pain.
Answer: C
Page Ref: 503
Skill: Factual
Objective: 19.3

33) Mr. Degerberger has terminal cancer. During the last week he has disengaged from most of his family and withdrawn. According to Kübler-Ross, he has reached which stage of dying?
A) anger
B) bargaining
C) denial
D) acceptance
Answer: D
Page Ref: 503
Skill: Applied
Objective: 19.3

34) Rather than stages, Kübler-Ross's observations on reactions to death are better viewed as
   A) steps through which the dying progress.
   B) an untested hypothesis with little validity in actual situations.
   C) reactions of the living as they watch their loved one dying.
   D) coping strategies that anyone may call on in the face of threat.
Answer: D
Page Ref: 504
Skill: Factual
Objective: 19.3

35) The most important criticism of Kübler-Ross's theory of dying is that it
   A) removes patients' reactions from their real-life contexts.
   B) was based on only a few interviews with dying people.
   C) cannot be applied to people who die unexpectedly.
   D) applies only to people without a sense of spirituality.
Answer: A
Page Ref: 504
Skill: Factual
Objective: 19.3

36) __________ is an alternative to Kübler-Ross's stages that theorists say makes sense in terms of the individual's pattern of living and values, preserves or restores significant relationships, and is as free of suffering as possible.
   A) Passive euthanasia
   B) Voluntary active euthanasia
   C) Assisted suicide
   D) An appropriate death
Answer: D
Page Ref: 504
Skill: Factual
Objective: 19.3

37) A terminally ill patient __________ experiences amplified pain, impaired immune system response, and poorer chances of survival.
   A) who lacks strong interpersonal relationships
   B) in the denial phase of dying
   C) with profound depression
   D) who receives hospice care
Answer: C
Page Ref: 504
Skill: Factual
Objective: 19.4

38) Treatment for profound depression for terminally ill patients should include
   A) therapy, antidepressant medication, and patient and family education.
   B) visitations with death counselors, pain medication, and family counseling.
   C) antidepressant medication, a "suicide watch," and education about their disease.
   D) options for disease treatment that allow patients to take control of their situation.
Answer: A
Page Ref: 504
Skill: Factual
Objective: 19.4

39) Which contextual factor can help family members and doctors appreciate the way that a dying person manages the dying process?
   A) pretending that the disease is not as bad as it is
   B) understanding the way that the individual viewed and coped with stressful life events in the past
   C) allowing them to die in a hospital rather than at home
   D) strictly following Kübler-Ross's stages

   Answer: B
   Page Ref: 504
   Skill: Factual
   Objective: 19.4

40) Mr. Sodhi is a terminally ill patient who states, "Because my future has been taken away, I feel like I'm already dead." According to your text, Mr. Sodhi views dying as
   A) a mandate to live ever more fully.
   B) imprisonment.
   C) part of life's journey.
   D) an experience to be transformed.

   Answer: B
   Page Ref: 504
   Skill: Applied
   Objective: 19.4

41) Mrs. Organakis is dying of lung cancer. She writes, "I plan to spend as much time with my grandchildren as I can, enjoying every second." According to your text, Mrs. Organakis views dying as
   A) a mandate to live ever more fully.
   B) imprisonment.
   C) part of life's journey.
   D) an experience to be transformed.

   Answer: A
   Page Ref: 504
   Skill: Applied
   Objective: 19.4

42) Mr. Kilpatrick has an inoperable brain tumor. He says, "I've had a lot of incredible experiences in my life. Because of my faith I don't fear death. It's just a prerequisite to the wonderful journey ahead of me." According to your text, Mr. Kilpatrick views dying as
   A) a mandate to live ever more fully.
   B) imprisonment.
   C) part of life's journey.
   D) an experience to be transformed.

   Answer: C
   Page Ref: 505
   Skill: Applied
   Objective: 19.4

43) Ms. McGaha is a terminally ill patient who states, "Every time the pain hits, I imagine that it's a test. I let my mind take me to the mountains of Narnia and just put the pain completely out of my thoughts. When it's over, I'll have passed the ultimate test." Ms. McGaha views dying as
   A) a mandate to live ever more fully.
   B) imprisonment.
   C) part of life's journey.
   D) an experience to be transformed.

   Answer: D
   Page Ref: 505
   Skill: Applied
   Objective: 19.4

44) The primary reason some caregivers join in a dying patient's denial by pretending that they will get better and continue to live is that
A) the patient seems so healthy they forget he or she is dying.
B) the patient becomes too angry whenever dying is mentioned.
C) it is difficult to face the impending death and to close off relationships.
D) they don't want to be bothered with discussing death.
Answer: C
Page Ref: 505
Skill: Factual
Objective: 19.4

45) Mrs. Aguillera is dying. Because of their cultural beliefs, her Mexican-American family will probably
A) avoid informing her of her condition because doing so hastens death.
B) forbid the doctors to talk to her about her condition because it will bring bad fortune to the family.
C) pretend there is nothing wrong in an attempt to avoid stress for the patient.
D) talk with her openly and honestly about her condition, so that she can focus on resolving family relationships before she dies.
Answer: A
Page Ref: 505
Skill: Applied
Objective: 19.4

46) __________ can reduce the dying person's sense of urgency to prolong life because it permits some incomplete tasks to be worked through.
A) Family contact
B) A religious conversion
C) Drawing up a living will
D) Administration of strong pain killers
Answer: A
Page Ref: 505
Skill: Factual
Objective: 19.4

47) The path of the hope trajectory for dying patients is typically:
A) hope that they can handle the death process, hope that their family will be all right, hope that they will not be forgotten.
B) hope for a cure, hope for prolonging life, hope for a peaceful death with as few burdens as possible.
C) hope that the medical results were a mistake, hope for a cure, hope for a miracle.
D) hope for longevity, hope for strength, hope for peace.
Answer: B
Page Ref: 505
Skill: Factual
Objective: 19.4

48) Mr. Yzquierdo has a strong sense of spirituality. When contemplating his impending death, his is likely to exhibit
A) less fear and more acceptance of death.
B) more anger at a God who should have prevented this.
C) confusion and distress at what dying really means.
D) anger and resentment at those who go on living.
Answer: A
Page Ref: 505
Skill: Applied
Objective: 19.4

49) Person X is dying. His friends and family read sutras to him, which he believes will help him to reach a state beyond the world of suffering. Person X is
   A) an African American.
   B) a Native American.
   C) a Buddhist.
   D) a member of the Maori tribe.
Answer: C
Page Ref: 505
Skill: Applied
Objective: 19.4

50) Person Z approaches death with stoicism taught at an early age, realizing the circular nature of the life–death relationship. Person Z is
   A) an African American.
   B) a Native American.
   C) a Buddhist.
   D) a member of the Maori tribe.
Answer: B
Page Ref: 506
Skill: Applied
Objective: 19.4

51) Person Y is terminally ill. Her family views this as a crisis, to which they all unite to care for their elder. Person Y remains an active member of the family until she can no longer carry out her role. Person Y is most likely
   A) an African American.
   B) a Native American.
   C) a Buddhist.
   D) a member of the Maori tribe.
Answer: A
Page Ref: 506
Skill: Applied
Objective: 19.4

52) What can be considered ironic about the places where most people die?
   A) About 70 to 80 percent of deaths occur in hospitals, a place that focuses on saving lives.
   B) Most people die at home, a place with very few medical supplies available to make the transition easier.
   C) Although most people say they want to die surrounded by loved ones, this situation is actually very stressful for the family members involved.
   D) Most people envision themselves dying away from home, when in reality 90 percent die in their own beds.
Answer: A
Page Ref: 506
Skill: Conceptual
Objective: 19.5

53) Most Americans and Canadians would prefer to die in
   A) their own home.
   B) a hospital.
   C) a hospice center.
   D) a child's home.
Answer: A
Page Ref: 506
Skill: Factual
Objective: 19.5

54) Modern medical care has affected the choice of dying at home primarily by
- A) shortening how long a person typically takes to die.
- B) extending life so that dying people are older, sicker, and have more difficulty living at home until the end.
- C) making medical equipment more lightweight and easier to move around, especially for spouses of elderly patients.
- D) training medical doctors to provide care at home.

Answer: B
Page Ref: 506
Skill: Factual
Objective: 19.5

55) One of the most essential factors in successful home care for dying individuals is
- A) an illness that causes death fairly quickly.
- B) a strong sense of spirituality or religiosity.
- C) adequate support for the home caregivers.
- D) the installation of specialized medical devices.

Answer: C
Page Ref: 506
Skill: Factual
Objective: 19.5

56) When patients die suddenly in an emergency room setting, their families usually need __________ in order to cope well.
- A) the opportunity to be with the patient at death
- B) to feel assured that every measure possible was taken to save the life
- C) information about the cause of death
- D) some type of crisis intervention services

Answer: D
Page Ref: 507
Skill: Factual
Objective: 19.5

57) The primary function of an intensive care ward is to
- A) allow the family privacy with the patient.
- B) provide for quality communication with the family regarding the patient's needs.
- C) prevent death in patients whose condition can worsen quickly.
- D) allow the patient to die with dignity.

Answer: C
Page Ref: 507
Skill: Factual
Objective: 19.5

58) __________ are particularly depersonalizing for patients who linger between life and death while hooked to machines for months.
- A) Intensive care wards
- B) Emergency rooms
- C) Hospices
- D) Home settings

Answer: A
Page Ref: 507
Skill: Factual
Objective: 19.5

59) Most of the cases of prolonged dying are caused by
A) AIDS.
B) cancer.
C) heart disease.
D) atherosclerosis.
Answer: B
Page Ref: 507
Skill: Factual
Objective: 19.5

60) Today, the term *hospice* refers to
A) a location providing specialized medical care to dying people.
B) a program of support services for dying people and their families.
C) alternative care for dying people that uses minimal medication.
D) medical care that is focused on prolonging a dying person's life.
Answer: B
Page Ref: 507
Skill: Factual
Objective: 19.5

61) The primary aim of the __________ is to provide a caring community sensitive to the dying person's needs so patients and family members can prepare for death in ways that are satisfying to them.
A) home-choice
B) intensive care unit
C) hospice approach
D) emergency room procedure
Answer: C
Page Ref: 507
Skill: Factual
Objective: 19.5

62) Estalee is near death and receiving palliative care. This means that she
A) will receive care aimed at relieving her pain and other symptoms, such as nausea and insomnia.
B) has agreed to life-saving measures, should her body begin to fail.
C) is probably being treated in an emergency room.
D) has no family or friends who can assist with her care.
Answer: A
Page Ref: 507
Skill: Applied
Objective: 19.5

63) Hospice care involves
A) a focus on the disease or disability to be overcome, rather than on the person.
B) keeping the patient at home or in a setting with a homelike atmosphere.
C) on-call services six days a week for approximately 20 hours per day.
D) follow-up bereavement services for the families for five years after a death.
Answer: B
Page Ref: 507
Skill: Conceptual
Objective: 19.5

64) Which of the following statements about hospice care is accurate?
- A) The majority of North Americans are familiar with the philosophy of hospice care.
- B) When it is described to them, only 10 percent of North Americans say it is the type of end-of-life care they want.
- C) Government health care benefits cover the costs of hospice care.
- D) The benefits of hospice care have not been validated through research.

Answer: C
Page Ref: 507–508
Skill: Conceptual
Objective: 19.5

65) Monica specializes in a type of music therapy that focuses on providing palliative care for the dying. Monica
- A) is a specialist in music thanatology.
- B) engages in a form of therapy unproven to be effective.
- C) probably sees no effects of her music on the patient, but rather on the patient's family members.
- D) knows that her music therapy works only on those who are feeling no pain.

Answer: A
Page Ref: 508
Skill: Applied
Objective: Box B&E: Music as Palliative Care for Dying Patients

66) Mrs. Dunn-Eagle, who is near death, has just taken part in an hour-long music vigil. Which of the following outcomes can we anticipate?
- A) a greater will to live
- B) increased wakefulness
- C) greater alertness
- D) slower, deeper, less agitated breathing

Answer: D
Page Ref: 508
Skill: Applied
Objective: Box B&E: Music as Palliative Care for Dying Patients

67) Which statement reflects the current right-to-die legislation in North America?
- A) Lack of controversy on the topic has allowed legislation to pass, guaranteeing the right to die for Canadians and Americans in a persistent vegetative state.
- B) No uniform right-to-die policy exists.
- C) Right-to-die legislation was initially passed in the 1950s, when the issue first gained national attention.
- D) Euthanasia is a practice that evolved as a result of the Terry Schiavo case.

Answer: B
Page Ref: 509
Skill: Factual
Objective: 19.6

68) __________ is the practice of ending the life of a person suffering from an incurable condition.
- A) Euthanasia
- B) Final-death experience
- C) Altruistic death fulfillment
- D) Withdrawing life support

Answer: A
Page Ref: 509
Skill: Factual
Objective: 19.6

69) When Mr. Jas slipped into a coma at the end of his battle with cancer, his family requested that his respirator and feeding tube be removed. In doing so, they were requesting
   A) durable power of attorney for health care.
   B) hospice care.
   C) passive euthanasia.
   D) voluntary active euthanasia.
   Answer: C
   Page Ref: 509
   Skill: Applied
   Objective: 19.6

70) In the United States today, passive euthanasia for patients whose death is imminent or who are in a permanent vegetative state is considered
   A) an ordinary part of normal medical practice.
   B) an unusual procedure that must be court ordered.
   C) immoral and unethical and almost never occurs.
   D) permissible only for patients who are very old.
   Answer: A
   Page Ref: 509
   Skill: Factual
   Objective: 19.6

71) __________ is a written statement of desired medical treatment should a person become incurably ill. Two types are recognized in most states.
   A) An advance medical directive
   B) A living will
   C) Durable power of attorney for health care
   D) A codicil
   Answer: A
   Page Ref: 510
   Skill: Factual
   Objective: 19.6

72) Alexa drew up a written document in which she specified the treatments she does and does not want in cases when she may be near to death. Alexa's document is a(n)
   A) durable power of attorney for health care.
   B) living will.
   C) health care plan.
   D) euthanasia directive.
   Answer: B
   Page Ref: 510
   Skill: Applied
   Objective: 19.6

73) One of Dr. Crabtree's terminally ill patients has a living will. However, Dr. Crabtree has decided not to follow it. This is common among medical professionals, primarily because
   A) of fear of legal action.
   B) the living will often lacks a formal signature.
   C) living wills are not recognized in most states.
   D) she doesn't know what a living will is.
   Answer: A
   Page Ref: 510
   Skill: Conceptual
   Objective: 19.6

74) Mr. Sainabou gave his doctors a signed and witnessed statement that appointed his daughter to make all health care decisions on his behalf, even though his death might ensue. This document was a(n)
   A) durable power of attorney for health care.
   B) living will.
   C) health care plan.
   D) euthanasia directive.
   Answer: A
   Page Ref: 510
   Skill: Applied
   Objective: 19.6

75) One important advantage of a durable power of attorney for health care over a living will is that the power of attorney
   A) will deal more flexibly with unexpected situations.
   B) will last longer than a living will without renewal.
   C) will ensure that your exact wishes are followed.
   D) is accepted in more states than living wills.
   Answer: A
   Page Ref: 510
   Skill: Factual
   Objective: 19.6

76) The durable power of attorney for medical care is particularly useful for ensuring the partner's role
   A) in states in which euthanasia is illegal.
   B) in situations other than terminal illness.
   C) in relationships not recognized or sanctioned by law.
   D) when mental as well as physical difficulties are present.
   Answer: C
   Page Ref: 510
   Skill: Factual
   Objective: 19.6

77) Jasper is a teenager with leukemia. His age prevents him from legally executing an advance medical directive, but he can utilize a __________ instead.
   A) living will
   B) health care proxy
   C) durable power of attorney
   D) treatment administrator
   Answer: B
   Page Ref: 510
   Skill: Applied
   Objective: 19.6

78) When an individual who is terminally ill requests that another person directly administer a treatment that will shorten his or her life, it is referred to as
   A) passive euthanasia.
   B) assisted suicide.
   C) voluntary active euthanasia.
   D) participatory death.
   Answer: C
   Page Ref: 510
   Skill: Factual
   Objective: 19.6

79) Which of these options for dealing with a painful terminal illness meets with the strongest resistance in the United States?

A) passive euthanasia
B) voluntary active euthanasia
C) comfort care
D) assisted suicide

Answer: D
Page Ref: 512
Skill: Factual
Objective: 19.6

80) The U.S. Supreme Court reinforced its policy of leaving assisted suicide in the hands of the states when it

A) rejected a challenge to Oregon's Death with Dignity Act.
B) overturned the right of other states to ban assisted suicide.
C) overturned the Oregon residents' vote to retain their assisted-suicide law.
D) handed down a ruling in favor of Oregon's Death with Dignity Act.

Answer: A
Page Ref: 512
Skill: Factual
Objective: 19.6

81) Which of the following statements, if true, could be used in an argument *for* assisted suicide?

A) There is no evidence of misuse of assisted suicide by doctors or caretakers, which should address the argument that people who want to live might mistakenly die.
B) Assisted suicide is less controversial than voluntary active euthanasia.
C) Thousands of Oregonians say they find comfort in knowing the option is available.
D) Thousands of Oregonians have taken advantage of their right-to-die law since its inception.

Answer: C
Page Ref: 512
Skill: Factual
Objective: 19.6

82) Which of the following statements, if true, could be used in an argument *against* assisted suicide?

A) The success rates of assisted suicides are low, resulting in terminally ill patients who are often left in more pain and discomfort after the attempt than before.
B) Only one-tenth of terminally ill patients surveyed seriously considered asking for assisted suicide; in a follow-up, many had changed their minds.
C) The most common reason for requesting assisted suicide is to relieve strain for the survivors.
D) Jack Kevorkian has recently renounced his earlier belief and advocacy for assisted suicide.

Answer: B
Page Ref: 512
Skill: Factual
Objective: 19.6

83) The experience of the death of a loved one is referred to as

A) bereavement.
B) morbidity.
C) mourning.
D) grief.

Answer: A
Page Ref: 512
Skill: Factual
Objective: 19.7

84) After Tia's sister died, she experienced intense physical and psychological distress. Tia was experiencing
A) bereavement.
B) grief.
C) a near-death experience.
D) mourning.
Answer: B
Page Ref: 512
Skill: Applied
Objective: 19.7

85) The specific expressions of the emotions associated with the death of a loved one that are specified by one's culture are called
A) bereavement.
B) grief.
C) mourning.
D) morbidity.
Answer: C
Page Ref: 512
Skill: Factual
Objective: 19.7

86) Which of the following statements about the grieving process is the most accurate?
A) People move through the three phases in a fairly orderly sequence.
B) The behavior and timing across each of the three phases is fairly consistent among people from different cultures, backgrounds, and SES levels.
C) The passage through the sequence is similar to a roller-coaster ride, with many ups and downs.
D) The recovery after someone has moved through the phases can actually happen quite quickly.
Answer: C
Page Ref: 513
Skill: Factual
Objective: 19.7

87) When Carmen first heard that her brother had died, she felt numbness and disbelief, as though she couldn't comprehend what she was told. This is typical of which phase of the bereavement process?
A) avoidance
B) accommodation
C) mourning
D) morbidity
Answer: A
Page Ref: 513
Skill: Applied
Objective: 19.7

88) Margery is experiencing the most intense grief she will feel when dealing with the death of her husband. Margery is in which phase of the grieving process?
A) restoration
B) confrontation
C) depression
D) resistance
Answer: B
Page Ref: 513
Skill: Applied
Objective: 19.7

89) Many of the reactions of the confrontation phase—such as anxiety, anger, frustration, sleeplessness, and loss of appetite—are symptoms of
   A) depression, an invariable component of grieving.
   B) avoidance.
   C) mourning, a necessary phase of grieving.
   D) poor coping strategies.
   Answer: A
   Page Ref: 513
   Skill: Factual
   Objective: 19.7

90) After her husband's death, Chevon was forced to adjust to other stressors that included handling the finances (a task that he had done) and raising their two boys alone. Once she began addressing these issues, Chevon moved into the __________ phase.
   A) accommodation
   B) avoidance
   C) confrontation
   D) restoration
   Answer: D
   Page Ref: 513
   Skill: Applied
   Objective: 19.7

91) According to the __________, effective coping requires people to oscillate between dealing with the emotional consequences of death and attending to life changes, which—when handled successfully—have restorative, or healing, effects.
   A) Lund Stages of Grief
   B) dual-process model of coping with loss
   C) anticipatory grieving phase
   D) emotional-applied theory of loss recovery
   Answer: B
   Page Ref: 513
   Skill: Factual
   Objective: 19.7

92) Which of these groups experiences a higher mortality rate?
   A) bereaved women
   B) bereaved men
   C) bereaved children
   D) parents whose child has died
   Answer: B
   Page Ref: 513
   Skill: Factual
   Objective: 19.7

93) Mrs. Waldschmidt's husband was killed in a carjacking. Because his death was so sudden and unanticipated, she would be expected to experience particularly traumatic stress during the __________ phase.
   A) accommodation
   B) avoidance
   C) confrontation
   D) mourning
   Answer: C
   Page Ref: 513
   Skill: Applied
   Objective: 19.7

94) Martha's mother is terminally ill and is expected to live for six more months. Because Martha can acknowledge that this loss is inevitable and even prepare for it emotionally allows her to engage in
A) near-death experience.
B) preliminary loss.
C) anticipatory grieving.
D) secondary mourning.
Answer: C
Page Ref: 514
Skill: Applied
Objective: 19.7

95) __________ complicate(s) grieving, particularly after acts such as suicide or a school shooting.
A) Feelings of anger
B) Prolonged avoidance
C) The concept of a "senseless" death
D) Large outpourings of support
Answer: C
Page Ref: 514
Skill: Factual
Objective: 19.7

96) Recovery from grief after a __________ is more prolonged than for other unanticipated deaths, due to feelings of __________.
A) school shooting; anger
B) suicide; guilt
C) terrorist attack; anger and fear
D) natural disaster; avoidance
Answer: B
Page Ref: 514
Skill: Factual
Objective: 19.7

97) Which sort of bereavement is typically the most intense and long-lasting?
A) death of a husband
B) death of a wife
C) death of a sibling
D) death of a child
Answer: D
Page Ref: 514
Skill: Factual
Objective: 19.7

98) One way in which children frequently cope with the death of close family members is to
A) think about and mentally speak to them regularly.
B) avoid thinking about or remembering them too often.
C) put the blame for the death onto some "bad" person.
D) imagine that they have just stepped out and will return.
Answer: A
Page Ref: 514
Skill: Factual
Objective: 19.7

99) Parents of young children who are dealing with the death of a loved one would be best advised to
   A) remove the children from the household until the death is over, and keep the truth from them even when they return.
   B) give them careful, repeated explanations assuring them that the person did not want to die and was not angry with them.
   C) keep the truth from them as long as possible so they will not worry.
   D) use comforting phrases such as "he's going to be with the angels."
Answer: B
Page Ref: 514
Skill: Factual
Objective: 19.7

100) Celeste's partner, Nadine, has just died. Nadine's family never approved of their relationship and will not allow Celeste to take part in or attend the funeral services. Without the opportunity to mourn publicly and benefit from others' support, Celeste is at risk for
   A) anticipatory grieving.
   B) unestablished bereavement.
   C) bereavement overload.
   D) disenfranchised grief.
Answer: D
Page Ref: 515
Skill: Applied
Objective: 19.7

101) Carson lost several members of his family in a recent flood. He is at risk for
   A) mourning failure.
   B) disenfranchised grief.
   C) bereavement overload.
   D) morbidity intensification.
Answer: C
Page Ref: 515
Skill: Applied
Objective: 19.8

102) When people you care about have recently experienced the death of a loved one, your best response is to provide
   A) privacy to be alone with their feelings.
   B) advice about how they should react.
   C) encouragement to return to normal life.
   D) sympathetic listening and simple presence.
Answer: D
Page Ref: 515
Skill: Factual
Objective: 19.8

103) Stephen witnessed the death of his teacher, who was killed in a school shooting. Effective intervention for Stephen should
   A) include reexposure to the incident to help him confront his fears.
   B) deemphasize cultural sensitivity, as this is not a factor.
   C) assist parents and teachers with their own distress so they can effectively offer comfort.
   D) provide him with lots of advice on how he should hasten his recovery.
Answer: C
Page Ref: 517
Skill: Applied
Objective: 19.8

104) Kelvin is undergoing grief therapy to help him deal with the death of his fiancée. His therapist will likely try to help Kelvin

A) see benefits of the grieving experience, perhaps by discovering his capacity to cope with adversity.
B) move through the grieving process quickly.
C) find a replacement relationship, such as a new friend or mentor.
D) develop a memorial to his girlfriend as a way of telling her all the things he didn't, but wishes he could.

Answer: A
Page Ref: 517
Skill: Applied
Objective: 19.8

105) One of the goals of death education is

A) training doctors in modern techniques for avoiding death.
B) encouraging an active approach, such as assisted suicide.
C) creating informed consumers of medical and funeral services.
D) promoting a more spiritual view of both life and death.

Answer: C
Page Ref: 517
Skill: Factual
Objective: 19.9

106) One primary function of all cultural rituals surrounding death is to

A) commemorate the deceased, providing social support for the bereaved.
B) help mourners achieve control and avoid expressing their grief.
C) reassure the assembled people of the reality of life after death.
D) remind the assembled people of their own impending mortality.

Answer: A
Page Ref: 516
Skill: Factual
Objective: Box CI: Cultural Variations in Mourning Behavior

107) A relatively new trend in memorials to the deceased on the Internet

A) is considered by most family members to be an impersonal way to remember someone.
B) allow mourners to convey their thoughts and feelings whenever they feel ready, at little or no cost.
C) appears to be losing its popularity.
D) has spawned an additional new trend where dying individuals request online memorials only, in hopes of sparing family members the costs of a large ceremony.

Answer: B
Page Ref: 516
Skill: Factual
Objective: Box CI: Cultural Variations in Mourning Behavior

108) Research indicates that the LEAST effective method of providing death education is

A) a program to help students confront their own mortality.
B) discussions with terminally ill patients and their families.
C) visits to mortuaries, cemeteries, and funeral homes.
D) lectures giving factual information about the dying process.

Answer: D
Page Ref: 517–518
Skill: Factual
Objective: 19.9

ESSAY

109) List three reasons why societies need a definition of death.

Answer: 1) To help doctors decide when life-saving measures should be terminated

2) To signal survivors that they must begin to grieve their loss and reorganize their lives

3) To establish when donated organs can be removed.

Page Ref: 500

110) Explain why some experts want to change the brain activity-related criteria that currently declare a person dead.

Answer: Today, brain death, defined as irreversible cessation of all activity in the brain and the brain stem (which controls reflexes), is used in most industrialized nations. The brain death standard, however, does not solve the dilemma of when to halt treatment. Consider an individual who, though not brain dead, had entered a persistent vegetative state. Doctors were sure they could not restore consciousness or body movement. Because thousands of North Americans are in a persistent vegetative state, with health care costs totaling many millions of dollars annually, some experts believe that absence of activity in the cerebral cortex should be sufficient to declare a person dead. Others, however, point to a few cases in which patients who were vegetative for months regained consciousness, although usually with very limited functioning.

Page Ref: 500

111) Mr. Caussanei is dying. Why is it important for his daughter to be honest with him about his condition? Why is it important for his doctors to also be candid regarding his condition?

Answer: Delivering candid information about death's certainty from loved ones and doctors is important for several reasons. Unless people are aware that they are dying and understand (so far as possible) the likely circumstances of their death, they cannot plan for end-of-life care and decision making and share the sentiments that bring closure to relationships they hold most dear.

Doctors and nurses can help dying people learn enough about their condition to make reasoned choices about whether to fight on or say no to further treatment. An understanding of how the normal body works simplifies comprehension of how disease affects it—education that can begin as early as the childhood years.

Page Ref: 500–501

112) Explain the concept of *appropriate death,* and what most patients would like when asked about a "good death."

Answer: An appropriate death is one that makes sense in terms of the individual's pattern of living and values and, at the same time, preserves or restores significant relationships and is as free of suffering as possible. When asked about a "good death," most patients mention the following goals: maintaining a sense of identity, or inner continuity with one's past; clarifying the meaning of one's life and death; maintaining and enhancing relationships; achieving a sense of control over the time that remains; and confronting and preparing for death.

Page Ref: 504

113) Mr. Wiata, who is terminally ill, is a member of the Maori tribe of New Zealand. How will his community respond to his condition?

Answer: Relatives and friends will gather around him to give spiritual strength and comfort. Elders, clergy, and other experts in tribal customs conduct a *karakia* ceremony, in which they recite prayers asking for peace, mercy, and guidance from the creator. After the ceremony, the patient is encouraged to discuss important matters with those closest to him—giving away of personal belongings, directions for interment, and other unfinished tasks.

Page Ref: 506

114) Briefly discuss considerations to take into account when considering a person's wish to die at home.
Answer: Because of dramatic improvements in medicine, dying people are sicker or much older than they used to be. Consequently, their bodies may be extremely frail, making ordinary activities—eating, sleeping, taking a pill, toileting, and bathing—major ordeals. For many people, the chance to be with the dying person until the very end is a rewarding tradeoff for the high stress of caregiving. But the advantages and disadvantages of home death should be carefully weighed before undertaking it. Adequate support for the caregiver is essential. A home health aide is often necessary—a service that hospice programs have made more accessible. When family relationships are conflict-ridden, a dying patient introduces additional strains, negating the benefits of home death. Finally, even with professional help, most homes are poorly equipped to handle the medical and comfort-care needs of the dying.
Page Ref: 506

115) List the main features of the hospice approach.
Answer: The patient and family as a unit of care

Emphasis on meeting the patient's physical, emotional, social, and spiritual needs, including controlling pain, retaining dignity and self-worth, and feeling cared for and loved

Care provided by an interdisciplinary team, including the patient's doctor; a nurse or nurse's aide; a chaplain, counselor, or social worker; and a pharmacist

The patient kept at home or in an inpatient setting with a homelike atmosphere where coordination of care is possible

Focus on protecting the quality of remaining life with palliative, or comfort, care that relieves pain and other symptoms (such as nausea, breathing difficulties, insomnia, and depression) rather than prolonging life

Regularly scheduled home care visits, as well as on-call services available 24 hours a day, 7 days a week

Follow-up bereavement services for families in the year after a death
Page Ref: 507

116) Explain why individuals in young and middle adulthood have a much harder time coping with the death of a spouse than their elder counterparts.
Answer: After a period of intense grieving, most widowed elders in Western nations fare well, but younger individuals display more negative outcomes. Loss of a spouse or partner in early or middle adulthood is a nonnormative event that profoundly disrupts life plans. Finding a positive new direction as a single person is harder than it is for widowed elders. Older widows and widowers have many more contemporaries in similar circumstances. In addition to dealing with feelings of loss, young and middle-aged widows and widowers often must assume a greater role in comforting others, especially children. They also face the stresses of single parenthood and rapid shrinking of the social network established during their life as a couple.
Page Ref: 515

STUDY QUESTIONS

How We Die

Physical Changes

1. True or False: Most people experience a quick, agony-free death. Explain your answer. (p. 499)

____

____

____

2. Describe physical and behavioral changes in the days or hours before death. (p. 500)

3. Describe the three phases of dying. (p. 500)

   Agonal phase:

   Clinical death:

   Mortality:

Defining Death

1. What definition of death is currently used in most industrialized nations? (p. 500)

2. Describe the definition of death used by doctors in Japan, citing cultural beliefs that have led Japan to use this definition. (p. 500)

3. Explain why the brain death standard does not solve the dilemma of when to halt treatment. (p. 500)

Death with Dignity

1. Summarize three ways that we can foster dignity in death. (pp. 500–501)

   A.

   B.

   C.

Attitudes Toward Death

1. Compared with earlier generations, today more young people reach adulthood (with / without) having experienced the death of someone they know well. (p. 501)
2. What is *death anxiety*? (p. 501)

____

____

3. Research reveals (few / large) individual and cultural differences in the anxiety-provoking aspects of death. (p. 501)
4. Identify two personal factors that minimize death anxiety. (p. 502)

   A. ____

   ____

   B. ____

   ____

5. Death anxiety (declines / increases) with age, reaching its (highest / lowest) level in late adulthood. What accounts for this trend? (p. 502)

____

____

6. Explain how death anxiety can motivate people in positive ways. (p. 502)

____

____

7. Regardless of age, cross-cultural studies show that (men / women) are more anxious about death. (p. 502)
8. Explain the link between death anxiety and mental health. (p. 502)

____

____

9. Children (frequently / rarely) display death anxiety. Cite exceptions. (p. 502)

____

____

Thinking and Emotions of Dying People

Do Stages of Dying Exist?

1. List and describe Kübler-Ross's five typical responses to dying, and explain how family members and health professionals can best react to the first four. (p. 503)

   A. ____

   Reactions: ____

   ____

   B. ____

   Reactions: ____

   ____

C. ______________________________

Reactions: ______________________________

____

D. ______________________________

Reactions: ______________________________

____

E. ______________________________

2. True or False: Kübler-Ross viewed the responses listed above as a fixed sequence that is universally experienced by all individuals. (p. 503)

3. Summarize criticisms of Kübler-Ross's theory. (pp. 503–504)

____

____

____

Contextual Influences on Adaptations to Dying

1. Describe an *appropriate death.* (p. 504)

____

____

____

2. Cite five goals that patients mention when asked about a "good death." (p. 504)

A. ______________________________

B. ______________________________

C. ______________________________

D. ______________________________

E. ______________________________

3. True or False: Dying people display similar reactions, regardless of the nature of their disease. (p. 504)

4. True or False: The way an individual views stressful life events and has coped with them in the past is likely to be closely related to the way the person manages the dying process. (p. 504)

5. A candid approach, in which those close to and caring for the dying person acknowledge the terminal illness, is (ill-advised / recommended). (p. 505)

6. True or False: In Asia and the Middle East, it is common for doctors to withhold information about a dying patient's prognosis. (p. 505)

7. Describe features of effective communication with dying people. (p. 505)

____

____

____

8. Explain how Buddhist practices and beliefs foster acceptance of death. (p. 505)

____

____

9. Describe beliefs and customs, guided by religious ideas, that shape dying experiences in the following cultures. (p. 506)

   Native-American: ____

   ____

   African-American: ____

   ____

   Maori of New Zealand: ____

   ____

A Place to Die

Home

1. True or False: Eighty to 90 percent of North Americans would prefer to die at home; however, only about one-fourth of Canadians and one-fifth of Americans experience home death. (p. 506)
2. Summarize the advantages and disadvantages of dying at home. (p. 506)

   Advantages: ____

   ____

   Disadvantages: ____

   ____

3. True or False: Family members report more prolonged psychological stress following a home death than a death that occurred elsewhere. (p. 506)

Hospital

1. How can emergency room staff help family members cope with the sudden loss of a loved one? (p. 507)

   ____

   ____

2. Patients with (cancer / cardiovascular disease) account for most cases of prolonged dying. (p. 507)
3. Explain the conflict of values between dying patients and health professionals in hospital settings, especially in intensive care units. (p. 507)

   ____

   ____

4. True or False: The majority of U.S. hospitals have comprehensive treatment programs to ease physical, emotional, and spiritual pain at the end of life. (p. 507)

The Hospice Approach

1. Describe the hospice approach, noting its seven main features. (p. 507)

   Description: ____

   ____

   A. ____

   B. ____

   C. ____

   D. ____

   E. ____

   F. ____

   G. ____

2. What is *palliative care*? (p. 507)

   ____

   ____

3. Hospice programs offer a continuum of care. Explain what this means. (p. 507)

   ____

   ____

   ____

4. Explain how hospice care contributes to improvements in family functioning. (p. 508)

   ____

   ____

5. The majority of North Americans (are / are not) familiar with the philosophy of the hospice approach. (p. 508)

Biology and Environment: Music as Palliative Care for Dying Patients

1. Define *music thanatology.* (p. 508)

   ____

   ____

2. How is music applied in palliative care? (p. 508)

   ____

   ____

3. True or False: Since hearing typically functions longer than other senses, an individual may be responsive to music until his or her final moments. (p. 508)

The Right to Die

1. The United States and Canada (do / do not) have uniform right-to-die policies. (p. 509)
2. Define *euthanasia,* and list its four forms. (p. 509)

   Definition: ______________________________

   ____

   A. ______________________________

   B. ______________________________

   C. ______________________________

   D. ______________________________

Passive Euthanasia

1. Define *passive euthanasia.* (p. 509)

   ____

   ____

2. True or False: When there is no hope of recovery, the majority of North Americans support the patient's or family members' right to end treatment. (p. 509)
3. Passive euthanasia (is / is not) widely practiced as part of ordinary medical procedure. (p. 509)
4. (Religion / Ethnicity) strongly contributes to people's views of passive euthanasia. (pp. 509–510)
5. Without a national consensus on passive euthanasia, how can people best ensure that their wishes will be followed if they become terminally ill or fall into a persistent vegetative state? (p. 510)

   ____

   ____

   ____

6. Name and describe two types of *advance directives* recognized in U.S. states and Canadian provinces. (p. 510)

   A. ______________________________

   ____

   B. ______________________________

   ____

7. Cite two reasons why living wills do not guarantee personal control over treatment. (p. 510)

   A. ______________________________

   ____

   B. ______________________________

   ____

8. The durable power of attorney for health care is (more / less) flexible than the living will. Explain your answer. (p. 510)

____

____

____

9. True or False: Over 70 percent of North Americans have executed a living will or durable power of attorney. (p. 510)

Voluntary Active Euthanasia

1. True or False: *Voluntary active euthanasia* is a criminal offense in most countries, including almost all U.S. states and Canada. (p. 510)
2. True or False: About 70 to 90 percent of people in Western nations approve of voluntary active euthanasia. (pp. 510–511)
3. Summarize the controversy over the legalization of voluntary active euthanasia. (p. 511)

____

____

____

Assisted Suicide

1. True or False: Assisted suicide is tacitly accepted in many Western European countries. (p. 512)
2. Describe Oregon's Death with Dignity Act. (p. 512)

____

____

____

3. True or False: 75 percent of North Americans approve of assisted suicide. (p. 512)
4. Briefly describe dilemmas associated with assisted suicide. (p. 512)

____

____

5. Public opinion consistently favors (active euthanasia/assisted suicide) over (active euthanasia/assisted suicide). (p. 512)

Bereavement: Coping with the Death of a Loved One

1. Distinguish among *bereavement, grief*, and *mourning*. (p. 512)

Bereavement: ____

____

Grief: ____

____

Mourning: ____

____

Grief Process

1. List four tasks of the grieving process that help people recover and return to a fulfilling life. (p. 513)

   A. ______________________________

   B. ______________________________

   C. ______________________________

   D. ______________________________

2. Match each of the following grief reactions with the appropriate description. (p. 513)

   _____ The bereaved individual must balance emotional consequences of his/her loss with attending to life changes associated with the loved one's death.
   _____ A numbed feeling serves as "emotional anesthesia."
   _____ The mourner confronts the reality of the loss and experiences a cascade of emotional reactions.
   _____ The bereaved individual yearns for the deceased and obsessively reviews the circumstances of the death.
   _____ The mourner may show a variety of behavioral changes, including absent-mindedness, poor concentration, self-destructive behavior, and/or depression.
   _____ Emotional energy shifts toward life-restoring pursuits.
   _____ The bereaved person experiences shock followed by disbelief and is unable to comprehend the death.

   1. Avoidance loss
   2. Confrontation
   3. Restoration

3. True or False: Grieving can accurately be described as a fixed series of three phases. (p. 513)

4. Describe the *dual-process model of coping with loss*. (p. 513)

   ____

   ____

   ____

Personal and Situational Variations

1. True or False: Compared with men, bereaved women typically express distress and depression less directly and seek less social support. (p. 513)

2. Explain differences in grieving when death is sudden and unexpected versus prolonged and expected. (pp. 513–514)

   Sudden and unexpected: ______________________________

   ____

   Prolonged and expected: ______________________________

   ____

3. What is *anticipatory grieving*? (p. 514)

   ____

   ____

4. Compared with survivors of other sudden deaths, people grieving a suicidal loss are (more / less) likely to blame themselves for what happened. (p. 514)

5. List three reasons why the death of a child is the most difficult loss an adult can face. (p. 514)

   A. ______________________________

   B. ______________________________

   C. ______________________________

6. Why is the loss of a family member likely to have long-standing consequences for children? (p. 514)

   ____

   ____

   ____

7. Briefly describe the physical symptoms often displayed by children who are grieving the loss of a family member. (p. 514)

   ____

   ____

   ____

8. True or False: When children maintain mental contact with a deceased parent or sibling by dreaming about or speaking to the loved one, this hinders the child's ability to cope with the loss. (p. 514)

9. Describe the link between cognitive development and children's ability to grieve, noting how adults can help young children better understand the person's death. (p. 514)

   ____

   ____

   ____

10. Grief-stricken (school-age children / adolescents) tend to keep their grieving from both adults and peers, often leading to depression and attempts to escape the grief through acting out behavior. (p. 515)

11. Younger adults display (more / fewer) negative outcomes than older adults following the death of a spouse. Explain your answer. (p. 515)

    ____

    ____

12. Describe the unique challenges that gay and lesbian partners face when they experience the death of an intimate partner, including disenfranchised grief. (p. 515)

    ____

    ____

    ____

13. Describe *bereavement overload*, and note how it influences one's ability to cope with grief. (p. 515)

    Description: ______________________________

    ____

    Impact: ______________________________

    ____

14. Identify three groups of individuals who are at risk for bereavement overload. (p. 515)

A. ______________________________

B. ______________________________

C. ______________________________

Cultural Influences: Cultural Variations in Mourning Behavior

1. Describe mourning behaviors and beliefs about death in the following religious and cultural groups. (p. 516)

Jews: ______________________________

____

Quakers: ______________________________

____

African Americans: ______________________________

____

Balinese of Indonesia: ______________________________

____

2. Summarize the benefits of Internet, or Web, memorials. (p. 516)

____

____

____

Bereavement Interventions

1. List five suggestions for resolving grief following the death of a loved one. (p. 517)

A. ______________________________

____

B. ______________________________

____

C. ______________________________

____

D. ______________________________

____

E. ______________________________

____

2. Self-help groups that bring together mourners who have experienced the same type of loss (are / are not) highly effective for reducing stress. (p. 517)

3. Describe characteristics of bereavement interventions for children and adolescents. (p. 517)

____

____

____

4. Cite four instances in which grief therapy may be necessary to help the mourner overcome his/her loss. (p. 517)

   A. ____

   B. ____

   C. ____

   D. ____

Death Education

1. List four goals of death education. (p. 517)

   A. ____

   B. ____

   C. ____

   D. ____

2. Compared to lecture-style programs, experiential programs that help people confront their own mortality are (less / more) likely to heighten death anxiety. (p. 518)

PUZZLE 19.1

Across

1. __________ death: irreversible cessation of all activity in the brain and brain stem
4. Persistent __________ state: cerebral cortex no longer registers electrical activity, but the brain stem remains active
6. __________ euthanasia: withholding or withdrawing life-sustaining treatment, permitting the patient to die naturally
8. __________ will: written statement specifying the treatments a person does or does not want in case of terminal illness, coma, or other near-death situation
9. Phase of dying in which an individual passes into permanent death
10. Durable power of __________ for health care: written statement that authorizes another person to make health care decisions on one's behalf in case of incompetence
11. Practice of ending the life of a person suffering from an incurable condition

Down

2. __________ medical directive: written statement of desired medical treatment should a person become incurably ill
3. Voluntary __________ euthanasia: practice of ending a patient's suffering, at the patient's request, before a natural end to life
5. __________ death: a death that makes sense in terms of the person's pattern of living and values, and at the same time, preserves or restores significant relationships and is as free of suffering as possible
7. __________ death: phase of dying in which heartbeat, circulation, breathing, and brain functioning stop, but resuscitation is still possible

PUZZLE 19.2

Across

2. Culturally specified expression of a bereaved person's thoughts and feelings
3. Comprehensive program of support services that focuses on meeting terminally ill patients' physical, emotional, social, and spiritual needs and that offers follow-up bereavement services to families
5. __________ care: aimed at relieving pain and other symptoms in terminally ill patients in order to protect the person's quality of life rather than prolonging life
6. Death __________: fear and apprehension of death
7. The experience of losing a loved one by death
8. __________-__________ model of coping: oscillation between dealing with emotional consequences of loss and attending to life changes

Down

1. __________ grieving: acknowledging that the loss is inevitable and preparing emotionally for it
4. Intense physical and psychological distress following a loss
9. Phase of dying in which gasps and muscle spasms occur during the first moments in which the body cannot sustain life anymore

CROSSWORD PUZZLE SOLUTIONS

PUZZLE 19.1

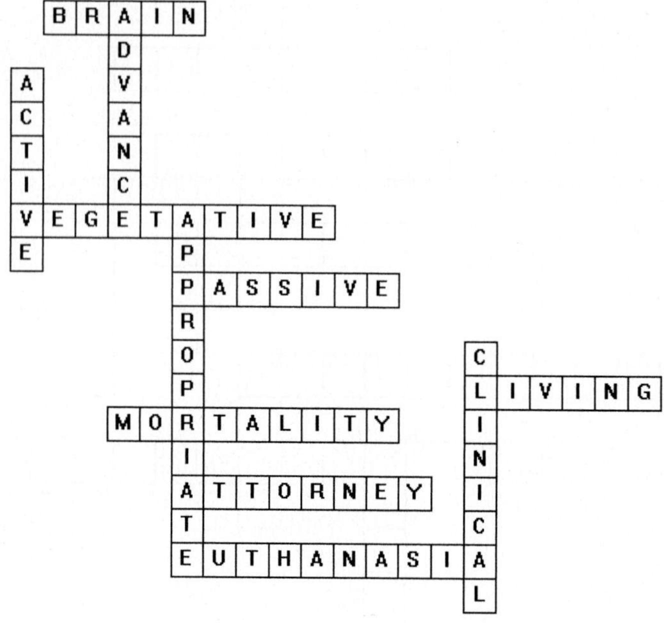

PUZZLE 19.2

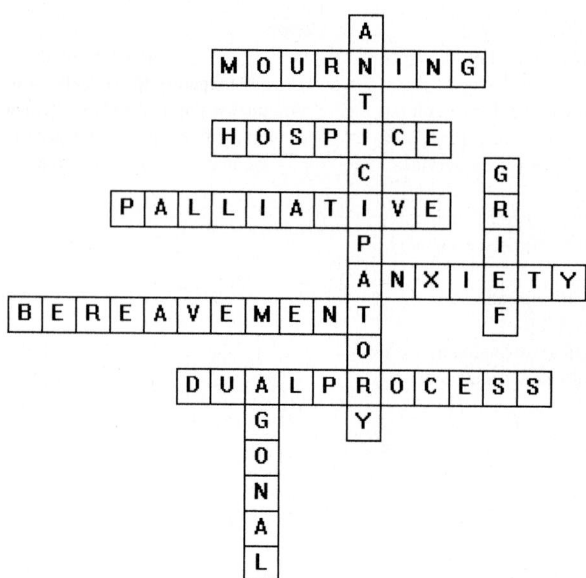

PRACTICE TEST #1

1. Death is long and drawn out for what percentage of people? (p. 499)
   a. 50%
   b. 66%
   c. 75%
   d. 90%

2. The definition of death that is currently used in most industrialized nations is (p. 500)
   a. loss of heartbeat and respiration.
   b. lack of activity in the cerebral cortex, even if the brain stem remains active.
   c. irreversible cessation of all activity in the brain and the brain stem.
   d. muscle spasms indicating that the body can no longer sustain life.

3. "Death with dignity" refers to (pp. 500–501)
   a. dying in one's sleep.
   b. receiving sufficient medication to ease pain during a prolonged death.
   c. dying at home, where one is likely to be most comfortable.
   d. being well informed about one's condition and receiving assurance of support and compassionate care.

4. Who among the following Westerns is LEAST likely to experience death anxiety? (p. 502)
   a. a religiously committed woman
   b. an adult with deep faith in a higher being
   c. an adult with contradictory religious beliefs and behaviors
   d. an adolescent with no personal philosophy on death

5. Death anxiety is largely limited to (p. 502)
   a. adolescence and adulthood.
   b. childhood.
   c. extreme old age.
   d. men of any age.

6. Elisabeth Kübler-Ross's stages of dying (p. 504)
   a. should be viewed as a fixed sequence displayed by all individuals.
   b. provide an exhaustive list of people's responses to death.
   c. are best viewed as coping strategies that individuals can call on in the face of threat.
   d. do not accurately represent people's reactions to their own impending death.

7. Which of the following statements accurately describes how those who are terminally ill cope with impending death? (pp. 504–505)
   a. They almost never come to accept their fate.
   b. They use diverse coping strategies, influenced by personality and by others' responses.
   c. At first, they are usually depressed.
   d. They rarely show anger about impending death.

8. When asked to describe a "good death," dying patients typically say that they hope to (p. 504)
   a. maintain a sense of identity, or inner continuity with their past.
   b. achieve financial autonomy before they die.
   c. avoid death as long as they possibly can.
   d. find spiritual guidance in their remaining days.

9. In communicating with a dying person, it is best to (p. 505)
   a. give only vague information about the diagnosis and the course of the disease.
   b. avoid any discussion of death-related issues.
   c. discourage the person from maintaining hope, because a favorable outcome is unlikely.
   d. foster a trusting relationship by listening attentively and accepting the person's feelings.

10. Which of the following statements about dying at home is true? (p. 506)
    a. Home is the least stressful place to care for a dying person.
    b. Although most older adults would prefer to die at home, they express concern about the burden placed on family members.
    c. A home death often leads to deterioration in relationships between the dying person and caregivers.
    d. Most homes are better suited than hospitals to handling the comfort-care needs of the dying.

11. One disadvantage of dying in a hospital is that (p. 507)
    a. a hospital death places high physical, psychological, and financial demands on caregivers.
    b. family members experience more prolonged psychological distress when a loved one dies in the hospital rather than at home.
    c. privacy and communication with family members are secondary to monitoring the patient's condition.
    d. hospitals tend to overemphasize palliative care.

12. Central to the hospice approach is that the dying person and his or her family be offered (p. 507)
    a. choices that guarantee an appropriate death.
    b. choices that guarantee an end to life free of death anxiety.
    c. an array of life-saving treatments regardless of cost.
    d. care at home, rather than in inpatient settings like hospitals and nursing homes.

13. The right of a dying patient or family members to choose passive euthanasia (p. 509)
    a. receives almost no support from Catholics because it is seen as a first step toward government-approved mercy killing.
    b. has similar levels of support across all North American ethnic groups.
    c. has very little support in North America because of controversial cases like that of Terri Schiavo.
    d. is supported by more than three-fourths of North Americans in cases where there is no hope of recovery.

14. The best way for people to ensure that they will have access to passive euthanasia should they desire it is by (p. 510)
    a. asking their doctors to record their wishes in their medical file.
    b. informing a close friend or relative.
    c. preparing and signing a living will.
    d. preparing and signing a durable power of attorney.

15. Assisting a suicide is (p. 512)
    a. legal in Canada.
    b. legal in all U.S. states.
    c. illegal in many, but not all, U.S. states.
    d. illegal in Germany.

16. Among the various forms of euthanasia, North Americans are LEAST supportive of (p. 512)
    a. voluntary passive euthanasia.
    b. voluntary active euthanasia.
    c. assisted suicide.
    d. all forms.

17. Theorists formerly believed that bereaved individuals moved through three phases of grieving. A more accurate account, however, compares grief to a (p. 513)
    a. roller-coaster ride, with many ups and downs.
    b. pinwheel, with many points of spinning emotions.
    c. washing machine, with anger, fear, and frustration all mixing together.
    d. rocket launch, with a huge surge of emotion followed by a settling-down period.

18. The major difference between a sudden, unexpected death and a prolonged death is that when dying is prolonged, the bereaved person has had time to engage in (pp. 513–514)
    a. restoration.
    b. dual-process coping.
    c. anticipatory grieving.
    d. confrontation.

19. Bereavement interventions typically (pp. 515, 517)
    a. advise people to reflect on their loss internally and privately.
    b. discourage people from involving themselves in self-help groups.
    c. encourage people to draw on their existing social network.
    d. are ineffective in relieving stress or anxiety about a loss.

20. Compared to lecture-format death education programs, experiential programs are (pp. 517–518)
    a. less likely to heighten death anxiety and may sometimes reduce it.
    b. more likely to result in gains in knowledge about the death process.
    c. less likely to help people confront their own mortality.
    d. more likely to heighten death anxiety by exposing people to the reality of death.

PRACTICE TEST #2

1. Technological advances have changed our thinking about death by (p. 499)
    a. providing reliable ways to restore functioning when an individual is in a persistent vegetative state.
    b. providing so many means of keeping death at bay that death has become a forbidden topic for many people.
    c. providing a clear, universally accepted definition of the end of life.
    d. easing the acceptance of death by providing increased scientific understanding of the death process.

2. About ___ percent of people experience a quick, agony-free death. (p. 499)
    a. 80
    b. 45
    c. 20
    d. 5

3. Resuscitation is NOT possible in (p. 500)
    a. brain death.
    b. clinical death.
    c. the agonal phase of death.
    d. a persistent vegetative state.

4. Compared with earlier generations, today's children and adolescents in industrialized nations are (p. 501)
    a. more comfortable dealing with death because they play a greater role in caring for dying family members.
    b. more accepting of death because they see frequent images of death in TV shows, movies and videos, and news reports.
    c. less likely to experience death anxiety because of their heightened religious awareness.
    d. more insulated from death because they are more likely to reach adulthood without experiencing the death of someone they know well.

5. Death anxiety (p. 502)
    a. increases with age, as individuals experience more deaths of family and friends.
    b. declines with age, reaching its lowest level in late adulthood.
    c. is greater in men than in women.
    d. is an individual trait that remains stable from childhood into late adulthood.

6. __________ predicts low death anxiety (p. 502)
   a. Terminal illness in children
   b. Physical health in adulthood
   c. Symbolic immortality
   d. Religiousness

7. A patient who __________ is most likely to cope well with dying and attain the goals of an appropriate death. (p. 505)
   a. feels she has much unfinished business to attend to
   b. has family members who participate in the patient's denial
   c. views dying as part of life's journey
   d. experiences an extended disease, accompanied by depression

8. Effective communication with the dying should include (p. 505)
   a. withholding information about the terminal nature of the illness, to reduce anxiety.
   b. gradually withdrawing social support, to help the dying person separate permanently from family members.
   c. avoiding family "unfinished business," to ease the stress of dying.
   d. building a trusting relationship that maintains hope as long as possible.

9. When a dying person feels a strong sense of spirituality, it tends to produce (p. 505)
   a. less fear of death.
   b. more anger at God for not preventing one's death.
   c. confusion and distress about what dying really means.
   d. anger and resentment toward those who go on living.

10. Today, about ______ percent of deaths in the United States and ______ percent in Canada take place in hospitals. (p. 506)
    a. 50; 40
    b. 60; 60
    c. 70; 80
    d. 80; 70

11. Eighty to 90 percent of North Americans say that they would prefer to die (p. 506)
    a. at home.
    b. in a hospital.
    c. in a hospice.
    d. in a doctor's office.

12. The central belief of the hospice approach is that (p. 507)
    a. medical choices should be made by an objective third party in order to ease the psychological strain on the dying person and his or her family.
    b. quality of life is the most important issue surrounding a person's journey toward death.
    c. terminally ill patients should always be able to die in their own homes.
    d. contact with family members should be secondary to monitoring the condition of the dying patient.

13. In North America, use of passive euthanasia for terminally ill patients and those in a persistent vegetative state is considered (p. 509)
    a. immoral and unethical.
    b. an extreme procedure that must be approved by the courts.
    c. permissible only for the most elderly patients.
    d. an ordinary part of normal medical practice.

14. In case of a terminal illness, coma, or other near-death situation, people specify the treatments they do or don't want in a(n) (p. 510)
    a. durable power of attorney for health care.
    b. living will.
    c. health care proxy.
    d. advance medical directive.

15. The U.S. state of ____________ has passed a law, the Death with Dignity Act, that allows physicians to prescribe drugs so that terminally ill patients can end their own lives. (p. 512)
    a. California
    b. New York
    c. Oregon
    d. Massachusetts

16. Grief refers to (p. 512)
    a. acknowledging that loss is inevitable.
    b. the experience of losing a loved one by death.
    c. culturally specified expressions of the bereaved person's thoughts and feelings.
    d. intense physical and psychological distress.

17. Adjusting to death is easier when (p. 514)
    a. the survivor understands the reasons for the death.
    b. the death is sudden and unanticipated.
    c. the death is the result of a suicide.
    d. a person experiences several deaths in close succession.

18. Compared to those grieving other types of loss, people who have lost a loved one to suicide are (p. 514)
    a. less likely to feel profound guilt and shame.
    b. more likely to conclude that they contributed to or could have prevented the death.
    c. likely to self-blame only if their religion condemns suicides as immoral.
    d. more likely to get over the bereavement period quickly.

19. Children who experience the loss of a parent or sibling (p. 514)
    a. adjust quickly because they cannot yet comprehend the permanence of the loss.
    b. respond best when adults tell them that the missing family member has merely gone to sleep.
    c. should be discouraged from maintaining mental contact with the deceased, such as by dreaming about or speaking to the person regularly.
    d. often display persistent mild depression, anxiety, and angry outbursts.

20. One of the best ways to help a grieving person is by (p. 515)
    a. giving advice aimed at hastening recovery.
    b. discussing one's own experiences with death.
    c. listening sympathetically and "just being there."
    d. encouraging the person to spend some time alone.

POWERPOINT SLIDES

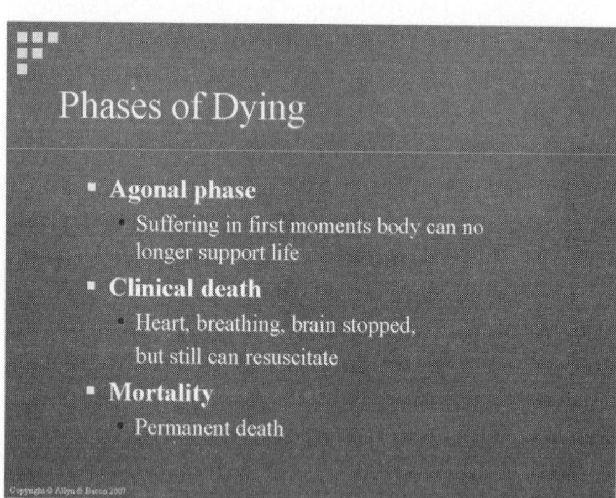

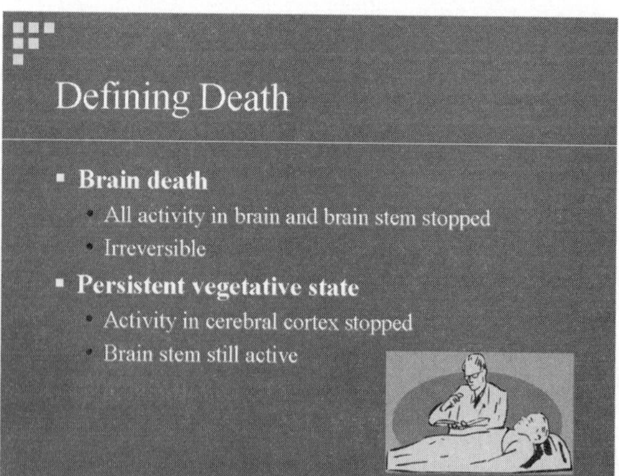

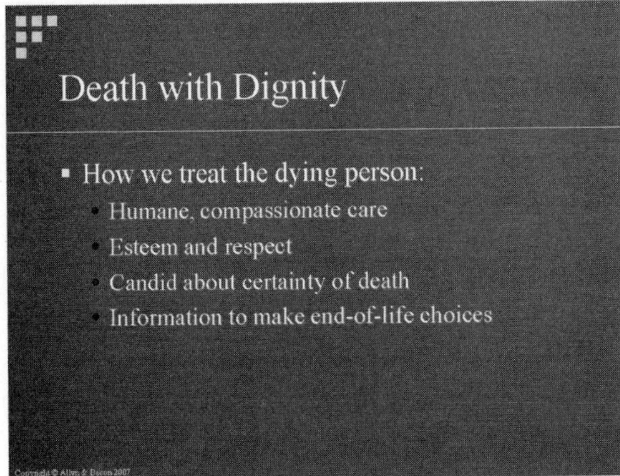
Death with Dignity
How we treat the dying person:
Humane, compassionate care
Esteem and respect
Candid about certainty of death
Information to make end-of-life choices
Copyright © Allyn & Bacon 2007

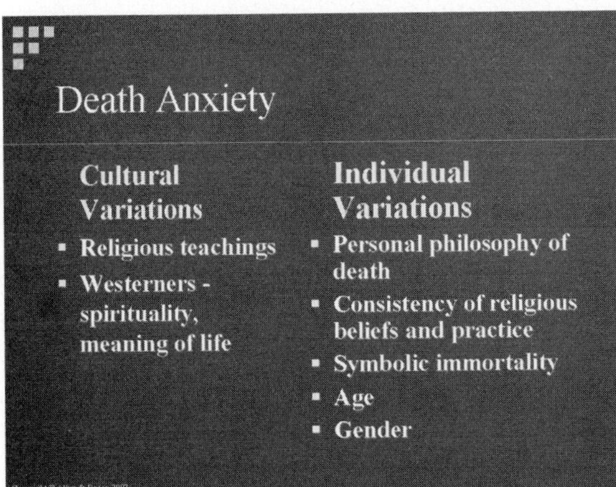
Death Anxiety
Cultural Variations
Religious teachings
Westerners - spirituality, meaning of life
Individual Variations
Personal philosophy of death
Consistency of religious beliefs and practice
Symbolic immortality
Age
Gender
Copyright © Allyn & Bacon 2007

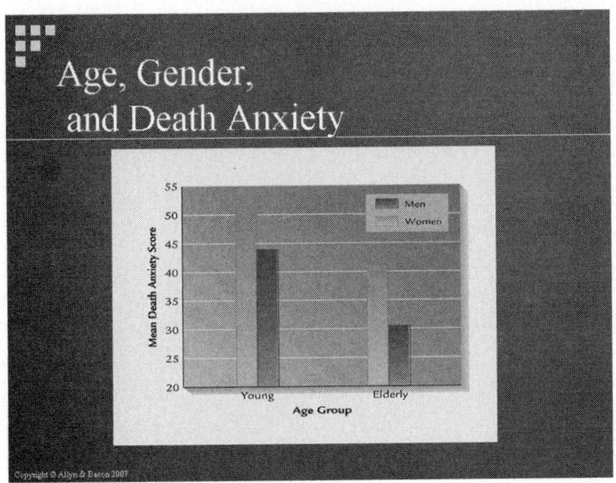
Age, Gender, and Death Anxiety
Mean Death Anxiety Score
55
50
45
40
35
30
25
20
Men
Women
Young
Elderly
Age Group
Copyright © Allyn & Bacon 2007

Kübler-Ross's Theory

- Denial
- Anger
- Bargaining
- Depression
- Acceptance

Appropriate Death

- Makes sense with person's pattern of living, values
- Preserves or restores significant relationships
- Free of suffering
  - As much as possible

Factors That Influence Thoughts About Dying

- Cause of death
  - Nature of disease
- Personality
- Coping style
- Family members' behavior
- Health professionals' behavior
- Spirituality and religion
- Culture

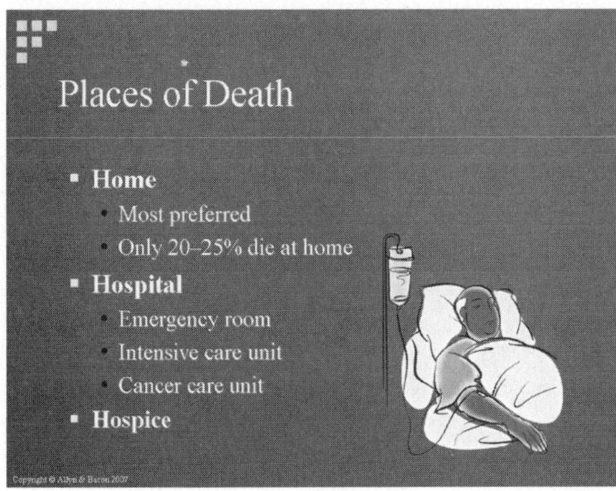
Places of Death
Home
Most preferred
Only 20–25% die at home
Hospital
Emergency room
Intensive care unit
Cancer care unit
Hospice

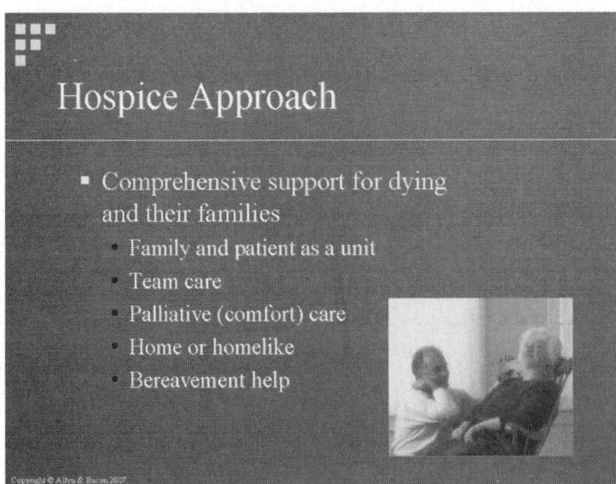
Hospice Approach
Comprehensive support for dying and their families
Family and patient as a unit
Team care
Palliative (comfort) care
Home or homelike
Bereavement help

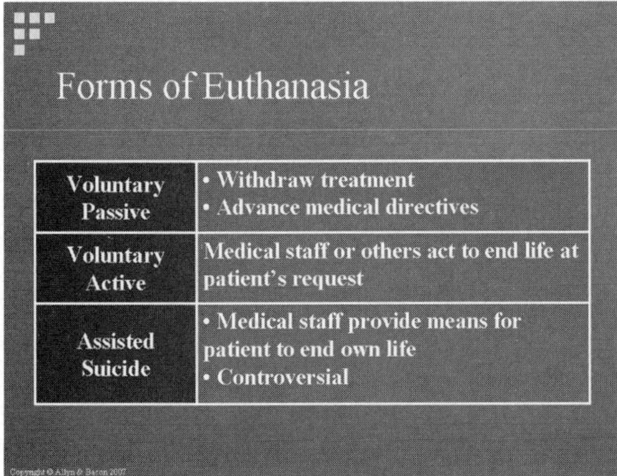
Forms of Euthanasia
Voluntary Passive
• Withdraw treatment
• Advance medical directives
Voluntary Active
Medical staff or others act to end life at patient's request
Assisted Suicide
• Medical staff provide means for patient to end own life
• Controversial

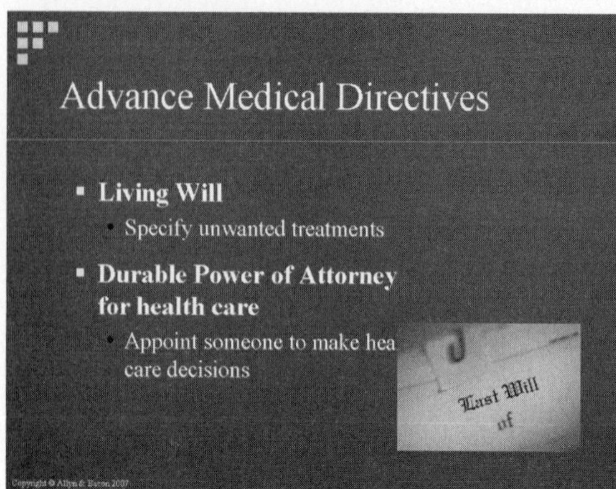
Advance Medical Directives
Living Will
Specify unwanted treatments
Durable Power of Attorney for health care
Appoint someone to make hea care decisions
Last Will of
Copyright © Allyn & Bacon 2007

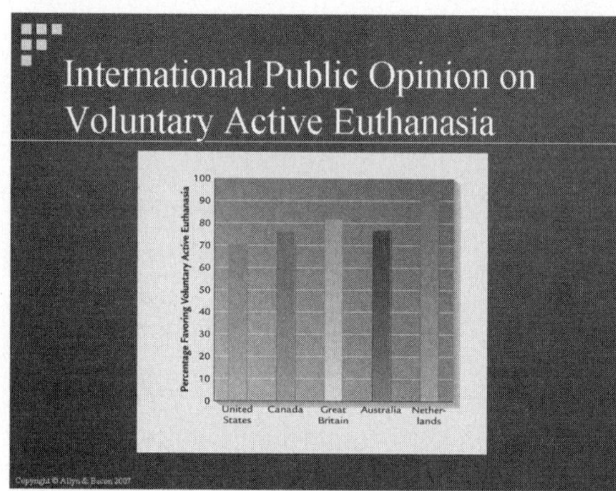
International Public Opinion on Voluntary Active Euthanasia
Percentage Favoring Voluntary Active Euthanasia
100
90
80
70
60
50
40
30
20
10
0
United States
Canada
Great Britain
Australia
Netherlands
Copyright © Allyn & Bacon 2007

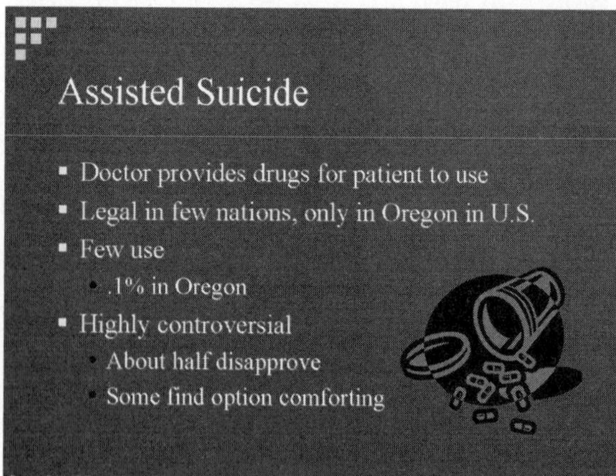
Assisted Suicide
Doctor provides drugs for patient to use
Legal in few nations, only in Oregon in U.S.
Few use
.1% in Oregon
Highly controversial
About half disapprove
Some find option comforting
Copyright © Allyn & Bacon 2007

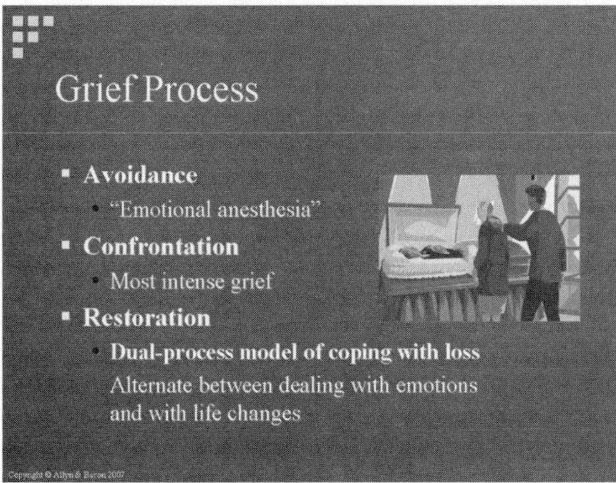

Grieving
Sudden or Prolonged Deaths

Sudden, Unexpected

- Avoidance from shock and disbelief
- May not understand reasons
- Suicide especially hard

Prolonged, Expected

- Anticipatory grieving
  - Allows emotional preparation
- Reasons usually known

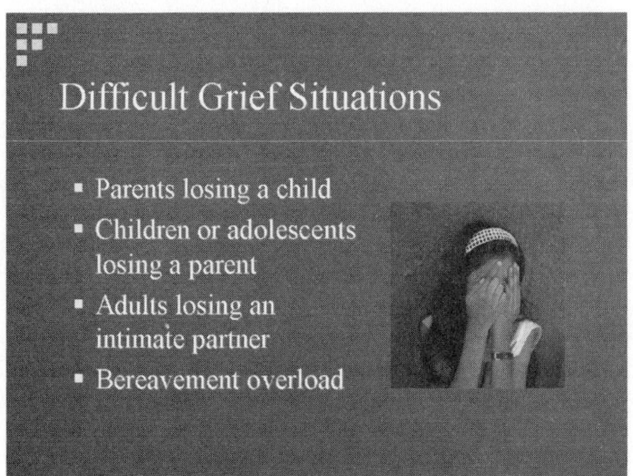

Bereavement Interventions
General Support
▪ Sympathy, understanding
▪ Patient listening, "being there"
Interventions
▪ Self-help groups
▪ Daily living help
Children & Adolescents
▪ After violent death, prevent unnecessary reexposure
▪ Help adults master own distress
Difficult situations
▪ Sudden, violent, unexplained, ambiguous deaths
▪ Grief therapy, individual counseling

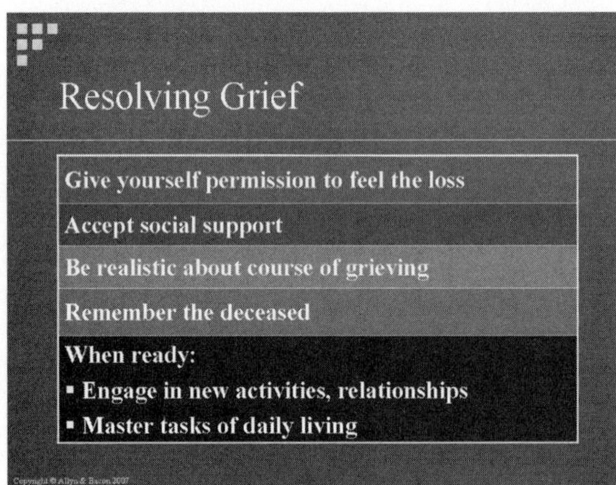
Resolving Grief
Give yourself permission to feel the loss
Accept social support
Be realistic about course of grieving
Remember the deceased
When ready:
▪ Engage in new activities, relationships
▪ Master tasks of daily living

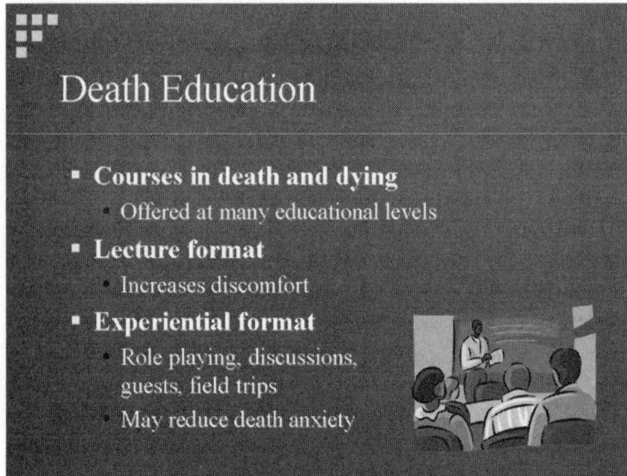
Death Education
▪ Courses in death and dying
Offered at many educational levels
▪ Lecture format
Increases discomfort
▪ Experiential format
Role playing, discussions, guests, field trips
May reduce death anxiety

Goals of Death Education

- Understand physical, psychological changes in dying
- Learn to cope with death of loved ones
- Inform consumers of medical, funeral services
- Understand social, ethical issues